WileyPLUS

WileyPLUS gives you the freedom **of mobility and provides a clear path to your course material and assignments, helping you stay** engaged and on track.

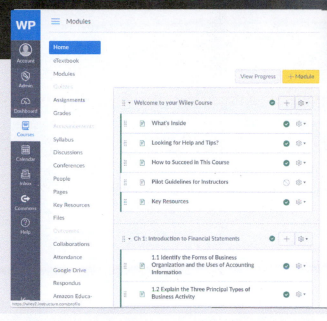

When course materials are presented in an organized way, you are more likely to stay focused, develop mastery, and participate in class. WileyPLUS provides you a clear path through the course material.

Starting with Wiley's quality curated content and adaptive practice questions, you can quickly access material most relevant to your course and understand topics that are most challenging to you. This easy-to-use, intuitive interface saves you time, helps you stay on track, and keeps you motivated throughout your course.

Customized Content

Your course has been customized with videos, documents, pages, and relevant links to keep you motivated.

Interactive eTextbook

You can easily search content, highlight and take notes, access instructor's notes and highlights, and read offline.

Adaptive Practice Questions

Quickly identify areas that are most challenging for you and then focus on material most relevant to your needs.

Linear Design and Organization

Course modules organized by learning objective include eTextbook content, videos, animations, interactives, and practice questions.

Calendar

The course calendar syncs with other features—like assignments and syllabus —so any updates from your instructor will immediately appear.

Student App

You can view due dates, submit assignments, read material, and communicate with your instructor all from your phone.

www.wileyplus.com/student-register

WILEY

Personal Finance

2nd Edition

VICKIE BAJTELSMIT, PhD, JD

Colorado State University

Fort Collins, Colorado

WILEY

DEDICATION

Dedicated to Ken, my partner in life and love

DIRECTOR AND VICE PRESIDENT	Michael McDonald
EXECUTIVE EDITOR	Emily Marcoux
INSTRUCTIONAL DESIGN LEAD	Ed Brislin
INSTRUCTIONAL DESIGNER	Jenny Welter
MARKETING MANAGER	Jenny Geiler
EDITORIAL ASSISTANT	Kirsten Loose
SENIOR CONTENT MANAGER	Dorothy Sinclair
SENIOR PRODUCTION EDITOR	Elena Saccaro
SENIOR DESIGNER	Wendy Lai
PRODUCTION MANAGEMENT SERVICES	Lumina Datamatics, Inc.
COVER IMAGE	pinstock/E+/Getty Images

This book was typeset in 9.5/12.5 Source Sans Pro at Lumina Datamatics and printed and bound by Quad/Graphics.
The cover was printed by Quad/Graphics.

Founded in 1807, John Wiley & Sons, Inc. has been a valued source of knowledge and understanding for more than 200 years, helping people around the world meet their needs and fulfill their aspirations. Our company is built on a foundation of principles that include responsibility to the communities we serve and where we live and work. In 2008, we launched a Corporate Citizenship Initiative, a global effort to address the environmental, social, economic, and ethical challenges we face in our business. Among the issues we are addressing are carbon impact, paper specifications and procurement, ethical conduct within our business and among our vendors, and community and charitable support. For more information, please visit our website: www.wiley.com/go/citizenship.

EPUB ISBN: 978-1-119-59243-3

The inside back cover will contain printing identification and country of origin if omitted from this page. In addition, if the ISBN on the back cover differs from the ISBN on this page, the one on the back cover is correct.

Library of Congress Cataloging-in-Publication Data
Names: Bajtelsmit, Vickie L., 1957- author.
Title: Personal finance / Vickie Bajtelsmit, Colorado State University.
Description: Second edition. | Hoboken, NJ : Wiley, [2020] | Includes index.
Identifiers: LCCN 2019036676 (print) | LCCN 2019036677 (ebook) | ISBN 9781119592471 (paperback) | ISBN 9781119600558 (adobe pdf) | ISBN 9781119592433 (epub)
Subjects: LCSH: Finance, Personal.
Classification: LCC HG179 .B2827 2020 (print) | LCC HG179 (ebook) | DDC 332.024--dc23
LC record available at https://lccn.loc.gov/2019036676
LC ebook record available at https://lccn.loc.gov/2019036677

Printed in the United States of America.

V10018394_050720

Brief Contents

From the Author

A course in personal finance offers essential skills and knowledge that will set students on the road to lifelong financial wellness. In this course, students learn how to set personal financial goals and develop a plan for achieving them. Unlike many college-level courses, Personal Finance focuses completely on real-world decisions, some of which will be immediately applicable to a student's personal situation (budgeting, credit management, insurance) and others that will be relevant shortly after graduation (paying student loans, buying a house or car, saving and investing). None of this is rocket science, but it does require a commitment to acquire the knowledge, skills, and decision-making tools that will help make dreams and goals a reality in the future. By the end of the course, students will have a personal financial plan that they can build on as they progress to their next life stages.

I love teaching this course and am delighted to continue sharing my expertise with faculty and students. You will see that my passion for this subject matter and for student success is infused throughout this second edition of *Personal Finance*. Designed for a one-semester introductory undergraduate course in personal finance, the text materials include significant online content and activities, making them equally appropriate for a traditional face-to-face environment, a completely online class, or a flipped classroom experience. The modular design allows faculty to easily assign content that fits their unique course emphasis. Because this course typically serves a diverse cross-section of college students from all majors and levels, the presentation assumes only a high school math background. Although financial math concepts are included where relevant, these topics are introduced both conceptually and mathematically to ensure that they are accessible to all learners.

Today's students are quite different from those of previous generations. They prefer a multimedia and interactive educational experience over a traditional text-and-lecture presentation. They want frequent performance feedback and more personalized learning opportunities. In this new reality of teaching, engaging students in the subject matter requires that the course materials both support and supplement the classroom experience, and that the course tools include multiple opportunities for review, practice, and immediate feedback on progress. With this goal in mind, *Personal Finance,* Second Edition is designed to be a learning tool rather than merely a textbook. The new edition has been carefully updated to integrate important changes in the legal and economic environment, new video materials, and enhanced assessment tools. As with the first edition, the writing style is student-friendly, and the material is reinforced by pedagogical features that make it easy for students to navigate: logical organization of content, clear learning objectives, well-designed graphics, demonstration problems with video walk-throughs, and case examples to illustrate key concepts. Student engagement is enhanced through the inclusion of Interactive Figures, Reflection Questions, and Personal Financial Planner assignments designed to reinforce core concepts and help students see the relevance to their own lives. Wiley's Adaptive Practice technology provides immediate feedback on their progress through each learning module. Faculty will especially enjoy the carefully constructed Test Bank and the multitude of author-written and assignable end-of-chapter questions, problems, and cases.

I hope that both faculty and students will enjoy the textbook and online materials as much I have enjoyed developing the content.

Vickie Bajtelsmit

VICKIE BAJTELSMIT is a Professor in the Department of Finance and Real Estate at Colorado State University, where she has taught a wide variety of undergraduate and graduate classes, including personal finance, financial planning, risk management and insurance, real estate, employee benefits, and investments. She has been the Director of the Master of Finance Program since 2011 and was the Department Chair from 2007 to 2012. She earned her Ph.D. from the University of Pennsylvania's Wharton School of Business and holds a J.D. from Rutgers University School of Law. In addition to her previous personal finance books, *A Busy Woman's Guide to Financial Freedom* (2001), *Personal Finance: Skills for Life* (2006), *Personal Finance: Managing Your Money and Building Wealth* (2008), and the first edition of *Personal Finance* (2016), she has authored numerous articles in academic and professional journals, focused on personal finance issues related to retirement, insurance, investments, and real estate. Previous professional accomplishments include service as the President of the American Risk and Insurance Association (2010), President of the Risk Theory Society (2010), and President of the Academy of Financial Services (2004) and service on the CFP-Board committee that developed the model curriculum for financial planning programs. She currently serves on the national Board of Trustees for the Jump$tart Coalition for Personal Financial Literacy and the Board of Directors for Junior Achievement of Northern Colorado, is an Associate Editor for several academic journals, and participates actively in several Society of Actuaries research groups.

Making Personal Finance Personal

The pedagogical approach of *Personal Finance,* Second Edition is to connect students with the content on a personal level, improving engagement and resulting in enhanced levels of learning. Written in a conversational style, relevant and interesting in-text examples are used to illustrate core concepts. Students are encouraged throughout to make connections to their own personal financial situations.

We have added current topics of interest to students, such as education financing, mobile payments, tax law changes, and cryptocurrency.

Features that help engage students include the following:

CHAPTER **5**

Managing Credit: Credit Cards and Consumer Loans

ArturVerkhovetskiy/Deposit Photos

Feature Story

Mason's dream job was to be a sound designer for a major film studio. During his senior year in high school, Mason was accepted into a highly selective film and video production program at a small private university. The program was expensive, but the school had strong job placement statistics and offered a generous scholarship that reduced Mason's tuition for his first year. He took out a federal student loan and got a part-time job to help cover his education costs.

Feature Story

Each chapter begins with a short vignette about a personal finance decision or challenge, meant to help students see the relevance of the chapter content.

Chapter Plan and Summary

Each chapter begins with a table that identifies the chapter learning objectives, topics covered in each section, and Demonstration Problems contained in the chapter. Students can use this roadmap to identify the key concepts to focus on while reading the chapter. At the end of the chapter, the Summary, which highlights key concepts and terminology, helps students review content in preparation for exams.

LEARNING OBJECTIVES	TOPICS	DEMONSTRATION PROBLEMS
5.1 Describe the role of consumer credit in your financial plan.	**5.1 What Is Consumer Credit?** • Types and Sources of Consumer Credit • The Advantages and Disadvantages of Consumer Credit • Applying for Consumer Credit	
5.2 Maintain your creditworthiness, and understand your consumer credit rights.	**5.2 Your Consumer Credit Plan** • Measuring Your Credit Capacity • When and How to Use Consumer Credit • Strategies for Reducing Debt • Your Consumer Credit Rights • Bankruptcy	**5.1** How Long Will It Take to Pay Off Your Balance?
5.3 Evaluate credit card choices based on terms and costs.	**5.3 Credit Cards** • Types of Cards • Common Credit Card Contract Terms	**5.2** Calculation of Credit Card Finance Charges
5.4 Evaluate consumer loan choices based on your financial needs, loan terms, and costs.	**5.4 Consumer Loans** • Common Types of Consumer Loans • Comparing Consumer Loan Alternatives	**5.3** How Much Can You Borrow with a Home Equity Loan? **5.4** Total Interest Paid on Loans with Different Maturities **5.5** Calculating Simple Interest Loan Payoffs

Reflection Questions

Particularly useful for flipped classrooms, Reflection Questions interspersed throughout the text encourage students to reflect on their own financial situations.

Reflection Question 1

How concerned are you about your consumer debt? In what ways can large debt repayment obligations negatively affect you and your graduation cohort in the future?

Case Studies

Each chapter includes one or more realistic mini-cases about a personal finance decision for an individual or family, with a detailed solution and discussion. These allow students to practice applying their new conceptual and analytical knowledge to real-world problems.

Case Study 10.2

Indigo Fish/Shutterstock.com

Funding Jake Johnson's College Education

Problem

Holly and Gary Johnson's son Jake is 12 years old in 2019 and hopes to attend an in-state public university at age 18. The Johnsons have saved only $2,000 for college so far, which means that they are getting a late start on their goal of establishing an education funding plan for Jake. His grandparents have set up a college fund for him that will be worth $20,000 by the time he starts college, and Jake plans to contribute $3,000 per year while he is in college from his savings and part-time employment. The Johnsons expect that Jake will receive $7,500 per year in scholarships and/or other financial aid. How much do they need to save per month in order to fund his remaining costs without borrowing?

Strategy

The Johnsons use Excel Worksheet 10.3 to calculate their funding objective and monthly savings amount.

Solution   Consulting **Figure 10.7** and assuming 3 percent annual inflation between now and when Jake goes to college, Holly and Gary estimate that the annual total cost of one year at a four-year public university will be approximately $30,000 when Jake starts college. They are conservative investors with a relatively short time horizon, so they estimate a 4 percent rate of return on their investments.

The Johnsons college funding calculations are shown in **Figure 10.8**. Assuming that Jake will use student loans for a small portion of the cost, they estimate that they will need to fund an additional $43,469 by the time Jake starts college. With only six years in which to save for this expenditure, they need to save $535 per month to reach that goal before Jake goes to college. Based on their finances, they doubt that they will be able to meet this goal, so it's likely that Jake will end up with more student loans than they have estimated in the worksheet.

FIGURE 10.8   Sample of Excel Worksheet 10.3: Education Funding Worksheet

	A	B	C	D
1	Number of years until child goes to college?	6		
2	After-tax return on college fund investments?	4%		
3				
4	**Step 1. Estimate total college costs for four years of college.**			
5	Estimated first year college costs	$30,000		
6	Total for all years = Annual cost × 4			$120,000
7				
8	**Step 2. Subtract other sources of funding.**			
9	Grants and scholarships	$30,000		
10	Child's own savings or employment income	$12,000		
11	Support from other family	$20,000		
12	Amount saved so far	$2,000		
13	Future value of current savings	$2,531		
14	Total from other sources			$64,531
15				
16	**Step 3. Additional college funding needed by the time child starts school**			
17	Total college costs minus total from other sources (Step 1 – Step 2)			$55,469
18	Student loans	$12,000		
19	Funding goal (after student loans)			$43,469
20				
21	**Step 4. Calculate monthly savings needed to reach funding goal.**			
22	(Note: You can use these inputs in your financial calculator.)			
23	FV = Additional college funding needed (Step 3)	$43,469		
24	N = Number of months to save	72		
25	I = After-tax monthly investment return (= Annual return / 12)	0.33%		
26	Solve for PMT			$535
27				

Ethics in Action

Ethics in Action

What's the Harm in Payday Loans?

You're a little short this month, and some of your bills are overdue. Payday is just a week away, and you saw an advertisement for a company that will give you a loan against your future paycheck. It seems like an easy and fast solution to your financial dilemma. All you have to do is write them a check for the amount of your loan plus the fee and they give you the cash on the spot. They agree to hold your check until payday.

Typical terms are $15 to $30 per $100 borrowed, with the loan due to be repaid quickly, usually in one to four weeks. So if you borrow $400 at a fee of $20 per $100, you'll have to repay $480 at the end of the loan period. If you don't pay it in full or if you roll over the loan, you'll have to pay the fee again. In fact, more than half of all payday loans are actually rollovers from previous loans.

Payday lending is controversial and is even illegal in some states, although most states do not place limits on fees as long as they are fully disclosed. Opponents say that these lenders take advantage of low-income and less educated consumers, exploiting their financial hardship and pushing them into a vicious cycle of debt. Others argue that these lenders provide a valuable service to consumers who do not have access to traditional banking services. They argue that although finance costs are high, they are not unreasonable, given the risks and costs the lenders must bear, such as fraudulent checks and failure to repay.

The Consumer Financial Protection Bureau (CFPB) released a special report on payday lending, available on the CFPB website (**www.consumerfinance.gov**). Although the report acknowledged the importance of providing for emergency loans, the data indicated that a fairly large percentage of payday loan consumers find themselves caught in a cycle of high-cost borrowing, paying extraordinarily high effective annual rates (averaging 392 percent). Borrowers average seven loans per year and often are unable to get out from under this debt burden.

There are many areas of personal finance where consumers may be taken advantage of or where they have to make difficult tradeoffs. Ethics in Action boxes present relevant ethical issues and discuss the various sides of these issues. Examples include payday loans (Chapter 5) and dog bite liability (Chapter 7).

End-of-Chapter Pedagogy

Personal Finance 2e includes many carefully-developed assessment materials for faculty to assign as homework or use for exams. Assignable elements include practice questions, end-of-chapter questions and problems, test bank questions, and video library questions. In the new edition, most quantitative questions are now algorithmic, allowing faculty to use assignments in different course sections and semesters.

Summary of Learning Objectives: At the end of each chapter, students are provided with a summary of the key chapter contents related to each of the learning objectives listed at the beginning of the chapter.

Practice Questions in WileyPLUS: Within every learning module in WileyPLUS, students can test their knowledge of key concepts from that section by answering several practice questions with automatically provided feedback.

Concept Review Questions: These essay-style questions review the major topics covered in the chapter.

Application Problems: These more quantitative questions require students to solve problems similar to those that are explained in text examples.

Case Applications: These mini-cases require students to synthesize chapter content while applying concepts from multiple learning objectives within the chapter.

Personal Financial Planner Worksheets in WileyPLUS: A series of worksheets are available to help students develop their own personal financial plan.

Improved Learning Outcomes with WileyPLUS

As with any course you take, the more effort you put into your studies, the more benefit you will get out of them. This second edition of *Personal Finance* and the online resources in WileyPLUS are designed to make the learning process easy and interesting, regardless of a student's learning style. Those who prefer to focus on reading the text will find that the writing style is very student-friendly, and the material includes plenty of relatable examples. Visual learners will enjoy the Interactives and video resources in WileyPLUS. Each chapter also includes flash cards and crossword puzzles for terminology review. As students progress through the various topic areas, they can easily check their understanding and track their progress using the Adaptive Practice technology in WileyPLUS.

The online materials in WileyPLUS provide students with a roadmap for success, multiple opportunities for practice and progress assessment, and many study aids. These include the following:

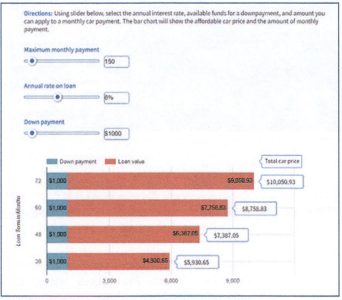

Interactives

Innovative interactives help students develop a better understanding of chapter concepts in a fun way. There are several types of activities in each chapter, including personal self-assessments, concept applications, and interactive visual tools.

Online Calculator Video Demonstrations

Taking advantage of the multitude of online resources that are available today, the new edition includes a video in each chapter that highlights particularly useful online calculators and walks students through how to use them to make financial decisions relevant to the chapter content.

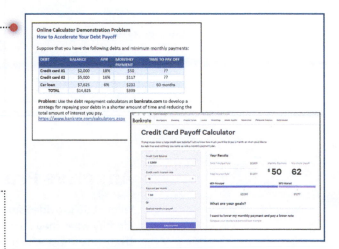

Peer-to-Peer Videos

Videos featuring actual students and professionals illustrate the impact of financial decisions and act as a catalyst for deeper discussion.

Demonstration Problems and Videos

Within each chapter, Demonstration Problems provide step-by-step directions for applying financial math calculations to specific personal finance problems, with solutions for multiple methods (formulas, financial calculator, and spreadsheet). In WileyPLUS, students can watch a Demonstration Problem Video in which the author works through the problem using light board technology and a financial calculator or spreadsheet visual where applicable.

Video Library

Curated videos with assignable questions for homework or discussion align with each chapter to provide more real-world context for students.

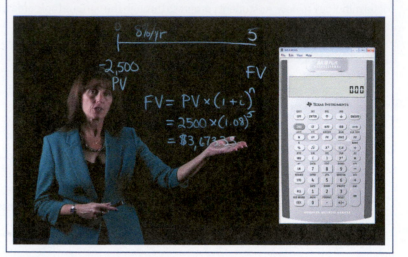

DEMONSTRATION PROBLEM 2.2 | Calculating the Future Value of a Lump Sum

Problem

You invest $2,500 today. How much will it be worth in five years if your account earns 8 percent interest per year, compounded annually?

Strategy

Use Equation 2.8, a financial calculator, or a spreadsheet to calculate the future value of a lump sum.

Personal Financial Planner Assignments

Instructors can assign to students the Personal Financial Planner Worksheets, along with reflection questions about their financial decisions, to incentivize students to develop their own personal financial plan.

Adaptive Practice

WileyPLUS provides students with a personal, adaptive learning experience, allowing them to identify what they know and don't know early, build their proficiency on topics, and use their study time most effectively. Faculty can use the performance reports to better identify student knowledge gaps. Classroom tests show that students who use the Adaptive Practice questions tend to have better course performance than those who do not.

- **Topical Coverage:** Topics of current interest to students have been updated, added, or expanded.

  - **Student Loans:** Student loans are introduced as a type of consumer loan in Chapter 5, as in the 1st edition, but the detailed discussion of financing options, types of student loans, and repayment planning has been expanded and moved to the education financing section in Chapter 10.

  - **Mobile Payments:** The discussion of banking and transaction accounts in Chapter 3 is expanded to include mobile payment options, with discussion of costs and benefits.

  - **Tax Law Changes:** Chapter 4 is completely rewritten to incorporate the changes to the US tax system that resulted from the Tax Cuts and Jobs Act of 2017, and other chapters are updated to reflect changes to retirement plan contribution limits, Social Security benefits, estate taxes, and other tax-related rules.

  - **Cryptocurrency:** In Chapter 13, the discussion of speculative investments is expanded to include cryptocurrency.

  - **Health Care:** As the health care and health insurance landscape continues to evolve, the new edition explains recent changes to employer plans and private health insurance options, as well as updates on the status of health care reform.

- **Chapter Plan and Summary:** Each chapter now begins with a table that identifies the chapter learning objectives, topics covered in each section, and Demonstration Problems contained in the chapter. Students can use this roadmap to identify the key concepts to focus on while reading the chapter.

- **Reflection Questions:** Particularly useful for flipped classrooms, Reflection Questions interspersed throughout the text encourage students to reflect on their own financial situations.

- **Peer-to-Peer Videos:** Videos featuring actual students and professionals illustrate the impact of financial decisions and act as a catalyst for deeper discussion.

- **Online Calculator Demonstration Videos:** Taking advantage of the multitude of online resources that are available today, most chapters in the new edition include one or more videos that highlight particularly useful online calculators and walk students through how to use them to make financial decisions relevant to the chapter content.

- **Algorithmic End-of-Chapter Questions in WileyPLUS:** Most quantitative questions are now algorithmic, allowing faculty to use questions in different course sections and semesters.

- **Algorithmic Testbank Questions in WileyPLUS:** Most quantitative testbank questions are now algorithmic, allowing faculty to use questions in different course sections and semesters.

- **Accessibility:** In WileyPLUS, accessibility is at the forefront of our design. All content and questions have been audited for accessibility, and anything that does not meet that standard has been flagged for awareness. WileyPLUS provides a learning path that complies with the Americans with Disabilities Act (ADA) and Web Content Accessibility Guidelines (WCAG 2.1).

Acknowledgements

The work, thoughts, ideas and recommendations of reviewers, focus group attendees, and ancillary authors, for this and the first edition, is deeply appreciated.

Janice Akao, *Butler Community College*

Norman Anderson, *Ivy Tech Community College*

Gail Austin, *Rose State College*

Kristine Beck, *California State University Northridge*

Connie Belden, *Butler Community College*

Melody Bell, *Portland State University*

Bryan Bouchard, *Southern New Hampshire University*

Walter Boyle, *Fayetteville Technical Community College*

Inga Chira, *California State University Northridge*

Ron Christner, *Loyola University of New Orleans*

Kevin Cochrane, *College of the Desert*

Thomas Coe, *Quinnipiac University*

Marc Condos, *American River College*

Christopher Coyne, *Saint Joseph's University*

Helen Davis, *Jefferson Community and Technical College*

Rob Diamond, *California State University Sacramento*

James Dow, *California State University Northridge*

Brenda Eichelberger, *Portland State University*

Mark Fronke, *Cerritos College*

Nicole Garrison, *Sam Houston State University*

Philip Gibson, *Winthrop University*

Terri Gonzales-Kreisman, *Delgado Community College*

Jennifer Eldridge, *Forsyth Technical Community College*

Howard Eskew, *San Diego Mesa College*

Frank Harber, *Indian River State College*

Sueann Hely, *West Kentucky Community & Technical College*

Alison Hollingsworth, *University of West Georgia*

Samira Hussein, *Johnson County Community College*

Charlotte Jacobsen, *Montgomery College*

John Jee, *Sacred Heart University*

Bruce Johnson, *South Dakota State University*

Carrie Johnson, *North Dakota State University*

Eddy Junarsin, *Southern Illinois University Carbondale*

Matthew Keyes, *Florida State College at Jacksonville*

Roberta Klein, *Rochester Institute of Technology*

Gregory Lattier, *Lee College*

Sharon Laux, *University of Missouri St. Louis*

John Mago, *Anoka Ramsey Community College*

Kenneth Mark, *Kansas City Kansas Community College*

Cheryl McGaughey, *Angelo State University*

Mike McGonigle, *New Mexico State University*

Earl Mitchell, *Santa Ana College*

Barry Mulholland, *Texas Tech University*

Tim Muth, *Florida Institute of Technology*

Joseph Newman, *Auburn University at Montgomery*

Nicholas Panepinto, *Flagler College*

Ohaness Paskelian, *University of Houston Downtown*

Dyan Pease, *Sacramento City College*

James Pettijohn, *Missouri State University*

Mike Phillips, *California State University Northridge*

Armand Picou, *Texas A&M Community College*

Jack Popovich, *Columbus State Community College*

KC Rakow, *Saint Xavier University*

Mitchell Ratner, *Rider University*

Deana Ray, *Forsyth Technical Community College*

Clarence Rose, *Radford University*

Murray Sabrin, *Ramapo College*

Andy Salcido, *Santiago Canyon College*

Timothy Sargent, *California State University Northridge*

Todd Saville, *Kirkwood Community College*

Diana Simpson, *Auburn University*

Alice Sineath, *Forsyth Technical Community College*

Edith Strickland, *Tallahasee Community College*

Diane Tanner, *University of North Florida*

Rhonda Thomas, *Butler Community College*

Roger Wallenburg, *Missouri State University*

Tiffany Willis, *American River College*

Scott Wright, *Ohio University*

Contents

8   Life Insurance and Long-Term Care Planning   8-1

9   Employee Benefits: Health, Disability, and Retirement Plans   9-1

10   Saving for Distant Goals: Retirement and Education Funding   10-1

CHAPTER 1

The Financial Planning Process

fstop123/iStock/Getty Images

Feature Story

Kayla and her friends, like most college students, saw college graduation as a big milestone, representing the beginning of their lives as independent adults. What they didn't anticipate was graduating in the middle of a major financial downturn, having trouble finding career employment, and moving back in with Mom and Dad.

Recent evidence suggests that as many as 20 percent of young adults are now living with their parents—about twice as many as did so in past decades. In fact, as more kids come home to roost with their Baby Boom parents, it's increasingly common to hear them called the "boomerang" generation.

The boomerang phenomenon in the United States is often the result of family financial decisions. Many college students have taken on significant debt in the form of credit cards, student loans, and car loans. In Kayla's case, she graduated college with $30,000 in student loans and a small car loan. Although her new job pays $40,000 per year, the student loan payment puts a big strain on her budget, so she's grateful that her parents are letting her live with them rent-free. Her plan is to put most of her earnings toward paying off her student loans as quickly as possible.

Personal financial success doesn't just happen—you have to put time and effort into educating yourself about important financial tools and products, and you need to take the time to put together a plan that can adapt to your changing life circumstances. This book will provide you with a roadmap for achieving your financial goals—everything from setting goals and developing a plan to buying insurance and investing for retirement. By the end of this course, you'll be able to put together a comprehensive financial plan that will take you from graduation to your future.

LEARNING OBJECTIVES	TOPICS	DEMONSTRATION PROBLEMS
1.1 Describe the personal financial planning process, and explain how the elements of a comprehensive financial plan fit together.	**1.1 What Is Personal Financial Planning?** • Why Study Personal Financial Planning? • The Personal Financial Planning Process • Elements of a Comprehensive Financial Plan	

(continued)

(continued)

LEARNING OBJECTIVES	TOPICS	DEMONSTRATION PROBLEMS
1.2 Describe how individual characteristics and economic factors influence personal financial planning.	**1.2 Factors That Influence Financial Planning Decisions** • Individual Characteristics and Your Financial Plan • Economic Factors and Your Financial Plan	**1.1** Calculating Percentage Change
1.3 Create a prioritized list of short-term and long-term personal financial goals.	**1.3 Setting Short-Term and Long-Term Financial Goals** • Why Goals Are Important • The Goal-Setting Process	**1.2** What Monthly Payment Is Necessary to Pay Off Your Debt?
1.4 Know when and how to find qualified financial planning professionals.	**1.4 Selecting Qualified Financial Planning Professionals** • When Do You Need a Financial Planner? • Factors to Consider in Choosing a Planner • How Are Planners Paid?	
1.5 Consider opportunity costs and marginal effects in making personal finance decisions.	**1.5 Making Effective Decisions** • Make Reasonable Assumptions • Apply Marginal Reasoning • Consider Opportunity Costs • Use Sensitivity Analysis • Decision-Making Styles	

1.1 | What Is Personal Financial Planning?

LEARNING OBJECTIVE 1.1

Describe the personal financial planning process, and explain how the elements of a comprehensive financial plan fit together.

INTERACTIVE

You can also take this quiz in **WileyPLUS.** See Interactive: **Financial Literacy Quiz.**

How much do you already know about personal finance? Complete **Interactive: Financial Literacy Quiz** to assess your financial literacy. If you know most of the answers, you're in better shape than the average person. Surveys show a relatively low level of financial literacy in the United States—with many people not even understanding basic concepts.

In this chapter, you will begin improving your financial literacy with some important background material. You'll learn about the importance of financial planning, the elements of a comprehensive financial plan, and the factors that influence financial decision making. After

INTERACTIVE **Financial Literacy Quiz** Test your knowledge of basic personal finance concepts by taking this quiz.

1.	For a person's standard of living to improve, expenses must decrease.	True	False
2.	If your total assets are $10,000 and your total debts are $11,000, your net worth is $21,000.	True	False
3.	If your taxable income falls in the lowest federal tax bracket, you pay no U.S. federal income tax.	True	False
4.	A Roth IRA allows tax-free withdrawals at retirement.	True	False
5.	Capital gains are taxed at a lower rate than ordinary income.	True	False
6.	Checking your account balance at an ATM is now considered an effective way of balancing your checking account.	True	False
7.	Making the minimum payment on a credit card bill each month is an effective way to be sure your balance will be paid back in a reasonable amount of time.	True	False
8.	Fixed-rate mortgage loans usually have lower rates of interest than adjustable-rate loans.	True	False
9.	Student loan debts cannot be discharged by a bankruptcy.	True	False
10.	Young male drivers pay higher auto insurance rates than young women because they tend to be worse drivers.	True	False
11.	If you are injured at work, your employer is required to pay your medical and rehab costs in most states.	True	False
12.	The major advantage of term life insurance over permanent life insurance for young, healthy people is that it is very inexpensive to buy a lot of coverage.	True	False
13.	A major difference between stock and bond investments is that bonds are usually less risky.	True	False
14.	When you buy stock issued by a company, you become an owner of the company.	True	False
15.	Index funds are generally expected to be low-risk investments.	True	False
16.	A divorcee or widow who never worked outside the home is not eligible for Social Security benefits because she never paid into the system.	True	False
17.	Money to be received in the future is not as available as money received today.	True	False

Answers: 1. F; 2. F; 3. F; 4. T; 5. T; 6. F; 7. F; 8. F; 9. T; 10. F; 11. T; 12. T; 13. T; 14. T; 15. F; 16. F; 17. T

reading this chapter, you'll know how to set goals, select financial planning professionals, and implement general strategies for making financial decisions.

Why Study Personal Financial Planning?

As a college student, you're likely to have made several important financial decisions already. **Table 1.1** includes a few of the questions you may already have asked.

These questions are all related to **personal finance**—a specialized area of study that focuses on individual and household financial decisions, such as budgeting, saving, spending, tax-planning, insurance, and investments. Understanding these topics will help you in many

TABLE 1.1 Common Personal Finance Questions

Simple Decisions	Complex Decisions
What is the best way to fund my college education?	Is graduate school a good investment?
How can I reduce my credit card debt?	How much should I contribute to my 401(k) retirement plan?
Can I afford to replace my car's transmission?	Should I start a savings plan to fund my child's college education?
Where should I go to buy my auto insurance?	How do I decide among the employee benefit options that my employer offers?

ways. You'll make better decisions when you buy an automobile, shop for a home mortgage, choose a career, and save for retirement. You may also be able to pay less in taxes and interest.

Personal financial planning is the process of developing and implementing an integrated, comprehensive plan designed to meet financial goals, to improve financial well-being, and to prepare for financial emergencies. In this course, you'll learn the elements of personal financial planning and how to prepare your own financial plan. Unlike many classes you'll take in college, this course will help you to gain knowledge, skills, and abilities that have immediate application to your own life situation. Furthermore, these benefits will continue throughout your life. In short, mastering the subject matter in this course will provide you with the knowledge and skills you need to achieve personal financial success.

What Are the Benefits of Personal Financial Planning?

The primary goal of personal financial planning is to develop and achieve financial goals, such as buying a home, making a major consumer purchase, supporting a growing family, and saving for retirement. But people who have their finances in order gain important social and psychological benefits as well. Generally, they feel less stressed and experience improved relationships with friends, family, and coworkers. As many couples know, financial difficulties can be a major contributor to marital problems. Most people also find that being financially self-sufficient improves their self-esteem.

Why Do People Avoid Financial Planning?

Surveys indicate that most people recognize the need to manage their finances, but fall short of that goal. Why does this happen? One or more of the following reasons are often given as explanations:

- They don't believe their math and finance skills are adequate.
- They fear failure.
- They expect someone else to take care of it.
- They aren't interested.
- They don't know whom to trust.
- They are too busy.
- They are overwhelmed with the quantity of information and don't know where to start.

Reflection Question 1

Are there aspects of your personal finances that you have avoided dealing with? If so, what are your reasons?

If you've used some of these excuses yourself, rest assured that you're not alone. You might be able to relate to the all-too-common situation of David Keller. During his first year in college, David used his credit card for extras such as concert tickets, occasional pizzas, movie tickets, and music downloads. David wasn't employed, so the credit card balances grew, and he began to have trouble meeting his minimum payments. With late charges and over-limit fees, his situation quickly got out of control. David was too embarrassed to tell his parents, even when he started getting stomachaches from the stress. Fortunately, on the advice of a friend, David signed up for a personal finance course at the beginning of his second year in college. By establishing a budget and taking a part-time job to pay down his credit card debt, David was able to get things in order.

What Problems Can Be Caused by Poor Financial Planning?

What happens to people who don't manage their finances well or at all? David's example illustrates just a few of the many unfortunate outcomes—stress, worry, embarrassment, and difficulty in meeting current obligations. Individuals and households experiencing financial distress have trouble handling a financial emergency or unexpected job loss. They can end up as the victims of "get rich quick" scams. Their children may be unintended victims, because high-quality educational opportunities and extracurricular activities may not be affordable without advance planning. Many people suffer from anxiety or depression related to their finances and may, as a result, have difficulty maintaining personal relationships. Spouses who lack an understanding of household finances often find themselves in serious trouble upon divorce or widowhood. And adult children who mismanage their finances may end up living with their parents well into their 20s and 30s. For all these reasons, mastering the financial planning process is well worth your investment of time and effort.

The Personal Financial Planning Process

Figure 1.1 illustrates the five steps in the financial planning process. This process is fundamental to all aspects of financial planning, so we'll revisit it throughout the text as we apply it to different financial planning decisions. In each area of your financial plan, applying this process will help you to make better financial decisions.

FIGURE 1.1 **The Financial Planning Process**   All personal financial decisions should be based on this process.

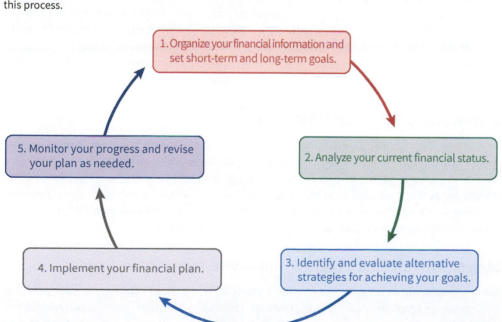

1. Organize your financial information and set short-term and long-term goals.

2. Analyze your current financial status.

3. Identify and evaluate alternative strategies for achieving your goals.

4. Implement your financial plan.

5. Monitor your progress and revise your plan as needed.

By the time you get to the end of this course, thinking in terms of the financial planning process will be second nature to you. You'll also know more about your own financial habits and attitudes. Personal financial planning will help you make better decisions about money, but its effect on your life will go much further than that. Nearly every aspect of life has a financial component.

Next, let's examine each of the steps in the personal financial planning process in a little more detail.

Step 1: Organize Your Financial Information and Set Short-Term and Long-Term Goals

Before you can move forward with your financial plan, you need to determine where you are starting from—where your money is coming from and where it is going. To do this effectively and efficiently, you first need to collect and organize your financial information. This step may be more difficult if you are "organizationally challenged," but you'll learn more about how to accomplish it in the next chapter.

The process of setting goals should involve some introspective assessment of *why* you have the goals that you do. For example, are your objectives focused on your own needs or the needs of others? Are your objectives related to pressures from family or peers? Keep in mind, too, that short-term and long-term goals change over time and may be influenced by changes in economic circumstances.

Step 2: Analyze Your Current Financial Status

After you've collected all of your financial information, you'll need to have some way of evaluating how well you're doing. In Chapter 2, you'll learn how to create personal financial statements and how to quantitatively assess your current financial position to establish a baseline against which you can measure improvement. This step will also help you identify which areas you need to work on and what funds you may have available to apply to achieving your goals. Once you have this process in place, it will be easy to track your progress over time.

Step 3: Identify and Evaluate Alternative Strategies for Achieving Your Goals

Although every person's goals and objectives are unique to that person's circumstances, the strategies for achieving them are similar. In general, in order to have more money available to attain current or future goals, you have to either reduce spending or increase income. You'll need to identify alternative strategies for achieving each of your goals and compare the costs and benefits of each strategy. In future chapters, we'll go into the details of specific strategies for each area of your financial plan. To effectively compare alternatives, you'll need to understand applicable tax rules and the time value of money.

Step 4: Implement Your Financial Plan

Using the information you developed in Step 3, you can decide on how best to achieve your goals. How do you make such decisions? How do you know which strategies are the best ones for achieving your goals? As you proceed through this course, you'll acquire fundamental knowledge and master analytical tools that will help you to make effective personal financial planning decisions. The result will be a personal financial plan that meets your basic household needs, builds wealth over time, and protects your income and assets.

Step 5: Monitor Your Progress and Revise Your Plan as Needed

Many changes will occur over the course of your life. Not only will changes in your personal circumstances (graduation, a new job, marriage, children) affect your financial planning objectives and strategies, but changes in economic conditions may also necessitate revision of your

Case Study 1.1

theboone/iStock/Getty Images

The Naughtons Revise Their Financial Plan after Job Loss

Problem

Jack and Sandy Naughton had stretched their finances a little to buy a house. They also were planning to increase their retirement account contributions and save for a vacation trip. Then, unexpectedly, Jack was laid off from his job. Jack and Sandy needed to drastically change their goals, returning to Step 1 of the financial planning process. Instead of saving for retirement and vacations, their new goals were to pay their bills and find employment for Jack.

Strategy

In applying Step 2 of the financial planning process, Jack and Sandy evaluated how long they could pay their household bills and where they could cut back on expenditures. Thankfully, they had a small emergency fund, which allowed them to meet expenses in the short run. Jack found a new job, though his new lower salary was not enough to cover the couple's monthly expenses. To achieve the goal of meeting expenses, the two made the following list of alternative strategies:

- Find Sandy a job.
- Sell or refinance the house to reduce payments.
- Sell other assets (car?).
- Dip into savings.
- Borrow money.

Each of these strategies has costs and benefits. For example, selling the house would reduce their expenses, but the selling price might not be high enough for them to pay off their mortgage and cover the selling costs. Furthermore, although mortgage interest rates had declined, the Naughtons' lower household income meant that they wouldn't be able to qualify for a new loan on a smaller house.

Solution   In the end, Sandy got a job as a cashier at a local retail store, and Jack took a second part-time job on the weekends.

plan. An effective financial plan must be adaptable to changing circumstances. Thus, Step 5 takes you continually back to Steps 1 through 4.

Interactive: Applying the Financial Planning Process will give you some practice in applying the financial planning process. To make the process a little more concrete, let's apply it to a specific household's situation in **Case Study 1.1**.

Although this is a hypothetical example, layoffs are common, particularly during economic downturns. Fortunately, the Naughtons had the financial capacity to make ends meet for a short period of unemployment, and both Jack and Sandy were able to find jobs. Many families live from paycheck to paycheck and have no emergency fund or savings to draw on in the event of a crisis.

INTERACTIVE

See Interactive: Applying the Financial Planning Process in WileyPLUS.

Elements of a Comprehensive Financial Plan

In this course, you'll begin the process of building a comprehensive, integrated financial plan. Critical to the success of this plan is that you approach its creation in a logical order. The steps to success in **Figure 1.2** illustrate the elements of a comprehensive financial plan.

These steps, and how they relate to the material presented in this book, are as follows:

1. **Establish a firm foundation.**   Setting goals, acquiring necessary tools and skills (Chapters 1–4).
2. **Secure basic needs.**   Short-term planning for security and liquidity (Chapters 5–6).
3. **Build and protect wealth.**   Long-term planning to protect income and wealth against losses (Chapters 7–9) and to meet future needs (Chapters 10–14).

Your first step toward success in reaching your personal financial goals will be to establish the necessary foundations by learning about the personal financial planning process, acquiring

FIGURE 1.2 **Elements of a Comprehensive Financial Plan**   To have the greatest chance of success, you should build your financial plan from the bottom up, completing the necessary activities for each part of your plan before jumping to the next.

the necessary tools, and considering the tax effects of your financial decisions. The second step involves securing your basic needs, such as a car and housing, setting aside funds for financial emergencies, and buying insurance. Once your basic needs have been taken care of, you can begin to think about long-term planning. This will include building wealth to meet future needs, such as retirement and college funding, as well as protecting wealth and income through life insurance, disability insurance, long-term care insurance, and estate planning.

1.2   Factors That Influence Financial Planning Decisions

LEARNING OBJECTIVE 1.2
Describe how individual characteristics and economic factors influence personal financial planning.

As you build your financial plan, you'll need to consider many factors that influence spending and saving. Some of these factors are unique to your household, such as your life cycle stage, your family makeup, your values, and your attitudes.

In addition, economic factors, such as inflation and interest rates, are important consider-ations for everyone who is developing and implementing financial plans. Both individual and economic factors can be expected to change over time, so your financial plan will need to be adaptable to new circumstances. In this section, we'll first discuss individual characteristics that influence financial planning and then describe some important economic factors that you should consider.

Individual Characteristics and Your Financial Plan

Every household is different and therefore has unique financial needs. A financial plan has to be tailored to your life cycle stage and the number of people in your family. It also needs to be consistent with your values and attitudes.

Life Cycle Factors

Your household will go through several phases over your life cycle, and your financial situation will change as well. **Figure 1.3** illustrates how a person's income and wealth can be expected to change over the life cycle.

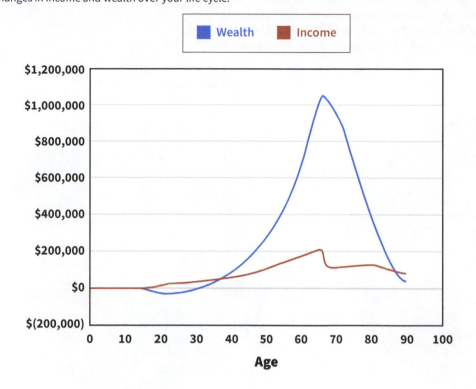

FIGURE 1.3   **Household Income and Wealth over the Life Cycle**   Your financial plan must adapt to changes in income and wealth over your life cycle.

The graph is not intended to imply that everyone's situation is the same. Rather, it is meant to illustrate the significant differences in planning needs over the life cycle. In general, your income level through your early 20s will be lower than it will be later, and your wealth may even be negative—that is, you may have more debts than assets at this point in your life. That's because you're currently making investments in your education that have not yet paid off.

Marriage, career development, the purchase of a home, and investments in your children's education will likely occur from your late 20s through your 40s. During this time, you will focus on setting goals, establishing savings, and protecting your family from unexpected negative events, such as a premature death or job loss due to illness or disability. This is also the beginning of the wealth accumulation phase, which continues through your 50s to late 60s.

As retirement approaches, most people in their 50s and 60s pay closer attention to planning for retirement income, managing health care, and preserving wealth for their heirs. The earlier you plan for these needs, the better off you will be once you get to that stage in the life cycle. During retirement, most likely starting in your mid- to late-60s, you'll begin to spend down your accumulated wealth. Your goals during retirement may include maintaining an active lifestyle, enjoying travel and leisure activities, and having sufficient income to support your needs. Without good planning, you risk running out of money in old age.

Demographic Characteristics

Family makeup and demographic characteristics—such as age, family size, income, and wealth—significantly affect financial planning. During child-rearing years, families tend to have higher expenses and, therefore, less ability to save. Over time, due to inflation and other factors, the increasing costs of health care, child care, and especially education have made it more expensive to raise a child.

How much do you think it costs for a middle-class family to raise one child from birth to age 17? **Figure 1.4** compares the breakdown of these costs in 1960 and 2015. Relative to 55 years ago, the cost of raising a child is about 16 percent higher, after adjusting for inflation. Most of the increase has been due to child care and health care expenses.

Given the extra expenses associated with having children, it isn't surprising that double-income couples without children tend to be financially better off than singles. Childless adults

FIGURE 1.4 **The Total Cost of Raising a Child and Breakdown of Expenditures, 1960 vs. 2015**

The average total cost for a middle-income, two-parent household to raise a child from birth to age 17 was $25,229 in 1960. After accounting for inflation, that would be the equivalent of $202,020 in 2015 dollars. According to the U.S. Department of Agriculture, the cost for a child born in 2015 is $233,610,—an increase of 16 percent over the 1960 amount. The graphs below show the breakdown of these costs.

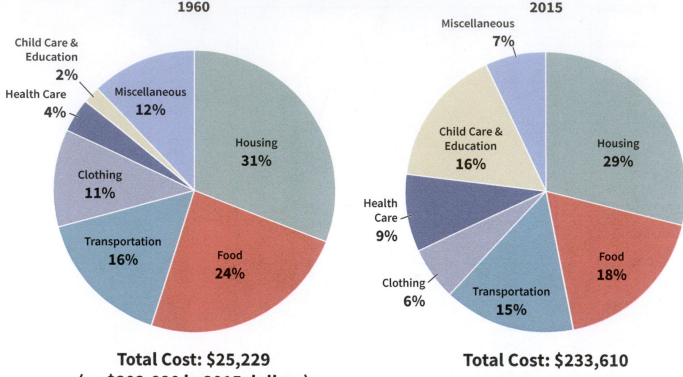

Source: USDA Center for Nutrition Policy and Promotion, Expenditures on Children by Families, 2015, Miscellaneous Report No. 1528-2015 (January 2017).

are able to focus on career goals and may move up the employment ladder more quickly. However, the financial and social support provided by children to their elderly parents may eventually be an offsetting benefit.

Most estimates of the cost of raising children do not count one of the biggest expenditures—higher education. As we'll see in a later chapter, a college education at a public university can easily run $50,000 per child or more, and private schools cost several times as much. This may be the most important investment a family can make, though, because education plays such a critical role in future financial success. College-educated people, particularly those with specialized skills (such as business, education, and engineering), tend to receive higher starting salaries and larger wage increases during their careers. They are also more likely to have retirement plans and fringe benefit packages.

Values and Attitudes

People have different values and attitudes regarding money and its use. Your money management style generally is the result of both learned behaviors and inherent tendencies. For example, if you were raised in a household where money was tight and consumer purchases were made with careful deliberation, you might carry the money skills learned from your parents' example into your adult life. Whether your parents were spendthrifts or tightwads, however, your own genetic makeup will also influence your personal money style. Individuals who are impulsive by nature often have difficulty controlling their spending, just as those with a tendency to orderliness are more likely to have their finances under control. Thus, both "nature and nurture" help to form your values and attitudes concerning money. In fact, it is not uncommon for siblings raised in the same households to have very different money management styles.

Values are fundamental beliefs about what is important in life. What do you think is most important: family, friends, possessions, education, religious faith, financial success, fame, health, self-sufficiency? The weight you place on each will influence the goals that you set and the strategies that you develop to achieve your goals.

Attitudes are opinions and psychological differences between people that affect their decisions. Are you an optimist or a pessimist? Do you consider yourself a conservative or a liberal? Do you like to have everything planned out in advance or just go with the flow? Spontaneous and generous people may have more difficulty controlling spending than those who are more analytical. People who are natural "planners" are more inclined to set goals and follow through on their strategies for achieving them.

What if you already know that you have a problem with money? Is it possible to overcome your biological makeup and your learned values and attitudes? Of course it is! To do this, though, you must first recognize what your values and attitudes are, particularly where they may run counter to achieving your goals. Remember David Keller from earlier in the chapter? David's credit card problems in college didn't come about by accident—he had learned bad money habits as a child. He grew up in a wealthy household with parents who were "spenders." When he was a child, his parents bought him toys whenever they set foot in a store. As a teen, he didn't need a part-time job like most of his friends, and he always had the latest video games and sports gear. When he went away to college, he didn't really know *how* to control his spending. If you're a spender like David, you will likely need to approach your budget differently than someone who is naturally inclined to be more conservative about spending.

Of particular importance to financial planning is your attitude toward **risk**, or uncertainty about the potential outcome of a decision. Although outcomes can be either good or bad, your financial plan needs to take into consideration the risk of *negative* outcomes, such as being injured or losing money on an investment. As we saw in Case Study 1.1, families also need to be prepared for unexpected job layoffs.

Are you a risk taker, or do you tend to avoid risk? We'll look more closely at risk attitudes and how they impact personal financial decisions in later chapters. If you're a natural risk taker, you'll approach investing quite differently than someone who tends to avoid risk. To help you understand your own inclinations, answer the questions in **Excel Worksheet 1.1** (Personal Financial Planner: Money Attitudes Questionnaire). You may also find it interesting to compare your answers to those of other family members.

Demographic factors such as gender, age, income, and education have often been linked to risk attitudes. Researchers have looked at many dimensions of behavior to identify people who are inclined to take risks. While findings are not entirely consistent, some relatively consistent trends have emerged. In **Interactive: Socioeconomic Differences in Risk Attitudes**, you can find out whether your intuition regarding which types of people are more likely to be risk takers is correct.

EXCEL WORKSHEET

See **Excel Worksheet 1.1 (Personal Financial Planner: Money Attitudes Questionnaire) in WileyPLUS.**

INTERACTIVE

See **Interactive: Socioeconomic Differences in Risk Attitudes in WileyPLUS.**

Economic Factors and Your Financial Plan

A fundamental truth about the economy is that it's very unpredictable. Even the experts cannot say with certainty what the future may hold. Nevertheless, some economic factors have a known influence on personal finances, and it's important for you to recognize these factors and incorporate them in your financial planning decisions. Throughout this course, you'll be developing your knowledge about economic factors that affect financial planning. Some factors that are highly likely to affect your future are inflation, interest rates, employment conditions, political unrest, and global issues. We'll discuss each of these in this section.

Inflation

Everyone has at one time or another heard an older person say, "When I was a kid, it was a lot less expensive to . . . ." Such statements describe the effects of **inflation**, the change in general price levels over time. Normally, inflation refers to an *increase* in prices, like the inflating of a balloon. As prices of goods and services go up, the spending power of your money goes down—a dollar will not purchase as much as it previously did. If the prices of goods and services decline over a period of time, a rare event, we call this decline "deflation."

Inflation affects nearly every aspect of your finances. Your grocery bills are probably higher this year than they were last year. You might be paying more for gasoline than in the past. Your monthly rent will probably go up next year, too. As prices get higher over time, you can only maintain your standard of living if your income also increases at a similar rate. For your standard of living to *improve*, your income must increase at a greater rate than the inflation rate. Inflation affects your investments as well. If the prices of goods and services rise at a rate of 3 percent, but your savings account is only paying an interest rate of 1 percent, then you are actually losing spending power.

In the United States, inflation is typically measured by the change in the **consumer price index (CPI)**, reported monthly by the Bureau of Labor Statistics. The CPI tracks prices of a representative basket of more than 400 goods and services used by urban households, including food, housing, consumer goods, gasoline, and clothing. **Table 1.2** illustrates the changing costs of various goods and services over the last three decades. Note that while costs have gone up in general, the cost of a college education at a public four-year institution has skyrocketed. Inflation has a serious impact on household budgets, particularly when prices rise faster than wages. You can see the effects of inflation over time by using **Excel Worksheet 1.2** (Personal Financial Planner: Inflation Calculator). Watch **Online Calculator Demonstration Video: Buying Power** to learn more about changes in costs over time.

Depending on various factors, you may experience a larger or smaller change in expenses than the price changes indicated by the CPI. For example, some areas of the country have higher rates of inflation than average, primarily because of higher fuel and housing costs. Housing in high-demand areas of the country is more expensive than housing in less popular locations.

You'll also need different goods and services at different stages in the life cycle. For example, health care costs, which have risen at a much faster rate than the costs of other elements of the CPI, are a bigger component of a retiree's expenses. Housing costs, in contrast, have less importance for retirees, because many of them have paid off their home mortgages. Furthermore, inflation can be particularly problematic for people on fixed incomes. If your retirement income doesn't increase over time, but your expenses do, your standard of living will gradually decline.

The CPI Index in May 2019 was 256.1, compared with 251.6 in May 2018. Normally, when people talk about inflation, they are referring to the *percentage change* in the index, not the

EXCEL WORKSHEET

See **Excel Worksheet 1.2 (Personal Financial Planner: Inflation Calculator)** in **WileyPLUS**.

ONLINE CALCULATOR DEMONSTRATION VIDEO

See **Online Calculator Demonstration Video: Buying Power** in **WileyPLUS**.

TABLE 1.2   **Changes in Income and Prices over Time**

Year	Median Household Income	Gallon of Gas	Loaf of White Bread	Dozen Grade A Eggs	College Tuition, Fees, Room & Board
1980	$21,023	$1.13	$0.50	$0.88	$ 2,330
1985	27,735	1.15	0.55	0.75	3,680
1990	35,353	1.34	0.69	1.22	4,720
1995	40,611	1.08	0.77	0.88	6,620
2000	50,732	1.39	0.91	0.98	8,080
2005	56,194	2.19	1.05	1.35	11,380
2010	61,521	3.02	1.39	1.77	15,240
2015	58,476	2.77	1.46	1.96	18,930
2019	62,786*	2.90	1.29	1.36	21,370
% Increase					
1980 to 2019	199%	157%	158%	55%	817%
Annual Rate	2.8%	2.4%	2.5%	1.1%	5.8%

Sources: U.S. Census Bureau, U.S. Bureau of Labor Statistics, trends.collegeboard.org.

* Estimated from most recent reported census data.

index number itself. To calculate the percentage increase over a period of time, you can use either form of **Equation 1.1**:

$$\text{Percentage change} = \frac{\text{New value} - \text{Old value}}{\text{Old value}} \tag{1.1}$$

$$\text{Percentage change} = \frac{\text{New value}}{\text{Old value}} - 1$$

Thus, we can calculate inflation between 2018 and 2019 as follows:

$$\text{Percentage change} = \frac{256.1 - 251.6}{251.6} = 0.018, \text{ or 1.8 percent}$$

If you're looking at changes over several years, you may want to convert the percentage change to an *annual percentage change* for the time period, as given in **Equation 1.2**:

$$\text{Annual percentage change} = (1 + \text{Percentage change})^{1/N} - 1 \tag{1.2}$$

$$\text{where } N = \text{Number of years}$$

Being able to calculate percentage change is useful not only for calculating inflation but also for calculating percentage increases in your salary and investments over time. **Demonstration Problem 1.1** gives you an opportunity to try this type of calculation.

Although inflation has averaged less than 4 percent per year since 1980, the annual rates of inflation have ranged from close to zero to more than 13 percent. Over that same period, the federal minimum wage rate increased from $1.60 to its current rate of $7.25, the equivalent

DEMONSTRATION PROBLEM 1.1 | Calculating Percentage Change

Problem

Your starting salary in Year 1 was $24,000, and your new salary for Year 3 is $27,500. What is the percentage change in your salary since you started working, and what is the annual percentage change?

Strategy

Use either form of Equation 1.1 to calculate the percentage change, and use Equation 1.2 to calculate the annual percentage change.

Solution

Calculate the percentage change by using either form of Equation 1.1—for example, as follows:

$$\text{Percentage change} = \frac{\text{New value} - \text{Old value}}{\text{Old value}}$$

$$= \frac{27,500 - 24,000}{24,000} = 0.1458, \text{ or } 14.58\%$$

Calculate the annual percentage change using Equation 1.2, with N equal to 2 (the number of years since you started working):

$$\text{Annual percentage change} = (1 + \text{Percentage change})^{1/N} - 1$$
$$= (1 + 0.1458)^{1/2} - 1$$
$$= 1.0704 - 1$$
$$= 0.0704, \text{ or } 7.04\%$$

Note: Most calculators will allow you to raise a number to any power using the key labeled y^x. Enter the number you want to raise to the power (for example, enter 1.1458), push the y^x button, and then enter the power (for instance, 1/2 or 0.5).

of only 3.9 percent per year. These statistics illustrate an important economic reality—wages don't always keep up with prices. This is particularly true during periods of high inflation. Fortunately, inflation has been fairly low over the last decade, and many states have taken action to increase the minimum wage above the federal requirement.

> **Reflection Question 2**
>
> In what ways do you expect that inflation will affect you in the next few years? Which of your expenses do you expect to increase at a faster rate than others?

Interest Rates

An **interest rate** is a cost of money. Interest is usually expressed as a percentage of the amount loaned or borrowed. When you *borrow* money, the interest rate is a cost to you. When you *invest* money, the interest is a measure of your earnings, or return, on that investment. When interest is earnings to you, it's a cost to whoever is paying you.

An interest rate can also be thought of as a cost of consumption. How much additional money will you need to receive in the future to be willing *not* to spend a certain amount today on consumption? For example, if your roommate asks you to lend him $1,000 and promises to pay you back exactly one year from now, how much will you require him to pay you at that time? If you would have to take the money out of a savings account that pays you 2 percent interest per year, you would probably want him to pay you at least the $1,000 plus the interest you would have earned. But what if lending him the money means that you will have to forgo that trip to Mexico over spring break? How much additional money in the future will it take to convince you to give up spending the money on the trip?

Like the prices of goods and services, interest rates are driven by supply and demand. When there is a lot of demand for borrowing, but not a lot of money available to borrow, interest rates go up. In recessions, when businesses do not need or want to invest in growth, the demand for borrowing is lower, and interest rates may go down.

In the United States, the **Federal Reserve** (commonly called the Fed) is the central banking system. The Fed controls the money supply in the economy in order to manipulate the rate of interest. For example, from 2008 to 2018, the Federal Reserve kept the **federal funds rate**, the rate that banks charge each other for short-term loans, near zero in an attempt to stimulate the economy out of recession. This kept business and mortgage loan rates at historic lows, making it easier for businesses to expand and people to buy homes. When the economy looked like it was on track for recovery, the Fed gradually took action to push interest rates up to more normal levels.

As you can see in **Figure 1.5**, the interest rates on different types of borrowing tend to track each other and the inflation rate. This occurs because they are all affected similarly by economic conditions.

Although the ups and downs in interest rates tend to track each other, there are always differences in interest rates on different types of loans at any given time. Why are some rates higher than others? The higher the risk of nonpayment, the higher the rate charged by lenders. Lenders consider the risk that payments will be late or that the loan will not be repaid. They also consider whether they have any way of collecting from borrowers if loans are not repaid as agreed. For example, credit card rates are always higher than car loan rates or home loans because the bank has the right to take back the car or the house in the event of nonpayment.

The Economy and the Job Market

Your personal finances will also be affected by cyclical business and employment conditions. Historically, the U.S. economy has experienced a pattern of ups and downs, commonly referred to as the **economic cycle**, or business cycle. A low point in the cycle is called a **recession** (or, in the extreme, a depression) and is characterized by reduced business investment and high unemployment rates. Recent recessions are indicated on Figure 1.5 by shaded areas. Although most of the recessions have been fairly short, lasting only a few months, the recession that

FIGURE 1.5 **Inflation, Federal Funds Rate, and 30-Year Mortgage Rates, 1980–2019** This graph compares the 30-year mortgage rate, the federal funds rate (usually one of the lowest interest rates in the economy), and inflation. You can see that, even though rates changed a lot over the last three decades, all three rates tracked up and down together. The shaded periods on the graph indicate recessions.

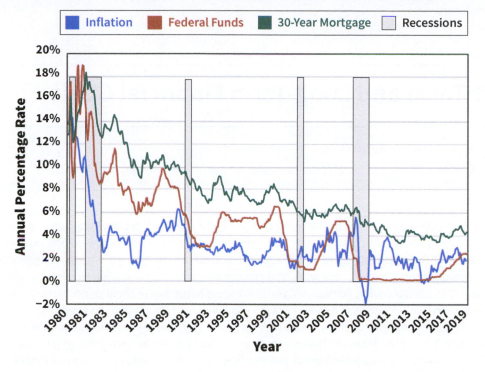

occurred between December 2007 and June 2009 lasted longer than average and is commonly referred to as the "Great Recession."

Periods of economic **expansion** are characterized by increased business investment and employment opportunities. In times of growth and low unemployment, salaries tend to rise more quickly, and there are better opportunities for advancement. Your future will be less sensitive to changes in employment conditions if you choose an area of study that is likely to have continuing strong demand over time. You can also minimize the risk of layoff by keeping your skills up-to-date.

Political Unrest and Global Issues

It should be obvious that political and global factors can affect your personal finances. The continuing threat of terrorism, the aftermath of the 2008 financial crisis and the Great Recession, ongoing uncertainty in the global marketplace for oil, political disagreements about immigration, and tariffs on foreign goods are all important issues that impact personal finances.

Here are some other examples of how political and global factors have affected college students and U.S. households in recent years:

- Interest rates on student loans and car loans have been low, due to the Federal Reserve's actions after the financial crisis, but are likely to rise as economic conditions improve.

- College tuition has been increasing, particularly at public institutions, which were subject to increasing costs and significant recession-related budget cuts by state legislatures.

- Changing immigration rules have impacted both undocumented students and exchange students from other countries.

- Families of military personnel have faced unexpected financial burdens due to repeated and lengthy deployments overseas.

- Due to the global oversupply of oil, gas prices have been low by historical standards, resulting in more money in consumers' pockets.

Because no one can predict what the future may hold, it is extremely important to have a financial plan that is adaptable to changing circumstances. In addition, you should attempt to keep informed on changing economic conditions—reading the newspaper regularly or subscribing to a news or financial magazine—so that you can take appropriate actions when necessary.

1.3 | Setting Short-Term and Long-Term Financial Goals

LEARNING OBJECTIVE 1.3
Create a prioritized list of short-term and long-term personal financial goals.

Have you ever noticed how a whole day can go by and you don't get anything accomplished? When you were a child, that was the best kind of summer day—nothing to do and no one to answer to. But now that you're an adult, and a student as well, you have many obligations—homework, housekeeping, yard work, and grocery shopping, to name a few. You have a million things you *should* do, but sometimes, you don't seem to get any of them done. In many cases, the reason that nothing gets done is because you didn't *plan* for anything to get done.

For many college students who are nearing graduation, one of the tasks that too easily slips to the bottom of the list is the job search. Even in a bad job market, students who invest a lot of effort in looking for a job are more likely to be employed at graduation. You can reduce the likelihood of having to move back in with your parents if you put more time into your job search and bolster your résumé with internships and volunteer activities.

Why Goals Are Important

For most people, the key to successfully accomplishing a set of tasks is to establish a set of specific goals and then to persistently plug away at achieving them. Have you ever looked at what some people accomplish on a regular basis and wondered if they somehow have more than 24 hours in a day? Such high productivity is just proof of the old saying "The more you do, the more you *can* do." Unfortunately, the opposite is also true—if you *don't* do much, you won't get much done. The reason these statements are both true is that people who are very busy have no choice but to be organized in using their time and setting their objectives. And as they succeed in their short-term endeavors, they find themselves motivated to do even more.

Those of you who are athletes can appreciate the importance of goals better than anyone else. Whether you're a runner, a body builder, or a member of a sports team, you know that success in athletics requires setting goals and making a plan to achieve those goals: running a little farther each day, bench-pressing a few more pounds, or increasing speed, endurance, and accuracy in your chosen sport. Small successes each day add up to large successes in the long run.

Achieving financial success requires a similar approach. Without some specific goals, it's very easy to get nothing accomplished. But if you have a prioritized list of specific goals with measurable outcomes and a plan for how to achieve them, you'll be able to make progress toward financial success.

The Goal-Setting Process

Although goals are an essential component of everyone's personal financial plan, there is no magic formula for identifying and prioritizing your goals. No one can set your goals for you, because they are unique to you and your household. However, most people's lists will have certain features in common. Categories that you may want on your list include:

- Consumer spending and borrowing
- Career advancement
- Education for yourself, your spouse, and your children
- Home purchase and maintenance
- Risk management
- Retirement planning
- Vacations and recreation
- Charitable giving
- Estate planning

Financial planning experts recommend that goals be specific, measurable, attainable, realistic, and time-specific. These characteristics are easy to remember because their first letters spell out the word SMART. **Figure 1.6** provides some guidelines to follow to help you develop SMART goals.

FIGURE 1.6   **SMART Goals: Guidelines**   The key to setting effective financial goals is to make them specific, measurable, attainable, realistic, and time-specific.

⑤ pecific

Clearly identify what you want to achieve, including the who, what, where, when and why. Instead of just setting a general goal to save up to buy a house, you could set this specific goal: Save $400 per month to accumulate $20,000 for a down payment on a house within five years.

Ⓜ easurable

How will you know if you have accomplished a goal? State each goal with a target so that you can measure progress, whether in money terms or by completion of certain activities. Example: Have your savings automatically deposited to a designated account. As you get your bank statements each month, you'll be able to track your progress.

Ⓐ ttainable

Setting impossible goals will only lead to discouragement. Evaluate your personal finances to determine what goals are within your means and time frame. Example: If you currently are barely able to cover necessary expenses, you can't set a goal to save $300 a month for your child's college fund. But you could set a goal of seeking a better-paying job or taking a second job to obtain funds to save.

Ⓡ ealistic

Your goals need to be set with your current circumstances in mind. Everyone has existing demands on their time and money, so new goals require difficult choices. Example: Setting a goal of going to graduate school full-time might not be realistic when you are supporting a family, but going part-time at night could be.

Ⓣ ime-specific

When you set goals with specific due dates, they are much more effective. Our natural inclination is to put off difficult tasks, so we need to set near-term and long-term targets to be sure we stay on track. Example: I will pay off my $2,000 credit card balance within two years by paying $100 more than the minimum payment each month.

FIGURE 1.7 **Process of Developing Personal Financial Goals** Follow these steps to identify and prioritize your financial goals.

Make a wish list. ●━━━━━━━━━━━━━━━━━━● Be specific and state in positive terms: "I will…." Include projected dates and a rough estimate of cost, in money and/or time.

Prioritize your list. ●━━━━━━━━━━━━━━━━━━● It's unlikely you'll be able achieve everything, so you need to decide which goals are most important to you and your family.

Break large goals into subgoals. ●━━━━━━━━━━━● You'll be more likely to stick to your plan if you can see progress more quickly.

Reevaluate regularly.

Figure 1.7 leads you through a series of steps for developing your personal financial goals: make a wish list, prioritize your list, break large goals into subgoals, and reevaluate your list regularly. After working through the process, you should have your own prioritized list of SMART personal financial goals. These should include:

- *Short-term goals* that can reasonably be accomplished within the next year, such as buying a car or taking a vacation
- *Intermediate-term goals*, like paying off debt or saving for a down payment on a home, which will take up to five years to accomplish
- *Long-term goals* that will take much longer to achieve—retirement funding or saving for your children's education, for example

Your goals will differ depending on your stage in the life cycle and your family makeup. Age, income, marital status, employment, and personal values will all influence your financial objectives. For example, a young couple's primary goal may be to buy their first home, whereas families with children may be more focused on building a college fund. Retired couples may dream of taking a cruise to the Bahamas or setting up a trust for their grandchildren. To give you some ideas, **Table 1.3** suggests several goals in each category with rough estimates of the cost. As you proceed through this course, you'll learn more about how to estimate the costs of attaining certain financial objectives, but a rough measure will be sufficient for now.

EXCEL WORKSHEET

See **Excel Worksheet 1.3** (**Personal Financial Planner: Prioritizing Goals**) in **WileyPLUS**.

Excel Worksheet 1.3 (Personal Financial Planner: Prioritizing Goals) will help you create your own list and prioritize your goals. You'll find that there will have to be trade-offs. The extra costs of having children may keep you from taking an annual vacation to Europe or buying a

TABLE 1.3 **Examples of Goals with Different Time Horizons**

Short-term (less than 1 year)		Intermediate-term (1–5 years)		Long-term (more than 5 years)	
Goal	**Cost**	**Goal**	**Cost**	**Goal**	**Cost**
Vacation	$1,000	Pay off credit cards	$200/month	Comfortable retirement	$1,000,000
Increase life insurance	$500	Down payment on new car	$3,000	Send kids to college	$50,000
Eat out once per week	$50/week	New roof for home	$3,000	Remodel the house	$30,000
Organize finances	–	Graduate school	$5,000/year	Provide for surviving spouse	?
Emergency fund	$40/week	Hire housecleaner	$50/week	Buy vacation home	$50,000
Create budget	–	Down payment on home	$20,000	Leave inheritance for kids	?
Make a will	$150	Learn about investing	–		
Work on career plan	–				

sports car. Your decision to go to graduate school may delay saving for retirement or purchasing a larger house. In some cases, you and your spouse may not agree on the relative priorities of different goals, so it's very important to discuss your list.

Once you have identified your most important goals, you can use **Excel Worksheet 1.4** (Personal Financial Planner: Breaking Large Goals into Subgoals) to break the larger goals into subgoals. **Case Study 1.2** gives a specific example of how a couple used the goal-setting process to help them make an important family decision.

EXCEL WORKSHEET

See Excel Worksheet 1.4 (Personal Financial Planner: Breaking Large Goals into Subgoals) in **WileyPLUS**.

Case Study 1.2

ESB Professional/Shutterstock.com

The Riveras Develop Prioritized Goals

Problem

Rosa and Mateo Rivera are both 34 years old. They have a son, age 14, from Rosa's previous marriage, and they are expecting a baby in the near future. Both currently work outside the home, and with the luxury of two incomes, they haven't worried much about financial planning. Now, though, they are trying to decide whether they can afford to live on one income after the baby is born. What should they do?

Strategy

Mateo and Rosa need to develop a prioritized list of short-term and long-term goals and subgoals. Developing and prioritizing goals will help them consider the costs, benefits, and trade-offs of having Rosa be a stay-at-home parent.

Solution A selected list of the Riveras' financial goals is shown in **Figure 1.8**. Mateo and Rosa have identified goals in all areas of their finances, but their highest priority is for Rosa to stay home with their new baby for a few years. Because they have a few months before the baby will be born, they decide to work on their other short-term goals while she is still working so they will be better able to live on only one income for a while.

FIGURE 1.8   **The Riveras' Financial Goals**   By breaking their larger goals into smaller, more easily completed subgoals, the Riveras increase the likelihood of accomplishing them.

Short-Term Goals

Goal 1. Rosa quits work in 6 months.
    a. Cut down on current expenses.
    b. Save money over the next 6 months.

Goal 2. Establish a household budget.
    a. Create a personal cash flow statement.
    b. Create a personal balance sheet.
    c. Estimate future income and expenses.

Goal 3. Reduce credit card debt.
    a. Calculate how much we need to pay.
    b. Stop using credit cards.
    c. Cut some of our other expenses and apply the money to the credit card debt.

Long-Term Goals

Goal 1. Increase retirement savings.
    a. Learn about tax rules for retirement saving.
    b. Start an IRA for Rosa.
    c. Determine how much we both need to be saving.

Goal 2. Send kids to college.
    a. Learn about college funding options.
    b. Start a college fund for the baby.

For many households, repayment of high-interest debt is an important financial goal. You can use **Table 1.4** to estimate the payments necessary to reduce an existing credit card debt to zero at various interest rates. To determine the amount more precisely using **Excel Worksheet 1.5** (Personal Financial Planner: Monthly Payment Necessary to Pay Off Debt), work through **Demonstration Problem 1.2**.

EXCEL WORKSHEET

See Excel Worksheet 1.5 (Personal Financial Planner: Monthly Payment Necessary to Pay Off Debt) in **WileyPLUS**.

TABLE 1.4 Monthly Payments Necessary to Pay Off Specific Debt Amounts

Months to Pay	Interest Rate	Monthly Payments Necessary to Pay Off Debt in the Amount of:			
		$1,000	$2,500	$5,000	$10,000
12	12%	$89	$222	$444	$888
	15%	90	226	451	903
	18%	92	229	458	917
	21%	93	233	466	931
24	12%	47	118	235	471
	15%	48	121	242	485
	18%	50	125	250	499
	21%	51	128	257	514
36	12%	33	83	166	332
	15%	35	87	173	347
	18%	36	90	181	362
	21%	38	94	188	377
48	12%	26	66	132	263
	15%	28	70	139	278
	18%	29	73	147	294
	21%	31	77	155	310
60	12%	22	56	111	222
	15%	24	59	119	238
	18%	25	63	127	254
	21%	27	68	135	271
72	12%	20	49	98	196
	15%	21	53	106	211
	18%	23	57	114	228
	21%	25	61	123	245

DEMONSTRATION PROBLEM 1.2 | What Monthly Payment Is Necessary to Pay Off Your Debt?

Problem

You have accumulated $4,000 in credit card debt, and although you've been making the minimum payments, you haven't been able to reduce the overall debt significantly. Your credit card interest rate is 18 percent per year. How much do you need to pay each month to eliminate the debt in two years?

Strategy

Use Excel Worksheet 1.5 to solve for the necessary monthly payment, given the amount of debt you want to repay, the number of months, and the interest rate on the debt.

Solution

As shown in the sample worksheet in **Figure 1.9**, you can enter information about your debt, including the balance owed ($4,000), annual interest rate (18 percent), and time in which you want to repay the debt in full (24 months). The worksheet solution tells you that you will need to pay about $200 per month to reduce your $4,000 debt to zero within 24 months.

FIGURE 1.9 Sample of Excel Worksheet 1.5: Monthly Payment Necessary to Pay Off Debt

	A	B	C	D	E	F	G	H	I
1			Debt #1		Debt #2		Debt #3		Totals
2	Creditor name		Credit card debt						
3									
4	Balance owed	PV	$4,000						$4,000
5									
6	Number of months to repay	N	24						
7									
8	Annual rate on the debt (APR)	I/YR	18%						
9									
10	Monthly payment	PMT	$199.70						$199.70
11									

1.4 # Selecting Qualified Financial Planning Professionals

LEARNING OBJECTIVE 1.4

Know when and how to find qualified financial planning professionals.

Although a course in personal financial planning will provide you with the basic tools and knowledge to handle many aspects of your finances, you will by no means be an expert when you have completed the course. Many areas of personal finance, such as tax and estate planning, are fairly specialized and have complex rules that change over time.

As your life and finances become more complicated, you may need to consult with experts about some issues. Fortunately, you have many choices. Lawyers, accountants, insurance agents, and stockbrokers can all assist with aspects of your financial plan that are within their areas of expertise. Alternatively, rather than obtaining piecemeal help for a single issue at a time, you may want to hire a financial planner who has a broad education in all areas of financial planning. This type of professional can help you develop your plan from the outset and implement strategies to achieve your financial goals. Because virtually anyone can claim to be a financial planner, you'll need to carefully evaluate the educational credentials and certifications of any professional you are considering hiring. If you do consider hiring a financial planner, you can use interview questions similar to those in **Excel Worksheet 1.6** (Personal Financial Planner: Questionnaire for Interviewing a Financial Planner).

> **EXCEL WORKSHEET**
>
> See **Excel Worksheet 1.6** (**Personal Financial Planner: Questionnaire for Interviewing a Financial Planner**) in **WileyPLUS**.

When Do You Need a Financial Planner?

Not everyone needs—or can afford—the services of a professional financial planner. A person who earns less than $50,000 a year, has little accumulated wealth, and has relatively uncomplicated taxes probably doesn't need to hire a professional. Even those with greater wealth and income may prefer to manage their own finances, hiring professionals only for special needs, such as drawing up legal documents or filing taxes.

Some people find that hiring a professional financial planner offers definite benefits. For wealthier people, if the advice given by the planner results in increased investment earnings or reduced taxes, these gains may offset the planner's fees. For others, the benefits may be largely psychological, because hiring a professional reduces the time and effort required to stay informed about financial matters such as investments, taxes, and insurance. Even if you hire a planner, though, you'll still have to be involved in the planning process to develop goals and decide among various strategies to achieve them.

The financial planning process followed by professional financial planners is much the same as the personal financial planning process that we outlined at the beginning of this chapter in Figure 1.1. The main difference is that planners have an additional step at the front end—they need to first establish and define the client–planner relationship. Don't be surprised if your first meeting with a planner requires sharing of a lot of information about your financial situation, personal goals, and risk attitudes. The planner can't do a good job for you without this background.

Factors to Consider in Choosing a Planner

In choosing a professional to help you with your personal finances, you should consider:

- Education
- Certification
- Experience
- Reputation
- Fees

Financial planners need a solid knowledge of law, finance, insurance, and tax accounting to ensure that they can handle all the components of your plan. Their education may have come from specific degree or certification programs, or it may have been gained through experience. In addition, any professional who sells financial products is required to pass examinations required by federal and/or state law.

Many organizations provide certifications attesting to the knowledge base of a professional planner, and new certifications are being created all the time. The most well-known certifications and the organizations that sponsor them are summarized in **Table 1.5**.

The best-known and most rigorous certification is the Certified Financial Planner (CFP®) designation. Planners who have a CFP® mark after their names have passed a comprehensive examination covering all the topics considered necessary in the practice of financial planning, and they have at least three years' work experience in the field. To maintain their certification, they must adhere to a rigorous code of ethics and fulfill regular continuing education requirements.

Because the integrity of the profession is essential to its long-term success, the Certified Financial Planner Board of Standards adheres to a stringent code of ethics to promote the highest principles and standards for certified financial planners, applicable to all their interactions with clients and others. Similar standards are required of Certified Public Accountants (CPAs), Chartered Financial Analysts (CFAs), and attorneys. Having a code of ethics doesn't guarantee that all professionals are beyond reproach, but since the penalty for violation is loss of the professional credential, the code helps to minimize the risk of unethical behavior. Common examples of such behavior include steering a client to products and services that generate the highest commissions for the advisor rather than those that are best for the client and encouraging a client to replace existing insurance contracts when there is no net benefit to switching.

How Are Planners Paid?

With so many different types of professionals calling themselves financial planners, it should come as no surprise that there is some variation in the ways in which planners are paid. The two basic methods of compensation are commissions and fees. The most common arrangements are described in more detail here.

- **Fee only**   The planner charges a fee to the client based on services provided. This may be a set fee for a particular service (such as $150 to write a will), or an hourly fee for services rendered ($50–$200 per hour), or a percentage fee (1 percent per year of your investment portfolio).

TABLE 1.5   Financial Planning Organizations and Certifications

Sponsoring Organization	Designation	Requirements					Contact Information
		Courses (#) and Certification	Work Experience	Comprehensive Exam	Ethics Code	Continuing Education	
American Association of Certified Public Accountants	Certified Public Accountant (CPA)	Yes Undergraduate degree	Yes	Yes	Yes	40 hrs per year	www.aicpa.org
	Personal Financial Specialist (PFS)	Self-study	Yes (CPA)	Yes (or CFP, ChFC)	Yes (CPA)	60 hrs per 3 years	
American College	Chartered Financial Consultant (ChFC)	Yes (11)	Yes		Yes	30 hrs per 2 years	www. theamericancollege. edu
	Chartered Life Underwriter (CLU)	Yes (12)	Yes		Yes	30 hrs per 2 years	
	Retirement Income Certified Professional	Yes (3)	Yes		Yes	30 hrs per 2 years	
	Registered Health Underwriter (RHU)	Yes (3)	Yes		Yes	30 hrs per 2 years	
American Institute for CPCUs	Chartered Property and Casualty Underwriter (CPCU)	Yes	Yes	Yes	Yes		www. theinstitutes.org
CFA Institute	Chartered Financial Analyst (CFA)	Yes	Yes	Yes (3)	Yes	20 hrs per year	www.cfainstitute. org
Association for Financial Counseling and Planning Education (AFCPE)	Accredited Financial Counselor (AFC)	Yes (2)	Yes	Yes	Yes	30 hrs per 2 years	www.afcpe.org
CFP® Board of Standards	Certified Financial Planner, CFP®	Yes Undergraduate degree	Yes	Yes	Yes	30 hrs per 2 years	www.cfp.net
College for Financial Planning	Accredited Asset Management Specialist (AAMS)	Yes (1)		Yes	Yes	16 hours per 2 years	www.cffp.edu
	Accredited Wealth Management Advisor (AWMA)	Yes (1)		Yes	Yes	16 hours per 2 years	
	Chartered Retirement Planning Counselor (CRPC)	Yes(1)		Yes	Yes	16 hours per 2 years	
	Chartered Mutual Fund Counselor (CMFC)	Yes (1)		Yes	Yes	16 hours per 2 years	
Financial Industry Regulation Authority (FINRA)	Series 6 (Mutual Funds and Var. Annuities Representative)		Yes	Yes		Regulatory update every 3 years	www.finra.org
	Series 7 (General Securities Representative)		Yes	Yes		Regulatory update every 3 years	
International Association of Registered Financial Consultants	Registered Financial Consultant (RFC)	AAMS, CFA, CFP, ChFC, CLU, CPA, EA, JD	Yes		Yes	40 hrs per year	www.iarfc.org
Investment Management Consultants Association	Certified Investment Management Analyst (CIMA)	Yes	Yes	Yes		40 hrs per 2 years	www.imca.org
National Association of Personal Financial Advisors	Registered Financial Advisor (RFA)		Yes (must be fee-only planner)	Case or financial plan	Yes	60 hours 2 years	www.napfa.org
National Association of Estate Planners and Councils	Accredited Estate Planner, AEP	Yes (2) +JD, CFP, CPA, CFA, CLU, or ChFC	Yes		Yes	30 hrs per 2 years	www.naepc.org

- **Fee-based**   The planner can charge fees for services, as in the fee-only example, but also can receive commissions for selling you investment and insurance products.

- **Commission only**   The planner receives no payment for helping you develop your financial plan or managing your portfolio, but receives a commission when you buy or sell a financial product, such as mutual fund shares or an insurance policy. Although this may be the cheapest way to get a professional to help you with your financial plan, the planner has an inherent conflict of interest. That is, the planner may have an incentive to sell you high-commission products or to buy and sell more often than necessary. You must take this possibility into account before acting on the planner's recommendations.

- **Fee plus commission**   The planner charges a fee for developing your financial plan and also receives commissions on any financial products sold to you. The fee for the plan may be lower than that charged in a fee-only arrangement.

- **Fee offset by commission**   The planner charges a fee for services, as in a fee-only arrangement, but reduces the fee if commissions are later earned on products purchased by the client. This reduces the conflict of interest inherent in the commission-only arrangement, because the planner does not make extra money by selling you the financial products.

1.5 | Making Effective Decisions

> **LEARNING OBJECTIVE 1.5**
>
> Consider opportunity costs and marginal effects in making personal finance decisions.

As you work on your financial plan, you'll be making many important decisions. Once you've identified your goals, you'll need to make decisions about consumption, education, savings, and investment alternatives. These decisions will help you achieve your goals more effectively if you use these decision-making strategies:

- Base your decisions on reasonable assumptions.
- Apply marginal reasoning.
- Consider opportunity costs.
- Use sensitivity analysis.

In this section, we'll examine each of the strategies in more detail.

Make Reasonable Assumptions

Most financial decisions require you to forecast, or predict, future events and economic circumstances: What will your needs be 5, 10, or 20 years from now? What will your family circumstances require from you financially? When will you retire? How long will you live? Which investments will perform better over time? What will the rate of inflation be in the future? What rate of return will you earn on your investments? What kinds of risks will you face?

Life is, of course, unpredictable. But even if you don't know an outcome with certainty, you can still use available information to come up with a reasonable assumption. Being able to make reasonable assumptions is a critical component of successful decision making.

One of the biggest mistakes people make in their finances is that they are too optimistic in their assumptions. After the recession that ended in 2009, for example, the stock market enjoyed a long period of strong growth. Investors who had never experienced a market downturn thought their investments would continue to earn high rates of return indefinitely. The following example illustrates the impact this flawed reasoning had on a married couple nearing retirement during that period.

Karen and Luke Amato were planning to retire at the end of 2018, when both would reach the age of 65. Through regular monthly contributions to Luke's retirement plan at work, they had invested 4 percent of Luke's salary in the stock market throughout his working career. By mid-2018, the Amatos reached their retirement savings goal of $1 million, an amount that they believed would allow them to maintain their standard of living in retirement. But late in 2018, investment values plummetted, and the Amatos' savings were substantially reduced. **Figure 1.10** shows the value of their portfolio beginning in 2009 after the financial crisis and going through the end of 2018. Although the 2018 market downturn was not as bad as the one in 2008, the Amatos' nest egg decreased by $200,000 in the last three months of 2018.

Although the Amatos probably could have limited their losses by having a more diversified portfolio or by moving their money out of stocks at the first sign of trouble, they, like many other investors, had unrealistically clung to the hope that the stock market would recover. As a result of their overly optimistic assumptions, they had to retire a year later than originally planned.

Apply Marginal Reasoning

In choosing among potential strategies to achieve your financial goals, it is important to apply **marginal reasoning**. The term "marginal" refers to the *change* in outcome, or the *additional* benefit or cost, that will result from the decision you make. For example, suppose you and your spouse share a car, and you're considering buying a second car. In applying marginal reasoning, you will consider only the additional benefits that the second car brings and not the general benefits of having a car in the first place. Similarly, if you're choosing between two possible cars, you'll consider how much *extra* benefit you would get from the more expensive of the two and balance that against the extra cost.

FIGURE 1.10 **The Amatos' Retirement Fund (Invested 100% in Stocks)**   The Amatos optimistically assumed that strong stock market performance after the Financial Crisis would continue indefinitely.

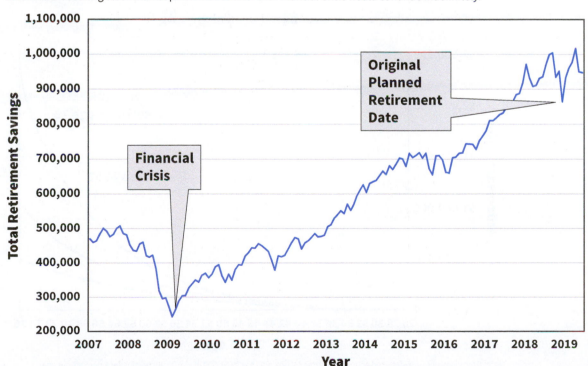

Consider Opportunity Costs

Every financial decision you make has an **opportunity cost**—a measure of what you have to give up in order to take a particular action. The opportunity cost often is measured in dollars but may also include less quantifiable costs, like your time and effort. For example, suppose you must decide whether to take money from savings for your college education or to work while attending school to earn the money. If you choose to take money from savings, you'll be giving up what you could have earned on that investment—this is a quantifiable opportunity cost. Other types of opportunity costs might be less tangible. For example, if you decide to work while attending school instead of taking money from savings, your cost will be the time you spend working instead of studying or taking part in other activities. Evaluating opportunity costs carefully results in better decisions.

Use Sensitivity Analysis

Suppose you are deciding on the purchase of a new home. Although the loan payment will be a bit of a stretch for you the first year, you anticipate getting a good raise next year, which will make the payment affordable. But what if this assumption is wrong—what if you do *not* get the raise or, even worse, are laid off from your job?

    Sensitivity analysis asks the question "What effect would it have on my personal finances if my assumptions turn out to be wrong?" By considering the outcomes under different assumptions, you can reduce the risk that your plan will have an unexpected impact on your finances.

    Sensitivity analysis can often be illustrated with a table or graph, showing the results under different sets of assumptions. For example, **Figure 1.11** shows the growth of a retirement portfolio over time under different assumptions about the rate of return on investment. Suppose you have decided that you need $1 million to retire. The figure shows that you might be able to retire at age 67 or you might have to wait until age 75, depending on how well your investments do. Alternatively, you could invest more money each year to reach your $1 million goal sooner.

FIGURE 1.11 **Sensitivity of Investment Portfolio to Rate-of-Return Assumptions** The greater your return on investment, the quicker you can reach your financial goals.

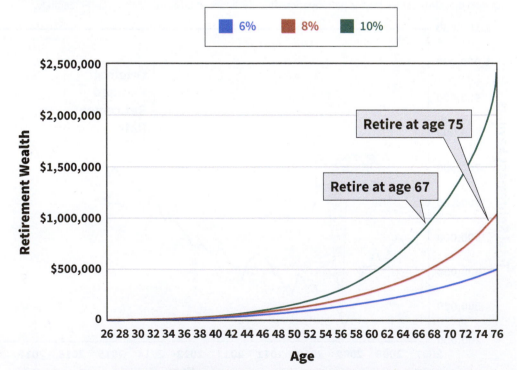

Note: Graph assumes tax-deferred annual investments, beginning with $1,500 at age 25, increasing by 4 percent per year.

TABLE 1.6   **Decision-Making Styles**

Type of Decision Maker	Common Characteristics
• Rational decision maker	• Uses a systematic approach to making decisions • Weighs the pros and cons, often making careful lists for comparison
• Intuitive decision maker	• Spontaneous • Often makes "gut" decisions
• External decision maker	• Obtains opinions and confirmation from others before making decisions • Has trouble making decisions independently
• Agonizer	• Puts off making decisions as long as possible • Spends a lot of time thinking over alternatives, even for relatively inconsequential decisions • Is uncomfortable with change
• Avoiders	• Can't or won't make decisions • Delegates decision to others or ignores the problem, hoping it will go away

Decision-Making Styles

People exhibit different decision-making styles, and many of them result in less than optimal outcomes. Your style of decision making can have a big impact on how you approach your finances and on whether you are likely to get into financial trouble. Even if you are naturally inclined to make suboptimal financial decisions, you can still learn to apply the strategies and tools discussed in this section and throughout this course in order to make more effective decisions.

Psychologists often classify people on a continuum based on how they approach and solve problems. Some people have a natural inclination to think through decisions carefully before they take action, whereas others tend to make snap decisions without carefully considering the alternatives or the consequences. There are also people who prefer to avoid making decisions as much as possible. Several decision-making styles are described in **Table 1.6**. You can take the assessment in **Interactive: What is Your Financial Decision-Making Style?** to help determine which one best describes you.

Although no method of decision making is perfect for everyone, there are advantages and disadvantage to each type. If you're an avoider or if you're overly spontaneous in making financial decisions, you may have trouble sticking to a budget, have too much debt, pay too much for major purchases, or incur personal costs from taking too many wrong turns in life. If you're an overly "rational" decision maker or an agonizer, you may also suffer negative consequences. Taking too long to make a decision can result in reduced investment returns, missed career advancement opportunities, and increased personal costs.

INTERACTIVE

You can assess your own financial decision-making style using **Interactive: What is Your Financial Decision-Making Style?** in **WileyPLUS.**

Reflection Question 3

Based on your decision-making style, which aspects of financial planning are likely to be most difficult for you and why? What strategies could you use to overcome your difficulties?

Summary

Learning Objectives Review

LEARNING OBJECTIVE 1.1   Describe the personal financial planning process, and explain how the elements of a comprehensive financial plan fit together.

Personal finance is the study of individual and household financial decisions. It includes such topics as budgeting, saving, tax planning, financing major purchases, buying insurance, and investing to achieve long-term goals.

- The **personal financial planning** process includes five steps: (1) Organize your financial information and set short-term and long-term goals, (2) analyze your current financial status, (3) identify and evaluate alternative strategies for achieving your goals, (4) implement your financial plan, and (5) monitor your progress and revise your plan as needed.

- To build a comprehensive financial plan, you need to (1) establish a firm foundation by acquiring necessary tools and skills; (2) secure your basic needs for security and liquidity though sound management of cash, credit, and insurance; and (3) develop a long-term plan for building and protecting wealth through saving, investing, insurance, and estate planning.

LEARNING OBJECTIVE 1.2   Describe how individual characteristics and economic factors influence personal financial planning.

Personal financial planning decisions are affected by both individual characteristics and general economic conditions.

- Individual characteristics that influence financial plans include individual differences in life cycle stage, demographic characteristics, and **values** and **attitudes**, including tolerance for **risk**.

- General economic conditions that affect household finances include inflation, interest rates, and economic cycles.

- **Inflation** in prices, which is measured by the annual percentage change in the **Consumer Price Index (CPI)**, can make it more difficult to maintain your standard of living over time. You can calculate the percentage change using **Equation 1.1**:

$$\text{Percentage change} = \frac{\text{New value} - \text{Old value}}{\text{Old value}}$$

$$\text{Percentage change} = \frac{\text{New value}}{\text{Old value}} - 1$$

You can use **Equation 1.2** when you need to convert the percentage change into annual percentage change to make comparisons over different periods:

$$\text{Annual percentage change} = (1 + \text{Percentage change})^{1/N} - 1$$

where N = Number of years

- **Interest rates** determine your cost of borrowing and your rate of investment return. They are strongly influenced by actions of the U.S. **Federal Reserve**, which controls the short-term interest rate called **federal funds rate**. Because this is the rate that banks charge each other for short-term loans, other loan rates, such as car loans and mortgages, are affected by it.

- The U.S. economy varies with stages in the **economic cycle**, which includes periods of **recession** and **expansion** that impact employment conditions and business performance.

LEARNING OBJECTIVE 1.3   Create a prioritized list of short-term and long-term personal financial goals.

Nothing happens without a plan.

- You should develop a list of personal financial goals that are SMART: specific, measurable, attainable, realistic, and time-specific. Your short term, intermediate-term, and long-term goals will change over your life cycle.

- The goal-setting process includes four general steps: (1) make a wish list, (2) prioritize your list, (3) break large goals into manageable subgoals, and (4) reevaluate your goals regularly.

- If your goals include debt reduction, you can use a table or worksheet to estimate the monthly payments necessary to pay off a debt in a specified period of time.

LEARNING OBJECTIVE 1.4   Know when and how to find qualified financial planning professionals.

Although you don't necessarily need professional help for personal financial planning, if you do decide to hire a financial planning professional, you should be sure that the planner fits your needs.

- Evaluation criteria include educational credentials, certifications, experience, reputation, and fee structure.

- A Certified Financial Planner (CFP®) will have completed specific coursework, passed a rigorous examination, and be subject to minimum professional experience and continuing education requirements.

- Financial advisors are compensated through some combination of fees for services rendered and commissions for products bought or sold.

LEARNING OBJECTIVE 1.5   Consider opportunity costs and marginal effects in making personal financial decisions.

You'll be more likely to achieve your personal financial goals if you use effective decision-making strategies.

- Base your decisions on reasonable assumptions.
- Use **marginal reasoning** to weigh the additional benefit to be received from one possible alternative action compared with another.
- In comparing multiple alternatives for achieving the same goal, always consider the **opportunity cost**, whether in time, effort, or money.

- Your decisions will also benefit by the application of **sensitivity analysis**, in which you evaluate what would happen if your initial assumptions are incorrect.

Excel Worksheets

1.1 Personal Financial Planner: Money Attitudes Questionnaire

1.2 Personal Financial Planner: Inflation Calculator

1.3 Personal Financial Planner: Prioritizing Goals

1.4 Personal Financial Planner: Breaking Large Goals into Subgoals

1.5 Personal Financial Planner: Monthly Payment Necessary to Pay Off Debt

1.6 Personal Financial Planner: Questionnaire for Interviewing a Financial Planner

Key Terms

attitudes   1-11
consumer price index (CPI)   1-12
economic cycle   1-14
expansion   1-15
federal funds rate   1-14
Federal Reserve   1-14

inflation   1-11
interest rate   1-14
marginal reasoning   1-25
opportunity cost   1-26
personal finance   1-3
personal financial planning   1-4

recession   1-14
risk   1-11
sensitivity analysis   1-26
values   1-11

WileyPLUS

Practice Questions to check your understanding, Peer-to-Peer Videos, Interactives, and many other resources are available in WileyPLUS.

Concept Review Questions

1. Allen has just graduated from college and is considering the purchase of a new or used car. Describe how Allen can use the personal financial planning process in making this purchase.

2. For each component of a comprehensive financial plan, identify a decision that must be made.

3. Why is it important to establish a firm foundation and secure your basic needs before beginning to invest?

4. Under what circumstances might the Federal Reserve take action to increase short-term interest rates?

5. What are the steps in the goal-setting process?

6. What factors should you consider in selecting a financial planning professional?

7. What are the advantages of using a fee-only planner compared with a commission-based planner?

8. Kenny and Ellen were married during their senior year in college. They planned and saved $3,000 for a honeymoon trip to Europe after graduation. They both have offers for jobs that begin in July. Two months before graduation, they discover that Ellen is pregnant. How might this change in life circumstances affect their current financial plan? If you were in their situation, would you change your honeymoon plans? Why or why not?

9. Identify three areas of your personal financial plan that you expect will change when you graduate from college. For each area, give a specific example.

10. How does your attitude toward risk affect your financial decisions?

11. Give two examples of how general economic conditions can have a beneficial or adverse impact on your personal finances.

12. For a college student who is single, what are two areas of financial planning that are particularly important?

13. For a young married couple with two children under the age of 5, what are two areas of financial planning that are particularly important?

14. For a double-income couple with children in college, what are two areas of financial planning that are particularly important?

15. For a recently retired couple, what are two areas of financial planning that are particularly important?

Application Problems

1. Your school just announced a tuition increase of 20 percent for next year. The annual tuition will increase from $8,000 to $9,600. If you expect that your other college-related expenses will increase with inflation from $10,000 to $10,400, what is the expected percentage increase in your total college costs for next year?

2. If your expenses total $20,000 in Year 1 and you expect the inflation rate to be 3 percent, how much more will you have to spend to buy the same goods and services in Year 2, assuming that all your expenses increase at the same rate as inflation?

3. If the Consumer Price Index rose from 250 to 255 in one year, what was the approximate annual inflation rate for that year?

4. Your starting salary in Year 1 is $30,000. If you receive a raise of $5,000 for Year 2, what is the percentage change in your salary?

5. Use the inflation calculator in Excel Worksheet 1.2 to find out what a $20,000 annual salary in 1983 would have been worth in 2019 dollars.

6. Use the inflation calculator in Excel Worksheet 1.2 to find out what a movie ticket that cost 25 cents in 1970 would have cost in 2019 dollars. Have movie ticket prices increased at a faster or slower rate than other prices?

7. The original Volkswagen Beetle sold for $2,000 in 1970. Assuming that a new Beetle cost $20,000 in 2012, did the price increase more or less than inflation? Use the inflation calculator in Excel Worksheet 1.2 to see what the inflation-adjusted price would have been in 2012.

8. Janelle has asked her friend Danny to drive her to the airport, which is a 60-mile, two-hour round trip, so that she can save the $20 cost of the shuttle bus. Danny will have to miss his personal finance class in order to take her there. If Janelle is willing to pay Danny for this service, should Danny charge her more or less than the cost of the shuttle bus, taking into account his time in addition to the price of gas?

9. Jamal would like to buy a car one year from now. He anticipates making a down payment of $1,200 and borrowing the remaining $10,000. Show how he can break this larger goal into several specific, smaller subgoals. Be sure to include an estimate of his required monthly allocation of funds to this goal.

10. You have a friend who just graduated from college as a liberal arts major. He has a new job as a financial planner at a local brokerage firm. You are thinking of hiring a professional to help with your financial planning needs. Would your friend be a good choice? Why or why not?

11. Your employer has just given you a 4 percent annual raise. You learned the following two pieces of information: (1) the average raise in the United States for people working in your profession was 3 percent this year, and (2) prices of goods and services, as measured by the national inflation rate, increased 5 percent since last year. Explain how your raise relates to these two pieces of information.

12. Your friend tells you that her only financial goal is to become a millionaire. In what ways does this goal violate the requirements for SMART goals (Specific, Measurable, Attainable, Realistic, and Time-specific)?

13. Fernando owes $10,000 on a credit card that charges 18 percent interest. Use Table 1.4 to determine the monthly payment Fernando will have to make in order to pay back the debt within four years. If Fernando doubled the payment, would he be able to pay off his debt in 2 years? Why or why not?

Case Applications

1. Miranda is a single mother of two, struggling to make ends meet. Her salary of $40,000, after taxes and child-care expenses, doesn't go very far. Miranda is a careful budgeter, and she has been setting aside $40 per month for Christmas presents for her kids. By October, she is proud to have $400 in her savings account. And then disaster strikes. Her car breaks down, and the mechanic tells her the cost of fixing it will be $350. What are Miranda's options? What are some ways that Miranda might lessen the impact of financial emergencies in the future?

2. Sanjay is currently employed as an engineer at a major technology firm and earns $50,000 a year. He thinks that an MBA will increase his chances of being promoted to a management position. He is trying to decide whether to enroll in a part-time evening MBA program that will take two years or in a one-year full-time MBA program.

a. Identify the factors that Sanjay should consider in making this decision.

b. What are the opportunity costs that Sanjay needs to consider?

c. Does Sanjay need any additional information to make an effective decision? If so, what information?

d. How can marginal reasoning be applied to this analysis?

3. Lucy and Desi are expecting their first child. Although they had previously developed a prioritized list of personal financial goals, they expect that their new family circumstances will necessitate some changes.

a. Identify three goals that they are likely to add to their original list.

b. How might their priorities change after the birth of their child?

CHAPTER 2

Financial Planning Tools: Personal Financial Statements and the Time Value of Money

Jupiterimages/Stockbyte/Getty Images
pjmorley/Shutterstock.com

Feature Story

In order to jump-start his financial future, Roberto took his $5,000 student loan and invested it in the stock market. He was excited to have earned 10 percent on his investments in one year. During this time, he used his credit card to pay for $5,000 in school expenses. Unfortunately, Roberto wasn't very good about making his payments on time, and the bank raised the interest rate on his credit card to 22.9 percent.

As you learned in Chapter 1, the first step in the personal financial planning process is to evaluate your current finances. For many people, this step is a stumbling block that prevents them from getting started on their financial plan because they don't know where to start or how to perform the evaluation. Although it may be tempting to avoid this step, you're likely to make some serious mistakes if you do so. In our example, Roberto earned 10 percent on his stock portfolio, but had to pay 22.9 percent on his credit card debt. This means he actually lost money over the year. If Roberto had evaluated his cash flow and developed a budget, he might have been able to find a way to invest in the stock market (although on a much smaller scale) and avoid building up so much debt. He would also have better understood that his focus should be on building his net worth, not just his stock account balance.

Roberto mistakenly focused his attention on one component of his financial plan, while ignoring other important steps in the process. This chapter describes many of the tools you'll need to establish a strong foundation for your financial plan so that you can avoid making the same kind of mistake. You'll learn how to organize your financial information and evaluate your current finances by developing personal financial statements and using financial ratios. The chapter also introduces a key concept in financial planning—the time value of money. You'll be able to estimate how much money you'll need in the future for specific purposes and how much it will cost you now. In later chapters, you'll apply all these tools to achieve your spending, saving, and investing goals.

LEARNING OBJECTIVES	TOPICS	DEMONSTRATION PROBLEMS
2.1 Develop a system for financial record keeping, and prepare a personal balance sheet.	**2.1 Organizing Your Financial Information** • What Financial Records Do You Need to Keep? • Summarizing Your Financial Condition	**2.1** Calculation of Net Worth
2.2 Prepare a personal cash flow statement, and evaluate your financial situation using financial ratios.	**2.2 Evaluating Your Personal Financial Situation** • The Personal Cash Flow Statement • Net Cash Flow • Using Financial Ratios	
2.3 Explain how compound interest benefits investors.	**2.3 The Time Value of Money** • The Power of Compound Interest • Time Value of Money Calculation Methods • Future Value: How Much Will My Money Grow?	**2.2** Calculating the Future Value of a Lump Sum **2.3** Calculating the Future Value of an Annuity (Series of Equal Payments)
2.4 Calculate present value of funds to be received or paid in the future.	**2.4 Present Value: How Much Do I Need Today to Reach a Future Goal?** • Present Value of a Lump Sum • Present Value of an Annuity • Loan Payments	**2.4** Calculating the Present Value of a Lump Sum **2.5** Calculating the Present Value of an Annuity **2.6** Estimating Student Loan Payments

2.1 | Organizing Your Financial Information

LEARNING OBJECTIVE 2.1
Develop a system for financial record keeping, and prepare a personal balance sheet.

In this section, you'll learn how to organize your financial records and use the information they contain to summarize your current financial condition.

What Financial Records Do You Need to Keep?

Although some people simply love to file and organize, most of us do not. The older you get, the more "stuff" you're likely to accumulate. If you save every piece of paper sent to you by all of your creditors and service providers, you'll eventually have to build on a room in your house to fit it all. The earlier you can develop a system for organizing your financial records, the easier it will be to maintain order as your life becomes more complex.

Will You Need Them in the Future?

The first rule of organization is that there should be a particular purpose for everything you save and file. Although this list is not exhaustive, some possible reasons for keeping particular documents include the following:

- Paying bills
- Tracking your budget
- Preparing tax returns
- Making investment decisions
- Making insurance or warranty claims
- Ensuring prompt access to essential records
- Proving ownership of assets

How Long Should You Keep Them?

You don't have to keep financial records forever. How long you should save each item depends on what you will use it for. Documents that are necessary for bill paying and budgeting have only short-term usefulness. Receipts for ATM withdrawals and deposits and for cash or credit purchases thus need only be saved until you receive a statement verifying that your account was correctly charged. Bills for utilities, telephone, car expenses, and other irregular expenses that are not tax-deductible should be kept for a full year so that you can accurately report the costs in your budget and personal cash flow statements. Any documents that support tax deductions should be filed with your tax records. Although most Internal Revenue Service (IRS) audits occur within three years of the filing of the return, they can also occur later, so it's generally recommended that you keep tax records for seven years to be safe. The IRS audits about 1 percent of individual tax returns, and most audits occur in the first year following filing. Audits in later years are usually the result of irregularities discovered in auditing earlier returns.

Where Should You Keep Them?

You can keep your personal financial documents anywhere, as long as you can easily access them when necessary. A system of file folders kept in a file cabinet or box can be effective and simple, but many people today keep most of their records on their computer. Banks and creditors offer online statements dating back several years, and many creditors offer the option of electronic billing and payment. To ensure that you have easy access to important documents when you need them, you should download and save the files to your computer. The most important advice for financial record keeping: Keep it simple. If your filing system is too complex, you'll probably get behind on your filing.

Important personal documents and valuables, particularly those that are difficult to replace, should be kept in a safe deposit box or fireproof lockbox. A **safe deposit box** is a secure, private storage area (usually a small locking drawer) maintained at a remote location, usually at a financial institution's place of business. Examples of items to be stored in safe deposit boxes include passports, birth and marriage certificates, wills, and deeds. A **lockbox**, which is a fireproof, lockable safe kept in your home, is not as secure as a safe deposit box, because it's usually moveable and may be the first thing thieves look for when they break into a house. The primary purpose of a lockbox is to prevent loss or damage to the contents in the event of a fire. Insurance policies and important family photos are examples of items to be stored in lockboxes.

If you use your home computer for managing your finances, you should regularly back up the information on a remote "cloud" server or on a disk stored in a separate location, such as a friend's house, your place of employment, or a safe deposit box. In the event of theft, fire, electrical outage, or water damage, you need to be sure that your electronic records are safe. The best way to ensure this is to back up your records immediately or have them automatically stored in a cloud whenever you make any major changes to the files, such as when you pay bills or revise your budget.

With so much financial information and transactions being stored or carried out online, it's also a good idea to maintain a record of account numbers, user IDs, and passwords. This information can be kept in a spreadsheet or in a file, but a copy should be kept in a secure location. It's also important that your loved ones know where to find it in the event that something happens to you.

EXCEL WORKSHEET

See **Excel Worksheet 2.1**
(Personal Financial Planner:
My Financial Records) in
WileyPLUS.

You can use **Excel Worksheet 2.1** (Personal Financial Planner: My Financial Records) to organize information about your financial records, including user IDs and passwords for online accounts and information about where your financial records are stored. **Table 2.1** offers examples of which financial documents and records to store and where to store them.

TABLE 2.1   Where Should You Store Financial Records?

Financial Record General Category	Specific Items Within Category	Filed	Lockbox	Safe Deposit
Auto	Insurance policy		x	
	Title information			x
	Repairs and expenses	x		
	Auto loan and lease Information	x		
Bank	Checking statements and records	x		
	Savings statements and records	x		
Credit	Records for each loan or credit account	x		
	Credit reports	x		
	Applications for credit	x		
Home	Mortgage documents and records		x	
	Homeowners insurance policy		x	
	Receipts for repairs and capital improvements	x		
	Rental contracts	x		
Children	Report cards		x	
	School photos		x	
	School policies and procedures manual	x		
	Records of child care expenses	x		
	Birth/adoption certificates			x
Estate planning	Life insurance policies		x	
	Billing records	x		
	Wills		x	x
	Estate planning documents		x	
Medical	Billing and insurance records	x		
	Prescription drug records	x		
	Health insurance policy		x	
	Health/immunization records		x	
Employee benefits	Periodic reports from retirement plans	x		
	Employer information	x		
	Other insurance and benefits	x		
Taxes	Tax statements from employer(s)	x		
	Tax statements from investments and loans	x		
	Tax returns	x	x	
	Receipts for next tax year	x		
Household budget	Current bills payable	x		
	Bill receipts	x		
	Budget records	x		
Investments	Records of purchases and sales		x	
	Account activity statements	x		

Summarizing Your Financial Condition

Once you've collected and organized your financial information, you can use it to help you make better financial decisions. **Personal financial statements** summarize your financial information in a way that makes it easy to see where you stand and to plan for where you want to be in the future. Just as companies report on their financial status to their shareholders, you can use a personal financial statement to make a financial report to yourself. You may need to provide financial information to others as well, such as banks considering your application for a loan or organizations evaluating your qualifications for a scholarship. So having the information organized in advance can be a real time-saver.

How Much Are You Worth Today?

In other words, how wealthy are you? This calculation is a good starting point for financial planning. A **personal balance sheet** is a financial statement that details the value of everything you own and subtracts what you owe to others to arrive at your *net worth*. The things you *own*, such as cash, cars, investment accounts, and real estate, are called **assets**. The amounts you *owe* are called **debts**, or liabilities. Debts can be short-term obligations, such as unpaid bills and credit card debt, or long-term obligations, such as student loans, car loans, and home mortgages. Household net worth is calculated by using **Equation 2.1**:

$$\text{Net worth} = \text{Total assets} - \text{Total debts} \tag{2.1}$$

This calculation is illustrated in **Demonstration Problem 2.1**.

DEMONSTRATION PROBLEM 2.1 | Calculation of Net Worth

Problem

You have $3,000 in a checking account, and you own a car worth $7,000 and a condo valued at $115,000. Your debts total $120,000. What is your net worth?

Strategy

Use Equation 2.1 to calculate your net worth.

Solution

Using Equation 2.1, you can see that your net worth is equal to $5,000. As shown in **Figure 2.1**, your net worth is positive.

$$\text{Net worth} = \text{Total assets} - \text{Total debts}$$
$$= (\$3,000 + \$7,000 + \$115,000) - \$120,000$$
$$= \$5,000$$

FIGURE 2.1   **Positive Net Worth**   Net worth is positive when assets outweigh liabilities.

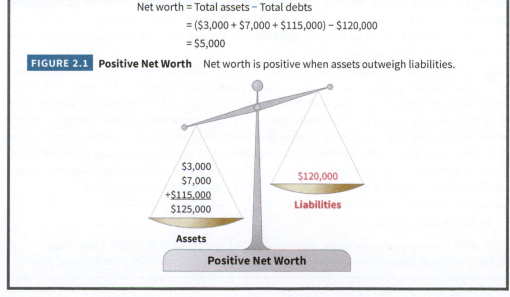

INTERACTIVE

To test your knowledge of asset and debt terminology, go to **Interactive: Which Are Assets?** in **WileyPLUS.**

Net worth is a measure of wealth. If your net worth is positive, it represents how much you would have left over after you've paid off all of your debts. If your net worth is negative, it means that you don't have enough assets to pay off your debts. There is no "magic number" representing the ideal amount of net worth, because it depends on your life cycle stage and personal goals. However, in general, the larger your net worth, the better off you are financially. (For practice in distinguishing assets from debts, see **Interactive: Which Are Assets?**)

Organization of the Personal Balance Sheet

To prepare a personal balance sheet, start by making a list of everything you own, beginning with the most **liquid assets**—cash and near-cash assets that can easily be converted to cash without loss of value—and ending with the least liquid. Checking and savings accounts are examples of liquid assets. In contrast, your home is not very liquid because it cannot be sold quickly.

EXCEL WORKSHEET

See **Excel Worksheet 2.2** (Personal Financial Planner: Personal Balance Sheet) in **WileyPLUS.**

The next step in constructing your personal balance sheet is to make a list of your debts. Similar to how you listed assets from most liquid to least liquid, your debts should be listed from short-term to long term. Start with short-term debts, such as currently unpaid bills, and end with long-term debts, such as your student loans and home mortgage. You can create your own personal balance sheet using **Excel Worksheet 2.2** (Personal Financial Planner: Personal Balance Sheet). The individual line items are explained in more detail below, and you'll see an example of a personal balance sheet later in this section.

Valuing Your Assets and Debts

How do you assign a dollar value to each asset and debt? Your most recent bank financial statements will give you the value of your checking and savings accounts. For other assets, you need an estimate of **market value**, or the price you could sell the asset for today. This is usually not the same as what you paid for the asset. For example, if you just bought a new car, it's already worth less than what you paid. In contrast, you may own some assets that have increased in value since you purchased them. Investments in stocks, bonds, mutual funds, and real estate can increase in value over time.

For some assets, such as your car or home, there may be corresponding debts. If so, enter the market value in the asset section of your balance sheet and the loan balance in the debt section. If you lease a car, your payment obligations are a debt, but you don't own the car, so you shouldn't include it as an asset.

Real estate values are determined by the values of comparable properties in the area, which usually change with time and economic conditions. If you're unsure about recent sales of similar properties, you can consult a real estate professional to help you determine the value of your home or other real estate investment. In general, real estate values increase over time, but during the 2009 recession, housing values in most areas of the country declined, putting many homeowners "under water." Their homes were worth less than the remaining balance of their mortgage. Whenever an asset is worth less than the amount you owe on it, ownership of that asset actually reduces your net worth.

An insurance policy is counted as an asset only if it's a policy that accumulates cash value over time. If you cancel an insurance policy that has a **cash surrender value**, the insurer will return that amount of money to you. Because this is an available source of cash to you, you should count it as an asset. Various types of insurance are explained in more detail in later chapters. At this point, simply note that homeowner's, auto, and health insurance don't accumulate cash value, but some types of disability and life insurance policies may have cash value, as specified by the contract terms. In addition, if you have borrowed against the cash value of an insurance policy, you'll need to include the amount owed as a debt on your personal balance sheet.

> **Reflection Question 1**
>
> In what ways do you expect your balance sheet 10 years from now to differ from your balance sheet today? What goals could you set for this component of your financial plan?

To illustrate the process of creating personal financial statements and using them to evaluate your personal finances, we next look at an example. **Case Study 2.1** introduces Danelle Washington, a college student who is about to graduate and begin her career.

Case Study 2.1

sirtravelalot/Shutterstock.com

Danelle Washington Develops a Balance Sheet

Danelle Washington will graduate in a few months with a major in biology and plans to be a high school teacher. Her parents helped with her first two years of college, but she is now supporting herself with a part-time job, financial aid, and student loans. She knows she needs to do a better job with her personal finances. Her credit card balances have been getting higher, and she's worried about how she'll pay them off in addition to making payments on her student loans.

Problem

Danelle has summarized her financials in a personal balance sheet, provided in **Figure 2.2** below. What is her net worth?

FIGURE 2.2   **Sample of Excel Worksheet 2.2: Danelle Washington's Personal Balance Sheet, December 31**

	A	B	C	D
1	**Assets**		**Debts**	
2	Checking accounts	$ 500	Current bills	
3	Savings accounts	$ 1,000	1. Rent	$ 500
4	Money market accounts		2. Credit cards	$ 150
5	U.S. savings bonds		3. Utilities and other bills	$ 130
6	Cash value of life insurance		**Total current bills**	$ 780
7	Other short-term investments			
8	**Total liquid assets**	$ 1,500	Credit card balances	
9			1. MasterCard	$ 4,200
10	Market value of automobile(s)	$ 5,000	2. JC Penney	$ 1,000
11	Home furnishings	$ 1,200		
12	Jewelry/art/collectibles	$ 500	**Total credit card balances**	$ 5,200
13	Clothing/personal assets	$ 3,000		
14	**Total personal property**	$ 9,700	Alimony/child support owed	
15			Taxes owed (above withholding)	
16	Market value of investments		Automobile loans	$ 3,000
17	Employer retirement plan(s)		Personal loans	
18	Individual retirement account(s)		**Total short-term debts**	$ 3,000
19	Other retirement savings			
20	College savings plan		Home mortgage	
21	Other savings plans		Home equity loans	
22	**Total investment assets**	$ –	Other real estate loans	
23			Student loans	$ 18,000
24	Market value of home		Other investment loans	
25	Market value of investment real estate		Other liabilities/debts	
26	**Total real property**	$ –	**Total long-term debts**	$ 18,000
27				
28	**Total assets**	$ 11,200	**Total debts**	$ 26,980
29				
30			**Net worth =** **Total assets – Total debts =**	$ (15,780)

Strategy

Use Equation 2.1 to calculate Danelle's net worth.

Solution

Danelle has a negative net worth of $15,780:

$$\text{Net worth} = \text{Total assets} - \text{Total debts}$$
$$= \$11,200 - \$26,980$$
$$= -\$15,780.$$

Net Worth and Life Changes

When you're in the accumulation phase of your life cycle, you're developing skills and abilities that will hopefully lead to greater income and wealth in the future. Like Danelle in Case Study 2.1, college students commonly have student loans and car loans, but little in the way of financial investments. Even if it's okay for a short period of your life, your net worth can't stay negative for long without risking **insolvency**—the inability to pay your debts as they come due—and possibly bankruptcy, which is explained in a later chapter.

Unexpected changes in life circumstances, such as an extended illness or loss of a spouse, can also cause net worth to decline. As discussed below, divorce can have serious financial impact, particularly for a stay-at-home spouse. One of the purposes of developing and evaluating personal financial statements is to identify ways to improve your situation so that you can be better prepared to deal with problems. As you proceed through the financial planning process, you should keep this in mind and conscientiously attempt to reduce debt and increase assets over time. **Online Calculator Demonstration Video: Net Worth** will show you how to compare your own situation to others in your age and income group.

ONLINE CALCULATOR DEMONSTRATION VIDEO

See **Online Calculator Demonstration Video: Net Worth** in **WileyPLUS.**

Cash Flow and Balance Sheet Impacts of Divorce

Although the divorce rate has declined from its peak, a substantial percentage of marriages still end in divorce. For most married couples, divorce results in reduced standards of living for both spouses. Consider, for example, the situation faced by Cameron and Annette Worth, who decided to divorce after 15 years of marriage. When their first child was born seven years ago, Annette had quit her job as an executive secretary, and her secretarial skills were somewhat rusty. The best she could hope for without further education was a low-wage job. With very little savings, Annette wasn't sure how she would be able to pay the bills without Cameron's support. His after-tax income is $6,000 per month, and the household expenses, not including saving, total $5,500. After consulting with a divorce attorney, the couple put together the following list of household assets and debts:

The Worths' Household Assets and Debts

Assets	Debts
House: $300,000	Mortgage: $250,000
Cameron's Toyota Prius: $10,000	Car loan on Prius: $5,000
Annette's Honda Odyssey: $15,000	Car loan on Odyssey: $12,000
Cameron's retirement account: $200,000	Credit cards: $10,000
Annette's Roth IRA: $15,000	Cameron's student loan: $15,000
Checking and savings: $3,000	

Two Households Cost More Than One   Cameron's $6,000 take-home pay will not be sufficient to cover the expenses of two households. Even if Annette gets a job, her earnings will be insufficient to maintain the lifestyle she and Cameron enjoyed as a couple. Annette's situation as a nonworking spouse is not unique. If she is the primary custodial parent, she will usually be entitled to child support until the children reach the age of majority and, in some cases, may be awarded a period of alimony. In the meantime, while the courts review their case, household resources could quickly be depleted.

Splitting Up the Assets Although divorce laws differ by state, in the absence of a prenuptial agreement specifying otherwise, most states divide assets fairly evenly between spouses. But because you can't split a house or car, it's up to the parties to decide who should get what. The family home may have to be sold to reduce household expenses. Retirement funds can be split, but will be subject to taxation if money is taken out prior to retirement age.

Special Issues for Women   Although both spouses may suffer financially, recent studies have shown that divorce tends to have a more negative financial impact on women. Divorced women are more likely to be living below the poverty level than other women their age and to be inadequately prepared for retirement. In the process of divorce, women often choose to give up rights to important financial assets, such as employer-sponsored retirement plans and individual retirement accounts (IRAs), in return for keeping the family home and the car, which may have little net value if they are debt-financed.

Given the relatively high incidence of divorce, both husband and wife should take the time to understand their family finances. When one spouse is out of the workforce during child-rearing years, financial planners recommend that they make an effort to maintain job skills. If necessary, a divorce agreement can also be structured to include payment of educational expenses for the nonworking spouse.

2.2 Evaluating Your Personal Financial Situation

> **LEARNING OBJECTIVE 2.2**
> Prepare a personal cash flow statement, and evaluate your financial situation using financial ratios.

An important starting point for improving your financial situation is to carefully evaluate your spending and saving. These two factors have a large impact on your net worth and your future financial well-being. If you consistently spend more than you earn, you'll end up with increasing debt. In contrast, if you're a regular saver, you'll accumulate wealth over time. In this section, we'll identify and explain some methods for getting and keeping your personal finances on track.

The Personal Cash Flow Statement

A **personal cash flow statement** is a financial statement used to evaluate the relationship between your income and your spending. Whereas your personal balance sheet is like a snapshot of your finances at a certain point in time, your personal cash flow statement shows inflows and outflows of cash over a period of time, often one month or one year. In this financial statement, you carefully itemize the amounts of money that come into your household from various sources, as well as the amounts of money that go out over the same period.

The cash flow statement is prepared on a "cash basis," which means that cash flows are recorded when they are received or paid. Thus, if you receive a bill on January 5 but don't pay it until February 1, you will record it as an expense in February, not in January. If certain amounts are deposited directly to or withdrawn directly from your checking account, such as paycheck deposits or car payments, you will record them when they occur.

Cash Inflows

When you create a personal cash flow statement, you should include as *cash inflows* all amounts of money you receive during the period in question. Obviously, you'll include all your employment earnings—wages, salaries, tips, and commissions. But your other sources of income may include one or more of the following:

- Scholarships
- Cash allowances or gifts from your parents or others
- Proceeds from the sale of assets
- Alimony or child support
- Government benefits such as welfare, unemployment, or Social Security payments
- Investment earnings (income from dividends and interest)
- Gambling winnings

Note that you should record your annual **gross income**—that is, income before taxes and expenses. You'll then record the taxes paid during the year as a *cash outflow*.

Cash Outflows

INTERACTIVE

To check your understanding of expenses, see **Interactive: Fixed and Variable Expenses** in **WileyPLUS**.

Whereas income is generally easy to identify and calculate, expenditures are more difficult to track accurately. It's not too hard to identify the big **fixed expenses**—items that are the same from month to month, such as rent and car loan payments. But very few people do a good job of keeping track of their **variable expenses**, such as grocery bills and gas money, even though these can be a big portion of total cash outflows. (See **Interactive: Fixed and Variable Expenses** to check your understanding of fixed versus variable expenses.)

If you spend money primarily by using a debit card or writing checks, it's a little easier to track your cash outflows, because your bank statement and check register are useful sources of information. Alternatively, you can track your expenditures on a daily basis using the spending log provided in **Excel Worksheet 2.3** (Personal Financial Planner: Spending Log). The example shown in **Figure 2.3** tracks spending for a week, but you'll need to do this for at least a month to be sure that you've included even irregular cash outflows. At the end of the time period you have chosen, you can total the amounts entered in your spending log to put into your personal cash flow statement.

EXCEL WORKSHEET

See **Excel Worksheet 2.3** (Personal Financial Planner: Spending Log) in **WileyPLUS**.

FIGURE 2.3 Sample of Excel Worksheet 2.3: Spending Log

	A	B	C	D	E	F
1	Monday		Tuesday		Wednesday	
2	Description	Amount	Description	Amount	Description	Amount
3	Starbucks latte	$ 4.00	Starbucks latte	$ 4.00	Starbucks latte	$ 4.00
4	Gas	$ 60.00	Bookstore	$ 12.00	Rent payment	$ 400.00
5	Lunch	$ 7.50	Lunch	$ 12.00	Snacks	$ 4.00
6	Parking	$ 5.00	Birthday present for Jill	$ 25.00		
7						
8						
9	Total for day	$ 76.50	Total for day	$ 53.00	Total for day	$ 408.00
10						
11	Thursday		Friday		Saturday/Sunday	
12	Description	Amount	Description	Amount	Description	Amount
13	Starbucks latte and donut	$ 6.50	Starbucks latte	$ 4.00	Church offering	$ 5.00
14	Lunch	$ 8.00	Pizza	$ 10.00	Clothes shopping	$ 45.00
15	Netflix bill	$ 8.95	Grocery store	$ 85.00	Movies	$ 10.00
16	Concert ticket	$ 50.00			Dinner	$ 15.00
17						
18						
19	Total for day	$ 73.45	Total for day	$ 99.00	Total for weekend	$ 75.00

Be careful not to alter your normal spending behavior temporarily simply because you're recording everything. Suppose, for example, that you never realized how much money you spent on lattes until you began keeping your spending log. (See **Interactive: It's Just a Latte** to find out how spending on lattes can add up.) Even if you plan to reduce your latte spending in the future, you need to incorporate this expense in your log so that you can more realistically evaluate your *current* finances. At this stage, it's better to be brutally honest with yourself and record all of your spending, regardless of whether you plan to make changes in the future.

INTERACTIVE

To find out how much difference small expenses can make, see **Interactive: It's Just a Latte** in **WileyPLUS.**

Net Cash Flow

Once you've entered and totaled your cash inflows and outflows on the personal cash flow statement, you can calculate your net cash flow using **Equation 2.2**:

$$\text{Net cash flow} = \text{Total cash inflows} - \text{Total cash outflows} \qquad (2.2)$$

We'll illustrate the preparation of a personal cash flow statement in **Case Study 2.2**, which again focuses on Danelle Washington's finances. You can create your own personal cash flow statement using **Excel Worksheet 2.4** (Personal Financial Planner: Personal Cash Flow Statement).

In the case study example, you might be tempted to explain Danelle's negative net cash flow by pointing to her low income. However, you need to look at her spending as well. In addition to taking on more student loan debt, Danelle spent $1,912 more than her cash inflows last year, so these expenditures must have been made on credit. The increased debt resulted in a negative net worth, as we saw earlier.

An interesting economic fact is worth noting here: Those who have more income also tend to spend more. A movie star earning millions of dollars each year likely has more than one extravagant home, entertains lavishly, and buys only designer clothes. But just because that movie star has a high income doesn't mean that her finances are in good shape. There are numerous examples of seemingly well-off people who have had to declare bankruptcy.

EXCEL WORKSHEET

See **Excel Worksheet 2.4** (Personal Financial Planner: Personal Cash Flow Statement) in **WileyPLUS.**

Case Study 2.2

sirtravelalot/Shutterstock.com

Danelle Washington's Personal Cash Flow Statement

Problem

Danelle has reviewed her financial records for the past year and summarized her cash inflows and outflows, as shown in **Figure 2.4**. Last year, she earned $9,500 from a part-time job and received a $1,300 scholarship and gifts of $200. She also took out a student loan in the amount of $6,000. Her total cash inflows are therefore $17,000 for the year. You can see on Danelle's personal cash flow statement that $2,052 for groceries was one of her largest annual expenditures, exceeded only by her rent at $3,600 and her college expenses at $3,996.

What is Danelle's net cash flow?

FIGURE 2.4   Sample of Excel Worksheet 2.4: Danelle Washington's Personal Cash Flow Statement

	A	B	C	D	E	F
1	Cash Inflows			Cash Outflows		
2		Monthly	January to December		Monthly	January to December
3	Salary/wage income	$ 792	$ 9,500	Income and payroll taxes	$ 71	$ 852
4	Interest/dividend income			Groceries	$ 171	$ 2,052
5	Other income (self-employment)			Housing		
6	Net rental income			Mortgage or rent	$ 300	$ 3,600
7	Cash from sale of assets			Property tax		
8	Student loans	$ 500	$ 6,000	Insurance		
9	Scholarships	$ 108	$ 1,300	Maintenance/repairs		
10	Other income			Utilities		
11	Gifts	$ 17	$ 200	Heating	$ 40	$ 480
12	**Total cash inflows**	**$ 1,417**	**$ 17,000**	Electric	$ 25	$ 300
13				Water and sewer		
14				Cable/phone/satellite	$ 15	$ 180
15				Car loan payments	$ 113	$ 1,356
16				Car maintenance/gas	$ 80	$ 960
17				Credit card payments	$ 125	$ 1,500
18				Other loan payments		
19				Other taxes		
20				Insurance		
21				Life		
22				Health	$ 42	$ 504
23				Auto	$ 67	$ 804
24				Disability		
25				Other insurance		
26				Clothing	$ 25	$ 300
27				Gifts	$ 30	$ 360
28				Other consumer goods		
29				Child-care expenses		
30				Sports-related expenses	$ 13	$ 156
31				Health club dues		
32				Uninsured medical expenses	$ 17	$ 204
33				Education	$ 333	$ 3,996
34				Vacations and travel	$ 25	$ 300
35				Entertainment	$ 84	$ 1,008
36				Alimony/child support		
37				Charitable contributions		
38				Required pension contributions		
39				Magazine subscriptions and books		
40				Other expenses		
41				**Total cash outflows**	**$ 1,576**	**$ 18,912**
42						

Strategy

Calculate Danelle's net cash flow using Equation 2.2.

Solution

Net cash flow = Total cash inflows − Total cash outflows

= $17,000 − $18,912

= −$1,912

Using Financial Ratios

Financial ratios provide another important tool for evaluating your financial condition. You can calculate your financial ratios from the information you've collected on your personal financial statements, compare your ratios to recommended targets, and track your ratios over time as a measure of progress toward achieving your financial goals. In this section, we examine ratios designed to measure three aspects of your finances: liquidity, debt management, and savings adequacy. The individual ratios and their calculations will be illustrated using Danelle Washington's financial information.

Measuring Liquidity

If you experience a total loss of income—for example, if you're temporarily disabled or laid off—you may need to meet your expenses without having the regular income that you normally rely on for this purpose. The **liquidity ratio** tells you how many months you could pay your monthly expenses from your liquid assets. This ratio is calculated as shown in **Equation 2.3**:

$$\text{Liquidity ratio} = \frac{\text{Liquid assets}}{\text{Monthly expenses}} \qquad (2.3)$$

For example, Danelle Washington's personal balance sheet (Figure 2.2) shows that her liquid assets—checking and savings accounts—total $1,500. Based on her personal cash flow statement (Figure 2.4), her annual expenses are $18,912, and her monthly expenses total $1,576. Thus, Danelle's liquidity ratio is

$$\text{Liquidity ratio} = \frac{\$1,500}{\$1,576} = 0.95$$

This means that, without her regular income, Danelle could pay less than one month's expenses.

Financial planners often recommend that you have liquid assets sufficient to cover your expenses for three to six months, so liquidity is definitely a concern for Danelle, particularly at the end of the school year, when she has depleted her student loan and scholarship funds. A low liquidity ratio, however, does not necessarily mean that she needs to allocate more funds to liquid assets. She may have other sources of funds that can be tapped in an emergency, such as family loans or credit cards.

Measuring Debt Usage

Everywhere you turn, it seems there's someone inviting you to borrow money to buy something today instead of waiting until you've saved enough to pay cash. Small wonder that one of the biggest financial problems facing U.S. households is that they have too much debt. If your money style is to spend impulsively or if you tend to avoid financial matters altogether, you may already understand the problems associated with credit card debt. Although borrowing money isn't inherently bad, payments made to lenders include interest charge and fees—funds that could be better used to build your wealth, as will be discussed in later chapters.

Financial institutions such as banks and mortgage companies use a variety of debt ratios when they evaluate you for mortgage or car loans. You can use them to evaluate your own debt management. The three ratios explained in this section—the debt ratio, the debt payment ratio, and the mortgage debt service ratio—are the ones most commonly used by financial institutions in their mortgage lending process.

The **debt ratio** measures the percent of your total assets that you've financed with debt. It is calculated as shown in **Equation 2.4**:

$$\text{Debt ratio} = \frac{\text{Total debts}}{\text{Total assets}} \tag{2.4}$$

As your credit card balances increase, so will your debt ratio. This occurs because credit cards are commonly used to purchase consumer goods that add little if any value to your assets. For example, suppose you use a credit card to pay for a $50 dinner for you and a friend. This will cause your debts to increase by $50, but your assets won't increase at all. Therefore, your debt ratio goes up. Your debt ratio will generally decline as you get older, because your investments and home equity will increase in value.

The debt payment ratio and the mortgage debt service ratio measure different aspects of your ability to pay your financial obligations. The **debt payment ratio** estimates the percentage of *after-tax income* that is used to cover required monthly minimum debt payments of all types, including mortgage loans, student loans, car loans, and credit card payments. The debt payment ratio is calculated using **Equation 2.5**:

$$\text{Debt payment ratio} = \frac{\text{Total monthly debt payments}}{\text{After-tax monthly income}} \tag{2.5}$$

Note that this ratio uses *after-tax* income in the denominator, because the purpose is to assess your ability to pay.

To calculate the debt payment ratio for Danelle, you'll need to consult her personal cash flow statement (Figure 2.4). She has after-tax income of $1,346 (calculated as monthly gross income of $1,417 less $71 in income and payroll taxes). Her monthly debt payments total $238 per month ($125 for credit cards plus $113 for her car loan). Using this information, we can calculate Danelle's debt payment ratio as follows:

$$\text{Debt payment ratio} = \frac{\$238}{\$1,346} = 0.177, \text{ or } 17.7\%$$

Danelle's 17.7 percent debt payment ratio is not very high, and this is a good thing. However, she will have to begin paying her student loan a few months after graduation, so a lot more of her after-tax income will have to be used for debt payments in the future.

Rent or mortgage payments are often a household's largest monthly expenditure. The total monthly cost of a mortgage, including the principal and interest paid to the lender, property taxes, and homeowner's insurance premiums, is called the **mortgage debt service**. Mortgage lenders commonly require that borrowers make a single monthly payment to cover all these expenses. Because the lender can lose money if you don't pay your mortgage, it carefully evaluates whether you make enough money to do so. The **mortgage debt service ratio** measures the percentage of your gross income that you pay out in mortgage debt service alone and is calculated using **Equation 2.6**:

$$\text{Mortgage debt service ratio} = \frac{\text{Principal} + \text{Interest} + \text{Taxes} + \text{Insurance}}{\text{Gross monthly income}} \tag{2.6}$$

Since Danelle doesn't have a mortgage, the mortgage debt service ratio does not apply to her situation.

In determining your creditworthiness, lenders commonly compare your ratios to predetermined maximums. For example, mortgage lenders require that total debt payments not exceed a certain percentage (commonly 33 to 38 percent) of *gross income*. (This, of course, implies that the maximum debt payment ratio based on *after-tax income* would be higher.) Lenders also set maximums for the mortgage debt service ratio.

The pie chart in **Figure 2.5** illustrates how the debt payment ratio and the mortgage debt service ratio might represent proportions of a household's income.

FIGURE 2.5 **Debt Payments as a Share of Gross Income for a Hypothetical Household with Gross Income of $40,000 and After-Tax Income of $36,000**   Total debt payments ($10,000 + $4,000) are 35% of gross income and almost 39% of after-tax income.

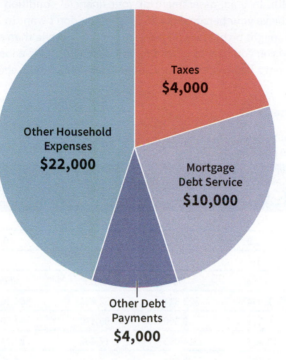

Taxes
$4,000

Other Household Expenses
$22,000

Mortgage Debt Service
$10,000

Other Debt Payments
$4,000

Reflection Question 2

If interest rates increase significantly in the future, in what ways will your borrowing decisions and financial ratios will be impacted?

Measuring Savings Adequacy

The **savings ratio** measures the percentage of your after-tax income that is being allocated to savings. It is calculated using **Equation 2.7**:

$$\text{Savings ratio} = \frac{\text{Monthly savings}}{\text{After-tax monthly income}} \qquad (2.7)$$

You can assess how well you're implementing your savings goals by tracking the savings ratio over time. Financial advisors commonly recommend that you have a savings ratio of at least 10 percent and that you try to increase this ratio over time.

Because the amount you have available for savings is what's left over from your income after you've paid all your expenses and taxes, it's quite possible to have negative savings. This will happen whenever cash outflows exceed cash inflows. If you have negative cash flow, your savings ratio will be negative as well. Using Equation 2.7, you can calculate Danelle Washington's savings ratio:

$$\text{Savings ratio} = \frac{-\$159}{\$1,346} = -11.8\%$$

A negative savings ratio means that, rather than saving, Danelle is accumulating more debt. This financial situation cannot continue for long, or Danelle will experience more serious financial problems.

Interactive: Using Financial Ratios will give you some practice in applying the ratios discussed in this section.

INTERACTIVE

For more practice with financial ratios, see Interactive: Using Financial Ratios in WileyPLUS.

How Do You Compare?

Just as "beauty is in the eye of the beholder," there isn't an established standard for household financial health. Instead, assessment of your financial condition should be motivated by the desire to achieve your personal goals. Clearly, you don't want to be just barely making ends meet, but you might be happy with a less expensive lifestyle than another person would choose. To see how you compare to other similar households, take a look at **Table 2.2**, which summarizes data from a large federally sponsored survey of U.S. households.

TABLE 2.2   How Do You Compare to Other U.S. Households?

The right-hand columns in the table show the budget amounts for households by income quintile (lowest 20 percent of all households by income to highest 20 percent).

Household Characteristic	All Households	By Income Group				
		Lowest	2	3	4	Highest
Number in household	2.5	1.5	2.2	2.5	2.9	3.1
Number of children under 18	0.6	0.3	0.5	0.6	0.7	0.8
Number of vehicles owned	1.9	1.0	1.6	1.9	2.3	2.8
Percent homeowners	63%	41%	55%	61%	72%	86%
Income before taxes	$73,573	$11,394	$29,821	$52,431	$86,363	$188,103
Annual expenditures	60,060	26,019	39,300	50,470	67,604	116,988
Housing expenditures	19,884	10,413	14,095	17,462	22,244	35,234
Food at home	4,363	2,582	3,622	4,038	4,893	6,677
Food away from home	3,365	1,488	2,049	3,023	3,863	6,492
Clothing	1,833	878	1,252	1,348	2,052	3,633
Transportation	9,576	3,497	6,572	8,532	11,099	18,190
Charitable contributions	1,873	650	1,192	1,485	1,873	4,170
Entertainment	3,203	1,270	1,873	2,517	3,470	6,889
Health care	4,928	2,492	3,889	4,642	5,764	7,857

Source: U.S. Bureau of Labor Statistics, Consumer Expenditure Survey, December 2017. www.bls.gov.

2.3   The Time Value of Money

LEARNING OBJECTIVE 2.3
Explain how compound interest benefits investors.

Personal financial planning is all about making choices. How will you spend your money? Where will you invest your savings? How will you finance a major purchase? For every financial choice you must make, there is inevitably a trade-off. For example, if you want to send your children to college, you may have to delay saving for retirement or reduce spending so that you can save for this important goal. In this section, we'll explain an important benefit of saving and investing: the **time value of money**. This tool will help you evaluate and compare various alternatives for achieving your financial goals.

The Power of Compound Interest

The basic idea of the time value of money is this: Money received today is worth more than the same dollar amount to be received in the future. This is true because, if you get an amount of money today, you can invest it to earn compound interest so that it will grow over time. **Compounding** occurs when you earn interest on your investment balance and then leave the interest in the account so that you earn future interest on the original balance plus the accumulated interest earnings. The time value of money is also the reason you shouldn't keep your savings in a piggy bank or under your mattress. Aside from the risk of fire or theft, money that isn't invested in interest-earning or growth assets will actually lose purchasing power over time because of the eroding effects of inflation, as discussed in Chapter 1.

To illustrate the concept of compounding, suppose you're offered an investment opportunity on which you'll earn 10 percent interest per year, payable at the end of each year. If you keep $10,000 in the investment account for one year, you'll receive 10 percent of $10,000, or $1,000, in interest at the end of the year. Now suppose you leave both the original amount and the earned interest, a total of $11,000, in the account. At the end of the next year, you'll receive interest on the full $11,000. Thus, your interest earnings at the end of the second year will be 10 percent of $11,000, or $1,100. At the end of the third year, your interest earnings will be $1,210 (10 percent of $12,100), and so on. The longer you leave your money in the account, the greater the dollar interest earnings each year will be. As illustrated in **Figure 2.6**, your investment account will also grow faster if you can earn a higher rate of interest on the invested amounts.

FIGURE 2.6   **The Power of Compounding at Different Interest Rates**   The higher the rate you earn on your investments, the more their value will grow over time.

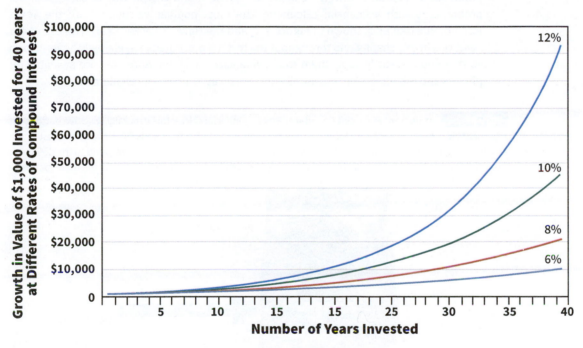

All financial calculations are based on this simple concept, although the problems can become more complicated when interest is compounded more frequently (monthly or daily) or when you add to your account balance on a regular basis. Once you've mastered time value of money calculations, you can use them to answer important personal finance questions such as these:

- How much do I need to save today to reach a particular savings goal?
- How much will my car loan payment be?
- How much will my investment grow over time?
- How long will it take me to pay off a debt?

Time Value of Money Calculation Methods

The purpose of this section is to familiarize you with the basic time value of money calculations used in this text—calculations of present value and future value—and the most common personal finance applications of these calculations. Nearly all financial decisions involve cash inflows and outflows over time, so it's important to master these concepts.

Three Ways to Calculate the Time Value of Money

You can perform the calculations in this section using three different methods, described below. Although your instructor may have a preference for one, all three will result in the same answer to a particular question, with only small differences due to rounding errors.

- **Mathematical formula solution** The solution to most financial problems can be reached through the use of a mathematical formula, or equation. When using equations, be certain to express all interest rates in decimal format (for example, 5% is expressed as 0.05). This can be a bit confusing, because financial calculator solutions require that you enter information in integer form (simply 5 rather than 5% or 0.05). Mathematical calculations can sometimes produce rounding and other errors. Although you should check with your instructor about his or her preferences with regard to rounding, it's generally recommended that you round only after completely solving an equation and that you round to two decimal places, representing the cents of a financial amount.

- **Financial calculator solution** Usually the quickest and easiest way to solve financial problems is with a financial calculator. The most popular calculators are the Texas Instruments BAII Plus, shown in **Figure 2.7**, and the Hewlett Packard 10B. The calculator solutions in this chapter and throughout the text are presented in a relatively generic form so that you can easily apply them to any financial calculator. Apps that are available for phones and tablets work in essentially the same way as financial calculators.

FIGURE 2.7 **Important Financial Calculator Keys** Financial calculators generally have five buttons representing the inputs necessary for time value calculations: number of periods (N), periodic interest rate (I), present value (PV), payment (PMT), and future value (FV). These buttons correspond to the definitions used in mathematical formulas and are arranged in a consistent order regardless of the manufacturer.

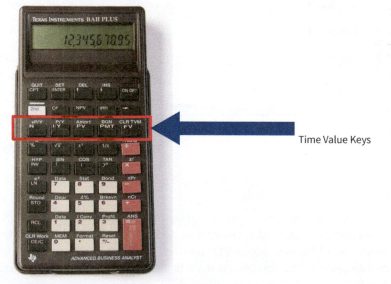

Time Value Keys

Source: David R. Tribble/WikimediaCommons

- **Spreadsheet solution** Electronic spreadsheet programs, such as Microsoft Excel, include built-in formulas for solving financial problems. If you have easy access to a personal computer, you may find that this method will be the best one for you. However, if you will not be allowed to use a computer during exams, you'll still need to be able to solve problems using one of the other methods. Throughout this text, you'll be able to access Personal

Financial Planner Excel Worksheets that will allow you to solve various types of time value of money problems without having to enter an equation.

Using Timelines to Clarify the Timing of Cash Flows

You'll find time value of money problems easier to visualize if you first draw a timeline that shows each of the cash flows for the problem you're solving. A timeline is simply a graphical representation of time going from today (time 0) to some future date in appropriate increments. For each of the examples in the remainder of the chapter, we'll draw a timeline to visually illustrate the cash flows.

Future Value: How Much Will My Money Grow?

Investing funds for future growth is an important aspect of financial planning. If you invest a sum of money today at a certain rate of interest, how much will it be worth at some point in the future? In this section, we'll use each of the three calculation methods described in the preceding section to determine the future value of invested funds.

Future Value of a Lump Sum

The **future value (FV)** of a lump sum is its value at a particular time in the future if it is invested today at a given rate of interest. For example, suppose that you invest $1,000 today in an account that earns 5 percent interest per year, compounded annually. *Annual compounding* means that the interest on the balance is calculated once per year at the end of the year. How much will you have at the end of one year? At the end of two years? The timeline for the problem is shown in **Figure 2.8**. In the figure, FV stands for future value, and PV stands for present value—the value of the cash flow today.

FIGURE 2.8   **Timeline for Future Value of a Lump Sum**   How much will a $1,000 investment (PV) be worth at the end of year 1 (FV_1) and year 2 (FV_2) if it earns 5% (i) per year?

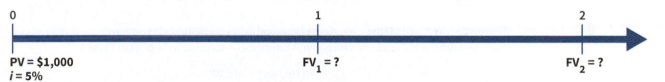

0   1   2

PV = **$1,000**
i = **5%**

FV_1 = ? FV_2 = ?

Mathematical Formula Solution   The future value (FV) of a lump sum is the present value (PV), or the amount invested today, plus the compound interest earned on that present value for the period. In this case, we're looking for the value in one year and in two years. We know that the present value is $1,000 and the interest rate is 5 percent. Thus, we can easily see that after one year, you'll have the original $1,000 plus $50 in interest ($1,000 × 0.05 = $50), for a total of $1,050. Notice that this is the same result you would get if you multiplied the original $1,000 times 1 plus the interest rate: $1,000 × 1.05 = $1,050.

Now suppose you leave the $1,050 in your account for another year. At the end of year 2, you'll have the $1,050 from the end of year 1 plus $52.50 in interest for the second year ($1,050 × 0.05 = $52.50), for a total of $1,102.50. This is the same result you would get if you multiplied the original $1,000 times $(1.05)^2$: $1,000 × $(1.05)^2$ = $1,000 × 1.1025 = $1,102.50. We can therefore generalize the equation for future value as shown in **Equation 2.8**:

$$\text{Future value of a lump sum (FV)} = PV \times (1 + i)^n \qquad (2.8)$$

where FV = Future value; PV = Present value, or the amount invested today; i = Interest rate for one period; and n = Number of periods.

To solve the two-year future value problem, just substitute the appropriate values for i and n in Equation 2.8 and solve for the future value:

$$FV = PV \times (1 + i)^n$$
$$= \$1,000 \times (1 + 0.05)^2$$
$$= \$1,102.50$$

Financial Calculator Solution   To solve a time value problem using a financial calculator, you'll enter the values that you know and solve for the one that you don't know. With most financial calculators, you key in the value of a variable and then push the appropriate button to enter it in the memory of the calculator. For our two-year future value problem, we know the present value, the interest rate, and the number of periods. Thus, to solve the problem, we use the following keystrokes:

1. Key in 2 and then press N.
2. Key in 5 and then press I.
3. Key in –1,000 and then press PV.
4. Key in 0 and then press PMT.
5. Press CPT (the "compute" button on the TI BAII Plus) and then FV.

The order of entry of the variables doesn't matter as long as you've entered all the necessary information before you compute the answer. If one of the keys is not relevant to the problem you're solving—as in the case of our sample problem, where there is no payment (PMT)—you can enter zero for that variable. However, if you've cleared the memory before starting a new problem, each variable will already be reset to zero, so you don't have to enter 0 again. Check your calculator manual for the proper way to clear memory. On the TI BAII Plus, for example, the keystrokes are [2nd] [CLR TVM].

You may wonder why the present value is entered as a negative number. For financial calculators and spreadsheets, you must enter cash *inflows* as positive numbers and cash *outflows* as negative numbers, using the +/− key to change the sign before entering the value. Because in this problem you're *investing* the original $1,000, it's a cash *outflow* to you, since it is going into an investment, and so it's entered as a negative value.

You can use the built-in calculator in **Excel Worksheet 2.5** (Personal Financial Planner: Future Value: How Much Will My Money Grow?) to solve all types of future value problems if you do not have a financial calculator.

EXCEL WORKSHEET

See **Excel Worksheet 2.5 (Personal Financial Planner: Future Value: How Much Will My Money Grow?)** in **WileyPLUS**.

Spreadsheet Solution   Microsoft Excel and other spreadsheets come with built-in formulas for many different purposes. The general future value formula in Microsoft Excel is

=FV(rate,nper,pmt,pv,type)

To solve a future value problem, set your cursor in any cell in a spreadsheet and type this formula, entering values for each of the variable names, in the order given and separated by commas (no spaces), and a zero for any variable that isn't applicable to the problem. As you can probably guess, the variables employed in Microsoft Excel correspond to those we use in the mathematical formula and financial calculator methods:

rate = Periodic interest rate i (in decimal format)
nper = Number of periods n
pv = Present value PV
pmt = Dollar amount of a regular periodic payment of money
"type" refers to the timing of payments and compounding (for beginning-of-period payments, enter 1; for end-of-period payments, enter 0)

To solve our two-year future value problem using the spreadsheet method, we type the following into a cell, with no spaces:

=FV(.05,2,−1000,0,0)

We then hit Enter on the keyboard. The solution, $1,102.50, will immediately appear in the cell.

Demonstration Problem 2.2 shows how to use each method to solve a future value problem.

DEMONSTRATION PROBLEM 2.2 | Calculating the Future Value of a Lump Sum

Problem

You invest $2,500 today. How much will it be worth in five years if your account earns 8 percent interest per year, compounded annually?

Strategy

Use Equation 2.8, a financial calculator, or a spreadsheet to calculate the future value of a lump sum.

Solution

1. **Mathematical formula solution**

$$FV = PV \times (1 + i)^n$$
$$= \$2,500 \times (1.08)^5$$
$$= \$2,500 \times 1.4694$$
$$= \$3,673.35 \text{ (rounded)}$$

2. **Financial calculator solution**

Enter:	5	8	−2,500	0	
	N	I	PV	PMT	FV
Compute:					3,673,32

3. **Spreadsheet solution**

The Excel future value formula is =FV(rate,nper,pmt,pv,type). Substituting values gives us =FV(.08,5,0,−2500,0).

A1			fx	=FV(.08,5,0,−2500,0)	
A	**B**	**C**	**D**	**E**	**F**
1	$3,673.32					
2						
3						
4						
5						

Future Value of an Annuity

What if, instead of saving a single lump sum today, you'd like to invest a certain amount each year (or each month) to arrive at your savings goal? An **annuity** is a series of payments of equal dollar amounts made at regular intervals for a period of time. An **ordinary annuity** is one in which each payment occurs at the *end* of the period. An **annuity due** is one in which each payment occurs at the *beginning* of the period. Your monthly paycheck is an ordinary annuity, whereas your monthly rent payment is an annuity due.

The amount an annuity will grow to, at a given rate of interest and with a certain number of payments, is called the **future value of an annuity (FVA)**. Calculating the future value of an annuity is the equivalent of calculating the future value for each of the payments considered as a lump sum and then adding all the future values. Finding the solution in this way, though, can be fairly tedious for longer investment periods.

Consider a simple example: You plan to make two payments of $100, one invested one year from now and one invested two years from now, and you expect your investment to earn

5 percent per year, compounded annually. Because each payment is made at the *end* of the year, this is an ordinary annuity. If you reinvest all your interest earnings, how much will the total be worth at the end of two years? First, we draw the timeline for the problem in **Figure 2.9**.

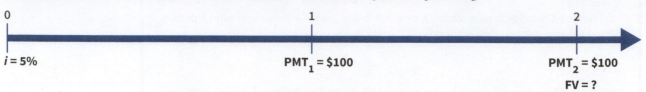

FIGURE 2.9 **Timeline for Future Value of an Ordinary Annuity** At an annual rate of 5% (i), what is the future value (FV) of two $100 payments made at the *ends* of two successive years (PMT$_1$ and PMT$_2$)?

At the end of the two-year period, the first $100 payment, PMT$_1$, will have been in the account for only one year, so it will have grown to $100 \times (1.05 = \$105$. The second $100 payment, PMT$_2$, will be invested at the end of year 2 and therefore will not have earned any interest yet. So it's still worth only $100 at the end of the second year. Altogether, you'll have $205, so that's the FV at the end of year 2.

What if you paid $100 at the end of each year *for three years*? At the end of the third year, you'd have

$$[100 \times (1.05)^2] + [100 \times 1.05] + 100 = \$315.25$$
$$\text{PMT}_1 \qquad\qquad \text{PMT}_2 \qquad\qquad \text{PMT}_3$$

But what if you wanted to invest $100 per year each year all the way to retirement? You can see what a chore it would be to calculate this future value with separate lump sums. Fortunately, there's a single formula that combines all the compounding calculations. As with the future value of a lump sum, you have a choice of mathematical, financial calculator, or spreadsheet methods of calculation.

Mathematical Formula Solution We can calculate the future value of an ordinary annuity (FVA) mathematically as shown in **Equation 2.9**:

$$\text{Future value of an annuity (FVA)} = \text{PMT} \times \frac{(1+i)^n - 1}{i} \qquad (2.9)$$

where PMT is the payment per period.

Let's use the equation to solve for the future value of the annuity after three years. Since we know that PMT = $100, i = 0.05, and n = 3, we can substitute these values into the equation and solve for FVA:

$$\text{FVA} = \$100 \times \frac{(1.05)^3 - 1}{0.05}$$

$$\text{FVA} = \$100 \times \frac{0.157625}{0.05}$$

$$= \$100 \times 3.1524$$

$$= \$315.25$$

Financial Calculator Solution The calculator button for annuity payments is PMT. You should use it only when there is a series of *equal* cash inflows or outflows in the problem you are solving. As before, you'll enter the values you know and solve for the one you don't know. After clearing the calculator's memory, use the following keystrokes to solve for the future value of the ordinary annuity:

1. Key in −$100 and then press PMT.
2. Key in 3 and then press N.
3. Key in 5 and then press I.
4. Press CPT and then press FV.

The answer should be $315.25, regardless of the order in which you enter the variables.

Reflection Question 3

In what ways do you think that understanding future value concepts will help you make better personal financial decisions over your lifetime?

So far, we've been working with an ordinary annuity, in which payments are made at the end of each period. But suppose that you make an investment contribution at the *beginning* of each year instead of at the end—an annuity due. Compare the annuity due timeline in **Figure 2.10** with the ordinary annuity timeline in Figure 2.9. Note that making beginning-of-period payments means that you gain an extra year of interest compounding for each payment.

FIGURE 2.10   **Timeline for Future Value of an Annuity Due**   At an annual rate of 5% (i), what is the future value (FV) of two $100 payments made at the *beginnings* of two successive years (PMT$_1$ and PMT$_2$)?

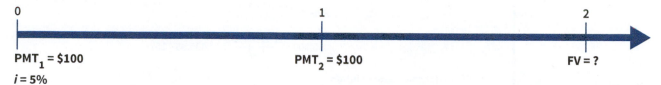

You can use your financial calculator to solve for the future value of an annuity due by adjusting a setting. For the TI BAII Plus calculator, the keystrokes for toggling between end-of-period (END) and beginning-of-period (BGN) settings are [2nd][BGN] [2nd][SET]. The END setting is the default, so an indicator BGN will appear in the LCD display if you are set for beginning-of-period payments. Once you've switched to the BGN setting, you can solve the problem using the same keystrokes you used to solve the ordinary annuity problem earlier in this section. The correct solution is $331.01, a little more than the $315.25 that resulted for the future value of the ordinary annuity. The difference is the extra interest received.

Spreadsheet Solution   The Microsoft Excel formula for the future value of an annuity is the same as the one used for the future value of a lump sum:

=FV(rate,nper,pmt,pv,type)

The difference is that you must input a value for *pmt* instead of *pv* because you are solving an annuity problem rather than a lump sum problem. You can calculate the future value of $100 invested annually for three years at 5 percent interest by typing the following formula into a cell on the spreadsheet:

=FV(.05,3,−100,0,0)

When you press Enter on your keyboard, the solution that appears in the cell should be the same as the calculator solution: $315.25. To solve for the future value of an *annuity due*, enter 1 instead of 0 for the variable "type":

=FV(.05,3,−100,0,1)

The result should be $331.01, again the same as the calculator solution.

Demonstration Problem 2.3 provides a worked-out example of how to calculate the future value of an annuity using each of the three alternative methods. You can test your understanding of future value in **Interactive: Future Value**.

INTERACTIVE

To test your knowledge of future value concepts, see **Interactive: Future Value** in **WileyPLUS**.

DEMONSTRATION PROBLEM 2.3 | Calculating the Future Value of an Annuity (Series of Equal Payments)

Problem

In thinking about your future, you decide to start making annual payments to your retirement account. You plan to make end-of-year payments of $5,000 every year for 40 years into the account, which earns 12 percent interest. How much will you have accumulated by the time you retire?

Strategy

This is a future value of an annuity problem. Use Equation 2.9, a financial calculator, or a spreadsheet to solve it.

Solution

1. **Mathematical formula solution**

$$FVA = PMT \times \frac{(1 + i)^n - 1}{i}$$

$$= \$5,000 \times \frac{(1.12)^{40} - 1}{0.12} = \$3,835,457.10$$

2. **Financial calculator solution**

Enter:	40	12	0	−5,000	
	N	I	PV	PMT	FV

Compute: 3,835,457.10

3. **Excel worksheet solution**

The Excel formula is =FV(rate,nper,pmt,pv,type) =FV(.12,40,−5000,0,0).

A1		fx	=FV(.12, 40,−5000,0,0)		
A	**B**	**C**	**D**	**E**	**F**
1	$3,835,457.10				
2					
3					
4					
5					

2.4 Present Value: How Much Do I Need Today to Reach a Future Goal?

LEARNING OBJECTIVE 2.4

Calculate present value of funds to be received or paid in the future.

You now know how to calculate the future value of an amount of money you invest. But suppose you already know that you need a certain amount of money in the future. How much would you need to invest today in order to reach that goal? In other words, what is the **present value (PV)** of the amount you need in the future? In this section, you'll learn how to calculate present value. Because a present value will always be less than its future value, we often use the word **discounting** to describe the process of calculating present value.

Present Value of a Lump Sum

As with future value, we can calculate the present value of a lump sum or a series of regular payments. We'll start with a lump sum. Suppose that you want to have $10,000 to buy a car four years from now. You would like to set aside enough money today so that, if you earn 5 percent interest over the four years, you'll have exactly $10,000 to buy the car at the end of the fourth year. We'll use each of the three time value calculation methods to solve this problem.

Your timeline for the problem should look like the one in **Figure 2.11**.

FIGURE 2.11   **Timeline for Present Value of a Lump Sum**   If the future value (FV) is $10,000 and the interest rate (i) is 5%, what is the present value (PV)—the amount that has to be invested today?

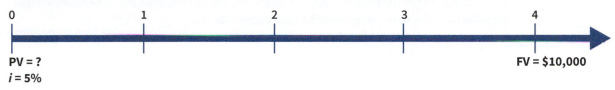

Mathematical Formula Solution

Recall from the previous section that $FV = PV \times (1 + i)^n$. You can turn that equation around—dividing each side by $(1 + i)^n$—to arrive at the formula for present value. The result is **Equation 2.10**:

$$\text{Present value of a lump sum (PV)} = FV \times \left(\frac{1}{1+i}\right)^n \qquad (2.10)$$

We enter the values for the car-purchasing problem to find the solution:

$$PV = \$10,000 \times \left(\frac{1}{1.05}\right)^4$$
$$= \$10,000 \times (0.9524)^4$$
$$= \$10,000 \times 0.8227$$
$$= \$8,227$$

If you use a calculator to solve this equation, it's best to enter the information in parentheses first. Then, without rounding the answer, raise it to the power of 4 by keying $[y^x]$ [4]. Finally, multiply that result by 10,000. Based on this calculation, if you deposit $8,227 in an account earning 5 percent per year, compounded annually, and leave it and all accumulated interest there for four years, you'll have $10,000 in the account at the end of the four years.

Financial Calculator Solution

To solve present value problems with a financial calculator, you enter the values that you know, enter zero for those that don't apply, and compute the result. After clearing the calculator's memory, use the following keystrokes to solve for the present value of a lump sum in the car-purchasing problem:

1. Key in 4 and then press N.
2. Key in 5 and then press I.
3. Key in 10000 and then press FV.
4. Press CPT and then press PV.

Regardless of the order in which you enter the variables, the answer will be −8,227. Note that this is a negative number, because it represents a cash outflow for you. You can also use the built-in calculator in **Excel Worksheet 2.6** (Personal Financial Planner: Present Value: How Much Do I Need Today to Reach a Future Goal?) to solve present value problems.

EXCEL WORKSHEET

See **Excel Worksheet 2.6** (**Personal Financial Planner: Present Value: How Much Do I Need Today to Reach a Future Goal?**) in **WileyPLUS.**

Spreadsheet Solution

The Microsoft Excel formula for present value of a lump sum is

$$=PV(rate,nper,pmt,fv,type)$$

As with the future value formula, you set your cursor in an empty cell in the spreadsheet and type in the formula, entering the appropriate values for the variables in the order indicated. For this problem, you enter

$$=PV(.05,4,0,10000,0)$$

The solution that appears in the cell, rounded to the nearest dollar, is −$8,227, which corresponds to the solution obtained using the mathematical formula and the financial calculator. Consistent with the financial calculator solution, the answer will appear as a negative number, because the present value represents a cash outflow for you.

    Demonstration Problem 2.4 shows you how to solve an example problem using each of the three alternative methods.

DEMONSTRATION PROBLEM 2.4 | Calculating the Present Value of a Lump Sum

Problem

Suppose you expect to receive $5,000 10 years from now. How much is that future amount worth today, assuming an interest rate of 7 percent, compounded annually?

Strategy

Use Equation 2.10, a financial calculator, or a spreadsheet to calculate the present value of a lump sum.

Solution

1. **Mathematical formula solution**

$$PV = FV \times \left(\frac{1}{1+i}\right)^n$$

$$= \$5,000 \times \left(\frac{1}{1.07}\right)^{10}$$

$$= \$2,541.75$$

2. **Financial calculator solution**

Enter: 10   7   0   5,000

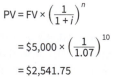

| N | I | PV | PMT | FV |

Compute: −2,541.75

3. **Spreadsheet solution**

The general Excel formula for the present value of a lump sum is =PV(rate,nper,pmt,fv,type). Substituting the given values for this problem, we enter =PV(.07,10,0,5000,0).

A1				fx	=PV(.07, 10,0,5000,0)	
	A	**B**	**C**	**D**	**E**	**F**
1	-$2,541.75					
2						
3						
4						
5						

Present Value of an Annuity

Earlier, you learned how to use the future value of an annuity (FVA) calculation to determine the future value of a series of steady payments into an investment account. Conversely, the **present value of an annuity (PVA)** is the amount you would have to set aside today to be able to withdraw a particular amount of money each period for a given number of periods.

For example, if you know you will need to withdraw a certain amount of money from savings each year once you have retired, you might want to know how much money you will need to have in your retirement account by the time you retire to be able to do so. The amount you'll need to start with to meet this goal will be less than the total of the payments you expect to take out, because the account will continue to earn interest each period on the gradually declining balance. Thus, if you want to take $10,000 per year from an account for 10 years, you don't need to start with $100,000. Instead, you need to deposit a smaller amount that, together with compound interest, will be sufficient to allow you to withdraw the $10,000 per year, leaving you with a zero balance at the end of the tenth year. In this section, we'll calculate the present value of an annuity, which is the amount you would need to deposit.

As an example, suppose you're considering the purchase of an annuity contract in which your bank promises to pay you $2,000 at the end of every year for the next three years. Note that this is an ordinary annuity, because the payments are made at the *end* of each year. The timeline for this annuity is illustrated in **Figure 2.12**. How much will you have to pay the bank today for this annuity? The answer depends on the rate of interest that the bank is able to earn. Let's assume that the interest rate is 10 percent.

FIGURE 2.12 **Timeline for Present Value of an Ordinary Annuity** What is the present value (PV) of three $2,000 payments received at the ends of year 1 (PMT$_1$), year 2 (PMT$_2$), and year 3 (PMT$_3$)?

0	1	2	3
PV = ?	PMT$_1$ = $2,000	PMT$_2$ = $2,000	PMT$_3$ = $2,000
i = 10%			

Mathematical Formula Solution

Recall that we calculated the present value of a lump sum by using Equation 2.10. An annuity is just a series of lump sum payments, in this case the three payments PMT$_1$, PMT$_2$, and PMT$_3$. The long way to calculate the present value of series of payments is to find the present value of each payment separately and then add those present values. Using this method, the present value of the annuity in Figure 2.12 is

$$PVA = \left[PMT_1 \times \left(\frac{1}{1+i}\right)^1\right] + \left[PMT_2 \times \left(\frac{1}{1+i}\right)^2\right] + \left[PMT_3 \times \left(\frac{1}{1+i}\right)^3\right]$$

$$= \left[\$2,000 \times \left(\frac{1}{1.1}\right)^1\right] + \left[\$2,000 \times \left(\frac{1}{1.1}\right)^2\right] + \left[\$2,000 \times \left(\frac{1}{1.1}\right)^3\right]$$

$$= (\$2,000 \times 0.9091) + (\$2,000 \times 0.08265) + (\$2,000 \times 0.7053)$$

$$= \$4,974$$

This result means that if your bank receives $4,974 and invests it to earn 10 percent interest per year, it will have exactly enough, with interest, to pay you $2,000 at the end of each year. To see that this is so, consider the bank's account balances over this three-year period, shown in Table 2.3.

The few cents that are left as the ending balance at the end of year 3 are the result of rounding the payment to the nearest dollar. Notice again that the present value of a series of payments will always be less than the sum of those payments. The difference is the interest earned on the gradually declining balance.

TABLE 2.3   **Example of Annuity Payments and Balances**

Year	Beginning Balance	Interest	Payment	Ending Balance
1	$4,974.00	$497.40	−$2,000.00	$3,471.40
2	$3,471.40	$347.14	−$2,000.00	$1,818.54
3	$1,818.54	$181.85	−$2,000.00	$0.39

Given the complexity of calculating present values for each annuity payment, you'll be happy to hear that there's a shortcut formula for the present value of an annuity, as given in **Equation 2.11**:

$$\text{Present value of an annuity (PVA)} = \text{PMT} \times \frac{1 - \left(\frac{1}{1+i}\right)^n}{i} \tag{2.11}$$

We can solve for the present value of the three $2,000 annuity payments as follows:

$$\text{PVA} = \$2,000 \times \frac{1 - \left(\frac{1}{1.1}\right)^3}{0.1}$$

$$= \$2,000 \times \frac{1 - 0.7513}{0.1}$$

$$= \$2,000 \times 2.4869$$

$$= \$4,973.70$$

Financial Calculator Solution

This type of problem is where a financial calculator really comes in handy. It's much easier to solve for the present value of an annuity using a financial calculator than using a formula. Again, you enter the information you know, enter zero for variables that don't apply, and solve for what you don't know—the present value.

1. Key in 2000 and then press PMT.
2. Key in 10 and then press I.
3. Key in 3 and then press N.
4. Press CPT and then press PV.

The answer should be the same as the mathematical formula solution—$4,973.70—except that it will be presented as a negative number, because it represents a cash outflow for you.

Spreadsheet Solution

The Microsoft Excel formula for the present value of an annuity is the same as that for the present value of a lump sum:

=PV(rate,nper,pmt,fv,type)

The difference is that, because an annuity is a series of equal payments, you'll input a value for pmt instead of for fv. For this problem, type the formula into a cell or in the formula toolbar in the spreadsheet as follows:

=PV(.1,3,2000,0,0)

The solution that appears ($4,973.70) is a negative number, just as for the calculator solution, because the spreadsheet shows cash outflows as negative values.

Demonstration Problem 2.5 walks you through an example using each of the alternative methods for solving a problem involving the present value of an annuity.

DEMONSTRATION PROBLEM 2.5 | Calculating the Present Value of an Annuity

Problem

You want to be able to draw $20,000 at the end of each year for 15 years to fund your estimated retirement needs. If your investment account earns 6 percent per year and you want the account balance to be zero at the end of the 15 years of retirement, how much do you need to have in your account when you retire?

Strategy

Use Equation 2.11, a financial calculator, or a spreadsheet to calculate the present value of an annuity.

Solution

1. **Mathematical formula solution**

$$PVA = PMT \times \frac{1 - \left(\frac{1}{1+i}\right)^n}{i}$$

$$= \$20,000 \times \frac{1 - \left(\frac{1}{1.06}\right)^{15}}{0.06}$$

$$= \$20,000 \times 9.71225$$

$$= \$194,245$$

2. **Financial calculator solution**

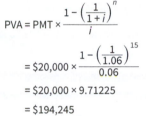

Enter: 15 [N]   6 [I]   [PV]   -20,000 [PMT]   0 [FV]

Compute: 194,245

3. **Spreadsheet solution**

The present value of this series of payments is found by entering =PV(.06,15,–20000,0,0).

	A	B	C	D	E	F
			fx	=PV(.06, 15,-20000,0,0)		
1	-$194,244.98					
2						
3						
4						
5						

You will find that there are many useful applications for the present value of an annuity. The more obvious ones are related to estimating how much you need to have saved to meet future income or payment obligations. In the next section, you'll use this concept to calculate how much money you have to pay each month on a loan. As a college student, have you ever

INTERACTIVE

Apply present value concepts using **Interactive: Present Value of a College Degree** in **WileyPLUS.**

thought about how much your education is worth? **Interactive: Present Value of a College Degree** shows how you can use present value to measure the worth of a college degree.

Loan Payments

Now you're ready to tackle a very practical personal financial planning problem: calculating monthly payments on a loan. Loan payments represent one of the most common types of annuities, and when you calculate loan payments, you directly apply what you've learned about the present value of an annuity.

Amortization is the financial term for the process of paying interest on a declining loan balance in addition to repaying some of the face value of the loan with each payment. The payments on an amortized loan are calculated so that by the time you make your last payment, you've paid off the total loan balance. Sound familiar? It should, because the process is the same as the one just described in the discussion of calculating the present value of an annuity. Instead of solving for the present value, though, you solve for the payment.

Let's consider an example similar to the one used to illustrate the present value of an annuity. Earlier, we found that it would cost you $4,973.70 to purchase an annuity that would pay you $2,000 per year for three years if the bank earned 10 percent on its funds. Now, suppose instead that you want to buy a used car and your bank is willing to lend you $4,973.70 at 10 percent interest for three years (a bit steep by today's standards, but maybe you're a risky customer). How much would your payments be per year? You may already have guessed that the answer is $2,000 per year, but let's see how you could arrive at that answer using time value of money calculation methods. **Figure 2.13** illustrates the problem.

FIGURE 2.13 **Timeline for Loan Payments**   With a present value (PV) of $4,973.70 and an interest rate (i) of 10%, what is the amount of each payment (PMT)?

PV = $4,973,70
i = 10%

Mathematical Formula Solution

The equation for the present value of an annuity was introduced in the previous section:

$$PVA = PMT \times \frac{1 - \left(\frac{1}{1+i}\right)^n}{i}$$

With a little algebra, you can solve that equation for PMT, as shown in **Equation 2.12**:

$$\text{Payment on amortized loan: PMT} = PVA \times \frac{i}{1 - \left(\frac{1}{1+i}\right)^n} \tag{2.12}$$

Equation 2.12 admittedly looks a bit intimidating, but if you take it step by step and don't round any numbers until the end, you'll find that the solution is $2,000:

$$PMT = \$4,973.70 \times \frac{0.1}{1 - \left(\frac{1}{1.1}\right)^3}$$

$$= \$2,000$$

Financial Calculator Solution

In contrast to the mathematical formula solution, it's particularly easy to solve for loan payments with a financial calculator. In fact, this may be the most useful thing you'll learn in your personal finance course. The calculator keystrokes for the example we are considering are as follows:

1. Key in 4973.70 and then press PV.

2. Key in 3 and then press N.

3. Key in 10 and then press I.

4. Press CPT and then press PMT.

The answer, rounded to the nearest dollar, should be –$2,000. Once again, it's a negative number because car loan payments are cash outflows for you.

If you don't have a financial calculator, you can solve for loan payments using the built-in calculator in **Excel Worksheet 2.7** (Personal Financial Planner: How Much Is the Loan Payment?).

Spreadsheet Solution

Calculating loan payments in Microsoft Excel requires a formula different from those we used previously. The formula used to solve for a payment is called PMT, conveniently the same abbreviation we've been using. It is as follows:

$$=PMT(rate,nper,pv,fv,type)$$

As always, you type the formula into the spreadsheet and then hit the Enter key. Note that for all amortized loan payment problems, the future value is always zero, because the loan will have been paid off when the last payment has been made:

$$=PMT(.1,3,4973.70,0,0)$$

The answer, $2,000, should appear in the cell as a negative value.

Monthly Loan Payments

We've so far assumed that interest is compounded annually. On most loans today, however, payments are made on a monthly basis, and interest is compounded monthly. If you review the equations presented in this chapter, you'll notice that we've consistently expressed interest and payments as per period amounts. Therefore, all you need to do to solve a problem involving monthly payments is to enter the interest rate as a monthly rate (divide i by 12 before entering) and enter the number of months instead of the number of years as n.

You can use any of the three methods of calculation for solving problems with nonannual payments, but the financial calculator and the spreadsheet methods are considerably simpler than the mathematical formula method. To illustrate, let's use a financial calculator to calculate how much you would have to pay per month for the three-year car loan of $4,973.70.

To solve this problem using a financial calculator, use the following keystrokes:

1. Key in 10/12 = and then press I.

2. Key in 3 × 12 = and then press N.

3. Key in 4973.70 and then press PV.

4. Press CPT and then press PMT to get the solution: –160.49.

Although you could simply enter the value for the interest rate (0.8333), as well as the number of periods (36), you will avoid rounding errors on future problems if you use this method. As before, the solution, –$160.49, will be a negative number, because it represents a cash outflow for you.

> ## Reflection Question 4
>
> Which of your future financial goals are likely to involve a series of regular payments, either to be paid or to be received? Why will it be valuable to you to be able to estimate their future value?

EXCEL WORKSHEET

See **Excel Worksheet 2.7** (Personal Financial Planner: **Future Value: How Much Is the Loan Payment?**) in **WileyPLUS.**

Before you take on future debt, it's important to be sure that you can afford to repay it. Although we'll discuss loans in more detail in later chapters, **Demonstration Problem 2.6** illustrates the use of time value of money concepts to estimate future payments on a student loan.

DEMONSTRATION PROBLEM 2.6 | Estimating Student Loan Payments

Problem

You are nearing graduation with $18,000 in total student loan debt. You want to be sure the income from your new job will be sufficient to cover your costs. Your salary will be $36,000, but, after taxes and expenses, you think you'll have only about $400 to apply to payments for your student loan and credit cards. The student loan will require monthly payments for 10 years at 6 percent interest. How much will your monthly payment be?

Strategy

Although it is possible to solve this problem with a mathematical formula, the calculation is quite messy, so it will be easier to use a financial calculator or Excel Worksheet 2.7 to answer this question.

Solution

Enter:	10 × 12 =120	6/12 = 0.5	18,000		0
	N	**I**	**PV**	**PMT**	**FV**
Compute:				−199.84	

This result means that you will have to make a student loan payment of $199.84 each month for 10 years. This will leave you about $200 per month to apply to paying off your credit cards.

Summary

Learning Objectives Review

LEARNING OBJECTIVE 2.1   Develop a system for financial record keeping, and prepare a personal balance sheet.

Evaluating and tracking your personal finances are activities that require you to have access to accurate financial information for planning, budgeting, and tax filing.

- You need to develop an effective system for organizing your financial records and safeguarding important documents in a **lockbox** or **safe deposit box**.

- Your **personal balance sheet** is a **personal financial statement** that lists the **market value** of everything you own (**assets**) and all the amounts you owe to others (**debts**, or liabilities) at a particular point in time. On these statements, assets are listed from most liquid to least liquid, and debts are listed according to length of term, from short-term to long-term.

- Using the information on your balance sheet, you can calculate your **net worth** using **Equation 2.1**:

  Net worth = Total assets − Total debts

  If your net worth remains negative for long, you may run the risk of future **insolvency** or bankruptcy.

LEARNING OBJECTIVE 2.2   Prepare a personal cash flow statement, and evaluate your financial situation using financial ratios.

Managing your personal finances requires that you fully understand your sources and uses of cash.

- A **personal cash flow statement** details inflows and outflows of cash over a period of time, often one month or one year. Cash inflows include your **gross income** as well as any other funds you receive during the period. Cash outflows may be **fixed expenses**, such as rent payments, or **variable expenses**, such as car repairs and doctors' bills.

- You can use the information on your personal cash flow statement to calculate net cash flow using **Equation 2.2**:

$$\text{Net cash flow} = \text{Total cash inflows} - \text{Total cash outflows}$$

Financial ratios allow you to evaluate your current financial position based on your personal balance sheet and cash flow statement. By comparing your ratios over time, you can track your progress toward achieving your financial goals.

- The **liquidity ratio (Equation 2.3)** measures your ability to pay your expenses from your current income.

$$\text{Liquidity ratio} = \frac{\text{Liquid assets}}{\text{Monthly expenses}}$$

- Debt management is often measured using the **debt ratio**, **debt payment ratio**, and **mortgage debt service ratio (Equations 2.4, 2.5**, and **2.6)**.

$$\text{Debt ratio} = \frac{\text{Total debts}}{\text{Total assets}}$$

$$\text{Debt payment ratio} = \frac{\text{Total monthly debt payments}}{\text{After-tax monthly income}}$$

$$\text{Mortgage debt service ratio} = \frac{\text{Principal} + \text{Interest} + \text{Taxes} + \text{Insurance}}{\text{Gross monthly income}}$$

- Lenders may use some or all of these ratios to determine your ability to pay your **mortgage debt service** costs, including principal, interest, taxes, and insurance premiums.
- The **savings ratio (Equation 2.7)** evaluates the percentage of after-tax income that is being saved.

$$\text{Savings ratio} = \frac{\text{Monthly savings}}{\text{After-tax monthly income}}$$

LEARNING OBJECTIVE 2.3   **Explain how compound interest benefits investors.**

The **time value of money** is an important concept in personal finance.

- The underlying principle of all time value calculations is that a dollar today is worth more than a dollar in the future due to the **compounding** of interest over time.
- There are three methods of solving time value of money problems: mathematical formulas, financial calculator, and electronic spreadsheet. All three will result in the same solution to a problem.

- **Future value (FV)** is the amount to which an amount invested today will grow. The future value of a lump sum is its value at a particular time in the future if invested today at a given rate of interest. You can calculate it using **Equation 2.8**.

$$FV = PV \times (1 + i)^n$$

- An **annuity** is a regular series of equal payments. With an **ordinary annuity**, payments are made at the ends of periods, and with an **annuity due**, payments are made at the beginnings of periods. The amount to which an annuity will grow if invested at a given rate of interest for a particular period of time is called the **future value of an annuity (FVA)**. You can calculate the future value of an ordinary annuity using **Equation 2.9**.

$$FVA = PMT \times \frac{(1 + i)^n - 1}{i}$$

LEARNING OBJECTIVE 2.4   **Calculate the present value of funds to be received or paid in the future.**

Present value (PV) calculations help you better understand the amounts you need today to meet future obligations.

- The present value of a lump sum tells you how much an amount to be received in the future is worth today or, equivalently, how much you should be willing to pay today to receive a certain amount of money in the future. You can calculate the present value of a lump sum using **Equation 2.10**.

$$PV = FV \times \left(\frac{1}{1+i}\right)^n$$

- The **present value of an annuity (PVA)** is the value today of a future stream of equal cash flows. The present value of an annuity can be calculated using **Equation 2.11**.

$$PVA = PMT \times \frac{1 - \left(\frac{1}{1+i}\right)^n}{i}$$

- You can also determine the payment on an amortized loan using time value of money concepts. Loan payments are generally equal payments over a period of time that are sufficient to pay the lender its required rate of interest in addition to paying off the amount borrowed over the loan term, a process called **amortization**. You can calculate loan payments using **Equation 2.12**.

$$PMT = PVA \times \frac{i}{1 - \left(\frac{1}{1+i}\right)^n}$$

- Time value problems with nonannual payments can be easily solved using a financial calculator or a spreadsheet. The interest rate used for the calculation is the periodic rate (such as the monthly rate, which is the annual rate divided by 12). The number of periods or payments is used instead of the number of years.

Excel Worksheets

2.1 Personal Financial Planner: My Financial Records

2.2 Personal Financial Planner: Personal Balance Sheet

2.3 Personal Financial Planner: Spending Log

2.4 Personal Financial Planner: Personal Cash Flow Statement

2.5 Personal Financial Planner: Future Value: How Much Will My Money Grow?

2.6 Personal Financial Planner: Present Value: How Much Do I Need Today to Reach a Future Goal?

2.7 Personal Financial Planner: How Much Is the Loan Payment?

Key Terms

amortization   2-30
annuity   2-21
annuity due   2-21
assets   2-5
cash surrender value   2-6
compounding   2-17
debt payment ratio   2-14
debt ratio   2-14
debts   2-5
discounting   2-24
fixed expenses   2-10

future value (FV)   2-19
future value of an annuity (FVA)   2-21
gross income   2-10
insolvency   2-8
liquid assets   2-6
liquidity ratio   2-13
lockbox   2-3
market value   2-6
mortgage debt service   2-14
mortgage debt service ratio   2-14
net worth   2-5

ordinary annuity   2-21
personal balance sheet   2-5
personal cash flow statement   2-9
personal financial statements   2-5
present value (PV)   2-24
present value of an annuity
   (PVA)   2-27
safe deposit box   2-3
savings ratio   2-15
time value of money   2-16
variable expenses   2-10

WileyPLUS

Practice Questions to check your understanding, Peer-to-Peer Videos, Interactives, and many other resources are available in WileyPLUS.

Concept Review Questions

1. Why is it important to have a system for organizing your financial records?

2. What options do you have for safeguarding your important records and documents? Explain which types of records each option is appropriate for.

3. What are personal financial statements, and why are they important for personal financial planning?

4. Explain the difference between short-term and long-term liabilities. Give an example of each.

5. When you are creating a personal balance sheet, what is the most appropriate measure of the value of your assets? Why?

6. Under what circumstances will net worth be negative?

7. How is net cash flow calculated? Under what circumstances is net cash flow negative?

8. Differentiate between fixed and variable expenses, and give an example of each.

9. What are the three aspects of your finances measured by personal financial ratios?

10. Give an example that illustrates the importance of the time value of money.

11. How does the interest rate affect the future value of an annuity?

12. How does the length of the investment period affect the future value of a lump sum invested today?

13. For each of the following types of financial activities, identify which time value of money concept could be used to help you select your best options.

    a. Estimate payments on a car loan

    b. Estimate monthly payments necessary to pay off a credit card

    c. Estimate how much to save for retirement

14. What is the purpose of saving each of the following types of financial records, and for what length of time should you save each one?

    a. Annual magazine subscription receipt

    b. Checking account statement

    c. Student loan statement

    d. Cell phone bill

    e. Credit card statement showing a zero balance

    f. Tax return

    g. College tuition, fees, and housing bill

15. List the primary categories of assets and the primary categories of debts.

Application Problems

1. You have estimated your total assets to be $10,000 and your total debts to be $11,000. What is your net worth?

2. Identify whether each of the following is an asset, a debt, or neither.

   a. Credit card balance

   b. Weekly employment earnings

   c. Car

   d. Rent paid to landlord

   e. Checking account

3. Assess Jason's personal finances using the following balance sheet information.

Assets		Debts	
Bank accounts	$3,000	Current bills	$1,500
Car	$5,000	Student loan	$10,000
Personal assets	$2,000	Car loan	$3,000

   a. What is Jason's net worth?

   b. How much does Jason have in liquid assets?

   c. Calculate Jason's debt ratio.

   d. Calculate Jason's liquidity ratio, assuming that his monthly expenses total $1,200.

4. Holly is putting together her end-of-the-year financial statements. She isn't sure how to classify some of her financial data. Identify whether each of the following financial transactions represents an asset, a liability, income, or an expense.

   a. She borrowed $1,000 from her parents this year, but will not begin to pay it back until she graduates from college in two years.

   b. She deposited her tax refund in her checking account.

   c. She receives $200 per month from a trust fund.

   d. She rents an apartment for $800 per month in her name.

   e. Her roommate has not yet paid her half of the December rent.

5. Lucin earns $30,000 per year. She pays 20 percent of her gross income in taxes. She has fixed expenses of $1,000 per month and variable expenses that average $900 per month. What is her net cash flow for the year?

6. Masako would like to buy a new car. She currently has after-tax monthly income of $2,000. Her monthly expenses are as follows:

   Car insurance $100

   Rent $900

   Groceries $300

   Entertainment $200

   Utilities $200

   Credit card payment $100

   Other $100

   a. What is Masako's net cash flow per month?

   b. Can Masako afford to buy a car? Why or why not?

7. The Sandell family reports the following financial information:

   Checking and savings account: $3,000

   Monthly after-tax income: $2,500

   Total monthly expenses: $2,000

   Monthly savings: $500

   Total debt: $10,000

   Total assets: $40,000

   a. Calculate the Sandells' liquidity ratio.

   b. Calculate the Sandells' debt ratio.

   c. Calculate the Sandells' savings ratio.

8. Use the following balance sheet and cash flow statement information to assess Carmelo's finances using personal financial ratios.

   Liquid assets: $5,000

   Total assets: $180,000

   Current bills: $1,500

   Short-term debt: $4,500

   Long-term debt: $160,000

   Monthly gross income: $10,000

   Monthly after-tax income: $7,000

   Monthly mortgage payment (principal, interest, taxes, and insurance): $1,300

   Monthly non-mortgage debt payments: $450

   Total monthly expenses (not including taxes or current savings): $6,200

   Current monthly savings: $700

   a. Calculate Carmelo's liquidity ratio.

   b. Calculate Carmelo's debt ratio.

   c. Calculate Carmelo's mortgage debt service ratio.

   d. Calculate Carmelo's debt payment ratio.

   e. Calculate Carmelo's savings ratio.

   f. Calculate Carmelo's net worth.

   g. Calculate Carmelo's net cash flow.

9. You would like to begin saving for a down payment on a home. If you want to buy the home five years from now, and you will make annual end-of-year payments into savings, how much will you have for your down payment if you save $500 per year and earn 10 percent on your investment, compounded annually?

10. Using one or more of the methods presented in this chapter, calculate the future value of $2,500 invested today at a 3 percent rate and held for six years.

11. Using one or more of the methods presented in this chapter, calculate the future value of $2,000 invested at the end of each year for six years at 8 percent interest.

12. Using one or more of the methods presented in this chapter, calculate the present value of $200,000 to be received 30 years from today, discounted at 12 percent.

13. Using one or more of the methods presented in this chapter, calculate the present value of $50,000 to be received 10 years from today, discounted at 8 percent.

14. Using one or more of the methods presented in this chapter, calculate the present value of $1,000 to be received at the end of each year for 10 years, assuming a 5 percent discount rate.

15. You've just won $10 million in a lottery, and the payout is 1/25 of the jackpot ($400,000) payable at the end of each year for 25 years. Alternatively, you have the option of receiving your payout as a $3 million lump sum.

   a. What is the present value of the annuity if your investments earn 8 percent?

   b. What is the present value of the annuity if your investments earn 10 percent?

   c. Based on the present value calculations, is it better to take the lump sum or the annuity?

16. Miguel would like to save money to pay for his daughter's college expenses. He estimates that he will need to accumulate $40,000 over the next 10 years. How much will he need to invest at the end of each year for 10 years to achieve his savings goal if he can earn 6 percent per year on the investment and he makes end-of-year payments?

17. You are borrowing $50,000 to buy a condo. If mortgage rates are currently at 6 percent and you take out a 30-year loan with fixed payments, how much will your monthly mortgage payment be, assuming you make fixed payments at the end of each month?

18. Jerry wants to buy a new car. He has $2,000 for a down payment, and he estimates that he can afford to make a loan payment of up to $300 per month. The current rate for a 36-month car loan is 6 percent.

   a. How much can Jerry borrow for a loan payment of $300?

   b. What is the maximum total cost that Jerry can afford, including taxes and dealer charges?

   c. How much difference will it make if the dealer offers Jerry zero percent financing?

Case Applications

1. As their daughter Lisa starts high school, Homer and Marge decide that it's time to take stock of their family finances to see how they will be able to pay for Lisa's education. They have constructed the following personal balance sheet and cash flow statements.

Cash Inflows (Monthly)		Cash Outflows (Monthly)	
Homer's gross income	$5,400	Income/payroll taxes	$2,000
Interest income	500	Groceries	600
		Mortgage payment	750
		Property taxes	190
		Homeowner's insurance	60
		Utilities	150
		Car loan payment	240
		Car expenses	125
		Auto insurance	60
		Credit card payments	215
		Clothing/gifts	170
		Entertainment	235
		Vacations	300
		Retirement funds	400
		Church donations	80
		Other expenses	160
Total Cash Inflows	$5,900	Total Cash Outflows	$5,735

Assets		Debts	
Bank accounts	$3,000	Current bills	$1,200
Car	5,000	Credit cards	10,000
Personal assets	20,000	Car loan	8,000
Homer's retirement account	50,000	Mortgage	100,000
Marge's IRA	9,000	Total Debts	$119,200
Market value of home	150,000		
Total Assets	$237,000		

   a. Describe how Marge and Homer most likely determined the values of their car and home.

   b. Calculate the family's net worth and net cash flow.

   c. After calculating their net cash flow, Marge is surprised to find that they should have a little money left over every month. She has usually found that they are down to their last dollar by the end of the month. "Doh!" says Homer, "I forgot to count my tab at Moe's." If the couple recorded all their other expenses accurately, how much is Homer spending each month on beer at Moe's, and should they revise their cash flow statement to reflect this expenditure?

   d. How will Marge and Homer's net cash flow and net worth change after they adjust their statements to reflect Homer's extra entertainment expenditures?

   e. Evaluate Homer and Marge's financial status with respect to liquidity, debt, and savings using personal financial ratios.

   f. Based on your analysis of Homer and Marge's household finances, do you think they are sufficiently prepared to send Lisa to college in four years? What suggestions do you have for improving their personal finances?

2. Melody and Charles Verona have been married for less than one year and currently live in a one-bedroom apartment. They would like a bigger place, and with two incomes, they think they could afford to pay a mortgage on a small house or condominium. Unfortunately, they don't have enough for a down payment yet, so they want to begin saving for this purpose. Over the last few months, Melody has been dismayed to find that they always seem to be a little short on cash at the end of the month. She decides to sit down with Charles to look more carefully at their spending habits and begin making a plan that will enable them to buy a house. The Veronas collect the following financial information in preparation for evaluating their current finances and determining how much to save:

Cash Inflows	Gross Income	After-Tax Income
Melody	$32,000	$25,000
Charles	35,000	27,000

Cash Outflows	Monthly
Groceries	$500
Eating out	250
Rent	1,250
Credit card payments	200
Telephone	100
Utilities	116
Car loan payments	560
Car expenses and fuel	260
Clothing	150
Entertainment	200
Health club membership	60
Travel and vacations	200

  a. Assuming that the cash flows above are accurate and complete, calculate the Veronas' net monthly cash flow.

  b. If the Veronas could allocate their net cash flow to savings each month and could earn 4 percent after taxes, how much would they have in the account after two years?

  c. What is a possible explanation for why the Veronas are having cash flow problems each month? What would you suggest they do to identify the reasons for this problem?

  d. Are there any categories of expenditures that the Veronas may have neglected to include on the list?

  e. Calculate the couple's debt payment ratio. What does this say about their ability to manage additional debt?

  f. Assuming that Melody and Charles receive 4 percent raises each year for the next two years and that their income tax rate is 20 percent, what will be the total of their after-tax income for the second year? How will the increased income affect their debt payment ratio?

3. Kristopher Stephens is a 19-year-old college student. His parents pay his college tuition, buy his books, and cover his room and board expenses, but they expect him to earn enough to cover all his incidental expenses while he is in school. He estimates that these total about $60 per week for the 40 weeks that he isn't home for the summer. He nets $2,600 after taxes from his summer job, and he has a part-time job at the university from which he earns $50 per week after taxes. Kristopher would like to buy a used car that costs $5,000. He estimates that he can obtain a car loan at 6 percent interest for three years. He expects to make a down payment of $500.

  a. What is Kristopher's annual net cash flow?

  b. What will the monthly payment on his car loan be under these terms? How much will he pay each year (round to the nearest dollar)?

  c. Are there any additional car expenses that Kristopher should take into account?

  d. Can he afford to buy the car? Why or why not?

CHAPTER 3

Budgeting and Cash Management

Feature Story

Alicia couldn't understand why she always seemed to be running out of money at the end of the month. On the advice of a friend, she decided to record all her out-of-pocket expenses for several months. What she discovered turned out to be an eye-opener. Although she didn't splurge on herself, Alicia found that she was a sucker for a good cause. In addition to regular tax-deductible contributions to the local animal shelter and the food bank, she was frequently solicited by members of her large circle of artistic friends to support their latest projects. Her friend Marlo was working on a documentary. Another friend, Katrina, had started a GoFundMe campaign to help her pay for a professional studio to record her first original album. After Alicia had helped out one friend, she felt she couldn't say "no" when others asked. Even though she didn't give a lot to any single project, a few dollars here and there added up to a cash management problem. Charitable giving can certainly be part of a comprehensive financial plan—but Alicia's donations did not generate any investment return to her, were not tax-deductible, and were stretching her budget.

LEARNING OBJECTIVES	TOPICS	DEMONSTRATION PROBLEMS
3.1 Develop, implement, and monitor a household budget.	**3.1 Developing, Implementing, and Monitoring a Household Budget** • Factors Affecting Household Budgets • The Budgeting Process • Money Attitudes and Household Budgeting	
3.2 Explain why cash management is an important component of your financial plan.	**3.2 The Role of Cash in Your Financial Plan** • Costs and Benefits of Holding Cash • How Much Should You Hold in Cash? • Rules of Effective Cash Management	

(continued)

(continued)

LEARNING OBJECTIVES	TOPICS	DEMONSTRATION PROBLEMS
3.3 Identify and evaluate the types of financial institutions that provide cash management services.	**3.3 Providers of Cash Management Services** • Depository Institutions • Nondepository Institutions • Evaluating Financial Institutions	
3.4 Evaluate checking and savings account choices based on liquidity, safety, and cost.	**3.4 Evaluating Cash Management Products and Services** • Criteria for Evaluating Cash Management Accounts • Checking Accounts • Savings Accounts • The Rule of 72	**3.1** Using the Rule of 72
3.5 Select appropriate tools for dealing with cash management problems, and protect yourself from identity theft.	**3.5 Resolving Cash Management Problems and Avoiding Identify Theft** • Cash Management Problems and Solutions • Identity Theft	

3.1 Developing, Implementing, and Monitoring a Household Budget

LEARNING OBJECTIVE 3.1
Develop, implement, and monitor a household budget.

You now know how to set financial goals and evaluate your personal financial situation. Unplanned small cash outflows, such as Alicia's contributions to her friends' projects in the Feature Story, can interfere with your ability to achieve those goals—that is, *unless* you've included those outflows in your financial plan and budget.

In the last chapter, you created a personal balance sheet and a personal cash flow statement in order to evaluate how well you've managed your money *in the past*. In this chapter, you'll learn how to create a **budget**, which is a plan for *future* spending and saving that will enable you to achieve your financial goals. The budgeting process is critical to the success of your financial plan.

If charitable giving is a priority, you can include it in your annual budget, but you'll also want to consider the tax consequences. Even if, like Alicia, you consider gifts to aspiring artist friends to be charitable contributions, those contributions won't be tax-deductible. You may want to focus instead on other types of donations in your budgeting plan.

Factors Affecting Household Budgets

Many factors affect household budgets and the allocation of funds to specific categories of expenditures. Family size and makeup, age and education of household members, sources and amounts of income, and money attitudes all have an impact on budget decisions. **Figure 3.1** shows how people in different age groups allocate their funds across several budgetary categories. **Table 3.1** shows corresponding budget amounts.

FIGURE 3.1 **Average Household Budget Allocations for Different Age Groups**   Your allocation of funds among various categories of expenditures is likely to change as you get older.

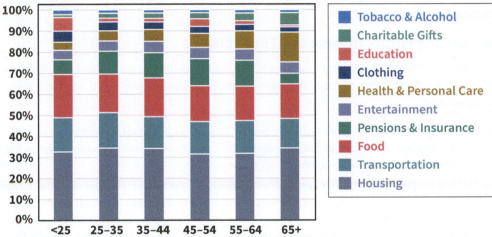

Source: U.S. Bureau of Labor Statistics, *Consumer Expenditure Survey 2017*, www.bls.gov.

TABLE 3.1   **Average Household Budget Amounts for Different Age Groups**

Age	Housing	Trans-portation	Food	Pensions & Insurance	Enter-tainment	Health & Personal Care	Clothing	Edu-cation	Chari-table Gifts	Tobacco & Alcohol	Total
<25	$11,255	$ 6,655	4,759	$2,567	$1,488	$2,020	$1,315	$2,333	$ 299	$ 537	$33,228
25–35	19,927	9,115	7,390	6,590	2,644	3,806	2,042	1,234	949	896	54,593
35–44	23,805	11,054	9,376	8,341	4,001	5,307	2,377	1,004	1,580	990	67,835
45–54	23,205	11,755	9,270	9,622	4,064	5,894	2,308	3,213	2,218	1,043	72,592
55–64	20,127	10,185	7,894	8,705	3,444	6,527	1,720	1,644	2,357	1,038	63,641
65+	16,668	7,513	6,326	3,230	2,636	7,290	1,193	388	2,430	678	48,342

Source: U.S. Bureau of Labor Statistics, *Consumer Expenditure Survey 2017*, www.bls.gov.

If you're a full-time student, it's likely that your allocation of funds to educational expenses is high, but that you're not yet allocating funds to savings. Families with young children spend more on housing and child care, whereas retirees have relatively high health care expenditures. Even within each category, however, you'll find wide variation across households.

The Budgeting Process

The budgeting process is the process of planning for future income and expenditures and tracking your actual cash flows over time. The process includes four steps:

1. Forecasting
2. Implementing
3. Monitoring
4. Reevaluating regularly

If you haven't already organized your financial data, as explained in Chapter 2, then you'll need to do so before proceeding with the budgeting process. In this section, we discuss this process and provide an example.

Forecasting Future Income and Expenditures

Because your budget is a plan for future spending, you'll need to forecast your future income and expenditures as a part of the budgeting process. Before you begin, you'll need to answer two questions:

- **What time period will your budget cover?** Although an annual budget can help with the big picture, most people find it necessary to budget on a monthly basis covering the entire year to coincide with payment obligations.

- **How will you keep your records?** You need to decide at the outset about the record-keeping format that you'll employ. You can use your personal cash flow statement as a starting point, but you may want to condense or expand on the categories of income and expenses used in that financial statement to develop a budgeting system that works for you. The process of recording day-to-day expenditures can be tedious but is absolutely necessary, so you should make it simple enough to ensure that you'll do it on a regular basis. You can use **Excel Worksheet 3.1** (Personal Financial Planner: Household Budget) as the starting point for your budget. Alternatively, you can purchase a home budget ledger at an office supply store or install budget software on your home computer.

EXCEL WORKSHEET

See **Excel Worksheet 3.1 (Personal Financial Planner: Household Budget)** in **WileyPLUS**.

Now it's time to tackle the key forecasting question: How much do you expect your income and expenses to change over time? In preparing your forecasting estimates, the best approach is to make two passes. In the first pass, go through each income or expense item on your financial statements and estimate its amount for the coming year based on past spending patterns and your reasonable expectations of the future. At this stage, don't add any expenditures for your new financial goals—we'll incorporate those changes in the second pass.

The starting point of your forecast is to estimate future changes in your income. A salary change will be easy to identify if you already know what your raise will be. Perhaps your employer has announced raises or you have a union-negotiated salary scale. Tips and bonuses are not as easy to estimate, but you should make a best (conservative) guess and plan to revise this part of your budget as you obtain new information.

Next, estimate your expenses. Fixed expenses such as loan payments are, by definition, going to remain about the same. Even fixed expenses can change year to year, however. For example, rent is usually a fixed expense for one year, but your landlord may raise your rent next year. Variable expenses, such as food and clothing, may be more difficult to estimate. One approach is to take current variable expenses and increase them by the expected rate of inflation. For example, if you spent $600 on clothing last year and you anticipate 4 percent inflation, your clothing expenditures for the coming year can be estimated as $600 × 1.04 = $624. Note that this is the calculation for the future value of a lump sum for one period at 4 percent interest.

Implementing Your Budget

Once you've estimated all the line items in the first pass, you can calculate your estimated net cash flow—total cash inflows less total cash outflows. If this value is negative, you'll need to come up with a plan for increasing your income or reducing your expenditures to reconcile your budget. **Reconciling a budget** is the process of adjusting income and spending so that your expenses do not exceed your income. Variable expenses can be changed most easily in the short run, but even fixed expenses can be reduced in the long run. For example, you could look for a less expensive apartment or change your phone plan.

After determining your net cash flow, you'll adjust your budget in a second pass, to reflect anticipated changes in spending and saving that will result from your new budget plan. Most important, in the second pass you should include the estimated costs associated with your new financial goals. If your second pass reveals that you won't be able to fully cover the new costs, you'll need to make additional changes to reduce expenses, increase your income, or adjust your financial goals to be more realistic, given your financial constraints.

To observe the budgeting process in action, we'll walk through Rosa and Mateo Rivera's income and expenditures from the current year and their forecasts for next year in **Case Study 3.1**.

ONLINE CALCULATOR DEMONSTRATION VIDEO

See **Online Calculator Demonstration Video: Using a Budget App** in **WileyPLUS.**

Case Study 3.1

ESB Professional/Shutterstock.com

The Riveras Develop a Budget

Problem

Rosa and Mateo Rivera, who have a son from Rosa's first marriage and are expecting a baby, want to develop a budget that will allow them to achieve several financial goals. They would like to increase saving for college and retirement, and they would like Rosa to be able to quit work after their baby is born.

Strategy

Using their current year personal financial statements and Excel Worksheet 3.1, Rosa and Mateo put together a forecast for the following year to determine whether Rosa can quit work to become a full-time homemaker.

Solution   **Figure 3.2** shows the Riveras' budget forecast. Notes in the "Comments" column explain how they arrived at their forecast amounts for each line item. For income, they entered Mateo's expected after-tax income based on his anticipated 10 percent raise. For most variable expenses in the first pass, Rosa and Mateo simply assumed an increase of 4 percent due to inflation.

The first pass at next year's budget shows that, without Rosa's income, the Riveras will not be able to meet their expenses without a change in spending behavior to cover a shortfall of $5,040. And keep in mind that they still haven't put any money toward their other financial objectives.

FIGURE 3.2 Sample of Excel Worksheet 3.1: The Riveras' First-Pass Household Budget

	A	B	C	D
		Actual Current-Year Cash Flows	First-Pass Budget for Next Year	Comments
1				
2	**Cash Inflows**			
3	Mateo's after-tax income	$48,000	$52,800	Raise
4	Rosa's after-tax income	18,000	0	Rosa quits work
5	Interest/dividend income	50	51	
6	Child support from Rosa's ex-husband	5,200	5,200	
7				
8	**Total Income**	**$71,250**	**$58,051**	$13,199 difference
9				
10	**Cash Outflows**			
11	Groceries and eating out	10,400	10,816	Inflation
12	Housing			
13	Mortgage principal and interest	10,800	10,800	
14	House repairs/expenses	2,000	2,080	Inflation
15	Property taxes and insurance	3,000	3,100	Inflation
16	Utilities			
17	Heating	1,200	1,248	Inflation
18	Electric	600	624	Inflation
19	Water and sewer	420	437	Inflation
20	Cable/phone/satellite	600	624	Inflation
21	Car loan payments	2,851	2,851	4 years to go
22	Car maintenance/gas	3,180	3,307	Inflation
23	Credit card payments	1,440	1,440	
24	Insurance			
25	Life	150	156	Increase in premium
26	Health	1,800	2,300	Increase in premium
27	Auto	1,200	1,320	Increase in premium
28	Disability			
29	Clothing	1,000	1,040	Inflation
30	Gifts	2,000	2,080	Inflation
31	Other consumer goods (e.g., TVs)	1,800	1,872	Inflation
32	Child-care expenses	2,700	1,140	Rosa provides most care
33	Sports-related expenses	180	204	
34	Health club dues	420	420	
35	Uninsured medical expenses	540	1,000	Baby costs
36	Education/training	600	600	Mateo's continuing education
37	College fund and other saving			
38	Vacations	6,000	6,240	Inflation
39	Entertainment	2,040	2,124	Inflation
40	Charitable contributions	1,200	1,248	
41	Non-employer retirement contributions	3,000	3,300	
42	Magazine subscriptions/books	120	120	
43	Other payments/expenses	600	600	
44				
45	**Total Expenses**	**$61,841**	**$63,091**	
46				
47	**Net Personal Cash Flow**	**$9,409**	**−$5,040**	
48				

The "Final Budget" column in **Figure 3.3** shows the Riveras' second-pass budget, in which they've carefully considered all their expected cash flows and decided on ways to reduce discretionary spending (indicated by peach highlighting in the that column). They also estimate that they can reduce expenses by refinancing their home and paying off their credit card debt while Rosa is still working.

As a result, the Riveras find that they will have sufficient extra cash flow to apply some funds to their other financial objectives, as indicated by light blue highlighting in the "Final Budget" column. Now the challenge will be for the Riveras to stick to their plan!

FIGURE 3.3   **Sample of Excel Worksheet 3.1: The Riveras' Second-Pass Household Budget**

	A	B	C	D	E
1		Actual Current-Year Cash Flows	First-Pass Budget for Next Year	Final Budget for Next Year	Comments
2	**Cash Inflows**				
3	Mateo's after-tax income	$48,000	$52,800	$52,800	Raise
4	Rosa's after-tax income	18,000	0	0	Rosa quits work
5	Interest/dividend income	50	51	51	
6	Child support from Rosa's ex-husband	5,200	5,200	5,200	
7					
8	**Total Income**	**$71,250**	**$58,051**	**$58,051**	$13,199 difference
9					
10	**Cash Outflows**				
11	Groceries and eating out	10,400	10,816	9,400	Eat out less
12	Housing				
13	Mortgage principal and interest	10,800	10,800	9,600	Refinance at lower rate
14	House repairs/expenses	2,000	2,080	1,000	Delay maintenance
15	Property taxes and insurance	3,000	3,100	3,100	Inflation
16	Utilities				
17	Heating	1,200	1,248	1,248	Inflation
18	Electric	600	624	624	Inflation
19	Water and sewer	420	437	437	Inflation
20	Cable/phone/satellite	600	624	624	Inflation
21	Car loan payments	2,851	2,851	2,851	4 years to go
22	Car maintenance/gas	3,180	3,307	3,000	Rosa drives less
23	Credit card payments	1,440	1,440	0	Pay off balances
24	Insurance				
25	Life	150	156	300	Insure Rosa
26	Health	1,800	2,300	2,300	Increase in premium
27	Auto	1,200	1,320	1,320	Increase in premium
28	Disability			600	For Mateo
29	Clothing	1,000	1,040	700	Reduce spending
30	Gifts	2,000	2,080	1,000	Careful shopping
31	Other consumer goods (e.g., TVs)	1,800	1,872	1,500	Reduce spending
32	Child-care expenses	2,700		1,140	Rosa provides most care
33	Sports-related expenses	180	204	204	
34	Health club dues	420	420	420	
35	Uninsured medical expenses	540	1,000	1,000	Baby costs
36	Education/training	600	600	600	Mateo's continuing ed.
37	College fund			2,400	For the children
38	Vacations	6,000	6,240	3,000	Reduce spending
39	Entertainment	2,040	2,124	1,000	Reduce spending
40	Charitable contributions	1,200	1,248	1,248	
41	Non-employer retirement contributions	3,000	3,300	6,300	IRA for Rosa
42	Magazine subscriptions/books	120	120	120	
43	Other payments/expenses	600	600	600	
44					
45	**Total Expenses**	**$61,841**	**$63,091**	**$57,636**	
46					
47	**Net Personal Cash Flow**	**$9,409**	**–$5,040**	**$415**	
48					

As you can see from Case Study 3.1, careful consideration of your pattern of expenditures can help you identify ways to reallocate funds to achieve your financial objectives.

Monitoring Your Budget

Planning to reduce your expenditures is an excellent start, but following the plan is often more difficult. Old spending habits are sometimes hard to break. After you've implemented a new budget, you'll need to keep track of how well you're sticking to it.

A **budget variance** occurs when your actual expenses are different from your budgeted expenses. There are two main reasons for tracking budget variances:

- To identify small cash leakages as soon as possible so that you can change your behavior before you have a major budget shortfall.
- To ensure that large irregular cash expenses do not cause financial hardship. Income often comes in regular, predictable amounts, whereas some expenses, such as unexpected car and home repairs, tuition bills, or tax payments, may come in chunks and must be budgeted for in advance.

A good way to track variances from your budget is by creating a monthly spending plan and tracking your actual spending to see how much it varies from your projections. You can do this using **Excel Worksheet 3.2** (Personal Financial Planner: Budget Tracker). In **Case Study 3.2**, the Riveras use this worksheet to track their budget for several months and evaluate their budget variances.

Household budgets can experience some variance from month to month due to large one-time expenditures. Many household expenses, such as health club dues and magazine subscriptions, are paid one time and cover the whole year. If such expenses are incurred early in the year, the family budget may be strained for a bit. For example, in Case Study 3.2, the Riveras' uninsured medical expenses were larger than budgeted in January, in part because their $500 health care insurance deductible must be paid out-of-pocket before the insurer begins to cover medical costs.

EXCEL WORKSHEET

See **Excel Worksheet 3.2 (Personal Financial Planner: Budget Tracker)** in **WileyPLUS**.

Case Study 3.2

ESB Professional/Shutterstock.com

The Riveras Track Their Budget Variances

Problem

Rosa and Mateo Rivera developed a new budget that they hoped would allow them to achieve some of their financial goals. Now they want to find out whether they are on track.

Strategy

Rosa and Mateo keep track of their monthly expenses for the first three months of the year. They record all their income and expenses for those months in Excel Worksheet 3.2.

Solution   The Budget Tracker worksheet that the Riveras completed is shown in **Figure 3.4.** The first column in the worksheet shows the budgeted monthly amount, which is the annual amount from their budget ($58,051, as shown earlier in Figure 3.3), divided by 12. The actual expenditures are shown for each month, and the "Variance" column shows how much actual expenses deviated from budgeted expenses, with negative numbers indicating that the Riveras spent more than they budgeted. For example, in the month of January, they spent $117 more than they had budgeted on groceries and eating out. To sum up, the Riveras had a small budget shortfall in January (–$32) but were ahead in February (+$398) and March (+$478) for a total cumulative variance of $845 by the end of March.

FIGURE 3.4 Sample of Excel Worksheet 3.2: The Riveras' Budget Tracker, January to March.

	A	B	C	D	E	F	G	H
1		**Actual Expenditures and Variance from Budgeted Amount**						
2		Monthly Budget	Actual, January	Variance	Actual, February	Variance	Actual, March	Variance
3	**Cash Inflows**	$4,837	$4,837	0	$4,837	0	$4,837	0
4								
5	**Cash Outflows**							
6	Groceries and eating out	783	900	−117	800	−17	750	33
7	Housing		0					
8	Mortgage principal and interest	800	800	0	800	0	800	0
9	House repairs/expenses	83	0	83	0	83	300	−217
10	Property taxes and insurance	258	258	0	258	0	258	0
11	Utilities							
12	Heating	104	150	−46	170	−66	130	−26
13	Electric	52	45	7	50	2	35	17
14	Water and sewer	36	36	0	36	0	36	0
15	Cable/phone/satellite	52	52	0	52	0	52	0
16	Car loan payments	238	238	0	238	0	238	0
17	Car maintenance/gas	250	190	60	230	20	200	50
18	Credit card payments	0	0	0	0	0	0	0
19	Insurance							
20	Life	25	25	0	25	0	25	0
21	Health	192	192	0	192	0	192	0
22	Auto	110	110	0	110	0	110	0
23	Disability	50	50	0	50	0	50	0
24	Clothing	58	0	58	75	−17	50	8
25	Gifts	83	50	33	0	83	0	83
26	Other consumables (TVs, etc.)	125	0	125	0	125	0	125
27	Child-care expenses	95	75	20	75	20	75	20
28	Sports-related expenses	17	50	−33	0	17	0	17
29	Health club dues	35	400	−365	0	35	0	35
30	Uninsured medical expenses	83	200	−117	30	53	30	53
31	Education/training	50	0	50	250	−200	0	50
32	College fund	200	200	0	200	0	200	0
33	Vacations	250	0	250	0	250	0	250
34	Entertainment	83	120	−37	60	23	100	−17
35	Charitable contributions	104	104	0	104	0	104	0
36	Non-employer retirement contributions	525	525	0	525	0	525	0
37	Magazine subscriptions/books	10	0	10	30	−20	30	−20
38	Other payments/expenses	50	65	−15	45	5	35	15
39	**Total Cash Outflows**	$4,803	$4,835		$4,405		$4,325	
40								
41	**Net Personal Cash Flow**	$34	$2		$432		$512	
42								
43	**Total Monthly Variance**			($32)		$398		$478
44								

Fortunately, the Rivera household's income was sufficient to cover their out-of-pocket medical costs at the beginning of the year. Many households are not as fortunate and must plan in advance to cover large irregular expenses. You can deal with this problem in various ways:

- Build a fund for this purpose (over the course of the previous months). If, for example, you pay your health club dues every January, then starting in February you could begin to set aside the money for the following year's dues so that, by the following January, you would have the funds and it wouldn't be a big hit to your budget for that month.

- Use emergency funds (and replace them in later months). In Chapter 1, we discussed the importance of having an emergency fund. One of the purposes of such a fund is to help you manage monthly budget fluctuations.

- Obtain a short-term loan (but be sure to include financing costs in your budget). Some households use credit cards to cover unexpected expenses, but this strategy can be dangerous if you don't have a clear plan to pay back this borrowing promptly.

Revising Your Budget

After tracking your budget for several months, you might find that you have been too conservative in estimating certain expenses or that you have forgotten to make allowances for unexpected expenses, such as car repairs or medical bills. In either case, you need to go back to the original budget and revise it so that, going forward, you'll be able to meet your expenses.

Reflection Question 1

Based on your own experience, which categories of your budget are you most likely to underestimate, and why?

INTERACTIVE

To test your understanding of the budgeting process, see **Interactive: The Budgeting Process** in **WileyPLUS**.

If the reason you're exceeding your budget is that you've failing to control your discretionary spending in certain areas, you should take the time to review your financial goals, evaluate your progress toward meeting them, and carefully weigh the benefits and costs of the purchases that are interfering with your plan. Research also shows that unexpected events, such as layoff, illness, and divorce, often lead to household financial distress. Even though you can't necessarily anticipate these problems, you can lessen the impact by maintaining an emergency fund. Some advice for dealing with these and other common budget problems is offered in **Table 3.2**. To practice identifying where various activities fit in the budgeting process, go to **Interactive: The Budgeting Process**.

TABLE 3.2   **Solutions for Common Budget Mistakes**

Common Budget Mistakes	Budget Solution
1. Having too little emergency cash. Many families live from paycheck to paycheck. A layoff, a car breakdown, or an unexpected bill can lead to financial crisis.	Budget for an emergency fund using an automatic transfer from your paycheck to a liquid savings account. Also, deposit any windfalls or unexpected refunds into this account.
2. Supersizing your house. People are often tempted to buy the largest house they can afford. They assume that their income will rise, making it gradually easier to pay the fixed mortgage payment. Expensive houses come with increased costs for maintenance, taxes, and insurance. Too much debt and you won't be able to survive a break in employment.	Downsize. Even though lenders may allow you to borrow more, keep your housing expenditures under 25 percent of your pretax income.
3. Buying stuff you don't need. Everyone is guilty of doing this at times. But when money is tight, many don't know how to stop.	Having a budget will help, but if you have a serious spending problem, you can try leaving credit cards at home, require another family member to sign off on all purchases above a specified dollar limit, or stick to a "need" list.

(continued)

TABLE 3.2   Solutions for Common Budget Mistakes *(continued)*

Common Budget Mistakes	Budget Solution
4. Being too generous. Whether it's charity, gift giving, or lavish birthday parties for your kids, it makes no sense to be generous with money you can't afford to give away.	Budget for such expenditures and avoid making impulse purchases or donations. Consider ways to give your time and talents instead of money. Create an account to save for next year's donations and gifts. Spend only from that account the following year. When the money's gone, no more gifts.
5. Getting used to living on two incomes. Once you get used to living on two incomes, it's much more difficult to go back to one in the event of illness, childbirth, or layoff.	Even if you are a double-income family, you should try to live on only one, saving and investing the remainder and using it for extras like vacations or special purchases. This will increase your financial flexibility to deal with the unexpected.
6. Overusing credit cards. If you're not paying your balance in full each month, then you likely have not fully accounted for credit card expenditures in your budget. Your overall financial position will decline as debt increases.	Always keep track of total expenditures, including those that were on credit. Try to pay the balance in full each month. If it's already too much, make a plan for paying it off over as short a period of time as possible, and don't use your cards for new purchases.
7. Underinsuring. Even though health insurance can be a large monthly expense if your employer doesn't cover all the premiums, it's a mistake to be uninsured. Twenty percent of bankruptcies are triggered by medical bills.	Budget to be able to afford at least a catastrophic health plan (with a large deductible). Shop on a state or federal health exchange and look into deals with organizations such as the AARP or AAA.
8. Delaying education saving. Preschool, private K–12, and college costs are all increasing faster than inflation. The longer you wait to start saving for these expenditures, the more you'll need to put in each month.	Set up an education savings plan as soon as a child is born, and include it in your budget. Never borrow to pay for elementary or secondary education. Consider less expensive options for college, including community colleges and in-state universities. Plan for your child to pay for a share of the costs.
9. Underestimating the cost of divorce. Two households are more expensive than one, so a divorce usually has negative financial consequences for both ex-spouses.	A prenuptial agreement can reduce the risk of a costly court battle. Go to counseling before making the decision to divorce. If divorce is inevitable, close joint accounts and refinance mortgages to avoid getting tangled in your ex-spouse's financial issues.

Money Attitudes and Household Budgeting

Our consideration of budgeting would be incomplete without some discussion of the relationship between budgeting and money attitudes. Individual differences in money attitudes and spending behavior are a major cause of conflict in relationships, not only for families who are struggling to meet a minimum standard of living, but also in affluent households. If you are a saver and your spouse is a spender, your family may have difficulty developing and sticking to a household budget. As discussed in **Ethics in Action**, these differences may also create conflicts among family members and incentives for deceptive behavior.

Ethics in Action

Financial Infidelity

Do you and your spouse or partner ever have arguments about money? If so, you're certainly not alone. A survey of more than a thousand adults by the American Institute of CPAs (AICPA) in March 2012 found that married couples averaged three to four disagreements over financial issues per month! Unexpected expenses, insufficient savings, and differing opinions over "needs" versus "wants" were identified as common sources of trouble.

Have you ever hidden purchases from your spouse or partner? Made a major purchase without consulting with your spouse or partner? Given the high incidence of money-related arguments, it probably shouldn't be surprising that the AICPA study also found that many married people had engaged in deceitful behavior related to their finances. After all, if your spouse doesn't know about it, he or she can't get mad, right?

A few years ago, the National Foundation for Financial Education (NEFE) commissioned a Harris Interactive poll of 1,339 U.S. adults. As you can see in **Figure 3.5**, three in ten of the respondents admitted to some sort of financial infidelity. Hiding cash and minor purchases were the most common deceptions. Women were slightly more likely to have committed each of the types of deceptions.

FIGURE 3.5 Financial Infidelity Among Adults Who Have Combined Finances with a Spouse or Partner

About one-third of survey respondents had deceived their partner or spouse about a financial issue.

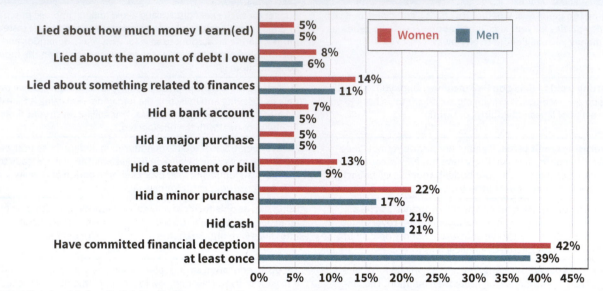

Source: Based on data from Harris Interactive Survey commissioned by National Endowment for Financial Education, January 2018, www.nefe.org.

Committing financial deception can negatively affect relationships in many ways. **Figure 3.6** details, by gender of the respondent, the ways in which the respondents' financial infidelity impacted current or past relationships.

FIGURE 3.6 Effect of Financial Deception on Current and/or Past Relationships

Financial deception can have serious negative consequences on a couple's relationship.

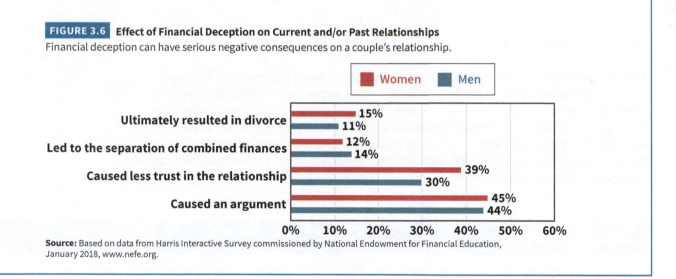

Source: Based on data from Harris Interactive Survey commissioned by National Endowment for Financial Education, January 2018, www.nefe.org.

Clearly, it is essential to have a frank discussion about money with your partner, preferably before you marry or move in together. In general, you can reduce the risk of future problems by setting at the beginning ground rules that are agreeable to both of you. These should be established after careful consideration and open discussion. **Table 3.3** identifies financial issues you may want to resolve in advance and outlines some possible strategies.

TABLE 3.3	Financial Issues to Resolve Before Marriage
Household Financial Management Issues	**Possible Strategies**
Who will manage the finances in the household, pay regular bills, and make investment decisions?	Couples can split up the regular financial tasks, manage them jointly, or decide that one person will take charge.
Will each person retain individual control over some of the money?	Couples can decide to pool everything, maintain a household account, or keep everything separate. Experts recommend that, even when household funds are pooled, each person should have control over some discretionary funds.
Which household expenditures require joint agreement?	Couples should discuss a dollar threshold for expenditures that require joint agreement.
When is it okay to use debt to finance purchases?	Agreement should be reached on the appropriate use of credit cards and other borrowed funds. If one person wants to maintain a more expensive lifestyle by borrowing and the other can't stand debt, this could create future strife. A compromise might be to use borrowed funds only for large-ticket items like cars and houses.
How much should be saved?	Saving for the future necessarily means less money for current consumption. Couples should agree in advance on the goals they will work toward and the degree of sacrifice they are willing to incur to achieve those goals.
How much should be allocated to gift giving?	Families differ widely in their gift-giving traditions. To avoid future conflict, it will be necessary to compromise somewhere in the middle, limiting the occasions on which gifts are given and the dollar amounts per gift.
Who pays expenses associated with children from previous marriages?	Court-ordered child support and maintenance, costs for children living in your home, and future college-funding costs can all be significant drains on household funds and should be discussed in detail with a future spouse in advance.
Who pays for the debt that precedes the marriage?	Even if you buy into the "yours, mine, and ours" philosophy of marriage, if one partner brings a lot of debt to the marriage, it may not be fair to expect the other to pay for it. In numerous cases, a starry-eyed newlywed has paid off her or his new spouse's debts only to have the spouse leave the marriage shortly thereafter—with no debt. Having a plan will reduce this problem.
What will happen to assets in the event of a divorce?	With the prevalence of divorce, individuals who bring substantial assets to a marriage often enter into a **prenuptial agreement**, a written contract in that specifies how the assets will be distributed in the event of a divorce. Although it may seem very unromantic to anticipate divorce when you aren't even married yet, the process of discussing the prenuptial agreement may open the door to discussing and resolving differences in money attitudes.

3.2 The Role of Cash in Your Financial Plan

LEARNING OBJECTIVE 3.2

Explain why cash management is an important component of your financial plan.

Many people are guilty of occasionally, or not so occasionally, neglecting to balance their checkbook or paying a bill late. Keeping track of account balances and paying bills on time are both important tasks associated with **cash management**, a foundation component of your financial plan.

Cash management includes all decisions related to cash payments and short-term (one year or less) liquid investments. As discussed in Chapter 2, liquid investments are those that can

INTERACTIVE

For more practice with these concepts, see Interactive: **Liquid Assets** in **WileyPLUS**.

easily be converted to cash without loss of value, such as funds in a checking or savings account. (To test your understanding of liquidity, see **Interactive: Liquid Assets**.) Although you can, of course, leave money in these accounts for longer periods, they are not generally the best choice for long-term savings.

Costs and Benefits of Holding Cash

When you hold cash, whether it's in a bank checking or savings account, your mobile money account, or in your pocket, you incur certain costs. For one, you give up the opportunity to invest those dollars in a way that will earn you a higher rate of return, and some types of accounts require that you pay additional fees. What is the cost of keeping funds in a Venmo or Square Cash account on which you earn no interest? If you carry an average balance of $1,000 in your Venmo account for a year, and you could instead have invested those funds to earn 5 percent interest, you've effectively given up $50 in interest (5 percent of $1,000). The convenience of easy transfer of money between friends that a Venmo account represents may make it worth the $50 cost. However, you should definitely avoid services that charge you a fee for making payments. These can easily add up to a substantial annual cost.

An additional cost of holding cash is psychological—if you have money sitting in your Venmo or checking account, it's very easy to spend. It would be a shame if all your hard work in developing your budget went to waste because you couldn't resist the temptation of buying something that wasn't in your budget plan. In contrast, if you keep your cash in an account that's not as easy to access, such as a savings account, you'll be more likely to stick to your plan.

Given that cash accounts pay less interest and increase the risk of overspending, why are we willing to incur these costs? There are three general reasons for holding cash:

- managing transaction needs
- preparing for cash emergencies
- making a temporary investment

All these purposes are related to managing liquidity. Money held in less liquid investments, such as bonds, stocks, and real estate, provides a better investment return than money held in checking and saving accounts, but it's also more difficult to access on short notice. Next, we examine each of the reasons for holding cash.

Managing Monthly Transactions

Everyone has bills. Rent, food, utilities, car payments, and other expenses must be paid as they come due. A transaction account, such as a checking account or Venmo account, allows you to easily deposit and withdraw funds, as well as make electronic payments in a timely fashion and at minimal cost.

Many people find it convenient to deposit their paycheck each month into a checking account from which they can pay their bills. Whether you use your bank's bill-paying service or sign up with your creditors for automatic payments, you'll need to have sufficient funds in the account each month to cover recurring monthly expenses. However, if your paycheck is normally *greater* than the total monthly payments you make from the account, then it makes sense to carefully estimate your transaction needs and to have the extra amount automatically transferred to an interest-earning account each month.

Preparing for Cash Emergencies

Life is full of unpredictable events. Maybe the car needs a new $2,000 transmission. Or your son breaks his arm playing football and you have to pay $400 in doctors' bills. More serious emergencies might involve loss of a job or temporary disability. In order to meet your emergency cash needs, it's important to manage your financial assets so that you can access cash when needed. Most households should have a **cash reserve**—a fund that you can turn to in the event of an emergency.

In your grandparents' day, a family's emergency fund might have been a few hundred dollars hidden in the bottom of a cookie jar or under a mattress. Today there are many other options for emergency cash needs. In addition to traditional checking and savings accounts, you can arrange for credit card and home equity lines of credit that can be accessed in the event of an emergency but that otherwise incur no interest. In Chapter 5, you'll see that you should avoid using credit cards as much as possible because of their high interest costs. However, it's worth noting here that they can be a source of short-term liquidity as long as you anticipate having the funds to repay the borrowed amounts in the near future.

Making a Temporary Investment

The third reason you might hold cash is in anticipation of a near-term need for the funds. Perhaps you're saving for a vacation or a new car. Maybe you're planning to apply the funds to the purchase of a new home or next semester's tuition bill. Or you may have sold some other assets recently and haven't yet decided how to reinvest the funds. All of these are situations that may justify temporarily holding excess cash in a liquid account.

How Much Should You Hold in Cash?

There's considerable debate among financial experts regarding how much money a typical household should hold in cash. Minor cash emergencies such as a car repair can be handled with a relatively modest emergency fund. In contrast, being out of work for a few months can have much more serious effects. Conservative financial advisors suggest that you should have sufficient liquid assets to cover five to eight months of regular expenses. Others suggest that two months is more than enough and recommend investing anything in excess of that amount for higher returns. For an average household with expenses of $2,000 per month, these rules of thumb would imply that from $4,000 to $16,000 should be held in cash or liquid assets.

Suppose you split the difference between the two positions and hold $10,000 in liquid assets. With that reserve, the risk of cash shortfall in the event of a big shock to your household income will be greatly reduced. But the cost can also be significant. Just how much would it cost you to be so "safe"?

Suppose that you hold $10,000 in an account that earns no interest and your alternative would be an investment that earns 8 percent per year. The opportunity cost of holding this large amount in cash is the average annual account balance multiplied by the difference between the interest you could earn on an alternative investment and the interest you are earning on the cash account. In this case, you would lose 8 percent on $10,000, or $800 per year. The reduction in risk may not be worth that much lost interest earnings. You could, however reduce the loss, by keeping some of the funds in cash and investing some in lower risk assets.

As part of your personal financial plan, you should assess your cash needs for transactions and emergencies, taking into consideration alternative sources you can tap into in the event of an emergency. You can use **Excel Worksheet 3.3** (Personal Financial Planner: Cash Needs Analysis) for this purpose. If you have a high risk of job loss, you might consider holding a relatively large amount in cash. In contrast, if you have a secure job and alternative sources of funds for emergencies, then you might hold only enough cash to meet your transaction requirements.

EXCEL WORKSHEET

See Excel Worksheet 3.3 (**Personal Financial Planner: Cash Needs Analysis**) in **WileyPLUS.**

Rules of Effective Cash Management

We've seen that most people need to hold cash for transaction needs, cash emergencies, and temporary investments. Cash management is, thus, an important part of your financial plan. Effective cash management will minimize the risk of bank charges for overdrafts and extra interest or penalties on overdue payments. Keeping careful track of cash flow is also necessary for budgeting expenditures. In this section, we consider four rules that, if followed, will result in better cash management outcomes:

1. Keep track of your cash by balancing your transaction accounts every month.
2. Develop a system to ensure that you pay your bills on time.
3. Stick to your financial plan by paying yourself first.
4. Use sound criteria to evaluate financial institutions and select products or services.

Balance Your Transaction Accounts Every Month

Regularly balancing your transaction accounts (checking and/or Venmo) is important for several reasons. With the increasing use of electronic payments, it's very easy to lose track of how much you spend every month, particularly if your household is one where more than one person is using the same account for transactions. If you don't balance your accounts regularly, you're more likely to exceed your budget or, worse yet, incur overdraft charges.

You should always record your transactions as they occur, keeping a running balance of the amount left in an account. It is often most convenient to keep a record in your smartphone of your checks, debit transactions, and electronic transfers, but any method of keeping track of your transactions will work. You should regularly check to be sure that your account balance correctly reflects the transactions you have made.

Reflection Question 2

What factors make you more or less likely to do a good job of keeping track of your account balances? What problems can result from failure to do so?

With computerized account records, it is highly unlikely that a bank statement will contain a mathematical error. There is, however, the possibility of errors in automatic withdrawals or ATM transactions. In rare cases, you may even find that someone has fraudulently accessed your account. It's important that you identify such errors promptly, because delay in discovering and reporting them makes it more difficult to get them corrected. The last section in this chapter discusses this and several other cash management problems and describes some methods for dealing with them.

Pay Your Bills on Time

Timely payment of bills will not only reduce your costs, but also minimize the risk that your credit rating will be adversely affected. As will be discussed in more detail in a later chapter, a history of late payments will make you a less attractive credit risk to financial institutions. As a result, you may not be able to qualify for loans, you may have to pay higher rates of interest, and you may have increased insurance premiums. By paying your bills on time, you'll also avoid getting annoying phone calls and emails from your creditors. One of the best ways to ensure that bills are paid on time is to arrange for automatic payment. This can usually be arranged directly with your creditors, or you can set up a bill-paying service through your bank.

Pay Yourself First

The single most common advice given by financial planners to their clients is "pay yourself first." What this means is that you should set aside the money necessary for achieving personal goals *before* you do anything else. If you wait until the end of the month to see how much is left to put into savings, inevitably there will be none left. If, instead, you treat savings as a primary expenditure and take it off the top before paying any other expenses, you are more likely to stick to your financial plan and avoid casual erosion of your cash flow.

There are many convenient ways to pay yourself first. Most banks and financial institutions offer the option of automatic funds transfer. Here, you arrange with your bank to have a certain amount of money automatically transferred from your checking to your savings or investment account as soon as your paycheck is deposited each pay period.

How much should you pay yourself first? In previous sections, you learned how to forecast your income and expenses to determine how much you will have left over each month. This is the amount that you should set aside at the beginning of the month or apply to meeting your financial goals.

Evaluate Alternative Accounts and Providers

Effective cash management requires that you carefully evaluate your alternatives and select the services and service providers that best meet your needs. You have many providers and services to choose from, and they vary widely in a number of ways: interest paid on similar accounts, fees charged for particular services, safety, and customer service. In the remaining sections of this chapter, we'll look more closely at different types of financial institutions and the variety of cash management products and services they offer.

3.3 | Providers of Cash Management Services

LEARNING OBJECTIVE 3.3
Identify and evaluate the types of financial institutions that provide cash management services.

At one time, cash management services could be obtained only at certain types of financial institutions. Today, however, many different types of financial institutions provide such services. This is the result of legislation introduced over the last two decades to foster competition. The good *and* bad news is that you now have many choices for cash management services. It's good news because competition often results in higher interest paid on accounts and lower interest charged on loans. It's bad news because having more choices means that it will take more time and effort to thoroughly investigate your alternatives.

The various types of financial institutions are identified by the general characteristics described in this section, but it's important to recognize that these differences are, for the most part, small and they are becoming less important over time. In general, financial institutions are classified according to where they primarily get their funds and what they primarily invest in. Financial institutions that get their funds from customer deposits are called **depository institutions**. Financial institutions that get their funds from other sources are called nondepository institutions.

Depository Institutions

Depository institutions include commercial banks, several types of savings institutions, and credit unions. All these types of firms are similar in two major ways:

- Their primary source of funds comes from customer deposits.
- Their primary source of income is interest earned on loans made to customers.

Personal accounts held in these institutions are insured for up to $250,000 per depositor by the **Federal Deposit Insurance Corporation (FDIC)**, a government-sponsored insurance agency. FDIC insurance applies to checking accounts, savings accounts, money market deposit accounts, and certificates of deposit (CDs) held in any insured bank or savings institution.

Commercial Banks

Often simply called a "bank," a **commercial bank** is a depository institution that gets its funds from checking and savings account deposits and uses the money to provide a wide array of financial services, including business and personal loans, mortgages, and credit cards.

Savings Institutions

There are a number of types of savings institutions, including **savings and loan associations (S&Ls)**, thrift institutions, and savings banks. All of these were originally designed to give individuals access to banking services that had previously only been available to business customers of commercial banks. For this reason, savings institutions were at first limited to offering savings accounts and making home and personal loans to individuals. More recently, however, savings institutions have been able to offer a more competitive selection of checking and savings accounts. They can even offer credit cards, business loans, and financial planning services. However, they still are primarily home mortgage lenders. In fact, S&Ls are required to use at least 70 percent of their money to make home mortgage loans, as opposed to other types of loans.

Although the various types of savings institutions are likely to offer similar products and services, one distinction among them is their form of ownership. A **mutual company** is one that is owned by its customers (in this case, depositors). A **stock company** is owned by stockholders. If you have an account in a mutual savings institution, even though the rates of return will be competitive, the earnings you receive on your investments will be called "dividends" rather than "interest." If the mutual company is very profitable in a given year, you'll receive a higher dividend that year, because the dividend is the way the company passes on the profits to its owner-depositors.

Credit Unions

A **credit union** is a special form of mutual depository institution. It gets its funds from checking and savings deposits and makes loans to its depositors, who are also the owners of the institution. An important distinction between credit unions and other depository institutions is that credit unions have nonprofit status and often make use of a partially volunteer labor force, giving them a cost advantage over other institutions. Their reduced costs of operation often mean that credit unions can offer lower loan rates and higher interest on deposits than other institutions. Depositors in credit unions are insured for up to $250,000 by the National Credit Union Association, which operates the National Credit Union Share Insurance Fund (NCUSIF).

At one time, credit union members were supposed to have a common bond, such as a religious or employment affiliation. For example, the federal government has a credit union for government employees and their families. Today, however, the common bond requirement is defined fairly loosely so credit unions can now be just as large as competing banks and offer a similar selection of products and services, including credit cards and mortgage loans.

Internet-Based Financial Institutions

A relatively new phenomenon among financial institutions is the increasing number of online financial institutions. Although all banks have an online presence for customer account management, internet-based financial institutions have no physical location but offer a menu of cash management accounts, loans, and investments. Presumably, these firms should have a cost advantage over traditional depository institutions, but consumers seeking higher interest and lower loan rates are cautioned to check out an institution's credentials before sending money to it. At the FDIC website, you can find out whether a bank is legitimate and whether it's insured.

Nondepository Institutions

Nondepository institutions include mutual fund companies, life insurance companies, brokerage firms, and other financial services firms. Although such institutions have always offered loans in competition with banks, savings institutions, and credit unions, only more recently have they begun to provide cash management services. Nondepository institutions now compete with other types of institutions for customers by offering a full range of products and services. For the consumer, this means more choices and potentially lower prices. None of the accounts offered by these firms are federally insured.

Mutual Fund Companies

A **mutual fund** is an investment company that sells shares to investors and then invests the pool of funds in a selection of stocks, bonds, or other assets. Some mutual fund companies have low-risk investment account options that also allow limited check writing.

Life Insurance Companies

A **life insurance company** sells products, called life insurance policies, intended to provide financial security for dependents in the event of the death of the policy owner. Such a firm's primary source of funds is the policy premiums paid to purchase the insurance policies. These companies invest the collected premiums in stocks, bonds, and other financial assets. Many life insurance products include savings and investment features. In addition, life insurers are active lenders in the home mortgage market. Life insurance companies may also sell annuities, whereby consumers give the company a lump sum of cash in return for a guaranteed amount of income each month for life.

Brokerage Firms

A **brokerage firm** is a company that facilitates investors' purchases of stocks, bonds, and other investments. An investor generally keeps money in an investment account with a brokerage firm which is authorized to make trades on behalf of the investor. Electronic trades and record-keeping services speed the transaction process by eliminating the need for physical transfer of the shares for cash. The brokerage firm usually makes its money by charging a commission for each purchase and sale. Today, more banks are competing for the brokerage business. In turn, traditional brokerage firms are offering a variety of cash management services and products.

Financial Services Firms

Recently, many financial institutions that had previously fit into one category or another have been trying to redefine themselves as multiservice financial institutions in an attempt to provide "one-stop shopping" for their customers and to take advantage of their existing market penetration. For example, State Farm Insurance, previously a large insurance company, has added mutual funds and cash management products to its offerings. Post-Great Recession, most major brokerage firms have affiliated with banks. For example, Merrill Lynch, formerly a brokerage firm and investment bank, is now owned by Bank of America, and previously non-bank financial services firms such as Goldman Sachs, Morgan Stanley, and Charles Schwab all operate FDIC insured depository banks. These firms all offer a complete menu of checking and savings accounts, insurance products, consumer and mortgage loans, and mutual fund investments.

Online Payment Processors

Online payment processors, such as Venmo, Square Cash, and Zelle, provide a more limited set of cash management services. Their primary role is to facilitate transfer of funds between bank accounts, for example from your bank account to a merchant's account or from your friend's account to yours. The transfers are often made directly from your checking account, but these processors also allow you to maintain a deposit of funds from which to make transfers. Any funds you hold in an online payment account are not federally insured, even if they originated from an insured account.

Evaluating Financial Institutions

With so many different financial institutions to choose from, how should you decide which to use? This decision should be based on how each financial service provider is rated based on the "Four Ps": products, price, people, and place.

Products

The ideal financial institution will provide you with all the products you need to manage your cash effectively. These products include not only checking and savings accounts but also many others, which you'll read about later in this chapter. In choosing among financial service providers, it's a good idea to begin with a list of the products and services you'd like to have. You'll want to find out which institutions offer the greatest number of products and services you want, and you'll also want to compare the products and services qualitatively. As with most decisions, you may not come up with a clear-cut winner—you'll have to weigh a variety of pluses and minuses for each financial institution. You may be willing to live with a smaller selection of products in return for the more personal touch offered by a smaller local institution.

Price

Price includes both the interest you earn on liquid asset accounts and the fees you pay for cash management services. Whereas many financial institutions offer similar selections of products, the pricing of these products may vary dramatically. Interest rates on demand savings accounts—that is, accounts that allow you to withdraw your funds at any time "on demand"—are usually much lower than those for other types of saving. For example, the average annual rate on demand savings accounts was only 0.8 percent in January 2019, whereas five-year certificates of deposit, which require that you leave your money on deposit for the full five years, at that time averaged 1.44 percent.

Financial institutions also differ substantially in the fees they charge for various services. For example, some require that you maintain a minimum balance in your checking account and others don't. It's fairly common for accounts to be subject to a monthly fee if the balance drops below a stated minimum, such as $100 or $1,000. Bounced check fees can range from $10 to $50.

People

Although customer service is somewhat less important today given the trend toward electronic transactions, it should still be an important factor in your decision. Are the lines long? When you call with questions, do you get to speak to a knowledgeable person? Are your phone calls returned promptly and courteously?

Place

Finally, you should consider the location of the institution. Although Internet-based financial institutions may offer higher interest, you may not want to give up the convenience of being able to transact business in person. Where are the ATMs located? Are the hours convenient to your schedule?

You can apply the decision-making tools from Chapter 1 to select the best cash management provider to meet your needs. After identifying your needs, collect information from several financial institutions and see how they stack up against one another. Keep in mind that although you're by no means limited to using only one financial institution for all your banking needs, it may be more cost-effective to do so. Not only will you save time by dealing with just one firm, but you may be entitled, as a depositor, to receive better consumer and home loan rates.

An easy way to summarize the information you gather about several financial institutions is to create a comparison worksheet such as the one in **Excel Worksheet 3.4** (Personal Financial Planner: Evaluating Financial Service Providers). A sample comparison of three hypothetical financial institutions is shown in **Figure 3.7**.

EXCEL WORKSHEET

See **Excel Worksheet 3.4** (**Personal Financial Planner: Evaluating Financial Service Providers**) in **WileyPLUS**.

FIGURE 3.7   **Sample of Excel Worksheet 3.4: Evaluating Financial Service Providers**

	A	B	C	D
1	How well does your current financial institution rate on the Four Ps?			
2	**PRODUCTS:**	Does the financial institution offer the selection of products you need?		
3		Do the products have the features you need?		
4	**PRICE:**	Are the financial products competitively priced?		
5	**PEOPLE:**	Does the financial institution provide the desired level of customer service?		
6	**PLACE:**	Is the financial institution located conveniently for your needs?		
7	**Financial Institution Name**	**Financial Institution #1**	**Financial Institution #2**	**Financial Institution #3**
10	PRODUCTS			
11	Free checking		✓	
12	Unlimited checks	✓	✓	
13	Online account review	✓	✓	✓
14	Bill-paying service		✓	✓
15	Debit card	✓	✓	✓
16	Overdraft protection		✓	✓
17	IRAs		✓	✓
18	Home equity loans		✓	✓
19	PRICE			
20	Checking account fees	0	0	$5/month
21	Checking account interest	0	0	0.25%
22	Fee for using other ATM	$1.50	$1.00	$2.50
23	Savings account interest	0.52%	0.45%	0.57%
24	PEOPLE			
25	Prompt/courteous service	A–	A+	B+
26	Knowledgeable staff	B+	A	A–
27	PLACE			
28	Convenient	✓	✓–	✓
29	Sufficient free ATMs	10	5	15
30	Online presence	✓	✓	✓

3.4   Evaluating Cash Management Products and Services

LEARNING OBJECTIVE 3.4

Evaluate checking and savings account choices based on liquidity, safety, and cost.

In addition to having a large selection of providers, you also have a choice among many different products and services to use for cash management. How do you decide which are most appropriate for your needs? What are the most important factors to consider in choosing your cash management accounts? How can you compare checking and savings alternatives? In this section, we'll explain what to look for in selecting checking and savings accounts.

Criteria for Evaluating Cash Management Accounts

Recall that the basic purposes of cash management are to meet transaction needs, develop a cash reserve for emergencies, and have a safe place to keep money in anticipation of a planned need for cash. Because all of these needs require that the account have minimal risk and be easy to access, your primary concerns in evaluating account choices should be liquidity, safety, and cost. Once you've narrowed your choices to the accounts that meet these initial criteria, you can make your final decision based on differences in costs and after-tax interest earnings.

Liquidity

Can you withdraw money from the account without incurring fees or losing any of your original investment? In evaluating your account options, pay careful attention to features that limit the account's liquidity, such as minimum balance requirements, limitations on withdrawals, and number of transactions or checks allowed each month.

Safety

Does the cash management account expose you to any risk of default by the financial institution? Is there any risk of losing your money? If the account pays interest, is the interest rate guaranteed, or does it fluctuate with market conditions?

    Because cash management accounts are a component of your finances that you can't afford to risk, you should consider limiting your choices to insured deposits and federally guaranteed investments. Recall, for example, that the FDIC insures accounts in many depository institutions. Notably, any balance you carry with an online payment processor, such as Venmo or Square Cash, is not insured.

Costs and After-Tax Interest

When you're deciding between savings alternatives, you'll inevitably have to make tradeoffs. Generally, the safer the investment and the institution, the lower the rate of interest paid on investments. Accounts that are more liquid will usually pay lower rates of interest and may have higher costs, such as monthly service charges, fees, and penalties. It's not uncommon for an account advertised as "free" to include many hidden costs that are very profitable to the institution, such as fees for check printing, overdrafts, stop payments, and debit cards. Many payment service companies allow you to make cash transfers for free, but charge fees for transactions made through linked credit cards. A number of different websites allow you to comparison-shop based on rates, fees, and other criteria.

    In comparing the interest that you can earn on each type of account, you may find that the accounts have different rules regarding when interest is credited. Recall from Chapter 2 that the frequency with which interest is calculated and added to an account is called compounding. The more often the interest compounds—daily instead of monthly, for example—the more you get the advantage of interest paid on interest. The difficulty in comparing accounts is that the stated, or nominal, interest rate is not directly comparable between accounts with different rates of compounding. The interest earnings on an account may also be eroded by fees, so that the actual annual rate of return on your invested funds may be lower than the quoted rate of return.

    Fortunately for consumers of financial services, the Truth in Savings Act requires that financial institutions report the **annual percentage yield (APY)** on all interest-earning accounts, in addition to the nominal rate. APY adjusts for different compounding periods to make it possible to compare "apples with apples." However, fees for specific services (debit cards, checks, and the like) aren't factored into this calculation, so you'll still need to consider those in your evaluation of account options.

    The formula for calculating APY is given in **Equation 3.1**:

$$\text{Annual percentage yield (APY)} = \left(1 + \frac{\text{Nominal rate}}{m} \right)^{m} - 1 \tag{3.1}$$

where m = number of compounding periods per year

INTERACTIVE

To see the impact of nominal rates and compounding on APY, see **Interactive: Annual Percentage Yield** in **WileyPLUS**.

    Although you can use this equation to calculate the APY yourself, in most cases this won't be necessary. You can easily compare your savings account alternatives based on the APY because financial institutions are required to provide it to you with any materials about their account offerings. In addition, all financial calculators include a function key that can convert a nominal rate to the APY. (Try your hand at comparing APYs in **Interactive: Annual Percentage Yield.**)

APY is most important to consider for larger investments and higher rates of return. For small account balances with low nominal rates, the compounding periods won't make a big difference in interest earned. With a $10,000 investment, the dollar difference between two accounts compounding at different intervals is only a few dollars per year. However, with small accounts, you should pay very close attention to differences in fees, because they could represent a larger percentage of your balance. For example, if you keep an average balance of $500 in a savings account, a $25 fee is 5 percent of your balance, several times more than the entire year's interest.

The taxability of interest will result in lower after-tax earnings on your invested funds. Because rates of return on short-term savings accounts are already low, as shown in **Figure 3.8**, the additional costs of federal, state, and local income taxes can erode your yield to a very low level. For example, if the APY on a regular savings account is 1 percent and your marginal tax rate is 40%, after paying taxes on your interest earnings, you'll earn only 0.6 percent [1 × (0 − 0.4)].

FIGURE 3.8   **One-Year Certificate of Deposit Rates, 2001–2019**   The APY on certificates of deposit (CDs), a type of short-term savings account, has averaged less than 1 percent since mid-2009.

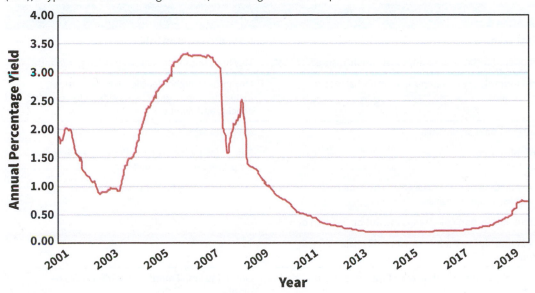

Source: Based on data from Federal Reserve Bank of St. Louis, research.stlouisfed.org.

To best meet your overall cash management needs, you may at some point want to consider having several accounts that vary in liquidity, cost, and interest. Many people have a transaction account for regular bill paying and a highly liquid savings account for short-term emergency needs, for example. Once you've built your emergency fund to the desired level, you may attempt to increase your interest earnings by spreading your funds among higher-yield savings options, such as U.S. savings bonds and CDs with varying maturities. Such an allocation makes sense because, in most financial emergencies, you won't need all of your cash holdings immediately. For example, if you lose your job, you'll only need to cover one month of expenses at a time.

Next, we turn our attention to the types of checking and savings accounts you can choose from to meet your cash management needs, as well as the costs and benefits of various features.

Checking Accounts

As we've seen, one of the reasons for holding cash is to manage transaction needs. A checking account allows you to make deposits and pay bills easily. Before opening a checking account, you should find out the following about any account you are considering:

- Will you earn interest on your balance? If so, at what rate?
- Will you be required to keep a minimum balance in the account? If so, how much is it, and what is the penalty for going below that minimum?

- Is there a monthly fee? If so, how much?
- Can you access the account with a debit card, and if so, is there a fee?
- Does the account offer overdraft protection?
- Are there any other fees?

All checking accounts are **demand deposits**, which means that you have the right to "demand" withdrawal of your deposited funds with little or no notice to the financial institution. For the purposes of cash management, the most important distinction between types of checking accounts is whether they pay interest. **Table 3.4** compares the different types of checking accounts.

TABLE 3.4   Comparison of Checking Account Alternatives

Type of Account	Advantages	Disadvantages
Regular Checking	Highly liquid.	No interest paid on balances.
	If offered by bank or savings institution, insured by FDIC.	May limit number of checks written per month.
	No monthly fee if minimum monthly balance is maintained.	May impose higher fees for various services, including stop payments, fund transfer, certified checks, and debit cards.
Interest-Earning Checking	Interest paid on balance.	Rates are very low.
	Highly liquid.	Rates may be reduced or eliminated if account drops below stated minimum.
	May include other services, such as debit cards, certified checks, and fund transfer.	May charge fees for some services.
	If offered by bank or savings institution, insured by FDIC.	
	No monthly fee if minimum monthly balance is maintained.	
Money Market Account	Pays higher interest than other checking alternatives.	Limited to small number of withdrawals per month.
		Higher minimum balance than other checking alternatives.
		Not FDIC-insured.

Regular Checking Accounts

The key feature of a **regular checking account** is that it pays no interest. In some cases, a bank may advertise this type of account as "free checking," because it waives the monthly service charge if you keep a minimum balance in the account. Not all regular checking accounts require a minimum balance. For those that do, the minimum can range from $100 to $1,000 or more. Regular checking accounts usually also limit the number of checks you can write each month, and there may be a fee for additional services, such as debit cards.

Financial institutions generally lose money on regular checking accounts. The average cost to a bank, including advertising, ATMs, payment processing, and security, is estimated to be about $350 per year. Institutions rely on this type of account to entice people to use other services they offer—services on which they can make more profit. In university towns, financial institutions often compete actively for student accounts, offering regular checking options with low minimum balance requirements, free mobile apps, and no monthly service charges. If available, such accounts may be good choices for students who do not need accounts that provide more "bells and whistles."

Interest-Earning Checking Accounts

Because regular checking accounts offer minimal services, to better meet your needs, you may want to consider a checking account that pays interest and includes other features, such as debit cards and unlimited check writing. If you plan to hold your cash reserves in this type of account, make sure you can meet the higher minimum balance requirements. If your balance falls below the minimum, the interest on the account is usually forfeited, and you may even have to pay a fee—typically $5 to $10 per month. Consider, too, that checking accounts generally pay lower interest than savings accounts. If your account balance is large, you'll need to determine the opportunity cost of keeping the entire amount in the interest-paying checking account rather than putting some of it in a savings account.

Savings Accounts

Whereas checking accounts vary in whether they pay interest, all savings accounts pay interest. The rate of interest depends on the type of account. Savings accounts can be classified as either demand deposit accounts or time deposit accounts.

Demand Deposits versus Time Deposits

Like a checking account, a demand deposit savings account allows you to withdraw your money at any time. In contrast, a **time deposit** account requires that you keep the money in the account for a minimum period of time and may specify a waiting period before you can withdraw funds. Because demand deposits are more liquid than time deposits, they are less risky to you. Therefore, they pay a lower rate of interest as well, often similar to that paid on interest-bearing checking accounts. Recall from Chapter 1 that the riskier the investment or loan, the higher the interest rate. You can see this important investment principle clearly illustrated in **Table 3.5**, which compares features of different savings account alternatives.

TABLE 3.5   **Comparison of Savings Account Alternatives**

Type of Savings	Advantages	Disadvantages	National Average Rate January 2019
Regular Savings	Low minimum balance.	Low rate of interest.	0.10%
	Highly liquid.		
	Insured by FDIC.		
Certificates of Deposit	If offered by depository institution, insured by FDIC.	Requires minimum balance.	
	Guarantees the rate of interest for the period.	Subject to reduced rate and/or penalty for early withdrawal.	12-month, 0.88%
	Interest higher than for regular savings, increasing with maturity.	Federal, state, and local income tax owed on interest.	5-year, 1.44%
Money Market Mutual Funds	Higher rates of interest than regular savings; rate changes with market.	Not FDIC-insured.	2.04%
	Usually allows limited check writing.	Requires minimum balance.	
Money Market Accounts	If offered by depository institution, insured by FDIC.	Requires minimum balance.	0.21%
	Higher rates than regular savings; rate changes with market.	Federal, state, and local income tax owed on interest.	

(continued)

TABLE 3.5 Comparison of Savings Account Alternatives *(continued)*

Type of Savings	Advantages	Disadvantages	National Average Rate January 2019
U.S. Series EE Savings Bonds	Low minimum investment ($25).	Cannot be redeemed in first 6 months.	0.10%
	Higher rate than regular savings; rate changes with market.	Lower interest paid if redeemed in less than 5 years.	
	Government guaranteed.		
	Exempt from state and local income tax.		
	Exempt from federal income tax if used for qualified educational expenses.		
U.S. Series I Savings Bonds	Same advantages as series EE above.	May pay lower interest than other types of accounts if inflation is low.	0.5% + inflation (=2.83%)
	Pays the inflation rate plus the stated rate.		

Sources: Information from fdic.gov and treasurydirect.gov.

Regular Savings Accounts

Regular savings accounts are demand deposit accounts, and as you can see in Table 3.5, the interest rate they pay is quite low. Many people find it convenient to have a regular savings account at the same institution where they have a checking account. That makes it easier to transfer funds between the accounts as necessary.

Certificates of Deposit

A **certificate of deposit (CD)** is the most common type of time deposit account. You agree to leave your money on deposit until the **maturity date** of the CD. CDs offered by depository institutions are very safe, because they are federally insured. Rates are higher for CDs of longer duration and for larger deposit amounts. For example, you can see in Table 3.5 that an average five-year CD paid about twice as much interest as an average one-year CD. At any given point in time, the actual difference in these rates might be smaller or larger, and rates can also differ between financial institutions. So it definitely pays to shop around. Although the average five-year rate in January 2019 was 1.44 percent, some institutions were offering as much as 3.1 percent.

If you have to withdraw funds before the maturity date of the CD, commonly called "breaking the CD," you'll incur a penalty in the form of a sharply reduced interest rate, usually equivalent to a demand deposit rate. If you cash out a CD within a short time of making the deposit, you may even have to pay a penalty fee in addition to the reduction in interest. Let's say that you have $10,000 in a five-year CD, which is paying 2.5 percent interest ($250 per year) when demand deposits are only paying 0.5 percent ($50 per year). If you get into a financial pinch and need this money prior to maturity, you'll probably lose $200 in interest, the difference between the CD rate and the lower demand deposit rate. For this reason, you should put money in longer-maturity CDs only if you are fairly certain you won't need access to it before the maturity date.

You can minimize he problems caused by early withdrawal by separating your investments into several smaller CDs maturing at different times, a strategy called "laddering." Instead of putting $10,000 in a CD that matures in five years, for example, you might put $5,000 in the five-year CD, $3,000 in a two-year CD, $1,000 in a twelve-month CD, and $1,000 in a six-month CD. Although you'll earn lower rates on the shorter-term CDs, the opportunity cost may be outweighed by the reduced risk of incurring an early withdrawal penalty should you need the funds prior to maturity.

When CDs mature, or come to the end of their term, your financial institution will usually automatically roll over the funds into a comparable account unless you file the necessary paperwork to change your investment plan. For example, if you have your money in a one-year CD, the institution will roll it into another one-year CD at maturity. Although this makes things simpler for you, it can cause problems as well.

Consider what happened to Joseph Gianetti, a retiree with three adult children. As part of his estate planning, he decided to give a tax-free gift to each of his children funded by a $40,000 five-year CD that was maturing at the end of the year. Unfortunately, when he went to his bank in December to withdraw the funds, he discovered that the CD had actually matured in October. Joseph had apparently overlooked the bank's notification letter and, when he didn't respond, the bank rolled the proceeds into another five-year CD. Joseph had to pay a penalty to cash in the CD. The moral of this story is that you should keep careful track of maturity dates and be sure to read any documentation sent to you by your bank.

In addition to offering CDs with different maturity dates, your financial institution may offer special types of CDs, including CDs that pay interest based on the performance of the stock or bond market. Obviously, with so many alternatives to consider, you need to make sure you fully understand the terms of a CD before you invest. The FDIC website (**www.fdic.gov**) offers several tips for investors to consider in deciding what CD features make sense for them.

Reflection Question 3

In what types of account(s) do you currently hold (or plan to hold in the future) your cash reserve or emergency fund? Should you consider putting it in a longer-term CD to get a higher rate of interest? Why or why not?

Money Market Mutual Funds

Mutual funds are financial companies that pool investors' funds and use the money to purchase a wide variety of financial assets. Most of these investment companies now offer money market mutual funds with characteristics (such as limited check-writing privileges) that make them good alternatives to other liquid savings accounts. A **money market mutual fund (MMMF)** is a fund that invests in short-term, low-risk financial assets, usually short-term debt securities issued by the federal government, federal agencies, and large public corporations. These types of investments are generally referred to as money market securities, and the funds are called money market mutual funds. When you buy shares of a money market mutual fund, the interest you earn will depend on the interest that the mutual fund is earning on its portfolio of investments.

MMMFs are riskier than some other savings alternatives. Although money market mutual funds may be sold by your financial institution and may look similar to other bank products, they are not federally insured, nor are their interest rates guaranteed. If interest rates go down, you'll earn less than you originally expected on the account. If the mutual fund goes bankrupt, you could lose everything you put in. Retirement plans typically offer MMMFs in their menu of investment choices, but their low rate of return makes them a fairly unattractive choice for long-term investment.

Money Market Deposit Accounts

A **money market deposit account (MMDA)** is similar to a money market mutual fund in that it pays interest that fluctuates with market rates on money market securities. Like money market mutual funds, MMDAs usually allow some check-writing privileges. Although at one time you'd have been limited to writing three to five checks per month, today you can sometimes get unlimited check writing. On the negative side, you must usually keep a fairly high minimum balance in a money market account, so, as with interest-earning checking accounts, you need to consider the opportunity cost of holding more in the account than you would otherwise. Finally, it's important to note that MMDAs offered by depository institutions are federally insured, whereas those offered by insurance companies and brokerage firms are not.

U.S. Savings Bonds

Individual savers should also consider **U.S. savings bonds** for short-term, low-risk investing that is exempt from state and local income taxes. The bonds must be held for a minimum of one year and are subject to a three-month interest penalty if redeemed in less than five years.

The U.S. Treasury issues two series of savings bonds: Series EE and Series I. Both can be purchased electronically through **www.treasurydirect.gov**.

- **Series EE bonds** Series EE bonds carry a fixed rate of interest and can be purchased in any amount from $25 to $10,000. At the time of issue, the rate of interest will be similar to that on ten-year U.S. Treasury securities. Interest accrues monthly for a maximum of 30 years and is compounded semiannually on May 1 and November 1 of each year. Regardless of the interest rate, these bonds are guaranteed to double in value in 20 years. In addition to paying no state or local income tax on the interest earned, federal income tax on the interest is not paid until you cash in the bond. For lower- and middle-income families, the interest income is exempt from federal income taxes if it is used to pay for qualified higher education expenses. If you live in an area with high state and local tax rates, the tax advantages may make this saving alternative preferable to taxable cash accounts offered by financial institutions.

- **Series I Bonds** Series I savings bonds are similar to EE bonds in their tax features but are designed to provide protection from inflation. The semiannual interest rate is fixed when you purchase the bond, but the face value on which the interest is calculated adjusts semiannually for inflation, measured by the change in the CPI. Suppose, for example, that you have a Series I bond with a face value of $1,000 that promises to pay an annual rate of 1.5 percent more than the current rate of inflation. The bond will earn $7.50 in interest the first six months (half of the annual interest rate of 1.5 percent, or 0.75 percent, on the face value of $1,000). Now suppose the CPI goes up 3 percent during that same time. The face value of your bond will increase by 3 percent, to $1,030. Over the next six months, you'll earn half of 1.5 percent on the new face value of $1,030. In fact, you'll always earn 1.5 percent more than the inflation rate—even if the inflation rate returned to double digits, as in the 1980s.

The Rule of 72

Although the stated interest rate is quite low, Series EE U.S. savings bonds are guaranteed to double in value in 20 years. Is that a good deal for you? A simple, and often useful, rule of thumb you can use to determine the answer is called the "**Rule of 72**." This rule will help you determine how long an investment will take to double in value at a given rate of interest. To approximate the number of years to double your money, take 72 and divide by the rate. For example, at 6 percent interest, it will take approximately 72/6 = 12 years to double your money. You can use this method with any investment. **Demonstration Problem 3.1** applies this rule to an investment in a Series E savings bond, and **Interactive: Double Your Money** shows how the Rule of 72 can make certain types of financial problems easier to solve.

INTERACTIVE

Get more practice using the Rule of 72 with **Interactive: Double your Money** in **WileyPLUS.**

DEMONSTRATION PROBLEM 3.1 | Using the Rule of 72

Problem

You have invested $5,000 in a U.S. Series EE savings bond at 1.2 percent fixed interest. At that rate of interest, how long would it take for your $5,000 to double in value without the government guarantee? How important is the government guarantee that it will double in 20 years?

Strategy

Apply the Rule of 72.

Solution

To apply the Rule of 72, divide 72 by the interest rate: 72/1.2 = 60. This means that it would take 60 years to double your $5,000 investment to $10,000 if it earned 1.2 percent per year. In order for it to double in 20 years, the rate of interest per year would have to be 3.6 percent (72/3.6 = 20). Thus, the government guarantee is actually the equivalent of a guarantee that the bond will earn 3.6% per year if you hold it for 20 years.

3.5 | Resolving Cash Management Problems and Avoiding Identify Theft

LEARNING OBJECTIVE 3.5

Select appropriate tools for dealing with cash management problems, and protect yourself from identity theft.

If you're like most people, at some point in your life you will have unexpected cash management problems. Such problems can result from your own cash management mistakes, as in the case of an overdrawn account or a seriously overdue bill. Or they can be someone else's fault—you deposit a check in your account, but the person who wrote it didn't have the funds to cover it. Worse yet, you may have your identity stolen. In this section, we consider how to deal with these problems.

Cash Management Problems and Solutions

Cash management problems are often related to shortfalls in your transaction account or temporary lack of access to your funds. In this section, we consider several such situations.

If You Overdraft Your Account . . .

Your online account balance was given as $200, so you used your debit card to buy groceries. Unfortunately, you forgot about an electronic payment of your cell phone bill that was due to be withdrawn from your account the next day. If you write a check or use your debit card when there isn't enough money in your account to cover the payment, you can end up owing penalty fees to your financial institution and to any retailer that ends up having a payment rejected. Because many transactions are processed overnight, there may still be pending withdrawals that do not yet show up in your ATM or online account balance. Many banks process payments from largest to smallest, so a single large payment may cause many smaller payments to overdraft, resulting in additional fees.

The best way to avoid the inconvenience, embarrassment, and cost of overdrafts is to keep careful track of your cash flows so that you have an accurate estimate of your account balance, paying particular attention to the timing of automatic payments. Just in case the unexpected occurs, you can arrange in advance with your financial institution to link your account to another account (for example, your savings account), or you can sign up for **overdraft protection** on your account, effectively providing you with an automatic loan in the amount of an overdraft. Debit transactions and checks will usually be disallowed when there are insufficient funds in an account unless you have specifically opted for overdraft protection.

If you opt for overdraft protection, the bank will honor your checks and debit transactions even when you don't have funds in your account. However, you need to have a plan for paying back the loan quickly because the rate charged on the borrowed amount is usually quite high, similar to the interest rate on a credit card balance. If you don't have overdraft protection, your debit transactions and checks will be disallowed, you will be charged a fee by the bank, and you may also owe penalties to retailers or creditors who have received bad checks.

If You Receive a Bad Check . . .

You can also run into trouble by being the victim of a bad check. If you deposit a check from someone else and it is rejected due to insufficient funds, your financial institution will often charge you a fee, even though you were not at fault. This fee is comparable to the fee charged to the person who wrote the bad check ($25 to $35). If, as a result of the bad check you deposited, you end up overdrafting your own account, you may incur additional penalties as well unless you have overdraft protection. Although you can try to get the wrongdoer to pay you back, you're unlikely to be successful. Therefore, the best way to avoid the problem is to take checks only from reliable sources and not to write checks against funds that have not yet been credited to your account.

If you use an online resale site, such as eBay or Craigslist, it is advised that you never take checks or money orders in payment for your goods. Many sellers have had an unpleasant surprise when they found out that the bank money order or cashier's check they accepted from a buyer was a fake.

If You Want to Stop Payment . . .

In some cases, you may want to keep a person or business from cashing a check that you have given them or from accessing funds transferred electronically. For example, you might have paid a contractor to do some work on your house but realized soon after he left that he hadn't actually finished the job you paid him for. In this circumstance, you can request that your financial institution issue a **stop payment order** on the check, which will involve a fee between $30 and $35. Although this request can be made over the phone, or sometimes online, you should follow up in writing to protect your rights in the event that the check slips through. Stop orders can be extended beyond their usual two-week period for an additional fee.

If You Need Money in a Hurry . . .

Nearly every dependent college student has had the experience of calling home for money, particularly late in the semester when the money earned at a summer job is all gone. If you're in a serious financial bind and need money in a hurry, a mailed check will take too long. With electronic banking, it's fairly easy to transfer money from one account to another if both accounts are in the same financial institution. These transfers result in funds being immediately available to the holder of the receiving account.

If the sending and receiving accounts are in different banks, you can still arrange for a **wire transfer** of funds if you know the routing number and the account number at the other bank. This is also the process that is used when you make electronic payments to pay your landlord or creditor. Similarly, when you use a payment service company such as Venmo or Square, you are giving them permission to facilitate a transfer on your behalf. In most cases, the funds will not be available until the next day. In some cases, the sending bank may charge a small fee for this service, and the fee will be higher if the funds are coming from a credit card account. **Figure 3.9** shows the usual location of the routing number and account number on a printed check.

What if you're traveling in a less-developed country? In that case, you may need to use a cash delivery service such as Western Union, MoneyGram, Walmart2Walmart, or PayPal. In general, this method of sending cash is quite expensive, since the cost is a percentage of the

FIGURE 3.9 **Routing Number and Account Number for Electronic Transfers Between Accounts**
This printed check shows the usual location and order of routing, account, and check numbers. Occasionally, though, the account number and check number are in the reverse order.

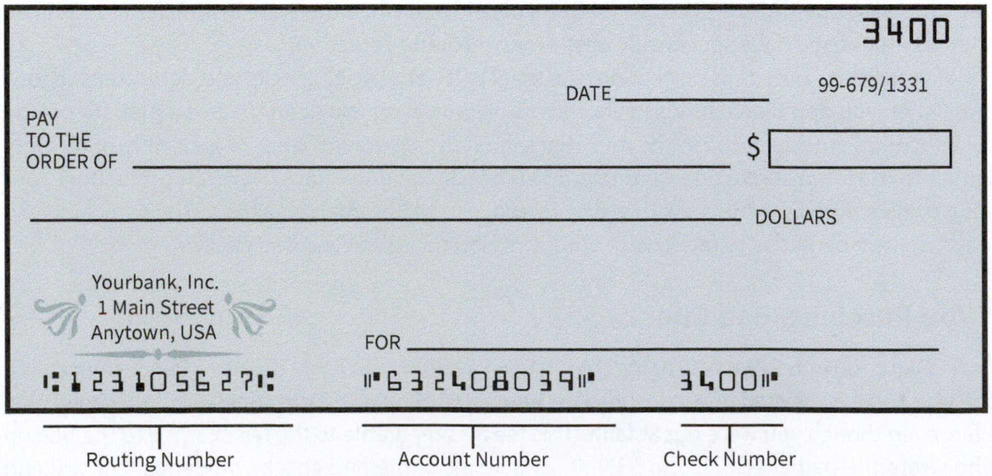

amount being sent. The sender is charged a flat fee, but for international deliveries, there may be an additional charge in the other country, as well as unfavorable currency exchange rates. Walmart offers competitive rates for cash delivery at its stores in the United States and through Moneygram offices in over 200 countries. In 2019, the Walmart2Walmart fees were $4 for up to $50, $8 for amounts $51 to $1,000 and $16 for amounts $1,001 to $2,500. But if you're a Peace Corps volunteer in Ethiopia or a student spending spring break in Mexico, you may consider using one of these companies' services to receive money from the United States when needed. Many immigrants use Western Union or Walmart2Walmart to send cash to their families in South America, Asia, and Africa. With the increased prevalence of smartphones in developing countries, it is expected that payment services such as Venmo and Square Cash may become the norm for transactions, making it much easier for both locals and visitors to meet their cash needs.

If You Are Unbanked . . .

What if you don't have a bank account that can send or receive funds? Despite significant improvements over time, national statistics from the FDIC suggest that 5 percent of U.S. adults, generally younger, lower-income, and nonwhite, are "unbanked." These individuals do not have a checking or savings account and operate on a primarily cash-basis system, relying on costly alternative financial services such as check cashers, payday loan firms, and pawn shops. Another 18 percent are "underbanked," in that they have a checking or savings account but continue to access alternative financial services. It is estimated that unbanked and underbanked households spend 5 percent of net income on unnecessary fees. There are a variety of reasons why individuals are unbanked, including distrust of banks, prior financial problems, questionable immigration status, immediate need for cash, and lack of knowledge. The federal government has recently launched an initiative to make it easier for the unbanked to gain access to financial services.

Identity Theft

Here's an increasingly common occurrence. You receive your credit card billing statement and see one or more charges that you know you didn't make—an indication that someone has stolen your credit card information. Or you check your credit bureau report after a credit denial and see a loan listed that you never applied for—an indication that someone masquerading as you has applied for a loan.

Both scenarios are commonly referred to as **identity theft**, which is the use of another person's personal or financial information—such as Social Security or credit card number—to commit fraud or other crimes. In 2017, nearly 17 million Americans were the victims of some type of identity fraud, or about 1 in 15 people.

It takes very little information to steal your identity. With your Social Security number, name, and address, a thief can apply for credit cards, cell phones, loans, bank accounts, apartments, and utility accounts. This is the reason that universities no longer use Social Security numbers for student and faculty IDs. To use your credit card, a thief only needs your credit card number, the expiration date, and sometimes the code on the back of the card.

According to the FTC, common methods used by identity thieves to obtain your information include the following:

- **Dumpster diving** Thieves often go through trash to find copies of bills and other documents containing personal information.
- **Skimming** Your credit/debit card numbers and PINs can be recorded using a special storage device attached to an ATM or other card-processing unit.
- **Phishing** You may be prompted to reply to a fraudulent email that seems to be coming from your financial institution. For example, it may say that your bank needs you to confirm some personal information.
- **Rerouting the victim's address** By filing a change of address form in your name, thieves may divert your mail to another location.

- **Old-fashioned stealing** Stealing wallets and purses is common, but thieves also steal personnel records to obtain Social Security numbers or mail, looking for preapproved credit, new checks, or tax information.
- **Pretexting** Thieves use false pretenses to obtain your financial information. For example, they may pretend to be calling for a research survey and then use the information you provide to masquerade as you in order to obtain information from your bank.
- **Data breaches** Sophisticated hackers routinely attempt to break into large corporate and government databases to obtain personal information that can be easily sold on the dark web. In 2018 alone, there were 668 reported data breaches exposing 22 million records.

Fraudulent credit card charges often arise through online or telephone orders, because it's easier to use someone else's identity in a venue where no additional identification, such as a driver's license with a picture, is required. The negative outcomes, of course, can be severe. Your credit may be damaged, and it takes time and effort to correct the fraudulent charges. And it's not just credit card information that is at stake. Victims of identity theft have been denied loans, lost out on job opportunities, spent time and money clearing their record, and even been arrested for crimes they didn't commit.

> **Reflection Question 4**
>
> Consider which of your activities expose you to the greatest risk of identity theft. What are some strategies you can use to minimize this risk in the future?

Most credit card issuers now use sophisticated software to track card usage patterns and look for suspicious card activity. If your lender thinks you've been the victim of fraud, it will contact you to verify purchases, cancel your card, and issue one with a new number. Although you certainly benefit from these antifraud mechanisms when they result in the early detection of fraudulent card usage, it's also possible that your own behavior could trigger the antifraud system. This might happen, for example, if you use your card at the same retailer more than once on the same day (because that could be an indication that a store employee stole your number when you used the card to make a purchase) or if you use a card that has been inactive for a period of time.

Identity theft affects people of all types. Past celebrity victims include popular television personality Oprah Winfrey, author J. K. Rowling, clothing designer Tommy Hilfiger, and golf legend Tiger Woods. You might even be the victim of someone you know. The Federal Trade Commission says that about 6 percent of the complaints they receive involve family members. In some cases, parents who have botched their own finances have used their children's identities to open credit card accounts.

INTERACTIVE

Take the quiz **Interactive: What's Your Risk of Identity Theft?** in **WileyPLUS.**

Table 3.6 offers some tips about how to avoid identity theft. To test your own knowledge about identity theft, take the quiz in **Interactive: What's Your Risk of Identity Theft?**

TABLE 3.6   How to Avoid Identify Theft

• Always use security software with firewall and antivirus protections.	• Do not click on links in or download attachments from suspicious emails.
• Check your credit card statements for accuracy before paying the bill. Shred all financial statements before throwing them away.	• Never give out your credit card number or personal information over the phone or online unless you are the one who made the contact and you trust the security provided by the business or website.
• Check your credit report regularly, and cancel unused credit card accounts.	• Do not give out your Social Security number, and don't print it on your checks.
• Do not access sensitive information using public wifi networks.	• Mail bill payments at the post office or from a locked mailbox.
• Do not carry extra credit cards and IDs.	• Use strong passwords and change them regularly.

Summary

Learning Objectives Review

LEARNING OBJECTIVE 3.1 Develop, implement, and monitor a household budget.

A **budget** is a plan for future spending and saving in order to achieve your household financial goals.

- Family size and makeup, age and education of household members, sources and amount of income, and money attitudes all have an impact on budget decisions.
- The steps in the budgeting process are: (1) forecasting future income and expenses, (2) implementing the plan, (3) monitoring income and expenses over time to reduce budget variances, and (4) reevaluating regularly.
- If a first-pass budget forecast yields an expected net cash flow that is negative, you'll need to **reconcile the budget** by determining strategies for reducing future cash outflows or increasing cash inflows. Positive net cash flow should be allocated to achieving your financial goals.
- A budget needs to be monitored to identify whether actual expenditures are in line with the budget. If a **budget variance** is identified, spending should be adjusted or the budget should be revised.
- People differ in their attitudes toward spending and saving. Since this can be a major cause of stress in relationships, it is important for household members to talk about money issues and establish mutually agreeable ground rules. In some cases, a couple planning to marry may need to have a **prenuptial agreement** that specifies how assets and income will be divided in the event that their marriage ends in divorce.

LEARNING OBJECTIVE 3.2 Explain why cash management is an important component of your financial plan.

Cash management includes all decisions related to cash payments and short-term liquid investments.

- People hold cash for three general reasons: (1) to manage transaction needs, (2) to prepare for cash emergencies, and (3) to make temporary investments.
- It is important to have an adequate **cash reserve**, or emergency fund, to meet cash needs. This should usually be enough to cover several months of required household expenses.

Following several rules will result in better cash management outcomes:

- Keep track of your cash by balancing your accounts every month.
- Develop a system to ensure that you pay your bills on time.
- Stick to your financial plan by paying yourself first. This means you should allocate funds to your financial goals at the beginning of the month rather than waiting to see how much is left at the end.
- Use sound criteria to evaluate financial institutions and to select cash management products and services.

LEARNING OBJECTIVE 3.3 Identify and evaluate financial institutions that provide cash management services.

Cash management services are offered by depository and nondepository institutions. Recent deregulation has made it possible for most types of financial institutions to offer a diverse menu of financial products and services.

- **Depository institutions**, which include **commercial banks, savings and loan associations (S&Ls)**, and **credit unions**, use funds from customer deposits to make loans of various types. Deposits in these institutions are insured by the **Federal Deposit Insurance Corporation (FDIC)** for $250,000 per depositor.
- Nondepository institutions, which include **life insurance companies, mutual funds, payment processing companies, brokerage firms**, and **online payment processors**, get their investment funds from other sources. Funds held by these types of firms are not FDIC-insured.
- Financial institutions can also be distinguished by whether they are organized as a **mutual company**, which is owned by customers, or a **stock company**, which is owned by outside investors or stockholders.
- In deciding among different financial institutions, you should consider the Four Ps: (1) whether they have what you need (products), (2) whether they are competitive in costs imposed and interest rates paid (price), (3) whether they provide high-quality customer service (people), and (4) how convenient their locations are (place).

LEARNING OBJECTIVE 3.4 Evaluate checking and savings account choices based on liquidity, safety, and cost.

Because the primary purpose of cash management accounts is to provide a liquid source of funds to meet cash emergencies, liquidity and safety are of utmost importance in selecting a cash management account.

- When evaluating comparably safe account alternatives, you should consider the differences in costs, such as monthly fees and penalties for early withdrawal, and the taxability of the interest earned.
- **Annual percentage yield (APY)** is used to compare interest rates across accounts with different compounding frequencies. The APY can be calculated using **Equation 3.1**:

$$APY = \left(1 + \frac{\text{Nominal rate}}{m} \right)^{m} - 1$$

where m = the number of compounding periods per year

- All checking accounts are **demand deposits**. Checking account choices include **regular checking accounts**, which pay no interest on the account balance, **interest-earning checking accounts**, and **money market deposit accounts (MMDAs)**, which interest at fairly low rates. Checking accounts also differ in monthly service charges, minimum balance requirements, and fees for additional services.

- Savings accounts may be demand deposits or **time deposits**. Thus, these accounts differ in liquidity and risk, with higher rates of interest paid on riskier accounts and those with more restrictions on withdrawals. The most common types of savings vehicles include regular savings accounts, **certificates of deposit (CDs)**, **money market mutual funds (MMMFs)**, and **U.S. savings bonds**. When you purchase a CD, you agree to leave your money on deposit until the CD's **maturity date**.

- According to the **Rule of 72**, dividing the number 72 by the rate of interest gives the number of years it will take for a lump sum of money to double in value.

LEARNING OBJECTIVE 3.5 Select appropriate tools for dealing with cash management problems, and protect yourself from identity theft.

Dealing with cash management and identity theft problems will often cost you time and money, so it's important to take steps to reduce your risk.

- Cash management problems can result from your own errors, as in the case of overdrafts and late payments, or they can be due to the carelessness or intentional actions of others, as when you receive a bad check.

- Financial institutions offer various services to help with cash management problems, including **overdraft protection**, **stop payment orders**, and **wire transfer**.

- **Identity theft** occurs when someone uses your personal or financial information to commit fraud or other crimes.

Excel Worksheets

3.1 Personal Financial Planner: Household Budget

3.2 Personal Financial Planner: Budget Tracker

3.3 Personal Financial Planner: Cash Needs Analysis

3.4 Personal Financial Planner: Evaluating Financial Service Providers

Key Terms

annual percentage yield (APY)   3-22
brokerage firm   3-19
budget   3-2
budget variance   3-8
cash management   3-13
cash reserve   3-14
certificate of deposit (CD)   3-26
commercial bank   3-18
credit union   3-18
demand deposit   3-24
depository institution   3-17

Federal Deposit Insurance Corporation (FDIC)   3-17
identity theft   3-31
life insurance company   3-19
maturity date   3-26
money market deposit account (MMDA)   3-27
money market mutual fund (MMMF)   3-27
mutual fund   3-19
mutual company   3-18

overdraft protection   3-29
prenuptial agreement   3-13
reconciling a budget   3-5
regular checking account   3-24
Rule of 72   3-28
savings and loan association (S&L)   3-18
stock company   3-18
stop payment order   3-30
time deposit   3-25
U.S. savings bond   3-27
wire transfer   3-30

WileyPLUS

Practice Questions to check your understanding, Peer-to-Peer Videos, Interactives, and many other resources are available in WileyPLUS.

Concept Review Questions

1. You have estimated your budget for next year. Based on your first pass, your net cash flow is negative. What are your choices for reconciling your budget?

2. How does a budget differ from a personal cash flow statement?

3. What are the four steps in the budgeting process, and what activities should you undertake in each?

4. Why do so many financial advisors recommend that you "pay yourself first"?

5. Pat Johannsen earns $35,000 and takes home $2,300 per month after taxes. She has total monthly expenses of $1,800. How much of an emergency fund should she have? What factors should she consider in deciding how much is necessary?

6. What criteria should you use to select a financial institution to meet your cash management needs?

7. Why might a financial institution customer value "one-stop shopping"? What kinds of products or services would a customer most likely prefer to get from the same institution?

8. Explain the similarities and differences between regular checking accounts and interest-earning checking accounts. Is it always better to have an interest-earning checking account?

9. When a bank offers several certificates of deposit (CDs) with different maturities, which will have a higher APY, a five-year CD or a one-year CD? Why?

10. Why are financial institutions required to report APY, in addition to the nominal rate, for all of their account offerings?

11. Explain how using credit cards increases your risk of identity theft. What are some methods you can use to minimize this risk?

12. Sanjay has just completed an annual budget for his family. He has determined that his family has a very small positive net cash flow for the year. Explain to Sanjay why he should also evaluate his budget on a monthly basis and track the budget variances.

13. What are the differences and similarities between U.S. Series EE savings bonds and Series I savings bonds?

14. Which of the reasons for holding cash would be most important for a freshman college student, and which would be most important for a 40-year old single parent?

15. Discuss the pros and cons of keeping extra cash in a transaction account with an online payment processor such as Venmo.

Application Problems

1. Your bank pays a nominal rate of 3% interest on a savings account. If the interest is compounded monthly, what is the annual percentage yield (APY) of this account?

2. Your bank pays a nominal rate of 3% interest on a savings account. If the interest is compounded daily (365 days), what is the annual percentage yield (APY) on this account?

3. Erikka estimates that her take-home pay for the coming year will be $1,420 per month. She expects total monthly expenses to be as follows: housing and utilities, $800; food, $200; auto, gas, and insurance, $220; credit card payment, $60; and other expenses $100. The balance on her credit card is $3,000, and she currently pays 18 percent interest on this balance. Erikka would like to reduce her credit card debt. If she decides to budget all of her net monthly cash flow to this goal, how long will it take (in months) to pay off her credit card?

4. First National Bank requires a minimum balance of $1,000 in its interest-earning checking accounts. Account holders are paid 2 percent on the average balance if the balance stays above the minimum all month. If you normally have an average balance of $2,500, what is the annual opportunity cost of keeping the money in a First National checking account instead of a savings account that pays 3.5 percent?

5. You have estimated that you need $6,000 in liquid assets in an emergency fund. You currently have only $1,000, which is invested in a savings account earning 3 percent nominal interest, compounded monthly. Your current budget leaves $300 per month to apply to this goal. If you plan to add this money to your savings at the end of every month, how much will you have after one year?

6. You live in a college town and notice that a local financial institution is advertising "free checking" for students. After calling the bank, you find that the $10 per month service charge is waived as long as the account balance stays above $200 during the month. In addition, the number of checks is limited to 20 per month. Is this really a "free account"? Why or why not?

7. You have $10,000 invested in a five-year CD with an APY of 5 percent. It will mature four years from now. If you withdraw money from the CD prior to maturity, the interest rate drops to 3 percent.

    a. If you will pay 25 percent in taxes on the interest earnings, what is your after-tax yield on this investment, assuming that you leave the money in the account to maturity?

    b. What risks are you exposed to by holding this much cash in a CD? What are your alternatives?

8. As part of his cash management plan, José Ramirez invested money in a five-year CD paying 4 percent interest. Assume that two years after the purchase of the CD, the economy enters a boom period, and the prices of goods and services rise at an annual inflation rate of 5 percent.

    a. What rate is José actually earning on this investment if he has to pay 20 percent income tax on the interest.

    b. Explain inflation risk to José, and tell him why he is effectively losing money on this investment.

9. You currently have $6,000 invested in a savings account with an APY of 7 percent. Each year, you have to pay 20 percent tax on your interest earnings. Assuming that you leave the original investment in the account along with all the after-tax interest, use the Rule of 72 to estimate how many years it will take for you to have $12,000.

10. Kenneth Allen has collected the following information in order to develop a budget for his sophomore year of college. He has a football scholarship that covers his meals, tuition, fees, and books. He estimates that his monthly income from all sources will be $1,000. His monthly expenses are as follows: one-fourth of rent and utilities for an apartment shared with three friends, $450; auto expenses and insurance, $300; cell phone, $25; health insurance, $50; and entertainment, $150.

    a. Develop a budget based on his current expenditures, and calculate his net monthly cash flow.

    b. Kenneth has developed his budget, but when he tracks his actual income and expenses, he finds that he is always out of money. Use his budgeted and actual expenses for the months of September and October to calculate his budget variances. What areas of his budget does he need to work on?

Item	Budgeted	September Actual	Budgeted Variance	October Actual	Budget Variance
Housing	$450	$450	?	$470	?
Auto	300	280	?	320	?
Cell Phone	25	50	?	25	?
Health Insurance	50	50	?	50	?
Entertainment	150	220	?	175	?

11. Suppose that you have developed a budget for next year assuming that the costs of your variable expenditures on goods and services will increase by 2.5 percent from the previous year's levels. Your total variable expenditures were $1,000 per month last year. How much will your variable expenses be for the coming year, assuming no other changes?

12. You created budget for this year assuming that your variable expenses would be 3% higher than they were last year. If it turns out that inflation this year is actually 4% for the year, how much budget variance per month will this difference cause if your monthly variable expenses averaged $1,000 last year?

13. Robert and Jamie are newlyweds in their 20s. Both are employed, but Robert's monthly take-home pay is substantially more than Jamie's. Robert's take-home pay is $3,000 per month and Jamie's is $1,500 per month. When they sit down to pay their bills together for the first time, Robert suggests that they split the regular bills (rent, utilities, phone, and groceries) equally. Although Jamie makes enough to pay her half, she knows she'll have trouble covering her other monthly out-of-pocket expenses. Is this a fair way to manage their household finances? Why or why not? What are some other alternatives Jamie could suggest?

14. Clark, age 45, and Lois, age 40, are engaged to be married. Both of them have been married previously, and both have well-paying jobs. Under what circumstances would you advise them to have a prenuptial agreement?

Case Applications

1. Ron Harrington works for a large technology company as a software engineer and currently earns $120,000 per year. He and his wife, Nancy, live in a five-bedroom suburban home with their three children, ages 10 to 17. Although Nancy has a degree in business marketing, she has not worked outside the home since their last child was born. Ron's employer recently announced plans to lay off a substantial number of employees over the course of the following year as a cost-cutting measure, and Ron is worried that he might lose his job in the next three to six months. Although the company has not explicitly said anything about severance pay, the rumor is that laid-off workers will receive only one month's pay after they are fired. Ron will also be eligible for unemployment compensation for several months, but he is concerned that this amount will be insufficient to cover their household expenses, and he knows it will take a long time to find a comparable job. He estimates that he will have to take a lower-level job at a salary significantly lower than what he now earns. Ron and Nancy currently live comfortably on Ron's income, they have no credit card or student loan debt, and they have about $50,000 in home equity. They recently bought their current home, and it was financed with a $180,000 mortgage.

   a. Explain why the Harringtons need to develop a budget.

   b. What financial steps should Ron and Nancy be taking to prepare for the possible layoff?

2. Katie Stewart is a legal secretary at a major law firm in New York City, where she has worked for the last two years, since graduating from Brookdale Community College. It's too expensive to live in the city on her $38,000 salary, so Katie commutes from New Jersey at a cost of $50 per week. Katie is worried about her personal finances. In the two years she has worked in New York, she has spent more than she has earned, primarily to buy clothes for work. A few lunch-hour shopping sprees with coworkers have resulted in impulse purchases on credit cards, and Katie now has $4,500 in credit card debt. Katie is considering a legal secretary position with a small firm in New Jersey that will pay $3,000 less than her current job.

   a. Explain why Katie's first step should be to develop a budget.

   b. What are some alternatives Katie has for reducing her credit card debt?

   c. If Katie's credit card interest rate is 14 percent, and she wants to pay off her credit card debt over four years, how much should she pay each month?

   d. What factors should Katie consider in deciding whether to change jobs? How would taking the New Jersey job affect her finances?

3. Erica Whitman, a college junior, normally prides herself on keeping control of her finances. But the fall semester was a disaster. She contracted West Nile virus and was very sick for months. It was an effort just to keep up with her classes, let alone balance her checkbook. Because she had to quit her part-time job, she knew her checking account balance was getting a little low, but she didn't quite realize how low until she got a bank notice indicating that she had overdrawn her account. The disallowed transactions are as follows:

Payment to:	Amount	Purpose	Bank Action
Valley Electric Authority	$80.32	Electric bill	Paid
Corner Market	$94.28	Groceries	Returned check?
Hot Wok Café	$12.54	Take-out Chinese	Returned check
Johnny's Pizza	$17.68	Pizza	Returned check
Account Balance	−$24.77		

   a. Assuming that each retailer (but not the electric company) charges Erica a penalty of $20 and her bank charges $35 for the first overdraft, how much will this cash management mistake cost Erica in total?

   b. How much does Erica need to deposit in the account to have enough to pay all the retailers plus her penalties?

   c. Erica's current account balance is not the same as the total of her bounced checks, because Erica had at least some funds in her account when these checks came in. Assuming that the bank overdraft fee was already subtracted to arrive at the amount shown and she has no other bank charges, how much did she have in her account to start with?

   d. What advice would you offer to Erica that will help her avoid this problem in the future?

4. Phil and Kendra Gonzalez graduated from college last May and were married in December. Both work for the same high-tech company as software designers, and their combined take-home pay is $5,200 per month. With monthly expenses that average only $3,000,

they've been able to accumulate $14,000 over the last year in a joint savings account that currently pays 3 percent interest. They also generally keep a little more than the $500 minimum balance in a checking account that pays no interest. If their checking account drops below the $500 minimum in any given month, the bank assesses a monthly fee of $10. This happens to them about once every three months. At present, Phil and Kendra have no investment accounts other than their savings account and their employment-based retirement funds. Phil is trying to talk Kendra into putting $5,000 of their savings into a higher-interest CD and another $5,000 into a stock mutual fund. He has found an online bank that is offering 6 percent interest on five-year CDs, and he has been investigating several stock funds that have had good returns over the last year. Kendra is not sure about what they should do. To investigate their options, she calls their current bank and asks about cash management account alternatives that might provide them with better interest earnings. The bank officer suggests that they consider moving their checking to an interest-earning account that pays 2 percent per year and carries a $1,000 minimum balance. He suggests spreading their investments into several CDs with increasing maturities. The five-year CD at this institution pays 5.75 percent.

a. How much do you think the Gonzalezes should hold in liquid accounts? Explain your reasoning.

b. What are the risks of putting money in CDs or in stocks instead of keeping it in a regular savings account?

c. Based on your analysis of their needs and options, what course of action would you recommend to the Gonzalezes? What additional information do they need to consider in making their decision?

5. Felicia Kobayashi has been using the same financial institution since she moved to Springfield in 1995. Since that time, there's been a lot of consolidation in the banking industry, and her formerly local bank has been bought up by a national conglomerate. After the resulting layoffs in the small branch office where she usually conducts business, Felicia began to notice that it took much longer to make deposits and withdrawals, whether at the drive-through teller or inside the office. As a result, she's considering switching her business to a different financial institution. She currently maintains a regular checking account for paying bills and has a savings account with $15,000 in it. Based on what you've learned in this chapter, outline a plan for Felicia to use in choosing a new bank and deciding among alternative account choices.

CHAPTER 4

Tax Planning

Iakov Filimonov/Shutterstock.com

Feature Story

After Natalie had been working for about six months as a dental technician—her first professional employment—she was actually looking forward to doing her taxes because she thought that she'd be getting a big tax refund. In each of the previous three years, she had worked part-time while attending school and had received a refund of most of the taxes that had been withheld from her paycheck.

Assuming that more income meant more refund, Natalie already had a plan for how to use her expected windfall. In fact, she had made some purchases on credit, planning to pay off the debt when she received her refund check. After completing her federal and state tax returns, though, Natalie was dismayed to find out that she would need to find a different way to pay her credit card bill because, instead of getting a refund, she was going to owe a small amount of money to the IRS.

After the major changes to the U.S. income tax system that took effect in 2018, most taxpayers are paying proportionally less in federal income taxes than they did in prior years. But this tax cut doesn't necessarily mean bigger refunds because the savings are usually spread throughout the year in the form of reduced withholding from paychecks. If Natalie had understood the tax system better, she would not have found herself in this uncomfortable situation. In this chapter, you'll learn more about how the tax system works and how it affects you financially. You'll also discover there are many ways to reduce your tax burden legally by taking advantage of favorable tax rules. To provide background for our discussion of tax planning, we first explain the main features of the federal income tax system and the requirements for filing, calculating, and paying taxes. The better your understanding of the rules, the easier it is to use them to your advantage. After identifying the most common tax planning strategies, we conclude with a discussion of how tax laws are enforced and explain some recent trends in tax law.

LEARNING OBJECTIVES	TOPICS	DEMONSTRATION PROBLEMS
4.1 Understand the major features of the federal income tax system.	**4.1 The Federal Income Tax System** • The Progressive Nature of the U.S. Tax System • Marginal Tax Rates	**4.1** Calculating Average Tax Rate **4.2** Calculating the Marginal Tax Effect
4.2 Determine whether you need to file a federal income tax return and which forms you should use.	**4.2 Filing Requirements** • Filing Status • Adjusted Gross Income and Taxable Income • IRS Forms	

(continued)

(continued)

LEARNING OBJECTIVES	TOPICS	DEMONSTRATION PROBLEMS
4.3 Prepare a basic tax return.	**4.3 Federal Income Tax Calculation** • Reporting Income • Deductions • Calculation of Taxes Owed • Determining Taxes Due or Refund to Be Received	
4.4 Establish financial planning strategies to legally minimize the taxes you pay.	**4.4 Tax Planning Strategies** • Maximize Pretax Contributions to Qualified Benefit Plans • Reduce the Applicable Tax Rate on Certain Income • Make Use of Available Deductions and Credits • Avoid Audits and Penalties	**4.3** Calculating the Marginal Tax Advantage of Home Ownership

4.1 | The Federal Income Tax System

LEARNING OBJECTIVE 4.1

Understand the major features of the federal income tax system.

Taxes take a big bite out of most household budgets, but there are many ways to reduce the taxes you pay. Although the U.S. income tax system is very complicated, with statutes and regulations that fill literally thousands of pages, you shouldn't allow yourself to be overwhelmed by the complexity. As a result of the Tax Cuts and Jobs Act of 2017, which went into effect for the 2018 tax year, the system became a bit simpler. If you focus on the basics and learn some key tax planning strategies, you'll be able to make good decisions regarding this aspect of your financial plan. Even if you use a tax professional to help you prepare and file your taxes, you'll need to know enough to take advantage of beneficial tax rules.

In this section, you'll get an overview of the U.S. income tax system and the role of the Internal Revenue Service (IRS), which is the government agency that administers U.S. tax law. The IRS performs a truly amazing function each year. It administers the ever-changing set of tax rules imposed by Congress, processes 150 million individual income tax returns, collects $2 trillion in taxes, and issues $350 billion in refunds, most within a few short months. The IRS offers many free services to taxpayers. At **www.irs.gov**, you can find information on most tax topics, as well as downloadable tax forms, data, and directions. If you plan to file your own taxes, a must-have publication is *IRS Publication 17, Your Federal Income Tax*.

The Progressive Nature of the U.S. Tax System

Although there have been many changes in the tax law over time, the United States has always maintained a **progressive tax** on income. That means higher marginal tax rates are imposed on taxpayers with higher incomes. Consequently, lower- and middle-income families do not bear a large income tax burden in this country. In fact, about 44 percent of households pay no federal income tax at all. So where does all the federal income tax revenue come from? The top 10 percent of households by income account for about three-quarters of taxes collected.

In contrast to a progressive tax, a **regressive tax** places a disproportionate burden on taxpayers with lower incomes. A tax is regressive if the same tax rate is applied to all taxpayers—as is the case for some payroll and sales taxes. In other words, regressive taxes take a bigger bite out of low-income families' disposable incomes. Although rich people spend more on food, clothing, and other consumer purchases than poor people do, they spend a smaller proportion of their income on these items, so the sales tax affects them less.

The payroll tax that finances Social Security and Medicare, the federal systems for retirement income and health care, is a classic example of a regressive tax. If you look at your pay stub, you'll see the amount withheld for the **FICA** (Federal Insurance Contributions Act) **payroll tax**, which is your contribution to Social Security and Medicare. A total of 15.3 percent of a wage earner's gross pay goes to this tax, with the employer and the employee each paying half. The FICA tax is regressive not only because nearly everyone pays the same 7.65% rate, but also because there is an income cap ($132,900 in 2019) for the Social Security portion of the tax. The portion paid for Medicare is not subject to an income cap. High-income taxpayers pay an additional 0.9 percent Medicare tax on part of their income.

We noted previously that many people pay no federal income tax. Most of these people, however, still pay the FICA tax on their earnings and sales tax on their purchases, so they don't escape taxes entirely. **Figure 4.1** illustrates the breakdown of those who pay no federal income tax.

FIGURE 4.1 **Who Pays No Federal Income Tax?**   This chart shows the proportion of the 172 million U.S. tax units (either singles or couples filing joint tax returns) in 2019 who paid no income tax. About one-third of those who pay no income tax also do not pay the FICA payroll tax, but most of these people are either elderly or very poor.

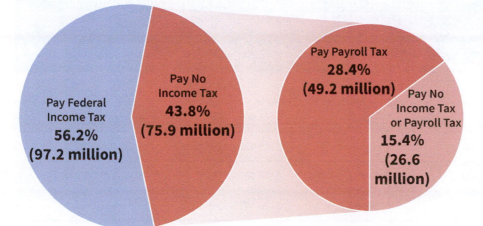

Source: Data from Urban-Brookings Tax Policy Center, www.taxpolicycenter.org.

Marginal Tax Rates

The U.S. income tax system maintains its progressive nature through a combination of increasing marginal tax rates, credits, and deductions. Not all of your income is taxable, and your **taxable income** is not all taxed at the same rate. A **marginal tax rate** is the rate that applies to your *next* dollar of taxable income. A **tax bracket** is the range of taxable income to which a particular marginal tax rate applies.

Tax Rate Schedules

Tax rate schedules tell you how income taxes will be calculated, based on filing status, tax bracket, and marginal tax rates. The tax rate schedules change each year as the brackets are adjusted for inflation. At times, the rates are changed by Congress. For example, the portion of the 2019 Tax Rate Schedule in **Table 4.1** includes Schedule X for single taxpayers and Schedule Y-1 for married taxpayers filing jointly. The marginal tax rates in effect in 2019 ranged from 10% to 37%. A single filer who, in 2019, told you that she was "in the 22 percent bracket" meant that her taxable income was between $39,475 and $84,200.

TABLE 4.1   **Marginal Tax Rates, 2019**

Schedule X. 2019 Tax Rate Schedule for Single Filers			
If your taxable income is:			
Over:	**But not more than:**	**You will owe:**	**Taxable income over:**
$ 0	$ 9,700	10% of	$ 0
$ 9,700	$ 39,475	$ 970 + 12% of	$ 9,700
$ 39,475	$ 84,200	$ 4,543 + 22% of	$ 39,475
$ 84,200	$160,725	$ 14,383 + 24% of	$ 84,200
$160,725	$204,100	$ 32,749 + 32% of	$160,725
$204,100	$510,300	$ 46,629 + 35% of	$204,100
$510,300	+	$153,799 + 37% of	$510,300

Schedule Y-1. 2019 Tax Rate Schedule for Married Filing Jointly			
If your taxable income is:			
Over:	**But not more than:**	**You will owe:**	**Taxable income over:**
$ 0	$ 19,400	10% of	$ 0
$ 19,400	$ 78,950	$ 1,940 + 12% of	$ 19,400
$ 78,950	$168,400	$ 9,086 + 22% of	$ 78,950
$168,400	$321,450	$ 28,765 + 24% of	$168,400
$321,450	$408,200	$ 65,497 + 32% of	$321,450
$408,200	$612,350	$ 93,257 + 35% of	$408,200
$612,350	+	$164,710 + 37% of	$612,350

As you can see, you pay lower tax rates on your first dollars of income and higher rates on later dollars of income. For example, Schedule X indicates that, for a single filer in 2019, the tax rate on the first $9,700 of taxable income is only 10 percent. A person who earned $9,700 or less in 2019 would be in the lowest tax bracket and would pay only 10 percent of her or his taxable income in taxes. A single person with 2019 taxable income of $39,475 would owe 10 percent on the first $9,700 ($970) plus 12 percent on the remaining $30,300 ($3,636), for a total of $4,606. This is about $900 less than that person would have owed if the marginal rates were those in effect before the 2017 tax reform.

The issue of whether tax rates should be higher or lower, particularly for those in higher tax brackets, has been the subject of vigorous debate over the years. In fact, tax rates today are historically quite low, as can be seen in **Figure 4.2**, which shows the top marginal tax bracket over time. Although the top rate is one factor that has changed over time, it's also important to compare the income level to which this marginal rate was applied. In 1936, the top rate was 79 percent on any income over $5 million, but it turns out that only one taxpayer qualified— John D. Rockefeller, Jr. In contrast, about 500,000 taxpayers are in the top bracket today, with taxable income over $510,300 for singles and $612,350 for married couples filing jointly. The figure also illustrates that the lowest marginal bracket is at one of its lowest levels in history. From the late 1970s to the mid-1980s, there was a 0 percent marginal rate, but that rate only applied to very low levels of income ($3,200 in 1977). For incomes above that level, the rate jumped to 14 percent or higher.

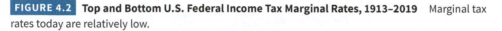

FIGURE 4.2   **Top and Bottom U.S. Federal Income Tax Marginal Rates, 1913–2019**   Marginal tax rates today are relatively low.

Source: Data from www.irs.gov.

Marginal versus Average Tax Rates

Because you can't do much about what tax bracket you're in, tax planning is aimed at minimizing your **average tax rate** for a given level of income. Your average tax rate is the percentage of total taxable income you pay in taxes and, and you can calculate it using **Equation 4.1**:

$$\text{Average tax rate} = \frac{\text{Taxes paid}}{\text{Taxable income}} \tag{4.1}$$

When a tax system is progressive, with higher rates on higher levels of income, your average tax rate will always be less than your marginal tax rate, as illustrated in **Demonstration Problem 4.1**.

DEMONSTRATION PROBLEM 4.1 | Calculating Average Tax Rate

Problem

You are single with taxable income of $40,000. Your marginal tax rate is 22 percent, and you owe $4,658.50 in taxes. What is your average tax rate?

Strategy

Use Equation 4.1 to calculate the average tax rate.

Solution

Although your marginal tax rate is 22 percent, your average tax rate is lower:

$$\text{Average tax rate} = \frac{\$4,658.50}{\$40,000} = 11.65\%$$

Figure 4.3 shows the breakdown of taxable income into taxes paid and after-tax income for taxpayers at various income levels, along with average tax rates for each level. The average tax rate for each income level except the lowest is 2 to 3 percentage points lower than it was before the 2017 tax reforms. **Figure 4.4** shows average tax rates and marginal tax rates for specific levels of taxable income based on filing status (single versus married filing jointly). You can use **Excel Worksheet 4.1** (Personal Financial Planner: Marginal and Average Tax Rates) to calculate these tax rates for different income levels.

EXCEL WORKSHEET

See **Excel Worksheet 4.1 (Personal Financial Planner: Marginal and Average Tax Rates)** in **WileyPLUS**.

FIGURE 4.3 **Taxes Owed, After-Tax Income, and Average Tax Rates** Each column in this graph shows the breakdown of taxable income into taxes owed and after-tax income for a single taxpayer in 2019, for different levels of taxable income. The percentage at the top of each bar is the average tax rate for that taxable income level.

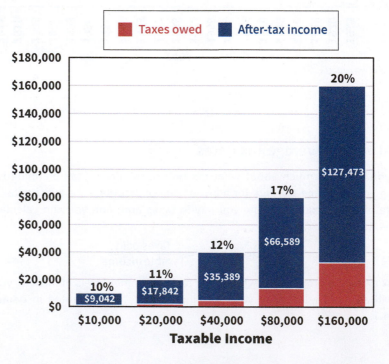

FIGURE 4.4 **Marginal and Average Tax Rates**   At almost all income levels, married taxpayers are subject to lower average and marginal tax rates.

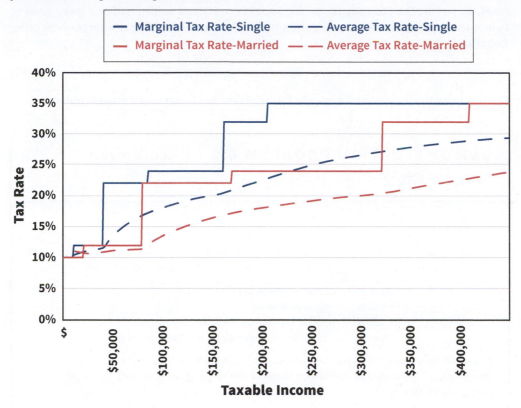

Our calculations of the average tax rate have been based on *taxable* income. Note that for some purposes, it may be useful to consider the proportion you pay in taxes out of your *total* income, before deductions. You may sometimes see this ratio referred to as your average tax rate. We'll examine the difference between total income and taxable income in more detail later in the chapter.

Inflation Indexing of Tax Brackets

Although federal income tax rates can only be changed by Congress, the levels of income that trigger each successive increase in tax rate are automatically increased each year to account for inflation. This feature of the tax system has been in place since 1981, following a period of very high inflation. Inflation indexing is a very important protection for taxpayers in lower tax brackets. As an example, suppose you're a single filer who had taxable income at the top of the 12 percent tax bracket. The next year, you received a raise equal to the inflation rate. If the brackets didn't change, your additional income would be taxed at the 22 percent marginal rate. But you wouldn't have had any additional purchasing power, because your income would have increased at the same rate as the cost of the things you need to buy. Due to the higher tax rate applied to your additional earnings, the net effect would be that you'd have a little *less* purchasing power than you had in the previous year.

Consider the Marginal Tax Effect in Making Financial Decisions

Tax laws include many rules that can allow you to pay lower taxes. For example, contributions to certain employer-provided retirement plans can be subtracted from your income before you calculate your tax. When deciding whether to take advantage of tax-saving opportunities, you should always consider the **marginal tax effect**—the reduction in taxes owed as a result of a financial decision. As discussed in Chapter 1, effective decision making requires that you always evaluate your alternatives based on the change in your financial circumstances that will result from the decision.

In estimating the marginal tax effect, you should apply an aggregate tax rate that includes all types of income and payroll taxes—most commonly, federal, state, and local income taxes, as well as the FICA payroll tax for Social Security and Medicare. For a given level of before-tax income, you can calculate the amount of income you will have after taxes by using **Equation 4.2**:

$$\text{After-tax income} = \text{Before-tax income} \times (1 - \text{Tax rate}) \tag{4.2}$$

Let's try using this equation for a specific financial decision in **Demonstration Problem 4.2**.

DEMONSTRATION PROBLEM 4.2 | Calculating the Marginal Tax Effect

Problem

You have taxable income of $40,000 (22 percent federal marginal tax bracket) and live in a state with a 5 percent state income tax. Your next dollar of taxable income will be subject to the following taxes:

22.00%	Federal income tax
+ 5.00%	State income tax
+ 7.65%	Social Security and Medicare payroll tax
34.65%	Total marginal tax rate on additional earnings

This results in a total of 34.65 percent paid in taxes. You have the opportunity to work overtime for your employer and expect to earn an additional $2,000 by doing so. How much better off will you be if you work overtime?

Strategy

Use Equation 4.2 to calculate the amount you will have left after paying your marginal tax rate on the additional income.

Solution

Because your additional earnings of $2,000 will be subject to the 34.65 percent marginal tax rate, you will have $1,307 left after taxes, as calculated by use of Equation 4.2:

$$\text{After-tax income} = \text{Before-tax income} \times (1 - \text{Tax rate})$$
$$= \$2,000 \times (1 - 0.3465) = \$1,307$$

Although this chapter covers only the basics of the tax system, later chapters will present more examples in which tax rules will make certain financial decisions more attractive than others. In each case, it will always be important to focus on the marginal tax effect in making these decisions.

4.2 | Filing Requirements

LEARNING OBJECTIVE 4.2

Determine whether you need to file a federal income tax return and which forms you should use.

The Internal Revenue Service receives about 150 million individual tax returns each year, about one-third from married households and two-thirds from singles. In general, it's pretty easy to determine whether you need to file a tax return. In this section, we'll go over the rules about who needs to file and which forms to use. If you use tax preparation software, it will ask you several questions at the outset to guide you through this process.

Filing Status

Your **filing status** identifies your household type. Because your filing status may change over time, you are required to identify your status each year as one of the following, based on your situation as of the last day of the year:

- **Single**   Unmarried or legally separated from your spouse.
- **Married filing jointly**   Married couple filing a single tax return, even if only one spouse had income.
- **Married filing separately**   Each spouse files an individual tax return.
- **Head of household**   Single person who lives with and pays more than half of the support for a **dependent** child or relative.
- **Qualifying widow(er) with dependent child**   Person whose spouse died within two years of the tax year and who lives with and pays more than half of the support for a dependent child.

Even if you're a dependent, you may have to file your own tax return, but this will depend on the types and amounts of income you receive, which will be discussed in the next section.

Adjusted Gross Income and Taxable Income

Along with your filing status, your taxable income is another major determinant of whether you must file a tax return. It will also determine the amount of taxes you pay. The IRS defines your **adjusted gross income (AGI)** as the total of your **earned income** (including salaries, wages, tips, bonuses, commissions, and self-employment income) plus your **unearned income** (interest, dividends, capital gains, rents, royalties, and net business income) minus certain allowed adjustments. From your adjusted gross income, you are also allowed to subtract the greater of the following two options:

- **Standard deduction**   In 2019, the allowed **standard deduction** was $12,200 for singles, $18,350 for heads of household, and $24,400 for married couples filing jointly. The allowed deduction increases each year by the same amount as inflation.
- **Itemized deductions**   If your annual expenses in certain allowed categories exceed, in total, the standard deduction for your filing status, you can choose to report **itemized deductions** instead of the standard deduction. Itemizing deductions involves filing an additional IRS form (Schedule A) on which you identify your deductions in accordance with the rules and limitations for each category.

The calculation of AGI and deductions is discussed in detail later in the chapter when we work through calculating federal income tax.

If your earned income is no more than your standard deduction or itemized deductions, then your taxable income is zero, and you aren't required to file a tax return. This means that single taxpayers could have earned up to $12,200 in 2019 without having to file a return. Married couples filing jointly had to file if they earned more than $24,400. Of course, if you made less than these amounts but had taxes withheld from your pay, you would still need to file a return in order to get a refund of the taxes you paid.

In addition to deductions, you can also use a **tax credit** to reduce the taxes you owe. Tax credits, unlike deductions, do not represent adjustments to your income. Rather, they are subtracted directly from the taxes you owe. You'll learn more about the specific application of all these tax rules later in this chapter.

As mentioned, even if your parent claims you as a dependent, you may still need to file a tax return, depending on the amount and type of income you received during the year. You need to file a return if any of the following apply:

- Your earned income was more than $12,200 (based on 2019 tax law).
- Your unearned income (such as earnings on investment accounts) was more than $1,100.
- Your total income was more than the larger of (1) $1,100 or (2) your earned income (up to $11,850) plus $350.
- Taxes were withheld from your income, and you want to get a refund.
- You qualify for a tax credit.

In some cases, families may decide to place certain income-earning property in their minor children's names in order to have the earnings escape taxation or be taxed at a lower marginal rate. If the unearned income is less than $2,200 (in 2019), it is taxed at the child's marginal rate. Amounts in excess of that limit will be subject to a higher rate which may even exceed the parents' normal marginal tax rate. This is commonly called the "kiddie tax," and applies to dependents who are children under the age of 19 or full-time students under age 24.

IRS Forms

The main federal income tax form is Form 1040. This postcard-sized form was greatly simplified as part of the tax reforms that took effect in 2018. Although most taxpayers will only file this form, many other schedules and forms may be required, depending on your circumstances. The most commonly required forms and schedules are identified and described in **Table 4.2**.

TABLE 4.2   **Additional Federal Income Tax Forms You May Need to File**

Form	Name	When You Need to Use It
Schedule 1	Additional Taxes and Adjustments to Income	If you need to report unearned income, such as alimony, investment earnings, and business income, or make adjustments to income, such as for educator expenses and student loan interest.
Schedule 3	Nonrefundable Credits	If you are claiming a tax credit, such as for education expenses, child-care expenses, or retirement savings.
Schedule 5	Other Payments and Refundable Credits	If you are claiming certain refundable tax credits.
Schedule A	Itemized Deductions	If your total itemized deductions are greater than the applicable standard deduction.
Schedule B	Interest and Ordinary Dividends	If you have interest and dividend income greater than $1,500. If you received tax-exempt interest. If you received interest from a seller-financed mortgage.
Schedule C	Profit or Loss from Business	If you have income and expenses from self-employment. (Use Schedule C-EZ if your expenses are $5,000 or less.)
Schedule D	Capital Gains and Losses	If you have gains or losses from the sale of investments.
Schedule E	Supplemental Income and Loss	If you have income and expenses from rental properties, royalties, partnerships, S corporations, estates, or trusts.
Schedule EIC	Earned Income Credit	If you are eligible for a credit because you have sufficiently low employment income.
Schedule SE	Self-Employment Tax	If you have self-employment income on which you owe FICA payroll taxes.
3903	Moving Expenses	If you are eligible to adjust your income for job-related moving expenses.
4562	Depreciation and Amortization	If you report depreciation or amortization expenses for your rental property or business assets.
4684	Casualties and Thefts	If you claim a deduction for uninsured personal casualty or theft losses.

(continued)

TABLE 4.2 **Additional Federal Income Tax Forms You May Need to File** *(continued)*

Form	Name	When You Need to Use It
4868	Application for Automatic Extension	If you want to extend the due date for filing your tax return by six months. You still must pay any taxes owed by the usual due date.
6251	Alternative Minimum Tax	If you are required to pay this tax because you have high income and claim a lot of deductions.
8283	Noncash Charitable Contributions	If you claim an itemized deduction for noncash charitable gifts of more than $500.
8615	Tax for Children Who Have Investment Income	If your dependent child has investment income in excess of the allowed limit.
8812	Additional Child Tax Credit	If you have sufficiently low income and have children.
8829	Expenses for Business Use of Your Home	If you claim a home office deduction on your Schedule C.
8863	Education Credits	If you have qualifying education expenses and meet income limitations.
8889	Health Savings Accounts	If you make contributions to or withdrawals from a health savings account.
8917	Tuition and Fees Deduction	If you pay qualified education expenses and do not take an education credit.
8949	Sales and Other Dispositions of Capital Assets	If you have gains or losses from the sale of investments.
1040X	Amended Return	If you make a mistake on any of the previous three years' tax forms.
1040ES	Estimated Tax	If you expect to owe taxes in the next tax year.

Source: www.irs.gov

Tax forms may be filled out by hand, typed, or completed electronically. You can also pay a professional tax preparer to complete your tax return for you, although you'll still need to collect the documentation necessary for him or her to complete the forms. Since 2011, professional tax preparers are required to e-file all of the returns they submit.

Reflection Question 1

What emotions do you feel when you think about completing your federal income tax return? If you had the power to make changes to the tax system, what would you do?

Tax software packages such as TurboTax® and Tax Cut® can often make it easier and faster to complete your return, identify the appropriate forms to file, and e-file the completed tax return. These programs walk you through entering information by asking specific questions to which you must respond. They then use this information to fill in the appropriate forms for you. If you previously used the same software, it will automatically transfer your information from previous years, making it less likely you'll forget potential deductions or credits. These programs can also help you avoid making some of the common filing errors identified in **Interactive: Common Filing Errors**.

INTERACTIVE

See Interactive: Common Filing Errors in **WileyPLUS.**

4.3 Federal Income Tax Calculation

LEARNING OBJECTIVE 4.3

Prepare a basic tax return.

As the April 15 tax-filing deadline approaches each year, many people whine and moan about filling out their tax forms. However, those who have their finances in order generally find that completing tax forms is a fairly painless task. In this section, we'll review key terminology and the steps in the process of calculating taxes owed. Then we'll apply this knowledge to the completion of the most important federal income tax forms. The steps involved in calculating how much tax you owe are illustrated in **Figure 4.5** and discussed in detail in this section.

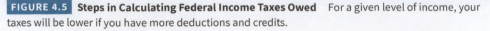

FIGURE 4.5 **Steps in Calculating Federal Income Taxes Owed** For a given level of income, your taxes will be lower if you have more deductions and credits.

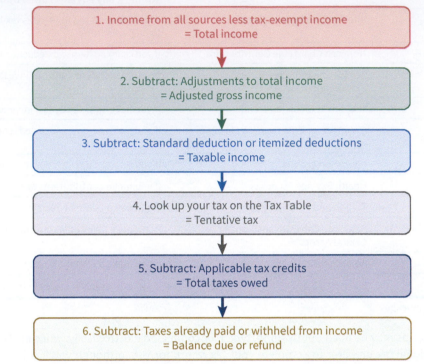

Reporting Income

In the next several sections, we'll illustrate the tax calculation steps by looking at a tax return prepared by Rosa and Mateo Rivera, a married couple with one child and another one the way. The first step is to accurately report income from all sources, less any exclusions.

Total Income

Gross income is your income from all sources. However, some categories of income are excluded to arrive at **total income** on your tax forms. **Table 4.3** details what must be included and what can be excluded in reporting total income. For example, you don't have to report scholarships used for tuition and course-related expenses, but scholarship funds applied to room and board expenses must be reported as income. Child support payments and alimony received from an ex-spouse are not reported as income, unless the divorce agreement was executed prior to 2019 and specified that alimony would be deductible by the payer and taxable to the recipient.

TABLE 4.3 **What Is and Is Not Included in Total Income on Your Federal Taxes**

Included	
Business or partnership income	Investment gains/losses
Commissions and fees	Moving expense reimbursement (if deducted)
Dividends	Pension income
Employer-paid disability income	Property rental income/loss
Gambling winnings and prizes	Royalties
Hobby income	Self-employment income
Income from tax-deferred retirement accounts	Unemployment compensation
Interest	Wages, salaries, tips, bonuses

(continued)

TABLE 4.3   What Is and Is Not Included in Total Income on Your Federal Taxes *(continued)*

Not Included (limitations apply to categories marked with *)

Annuities*	Long-term care benefits
Child support and alimony	Military cost-of-living allowance
Disability payments*	Qualified fringe benefits paid by employer*
Gifts	Required travel expenses paid by employer*
Inheritance	Roth IRA and Roth 401(k) distributions
Insurance claim payments	Scholarships and fellowships*
Jury awards	State and local bond interest
Life insurance proceeds	Welfare payments
Long-term capital gain on sale of home*	Worker's compensation payments

Rosa and Mateo's completed 1040 for 2019 is reproduced in **Figure 4.6**. You can see that they reported their combined $88,500 in salaries and $48 in taxable interest income to arrive at a total income of $88,548. For most people, the largest source of total income is earned income from employment—salaries, hourly wages, bonuses, tips, and commissions—all of which is included in gross taxable income. If you receive business income, investment income, unemployment compensation, or retirement benefits, this income must also be included in total income. Unearned income may include interest and dividends from investments, net business income, rents, and royalties you received during the year, annuity and pension income, awards for scientific and charitable achievement, gambling and lottery winnings, and scholarship funds spent on room and board. Note that Rosa does not report the child support she receives from her ex-husband as income for tax purposes.

Employers and financial institutions are required to report the amounts that they pay to you each year, and you'll generally receive an informational copy of this report in January following the tax year (Form W-2 for employment income and Forms 1098 and 1099 for other types of income). You're also required to report other income, such as cash tips you receive as a restaurant server, even if these amounts do not appear on your W-2. Your taxable income, as reported on the W-2, will exclude any payments made on your behalf for tax-qualified health insurance and retirement plans—in other words, those amounts are subtracted from your income before it is reported on the W-2 and are not subject to tax.

Adjusted Gross Income

For most taxpayers, such as Rosa and Mateo, wages and interest are their only sources of income. If you have other sources of taxable income, you must file Schedule 1 (Additional Income and Adjustments to Income) and attach it to your Form 1040. This schedule is used to report additional sources of income and any allowed adjustments to income. For example, you need to report unemployment benefits, taxable refunds, profits (or losses) from businesses or rental properties, and any **capital gain**, or increase in value, of taxable investments that you sold during the year. If you sold a rental property during the year for $100,000 and you had paid $80,000 for it, you will owe tax on the $20,000 capital gain (less the cost of improvements to the property and some allowed expenses for the sale). Note that even if you received the whole $100,000 in cash flow that year, you only report the $20,000 gain as taxable income. If you hold an investment longer than one year, the gain from its sale is subject to a lower capital gains tax rate—0 percent for those in the 10 or 12 percent tax brackets, 20 percent for those with taxable income over $434,550 (single) or $488,850 (married filing jointly) in 2019, and 15 percent for everyone else.

For some high-income taxpayers, net investment income is subject to an additional 3.8 percent Medicare tax, as mentioned earlier. The tax is owed on the lesser of (1) net investment income or (2) the amount by which adjusted gross income exceeds $250,000 for married couples or $200,000 for singles.

FIGURE 4.6 Completed 1040 for Rosa and Mateo Rivera

Form **1040** Department of the Treasury—Internal Revenue Service (99)
U.S. Individual Income Tax Return **2019** OMB No. 1545-0074 IRS Use Only—Do not write or staple in this space.

Filing status: ☐ Single ☑ Married filing jointly ☐ Married filing separately ☐ Head of household ☐ Qualifying widow(er)

Your first name and initial	Last name	Your social security number
Mateo S.	Rivera	1 1 1 1 1 1 1 1 1

Your standard deduction: ☐ Someone can claim you as a dependent ☐ You were born before January 2, 1954 ☐ You are blind

If joint return, spouse's first name and initial	Last name	Spouse's social security number
Rosa M.	Rivera	2 2 2 2 2 2 2 2 2

Spouse standard deduction: ☐ Someone can claim your spouse as a dependent ☐ Spouse was born before January 2, 1954
☐ Spouse is blind ☐ Spouse itemizes on a separate return or you were dual-status alien
☑ Full-year health care coverage or exempt (see inst.)

Home address (number and street). If you have a P.O. box, see instructions. Apt. no.
34 Main Street

City, town or post office, state, and ZIP code. If you have a foreign address, attach Schedule 6.
Anytown, NJ 12345

Presidential Election Campaign (see inst.) You Spouse
If more than four dependents, see inst. and ✓ here ►

Dependents (see instructions):

(1) First name Last name	(2) Social security number	(3) Relationship to you	(4) ✓ if qualifies for (see inst.): Child tax credit	Credit for other dependents
Kyle Larson	3 3 3 3 3 3 3 3	Child	☑	☐
			☐	☐
			☐	☐
			☐	☐

Sign Here

Under penalties of perjury, I declare that I have examined this return and accompanying schedules and statements, and to the best of my knowledge and belief, they are true, correct, and complete. Declaration of preparer (other than taxpayer) is based on all information of which preparer has any knowledge.

Joint return? See instructions. Keep a copy for your records.

Your signature *Mateo S. Rivera*	Date 4/15/2020	Your occupation **Computer system analyst**	If the IRS sent you an Identity Protection PIN, enter it here (see inst.)
Spouse's signature. If a joint return, **both** must sign.	Date	Spouse's occupation **Office manager**	If the IRS sent you an Identity Protection PIN, enter it here (see inst.)

Paid Preparer Use Only

Preparer's name	Preparer's signature	PTIN	Firm's EIN	Check if: ☐ 3rd Party Designee
Firm's name ► **Self-prepared**		Phone no.		☐ Self-employed
Firm's address ►				

For Disclosure, Privacy Act, and Paperwork Reduction Act Notice, see separate instructions. Cat. No. 11320B Form **1040** (2019)

Form 1040 (2019) Page **2**

Attach Form(s) W-2. Also attach Form(s) W-2G and 1099-R if tax was withheld.

1	Wages, salaries, tips, etc. Attach Form(s) W-2	**1**	88,500
2a	Tax-exempt interest . . . **2a**	b Taxable interest . . . **2b**	48
3a	Qualified dividends . . . **3a**	b Ordinary dividends . . . **3b**	
4a	IRAs, pensions, and annuities . **4a**	b Taxable amount . . . **4b**	
5a	Social security benefits . . **5a**	b Taxable amount . . . **5b**	
6	Total income. Add lines 1 through 5. Add any amount from Schedule 1, line22	**6**	88,548
7	Adjusted gross income. If you have no adjustments to income, enter the amount from line 6; otherwise, subtract Schedule 1, line 36, from line 6	**7**	88,548

Standard Deduction for—
- Single or married filing separately, $12,200
- Married filing jointly or Qualifying widow(er), $24,400
- Head of household, $18,350
- If you checked any box under Standard deduction, see instructions.

8	**Standard deduction or itemized deductions** (from Schedule A)	**8**	24,400
9	Qualified business income deduction (see instructions) . . .	**9**	
10	Taxable income. Subtract lines 8 and 9 from line 7. If zero or less, enter -0-	**10**	64,148
11	a Tax (see inst.) 7,307 (check if any from: 1 ☐ Form(s) 8814 2 ☐ Form 4972 3 ☐)		
	b Add any amount from Schedule 2 and check here ► ☐	**11**	7,307
12	a Child tax credit/credit for other dependents 2,000 b Add any amount from Schedule 3 and check here ► ☐	**12**	2,000
13	Subtract line 12 from line 11. If zero or less, enter -0-	**13**	5,307
14	Other taxes. Attach Schedule 4 . . .	**14**	
15	Total tax. Add lines 13 and 14	**15**	5,307
16	Federal income tax withheld from Forms W-2 and 1099	**16**	7,352
17	Refundable credits: a EIC (see inst.) b Sch. 8812 c Form 8863		
	Add any amount from Schedule 5	**17**	
18	Add lines 16 and 17. These are your total payments	**18**	7,352

Refund

Direct deposit? See instructions.

19	If line 18 is more than line 15, subtract line 15 from line 18. This is the amount you **overpaid**	**19**	2,045
20a	Amount of line 19 you want **refunded to you.** If Form 8888 is attached, check here ► ☐	**20a**	2,045
►b	Routing number _____ ►c Type: ☐ Checking ☐ Savings		
►d	Account number _____		
21	Amount of line 19 you want **applied to your 2019 estimated tax** ► **21**		

Amount You Owe

22	**Amount you owe.** Subtract line 18 from line 15. For details on how to pay, see instructions . . . ►	**22**	
23	Estimated tax penalty (see instructions) . . . ► **23**		

Go to *www.irs.gov/Form1040* for instructions and the latest information. Form **1040** (2019)

A special capital gains tax rule applies to profits made on the sale of your primary residence, defined as the place in which you lived for two of the last five years before the sale. You can exclude from your total income up to $250,000 of the gain on the sale of your home ($500,000 for married couples). In practice, this rule means that most people will never pay any tax on the profit they realize from selling their home.

Schedule 1 is also used to report certain expenses that are subtracted from total income to arrive at adjusted gross income. Although some of these adjustments are subject to income limitations, they can represent significant tax breaks for those who qualify. In addition, if you qualify for one of these adjustments, you can benefit from it even if you don't itemize deductions. Some of these adjustments include the following:

- For teachers of kindergarten through grade 12, unreimbursed educator expenses up to $250.
- Deductible individual retirement account contributions up to $6,000.
- Interest paid on student loans during the year up to $2,500.
- Unreimbursed moving expenses for those serving in the armed forces.
- Contribution to qualifying health savings account up to $3,500 ($7,000 for a family).
- One-half of Social Security taxes paid on business income.

The amount you have left after making all these adjustments is your adjusted gross income, as defined earlier. The Riveras' adjusted gross income is the same as their total income—$88,548—because they didn't qualify for any of the adjustments to total income.

Deductions

As already noted, once you've calculated your adjusted gross income, you can subtract either the standard deduction or itemized deductions from that amount to arrive at taxable income.

Standard Deduction

The amount of the standard deduction increases annually with inflation and depends on your filing status. You don't have to provide any proof or expense receipts to be able to take the standard deduction. For tax year 2019, the allowed standard deduction amounts were as follows:

- Single and married filing separately, $12,200
- Married filing jointly, $24,400
- Head of household, $18,350

Because the standard deduction amounts are so high, more than double what they were before the 2017 tax reforms, more than 90 percent of taxpayers now take the standard deduction instead of itemizing.

Itemized Deductions

If you have tax-deductible expenses that exceed the standard deduction for your filing status, you can reduce your taxes by itemizing deductions. The categories for itemized deductions include medical and dental expenses, taxes you paid, some types of interest you paid, gifts to charity, casualty and theft losses, and other itemized deductions. To determine whether you should itemize deductions, you need to total up your possible deductions to see if they are greater than your standard deduction would be. The Riveras did this by completing Schedule A, as shown in **Figure 4.7**. Each of the categories of deductions is described below. Since the Riveras itemized deductions totaled only $17,808, they will take the $24,400 standard deduction instead and will not file Schedule A.

Although you don't have to provide supporting documentation when you file your tax return, you must be able to produce proof of the actual expenses if the IRS requests it. For example, if you've made charitable contributions during the year, you should have a statement or receipt that acknowledges your donation.

- **Medical and dental expenses** You can deduct out-of-pocket expenditures for health insurance premiums, medical services (doctor, dentist, optometrist, nurses, hospitals), prescription drugs, eyeglasses, hearing aids, travel for medical purposes, special schooling for disabled children, nursing homes, alternative medicine (chiropractors, acupuncture), and other medical and dental expenses to the extent that the sum of these expenses adds up to more than 10 percent of your adjusted gross income. You cannot deduct medical or dental expenses paid or reimbursed by your health insurer, nor can you deduct health insurance premiums that have been deducted from your payroll on a pre-tax basis. To determine your deduction, you first total your medical and dental expenses and then subtract 10 percent of your AGI. The remainder is your deduction. Thus, the Riveras, who had an AGI equal to $88,048, would have been able to deduct medical and dental expenses only to the extent that they exceeded $8,805 (10 percent of $88,048). If you pay your own health insurance or long-term care insurance premiums, this may be a valuable deduction for you.

- **Taxes you paid** You're allowed to deduct up to $10,000 in state and local income taxes, real estate property taxes paid on your primary residence, and personal property taxes (imposed in some states on cars and other personal assets). If you take a deduction for state income taxes, you may have to make an adjustment to your income in a later year for tax refunds that you receive from the state. Rosa and Mateo paid state income taxes of $4,000 (reported on their W-2s) and $2,400 in property taxes on their home (reported to them by their mortgage lender).

- **Interest you paid** The mortgage interest deduction is now limited to interest on $375,000 of home mortgages ($750,000 for married couples filing jointly) on both first and second homes, as well as points and loan origination fees incurred in obtaining a mortgage loan. (If your mortgage originated before 2018, you can still deduct all the interest.) The Riveras report mortgage interest for the year in the amount of $9,958. Interest paid on credit cards, personal loans, and car loans is not deductible.

- **Gifts to charity** The tax laws allow you to deduct cash and noncash contributions made to charitable organizations. Noncash contributions can include food you've donated to the local food bank or a bag of used clothing given to a local charitable organization. Rosa and Mateo reported their regular cash contribution to their church, which totaled $1,200 for the year. Rosa took several bags of clothes and toys to the Goodwill drop-off and received receipts for her donations totaling $250. You can deduct only the current market value of the items you've donated. People who are actively involved in volunteer organizations can also deduct expenses incurred in their volunteer work, including mileage expenses. For example, if you took a group of Boy Scouts on a camping trip during the summer and incurred expenses for minivan rental, gasoline, and food, you can deduct your costs. For those who do not itemize deductions, there is no tax benefit from charitable contributions.

- **Casualty and theft losses** For an unreimbursed loss due to damage or theft attributable to a federally declared disaster, the tax law allows you to deduct the amount of the loss less $100 less 10 percent of your AGI. For example, suppose your car, which was worth $3,000, was destroyed in a flood or fire, but it wasn't insured. If your AGI is $25,000, you can deduct ($3000 − $100) − (0.1 × $25,000) = $2,900 − $2,500 = $400. The Riveras didn't have any deductions in this category.

FIGURE 4.7 **Schedule A: Itemized Deductions for Rosa and Mateo Rivera** The Riveras' itemized deductions are much less than the standard deduction.

SCHEDULE A (Form 1040)	**Itemized Deductions**	OMB No. 1545-0074
Department of the Treasury Internal Revenue Service (99)	▶ Go to *www.irs.gov/ScheduleA* for instructions and the latest information. ▶ **Attach to Form 1040.** **Caution:** If you are claiming a net qualified disaster loss on Form 4684, see the instructions for line 16.	**2019** Attachment Sequence No. **07**

Name(s) shown on Form 1040 | Your social security number

Mateo S. Rivera and Rosa M. Rivera

Medical and Dental Expenses

Caution: Do not include expenses reimbursed or paid by others.

1 Medical and dental expenses (see instructions).................**1**

2 Enter amount from Form 1040, line 7 **2**

3 Multiply line 2 by 7.5% (0.075).................**3**

4 Subtract line 3 from line 1. If line 3 is more than line 1, enter -0- **4**

Taxes You Paid

5 State and local taxes.

  a State and local income taxes or general sales taxes. You may include either income taxes or general sales taxes on line 5a, but not both. If you elect to include general sales taxes instead of income taxes, check this box . . . . ▶ ☐ **5a** 4,000

  b State and local real estate taxes (see instructions) **5b** 2,400

  c State and local personal property taxes **5c**

  d Add lines 5a through 5c **5d**

  e Enter the smaller of line 5d or $10,000 ($5,000 if married filing separately) **5e**

6 Other taxes. List type and amount ▶ -------------------------------- **6**

7 Add lines 5e and 6 . . . . **7** 6,400

Interest You Paid

Caution: Your mortgage interest deduction may be limited (see instructions).

8 Home mortgage interest and points. If you didn't use all of your home mortgage loan(s) to buy, build, or improve your home, see instructions and check this box . . . . ▶ ☐

  a Home mortgage interest and points reported to you on Form 1098 . . . . **8a** 9,958

  b Home mortgage interest not reported to you on Form 1098. If paid to the person from whom you bought the home, see instructions and show that person's name, identifying no., and address ▶ -------------------------------- **8b**

  c Points not reported to you on Form 1098. See instructions for special rules **8c**

  d Reserved **8d**

  e Add lines 8a through 8c **8e**

9 Investment interest. Attach Form 4952 if required. See instructions.................**9**

10 Add lines 8e and 9.................**10** 9,958

Gifts to Charity

If you made a gift and got a benefit for it, see instructions.

11 Gifts by cash or check. If you made any gift of $250 or more, see instructions.................**11** 1,200

12 Other than by cash or check. If any gift of $250 or more, see instructions. You **must** attach Form 8283 if over $500 . . . **12** 250

13 Carryover from prior year.................**13**

14 Add lines 11 through 13.................**14** 1,450

Casualty and Theft Losses

15 Casualty and theft loss(es) from a federally declared disaster (other than net qualified disaster losses). Attach Form 4684 and enter the amount from line 18 of that form. See instructions.................**15**

Other Itemized Deductions

16 Other—from list in instructions. List type and amount ▶ -------------------------------- **16**

Total Itemized Deductions

17 Add the amounts in the far right column for lines 4 through 16. Also, enter this amount on Form 1040, line 8.................**17** 17,808

18 If you elect to itemize deductions even though they are less than your standard deduction, check here . . . . ▶ ☐

For Paperwork Reduction Act Notice, see the Instructions for Form 1040.   Cat. No. 17145C   Schedule A (Form 1040) 2019

Calculation of Taxes Owed

Subtracting deductions from adjusted gross income gives you taxable income. You'll use this amount to calculate the taxes you owe. The resulting tax is only the tentative tax, because it may change once you consider credits you might qualify for and additional taxes that might apply to your tax situation. You can use **Excel Worksheet 4.2** (Personal Financial Planner: Federal Income Tax Estimator) to estimate your taxes owed.

EXCEL WORKSHEET

See **Excel Worksheet 4.2** (Personal Financial Planner: Federal Income Tax Estimator) in **WileyPLUS**.

Tax Table and Tax Schedules

As explained earlier, the tax rate schedules are useful for understanding how different layers of income are taxed. However, individual taxpayers are not expected to do that type of calculation themselves. Instead, the IRS precalculates the tax for many different ranges of taxable income. If you know your taxable income, you can look up the tax amount that you must pay on the Tax Table provided in the instruction booklet that comes with your tax forms or on the IRS website. **Table 4.4** shows an excerpt from the 2019 Tax Table.

TABLE 4.4   **Excerpt from 2019 Tax Table**

| If line 43 (taxable income) is ___ | | And you are ___ | | | |
At least	But less than	Single	Married filing jointly	Married filing separately	Head of a household
			Your tax is ___		
64,000					
64,000	64,050	9,944	7,795	9,944	8,524
64,050	64,100	9,955	7,301	9,955	8,535
64,100	64,150	9,966	7,307	9,966	8,546
64,150	64,200	9,977	7,313	9,977	8,557
64,200	64,250	9,988	7,319	9,988	8,568
64,250	64,300	9,999	7,325	9,999	8,579
64,300	64,350	10,010	7,331	10,010	8,590
64,350	64,400	10,021	7,337	10,021	8,601
64,400	64,450	10,032	7,343	10,032	8,612
64,450	64,500	10,043	7,349	10,043	8,623
64,500	64,550	10,054	7,355	10,054	8,634
64,550	64,600	10,065	7,361	10,065	8,645
64,600	64,650	10,076	7,367	10,076	8,656
64,650	64,700	10,087	7,373	10,087	8,667
64,700	64,750	10,098	7,379	10,098	8,678
64,750	64,800	10,109	7,385	10,109	8,689

Once you've determined your tentative tax, you're almost done. The final steps are determining eligibility for tax credits that can reduce taxes owed and determining applicability of the alternative minimum tax (AMT), which may result in an increase in the taxes owed. If you're self-employed, you'll also need to determine whether you owe Social Security and Medicare taxes on your business income. You'll then subtract what you've already paid through withholding during the year and determine whether you owe additional money or will receive a refund.

Using the applicable section of the Tax Table, shown in Table 4.4, Rosa and Mateo look down the left column to find their income level and then across the row to the column headed "Married filing jointly," which is their filing status. Their taxable income is between $64,100 and $64,150, so the amount of tax they owe, according to the table, is $7,307. This amount could change if the Riveras qualify for any tax credits or if they owe any additional taxes. The Riveras have already paid $7,352 in taxes through withholding from their paychecks. Based on the Tax Table, the Riveras estimate their tentative refund as $7,352 – $7,307 = $45. Their next step is to consider whether they are eligible for any tax credits.

Tax Credits

As mentioned earlier, tax credits directly reduce the taxes you owe. In 2019, credits were available for foreign taxes paid, child and dependent care expenses, elderly and disabled status, education expenses, retirement contributions, dependent children, and adoption. These are summarized in **Table 4.5**. You report tax credits on Schedules 3 and 5, but some also require another form to be filed as well. Because their AGI is less than $200,000, the Riveras determine that they're eligible for the child tax credit in the amount of $2,000, which will increase their refund to $2,045.

TABLE 4.5   **Summary of Common Tax Credits in Effect for 2019**

Tax Credit	Purpose	Amount and Conditions
Foreign Tax Credit	Avoid double taxation	Applies to taxes paid to another country
Child and Dependent Care Expenses	Cover the costs of child care necessary to allow you to work	20%–35% of actual expenses (up to $3,000 for one child, $6,000 for two or more); maximum credit is $600 for one child, $1,200 for two or more
Credit for Elderly and Disabled	Cover additional expenses due to working while disabled	15% of a base amount of income up to $7,500, depending on filing status, age, and disability; maximum credit $1,125
Child Tax Credit/Additional Child Tax Credit	Reduce tax burden on working parents	$2,000 per child; phased out for AGI above $200,000 single ($400,000 married); unused credit may be refundable up to $1,400
Earned Income Tax Credit	Help working poor	Credit increases with number of children. Maximum credit for married filing jointly with three children: $6,557 (maximum AGI $55,952); maximum credit for childless single: $529 (maximum AGI $21,370)
American Opportunity Credit (formerly Hope Scholarship Credit)	Encourage higher education	$2,500 of first $4,000 of qualified undergraduate education expenses; phased out for AGI $80,000–$90,000 single ($160,000–$180,000 married); 40% refundable credit
Lifetime Learning Credit	Encourage higher education	20% of first $10,000 of qualified education expenses to maximum $2,000 per family per year; phased out for AGI $58,000–$68,000 single ($116,000–$136,000 married)
Retirement Savings Contributions Credit	Encourage retirement saving	10%–50% of eligible retirement contribution; maximum credit $2,000 single ($4,000 married); phased out for AGI $19,251–$32,000 single ($38,501–$64,000 married)
Adoption Credit	Encourage adoption	Up to $14,080 for adoption of an eligible child; phased out for AGI $211,160–$251,160

There are specific guidelines for determining whether you qualify for each credit and how much it will reduce your tax. Several of the available credits are particularly helpful for working parents and contribute to the progressive nature of the tax system. In addition to a flat credit per child under the age of 17, you can take a tax credit for a portion of the costs of child care incurred while you are at work. For lower-income families, the earned income credit and child tax credits can significantly reduce taxes paid and may be refundable. With a **refundable tax credit**, if the credit is larger than the amount of tax owed, the taxpayer gets a cash payment for the difference. The American Opportunity Credit (formerly the Hope Scholarship Credit) and the Lifetime Learning Credit are important credits for college students and their families. Many of the currently available tax credits have income limitations, so it's advisable to use the applicable IRS worksheet to determine your eligibility and the amount of your credit.

Does the Alternative Minimum Tax Apply?

Some taxpayers end up owing more in taxes because of the **alternative minimum tax (AMT)**. This tax was originally designed to make sure that high-income people couldn't take advantage of too many special tax rules to avoid paying their fair share of taxes.

The AMT works this way: You are required to recalculate your taxes under a different set of rules in which many of the current deductions and special tax breaks do not apply. If the recalculated tax is larger than the one calculated in the normal way described above, then you must pay the higher amount. Some of the triggers for AMT liability in a given year include the following:

- A large number of credits
- Exercise of incentive stock options
- Long-term capital gains
- Unusually large itemized deductions, particularly for medical expenses, state and local taxes, or interest on home equity loans unless the loans were used for home improvements

If any of these apply to you, you should follow the IRS directions for calculation of the AMT to see whether it applies to your circumstances. The IRS automatically calculates the AMT based on your submitted tax form, so if you neglect to do so and therefore underpay your taxes, you may end up paying additional interest and penalties. However, tax preparation software and tax professionals will automatically calculate the AMT for you. The minimum income levels subject to the AMT were increased under the 2017 tax reforms, so fewer households will be impacted. The Riveras are thankful that they don't have to pay the AMT.

Additional Taxes Owed by the Self-Employed

If you're self-employed, you report total business revenues and certain deductible expenses on Schedule C. The difference between your revenues and expenses is taxable and therefore must be reported as business income (or loss) on your 1040 form. Because income tax and FICA (Social Security and Medicare) payroll taxes are not automatically withheld from this income, self-employed individuals are required to make quarterly estimated tax payments throughout the year. Any self-employed person who has not made estimated payments needs to pay the full amount of tax owed when filing Form 1040, along with a penalty.

Individuals who report self-employment income are also required to file Schedule SE (for self-employment) with their federal tax forms. This is a worksheet to determine the amount of Social Security and Medicare payroll taxes owed on business income. Whereas wage and salary workers split the 15.3 percent tax with their employer (each paying 7.65 percent), self-employed people are their own employers and thus must pay both portions of the tax. The combined effect of federal and state income taxes plus the Social Security and Medicare taxes take a hefty bite out of business income, sometimes more than 50 percent for those in the highest marginal income tax bracket.

Determining Taxes Due or Refund to Be Received

For earned income from employment, the payment of estimated taxes is usually accomplished through **payroll withholding**, whereby the employer takes money out of your income and sends it to the government. The amount of taxes withheld is calculated based on expected income and filing status.

If you're self-employed or have investment income that hasn't been subject to withholding, you must still pay your taxes by the April 15 due date. The law requires that you pay the tax in quarterly estimated tax installments during the tax year (on April 15, June 15, September 15, and January 15.) If you underpay, you'll be subject to penalties. To avoid underpayment penalties, make sure that the total of your withholding plus estimated tax payments is at least as much as 100 percent of your prior year's tax owed. **Online Calculator Demonstration Video: Withholding Estimator** shows how to use an IRS online calculator to estimate how much you should withhold to avoid paying penalties.

If the total withholding and estimated taxes paid during the year are less than the amount of taxes you owe for the year, you must include a check for the remainder with your submitted

ONLINE CALCULATOR DEMONSTRATION VIDEO

See **Online Calculator Demonstration Video: Withholding Estimator** in **WileyPLUS**.

tax form. If you've paid too much through withholding, you're entitled to a tax refund. Most people have more withheld than they'll owe in taxes, with about 75 percent receiving a tax refund when they file their taxes.

> **Reflection Question 2**
>
> When you're anticipating a tax refund, do you treat that money differently in your financial planning? Why are windfalls easier to spend (or save) than other funds in your budget?

4.4 | Tax Planning Strategies

LEARNING OBJECTIVE 4.4
Establish financial planning strategies to legally minimize the taxes you pay.

Understanding the fundamentals of income taxation is important to financial planning because it enables you to anticipate the tax consequences of your other financial decisions. Effective personal financial management requires that you attempt to minimize unnecessary cash outflows—and that includes any taxes that you pay unnecessarily. Of course, you must pay taxes that you legally owe. **Tax evasion**—the deliberate failure to pay taxes that are legally owed—is against the law.

An example of tax evasion is failure to report tip income. Because waiters and waitresses usually earn more in tips than they earn in wages, the IRS regularly audits these jobs to estimate average tips and requires that restaurant owners withhold sufficient taxes from employees' wage income, in some cases leaving employees with very little in their paychecks. However, it is generally the case that restaurant workers receive more in tips than the amounts reported by their employers in these audits, thus resulting in underwithholding.

Another example of tax evasion involves getting paid "under the table," which means working for someone who pays you in cash and doesn't withhold taxes. This is illegal. It is suspected that many farm and agricultural workers and their employers, particularly in areas near the U.S. borders, illegally evade taxes in this way. Because these workers are often transient, it's difficult for the government to find them and collect taxes owed.

Although tax evasion is illegal and can have serious consequences, there is nothing illegal about **tax avoidance**. When you use your knowledge of the tax rules to make financial decisions that reduce the taxes you owe, you're ensuring that you don't pay more taxes than you're legally obligated to pay. The money you save in taxes can be applied to achieving your other financial goals.

As an example, consider the choice between tax-deductible and nondeductible contributions to savings. Let's assume your marginal federal income tax rate is 24 percent and your state tax rate is 6 percent. A tax-deductible investment allows you to put the money into savings or investment without paying taxes on it first. In other words, $1,000 of income results in $1,000 saved or invested. If you invest instead in something that does not carry that tax benefit, then you'll pay 30 percent taxes on the $1,000 in income first, leaving you with only $700 to invest after taxes. We'll consider these investment choices in detail in later chapters.

Tax avoidance requires thoughtful planning. In general, tax planning is the ongoing process of using the provisions of the tax laws to reduce your taxes or defer them to later years. As you begin to work toward achieving long-term financial goals, you'll need to consider not just the current year's taxes, but tax liability for future years as well. Tax laws change frequently, so it's important to stay informed about new rules that might benefit your tax situation. In general, strategies for minimizing taxes fall into the four categories discussed in the sections below:

- Maximize pretax contributions to qualified benefit plans.
- Reduce the applicable tax rate on certain income.
- Make use of available deductions and credits.
- Avoid audits and penalties.

Maximize Pretax Contributions to Qualified Benefit Plans

There are several strategies for reducing taxable income without reducing gross income. Many employers offer the opportunity to make pretax contributions to employee benefit and retirement plans. These will be discussed fully in Chapter 10, but the basic concept is that the law allows you to use your pretax income to buy your benefits. Federal, state, and local income taxes are then calculated based on the income left after these expenditures have been made. You get the benefit of not paying taxes on the income that is used for buying the employee benefit or contributing to your retirement plan.

Let's consider an example. Suppose your employer offers you the opportunity to purchase dental insurance for your family with pretax dollars at a cost of $100 per month, or $1,200 per year, for the plan. Your friend Jonah, who earns the same salary at a competing firm, has no dental insurance through his employer but finds a comparable plan that he can purchase for his family, again at $100 per month. How much better off are you than your friend if you're both subject to a marginal tax rate of 30 percent? Your taxable income will now be lower by $1,200, so you'll be able to avoid paying $360 per year in taxes ($1,200 × 0.30). Jonah must pay taxes on his full earnings and then buy the dental insurance out of what's left over. In effect, the reduction in taxable income allows you to get a $360 discount on the cost of the dental insurance (equal to your tax savings), money that you can apply to one of your financial goals.

Many larger employers also allow employees to take advantage of a **flexible spending account**, a reimbursement account for qualified medical and child-care expenses. Each pay period, the employer subtracts a certain amount from your paycheck and deposits it in your flexible spending account. The amount deposited reduces your taxable income for the year. You can then obtain reimbursement from the account as you incur qualified expenses, such as money you pay to your child-care provider or for medicines and eyeglasses. Effectively, this allows you to pay for these items with pretax dollars, substantially reducing the out-of-pocket cost to you. For example, if your marginal tax rate is 20 percent and you normally pay $5,000 per year for child care, you would save about $1,000 in taxes ($5,000 × 0.2) for the year by using one of these accounts. If you had instead taken $5,000 in taxable earnings and paid taxes on it, you would have had only $4,000 left after taxes [$5,000 = (1 − 0.2) = $4,000]—not enough to pay for your child-care expenses. The maximum annual contribution to a health-care flexible spending account for 2019 was $2,700, which increases annually with inflation. The maximum annual contribution for child-care flexible spending accounts was $5,000.

If you aren't fortunate enough to have a retirement plan option at your current employer, tax rules allow you to set up an individual retirement account (IRA). Currently, there are two types of IRAs, which are defined here and will be considered in detail in Chapter 10. A **traditional IRA** allows you to deduct your annual contribution to the account from income and to defer the payment of taxes until funds are withdrawn from the account. Note that this type of IRA has a tax effect similar to that of employment-based retirement plans. In contrast, a **Roth IRA** does not allow you to take a current tax deduction, so you must make your contribution with after-tax dollars. However, assuming that you use the funds for retirement or other allowed purposes, you never have to pay tax on the money again—the account, including all accumulated investment earnings, can grow tax-free, and you can take the money out during retirement without paying any taxes on the investment earnings. The maximum contribution to both types of IRAs increases annually with inflation, but in 2019 was $6,000, with an additional $1,000 allowed for people aged 50 or older. To compare traditional and Roth IRA outcomes, go to **Online Calculator Demonstration Video: Traditional versus Roth IRAs**.

ONLINE CALCULATOR DEMONSTRATION VIDEO

See **Online Calculator Demonstration Video: Traditional versus Roth IRAs** in **WileyPLUS.**

Reduce the Applicable Tax Rate on Certain Income

In some limited circumstances, you may be able to shift income so that it is taxed at a lower rate by deferring it to future periods or to members of the family who are in lower tax brackets. Employer retirement plans may allow you to make investment contributions on a pretax basis and therefore avoid current income taxes on that income. But, in addition to reducing current taxable income, these plans also allow you to defer or, in some cases, avoid entirely, the payment of taxes on investment earnings. If you earn $1,000 in investment income in a taxable account—such as interest on your bank savings account—you'll owe income taxes on these earnings in the year they are received, the actual amount being a function of your marginal tax rate (including state and federal income tax). In a tax-deferred account, you won't pay tax on the income until you withdraw it, which may be many years in the future. At that point, you may be in a lower marginal tax bracket. But even if you're not, you will benefit from the time value of money. It's always better to pay taxes in the future than it is to pay the same amount today.

In some cases, it may be beneficial to defer the receipt of taxable income until a future tax year. For example, suppose a family friend hired you to build a deck for him in November of the current tax year. You know that your income this year is relatively high because you worked the whole year but you'll be attending college the following year, and thus expect to be in a lower tax bracket. If you can delay the receipt of payment for your deck-building services—for example, by waiting to bill your friend—you won't have to pay the tax until the following year, and you'll reduce the overall tax owed (because you'll be in a lower tax bracket). Certain professions—small businesses and consulting practices, for example—can more easily take advantage of this type of tax strategy.

Capital gains and certain dividends from long-term investments are taxed at a lower rate than ordinary income. To be taxed at the lower rate, you'll normally need to own the asset for at least one year before selling it. For long-term investment goals, you should focus on investments that provide returns in the form of increased value rather than interest or dividend income, which is taxable in the year it is received. Because a capital gain is not reported on your taxes until you sell the asset, you can accumulate substantial wealth without incurring any current tax. When you do realize a gain on a qualifying investment, you'll pay at a lower tax rate under current tax law. Your home provides an even greater advantage in this respect because most capital gains from the sale of your primary residence are tax-free.

Families can achieve lower taxes overall by shifting some income to household members who are in lower tax brackets. For example, you can give taxable investment accounts to your children. In 2019, you were allowed to make gifts of up to $15,000 tax-free to as many people as you wanted without being subject to the gift tax. Dependent children could have earned income up to the standard deduction ($12,200) or unearned income up to $2,200 in 2019 without triggering the "kiddie tax" mentioned earlier, in which their income is taxed at a higher rate.

For taxpayers in high tax brackets, it may be beneficial to consider investing in real estate properties that will produce a tax loss after expenses. As you'll see in Chapter 13, investment real estate owners are allowed some deductions that aren't actually out-of-pocket expenses. As a result, it's not unusual for a profitable investment property to produce a tax loss that can be applied against other income in order to reduce taxes.

Make Use of Available Deductions and Credits

In order to maximize your tax deductions, it is important to plan ahead for the recording and timing of expenditures. Careful record keeping will help to ensure that you are reporting all deductible expenses. When you have a choice as to when to incur an expense, you should consider how the timing will affect your taxes. To see that lots of people apply this rule to their finances, you need only go to an office supply or computer store on New Year's Eve. The store will probably be packed because December 31 is the last day to make purchases that can be deducted for the tax year. It's a good idea to roughly estimate your expected tax liability before that time. Any deductible expenditures will have a much lower effective cost to you, because you would otherwise be paying some of that money in taxes.

Another example of strategic end-of-year expenditures involves the timing of uninsured medical procedures. Let's say that in a given tax year, you've already incurred sufficient medical costs (greater than 10 percent of AGI) to qualify for the medical expense deduction. Any additional uninsured medical expenses—including out-of-pocket premiums, deductibles and copays, doctor visits, surgery, vision care, and prescriptions—can be itemized in that year, reducing the effective cost to you by the amount of your marginal tax rate. If, for example, you need a new pair of glasses, this is the time to get them.

Charitable contributions are another way to increase your deductions in a given tax year. Be sure to keep track of all the times you've taken a bag of used clothing to Goodwill or donated food to a food drive. Although it's always a good idea to get receipts, they're only required by the IRS for large contributions of cash or goods. In high-tax years, consider making an end-of-year contribution to your favorite charity. If you don't normally itemize deductions, a good strategy is to bundle several years of charitable contributions into one year if they will push your itemized deductions above the standard deduction.

Don't forget the tax-sheltering value of your home. In addition to the capital gains advantage described in the previous section, mortgage interest and property taxes are deductible, so your home is an incredible tax shelter. You might also consider using home equity loans as an alternative to other types of financing. The interest on the loan will be deductible if you use the funds to improve your home.

To see how home ownership can produce tax benefits, consider the difference between an otherwise similar renter and homeowner in **Demonstration Problem 4.3**.

DEMONSTRATION PROBLEM 4.3 | Calculating the Marginal Tax Advantage of Home Ownership

Peter Dazeley/Photographer's Choice/ Getty Images

Problem

You and your former college roommate Marissa have identical incomes and are both unmarried taxpayers subject to a 25 percent marginal tax rate. You are a renter and pay rent of $1,000 per month. Marissa is a homeowner, and her mortgage interest and property taxes total $16,000 for the year. What marginal effect does the difference in home ownership status have on your respective taxes, assuming that the standard deduction is $12,200 and neither of you has any other itemizable deductions?

Strategy

Estimate the marginal tax effect by applying the marginal tax rate to your respective housing expenses.

Solution

You cannot deduct any of your housing expenses if you are a renter. Therefore, you get no tax break from renting and will take just the standard deduction. Marissa, however, can deduct all her mortgage interest and property taxes. She gets an additional deduction of $16,000 − $12,200 = $3,800. This will save her an additional 25 percent of $3,800 = $950. Her marginal housing costs are therefore $950 less than yours, and she also has the advantage that her home can increase in value tax-free.

Child tax credits can also increase your after-tax income. Although no one would advise that you have more children just to increase your tax credits, it is not unusual for expectant parents to schedule a Caesarean section for December 31 (subject to the approval of their physician, of course) rather than waiting for a January 1 due date. One day makes a big difference in your taxes—an extra $2,000 child tax credit for the year ending on December 31.

Many people are eligible for various deductions and credits but don't claim them. This generally happens when they either don't know about them or haven't kept adequate records to claim them. Your tax planning strategies should therefore include a careful review of available credits and evaluation of your eligibility for each. If you use tax preparation software, it will prompt you with questions designed to determine your eligibility for tax credits.

Avoid Audits and Penalties

What happens if you don't pay your taxes or if you underreport income or exaggerate deductions? These actions are illegal under federal law. At a minimum, you'll be subject to interest and penalties on your underpayments. In the extreme, you can actually go to jail for tax evasion. Unfortunately, the threat of these adverse consequences isn't enough to deter some people. In fact, surveys have shown that most people think it's acceptable to cheat on their taxes a little. That kind of attitude, while perhaps not surprising, hurts everyone—we all pay higher tax rates to cover the lost revenue from tax cheats and the additional enforcement costs. In this section, we explain the enforcement process used by the IRS.

Enforcement of Tax Laws

The IRS employs several levels of scrutiny to investigate tax returns for errors and intentional omissions. A **tax audit** can range from a simple electronic screening of returns for errors all the way up to the dreaded visit from the "men in black." Although there have always been stories in the paper about people who claim to have avoided paying taxes for years, today's high-tech environment makes it fairly easy for the IRS to track down most tax cheats. All earned income, investment income, and interest expenses are independently reported to the government, so errors and omissions in reporting these items are usually caught within a few months of filing a return. You'll simply get a bill for the underpayment plus any applicable penalties.

In addition to automatically checking for and correcting errors, the IRS randomly selects returns for more careful scrutiny. In some cases, your return might be selected for evaluation in a truly random process. In others, your audit may have been triggered by screening programs designed to identify suspect returns based on key characteristics of income and deductions that have been correlated with tax fraud in the past. If you are audited, you may be asked to provide documentation for specific deductions. In rare cases, you may even have to appear at a local IRS office. Alternatively, an IRS agent may come to your home to investigate, most commonly to verify small business and home office deductions.

What Are the Odds of Getting Audited?

For the average taxpayer, the likelihood of being audited has never been lower. The IRS examines less than 1 percent of all individual returns, down from about 5 percent in the mid-1960s. Budget cuts and staff reductions, as well as a greater emphasis on customer service at the IRS, have reduced the number of tax returns subject to audits. **Interactive: What Is Your Audit Risk?** will give you a better idea of how likely you are to be audited, given your income level. Not surprisingly, high-income households are most at risk. Still, you can significantly reduce your chances of being audited by filling out your tax forms correctly and being sure to completely report income from all sources.

As the IRS has concentrated its attention on high income-taxpayers, the audit rate for filers with incomes below $100,000 has decreased. This doesn't imply that there's a zero chance of getting audited if your income is low, but it's not highly likely unless your tax return has one or more of the following audit "triggers":

- Reported income that doesn't agree with your W-2 and 1099 forms
- Married taxpayers filing separately who file inconsistent tax returns
- Taxpayers who should have paid the alternative minimum tax but didn't
- Receipt of substantial cash income (such as by doctors, lawyers, retail businesses, and restaurant servers)
- Large deductions relative to income, particularly charitable deductions and employee business expenses
- Schedule C business income greater than $100,000 and large business deductions relative to income

INTERACTIVE

See **Interactive: What Is Your Audit Risk?** in **WileyPLUS** to find out how likely you are to be audited.

- Complex investment or business transactions without clear explanations
- Earned income tax credit claimed
- Home office deduction claimed

Tax Reform

Many people have argued that the current tax system is unfair, in part because it's so complex that the average person can't understand his or her rights and obligations. The Internal Revenue Code and IRS Regulations are literally thousands of pages long, and they seem to undergo a major overhaul with every new presidential administration. A major change in 2017 was the reduction in marginal rates and increase in the standard deduction. As a result, most taxpayers will now file a simpler tax return. Congress had the opportunity to simplify many other aspects of the law, but it did not. Although the complexity of the tax system may seem daunting, much of it can actually be beneficial to you—as we've seen, the special rules offer opportunities to reduce the taxes you pay.

Periodically, politicians and taxpayer lobby groups suggest that our federal income tax system be simplified by imposing a flat tax, such as 15 percent, on every dollar of income. The simplicity of such a system is that all tax collection could be handled at the employer level, much as is currently done with Social Security payroll taxes and withholding. In such a system, there would be limited need for filing or processing tax returns, resulting in substantial savings for the government and reduced effort by taxpayers. Although requiring everyone to pay the same percentage of income in taxes seems fair, such a tax system would be quite regressive. That is, it would have a great impact on disposable income for poor and middle-class taxpayers, particularly if the tax applied only to wage income and not to business and investment income.

Summary

Learning Objectives Review

LEARNING OBJECTIVE 4.1 Understand the major features of the federal income tax system.

Understanding how the tax system works will help you make better financial decisions and pay lower taxes.

- The federal income tax is a **progressive tax**, which means that high-income taxpayers are subject to higher marginal tax rates than low-income taxpayers. In contrast, the **FICA payroll tax** that funds Social Security and Medicare is a **regressive tax** because it imposes the same rate on all wage income.
- Federal income tax is based on marginal tax rates that range from 10 percent to 37 percent for increasing ranges of taxable income, called **tax brackets**.
- Your **marginal tax rate**, the rate applicable on your next dollar of income, will always be greater than your **average tax rate**, calculated with **Equation 4.1**:

$$\text{Average tax rate} = \frac{\text{Taxes paid}}{\text{Taxable income}}$$

The **marginal tax effect** is the reduction in taxes resulting from a financial decision.

- You can calculate the amount of income you will have after taxes by using **Equation 4.2**:

$$\text{After-tax income} = \text{Before-tax income} \times (1 - \text{Tax rate})$$

LEARNING OBJECTIVE 4.2 Determine whether you need to file a federal income tax return and which forms you should use.

It's important to know whether you must file a federal income tax return and which forms you must use.

- Most people must file the Form 1040. Taxpayers are required to report their **filing status**, income, and **dependents**.
- Federal income tax returns are due by April 15 of the year following the tax year. Although you may file an extension to extend the deadline, you must still pay the taxes you owe by April 15.

- Your income and allowed deductions must be reported on official tax forms either on paper or electronically. The IRS defines your **adjusted gross income (AGI)** as the total of your **earned income** (including salaries, wages, tips, bonuses, commissions, and self-employment income) plus **unearned income** (interest, dividends, capital gains, rents, royalties, and net business income) minus certain allowed adjustments.

- AGI is reduced by the **standard deduction** or **itemized deductions** to arrive at **taxable income**.

- After you have calculated a tentative tax, you may still end up owing less if you qualify for a **tax credit**.

LEARNING OBJECTIVE 4.3   Prepare a basic tax return.

The process of calculating taxes owed or refund to be received is summarized in Figure 4.5.

- Generally, you must report all types of income, including earned income, business income, investment income, and **capital gains** from the sale of assets. Some categories of **gross income** are excluded to arrive at **total income** on your tax forms.

- Certain medical expenses, taxes paid, charitable contributions, and interest can be claimed as itemized deductions provided that you have receipts. You should itemize using Schedule A if your deductions total more than the standard deduction.

- After subtracting deductions, you can look up your tentative tax in the applicable section of the Tax Table.

- The actual tax you owe may be reduced if you qualify for tax credits. Sometimes you may even be eligible for a **refundable tax credit**, which you can receive in cash even if you owed no taxes. Your tax liability may be greater than the tentative tax if you're subject to the **alternative minimum tax (AMT)** or if you have self-employment income that is subject to additional tax.

- The amount of tax due or refund to be received is calculated by subtracting the amount you have already paid through **payroll withholding** or estimated tax payments.

LEARNING OBJECTIVE 4.4   Establish financial planning strategies to legally minimize the taxes you pay.

Although **tax evasion** is illegal, **tax avoidance** is not. Effective financial planning requires that you legally minimize the amount of tax you pay wherever possible. You can do this by using the following strategies:

- Maximizing pretax contributions to qualified benefit plans, such as retirement plans, **flexible spending accounts**, and individual retirement accounts, such as a **traditional IRA** or **Roth IRA**.

- Reducing the applicable tax rate on certain income. You can do this by deferring income to future periods in which you are subject to a lower marginal tax rate, by transferring income-earning assets to family members in lower tax brackets, and by investing in assets that are subject to favorable tax rules.

- Making use of available deductions and credits.

- Avoiding **tax audits** and penalties.

In all cases, tax planning should include careful record keeping so that you can show proof of deductions and credits claimed in the event that they are later challenged by the IRS.

Excel Worksheets

4.1 Personal Financial Planner: Marginal and Average Tax Rates

4.2 Personal Financial Planner: Federal Income Tax Estimator

Key Terms

WileyPLUS

Practice Questions to check your understanding, Peer-to-Peer Videos, Interactives, and many other resources are available in WileyPLUS.

Concept Review Questions

1. In what ways does our current federal income tax system more equitably distribute the tax burden among taxpayers?

2. What is the difference between a progressive tax and a regressive tax? Which type of tax is our federal income tax? Which type is the Social Security payroll tax?

3. What is the difference between your marginal tax rate and your average tax rate? In making financial decisions, which is more important to consider?

4. What is a tax bracket, and why is it important for tax brackets to be inflation-indexed?

5. Under what circumstances should you file a tax return even when you're not required to?

6. Under what circumstances does a person qualify as a dependent for tax purposes?

7. How are tax credits different from deductions? Assuming that a tax credit and a deduction are the same dollar amount, which is more advantageous to the taxpayer?

8. What is the purpose of the alternative minimum tax (AMT), and how does it accomplish that purpose?

9. What are the major categories of itemized deductions? Are there any limitations on expenses you may deduct in each of these categories?

10. Why is it beneficial to defer income to later tax years?

11. What are the tax advantages of saving for retirement by investing in an IRA? Does it matter which type of IRA you have?

12. In what ways is a person's home considered to be a tax shelter?

13. Which would you prefer—paying $100 less in taxes per month or receiving a $1,200 tax refund next year? Why do people often prefer getting a tax refund even though it is the equivalent of giving the federal government an interest-free loan?

14. How can a flexible spending account help reduce your out-of-pocket medical and child-care expenses?

15. Why do higher-income taxpayers often face a higher risk of audit than lower-income taxpayers?

Application Problems

1. You were single and had taxable income of $24,000 in 2019. What was your marginal tax rate?

2. You are single and have taxable income of $24,000 in 2019. How much tax did you owe, assuming that you didn't qualify for any tax credits?

3. You were single and had adjusted gross income of $37,000 in 2019. You calculated that your taxable income was $24,000 and that you owed $2,686 in federal income taxes. What is the average tax rate you paid on your adjusted gross income, and what was your marginal tax rate?

4. June's 15-year-old nephew has lived in her home for the entire tax year, and his parents are not providing funds for his support. Can she claim him as a dependent on her taxes?

5. Rashid has adjusted gross income of $40,000. He incurred the following expenses during the year: medical expenses, $1,200; property taxes, $1,900; mortgage interest, $8,400; and state income taxes, $1,600. If the standard deduction for a single filer is $12,200, should he itemize deductions? Why or why not?

6. You are in the 24 percent marginal tax bracket and itemize deductions. What impact will an additional $1,000 of itemized deductions have on your federal income taxes owed?

7. You are in the 24 percent marginal tax bracket and itemize deductions. What impact will an additional $1,000 tax credit have on your federal income taxes owed?

8. Jack Spratt has an investment that gives him $1,000 per year in interest income. His friend Peter Pumpkineater has been telling Jack that he should invest in something that provides him with capital gains instead of interest. This year, for example, Peter sold some shares of a mutual fund (which he had held for more than one year) for a $1,000 profit. Assuming that both Jack and Peter are in the 37 percent marginal tax bracket, how much difference did the type of income they received from these two investments make to the taxes owed on the income?

9. Assume that you are in the 24 percent marginal tax bracket and you normally itemize deductions. If you make an end-of-year contribution to your church in the amount of $1,000, what is the effective cost of that gift to you, taking into consideration the tax savings it will generate?

10. Carly Simmons is single and her adjusted gross income in 2019 is $65,000. She has the following expenses:

- Medical expenses $4,500
- Mortgage interest $10,400
- Property taxes $2,400
- State income tax $1,800
- Charitable gifts $1,500

a. Should Carly take the standard deduction ($12,200 in 2019) or itemize her deductions? Explain your reasoning.

b. Calculate Carly's taxable income.

11. Kristoff and Anna Svenson are a married couple who have adjusted gross income of $84,000 in 2019. They have the following expenses:

- Medical expenses $3,000
- Mortgage interest $8,100
- Property taxes $2,000
- State income tax $3,200
- Charitable gifts $730

a. Should the Svensons take the standard deduction ($24,400) or itemize their deductions? Explain your reasoning.

b. Calculate the Svenson's taxable income. What is their marginal tax rate?

c. If the Svensons contribute to a deductible IRA, what impact will this have on their taxes?

12. What potential strategies for minimizing taxes should a real estate investor in a high tax bracket investigate?

13. What potential strategies for minimizing taxes should working parents with preschoolers investigate?

14. What potential strategies for minimizing taxes should a college student who is independent of his or her parents investigate?

15. Consider your own personal tax situation for the coming year. In answering the following questions, it may be helpful to consult Excel Worksheet 4.2 to estimate your taxes owed.

a. What will your filing status be for this year?

b. What tax form will you file?

c. Will you itemize deductions or take the standard deduction?

d. Will you be eligible for any tax credits?

e. If you complete the tax estimator worksheet and have determined that you will owe additional taxes for the year, is there anything you can do now to reduce your tax liability?

Case Applications

1. Xiao Yang, a single woman with no children, graduated from college in 2019 with a degree in psychology. She had been working part-time at a local department store while in school and was offered a job as assistant manager starting in June following graduation. It is now February of the following year, and she is getting ready to file her taxes. This is the first year that she has been independent from her parents.

Xiao has collected the following information to use in preparing her return:

- The standard deduction for 2019 is $12,200.
- The W-2 form from her employer shows wages of $21,750 for the previous tax year, $1,200 in federal income taxes withheld, $600 in state income tax withheld, and FICA (Social Security) tax of $1,850.
- Rent, $4,200
- Groceries, $2,500
- Dress clothes for work, $1,000
- Out-of-pocket health insurance premiums, $2,000
- Unreimbursed medical expenses, $500
- Church offerings, $250
- Donation to Salvation Army, $150
- Graduation gifts received, $1,000
- Credit card interest payments, $900

a. Should Xiao itemize deductions for 2019? Why or why not?

b. What is Xiao's taxable income?

c. Is Xiao entitled to any tax credits? If so, which one(s)?

d. What is Xiao's marginal tax rate?

e. Would it be beneficial for Xiao to contribute to an IRA at this time? Explain.

f. How much are Xiao's federal income taxes for 2019?

g. What refund will Xiao be entitled to receive?

2. Christine Melinsky and her husband Jared have four children, ages 4 to 10. Chris works as a marketing executive for a cosmetics firm, and Jared is a stay-at-home dad who is not employed outside the home. Christine's salary is $75,000. They have collected the following information to use in preparing their 2019 federal income tax return:

- The standard deduction for 2019 is $12,200 for singles and $24,400 for married filing jointly.
- Unreimbursed medical expenses, $2,500
- Mortgage interest, $15,300
- Property taxes, $3,600
- Federal income tax withheld, $6,000
- State income tax paid, $2,750
- Traditional IRA contributions, $6,000
- Gambling winnings, $600
- Student loan interest, $420

a. Should they itemize deductions this year?

b. What is the Melinskys' taxable income for 2019, assuming that their filing status is married filing jointly?

c. Use the tax rate schedule in Table 4.1 to calculate the tentative tax they owe (before any credits), assuming that their status is married filing jointly.

d. Are the Melinskys eligible to take any tax credits? Explain.

ArturVerkhovetskiy/Deposit Photos

CHAPTER 5

Managing Credit: Credit Cards and Consumer Loans

Feature Story

Mason's dream job was to be a sound designer for a major film studio. During his senior year in high school, Mason was accepted into a highly selective film and video production program at a small private university. The program was expensive, but the school had strong job placement statistics and offered a generous scholarship that reduced Mason's tuition for his first year. He took out a federal student loan and got a part-time job to help cover his education costs.

Mason loved the program. Unfortunately, the school didn't renew his scholarship after his first year, and his mother was able to contribute only a small amount of money toward the cost. Mason didn't want to leave the program, so he signed up for more student loans in each of his remaining years. In addition to federal loans, he also took out private bank loans with his mother as a cosigner. Although he tried to use his credit card only for emergencies, Mason's credit card balance was about $5,000 by the time he graduated, and he accumulated $125,000 in student loan debt.

The good news was that Mason landed an entry-level job as an assistant sound engineer at a California studio. The bad news—the starting salary was only $35,000. On a 10-year repayment plan, his combined student loan and credit card payments would take a big bite out of his take-home pay. Mason was able to extend the repayment period on the loans, and his mother helped with the payments, but he knew his education costs would be a burden on both of them for many years to come.

This problem is not unique to Mason. Recent Federal Reserve research concluded that student loan debt has led to a drop in homeownership among Americans ages 24 to 32, as compared to the previous decade. Some of these people could not qualify for home loans because late student loan payments had hurt their credit scores. Others simply did not have enough income to cover both the student loan payment and the mortgage payment. Thus, it's important to plan for future repayment of a student loan and to borrow only what is needed.

In this chapter, we'll explore a variety of credit alternatives, including credit cards, auto loans, home equity loans, and student loans. Before making a decision to use debt financing, even if it's for education, you need to understand the costs and characteristics of all your alternatives.

LEARNING OBJECTIVES	TOPICS	DEMONSTRATION PROBLEMS
5.1 Describe the role of consumer credit in your financial plan.	**5.1 What Is Consumer Credit?** • Types and Sources of Consumer Credit • The Advantages and Disadvantages of Consumer Credit • Applying for Consumer Credit	
5.2 Maintain your creditworthiness, and understand your consumer credit rights.	**5.2 Your Consumer Credit Plan** • Measuring Your Credit Capacity • When and How to Use Consumer Credit • Strategies for Reducing Debt • Your Consumer Credit Rights • Bankruptcy	**5.1** How Long Will It Take to Pay Off Your Balance?
5.3 Evaluate credit card choices based on terms and costs.	**5.3 Credit Cards** • Types of Cards • Common Credit Card Contract Terms	**5.2** Calculation of Credit Card Finance Charges
5.4 Evaluate consumer loan choices based on your financial needs, loan terms, and costs.	**5.4 Consumer Loans** • Common Types of Consumer Loans • Comparing Consumer Loan Alternatives	**5.3** How Much Can You Borrow with a Home Equity Loan? **5.4** Total Interest Paid on Loans with Different Maturities **5.5** Calculating Simple Interest Loan Payoffs

5.1 What Is Consumer Credit?

LEARNING OBJECTIVE 5.1
Describe the role of consumer credit in your financial plan.

Any time you receive cash, goods, or services now and arrange to pay later, you are buying on **credit**. If you use credit to buy consumer goods or services, you're using **consumer credit**. The most common types of consumer credit are credit card accounts, automobile loans, home equity loans, and student loans. A common feature of all of these types of credit is that the lender is letting you have the use of the money now and is expecting you to repay it with interest in the future, often over a specified time period.

In the last decade, total household debt has more than doubled, rising much faster than income. A big chunk of this debt, in fact more than 70 percent, is in the form of home mortgages. The rest is consumer credit of various types, including student loans, auto loans, credit cards, and home equity lines of credit. The fastest-growing component of debt is student loan debt. It has more than quadrupled since 2003, totaling nearly $1.6 trillion at the end of 2018. **Figure 5.1** shows how much consumer credit has grown in recent years.

 **FIGURE 5.1**   **Household Consumer Credit in the United States, 2003–2018**   Consumer debt has nearly doubled in the last 15 years, an increase driven largely by growing student loan debt.

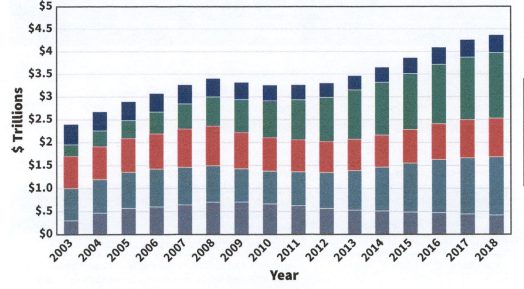

Source: New York Federal Reserve Board, *Consumer Credit Report*, 2019

> **Reflection Question 1**
>
> How concerned are you about your consumer debt? In what ways can large debt repayment obligations negatively affect you and your graduation cohort in the future?

Types and Sources of Consumer Credit

There are many different consumer credit alternatives and a variety of lenders competing for your business. In this section, we'll provide an overview of the general characteristics of these types of borrowing arrangements. The unique characteristics of the most common types of credit are discussed in more detail later in this chapter.

Closed-End versus Open-End Credit

Closed-end credit is credit that a lender approves for a specific purpose (such as the purchase of a television or a car). It must be paid back with interest either in a single payment or according to an installment agreement, with equal payments per period ending at a specific time. This type of credit is often called a consumer loan. Common examples of closed-end credit include car loans and student loans.

Open-end credit, also called **revolving credit**, is generally not earmarked for a particular purchase, and, although billing periods and requirements for minimum monthly payments are specified in advance, there isn't a maximum time period for full repayment of the debt. Instead, the lender preapproves an amount of credit, called a **credit limit** or **credit line**, in advance of any purchase. You can then use this credit as you wish until you've reached your credit limit. Credit cards, such as Visa and MasterCard, are familiar examples of this type of credit. Personal loans, home equity lines of credit, and other delayed-payment arrangements offered by retail and public service providers (such as utility, Internet, phone, and cable companies) are also open-end credit arrangements.

Table 5.1 summarizes the most common types of closed-end and open-end credit and gives examples of potential lenders. These are discussed in more detail in the following section.

TABLE 5.1 Types and Sources of Consumer Credit

Open-End Credit	
Type	**Offered by**
Credit Cards	
Bank Card	Visa, MasterCard
Retail Card	Home Depot, Target, JCPenney's, Macy's
Travel and Entertainment Cards	American Express, Diner's Club
Overdraft Protection	Depository institutions
Home Equity Line of Credit	Depository institutions
Other Secured Loans	Cash-value life insurance, pawn shops, brokerage firms

Closed-End Credit	
Type	**Examples and Issuers**
Home Mortgages	Depository institutions, insurance companies
Car Loans	Depository institutions, consumer finance companies (often affiliated with auto manufacturers such as Ford and Toyota)
Student Loans	Federal government, depository institutions
Installment Contracts	Consumer finance companies

Sources of Consumer Credit

Although consumer credit is available from many different lenders, depository institutions are the most common source. Recall from Chapter 3 that depository institutions, such as banks and credit unions, obtain funds from customer deposits into checking and savings accounts. They can lend at lower rates because they pay relatively low rates of return to their depositors. They also impose fairly strict standards for creditworthiness, so if you have very little experience with borrowing or have made late payments in the past, you might not qualify for a loan. Most will also require that you maintain a checking or savings account at their institution as a condition of obtaining a loan from them.

Consumers who cannot borrow from depository institutions, either because of poor credit or insufficient credit history, might consider borrowing from a **consumer finance company**. These firms obtain funds from investors and from short-term borrowing rather than from depositors. Because these companies specialize in making riskier loans, they tend to charge higher interest rates to borrowers. Their advantages include access and speed, with approvals often taking 24 hours or less. Consumer finance companies that specialize in debt consolidation loans may require home equity as **collateral** for such loans. When you pledge an asset, such as your home or car, as collateral for a loan, the lender has the right to take the asset from you if you do not repay the loan. While many of these firms are perfectly legitimate businesses, some are not, so you should never do business with an unfamiliar financial institution without checking on its status with appropriate authorities.

A **sales finance company** makes consumer loans to buyers of products offered through its parent company, usually a large retailer. For example, many automakers and large department stores have their own finance companies. The rates charged by sales finance companies are likely to be lower than those charged by consumer finance companies, particularly if the item being purchased, such as a new car, is pledged as collateral for the loan.

The federal government is a source for student loans (**www.studentaid.ed.gov**) and small business loans (**www.sba.gov**). You can also obtain short-term consumer loans through investment accounts at brokerage firms (discussed in Chapter 11), cash-value life insurance policies (discussed in Chapter 8), and retirement plans (discussed in Chapter 10). Borrowing from insurance, investment, or retirement accounts is not necessarily a good idea because it can jeopardize your ability to achieve other financial goals. For example, if you borrow against a life insurance policy and then die before you've repaid the loan, the proceeds of your life insurance policy will be reduced by the unpaid amount of the loan. If you borrow from a retirement account, your investment returns will be earned on a smaller principal balance, and you may owe income taxes on the amount you withdraw.

Certain types of businesses, such as pawnshops and payday loan shops, regularly provide short-term loans to people who don't have other, less costly, options. The pawnshop makes the loan in return for holding something of value as collateral, such as jewelry, electronics equipment, or a musical instrument. The maximum loan amount is usually a percentage of the resale value of the item being held, often 50 percent or less, and the pawnshop has the right to sell your valuable if you don't repay the loan within the allowed period of time. Payday lenders provide advances against future paychecks or tax returns. Because the time period between when you get the money and when the lender is repaid is so short, consumers end up paying very high rates of interest on these loans, as described in the **Ethics in Action** feature.

Ethics in Action

What's the Harm in Payday Loans?

You're a little short this month, and some of your bills are overdue. Payday is just a week away, and you saw an advertisement for a company that will give you a loan against your future paycheck. It seems like an easy and fast solution to your financial dilemma. All you have to do is write them a check for the amount of your loan plus the fee and they give you the cash on the spot. They agree to hold your check until payday.

Typical terms are $15 to $30 per $100 borrowed, with the loan due to be repaid quickly, usually in one to four weeks. So if you borrow $400 at a fee of $20 per $100, you'll have to repay $480 at the end of the loan period. If you don't pay it in full or if you roll over the loan, you'll have to pay the fee again. In fact, more than half of all payday loans are actually rollovers from previous loans.

Payday lending is controversial and is even illegal in some states, although most states do not place limits on fees as long as they are fully disclosed. Opponents say that these lenders take advantage of low-income and less educated consumers, exploiting their financial hardship and pushing them into a vicious cycle of debt. Others argue that these lenders provide a valuable service to consumers who do not have access to traditional banking services. They argue that although finance costs are high, they are not unreasonable, given the risks and costs the lenders must bear, such as fraudulent checks and failure to repay.

The Consumer Financial Protection Bureau (CFPB) released a special report on payday lending, available on the CFPB website (**www.consumerfinance.gov**). Although the report acknowledged the importance of providing for emergency loans, the data indicated that a fairly large percentage of payday loan consumers find themselves caught in a cycle of high-cost borrowing, paying extraordinarily high effective annual rates (averaging 392 percent). Borrowers average seven loans per year and often are unable to get out from under this debt burden.

The Advantages and Disadvantages of Consumer Credit

Although too much debt can obviously have an adverse impact on your household finances, credit is not inherently bad, and it may play an important role in your financial plan. In this section, we discuss the advantages and disadvantages of consumer credit. These are also summarized in **Table 5.2**.

TABLE 5.2 Advantages and Disadvantages of Consumer Credit and Credit Cards

Advantages

	All Consumer Credit	Credit Cards Only
Buy now, pay later	✓	✓
Convenient and safe alternative to cash	✓	✓
Source of emergency cash	✓	✓
Helps fuel the economy	✓	✓
Method of identification		✓
Record keeping for business expenses		✓
Ability to make remote purchases		✓
Easier to return merchandise		✓
Free credit		✓
Required to reserve rental cars, hotels		✓
May include other perks		✓

Disadvantages

	All Consumer Credit	Credit Cards Only
Financial statement impact	✓	✓
Increases cost of consumer purchases	✓	✓
Risk of overspending	✓	✓
May reduce credit rating	✓	✓
May increase insurance premiums	✓	✓
High cost of interest and fees		✓
Annoying marketing tactics		✓
Loss of privacy		✓
Risk of fraud and identity theft		✓
Interest not tax-deductible		✓

Advantages of Consumer Credit

Consumer credit offers the advantages of spreading the cost of purchases over time, limiting the need to carry cash, and providing a source of funds for emergencies.

- **Buy now, pay later** Most people strive to improve their standard of living over time. Being able to spread out the cost of more expensive items over time, but also getting to use them right away, makes it possible to fit purchases into your budget sooner. You don't have to save up the entire purchase price of a car, for example, before buying one. This type of arrangement is advantageous as long as: (1) you can afford the payments without sacrificing other worthy financial goals, and (2) the product you purchase lasts at least as long as the time period over which you make payments.

- **Convenience and safety** Instead of carrying large amounts of cash, you can simply carry a credit card. It's convenient and, although a card can be stolen, it's not as easy as cash for a thief to use. If you pay off your balance every month before the due date, you can take advantage of free credit offered by the card issuer and still have the convenience and safety of not carrying cash.

- **Source of emergency cash** Credit lines can be a source of funds to meet emergency needs. In deciding whether to use credit in this way, however, it's important to consider whether you'll be able to repay the debt in accordance with the credit terms as well as how the payments will affect your household cash flow.

Disadvantages of Consumer Credit

The primary reasons for limiting your use of credit include the additional cost of paying finance charges and the potential negative impacts on your household financials and spending behavior.

- **Increased cost**   Credit is hardly ever free. When you use credit to make a purchase, you'll pay more for that item because of the financing costs of the loan. Lenders charge interest for the use of their funds and commonly also charge additional fees and penalties. Even when retailers offer zero-interest financing, you can be sure that they're making money on fees or, alternatively, charging you more for their product than they would if they didn't offer the "free" financing.

- **Impact on household financials**   The more you borrow relative to your total wealth, the worse your liquidity and debt ratios will look. Too much credit can limit your financial flexibility. You may also expose your household to too much risk because you're committing your family to greater fixed expenses. If you or your spouse were laid off, for example, you might not be able to meet these expenses. In addition, if you're planning to buy a home, high levels of consumer debt may make it more difficult for you to qualify for a mortgage.

- **Risk of overspending**   The availability of consumer credit increases the risk that you will spend more than you earn. Without a credit card, if you don't have enough cash in your pocket or your checking account to buy something, you can't make the purchase. When you have a credit card, you may decide to make the purchase anyway. Or you may buy more than you need. Instead of buying one sweater at that great sale price, why not buy three? Why choose between those two e-books when you can buy both? Retailers even use advertising to reinforce the ease of making credit purchases. Next to the full price, you might see: "Only $25 per month if you take advantage of in-store credit."

- **Higher insurance premiums**   For the last several years, many insurance companies have been using consumer credit history as a factor in pricing individual auto and homeowner's insurance policies. Thus, if you have a lot of outstanding debt or a history of making late credit card payments, you may be paying a higher insurance premium than others with better credit.

Consumer Credit and the Economy

In addition to offering certain advantages to consumers, credit benefits the U.S. economy as a whole. When consumers spend more, businesses profit, employment increases, and the economic outlook improves. Keeping interest rates at historic lows was an important element of the federal government's strategy for revitalizing the U.S. economy in the aftermath of the Great Recession. Low loan rates encouraged more people to become homeowners, buy cars, go to college, and, ultimately, increase their spending.

Despite these benefits to the economy as a whole, many experts believe that the level of household debt in the United States, relative to income and wealth, is cause for concern. As a result of easy credit and changing attitudes about debt, the average household is relying on borrowed funds more than they have in the past.

Applying for Consumer Credit

You can apply for credit by filling out a credit application form or responding to an interview that requests information related to your creditworthiness—usually details about income, assets, and debts. If you've developed a personal income statement and balance sheet, the requested information will be easy to supply. You may receive a credit offer by telephone or mail. When this happens, it's possible the lender has already prescreened your income and credit using credit bureau information, as will be explained later in the chapter. In other cases, the lender will check your credit after receiving the signed application.

In some cases, it may seem that lenders are not carefully evaluating the creditworthiness of applicants. For example, despite a federal law that limits on-campus solicitation of credit card applications, college students are often inundated with credit card offers, especially if their schools sell mailing lists of enrolled students to card companies. Although unemployed students may not seem to be the best credit risks, the rates are generally high, and lenders know that parents often step in to pay their dependent children's debts.

Applications for consumer loans are usually more detailed than those for credit cards. This is because depository institutions charge lower rates of interest and prefer to make loans to the best credit risks. They'll therefore collect more information on your income and assets to better assess your creditworthiness.

5.2 | Your Consumer Credit Plan

LEARNING OBJECTIVE 5.2
Maintain your creditworthiness, and understand your consumer credit rights.

Recent college graduates, on average, are graduating with more student loan and credit card debt than those of previous generations. In some cases, required monthly payments exceed the new graduates' ability to pay. Before borrowing money, even if it's for an important objective such as higher education, it's important to have a plan for repaying the debt.

How much debt can you afford? How much will a lender let you borrow? These questions are related to your creditworthiness. In this section, we'll consider the factors that determine creditworthiness and provide some guidelines for determining how much debt you need and how much you can afford.

In addition to the personal financial statements we considered in Chapter 2, you should maintain a summary of your household debt usage. You can use an Excel worksheet, such as the one in **Excel Worksheet 5.1** (Personal Financial Planner: Household Credit Summary), to keep track of account numbers, Internet account logins, and customer service contact information.

EXCEL WORKSHEET

See **Excel Worksheet 5.1** (**Personal Financial Planner: Household Credit Summary**) in **WileyPLUS**.

Measuring Your Credit Capacity

Lenders commonly apply guidelines for credit capacity, and it's important for borrowers to understand these measures to better manage their credit.

Using Financial Ratios to Measure Credit Capacity

In Chapter 2, we identified several ratios that are useful in evaluating how debt usage affects your financial health—specifically, the debt payment ratio, the mortgage debt service ratio, and the debt ratio. In addition to their usefulness in assessing your current financial health, these ratios may be used to evaluate whether your finances can handle an increased level of debt.

Lenders commonly use ratio guidelines to assess the creditworthiness of potential borrowers. However, just because you meet a lender's guidelines does not automatically mean that your level of debt is acceptable from a financial planning perspective. For example, you may have less disposable income available for debt repayment than the average borrower because you spend more on certain budget categories or save more for retirement than the average household.

Recall, for example, that the debt payment ratio is calculated as follows:

$$\text{Debt payment ratio} = \frac{\text{Total monthly debt payments}}{\text{After-tax monthly income}}$$

Suppose that according to your lender's guidelines, total monthly debt payments are allowed to be 35 percent of your gross monthly income. If your gross income is $2,000 per month, the lender's 35 percent maximum would mean you could have total debt payments of $2,000 × 0.35 = $700.

But if your *take-home pay* is only $1,600, you'll be paying out 44 percent of it in debt payments ($700/$1,600 = 0.44), many times greater than the 10 to 20 percent maximum recommended by financial experts.

The reason that lenders allow such high ratios is that they're concerned only with your ability to make payments, not with your ability to achieve your other financial goals. But the dollars you spend on debt repayment are dollars that are not being allocated to savings and investment. Thus, in weighing the advisability of taking on more debt, even when you can technically afford the payments, you should consider the impact this decision will have on other aspects of your financial plan.

The following example illustrates the potential cost that additional debt can impose on your financial plan. Suppose you're currently saving all your extra income—$300 per month—in an account earning 5 percent interest, so that you can attend graduate school six years from now. You decide to buy a car by taking out a six-year loan with payments of $150 per month. This decision means that you'll have to reduce your monthly graduate school savings contributions by that same amount. At the end of the six years, your graduate school account will be $12,565 smaller than it would have been if you had continued with your original savings plan (the future value of six years of $150 monthly payments with compound interest).

The Five Cs of Credit

Although lenders use ratios as part of their assessment of your creditworthiness, they're concerned with much more than just your monthly cash flow. The factors they consider are often summarized using the "Five Cs of Credit"—capacity, capital, collateral, character, and conditions.

- **Capacity**   A lender's assessment of your ability, or capacity, to repay your debts is usually based on your household cash flow. Lenders may evaluate your capacity by looking at your sources of income and your expenses. They may use the debt payment ratio, the mortgage debt service ratio, or other measures that consider your expenses relative to your income.

- **Capital**   Lenders are also interested in your household's net worth, or capital. If total assets are greater than total debts, they will consider that you could, if necessary, liquidate other assets to pay back the loan. In addition, lenders know that you won't want to risk your other assets being taken to repay the debt.

- **Collateral**   If you don't make payments as promised, a lender can take any pledged collateral (such as a car or home) and resell it to pay off the loan. This factor makes a secured loan safer to the lender than an unsecured loan. The more valuable the collateral, the better the lender will like it.

- **Character**   Your previous credit, employment, and education history tell the lender about your character. Are you the type of person who honors an obligation? Do you have experience with making payments on debt? If you've previously borrowed money and repaid it on time, you'll be considered a better credit risk. Similarly, if you own a home, have held a job for a period of time, and have lived in the same area for a while, the lender will assume that you're less likely to default.

- **Conditions**   Every loan and every borrower represents a unique situation, and lenders will sometimes take individual factors into consideration. Low unemployment and a strong housing market significantly reduce the risk for a mortgage lender.

If you fail one or more of the Five Cs or have insufficient credit history, a lender might still approve your loan if you have a **cosigner**—a person who agrees to take responsibility if you don't make your payments as agreed. This significantly reduces the lender's risk, but it's fairly risky for the person who cosigns, since he or she is effectively taking responsibility for the debt. The lender can use the same collection methods against the cosigner as it can against the borrower, such as garnishing wages and suing in a court of law. And if the loan goes into default, the cosigner's credit will be adversely affected.

By understanding the Five Cs of Credit, you can take steps to improve your own creditworthiness. **Figure 5.2** summarizes questions creditors consider in determining how creditworthy you are.

FIGURE 5.2 **Assessing Your Creditworthiness Using the Five Cs of Credit** Ask yourself these questions to determine whether you satisfy the Five Cs of Credit.

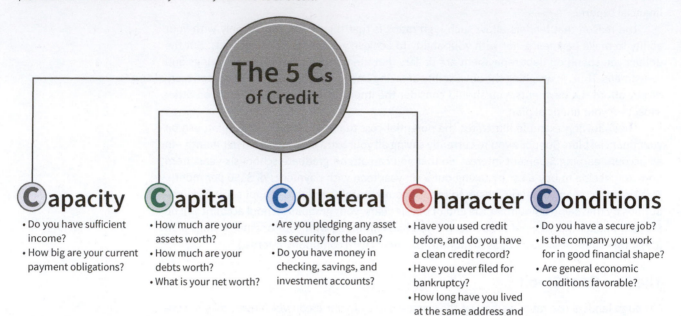

The 5 Cs of Credit

Capacity
- Do you have sufficient income?
- How big are your current payment obligations?

Capital
- How much are your assets worth?
- How much are your debts worth?
- What is your net worth?

Collateral
- Are you pledging any asset as security for the loan?
- Do you have money in checking, savings, and investment accounts?

Character
- Have you used credit before, and do you have a clean credit record?
- Have you ever filed for bankruptcy?
- How long have you lived at the same address and worked for your current employer?

Conditions
- Do you have a secure job?
- Is the company you work for in good financial shape?
- Are general economic conditions favorable?

Reflection Question 2

For each of the Five Cs of Credit, consider how your circumstances will be different five years from now. In what ways will you look better to a lender at that time, as compared to now?

Understanding Your Credit Score

Lenders evaluate your creditworthiness in part by checking your outstanding debt obligations and your history of making payments. This information is reported by your creditors and compiled by **credit bureaus**. The three major credit bureaus are Equifax (**www.equifax.com**), Experian (**www.experian.com**), and TransUnion (**www.transunion.com**). These firms collect relevant information and use mathematical models to arrive at a score that lenders can use to determine whether to lend to you and what interest rates to charge you. For a fee, credit bureaus will provide a credit report and a credit score to prospective lenders, landlords, employers, insurers, and others who are interested in doing business with you.

You may be surprised to find that your credit report contains more than just information on credit accounts. Typically, it includes previous, current, and future credit history; specific information about average balances, late payments, and over-limit charges; and home mortgage amounts and payments. Public information, such as judgments, liens, wage garnishments, and bankruptcies, will also be reported. Credit reports also identify recent consumer-initiated requests for your credit report by other lenders. If you've applied for a lot of other loans or credit cards, a lender may be concerned that you'll get into future credit trouble.

Based on the information in their files, credit bureaus classify you based on their estimate of your credit risk, commonly using a credit scoring system such as the FICO system developed by Fair Isaac Corporation. This system and others use statistical models to calculate your probability of repayment. The higher your score, the better your creditworthiness. **Figure 5.3** identifies the factors FICO uses to create these scores for each person and their relative weights. **Figure 5.4** shows a typical distribution of credit scores.

FIGURE 5.3 **FICO Credit Score Factors**   Although the FICO score measures many aspects of how you manage credit, the most important factor is whether you make payments on time.

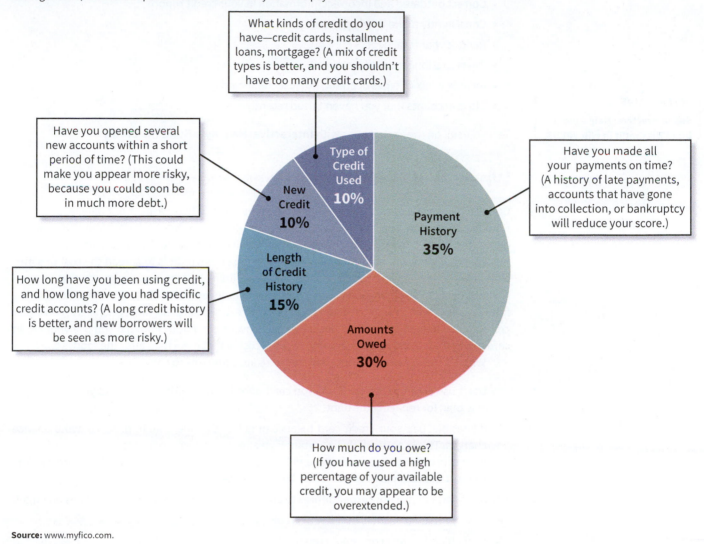

What kinds of credit do you have—credit cards, installment loans, mortgage? (A mix of credit types is better, and you shouldn't have too many credit cards.)

Have you opened several new accounts within a short period of time? (This could make you appear more risky, because you could soon be in much more debt.)

Have you made all your payments on time? (A history of late payments, accounts that have gone into collection, or bankruptcy will reduce your score.)

How long have you been using credit, and how long have you had specific credit accounts? (A long credit history is better, and new borrowers will be seen as more risky.)

How much do you owe? (If you have used a high percentage of your available credit, you may appear to be overextended.)

Type of Credit Used 10%

New Credit 10%

Payment History 35%

Length of Credit History 15%

Amounts Owed 30%

Source: www.myfico.com.

FIGURE 5.4 **National Distribution of Credit Scores**   More than half of Americans have FICO credit scores of 700 or above. How do you stack up?

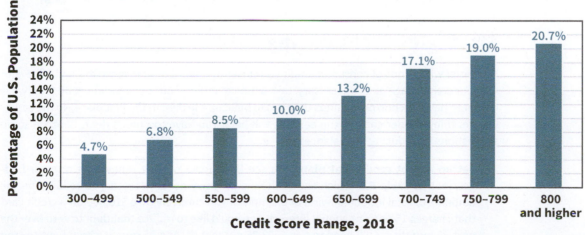

Source: www.myfico.com.

If your credit score is too low, you can use one or more of these methods to raise it:

- Correct outdated and incorrect information in your credit report.
- Consistently make timely payments.
- Reduce your total debt.
- Develop a longer credit history.
- Include a mix of types of credit, not just credit cards.
- Close accounts that you haven't used recently.

INTERACTIVE

See **Interactive: Help Kyle Build His Credit** in **WileyPLUS**.

Test yourself on these strategies with **Interactive: Help Kyle Build His Credit**.

When and How to Use Consumer Credit

Controlling the use of consumer credit is often the most difficult aspect of financial planning. No one can do it for you, and there isn't a one-size-fits-all answer to the question "How much debt is too much?" In fact, your own use of credit will likely change over your lifetime.

As noted earlier, an important advantage of consumer credit is to spread the cost of a purchase over time, allowing you to use the purchased item while making payments that you can easily budget for. Another good use of credit is to make investments that will earn a return in the future, such as investments in education or real estate. Unfortunately, most people use consumer credit to buy items that actually decline in value over time. For example, if you use your credit card to pay for a pizza, you'll be paying back the cost of that meal long after the food is gone.

When is the use of credit appropriate? Here are some tips to consider:

1. Don't use credit to pay for items you can't afford to buy with cash, unless you have a specific plan for repaying the debt.
2. If possible, pay your credit card balance in full by the due date in order to avoid finance charges. This is particularly important if you use consumer credit to pay for regular expenditures in order to take advantage of free frequent flier miles or discounts. Otherwise, the value of the card perks will be offset by the finance charges.
3. Keep track of monthly expenditures to ensure that your net monthly cash flow is on target.
4. Limit yourself to a small number of credit cards.
5. Avoid high-interest consumer credit.
6. Avoid consumer credit with annual fees.

INTERACTIVE

See **Interactive: Are You in Debt Danger?** in **WileyPLUS**.

Sometimes people don't realize they are in over their heads with debt until it's too late. If you want to evaluate your own debt risk, check out **Interactive: Are You in Debt Danger?**

Strategies for Reducing Debt

No matter what kinds of consumer credit you currently have, it makes sense to regularly evaluate your credit usage and, if necessary, take action to reduce your outstanding debt. It's always harder to pay back borrowed funds than it is to build up the debt in the first place, so the earlier you get things under control, the easier it will be. If you have too much debt, here are some suggestions for reducing the balances.

1. **Set up a debt repayment plan.** To see the impact of debt repayment on your budget, look at **Table 5.3**, which shows the monthly payments necessary to reduce specific amounts of total indebtedness. For example, if you currently owe $10,000 on a credit card that charges 18 percent annual interest, and you'd like to reduce that debt to zero over the next 48 months, you'll need to pay $293.75 per month. And of course, you'll have to stop using your credit card in the meantime. This is an application of the time value of money concepts you learned in Chapter 2; the loan balance owed is the present value of a series of payments, given the number of months and the interest rate.

TABLE 5.3 Monthly Payments Necessary to Achieve Debt Reduction Goals

Months	Interest Rate %	Amount of Total Indebtedness					
		$1,000	**$2,500**	**$5,000**	**$7,500**	**$10,000**	**$15,000**
12	6	86.07	215.17	430.33	645.50	860.66	1,291.00
	10	87.92	219.79	439.58	659.37	879.16	1,318.74
	14	89.79	224.47	448.94	673.40	897.87	1,346.81
	18	91.68	229.20	458.40	687.60	916.80	1,375.20
24	6	44.32	110.80	221.60	332.40	443.21	664.81
	10	46.14	115.36	230.72	346.09	461.45	692.17
	14	48.01	120.03	240.06	360.10	480.13	720.19
	18	49.92	124.81	249.62	374.43	499.24	748.86
36	6	30.42	76.05	152.11	228.16	304.22	456.33
	10	32.27	80.67	161.34	242.00	322.67	484.01
	14	34.18	85.44	170.89	256.33	341.78	512.66
	18	36.15	90.38	180.76	271.14	361.52	542.29
48	6	23.49	58.71	117.43	176.14	234.85	352.28
	10	25.36	63.41	126.81	190.22	253.63	380.44
	14	27.33	68.32	136.63	204.95	273.26	409.90
	18	29.37	73.44	146.87	220.31	293.75	440.62
60	6	19.33	48.33	96.66	145.00	193.33	289.99
	10	21.25	53.12	106.24	159.35	212.47	318.71
	14	23.27	58.17	116.34	174.51	232.68	349.02
	18	25.39	63.48	126.97	190.45	253.93	380.90
72	6	16.57	41.43	82.86	124.30	165.73	248.59
	10	18.53	46.31	92.63	138.94	185.26	277.89
	14	20.61	51.51	103.03	154.54	206.06	309.09
	18	22.81	57.02	114.04	171.06	228.08	342.12
120	6	11.10	27.76	55.51	83.27	111.02	166.53
	10	13.22	33.04	66.08	99.11	132.15	198.23
	14	15.53	38.82	77.63	116.45	155.27	232.90
	18	18.02	45.05	90.09	135.14	180.19	270.28

If you don't have extra cash in your budget to apply to debt reduction or if you're having trouble making minimum payments out of current cash flow, you'll have to take more drastic measures. You'll need to either reduce monthly cash outflows or increase monthly cash inflows.

2. **Obtain a debt consolidation loan at a lower interest rate.** A debt consolidation loan is a loan earmarked for repayment of higher-interest debt owed on multiple cards and/or

accounts. For instance, consider again the example above, in which you'd need to make monthly payments of $293.75 for 48 months to pay off a $10,000 credit card balance at 18 percent interest. If you could obtain a home equity loan at 6 percent, you could repay the debt in four years with a monthly payment of $234.85, a savings of $58.90 per month, or $2,827 over four years. If you also avoid an annual card fee, the savings could be even greater.

If you decide to consolidate your debts to reduce your payments, it's very important to stop using the cards you're paying off. If you couldn't afford the payments before, you certainly won't be able to make payments on both the new loan and new credit card debt. Another factor to consider is the term of the loan. Obviously, your monthly payment will be lower if you stretch out the payment schedule, but that will mean additional interest charges, and it will take you that much longer to get your finances back on track. For those reasons, it's best to take the shortest loan that you can reasonably afford to pay off.

3. **Take a second job specifically earmarked to pay down the debt.**   Although working two jobs may not sound like fun, it's often the fastest way to reduce your outstanding credit card debt. If you can work an extra 15 hours per week, at $9 per hour after taxes, you'll be able to get rid of your $10,000 debt in less than two years.

4. **Develop a zero-based budget.**   Zero-based budgeting is a strategy often recommended by financial planners. To construct a zero-based budget, you start with absolute necessities and debt payments and then add expenditures until you run out of cash. Thus, "fun" money for entertainment, eating out, and clothes shopping would have lower priority than payments to reduce your debt.

5. **Live with family or friends to reduce your expenses.**   Recent government statistics show that more than 25 percent of adult children move back in with their parents at some time during their 20s. Although this arrangement may not be ideal, it can be quite helpful as a means of reducing the debt load that many college students accrue during their years of education. Starting salaries for college grads are often insufficient to pay a student loan, car loan, and credit card bills while still putting food on the table. Sharing living expenses with additional roommates can also free up funds for debt repayment. Adult children who are considering moving back home should keep in mind that it is quite reasonable for parents to expect contribution toward household expenses and chores.

6. **Sell assets.**   Many families who get into consumer credit trouble have done so to finance a higher standard of living. If you can't afford to maintain that standard of living, then you need to cut back. You could buy a cheaper car or downsize your home, for example. If you have other marketable valuables, such as musical instruments, collectibles, or consumer electronics, these could be sold to pay off debts. It only makes sense to do so, however, if you will not need to replace the item in the future at a much higher cost.

No matter which method you choose to use for reducing your debt, you'll be more successful if you have a plan with specific goals, including a timeline for achieving them. **Demonstration Problem 5.1** shows how to calculate the time it will take to pay off a credit balance.

DEMONSTRATION PROBLEM 5.1 | How Long Will It Take to Pay Off Your Balance?

Problem

Robin signed up for a credit card when she was a freshman because her parents thought it would be good for her to learn to manage credit. As a student, Robin always found that she was running out of money at the end of the month, so she was thankful to have the card to pay for groceries and other expenses here and there. In the beginning, the minimum payments were small, so Robin was able to keep up. She was a little concerned about the increasing total balance and the interest rate on her debt (18%), but figured she'd be able to catch up once she had a real job. By the time she was a senior, Robin's credit card balance was $5,000, and it was difficult to make the minimum payment each month. She decided to make a plan for paying off the credit card by increasing her hours at her part-time job and applying the income to debt reduction. She estimates that she can pay $200 per month, and she plans to avoid using her card for any new purchases. How long will it take her to pay off the card?

Strategy

This is a time value of money problem in which you need to enter the information you know about the present value owed, the rate of monthly interest, and the monthly payment, and then solve for the number of months it will take to repay. You can solve this problem using a financial calculator, or you can use **Excel Worksheet 5.2** (Personal Financial Planner: How Long Will It Take to Pay Off Your Balance?).

Solution

The financial calculator solution: Enter PV = 5000, I = 18%/12, PMT = −200, and solve for N = 32. Note that your calculator entry for the payment must be entered as a negative number because it is a cash outflow to you. This means that it will take Robin 32 months, or almost three years, to pay off this debt.

EXCEL WORKSHEET

See **Excel Worksheet 5.2 (Personal Financial Planner: How Long Will It Take to Pay Off Your Balance?)** in **WileyPLUS.**

Your Consumer Credit Rights

Because financial transactions are complex, many consumers don't understand them very well. Therefore, Congress has passed a number of laws to protect consumers in credit transactions, including the Truth in Lending Act, the Equal Credit Opportunity Act, the Fair Credit Billing Act, the Fair Debt Collection Practices Act, the Fair Credit Reporting Reform Act, the Credit Card Accountability Responsibility and Disclosure (CARD) Act, and the Dodd-Frank Wall Street Reform and Consumer Protection Act. In 2011, the Consumer Financial Protection Bureau (CFPB) was launched as the first government agency solely dedicated to consumer financial protection. In this section, we summarize your most important rights under various consumer credit laws. You can learn more at the CFPB's website: **www.consumerfinance.gov**.

Full Information from Prospective Lender

Perhaps the most important consumer credit right is provided by the Truth in Lending Act. Under this act, lenders must provide you with full and truthful information, written in plain English, including the true cost of consumer credit as measured by annual percentage rate (APR, discussed later in this chapter), including finance charges, fees, and penalties. This information enables you to make better decisions when choosing between potential lenders and reduces the likelihood that you'll be taken advantage of by unscrupulous lenders.

Clear and Accurate Billing Statements

Lenders must provide you with full information related to all charges made to your account, and they must clearly explain any finance charges and how they are calculated. If you find an error on a bill, specific rules identify your right to contest the bill. Within 60 days of the billing error, you should:

- Send a written notice to the credit card issuer, including copies of verifying documents, explaining why you believe the item to be incorrect. The company must immediately credit your account by that amount, pending resolution of the dispute.
- Withhold payment for the disputed item. The issuer cannot charge you interest or penalties on this amount while it is in dispute.
- Check your credit bureau file to see whether a notice has been sent relating to this item or your nonpayment.

Limits on Interest Rate Increases and Fees

There are several important protections against unfair credit card practices related to interest rates and fees:

- Promotional rates must last at least six months.
- Interest rates cannot be increased in the first 12 months after you have opened a credit card unless you have been late in making your payments or the rate increase was disclosed when you first opened the card.
- Rate increases require 45 days notice.
- Rate increases apply to new purchases and not previous balances. However, if you are more than 60 days late on your credit card payments, they can apply to previous balances.
- Payments above the minimum must be applied to the highest interest rate balances.
- You cannot be charged a fee for making your payment online or by phone, unless the bill is being paid at the last minute.

Freedom from Discrimination

Lenders are not allowed to deny you credit based on race, sex, marital status, religion, age, national origin, or receipt of public benefits. However, they can deny credit based on insufficient income or credit history. Before this law was passed, women had difficulty getting credit in their own name either because they were homemakers with little or no income or because lenders worried they might quit their jobs in the future due to pregnancy. Upon divorce or the death of a spouse, many women found themselves without access to credit at all. Today, lenders can't consider either marital status or gender in making their credit decisions, so it's much easier for a woman to establish a credit history in her own name.

Credit discrimination may not always be blatant. It can be as simple as a lender discouraging you from applying for credit, treating you differently on the phone, or charging you a higher rate than the one you applied for. If you think you have been discriminated against, you can register a complaint on the CFPB website at **www.consumerfinance.gov**.

Privacy of Financial Information

One of the disadvantages of credit cards and other consumer loans is reduced privacy of financial information. Your credit card provider may sell your credit and financial information to other companies that wish to solicit you for magazine and product sales. However, your financial institution is required to inform you of its intent to share your information with others and offer you the opportunity to opt out. You also have protections against unwanted credit solicitation. The federal government and most states have passed legislation that specifically prohibits telephone calls to the phone numbers placed on "no-call lists." To have your number permanently added to the federal no-call list, call 888-382-1222 from your phone or go to **www.donotcall.gov**.

Know Why You Were Denied Credit

If you are turned down for credit, the lender must inform you in writing of the reason for the denial. This will usually be based on some aspect of your previous credit history, which lenders evaluate by checking with credit bureaus, discussed earlier. You have the right to one free copy of your credit report from each credit bureau per year and also whenever you are denied credit based on something in your credit report.

Fair and Respectful Debt Collection

You have an obligation to repay any debts you have incurred. However, even when you're in default on a debt, you're protected by the Fair Debt Collection Act against unfair, deceptive, and abusive practices on the part of debt collectors. The act applies only to debt collection agencies that collect debts on behalf of creditors, usually for a percentage of the amount owed.

Surveys suggest that many consumers are the victims of abusive and illegal debt collection practices such as those reported in **Figure 5.5**. The Federal Trade Commission (FTC), the federal agency charged with protecting consumers from unfair business practices, receives thousands of complaints about collection companies each year. No-call lists have significantly reduced the number of complaints of repeated calls.

FIGURE 5.5 **Debt Collection Complaints** Debt collectors receive a portion of what they collect, up to 50 percent of the amount originally owed, and sometimes engage in deceptive or abusive practices to get the money. Enforcement actions under the Fair Debt Collection Practices Act have significantly curtailed these illegal activities.

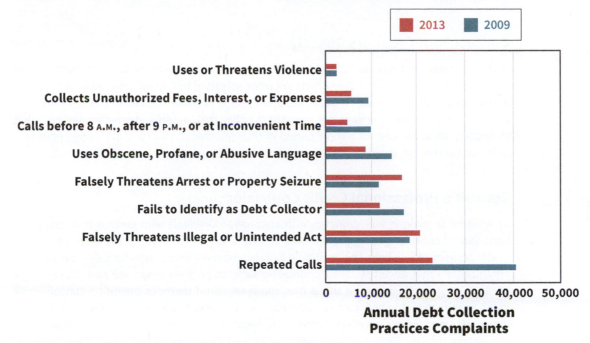

Source: www.consumerfinance.gov; Fair Debt Collections Practices CFPB Act Annual Report 2014.

Accuracy of Reported Credit Information

You have the right to have information reported fairly and accurately, so you should check your credit reports regularly. Credit reporting agencies must notify you whenever new negative information is added to your file. Negative credit information must be removed from your file after seven years, with the exception of bankruptcies, which remain on record for 10 years.

Correcting Information on Your Credit Report

When you notify a credit bureau about incorrect information in your file, it must investigate and make corrections, if warranted. Lenders must certify the accuracy of any negative information they report. Even if the negative information in your file is correct, you still have the right to add an explanatory statement of your own. For example, if you're notified that your credit card issuer reported late payments during a specific period of time, you can request that a note be included on your report explaining any extenuating circumstances, such as unemployment or illness.

Despite the extensive regulation of credit reporting, it is estimated that a large percentage of all reports contain some inaccurate, misleading, or outdated information. Furthermore, it's not always easy to get this misinformation corrected. If you have a common name, such as John Smith, you might find that your credit report includes negative information about a different John Smith's credit. After a divorce, you should be sure to notify credit bureaus so that your individual credit will not be affected by the possibly poor credit habits of your ex-spouse.

Bankruptcy

Earlier, we looked at some strategies for getting your debt under control before you get into serious credit trouble. But what if it's too late for that? What if you've already gotten so far behind on your payment obligations that you can't see any way to resolve your financial problems? Probably the most common strategy in this situation is avoidance—throwing the past due notices in a pile and refusing to answer the phone. This is *not* a good approach, and it increases the risk that your creditors will take more serious steps to collect the debt. Instead, you should contact your creditors directly and seek out consumer credit counseling. As a last resort, you might consider declaring bankruptcy, but doing so has serious long-term consequences. These options are discussed below.

Contact Your Creditors Directly

When you know that you can't pay your debts as agreed, you should immediately contact your creditors and let them know. Consumers are often surprised to find out that, although interest and late fees will still accrue, creditors are often willing to make alternative payment arrangements. Creditors much prefer to get something rather than nothing. If your budget crunch is temporary, as in the case of a short period of unemployment, this type of arrangement may help you get through it without becoming seriously delinquent.

Consult a Professional Credit Counselor

In addition to making arrangements with creditors, individuals with serious financial problems should consider getting professional consumer credit counseling. There are many reputable sources of free help, so you should avoid companies that charge for this service. Some organizations that advertise credit counseling services prey on desperate people, making a profit by charging high fees to those who can least afford them, or providing consolidation loans at unreasonably high rates of interest. The National Foundation for Consumer Credit (**www.nfcc.org**), an organization sponsored by large creditor firms, offers free consumer credit counseling through local nonprofit branches called Consumer Credit Counseling Services. In addition to providing educational materials, the certified counselors at these offices help millions of consumers each year to develop realistic budgets, plan for debt reduction, and negotiate with creditors. Large employers may offer financial counseling through their human resources departments, or you may be able to get free counseling through your financial institution, a county extension office, or an employee union.

File for Bankruptcy

Some people get so deeply in debt or experience such a reduction in income (for example, because of illness or injury) that repayment isn't a realistic option. In this situation, it's sometimes necessary to declare bankruptcy as a last resort. **Bankruptcy** is the legal right to ask a court of law to relieve you of certain debts and obligations. If a court grants you an ordinary bankruptcy, your creditors will divide up your assets in a fair and equitable process overseen by a trustee.

Around 800,000 people file for personal bankruptcy each year in the United States, and this number has declined steadily over the last decade. **Figure 5.6** shows the relationship between total bankruptcy filings and average debt payment ratios. In the early 2000s, households were more heavily in debt, as indicated by the debt payment ratios, and bankruptcies reached an all-time high. The stronger economy in recent years resulted in a decline in household debt payment ratios, and the total number of bankruptcies went down as well.

Bankruptcy appears on your credit report for 10 years and may affect your ability to obtain a home mortgage or other credit. The long-lasting impact may outweigh the benefits of debt reduction. So why are there so many personal bankruptcies? Bankruptcies are often initiated to deal with large uninsured medical expenses, but there's no doubt that the recession and high

FIGURE 5.6 **Bankruptcy Filings and Household Debt Ratios, 1989–2018**   The figure shows the relationship between total bankruptcy filings during the period, represented by bars, and average U.S. debt payment ratios, represented by the line.

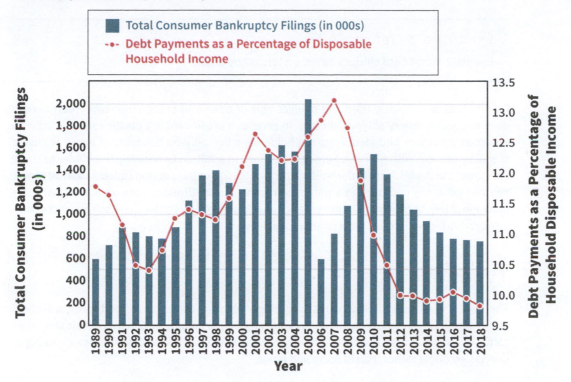

levels of unemployment have been recent factors. Many families had too much debt and too little liquidity to survive a period of unemployment.

Although most bankruptcy filers today are baby boomers, people of all ages can get into financial trouble. Most people who declare bankruptcy have low incomes, earning less than $20,000 per year, but bankruptcy isn't limited to the poor. Even some celebrities—NFL player Michael Vick and movie star Kim Basinger, for example—have declared bankruptcy in the past. However, you should consider bankruptcy only as your *last* alternative to resolving credit management difficulties.

Chapter 7 Bankruptcy

A Chapter 7 bankruptcy requires the liquidation, or sale, of most of your assets. Under current law, debtors are allowed to keep a small amount of home equity, Social Security and unemployment insurance payments, a vehicle, household goods, trade tools, and books. The proceeds of the sale of your remaining assets are used to pay creditors to the extent possible, and most of your financial obligations are then cleared. However, certain obligations—alimony and child support, student loans, and debts that were not disclosed in court—are unaffected by a Chapter 7 bankruptcy, and you must still pay them. In addition, debtors are not allowed to repay certain preferred creditors (such as family members) in anticipation of the bankruptcy.

Chapter 13 Bankruptcy

The Bankruptcy Abuse Prevention and Consumer Protection Act of 2005 makes it harder to declare Chapter 7 bankruptcy, particularly if you have sufficient income to pay some of your debts. Instead, most people are now required to opt for a Chapter 13 bankruptcy, under which you are protected from creditors' claims while you develop and implement a plan to repay your debts under court supervision, usually with reduced balances and payments. In a Chapter 13 bankruptcy, you generally can keep all of your assets. But if the repayment plan fails, you may eventually end up in a Chapter 7 liquidation.

5.3 | Credit Cards

> **LEARNING OBJECTIVE 5.3**
> Evaluate credit card choices based on terms and costs.

Credit cards are a widely used and familiar type of open-end credit. The term **credit card** is used to cover a variety of types of cards. In general, a credit card is a plastic card printed with an account number and identifying the holder as a person who has entered into a revolving credit agreement with a lender. Some credit cards, in addition to allowing the holder to make consumer purchases, permit the holder to borrow cash in a transaction called a **cash advance**. You can get a cash advance at a participating financial institution, from an automated teller machine (ATM), or by writing a **convenience check** supplied by the lender. Cash advances commonly have higher interest rates or additional fees.

Types of Cards

There are several types of credit cards, including bank credit cards, retail credit cards, and travel and entertainment cards. In addition to explaining these choices, we'll discuss debit and smart cards, which are similar to credit cards in some ways but offer users access to their checking or savings accounts rather than to borrowed funds.

Bank Credit Cards

A **bank credit card** allows the holder to make purchases anywhere the card is accepted. Although these cards carry a brand name from a particular service provider (primarily Visa, MasterCard, or Discover), the lender is usually a depository institution, such as a bank or credit union. Nearly all financial institutions offer credit cards, and they pay transaction fees to the service providers for managing payments to retailers and billing of account holders.

Many nonfinancial companies offer branded credit cards to encourage spending on their products. An example is the United Mileage Plus Visa card, which gives the holder miles in the United Airlines frequent flier program for all purchases made with the card. Alumni associations and other affinity groups (charitable organizations, political groups, fraternities, and sororities) commonly issue credit cards this way as well. Typically, the group will get a small percentage of the finance charge paid by the cardholders.

Some businesses don't accept credit cards, and others accept only certain cards. For example, a business might accept Visa and MasterCard but not American Express. This is because the retailer incurs a cost for accepting credit purchases, with the highest fees charged by American Express and Discover.

Retail Credit Cards

Some businesses offer **retail credit cards** that can only be used at their own outlets. Retailers ranging from Home Depot to Neiman Marcus offer such cards. Aside from earning interest on credit balances, retailers benefit from having branded cards because customers spend more. Cardholder mailing lists can also be used to advertise special sales and discounts. It's fairly common for a retailer to offer "10 percent off your first purchase" to entice new borrowers and to give special discounts to credit customers.

Travel and Entertainment Cards

Some types of cards are designed primarily to allow business customers to delay payment of travel and entertainment expenses to coincide with their company's reimbursement system.

A **travel and entertainment (T&E) card** is therefore a type of credit card, but one that generally requires outstanding balances to be paid in full each month. Diners Club and American Express are the best known of these cards, but financial institutions such as Citibank may issue them through contracts with specific large employers. Since holders who pay their accounts according to the terms of the agreement will never incur any interest charges, these types of accounts tend to carry significant annual fees and penalties in order to make them profitable to the issuers. These card issuers also typically charge higher fees to merchants.

Debit Cards

A debit card allows you to subtract the cost of your purchase from your checking or savings account electronically. Debit cards are not the same as credit cards because you're using your own money to pay for purchases. Unless you have overdraft protection, which works similarly to a credit card, the transaction will be denied when there isn't enough money in the account, and you may be required to pay a penalty fee. As illustrated in **Figure 5.7**, debit cards have surpassed cash as the preferred method of making payments. Although paper checks still account for 10 percent of all payments, they are less likely to be used for in-store transactions than they were in the past.

FIGURE 5.7 **Changes in Consumer Payment Choice, 2009–2017** Debit cards have become the preferred method of making payments for consumer items, and payments by check are declining.

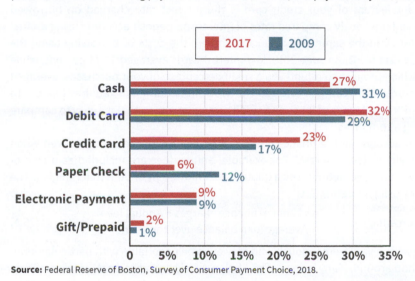

Source: Federal Reserve of Boston, Survey of Consumer Payment Choice, 2018.

Smart Cards and New Technology

Although credit cards are a fixture in our modern culture, new technologies could soon make them seem outdated. Already in use, with potentially unlimited applications, is the **smart card**, a card embedded with a computer chip that can store substantially more information than the magnetic strip on a traditional credit card. Unlike debit and ATM cards, smart cards actually store **electronic cash**. These funds have already been withdrawn from a bank account and are essentially "on deposit" in the card until used. Many universities have found smart cards to be a convenient way for students to access a variety of services on campus, from dining halls to copy machines. Prepaid cards such as Walmart or Starbucks gift cards operate on the same principle and are increasing in popularity. Gift card sales exceeded $160 billion in 2018, and there is now an active online resale market for these cards.

Although payments using credit or debit cards are still very common, it is possible that mobile payment will be the preferred method in the future. Smartphone apps such as Venmo and Square Cash, along with mobile payment options offered by Amazon, Apple, Google, and others, are favored by younger consumers.

Common Credit Card Contract Terms

Credit card agreements are legal contracts subject to numerous terms and conditions. You effectively agree to these terms and conditions when you apply for the card. If you own a credit card, you should be familiar with its important features. You should also understand your legal rights and protections under the Truth in Lending Act and the more recent Credit CARD Act, both mentioned earlier in the chapter.

Annual Fees

Some credit cards charge you an annual fee for the privilege of being a cardholder. Although competition has caused many lenders to eliminate these fees altogether, some cards charge as much as $300 per year. If possible, you should avoid cards that impose annual fees unless the cards offer other financial benefits that offset this cost. For example, suppose you have a card with a $1,000 balance, on which you pay 10 percent annual interest, or $100 per year. If you pay a $50 annual fee in addition to your interest charges, the total annual financing costs are $150, which is 15 percent of your balance (150/1,000 = 15%). Compensating features might include insurance, rebates, discounts, frequent flier miles, or other services provided to cardholders. In most cases, though, the value of the additional perks isn't enough to justify paying an annual fee.

Annual Percentage Rate (APR)

The most important feature of your credit card is the interest rate charged on borrowed funds. Recall that you previously compared rates of interest on deposit accounts using annual percentage yield (APY). In the same way, you can compare the costs of borrowing using the **annual percentage rate (APR)**. In June 2019, low-interest cards averaged 14.71 percent, while cash-back cards, which promise to refund you a small percentage of your purchases, averaged 17.68 percent, according to **creditcards.com**. The Truth in Lending Act requires lenders to clearly report the APR on all types of loans and credit arrangements so that it's easy to compare consumer financing alternatives.

APR takes into account all the finance charges associated with the account, even when they aren't technically called "interest." For example, annual fees are included as a cost of financing. That's why you'll sometimes see a quoted rate followed by an APR that is higher. The APR is calculated by using **Equation 5.1**:

$$\text{Annual percentage rate} = \frac{\text{Total annual finance charges} + \text{Annual fee}}{\text{Average loan balance over the year}} \tag{5.1}$$

Finance charges can vary tremendously and may even be negotiable with particular lenders, so it pays to shop around. Many issuers offer a below-market promotional, or "teaser," rate to attract new customers and to encourage current credit card holders to transfer balances from other cards. Although this might seem like it makes financial sense, the difficulty lies in the details. The rate on these cards after the teaser period is usually higher than other cards, and there may also be annual fees and higher penalty rates for late payments.

Transaction, Billing, and Due Dates

Credit card statements are issued once per month. The date you use your credit card to make a purchase is called the **transaction date**. The lender will close off reporting of transactions on a predetermined **billing date**—say, the 20th of the month. Any new charges you make after that date will appear on the next bill. Federal law now requires that the bill be mailed or delivered to you at least 21 days before the **due date**, which is the date on which partial or full payment on the account is due. If you find it more convenient to have your payments due on a different date—for example, to coincide with your paydays—you can request a change in your billing cycle from the lender.

With some credit cards, if you pay in full each month, no interest will accrue on new charges (other than cash advances) until the due date; this period of time from transaction to due date is therefore called the **grace period**. If you do not pay your previous balance in full by the due date, however, interest will begin to accrue on new purchases immediately. When you make payments, the lender will credit you as they are received. If you return purchases, these credits will appear on the next month's statement as a reduction in the total amount owed. The Credit CARD Act requires that payments in excess of the monthly finance charge be used first to pay off amounts that are subject to the highest interest rate, such as cash advances.

As an example of how these dates might affect you, suppose that you begin the billing cycle with a zero balance, and your billing date is March 20. You make a $100 credit purchase on March 21, and you receive your bill on March 24 with a due date of April 15. Your March bill will not include the March 21 transaction; it will appear on the April bill with a due date of May 15. Because you did not carry a balance from the previous billing cycle, you will get the benefit of a grace period. You will not be charged interest on the new transaction until the due date. Thus, if you pay the April bill by May 15, you will pay no interest on the $100 purchase.

Minimum Payment

Under the terms of most credit card agreements, you must make a **minimum payment** each month to be in good credit standing. This amount is calculated according to the terms of your agreement with the lender, but it will usually be the greater of $15 or a specific percentage of the outstanding balance. Under guidelines suggested by federal regulators and adopted by most credit card companies, the minimum payment is equal to the amount of interest and fees due on the account for the period plus 1 percent of the balance owed. At this rate, it can take several years to fully repay the balance. To develop a plan for paying off your debts more quickly, go to the **Online Calculator Demonstration Video: How to Accelerate Your Debt Payoff** in WileyPLUS.

ONLINE CALCULATOR DEMONSTRATION VIDEO

See **Online Calculator Demonstration Video: How to Accelerate Your Debt Payoff** in **WileyPLUS.**

Penalties and Fees

Credit card issuers penalize cardholders when they make late payments, exceed their credit limits, or write cash advance checks on accounts with insufficient credit availability. In addition, fees for cash advances and for ATM usage are relatively common. Penalties and fees, although specified in the terms of the original agreement, are subject to change upon written notification to cardholders.

Legal limits apply to some penalties and fees. For example, a late payment penalty cannot be greater than the minimum payment due and is limited to $25 ($35 if you had another late payment within the last 6 months). If you make charges that put your balance over your credit limit, the lender will assess an over-limit charge, but only one charge is allowed per billing cycle. Under the Credit CARD Act, you cannot be assessed an over-limit charge unless you have agreed to allow the card company to process over-limit transactions. Otherwise, the company must deny payment, and you will not be charged a fee. Because making a late payment and going over your credit limit are both violations of the terms of your loan agreement, these actions may affect your ability to get future credit.

Finance Charge

The **finance charge** is the dollar amount of interest charged by the lender in a particular billing cycle. It is calculated using **Equation 5.2**:

$$\text{Finance charge} = \text{Periodic rate} \times \text{Account balance owed}$$

$$= \frac{\text{Nominal rate}}{\text{Number of billing periods per year}} \times \text{Account balance owed} \quad (5.2)$$

For this calculation, the nominal rate is the quoted rate, not the APR. The number of billing periods per year is 12 because payments are monthly. Thus, if your nominal rate is 18 percent, your periodic rate is 18/12 = 1.5 percent per month. This rate will be specifically identified on your monthly bill.

The account balance on which the finance charge is assessed each month depends on the calculation method used by each lender. The most common method used is the **average daily balance**. The average daily balance is calculated by identifying how much you owed on each day of the billing period, adding these amounts together, and dividing by the number of days.

So, for example, if you owed $0 on your account for 29 days of the billing cycle and $300 for the last day, your average daily balance would be [(29 days × $0) + (1 day × $300)]/30 = $300/30 days = $10. If your card terms give you a grace period and you carry no balance forward from the previous billing cycle, new transactions will not be included in the daily balances. Although it is relatively uncommon, some credit cards use the previous balance method, which calculates interest based on the amount owed at the beginning of the billing cycle, excluding new purchases. This method produces lower finance charges if you usually pay your balance in full each month.

Demonstration Problem 5.2 shows how to calculate the finance charges on a typical credit card, and **Interactive: Understanding Your Credit Card Statement** shows you how to find and interpret important information on your credit card statement.

INTERACTIVE

See **Interactive: Understanding Your Credit Card Statement** in **WileyPLUS** to learn about your billing statement.

DEMONSTRATION PROBLEM 5.2 | Calculation of Credit Card Finance Charges

Problem

Your card has a nominal rate of 18 percent, and you end your billing cycle on July 31 with a balance of $1,000. Your card issuer calculates finance charges based on the average daily balance with a grace period. During the month, you have the following charges and payments:

August 1	$500 new charge
August 21	$1,000 payment

What is the average daily balance to which your finance charge will be applied in the following billing period, and how much interest will you owe?

Strategy

Calculate the average daily balance and the periodic rate. Apply Equation 5.2 to calculate the finance charge.

Solution

Because you carried a balance from the previous billing cycle, the grace period will not apply, so you'll need to calculate the balance owed on each day of the billing period, including new transactions, and subtract any payments received. Your daily balances are:

July 31 (1 day out of 31)	$1,000
August 1 to August 20 (20 days out of 31)	$1,500
August 21 to August 31 (10 days out of 31)	$500

These amounts result in an average daily balance of:
[(1 day × $1000) + (20 days × $1500) + (10 days × $500)]/31 days = $1,161.29. Your finance charge for the period will be:

$$\text{Finance charge} = \frac{\text{Nominal rate}}{\text{Number of billing periods per year}} \times \text{Account balance owed}$$

$$= \frac{0.18}{12} \times \$1,161.29 = 0.015 \times \$1,161.29 = \$17.42$$

EXCEL WORKSHEET

See **Excel Worksheet 5.3 (Personal Financial Planner: Comparing Credit Cards)** in **WileyPLUS**.

Before signing up for a credit card, it clearly pays to compare your choices based on terms, with careful consideration of finance charges and any benefits associated with the cards. You can use **Excel Worksheet 5.3** (Personal Financial Planner: Comparing Credit Cards) to compare credit card choices and to keep track of information on your current credit cards, as shown in the example in **Figure 5.8**.

FIGURE 5.8 Sample of Excel Worksheet 5.3: Comparing Credit Cards

	A	B	C	D	E
1		Financial Institutions Offering Credit Cards			
2	Credit Card Feature				
3	Annual fee	$0	$0	$35	$95
4	APR % on purchases	17.9%	18.9%	16.9%	14.9%
5	APR % on cash advances	24.9%	21.9%	18.9%	16.9%
6	Credit limit	$3,000	$5,000	$2,500	$3,500
7	Grace period	25 days	21 days	21 days	21 days
8	Frequent flier miles	N/A	N/A	1 mile per $1	2 miles per $1
9	Insurance included	accident	accident	accident, travel	accident, travel
10	ATM fees	$2	$3	$2	$2
11	Rebate on purchases	N/A	N/A	1%	N/A
12	Other: Teaser rate	N/A	10.9% for 1 year	N/A	N/A
13	Other:				
14	Other:				

5.4 Consumer Loans

LEARNING OBJECTIVE 5.4

Evaluate consumer loan choices based on your financial needs, loan terms, and costs.

Although credit cards are easy to apply for and use, they are usually more expensive than consumer loans. Financial institutions offer a variety of consumer loan products, many designed to be used for specified purposes. Assuming you meet lender guidelines, you can obtain a consumer loan for almost any consumer purchase.

Common Types of Consumer Loans

Most financial institutions offer automobile loans, home equity loans and lines of credit, and student loans. Each of these types of loans is designed to finance a specific type of consumer purchase.

Home Equity Loans

If you own a home, you'll gradually build up home equity as your property value increases and your mortgage is repaid over time. **Home equity** is the difference between the market value of your home and the remaining balance on your mortgage loan (discussed in more detail in Chapter 6). A home equity loan allows you to borrow against this valuable asset.

Like your primary mortgage loan, a **home equity loan** is secured by your home. However, the lender's right to the home in the event of nonpayment is secondary to that of the primary mortgage lender, so these loans are also referred to as "second mortgages." In the event of default, the first mortgage lender must be repaid from the proceeds of the sale of the home before the second mortgage lender gets anything.

In evaluating home equity loan applications, lenders apply a maximum loan-to-value ratio, commonly from 75 percent to 90 percent. This means that they will not allow total debt on the home, including the first mortgage and the home equity loan, to exceed that percentage of the current market value of the home. For example, suppose you own a home worth $150,000 and your mortgage balance is $100,000. Your home equity is therefore $150,000–$100,000 = $50,000. If you're approved for a home equity loan in the amount of $20,000, your total debt on the home will be $120,000, which amounts to 80 percent of the market value. **Demonstration Problem 5.3** shows how to estimate the amount you can borrow, given the ratio requirements of your lender and your current mortgage balance.

Home equity loans are usually installment loans payable over five to 15 years in equal monthly payments. They are often established as lines of credit that the borrower can access as

---

DEMONSTRATION PROBLEM 5.3 | How Much Can You Borrow with a Home Equity Loan?

Problem

Barbara and Matt Montoya own a home with a current market value of $180,000. When they bought their home five years ago, the value was $140,000, and they financed the purchase by taking a first mortgage for $112,000, with payments of $745 per month. Their current mortgage loan balance is $105,000. They would like to make some home improvements and want to know how much they could borrow using a home equity line of credit. The Montoyas determine that the lenders in their area require that the total amount of loans on a home cannot be more than 80 percent of the home's value and that they can expect $2,000 in loan-related costs, which will reduce the proceeds of the loan. What is the maximum the Montoyas will be able to net from their home equity credit line to pay for their home remodeling?

EXCEL WORKSHEET

See **Excel Worksheet 5.4** (**Personal Financial Planner: How Much Can You Borrow with a Home Equity Loan?**) in **WileyPLUS**.

Strategy

Apply the maximum loan-to-value ratio to determine the maximum total debt. Calculate the maximum credit line after subtracting the current loan balance. You can use **Excel Worksheet 5.4** (Personal Financial Planner: How Much Can You Borrow with a Home Equity Loan?) to calculate the Montoyas' maximum credit line.

Solution

Figure 5.9 shows the spreadsheet solution to the problem. Note that even though the maximum credit limit is $39,000, the Montoyas will not necessarily be approved for this much credit. The lender will also assess their ability to repay the debt before agreeing to lend them the money.

FIGURE 5.9 Sample of Excel Worksheet 5.4: How Much Can You Borrow with a Home Equity Loan?

	A	B	C	D
1	Home Value, Current Debt, and Loan Terms			
2				
3	Market value of home	$	180,000	
4				
5	Lender's maximum loan as a % of value		80%	
6				
7	Maximum total debt	$	144,000	
8				
9	Balance owed on current mortgage(s)	$	105,000	
10				
11	Total maximum credit line	$	39,000	
12				
13	Mortgage costs to be paid from loan principle	$	2,000	
14				
15	Home equity credit available after loan costs	$	37,000	
16				

needed. Generally, home equity loan proceeds can be used for any purpose. Interest on home equity loans used to be tax-deductible up to a limit, which made these loans advantageous for those in high tax brackets. After passage of the Tax Cuts and Jobs Act of 2017, interest on a home equity loan is tax-deductible only if it is used improve the home, and the total debt on the home cannot exceed $750,000.

Automobile Loans

An automobile or car loan is specifically for the purpose of buying a car. Lenders typically limit the amount of the loan to some percentage of the current market value of the car being purchased, and they require that the borrower pledge the car as security for the loan. In addition, borrowers must list the lender as an insured party under their auto collision insurance, as will be explained in Chapter 7. Because of the relatively short economic life of a car, car loan maturities are typically from two to seven years.

Both new car prices and rates on car loans have been unusually low in the last few years due to competition among auto dealers and generally low market interest rates. As a result, consumers have taken on significant car loan debt. It's worth noting, though, that getting a below-market interest rate from an auto dealer doesn't necessarily mean you've come out ahead. As will be explained in Chapter 6, dealers generally make up the difference in higher prices and fees.

Student Loans

A student loan is a loan made for the purpose of paying educational expenses. About two-thirds of all student financial aid comes from federal programs, including loan and grant programs. In addition, private student loans are available from a variety of financial institutions, but usually at less favorable rates and with shorter repayment periods than government loans. Although many people borrow to cover some of the costs of higher education, you should be cautious about taking on substantial debt for this purpose. Many student borrowers find that the repayment obligation will continue for many years after they leave school. Savings, scholarships, and grants are all less expensive alternatives than loans. Chapter 10 will discuss education financing and student loan repayment options in more detail.

Borrowing to pay educational expenses can sometimes make financial sense. After all, your education is an investment you hope will pay off later in the form of increased income. If a loan is necessary, a student loan is generally preferable to other types of consumer loans, because the rates are typically lower. In addition, some student loans are subsidized by the federal government. For parents and students interested in finding out more about educational funding, the first stop should be the Department of Education's well-designed and informational website at **studentaid.ed.gov**.

Comparing Consumer Loan Alternatives

Even though you can easily download an app that will calculate a loan payment, selecting the right consumer loan shouldn't be based solely on the rate or the payment. Like other financial contracts, consumer loans include a variety of features and terms. In choosing between different loans, you must therefore evaluate the characteristics of each and select the one that best meets your needs.

All the important loan terms are spelled out in the **promissory note**, the legal document that represents your promise to repay the loan amount. Consumer loans vary in the interest rates charged, payment arrangements, and collateral required. In this section, you'll learn more about each of these characteristics and how to compare loans based on key features.

Secured versus Unsecured Loans

A **secured loan** gives the lender the right to take certain assets or property if the loan is not repaid according to its terms. The pledged property is the collateral for the loan, as discussed earlier, and can be any valuable asset, such as an automobile or a home. The promissory note for a secured loan will include a description of the collateral pledged for the loan and specify the conditions under which the lender can take possession of the collateral. If you borrow money to buy a car, for example, the lender usually will hold title to the car until you repay the loan in full. If you don't repay the loan, the lender has the right to take the car from you.

Obviously, the right to take the collateral reduces the potential risk of default for the lender. Therefore, lenders commonly charge much lower rates of interest on secured loans than on unsecured loans, such as credit cards. For example, in June 2019, **bankrate.com** reported the average for four-year used car loans was 4.7%, about 1/4 of the average rate on credit cards. The difference at any given point in time is usually 9–11 percentage points. If you don't make your credit card payments, the lender has very few options for recovering your bad debt. But if you don't make your car payments, the lender can repossess, or take back, the car, sell it, and keep the proceeds.

When real property is used as collateral, as in the case of a home mortgage or home equity line of credit, the lender records a **lien** against the property at the county courthouse, putting the public on notice of its potential right to the property. This ensures that if you sell the home, the loan will be repaid before you can take any of the proceeds from the sale.

Student loans, credit cards, and some personal loans are unsecured, which is one explanation for why the interest rates charged on them are higher.

Interest Rates

Interest rates on consumer loans can be either fixed or variable. With a **fixed-rate loan**, the same interest rate applies throughout the life of the loan. With a **variable-rate loan**, the periodic rate fluctuates along with a predetermined measure, such as the prime rate or the Treasury bill rate. For example, suppose you took out a loan in June 2019, when the prime rate was 5.25 percent, and agreed to pay the prime rate plus 2 percentage points in interest. The interest rate on your loan would have started out at 7.25 percent.

A variable-rate loan generally carries a lower initial interest rate than a fixed-rate loan because the lender has the option of raising the rate later. However, a variable-rate loan can subject you to unexpected increases in payments if interest rates are rising—especially if they are rising rapidly. You must take this risk into account in evaluating your options.

Certain types of loans are more likely than others to have fixed rates. For example, it's relatively common for rates on automobile loans to be fixed, whereas rates on home equity loans can be either fixed or variable. The interest rates on credit cards, discussed earlier, can be either fixed or variable under the terms of the contract. In practice, revolving credit agreements are more often classified as variable-rate, since the issuer generally retains the right to change the rate at any time in the future.

Payment Arrangements

Loan agreements may be single-payment or, more commonly, installment arrangements. A **single-payment loan** requires that the balance be paid in full at some point in the future, including the **principal**—the original borrowed amount—and the interest owed on the borrowed funds. For example, many tax preparation firms offer to lend their customers money on the condition that it be repaid in full when the customers receive their income tax refunds. In contrast, an **installment loan** allows the borrower to repay over time, usually in monthly installments that include both principal and interest.

The repayment time period for consumer loans varies by type of loan and between lenders. In the case of a single-payment loan, the contract will specify the date by which the loan must be paid in full. For an installment loan, the contract will specify the monthly payment amount and the term of the loan—the amount of time the loan will cover. For example, a lender may offer 48-month and 60-month terms for its car loans, whereas student loans are normally paid back over 120 months. The date on which the last payment is due is called the maturity date.

An installment loan is said to be in **default** whenever a required payment is overdue. Loan agreements specify the consequences of defaulting, which may include late fees or even cancellation of the loan. Some loan agreements include an **acceleration clause** that makes the entire balance due and payable if you don't make payments as promised. A **prepayment penalty**—a fee charged for early repayment of the loan—can apply to certain loans.

The term of the loan affects both your monthly payments and the rate of interest you pay. The longer the term, all else being equal, the smaller your monthly payments. In addition, lenders usually charge higher rates of interest on loans with longer terms. Perhaps more important, you'll be paying more interest over the life of the loan. **Demonstration Problem 5.4** shows how much difference a longer term will make in total costs.

DEMONSTRATION PROBLEM 5.4 | Total Interest Paid on Loans with Different Maturities

Problem

You have been approved for a $10,000 car loan at 6 percent interest. The lender is willing to give you a 36-month loan or a 48-month loan. How much difference will it make in your payments and your total interest paid?

Strategy

This is a good application of the time value of money concepts introduced in Chapter 2. You can use your financial calculator to solve for the monthly payment. The total interest you'll pay over the life of the loan can be calculated as follows:

Total interest paid on loan = Total of monthly payments − Original loan amount

As an alternative to the calculator, you can use **Excel Worksheet 5.5** (Personal Financial Planner: Amortization of One- to Six-Year Loans).

EXCEL WORKSHEET

See **Excel Worksheet 5.5 (Personal Financial Planner: Amortization of One-to-Six-Year Loans) in WileyPLUS.**

Solution

1. Calculate monthly payments for each loan alternative:

   36-Month Loan:

   Enter N = 36, I = 6/12 = .5, PV = 10000 → Solve for PMT = $304.22

   48-Month Loan:

   Enter N = 48, I = 6/12 = .5, PV = 10000 → Solve for PMT = $234.85

2. Calculate the interest cost of each loan

36-Month Loan:	$304.22 × 36 = $10,951.92
	Minus $10,000.00
	Total Interest Cost $ 951.92
48-Month Loan:	$234.85 × 48 = $11,272.80
	Minus $10,000.00
	Total Interest Cost $ 1,272.80

   The difference in total interest cost between the two loans is therefore:
   $1,272.80 − $951.92 = $320.88

Reflection Question 3

Suppose you have a choice between a variable-rate auto loan with an initial rate of 5 percent and a fixed-rate loan with a rate of 6 percent. Would the variable-rate loan be a better option for you because of the lower monthly payment? What are the benefits and potential risks of the variable-rate loan?

Finance Charges

As with credit cards, there are alternative methods for calculating interest on consumer loans. Most common are the simple interest method, add-on interest method, and bank discount interest method. Most depository institutions use the simple interest method to determine finance charges on consumer loans, but you should always compare annual costs using the APR, which is the total annual finance charges divided by the average loan balance over the year. Lenders are required by law to clearly state the APR on the loan agreement and in any advertising materials.

To illustrate each type of interest calculation, let's consider an example in which you borrow $2,000 for one year at 12 percent interest and pay it back in equal monthly installments.

Simple Interest   Unlike credit cards, consumer loans usually don't require the payment of an annual fee, so the annual interest charges are the only finance charges. However, with some consumer loans, there may be an upfront fee, which results in a higher APR for the first year. For a simple interest loan with no fees, the quoted rate is also the APR. The amount of interest owed in each payment period for a simple interest loan is calculated using **Equation 5.3**:

$$\text{Interest} = \text{Remaining balance of loan} \times \text{Periodic rate} \tag{5.3}$$

$$= \text{Remaining balance of loan} \times \frac{\text{Nominal rate}}{\text{Payments per year}}$$

The periodic rate in our example is equal to 1 percent (12%/12 = 1%). The monthly payment on this loan will be $177.70. You can use your financial calculator to determine this: enter N = 12, I = 1, PV = 2000, and FV = 0 ; then solve for PMT = 177.70. The amount of interest you'll pay in the first month is:

$$\text{Interest} = \$2,000 \times 0.01 = \$20$$

Add-on Interest   If a lender uses the add-on interest method, the interest is added to the amount borrowed before the payments are calculated. The total is then divided by the number of payments to determine the payment amount, using **Equation 5.4**:

$$\text{Payment} = \frac{\text{Amount of loan} + (\text{Amount of loan} \times \text{Nominal rate} \times \text{Number of years})}{\text{Number of payments}} \tag{5.4}$$

For the $2,000 loan, the monthly payment calculated using the add-on interest method would be:

$$\text{Payment} = \frac{\$2,000 + (\$2,000 \times .012 \times 1)}{12} = \frac{\$2,240}{12} = \$186.67$$

Add-on interest will always result in a higher APR than simple interest because you'll always be paying interest on a higher balance than you actually still owe. Recall that we normally calculate APR as the total annual finance charge divided by the average monthly balance. Precise calculation of the APR for an add-on interest loan is a little tricky because the changing allocation of your payment dollars to interest and principal makes it more difficult to measure the average loan balance. You can roughly estimate the APR for an add-on interest loan using **Equation 5.5**:

$$\text{APR approximation for add-on interest loan} = \frac{\text{Total annual finance charges}}{\text{Original loan amount} \times 0.5} \tag{5.5}$$

The denominator (original loan amount × 0.5) is an approximation of the average loan balance, based on the idea that, because you're paying back the principal evenly over time, the average balance owed will be about half of the original amount borrowed. In our example, the total finance charge is 12 percent of $2,000, or $240, and the original loan amount is $2,000, yielding an APR approximation of 24 percent:

$$\text{APR approximation for add-on interest loan} = \frac{\$240}{\$2,000 \times 0.5} = 0.24, \text{ or } 24 \text{ percent}$$

Discount Interest   Like the add-on interest method, the discount interest method results in relatively expensive financing. With this method—which is more commonly used for single-payment loans, such as payday loans—the lender subtracts the interest due from the principal amount before the borrower gets the money. Then, at the maturity date, the entire principal amount is due. Because you pay the interest up front on the entire principal amount, but you receive only that amount less the interest, you again end up paying interest on funds that are not available to you.

Not surprisingly, the discount method also results in a higher APR than the simple interest method. Suppose in our example that you were repaying the $2,000 in a single payment instead of installments. Under the discount method, you'd receive $2,000 – $240 = $1,760 at the beginning of the loan, and repay the full $2,000 at the end of the year. Applying the APR formula to this scenario:

$$\text{APR} = \frac{\text{Total annual finance charges}}{\text{Average loan balance of the year}} = \frac{\$240}{\$1,760} = 0.136, \text{ or } 13.6 \text{ percent}$$

Note that the denominator in the equation is the amount of money that you actually have available to use, not the original borrowed amount. Because you don't repay any of the money until the end of the year with a single-payment loan, the average loan balance is constant throughout the period.

When the discount interest method is used for an installment loan rather than a single-payment loan, the APR is even higher. To approximate it, we use the same estimation method described for the add-on method. Here, your balance is $1,760 at the beginning of the loan. This amount will gradually be paid back over the life of the loan so that, on average, your balance is half the original amount. Thus, the approximate APR is $240/($1,760 × 0.5) = 27.3 percent.

Repayment of Principal

In order to completely pay back the loan over the loan term, your monthly payments necessarily must include some repayment of principal in addition to the interest. As you make principal payments, the remaining balance goes down, the amount of interest owed in that payment period goes down, and the amount of the payment going to principal increases.

As explained above, you can calculate the monthly payment on a simple interest loan with a financial calculator or spreadsheet if you know the periodic interest rate, the present value (the amount of the loan), and the number of payments (months to pay). In the simple interest example above, the monthly payment is $177.70 and the interest portion for the first payment is 1 percent of $2,000, or $20. The first payment therefore includes $20 in interest, with the remaining $157.70 going to reduce the principal balance owed to $1,842.30 ($2,000 – $157.70 = $1,842.30). This amount will be used to calculate the interest paid in the second month, with the difference again applied to repaying the principal of the loan.

Table 5.4 provides a complete amortization table of interest and principal payments for this 12-month installment loan. Note that although the payment stays constant, the portion allocated to interest declines and the portion that repays principal increases over the life of the loan. You can see that the total interest for the year is $132.37. The average monthly balance owed on the loan is $1,103.09. Based on the average loan balance for the year, you can confirm that the APR on a simple interest loan is equal to the nominal rate:

$$\text{APR} = \frac{\text{Total annual finance charges}}{\text{Average loan balance over the year}}$$

$$= \frac{\$132.37}{\$1,103.09} = 0.12, \text{ or } 12.0 \text{ percent}$$

Early Repayment of Installment Loans

If you want to pay off your installment loan balance before the maturity date, you can consult an amortization table for an approximation. Your lender will give you a more precise payoff

TABLE 5.4	Principal and Interest Payments for a Simple-Interest Loan ($2,000 loan, 12% annual rate, monthly payments)			
Month	**Beginning Balance**	**Monthly Payment**	**Monthly Interest**	**Principal Repayment**
1	$2,000.00	$177.70	$20.00	$157.70
2	1,842.30	177.70	18.42	159.27
3	1,683.03	177.70	16.83	160.87
4	1,522.16	177.70	15.22	162.48
5	1,359.68	177.70	13.60	164.10
6	1,195.58	177.70	11.96	165.74
7	1,029.84	177.70	10.30	167.40
8	862.44	177.70	8.62	169.07
9	693.37	177.70	6.93	170.76
10	522.61	177.70	5.23	172.47
11	350.13	177.70	3.50	174.20
12	175.94	177.70	1.76	175.94
Average Balance	$1,103.09			
Total Payments		$2,132.37		
Total Interest			$132.37	
Total Principal				$2,000.00

between monthly due dates by applying a daily interest rate (APR/365) to the additional days. You can use the amortization function in your financial calculator or spreadsheet to calculate the remaining balance at any point in time, as explained in **Demonstration Problem 5.5**.

DEMONSTRATION PROBLEM 5.5 | Calculating Simple Interest Loan Payoffs

Problem

Geoffrey Spinelli bought a car 3 years ago and financed it with a 60-month, simple interest car loan from his bank. The original loan balance was $15,000, with an APR of 6 percent. After making his 36th loan payment, Geoffrey wants to know what his remaining loan balance is because he's thinking about trading in his car for a new model.

Strategy

Most financial calculators include a built-in amortization table function that will allow you to find the balance owed after a given number of payments have been made. The directions below are for the Texas Instruments BAII Plus calculator, but if you have a different calculator, you should consult the instruction manual for help on the amortization function. Alternatively, you can again use Excel Worksheet 5.5 (Personal Financial Planner: Amortization of One- to Six-Year Loans).

Solution

1. Calculate the original monthly payment using the time value functions on the calculator.
   Enter N = 60, I = 6/12 = .5, PV = 15000; solve for PMT = 289.99.

2. Without clearing the information from step 1 above, push 2nd Amort. This will access the amortization table for the loan problem you entered in step 1. To calculate the balance owed, you will use the down arrow key to scroll through the variables and enter the number of payments you have already made as follows:

   a. The first screen will say P1 = 1. This is the indicator for the starting period of your loan, in this case, month 1. Do not change this. Push the down arrow key.

   b. The next item on the menu is P2 = 1. This is the indicator for the number of loan periods or payments you have already made. Because you've made 36 payments so far, type in 36 and push ENTER. Then push the down arrow key.

   c. The value that appears will be the balance owed on Geoffrey's loan after he has made 36 payments: BAL = $6,543.

Although it's not required for this problem, you can also use the amortization function to determine how much principal and interest Geoffrey has paid over the three years he has had this loan. After the balance is calculated, you can press the down arrow key again to find PRN, the total principal repaid between months 1 and 36 (P1 and P2), and once more to find the total interest (INT) paid in those 36 months. For this problem, PRN = $8,457 and INT = $1,983. Note that if you only wanted to know the principal and interest amounts for the 36th month, you could enter P1 = 36 and P2 = 36.

Other Loan Repayment Plans

A **balloon loan** is a special type of installment loan involving a final "balloon" payment that is substantially larger than the other installment payments. The amount of the balloon payment is usually calculated like the amount of an early repayment. For example, the payments on a simple interest balloon loan could be calculated using a 10-year amortization term, but require that the loan balance be paid in full at the end of three years. The balloon payment at the end is the same as what you would have paid if you had a 10-year simple interest loan and wanted to pay it off at the end of three years. Balloon loans are useful if you need the funds for only a short period of time but don't want to be burdened with a large monthly payment in the interim. Lenders like to issue this type of loan when interest rates are rising, because they prefer not to be locked into longer-term loans at low interest rates.

Although most loans require that you pay both principal and interest over the life of the loan, some lenders offer **interest-only loans**. These loans charge a stated APR on the balance owed in each period and require repayment of the full balance within a relatively short period of time, similar to a balloon loan. Construction loans for new homes are usually interest-only. When the home is completed, the owner or builder refinances the construction loan with a regular amortized mortgage.

Summary

Learning Objectives Review

LEARNING OBJECTIVE 5.1   Describe the role of consumer credit in your financial plan.

Any time you receive cash, goods, or services now and arrange to pay for them later, you are buying on **credit**. If you use credit to buy consumer goods or services, you're using **consumer credit**.

- Consumer credit allows you to spread the cost of more expensive purchases over time, but it also can have a negative impact on household financials due to the additional costs of interest and fees and the potential for overspending.

- The two major types of consumer credit are **closed-end credit**, which is usually a loan for a specific purpose that has a preset repayment period, and **open-end, or revolving, credit**, in which you are given a particular **credit limit or credit line** that you can borrow from and repay repeatedly.

- Consumer credit is available from a variety of financial institutions, including banks, credit unions, **consumer finance companies**, and **sales finance companies**.

- Obtaining consumer credit usually requires that you complete an application on which you will be asked to provide information that will allow the lender to assess your creditworthiness.

LEARNING OBJECTIVE 5.2   Maintain your creditworthiness, and understand your consumer credit rights.

In evaluating whether to extend credit to you, lenders commonly evaluate your creditworthiness in five areas, sometimes called the Five Cs of Credit: capacity, capital, collateral, character, and conditions.

- If your credit is substandard in one or more of these areas, you may still be able to qualify for a loan if you can get someone to be a **cosigner** on the loan, but you should take action to fix your credit problems.

- Strategies for reducing debt include: setting up a repayment plan, obtaining a debt consolidation loan, taking a second job, developing a zero-based budget, living with parents, and selling assets.

- Consumer credit laws give you the rights to obtain full information from prospective lenders regarding consumer credit terms and costs, to be free from discrimination, to receive clear and accurate billing statements, to have your financial information be private, to be treated fairly and respectfully by debt collectors, and to have your credit information reported accurately.

- **Credit bureaus** provide credit reports and credit scores to prospective lenders, employers, and landlords. You should check your credit report regularly for accuracy and take steps to improve your creditworthiness. It is important to avoid more serious financial difficulties that might lead to personal **bankruptcy**.

LEARNING OBJECTIVE 5.3   Evaluate credit card choices based on terms and costs.

The various types of **credit cards** include **bank credit cards**, **retail credit cards**, and **travel and entertainment cards**. A **smart card** is a card embedded with a computer chip that can store information and **electronic cash**.

- Credit cards commonly carry high rates of interest and may require the payment of an annual fee. Other costs include penalties for making payments late and exceeding the credit limit.

- The finance charge assessed on unpaid balances differs depending on the method used by the lender to calculate the account balance.

- The **APR** on credit cards is calculated using **Equation 5.1**:

$$\text{Annual percentage rate} = \frac{\text{Total annual finance charges} + \text{Annual fee}}{\text{Average loan balance of the year}}$$

This rate is usually higher than that for other forms of borrowing, although some cards will offer a low teaser rate to attract new customers.

- The **finance charge** for the billing period is calculated using **Equation 5.2**:

$$\text{Finance charge} = \text{Periodic rate} \times \text{Account balance owed}$$

where the periodic rate is 1/12 of the APR and the account balance owed is based on the **average daily balance**.

- The amount you pay in interest will also depend on whether you have a **grace period** between the **transaction date** and the **billing date**. You must at least make the **minimum payment** by the **due date** to avoid late payment fees.

LEARNING OBJECTIVE 5.4   Evaluate consumer loan choices based on your financial needs, loan terms, and costs.

Financial institutions offer a variety of consumer loan products. The most common types of consumer loans are **home equity loans**, automobile loans, and student loans.

- Consumer loans are typically **installment loans** and require repayment of interest and **principal** over a designated period of time in equal monthly payments. Secured loans allow the lender to take the **collateral** if you don't meet the repayment terms of the loan and sometimes involve a **lien** against your property.

- **Fixed-rate loans** charge the same rate of interest for the life of the loan, and **variable-rate loans** have rates that vary with market interest rates. Most loans are amortized, with payments including both interest and repayment of principal. Exceptions include **single-payment loans** and **interest-only loans**. **Balloon loans** are installment loans involving a final payment that is substantially larger than the other installment payments.

- It's important to shop around for loans, carefully comparing their features and costs. The details of your contractual obligation will be spelled out in the **promissory note**. Factors to consider include interest rate, term, and collateral requirements.

- The interest rates charged for consumer loans can vary dramatically among types of loans and different lenders. Furthermore, lenders use different methods of interest calculation, so you should always compare loans based on the APR. The interest on a simple interest loan is calculated according to **Equation 5.3** and is equal to the APR.

$$\text{Interest} = \text{Remaining balance of loan} \times \text{Periodic rate}$$

- In general, simple interest loans are a better alternative than add-on or discount loans, which will have a higher APR for a given nominal rate. The payment for an add-on loan is calculated based on **Equation 5.4**.

$$\text{Payment} = \frac{\text{Amount of loan} + (\text{Amount of loan} \times \text{Nominal rate} \times \text{Number of years})}{\text{Number of payments}}$$

The APR for an add-on loan can be estimated based on **Equation 5.5**:

$$\text{APR approximation for add-on interest loan}$$
$$= \frac{\text{Total annual finance charges}}{\text{Original loan amount} \times 0.5}$$

- Other important considerations in comparing loan alternatives include term of the loan, required fees, and the effect of early repayment. Some consumer loans may include an **acceleration clause** or a **prepayment penalty**.

Excel Worksheets

5.1 Personal Financial Planner: Household Credit Summary

5.2 Personal Financial Planner: How Long Will It Take to Pay Off Your Balance?

5.3 Personal Financial Planner: Comparing Credit Cards

5.4 Personal Financial Planner: How Much Can You Borrow with a Home Equity Loan?

5.5 Personal Financial Planner: Amortization of One- to Six-Year Loans

Key Terms

acceleration clause   5-29
annual percentage rate (APR)   5-22
average daily balance   5-23
balloon loan   5-33
bank credit card   5-20
bankruptcy   5-18
billing date   5-22
cash advance   5-20
closed-end credit   5-3
collateral   5-4
consumer credit   5-2
consumer finance company   5-4
convenience check   5-20
cosigner   5-9

credit   5-2
credit bureau   5-10
credit card   5-20
credit limit or credit line   5-3
default   5-28
due date   5-22
electronic cash   5-21
finance charge   5-23
fixed-rate loan   5-28
grace period   5-22
home equity   5-25
home equity loan   5-25
installment loan   5-28
interest-only loan   5-33

lien   5-28
minimum payment   5-23
open-end, or revolving, credit   5-3
prepayment penalty   5-29
principal   5-28
promissory note   5-27
retail credit card   5-20
sales finance company   5-4
secured loan   5-27
single-payment loan   5-28
smart card   5-21
transaction date   5-22
travel and entertainment (T&E) card   5-21
variable-rate loan   5-28

WileyPLUS

Practice Questions to check your understanding, Peer-to-Peer Videos, Interactives, and many other resources are available in WileyPLUS.

Concept Review Questions

1. Why is the availability of consumer credit good for the economy?

2. What is the difference between consumer credit and other types of borrowing? Give some examples of each.

3. Penny has just found out from her dentist that she needs to have her wisdom teeth removed. Because she has been experiencing some jaw complications, she cannot delay this expenditure, but she does not have dental insurance. Explain the advantages and disadvantages of using credit to pay for this expense.

4. Your friend tells you that he always makes the minimum payment on his credit cards. Explain to him why he should pay more than the minimum payment each month.

5. Describe the relationship between the maturity of a loan and the monthly payment.

6. If a lender assesses your credit capacity and determines that it will approve a loan to you, does that necessarily imply that you can afford the loan? Why or why not?

7. What are the Five Cs of Credit? Give an example of each.

8. Assume that one of your high-priority financial goals is to pay off your current credit card balance of $5,000. The rate of interest on this debt is 18%, and you have been making minimum payments only. What are some strategies you can employ to pay off this debt as soon as possible?

9. How is annual percentage rate (APR) different from and similar to annual percentage yield (APY), which was defined and explained in Chapter 3?

10. You currently have $10,000 in a savings account at a local financial institution earning 2 percent interest. Your outstanding consumer credit totals $3,000 and costs you 12 percent interest per year. Your monthly debt payment is $60. Should you take the money from your savings to repay the debt? Why or why not?

11. Explain why the rates charged on secured loans are usually lower than those for unsecured personal loans.

12. How can a debt consolidation loan help you to reduce your outstanding credit obligations?

13. Under what circumstances would you recommend that someone consult a consumer credit counselor?

14. Under what circumstances might it be advisable to declare bankruptcy? If you do so, what impact will the bankruptcy have on your personal finances?

15. Explain why lenders often charge lower rates of interest on loans with shorter maturities.

16. Distinguish between simple interest, add-on interest, and discount interest. Which type generally results in the lowest APR, given the same nominal rate of interest? Why are the APRs different?

17. If you discover an error on your credit report, what should you do to correct it?

18. If you discover a fraudulent or incorrect charge on a credit card bill, what should you do to correct it?

19. Perry's insurance agent recently notified him that his auto insurance premium is going to increase because his credit report shows so many late payments in the last six months. In addition, the agent noted that Perry had applied for several new credit cards during that time period. Perry complains to his friends that this treatment is totally unfair and argues that there is no possible relationship between his bad credit and his risk of having auto accidents or damaging his vehicle. Do you agree that it is unfair to use credit information in setting insurance premiums? What is the justification for this practice?

20. You have just received a credit card solicitation in the mail that offers you a 4 percent APR. Your current card, which has an outstanding balance of $5,000, has an APR of 14 percent. What factors should you consider in making the decision to transfer your balance?

21. Your younger sister is 18 years old and just starting college. At present, she has no credit history.

  a. What are some strategies you can suggest to help her build a credit history?

  b. How can you help her avoid getting into trouble with credit while she is a student?

Application Problems

1. The total annual finance charges on your credit card account are $200. You also pay an annual fee of $50. If your average outstanding balance during the year is $1,000, what is the annual percentage rate?

2. You have just received a credit card solicitation in the mail that offers you a 4 percent APR. Your current card has an APR of 14 percent. How much interest will you save the first month by switching cards, assuming you make no additional charges and both cards calculate interest based on the average daily balance of $5,000?

3. Your home is currently valued at $120,000. You have a first mortgage in the amount of $80,000. If your lender applies a 90 percent loan-to-value ratio for approving home equity lines of credit, what is the maximum amount you can borrow, assuming that you meet all other lender requirements?

4. Your credit card lender charges an annual rate of 15 percent on the average daily balance. Your balance on March 10, the end of the last billing cycle, was $5,000. The following transaction was posted to your account during the billing cycle:

3/15	New credit purchase	$500
3/20	Payment received	$750
4/1	New credit purchase	$1,000

The last day of the monthly billing cycle is April 10. Calculate the finance charge.

5. Your credit card lender charges an annual rate of 15 percent on the average daily balance. Your balance on March 10, the end of the last billing cycle, was $5,000. The following transaction was posted to your account during the billing cycle:

| 3/20 | Payment received | $750 |

The last day of the monthly billing cycle is April 10. Calculate the finance charge.

6. Suppose the average household in the United States pays $1,340 in interest and fees on credit cards each year. If a household could instead contribute this amount of money each year to a retirement savings account earning 6 percent per year compounded annually, how much money would be in the account 40 years from now?

7. If you owe $1,000 and the APR is 10%, what monthly payment would you need to make to reduce your debt to zero within two years?

8. Calculate the monthly payment, rounded to the nearest dollar, for a three-year $10,000 simple interest car loan if the loan terms specify a rate of 6 percent with monthly payments.

9. What is the APR for a $1,000, two-year, 10 percent simple interest installment loan with monthly payments?

10. What is the approximate APR for a $1,000, two-year add-on loan with a 10 percent quoted rate?

11. What is the approximate APR for a $1,000, two-year discount interest single-payment loan with a quoted rate of 10 percent?

12. For a $3,000, three-year loan, calculate the APR if the loan is an 8 percent simple interest single-payment loan.

13. For a $3,000, three-year 8 percent loan with monthly payments, how much will you pay in interest over the life of the loan?

14. For a $3,000, three-year 6 percent add-on interest installment loan, calculate the approximate APR.

15. Danny's original car loan amount was $13,000, and the loan is a 6 percent simple interest 48-month loan.

  a. What is the monthly payment?

  b. What is the APR?

16. Chuan took out a $13,000 car loan at 6 percent simple interest for 48 months. What is the remaining balance on his loan after two years, or 24 months? (Hint: Use the amortization function on your financial calculator or Excel Worksheet 5.5.)

17. Marie graduated from college with $20,000 in student loan debt. The annual simple interest rate on her loans is 5 percent, and she will make monthly payments for 10 years.

  a. What is the monthly payment?

  b. What is the APR?

18. Constanza graduated from college with $20,000 in student loan debt. The annual simple interest rate on her loan is 5 percent, and she will make monthly payments for 10 years. What is the remaining balance on her loan after five years, or 60 months? (Hint: Use the amortization function on your financial calculator or Excel Worksheet 5.5.)

19. You have after-tax monthly income of $1,200, and your monthly debt payments total $300. What is your debt payment ratio?

20. Ellen's gross monthly income is $2,500. Her take-home pay is 80 percent of her gross income. She currently pays $75 per month for credit cards and $310 per month for a car loan. She is considering the purchase of a $1,500 living room set, and the store has offered financing with payments of $50 per month.

   a. What is Ellen's debt payment ratio before the furniture purchase?

   b. If she borrows the money to buy the furniture, what will be her debt payment ratio?

   c. Assuming that she has already comparison-shopped for the living room set, what other factors should she consider before making this credit decision?

Case Applications

1. You are out shopping with your friend Andrea and find some wonderful bargains on last season's clothing. You are standing next to Andrea in the checkout line when both her credit cards are declined. She laughs it off and rummages around in her purse for her checkbook, saying that she probably just made a late payment. You are not so sure. You recall other instances in which her card has been turned down, and you know that she is always spending more on clothes than her income would seem to justify. When you ask Andrea about her credit, she confesses that she has gotten in over her head. In fact, she recently applied for a new credit card, figuring that she would be able to make overdue payments on her other cards using cash advances from the new one.

   a. Does Andrea exhibit any warning signs of credit trouble? (Hint: See Interactive: Are You in Debt Danger?)

   b. If Andrea asks for your advice, where would you suggest she go for more information? Would you suggest that she seek professional help? If so, where would you recommend she go?

   c. What are some strategies that Andrea might employ to dig herself out of this debt trap?

2. Mike and Allison Randall are middle-income baby boomers. Mike works as an engineer for a well-established company, and Allison works part-time so that they can afford to send their two children to a private elementary school. Although they have a combined pretax income of $120,000 and after-tax income of $90,000, the Randalls' budget has been a little tight ever since they decided to buy a larger home two years ago. As a result, they are not currently making contributions to savings other than those required by Mike's employer for his retirement account. Allison estimates that their debt ratio is about 90 percent and their debt payment ratio is 35 percent. One day, Allison is surprised to come across a bill for a credit card she did not know they had. According to the statement, the card is maxed out to the full credit limit of $10,000, and the minimum monthly payment is $200. When Allison confronts her husband, he confesses to her that he has a small gambling problem and has been too embarrassed to tell her about it. In addition to the amount he owes on the account she discovered, he owes an additional $5,000 on another. Mike tells his wife that he has been looking into the possibility of a debt consolidation loan.

   a. What risks do Mike and Allison face as a result of their high level of debt payments? If they have little in savings, what options would they have in the event that Mike lost his job?

   b. Why is it important that the Randalls confront the cause of their credit problems and not simply deal with the symptoms? Where would you suggest they go for help?

   c. What might be some problems associated with applying for and being approved for the debt consolidation loan?

   d. What are some strategies that this couple should consider for dealing with their debt problems?

3. Lana and Zack Worzala were married a year ago, and they are thinking about buying a home. They have saved $10,000 to put toward the down payment, but they are wondering if they should pay off some of their consumer debt instead. Their combined gross monthly income is $5,000, and their after-tax monthly income is $4,000. They have the following debts:

	Balance Owed	APR	Monthly Minimum Payment	Payments Left
Zack's car loan	$2,000	6%	$340	6
Lana's Visa	1,300	18	35	
Zack's MasterCard	4,200	21	110	
Lana's student loan	3,370	5	37	114
Zack's student loan	10,600	6	122	114

   a. What is the Worzalas' debt payment ratio, based on their current situation?

   b. Assume that mortgage lenders require that the mortgage debt service ratio for a new home purchase not exceed 28 percent of gross monthly income. Given Zack and Lana's gross income, what is the maximum mortgage debt service amount that would be allowed by a lender (including mortgage principal and interest, property taxes, and insurance)?

   c. If mortgage lenders require that total debt payments not exceed 36 percent of after-tax disposable income, will Zack and Lana have any trouble meeting this requirement? Explain.

   d. Zack and Lana estimate that, given the prices of homes in the area and the costs of property taxes and insurance, the minimum mortgage debt service they would have to pay is $1,000 per month (including mortgage principal and interest, property taxes, and insurance). If that is the case, will they be able to get a loan with their current debt obligations, assuming that the lender's maximum debt payment ratio is 36 percent? Should they consider applying some of their savings to debt repayment?

CHAPTER 6

Making Automobile and Housing Decisions

Sasha, CelebrityHomePhotos/Newscom; inset: Kristin Callahan/Everett Collection/Alamy Live New/Alamy Stock Photo

Feature Story

Most people have financial goals related to cars and housing. For some, it's the purchase of a new car. Others may be saving to buy their first home. For Taylor Swift, this was a condo with views of the Nashville skyline, purchased when she was just 20. Since that time, she has bought several homes in different areas of the country. The total value of her real estate holdings, including this $18 million seaside estate in Rhode Island, was estimated to be $81 million in 2019.

When you hear about celebrities spending millions on cars and homes, you might wonder how they can afford to be so lavish. Would it surprise you to know that the extremely wealthy usually spend less on housing as a percentage of income or wealth than do typical households? For example, Taylor Swift is one of the highest paid celebrities in the world, with annual income in 2019 of more than $100 million and estimated net worth of $360 million. Her total annual housing costs on this home, including mortgage, taxes, and insurance, are probably less than $1 million. Even adding the costs of decorating and furnishing, housing costs are a fairly small share of her total income.

For most of us, cars and houses are our largest purchases. Auto and housing expenses account for about 50 percent of the typical household budget. Furthermore, auto and home loans that finance these purchases represent the lion's share of household debt. For these reasons, your goals and decisions relating to the purchase or lease of automobiles and housing are extremely important components of your financial plan and deserve more careful deliberation than other purchase decisions. In this chapter, we'll outline the process to use for making auto and housing decisions, explain the pros and cons of renting versus buying, and review the contract and financing choices available to you.

LEARNING OBJECTIVES	TOPICS	DEMONSTRATION PROBLEMS
6.1 Evaluate your household automobile needs and budget.	**6.1 Making Auto Decisions on a Budget** • Making Smart Purchase Decisions • Assessing Needs and Affordability • Evaluating Vehicle Choices	**6.1** Calculating the Price You Can Afford to Pay for a Car **6.2** Will a Hybrid Save You Money?

(continued)

(continued)

LEARNING OBJECTIVES	TOPICS	DEMONSTRATION PROBLEMS
6.2 Decide whether to lease or buy a vehicle, and negotiate the terms for purchase and financing.	**6.2 Should You Lease or Buy a Car?** • Leasing versus Buying • Negotiating the Auto Purchase Price • Making Consumer Complaints	**6.3** Comparing the Costs of Leasing and Buying a Car
6.3 Evaluate your housing needs and budget.	**6.3 Making Housing Decisions on a Budget** • Housing Needs over the Life Cycle • The Rent-versus-Buy Decision • How Much House Can You Afford?	**6.4** Comparing the Costs of Renting and Buying a Home **6.5** Calculating an Affordable Home Price
6.4 Evaluate mortgage financing alternatives.	**6.4 Mortgage Financing** • What Is a Mortgage? • Factors That Affect Mortgage Payments • When to Refinance	**6.6** Calculating the Impact of APR on Monthly Mortgage Payments **6.7** Comparing 15-Year and 30-Year Mortgages **6.8** Should You Pay Points to Get a Lower Mortgage Rate? **6.9** Qualifying for a Mortgage Based on Lender Ratios
6.5 Identify factors that affect home prices, and explain the other costs of completing a real estate transaction.	**6.5 Completing a Real Estate Transaction** • Determinants of Real Estate Value • The Home-Buying Process • The Closing	

6.1 Making Auto Decisions on a Budget

> **LEARNING OBJECTIVE 6.1**
> Evaluate your household automobile needs and budget.

The decision process for evaluating large consumer purchases, such as autos and houses, is actually the same one that you should apply to most consumer purchases. In this section and the next one, we explain the process, which is illustrated in **Figure 6.1**, and discuss how to apply it to an automobile purchase.

FIGURE 6.1   **Decision Process for Consumer Purchases**   You can apply this decision process to any major consumer purchase.

Making Smart Purchase Decisions

Whenever you decide to buy something, you're also deciding *not* to spend the money on something else and *not* to save or invest those funds. Unfortunately, it has never been tougher to refrain from excess spending. Most people are bombarded daily with media ads intended to make them overcome their carefully developed financial plans and buy more "stuff." If you don't have the money right now, no problem—there are plenty of credit cards and offers of "zero-interest financing" or "no payments until next year." It's easy to see why so many families in the United States are in financial trouble—it's simply much easier to spend than it is to stick to a budget. And it's also easy to see why retailers would prefer that you forget your budget and buy their products—their companies' financial health depends on it. That's why it's important to carefully consider each major purchase.

Keep Your Financial Goals in Mind

Every purchase decision influences your ability to achieve your short-term and long-term goals. Therefore, consumer purchase and credit decisions should be directly related to your financial goals. Necessities—things you need in order to live, like food, clothing, and shelter—must have priority over luxuries, things you want to have but can live without, like a new car, a home theater system, or a spring break trip to Mexico. All spending decisions have a ripple effect on your financial plan. Money spent on one thing means less money to spend on another or to save for the future.

Your goals may change over time, so it makes sense to reevaluate as necessary. For example, the purchase of a car may not have been on your original list of goals because you had an older car that was working just fine. But if your car has just "died" and you have to have one to get to school or work, then you probably need to add a car to your list.

Don't Ignore the Small Stuff

Buying a car or a house is a major purchase decision, but large purchases aren't the only ones to which the decision process shown in Figure 6.1 applies. In fact, when people analyze their excess spending, they often find that the little stuff is to blame—clothes, books, food, and other less expensive consumer items that seem inconsequential alone but can add up to thousands of dollars each year. While you may not have included specific goals in your financial plan related to such purchases, you probably did include goals related to saving more or reducing household debt. Always keep in mind that every dollar spent on consumer purchases is one less dollar spent on these goals.

Why Auto and Housing Decisions Are Harder

For small purchases, researching and evaluating your alternatives can be a pretty simple process. In contrast, auto and housing decisions can be significantly more complex. They deserve more attention for several reasons, including the following:

- Houses and cars are more expensive than other consumer purchases, so they have a much larger impact on your budget.
- There is a wide selection from which to choose, including both new and used.
- You need to examine a car or a house in person, and you may need professional help to determine quality.
- There are hidden costs associated with ownership.
- The prices are often negotiable.
- There are many financing alternatives.

In the rest of this chapter, we'll apply the purchase process shown in Figure 6.1 to auto and housing decisions, identifying needs, assessing costs, determining affordability, and evaluating financing alternatives. With both auto and housing decisions, you'll usually have the choice of whether to lease or buy. We'll therefore explore the advantages and disadvantages of your financing choices in some detail.

Assessing Needs and Affordability

The first two steps in the consumer purchase decision process require that you determine what you need and what you can afford. In many cases, needs and affordability may be quite different from wants, particularly when you're just starting out on your own.

Do You Need a Car?

In most suburban and rural areas, having access to a car is a necessity. However, most families could get by with fewer cars, or less expensive cars. In urban areas, mass transportation can often be adequate for access to work, shopping, and recreation locations. Nevertheless, nine out of ten households in the United States own at least one vehicle, and the average household owns two.

If a vehicle is not a necessity, its purchase should be weighed against other luxury and convenience expenditures. If it will reduce or slow your ability to achieve more important goals, you might want to give serious consideration to alternative methods of meeting your transportation needs—such as carpooling, using mass transit, bicycling, walking, or renting a car for weekends and holidays. At fairly low daily rates and no maintenance obligations, occasional renting is a practical and often overlooked alternative to owning a car, particularly for urban consumers.

Can You Afford a Car?

Even if you need something, you may not be able to afford it. Therefore, it's important to evaluate your ability to meet your auto purchase goal in light of your household budget. Many people make the mistake of estimating the cost of automobile ownership based on their auto lease or loan payment alone. Many other costs should enter into the decision process and can amount to thousands of additional dollars per year. For a rough estimate, various websites provide calculators to help you determine the cost of owning a car.

Your automobile costs will include both fixed expenses and variable expenses. **Fixed expenses**—those that remain constant each month, such as loan or lease payments, insurance, and registration—are easy to keep track of. **Variable expenses**, such as gasoline and maintenance costs, differ from month to month and can therefore be more difficult to estimate.

To better estimate these expenses, you should keep a record of your auto-related expenses for a period of time, recording mileage, gasoline, and maintenance expenditures. If some or all of your auto expenses are tax-deductible as business expenses, it is absolutely necessary that you keep a written record for your tax accountant to justify the deduction in the event of an IRS audit. You can use **Excel Worksheet 6.1** (Personal Financial Planner: Auto Costs Log) to keep track of your auto costs. The various types of automobile costs are defined in **Table 6.1**.

EXCEL WORKSHEET

See **Excel Worksheet 6.1** (**Personal Financial Planner: Auto Costs Log**) in **WileyPLUS.**

TABLE 6.1   **Costs of Automobile Ownership**

Fixed Expenses	Expenses That Stay the Same Each Month
Insurance	State law usually requires that you have automobile liability insurance. This cost will increase each year, particularly if you have any traffic violations or accidents. Some makes and models of cars, such as high-performance vehicles, are more expensive to insure.
Finance charges	If you finance the purchase of your car, you will have to pay interest on the loan or lease. Payments are typically fixed for a period of months.
Depreciation	Loss in value due to wear and tear. You can estimate this as the initial value divided by number of months of useful life, but new cars often lose more value in the first year.
Registration and taxes	States may charge a fixed price per vehicle for registration or use a sliding scale, with more expensive vehicles being more expensive to register. All sales of motor vehicles are subject to sales tax, and a few states impose personal property taxes on vehicles.
Variable Expenses	**Expenses That Differ from Month to Month and May Depend on How Much and Where You Drive**
Fuel	Estimate this expense based on mileage driven in a typical year and average fuel costs, or keep a careful record for a period of time.
Repairs and maintenance	Typically, maintenance costs are very low for new cars but increase with vehicle age, particularly after the warranty period has expired.
Parking and tolls	These expenses can vary widely depending on where you live and work.

You can compare the costs of different vehicles by considering the total annual cost or the cost per mile. Because a portion of the total cost is fixed, the cost per mile decreases with mileage driven as the fixed costs are spread over a larger number of miles. **Case Study 6.1** illustrates an auto purchase decision.

Case Study 6.1

Monkey Business Images/Shutterstock.com

The Walkers Estimate the Costs of an Additional Vehicle

Problem

Caleb and Madison Walker currently own two vehicles and are considering the purchase of another vehicle for their teenage daughter Olivia. After carefully considering their budget, they estimate that they can put $2,000 from their savings toward a down payment on a car and $300 per month toward license, registration, and maintenance costs by reducing expenditures on food, entertainment, and vacations. Olivia will pay the regular operating expenses and insurance herself. The table below summarizes the Walkers' estimates of expected fixed and variable costs. A range of values for each category is included because some costs depend on their choice of vehicle.

Fixed Costs	Monthly	Annual
Insurance	$40–$60	$480–$720
License and registration	$10–$30	$120–$360
Variable Costs		
Gasoline, oil	$60–$100	$720–$1,200
Maintenance	$20–$50	$240–$600
Total Costs	$130–$240	$1,560–$2,880

Given the Walkers' budget limitations, how much can they afford to apply to a car lease or loan payment?

Strategy

First, estimate the range of additional costs for the vehicle. Then subtract this from the family's $300 monthly budget to determine how much they can apply to financing costs.

Solution   Because Olivia will pay the operating costs and insurance, the only expenses Caleb and Madison need to consider are the costs of license, registration, and maintenance. Using the higher estimates, these will not be more than $30 + $50 = $80 per month. With a budget of $300, they can allocate at least $220 per month to the financing costs.

Evaluating Vehicle Choices

The next step in the purchase process is to do your research by identifying your choices and comparing them based on attributes and price. The purchase of an automobile is a multidimensional decision. If cost were not a factor, you could purchase a new car with every option available. Most people, however, are not independently wealthy and therefore must make their purchase decisions based on predefined priorities.

What are the key vehicle features that will meet your needs? Although price is usually a major factor, practical considerations also may include safety and reliability, size, and fuel efficiency. You should be sure to test drive the vehicle under normal driving conditions to judge the smoothness of ride and degree of road noise. Qualitative features, such as comfort, color, and sportiness, may also be important to you.

Whatever your needs and wants, there are many sources of information on vehicles, their features, and their costs. Two good online sources are the Kelley Blue Book (**www.kbb.com**) and Edmunds (**www.edmunds.com**). In the following sections, we'll discuss factors that commonly play a role in vehicle decisions, including price, age, equipment, fuel economy, and safety.

Price

Unlike the prices of most consumer products, car prices are usually negotiable. Manufacturers provide a printed form for new cars that identifies the manufacturer's suggested retail price (MSRP) for the car with its accessories and options, often referred to as the **sticker price**. However, some dealers use the term "sticker price" to refer to their own sticker, which gives the total price as the MSRP *plus* additional charges for delivery, detailing, and other dealer-provided services. The **dealer's invoice price** is the price that the dealer paid to purchase the vehicle from the manufacturer and is an important piece of information to have in the negotiation process (discussed later in this chapter).

Used cars are sold by dealers and private owners. Although sellers will advertise an asking price, the actual price that you end up paying will depend on the motivation of the seller, the local market for the vehicle, and your ability to negotiate effectively.

The price you can afford to pay is directly related to your household budget and financial goals. If you plan to borrow money to buy a car and you know how much you have available for up-front costs and how much you can allocate to your total automobile costs each month, you can use time-value-of-money calculations to determine the price range you can afford. It doesn't make sense to waste your time looking at vehicles that are outside your price range. We work through the process of finding the price you can afford to pay in **Demonstration Problem 6.1**.

DEMONSTRATION PROBLEM 6.1 | Calculating the Price You Can Afford to Pay for a Car

Problem

You have $2,000 for a down payment on a car. After taking into consideration the additional fixed and variable costs of ownership, you have determined you can afford up to $220 per month for auto financing costs. Your bank has quoted you a 6 percent rate on a 48-month car loan.

a. What is the maximum loan you can afford?

b. How much difference does a longer-term loan make—say, six years instead of four—assuming the same interest rate?

Strategy

Because you will pay equal monthly payments for a set period of time and you're interested in the loan value *today*, this is a present value of an annuity problem, as explained in Chapter 2. Here, we'll use a financial calculator to solve the problem, but you can alternatively use **Excel Worksheet 6.2** (Personal Financial Planner: Maximum Affordable Car Price) to find the solution.

> **EXCEL WORKSHEET**
>
> See **Excel Worksheet 6.2 (Personal Financial Planner: Maximum Affordable Car Price) in WileyPLUS.**

Solution

a. Using your financial calculator, enter PMT = −$220, N = 48, and I = 6/12 = 0.5. Solve for PV = $9,368. The PV amount represents the *maximum loan you can afford*. Add this amount to your available down payment funds, to find the maximum total car price you can afford, including taxes and fees:

$$\$9{,}368 + \$2{,}000 = \$11{,}368$$

b. If you change the term of the loan from 48 months to 72 months, you can borrow more for the same monthly payment. You can calculate this by changing the number of periods and recalculating the PV. If you work this out using a calculator or Excel Worksheet 6.2, you'll find the maximum loan amount is $13,275 for the six-year loan, so the affordable car price is $15,275. **Interactive: What Car Can You Afford to Buy?** shows how your budget and different loan terms impact affordability.

> **INTERACTIVE**
>
> Go to **Interactive: What Car Can You Afford to Buy? in WileyPLUS.**

New versus Used

Based on what you can afford to pay, you may find that you can't consider a new car. If a used vehicle is an option, many attractive alternatives are available through both private sale and dealerships. You can often buy a low-mileage car that is one or two years old at a fraction of the cost of a new car. There is some risk to buying an older vehicle that may have hidden defects, but you can minimize that risk by taking the car to a mechanic for a systems checkup. In addition, dealerships usually offer a 30-day warranty. If you're buying from a private party, be sure to ask the seller why the car is being sold and what kind of maintenance has been done over its life. Although there's no guarantee that you'll get an honest answer, you might learn something useful, so it's worth asking. You should request that the seller provide you with a CARFAX Vehicle History Report from **www.carfax.com**. This report will include reported accidents, repairs, and regular maintenance visits for the vehicle.

Equipment

Depending on make and model, vehicles can differ substantially in standard equipment, options, and accessories. A checklist can be helpful for first deciding on your wants and needs and then checking available cars against your list. You can use **Excel Worksheet 6.3** (Personal Financial Planner: Auto Features Comparison), which provides a checklist for this purpose.

> **EXCEL WORKSHEET**
>
> See **Excel Worksheet 6.3 (Personal Financial Planner: Auto Features Comparison) in WileyPLUS.**

As you consider different vehicles, keep track of which ones satisfy your requirements. Keep in mind that some options are expensive, so you'll need to consider whether they are worth the cost. For example, would you pay $2,000 for a sunroof?

Size and Fuel Economy

All new car dealers are required by federal law to report the estimated mileage per gallon (MPG) for city and highway driving. Auto manufacturers are gradually improving the fuel efficiency of their vehicles. Obviously, larger and heavier cars are less fuel-efficient and are ultimately more costly to operate, particularly if you drive a lot.

You can calculate annual gasoline costs using **Equation 6.1**:

$$\text{Annual gasoline costs} = \text{Gallons per year} \times \text{Price per gallon} \qquad (6.1)$$

$$= \frac{\text{Annual miles driven}}{\text{MPG}} \times \text{Price per gallon}$$

For example, suppose you're trying to decide whether to purchase a fuel-efficient car (40 MPG) or a gas-guzzler (10 MPG) and the price of gas is $4 per gallon. If you expect to drive the car 10,000 miles annually, what will the difference in fuel efficiency cost per year? Using Equation 6.1, the annual gasoline costs for the gas guzzler would be (10,000/10) × $4 = $4,000, whereas the gas for the fuel-efficient car would cost only (10,000/40) × $4 = $1,000, a difference of $3,000 per year of ownership.

In Europe, where the price of gasoline is much higher than in the United States, consumers prefer to buy small, fuel-efficient cars, such as gasoline-electric hybrids and fully electric vehicles, or to use public transportation. Alternative-fuel vehicles sometimes cost more than their gasoline-powered alternatives, but the extra cost might be worth it if you save enough on gas or if government incentives are available. Smart consumers should apply their financial skills to figure out whether such a purchase makes good financial sense in addition to adding perceived social value. **Demonstration Problem 6.2** provides an example of this type of calculation.

DEMONSTRATION PROBLEM 6.2 | Will a Hybrid Save You Money?

Problem

How long will it take to recoup the $1,600 difference in price between a hybrid and a regular sedan, based on the fuel economy differences shown in the table below and assuming gas costs $3 per gallon and you drive 15,000 miles per year?

Feature	Honda Accord Hybrid	Honda Accord
MPG	48 highway	31 highway
MSRP (2019)	$26,215	$24,615
Tax Incentives	None	None
Warranty	3 years/36,000 miles limited warranty; 5 years/60,000 miles for power train; battery warranty varies by state (8–10 years)	3 years/36,000 miles limited warranty; 5 years/60,000 miles for powertrain

Source: www.honda.com

Strategy

Calculate the annual gasoline cost savings for the hybrid. Calculate the years to recoup the price differential.

Solution

Annual gasoline costs	= (Annual Miles Driven/MPG) × Price per gallon
Cost of gas for nonhybrid	= (15,000/31) × $3 = $1,452
Cost of gas for hybrid	= (15,000/48) × $3 = $938
Savings	= $1,452 − $938 = $514 per year
Years to recoup hybrid cost	= $1,600/514 = 3.1 years

Safety

The odds of having a minor accident, or fender bender, in any given year are fairly high, and they increase with the number of miles you drive each year. Given the high risk of accidents, or even fatalities, on the road, safety should be a factor in any automobile purchase.

Seat belts and air bags are required in all new autos, and auto manufacturers are continuously working to develop new ways to keep drivers and passengers safe. Most automobile manufacturers are incorporating technology designed to improve how you drive. For example, some cars now warn you when you're too close to another car. More advanced systems can even activate the car's brakes automatically in dangerous situations and tug your seat belt to wake you.

Reflection Question 1

How important is safety to your choice of vehicle? Would it make a difference if you were buying a car for your teenage son or daughter to use?

The National Highway Traffic Safety Administration sets criteria for auto safety ratings. Because manufacturers have focused greater attention on safety in recent years, most new vehicles achieve four- and five-star safety ratings on front, rear, and side crash safety. To compare auto safety ratings and view crash test photos, go to **www.iihs.org**/ratings, the website for the Insurance Institute for Highway Safety, which conducts the tests on which the star ratings are based.

Reliability and Warranties

Buying a new car doesn't guarantee that you'll have no maintenance or repair costs for the first several years. *Consumer Reports* (**www.consumerreports.org**) is a good source for reliability ratings based on customer surveys and maintenance records.

Most new vehicles and late-model used vehicles sold at dealerships come with both express and implied warranties. A **warranty** is a legal promise made by the seller, in this case with respect to the qualities of the vehicle being sold or the seller's obligation to repair or service the vehicle for a period of time. An express warranty is a promise made orally or in writing. Even without an express warranty, there is an implied warranty that a purchased vehicle is suitable for its intended use—unless it was explicitly sold "as is," which means that the seller makes no warranties at all.

Auto dealers and manufacturers usually offer a warranty on parts and labor for certain types of repairs limited to a specified number of years or miles driven, whichever comes first. These often cover the car "bumper-to-bumper" for the first three years or 36,000 miles, although some now offer coverage for 50,000 or even 100,000 miles. This type of warranty covers the costs of most problems you might experience with your vehicle, except for routine maintenance and accident damage. Power-train problems are usually covered for a longer period of time, sometimes up to 10 years, depending on the manufacturer. Used vehicles purchased from a dealer may or may not include a warranty.

In addition to a regular warranty, most manufacturers and dealers offer the opportunity to purchase an **extended warranty** or service contract. This type of agreement either extends the amount of time that your car is covered by the original limited warranty or adds services or coverage to your existing warranty. You should read the fine print on such a warranty carefully, because many extended warranties exclude coverage for the problems you're most likely to experience. It is also generally the case that the warranty contract price is greater than the expected costs of covered repairs.

6.2 | Should You Lease or Buy a Car?

> **LEARNING OBJECTIVE 6.2**
>
> Decide whether to lease or buy a vehicle, and negotiate the terms for purchase and financing.

You have many choices for financing the purchase of an automobile. If you buy the vehicle, you can finance the cost through a consumer loan. Another alternative is to lease the vehicle. In this section, we address the lease-versus-buy decision and explain the key features of automobile leases. Then we discuss the process of negotiating for the best price.

Leasing versus Buying

Generally, the up-front and monthly costs associated with buying a car are higher than the costs of leasing. This tends to make leases attractive to consumers who want to limit their monthly expenses. However, many of these advantages are negated at the end of the lease term, so it's important to read the fine print and carefully compare the costs.

What Is a Lease?

A lease is essentially a rental agreement between the owner of the car, the **lessor**, and you, the **lessee**, in which you agree to pay money for the right to *use* the vehicle for the period of your contract. Most commonly, the term of the lease is two or three years, although it can be longer. The newspapers are full of ads touting low monthly payments for new cars. Usually these are lease payments rather than loan payments. Why are leases so much cheaper? The reason is that the lessor can afford to charge a lower monthly payment during the lease term because it retains the ownership of the vehicle and can make additional money on the vehicle by selling it at the end. If you buy a vehicle instead of leasing, *you* are the one who benefits from selling the car because you own the **equity** in the car—the difference between the car's market value and the remaining amount of the loan. Leases are increasingly popular, with about a third of all new cars being leased rather than purchased, primarily because of the attractively low monthly payments and the option of exchanging the car for a new one every few years.

What Determines the Cost of an Auto Lease?

The cost of a lease is based on the difference between the initial value of the car and the resale value at the end of the lease—or, in other words, how much the car will depreciate in value over the term of the lease. If the car is worth $29,000 today and is expected to be worth $15,000 in two years at the end of your lease, then your lease payments must compensate the lessor for the $14,000 depreciation plus finance charges. This is why a lease payment can be half as much as a loan payment for the same vehicle. When you *buy* the car, you pay the whole purchase price and get to keep the car at the end. With a *lease,* you pay only for the expected depreciation over the time you have the car, because you have to give back the car at the end of the lease term.

Closed-End versus Open-End Leases

Auto leases are either closed-end or open-end. In the more common **closed-end lease**, the lessor takes the risk that the resale value of the car will be less than what was originally assumed. This type of lease is also sometimes called a *walk-away lease* because you can return the car in good condition and simply walk away from any further responsibilities. A disadvantage of closed-end leases is that you are committed to the full term of the lease and may be subject to a large penalty for canceling prematurely.

An open-end lease, which is not very common, requires you to bear the risk of greater than expected depreciation. The contract makes you responsible for any difference between the actual and estimated depreciation. However, the amount you may be charged is limited by the Federal Consumer Leasing Act to three times the monthly lease payment.

Lease Contracts

As with any financial contract, if you don't understand your rights and obligations under a lease agreement, you run the risk of being taken advantage of by the other party. Under the Federal Consumer Leasing Act, lessors are required to tell you all of the relevant information about your lease on a disclosure form. The most important terminology and common contractual clauses for automobile lease agreements are described in **Table 6.2**.

TABLE 6.2   Lease Terminology

Lease Term	Definition
Disposition fee	Fee charged if you choose not to purchase the vehicle at the end of the lease
Gross capitalized cost	The price you negotiate for the vehicle
Up-front fees	Credit report and/or application processing
Capitalized cost reduction	Down payment and/or rebate
Residual value	Expected depreciated value of the vehicle at the end of the lease term
Rent charge	Total finance charges for the term of the lease
Lease term	The number of months in the lease
Excess wear and mileage limits	If you exceed these limits, commonly 10,000 to 12,000 miles per year, you are charged a penalty at the end of the lease—10 cents to 30 cents per mile
Purchase option	Price to buy the car at the end of the lease; residual value used for calculation of the depreciation amount
Early termination	Penalty charged if the lease ends early or the car is stolen or destroyed in an accident, in addition to remaining payments on lease

Before deciding whether to lease or buy a car, you should carefully compare the costs. **Demonstration Problem 6.3** illustrates how to compare leasing and buying costs.

DEMONSTRATION PROBLEM 6.3 | Comparing the Costs of Leasing and Buying a Car

Problem

You have decided which new car you want, but you need to determine whether to lease it or buy it. You have the following information:

- The car's purchase price is $15,000 (including taxes and dealer fees), and you have saved $2,500 to put toward the purchase or lease.
- The dealer's three-year lease agreement requires a monthly payment of $199 with a capitalized cost reduction of $2,000 and a $500 security deposit. The mileage limit is 10,000 miles per year, and excess mileage at the end of the lease term is penalized at the rate of 10 cents per mile. Based on your past driving history, you typically drive 12,000 miles per year.
- The payment for a three-year car loan, assuming a $2,500 down payment, will be $375 per month.
- The estimated value of the car at the end of three years is $8,000.
- You earn 2 percent APY on savings per year.

Which will cost you more, leasing or buying?

Strategy

Use **Excel Worksheet 6.4** (Personal Financial Planner: Costs of Leasing versus Buying a Car) to compare the costs of these alternatives. Although the worksheet will make this calculation for you, note that you can also calculate forgone interest as the interest rate times the amount you could have earned interest on if you hadn't spent it on the car. Thus, in our example, if you did not use the $2,500 for the down payment, you could earn 2% × $2,500 = $50 per year, or $150 for the three-year period.

Solution

Based on the completed worksheet shown in **Figure 6.2**, the total cost of leasing will be $9,914, and the total cost of buying will be $8,277. It is better to buy the car even though you will have to spend more per month. The deciding factor is that you will still own the car at the end of the three years.

FIGURE 6.2 Sample for Excel Worksheet 6.4: Costs of Leasing versus Buying a Car

	A	B
1	**Cost of Leasing**	
2	Total up-front costs: Capitalized cost reduction plus security deposit	$ 2,500
3	Forgone interest on capitalized cost reduction and security deposit	150
4	Total lease payments	7,164
5	End-of-lease excess mileage charges	600
6	Less: Return of security deposit	500
7	**Total Cost of Leasing**	$ 9,914
8		
9	**Cost of Buying**	
10	Down payment	$ 2,500
11	Forgone interest on down payment	150
12	Forgone interest on difference in payments	127
13	Total loan payments	13,500
14	Less: Expected end-of-loan value	8,000
15	**Total Cost of Buying**	$ 8,277
16		

Negotiating the Auto Purchase Price

Whether you lease or buy, it's important to negotiate the best possible terms. A lower price will reduce the amount to be financed in the case of a purchase and reduce the depreciation charge in the case of a lease. Very few people pay the price originally asked by the seller, and those who do are paying too much. You should go into any negotiation process with as much information about the vehicle's value as possible so that you can negotiate effectively. If you purchase from a private party, the terms are fairly simple and there aren't many trade-offs. A better price for you is a worse deal for the seller. If you buy from an auto dealer, understanding the components of the dealer's profit will help you in the negotiation process.

Components of Auto Dealer Profit

It's a mistake to focus on price alone, since other factors, such as fuel efficiency, play a role in how expensive your car will be in the long run. Still, the negotiated price makes the most difference to your monthly budget. In negotiating, you need to be aware that many different factors can contribute to the auto dealer's profit. Sometimes, for example, dealers advertise that they'll sell vehicles for a set amount—say, $200—over their invoice price. (Recall that the dealer's invoice price is the price the dealer pays to purchase the vehicle from the manufacturer.) In essence, they're implying that this is the only profit they'll make on the sale. Although this may be true, the "invoice" they're using is often the dealer's invoice plus all of the dealer-installed options, on which they'll also earn some profit. Dealers may also receive a fee from the manufacturer for selling certain car models, which further adds to their profit. **Table 6.3** outlines several sources of profit for auto dealers. Some of these, such as preinstalled options and rebates, apply only to new cars.

TABLE 6.3	**Components of Auto Dealer Profit**
1.	Price paid by customer less dealer's invoice price
2.	Profit on preinstalled options (= list price less cost to dealer)
3.	Delivery and preparation fee to cover dealer's cost of getting the car to the lot and cleaning it up, often $1,000 or more
4.	Undercoating or rust-proofing
5.	Manufacturer incentives not passed on to the consumer, such as rebates, allowances, and discounts
6.	Extended warranties and service contracts purchased by consumer
7.	Finance charges and loan application fees
8.	Profit on vehicles traded in for less than resale value

Negotiation Strategies

As noted, the asking price for both new and used vehicles is rarely the price that is actually paid. When buying a car, you should be prepared to negotiate for the best price possible.

Figure 6.3 illustrates the process you should follow to effectively negotiate a new car purchase. For new cars, you can often get the best price by going through the dealer's online sales department. Because these orders usually don't require the payment of commissions to salespersons, dealerships can sell at lower prices and still make the same profit on the vehicles. Most of these steps also apply to used car negotiation. You should do your research on price; test drive the car and, if necessary, take it to a mechanic for a checkup; make a reasonable offer; and be prepared to walk away from the deal if the price is too high.

FIGURE 6.3 **Negotiation Process for Buying a New Car** If you do your homework, you'll be in a better position to negotiate a good deal for your auto purchase or lease.

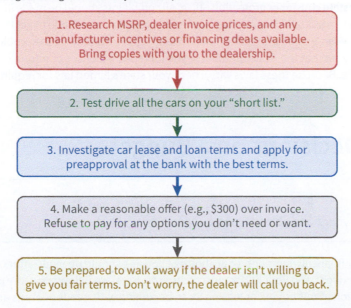

1. Research MSRP, dealer invoice prices, and any manufacturer incentives or financing deals available. Bring copies with you to the dealership.

2. Test drive all the cars on your "short list."

3. Investigate car lease and loan terms and apply for preapproval at the bank with the best terms.

4. Make a reasonable offer (e.g., $300) over invoice. Refuse to pay for any options you don't need or want.

5. Be prepared to walk away if the dealer isn't willing to give you fair terms. Don't worry, the dealer will call you back.

Marketing research shows that women tend to thoroughly research and comparison-shop before buying a car. In theory, this should put them in a good negotiation position. Even though more than half of all new and used cars are bought by women, women are generally more dissatisfied with their car-buying experience than men. This may be, in part, due to differences in women's preferences regarding the shopping experience. Women tend to feel that they receive less attention from salespeople. Many also say that the negotiation process makes them feel uncomfortable.

Reflection Question 2

How comfortable are you with price negotiation? Would you prefer cars to have fixed prices?

Fortunately, there are many websites with helpful content for female car buyers. For example, **bankrate.com** offers a "Bill of Rights" for female car buyers. Two useful tips for female buyers (or for anyone who is uncomfortable with the car-buying experience) are these:

- Bring along a relative or friend who is knowledgeable about cars. This will prevent the salesperson from trying to dazzle you with meaningless car jargon. And it's easier to make the salesperson worry that you might walk away from the deal when you have someone else to talk to. ("I don't know about this one, Dad—I really liked that car at the other dealership better.")
- Make sure the salesperson knows that you've done your homework and that you are well-informed about pricing and financing options. A simple way to do this is to come prepared with a printout from a website that gives the dealer invoice and other information on the vehicle.

Fortunately, it appears that the auto industry is recognizing that the auto-buying experience has to change in light of a new generation of customers who have grown up in an era of online price comparison and instant-click sales. A few auto companies have recently announced a streamlined buying process: advertising "true" sticker prices, reducing the number of salespeople, and eliminating the extended negotiation process. If this strategy succeeds in attracting more customers, we may see more dealers adopting these consumer-friendly practices in the future.

Making Consumer Complaints

Although no one likes to think about what can go wrong, you may find that the car you've purchased doesn't live up to your expectations. Most problems with a new car should be covered by the manufacturer's warranty. If you don't get satisfaction at the dealer's service department, you should go to the service manager or owner. The next level of complaint is the manufacturer, where you'll need to contact someone in the consumer affairs department. If this fails, you can contact your state consumer protection office. All complaints should be made in writing, and you should provide adequate documentation of each attempt you've made to get the defect fixed. In some cases, when a vehicle is clearly defective and repairs don't solve the problem, state **lemon laws** may require that the dealer reimburse you for repair expenses or refund the price you paid for the vehicle. Because these laws vary, check your state's lemon law for requirements.

6.3 | Making Housing Decisions on a Budget

LEARNING OBJECTIVE 6.3

Evaluate your housing needs and budget.

As with other financial decisions, your choice of housing should be made after careful consideration of your needs and your budgetary constraints. Here, we follow the same process we used for the decision about buying or leasing a car, beginning with needs analysis and affordability.

Housing Needs over the Life Cycle

Housing is generally a household's largest budget expenditure, accounting for about 30 percent of all household spending. Not surprisingly, housing expenditures tend to increase with income. With the exception of the mega-rich, the proportion of a household budget that is spent on housing is relatively consistent across income brackets. Although wealthy celebrities might spend several million dollars to buy and furnish a home, the amount they spend may actually be in line with their income. When you make $50 million per year, you can buy a mansion, too!

Over your life cycle and with changing life circumstances, your housing needs will probably change. Young single adults often rent small apartments and share living quarters with friends. Married couples tend to prefer to live on their own, and families with children often need more space, including a yard and proximity to schools. This usually means that they must consider more expensive options, either renting or buying single-family housing. Consistent with this logic, federal government statistics show that average housing expenditures are greatest for people during their child-rearing years, ages 35–44, averaging more than $20,000 per year. In contrast, retiree households spend about one-third of that amount because they commonly downsize and pay off their mortgages prior to retirement.

Spending more on housing necessarily involves a trade-off—the more you spend on any one thing, the less you have available for other uses. Because you have a wide variety of choices to meet your housing needs, it's up to you to make this decision in light of your other priorities. For example, if reducing your credit card debt is a high priority for you, it would make sense to rent a smaller apartment and live with a roommate until you've achieved that goal. It's also fairly common for new college graduates to live with their parents for a period of time after graduation so that they can pay off debt and increase savings before going out on their own.

The Rent-versus-Buy Decision

The decision whether to rent or buy housing depends on your preferences, budget, and creditworthiness. Although it usually costs more to buy than to rent equivalent space, this is not always the case. The cost of renting in some areas of the country has increased sharply in recent years. You should decide between renting and buying by weighing the relative costs and benefits, both financial and personal. Some advantages and disadvantages of renting are summarized in **Table 6.4**.

TABLE 6.4   **Advantages and Disadvantages of Renting**

Advantages	Disadvantages
• **Lower monthly payments.** Rent per month is usually less expensive than monthly costs for a comparably sized house.	• **Increasing costs over time.** Rent usually increases each year, whereas mortgage payments are often fixed for the life of the loan.
• **Mobility.** Leases commonly cover one year, so you can more easily make a change to accommodate a new job or family situation. Selling a home often takes a long time.	• **No investment value.** Renters don't benefit from the increase in value of the property over time, but homeowners do.
• **Less responsibility.** Renters of apartments usually have no responsibility for maintenance of lawns and gardens, clearing of snow, or exterior cleaning and painting.	• **No tax deduction.** Mortgage interest is tax-deductible, so the after-tax cost of home ownership may be lower than renting.
	• **Restrictions on use of the property.** Lease contracts often restrict how you can use your property—how many people may live in the unit, whether pets are allowed, etc.
	• **Uncertainty.** There are no guarantees that you'll be able to continue renting the property after the end of the lease term.

Types of Housing

In considering whether to rent or buy, you also will consider the type of property involved. There are several types of residential properties in addition to traditional apartment buildings and individual single-family homes.

Condominiums are a type of residential property in which the unit owner has control and use of his or her own unit but shares the common areas with other unit owners. Maintenance and repairs of the exterior building and landscaping are taken care of by the condominium association and each owner pays dues to cover those costs. Condominiums may also be used as rental properties.

Similarly, cooperative housing arrangements, in which a group of people own housing units together as a nonprofit organization, are gaining in popularity. With so many young people delaying marriage or never marrying, this type of housing can offer some of the advantages of family living, while still allowing each individual his or her own space. The owners of a cooperative have the right to approve others who want to buy into the cooperative.

EXCEL WORKSHEET

See **Excel Worksheet 6.5 (Personal Financial Planner: Costs of Renting versus Buying a Home)** in **WileyPLUS.**

The Costs of Renting versus Buying

A significant consideration in the rent-versus-buy decision is the difference in costs. There are online calculators that can help you with this comparison, or you can estimate the costs using **Excel Worksheet 6.5** (Personal Financial Planner: Costs of Renting versus Buying a Home), as illustrated in **Demonstration Problem 6.4**.

DEMONSTRATION PROBLEM 6.4 | Comparing the Costs of Renting and Buying a Home

Problem

You are considering whether to rent or buy a home. You have researched the costs of each alternative and have collected the following information.

- Costs of renting will include $600 rent per month plus $15 per month in renter's insurance. You will also have to make a $1,200 deposit.
- You can finance a $100,000 home purchase with a 30-year mortgage at 6 percent APR.
- Your down payment on the purchase will be $10,000, and since this is less than 20% of the purchase price, you will have to pay 0.5% of the loan value for private mortgage insurance. Other closing costs will add up to $3,000.
- Annual property taxes will be $1,500, and annual homeowner's insurance will be $500.
- You estimate that annual repairs and maintenance will cost $500 and that your home's value will appreciate at 5 percent per year.
- You earn 2 percent APY on your savings, and your marginal tax rate is 20 percent.
- You expect to take the standard deduction on your federal income taxes.

Based on this information, which alternative is less expensive? Does it make a difference if you compare costs for one year versus five years?

Strategy

Estimate the total costs of renting and the total costs of buying, for one year and for five years. You can use Excel Worksheet 6.5 (Personal Financial Planner: Costs of Renting versus Buying a Home) to help with the calculation.

Solution

After you enter the information in the worksheet, the worksheet will solve for the total cost for one year and for five years, as shown in **Figure 6.4**.

FIGURE 6.4   **Sample of Excel Worksheet 6.5: Costs of Renting versus Buying a Home**

	A	B	C
	Cost Comparison	**1 Year**	**5 Years**
2	Total rent payments	$ 7,200	$ 36,000
3	Renter's insurance	180	900
4	After-tax interest lost on security deposit	19	96
5	**Total Cost of Renting**	$ 7,399	$ 36,996
6	Total mortgage payments	$ 6,475	$ 32,376
7	Property tax	1,500	7,500
8	Homeowner's insurance	500	2,500
9	Private mortgage insurance	450	2,250
10	Repair and maintenance expenses	500	2,500
11	Down payment	10,000	10,000
12	Closing costs	3,000	3,000
13	Lost after-tax interest on down payment and closing costs	208	1,040
14	Subtotal: Costs	22,633	61,166
15	Savings from repaying principal	1,105	6,251
16	Increase in home value	5,000	27,628
17	Tax savings from deductibility of interest, mortgage points, and property taxes	0	0
18	Subtotal: Savings	6,105	33,879
19	**Total Cost of Buying**	$ 16,528	$ 27,286

Your first-year costs make buying about twice as expensive as renting, but over a five-year period, renting turns out to be the more expensive alternative.

Legal Issues for Tenants

If you choose to rent, you will generally sign a lease with the owner of the housing unit, also called the landlord. The important terms in the lease include the following:

- The amount of monthly rent and penalties for late payment
- The length or term of the lease (usually six months to one year)
- Description of the responsibilities and rights of the landlord and the tenant
- Procedures to be taken in case of nonpayment
- Procedures for renewal or lease termination (often, 30 to 60 days notice is required)
- The **security deposit**, an amount paid up-front to protect the landlord from losses due to nonpayment of rent and/or damage to the property (commonly one month's rent, but college students are sometimes required to pay more)
- Explanation of how the security deposit may be used

In most states by law, leases don't have to be in writing unless they're for a period of more than a year, but it's a good idea to have a written lease to guard against misunderstandings at a later date. Some leases specify exactly what the penalty will be for certain types of damage. For example, if you leave the unit at the end of the lease term without cleaning the oven, you might have $75 subtracted from your security deposit. These itemized lists are helpful to tenants in that they spell out what must be done to have their entire security deposit returned.

Even with a written lease, you can attempt to negotiate the terms if you find some of them unacceptable. For example, your lease might say that the landlord can cancel the lease with 30 days' notice to you, but you might try to have that changed to 60 days to give yourself enough time to find a new apartment. You should also carefully inspect the premises before signing the lease. You don't want to be held responsible for a cigarette burn in the carpet if it was there before you moved in. Take photos of any preexisting defects and give them to the landlord at the beginning of the lease.

All states have laws that govern landlord-tenant relations. If you don't pay your rent in a timely fashion, the landlord has the right to take legal action against you for nonpayment but generally cannot evict you without a court hearing. In addition, the law in most states requires that a landlord hold your security deposit in a separate account and return it to you within 30 days of the end of your lease, less any unpaid rent and deductions for damage—other than normal wear and tear—that you have caused to the property. Any rental unit, regardless of how inexpensive, must meet minimum standards of habitability, which include hot and cold running water, heat, electricity, and safe access. If you have requested in writing that your landlord make certain repairs, but your request has been ignored, you have the right to make the repair yourself and deduct the cost from your next month's rent.

How Much House Can You Afford?

Once you've identified your housing needs, you must consult your budget to determine what you can afford to spend. If you're anticipating a change, such as a new job or a change in family circumstances, you'll need to reestimate your budget as accurately as possible to accommodate any new cash inflows or outflows. If you're currently allocating funds to other financial goals, you should keep those in your budget so that you can better see how the housing decision might affect your other financial priorities.

Based on your budget, you'll first need to estimate the monthly amount you can allocate to housing. If you decide to rent, your monthly housing budget will have to cover your rent plus related costs, such as utility costs. If you decide to buy a home, the next step is to identify an affordable price range. To do this, you need to carefully consider the following factors:

- Your monthly housing budget
- The nonfinancing costs of home ownership
- The down payment you can make and the costs of closing
- The maximum loan amount for the relevant level of payment

The Nonfinancing Costs of Home Ownership

When comparing the costs of renting and buying, it's easy to make the mistake of assuming that the mortgage payment is the total monthly financial cost of buying. In addition to the principal and interest payments on the mortgage, homeowners also pay local property taxes, homeowner's insurance premiums, and the costs of repairs and maintenance on the property. Some home owners must pay a monthly fee to cover maintenance of neighborhood common areas. All these costs can vary substantially in different areas and for different properties but will likely constitute 20 to 25 percent of your total housing cost. They are explained in detail in this section.

- **Property taxes** Most local jurisdictions pay for community services such as roads, schools, and fire and police protection by levying a tax on real property. **Property tax** is proportional to the assessed value of the property, so the tax owed will increase as your property value increases. A property assessed at $300,000 will pay twice as much tax as one assessed at $150,000. You can look up the property taxes for a particular property at your local assessor's office or online. The tax rate can differ dramatically across jurisdictions and so should be a factor in your location decision.
- **Homeowner's insurance** All lenders require that borrowers carry homeowner's insurance on the property. The cost can range from $200 per year and up, depending on the value of the home and the riskiness of the area in which it is located. A real estate broker can generally give you an estimate of insurance costs in your area. You'll learn more about this type of insurance in Chapter 7.
- **Repairs and maintenance** Homeowners are responsible for routine maintenance costs for such things as lawns, sprinkler systems, and snow removal, although these costs are sometimes covered by association dues. You should also assume that you'll have to invest

in regular structural maintenance and repairs. These could be minimal for new homes, but can be quite substantial for older homes. For example, a new roof can cost several thousand dollars.

- **Association dues**   Condominiums and some residential communities require that homeowners pay dues to a homeowners' association. These cover the cost of maintaining common areas, such as gardens and sidewalks, as well as more expensive items, such as a neighborhood swimming pool. Although your mortgage costs are fixed by contract, association dues are usually determined by a volunteer board made up of a few homeowners. Well-managed associations will have a reserve for expected future maintenance projects. However, poor planning or unexpected maintenance issues can result in large one-time charges to everyone in the association, so it's important to look at association financial records before buying property that is part of an association.

- **Offsetting tax benefits**   Although home ownership often has higher monthly costs than renting, the tax savings from deductibility of mortgage interest and property taxes provide an offsetting benefit. In addition, subject to some limitations, your home can appreciate in value without triggering any tax liability for capital gains from its sale. Although federal income tax law places limits on deductions for both mortgage interest and property tax, these limits are a factor only for more expensive homes.

The Down Payment

The cash that you apply up front to a home purchase is called the **down payment**. The amount of your down payment is affected by the minimum imposed by the lender (often 10 to 20 percent), your available cash, and the opportunity cost of using cash for this purpose.

If possible, you should try to make a down payment of at least 20 percent. When you borrow more than 80 percent of the value of the home, lenders charge an extra amount to cover **mortgage insurance** in addition to the normal mortgage interest. This additional charge usually ranges from 0.25 percent to 1.0 percent of the loan value. Mortgage insurance protects the lender against the possibility that you will fail to pay back the mortgage as promised.

First-time home buyers can sometimes obtain mortgages with much smaller down payments, even as little as 3 percent. However, if home prices decline even a little, your home may end up being worth less than the amount you owe on your mortgage, a problem sometimes referred to as being "under water."

Even if you can't—or choose not to—make a 20 percent down payment, you'll eventually be able to stop paying the mortgage insurance. By law, lenders can't charge you extra for the premium once you've paid down your balance on a conventional loan to 80 percent of your home's *original purchase price.* This will take about 10 years on a typical 30-year mortgage financed with 5 percent down. Furthermore, if the market value of your home appreciates sufficiently, you can notify your lender to have the insurance removed. Unfortunately for those homebuyers who have FHA loans, which allow much lower down payments than conventional loans, mortgage insurance is required for the life of the loan.

Unless you receive a gift exclusively earmarked for helping you to buy a house, any cash you apply to the purchase of a home necessarily reduces your savings. Thus, you need to consider the opportunity cost of using it for this purpose. If you didn't use the money for a down payment, what would you do with it? For example, if you can earn 8 percent on your investments when mortgage rates are 5 percent, you will effectively lose 3 percent in interest over the life of your mortgage by using the money for a down payment. However, if your home appreciates more than 3 percent per year in value, then the home investment will have been worth it. For this reason, people tend to maximize their loan amounts when mortgage rates are low relative to investment returns or when home values are appreciating rapidly. In contrast, if your investments are earning less than your mortgage financing costs—such as when your money is held in bank checking or savings accounts—you're better off applying the money to reducing the amount you need to borrow.

First-time home buyers are permitted to withdraw funds from individual retirement accounts without incurring penalties if the funds are used to purchase a home. You may also be able to borrow funds from retirement plans or life insurance policies to apply toward a down payment. Financial planners usually recommend against doing either of these things because it takes funds away from other important financial goals.

Expected Closing Costs

When you buy a home, you'll also incur various costs associated with the real estate transaction. These are usually called **closing costs**, because the meeting where you sign all the required paperwork to finalize your purchase is called the **closing**. Closing costs, which we consider in more detail later in the chapter, can vary widely and can be a substantial drain on your available cash. Your realtor and lender will give you a better idea of what to expect, given the price range you're considering and the other common costs paid by the buyer at closing. Federal law also requires a closing statement (called a HUD-1) of estimated costs be provided to you well in advance of the actual closing so you know what charges you will have to pay.

Maximum Loan Amount and House Price

What you can afford to spend on purchasing a home depends on your financial situation and is limited by your available monthly cash flow and the amount of savings you can apply to the up-front purchase costs. You also have to meet lender requirements, which are explained later in this chapter. **Figure 6.5** illustrates how the house price you can afford increases with your budget for monthly housing expenses. This graph assumes that you will finance 80 percent of the home's value with a mortgage and that your monthly costs of ownership will be 75 percent financing costs and 25 percent nonfinancing costs.

FIGURE 6.5   **Maximum Affordable House Price and Loan Amount**   The graph shows how much house you can afford based on your monthly housing budget and assuming a 20 percent down payment, 30-year fixed-rate mortgage at 5 percent annual interest, and nonfinancing costs equal to 25 percent of the housing budget. As shown, with a monthly budget of $1,000, you could afford a mortgage loan amount of about $140,000 and a total home value of almost $175,000.

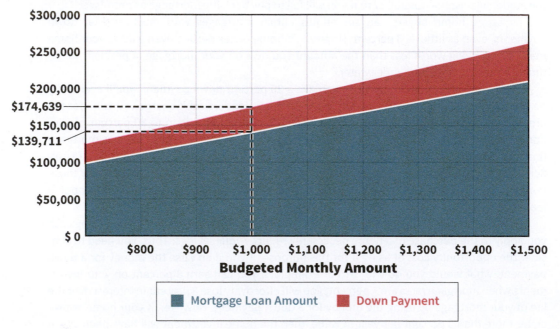

INTERACTIVE

See Interactive: Interest Rates and Home Affordability in **WileyPLUS**.

Note that if mortgage rates are higher, your monthly costs for principal and interest repayment will be higher, so your housing budget won't go as far. Use **Interactive: Interest Rates and Home Affordability** to see the impact that higher mortgage rates can have on home affordability.

Demonstration Problem 6.5 shows how to estimate the house price you can afford, taking into consideration all the costs of purchasing and owning a home.

DEMONSTRATION PROBLEM 6.5 | Calculating an Affordable Home Price

Problem

You have $10,000 available for a down payment and expect closing costs for your loan to total $3,000. You have $1,000 per month to allocate to housing costs. You estimate the following monthly nonfinancing costs:

- Property taxes, $150
- Homeowner's insurance, $30
- Repairs and maintenance, $60

You qualify for a 30-year mortgage at 5.5 percent APR, but will have to pay an additional 0.5% each year for private mortgage insurance (PMI) because you do not have enough cash to make a 20 percent downpayment. What is the maximum you can afford to pay for a home?

Strategy

Use **Excel Worksheet 6.6** (Personal Financial Planner: Calculating an Affordable Home Price) to solve this problem. Your completed worksheet should look like the one in **Figure 6.6**.

EXCEL WORKSHEET

See **Excel Worksheet 6.6** (Personal Financial Planner: Calculating an Affordable Home Price) in **WileyPLUS**.

FIGURE 6.6   **Sample for Excel Worksheet 6.6: Calculating an Affordable Home Price**

	A	B
1	**STEP 1. Enter Monthly Amount to Allocate to Housing**	
2		$ 1,000
3	**STEP 2. Estimate Funds Available for Financing Costs**	
4	a. Expected monthly cost of property taxes	$ 150
5	b. Expected monthly cost of homeowner's insurance	30
6	c. Expected monthly cost of repairs and maintenance	60
7	d. Expected monthly cost of association dues	–
8	e. Total monthly nonfinancing housing costs (a + b + c + d)	240
9		
10	**Total available for loan principal and interest**	$ 760
11	**STEP 3. Estimate Affordable Mortgage Amount**	
12	a. Mortgage annual percentage rate (APR), including PMI rate if required	6.00%
13	b. Mortgage period in months (e.g., for 30-year, enter 360)	360
14	c. Total available for financing costs (from Step 2)	760
15		
16	**Maximum affordable mortgage amount**	$ 126,762
17	**STEP 4. Other Relevant Financial Information**	
18	a. Down payment available	10,000
19	b. Gifts from parents or others	–
20	c. Expected closing costs	3,000
21		
22	**Maximum house you can afford**	$ 133,762

Solution

Your monthly nonfinancing costs (taxes, insurance, repairs, and maintenance) total $240, so even though you have $1,000 per month to apply to housing, you have only $760 ($1,000 – $240) to pay for principal and interest on a home mortgage. In Step 3, the worksheet does the financial math to figure out the amount of loan that would result in a $760 payment. Because you do not have enough for a 20 percent downpayment, you will have to pay the PMI, which increases your monthly financing costs. In Step 4, you take into consideration closing costs and the amount of down payment you have available. The maximum house price you can afford is estimated to be $133,762.

Note that even if you can afford to pay $133,762 for a home, that doesn't necessarily mean you should borrow that much. It would be better to consider saving a little more money for a larger down payment so that you don't have to pay for PMI.

Mortgage Financing

> **LEARNING OBJECTIVE 6.4**
> Evaluate mortgage financing alternatives.

Very few people pay for a home purchase in cash. Instead, they finance some of the cost with a long-term loan. In this section, we explore your home financing options.

What Is a Mortgage?

A **mortgage** is a long-term amortized loan that is secured by real property. As you learned in earlier chapters, a secured loan carries a lower interest rate than an unsecured loan because the lender has less risk. If you don't make your mortgage payments as promised, the lender has the right to take your home to pay off the debt, in a process called foreclosure.

Common Characteristics of Mortgage Loans

Most mortgages have these characteristics in common:

- **Lenders** Mortgages can be obtained from many different types of financial institutions, including depository institutions, such as commercial banks and S&Ls, and nondepository institutions, such as insurance companies.
- **Term** Mortgages are long-term contracts, usually lasting 15 to 30 years.
- **Collateral** Mortgage lenders require that borrowers give them the right to take the property in the event that the borrower fails to pay back the loan as promised. The property is the collateral that secures the mortgage.
- **Amortization** Most mortgages are amortized loans. This means that each monthly payment covers interest charges and some principal repayment. At the end of the mortgage term, you will have completely paid back the original loan with interest. During the early years of the mortgage, when the balance you owe is high, most of each monthly payment will go to pay interest. As you gradually pay back the loan, your payment may stay the same, but the interest charge will be a smaller proportion of the total payment, because the balance on which the interest is computed is lower. You'll see examples of how this works later in this section.

Resale of Loans in the Secondary Market

After contracting with you for a mortgage (also called "originating" the mortgage), your lender will most likely sell the loan to another financial institution in the **secondary mortgage market**. This allows your lender to recoup the cash and lend it out again. The lender makes money from the loan application and origination fees and from a profit on the sale of the loan. The lender may also be paid to service the loan, which consists of collecting and processing payments.

The secondary mortgage market is important because the buyers of loans in that market, such as the Federal Home Loan Mortgage Corporation (commonly called Freddie Mac) and the Federal National Mortgage Association (commonly called Fannie Mae), impose loan-to-value and other ratio restrictions on the mortgages that can be sold to them. Secondary mortgage market institutions raise money to buy the loans by selling mortgage-backed securities to investors—investments that are backed by the thousands of mortgages in their loan portfolios. The buyers of mortgage-backed securities receive a proportionate share of the interest and principal repayments made by borrowers.

Investors in mortgage-backed securities can lose a lot of money if borrowers default on their mortgages, as many did after the financial crisis in 2008–2009. More recently, stricter lending standards and regulations have made it more difficult for some people to qualify for loans.

Types of Mortgages

Many types of mortgages are available to home buyers today, but all fall into a few general categories that differ in their contractual terms related to interest rates, term to maturity, and type of payment. Key features of common types of mortgage are summarized in **Table 6.5** and discussed below.

TABLE 6.5 **Key Features of Different Types of Mortgages**

Mortgage Type	Rate	Payment	Term	Amortization
Conventional	Fixed	Fixed	Usually 15 or 30 years	Yes
Adjustable rate (ARM)	Variable	Fixed, usually for 5 or 7 years; then changes with market rates	Usually 15 or 30 years	Yes
Balloon	Fixed	Fixed for period of years, at which time full balance is due	Balloon period of 5–10 years	Usually amortized over 30 years
Graduated payment	Fixed	Increases over life of loan, often in 2-year increments	Usually 30 years, but can be shorter	Negative in early years
Growing equity	Fixed	Can be fixed or increasing; often accomplished by borrower making extra payments	Loan is repaid sooner by making extra principal payments	Amortized over 30 years; additional payments applied to principal repayment
Reverse annuity	Fixed	Can be fixed or variable; payment made to homeowner	Negotiable	Yes
Interest only	Fixed or variable	Fixed or variable with market rates; does not include any repayment of principal	Usually shorter term; commonly used for home equity loans	No

- **Conventional mortgages** A **conventional mortgage** is a fixed-rate, fixed-term, fixed-payment loan with monthly payments. Rates vary with market conditions and borrower qualifications but, once contracted for, are fixed for the life of the loan, which is commonly 15, 20, 25, or 30 years. **Figure 6.7** illustrates the annual breakdown of principal and interest for a $100,000, amortized, 30-year conventional mortgage at 6 percent interest.

FIGURE 6.7 **Annual Interest and Principal Payments for a 30-Year Mortgage** The graph assumes an amortized $100,000 mortgage at a fixed interest rate of 6 percent per year. Monthly payments are $599.55 per month, or $7,195 per year.

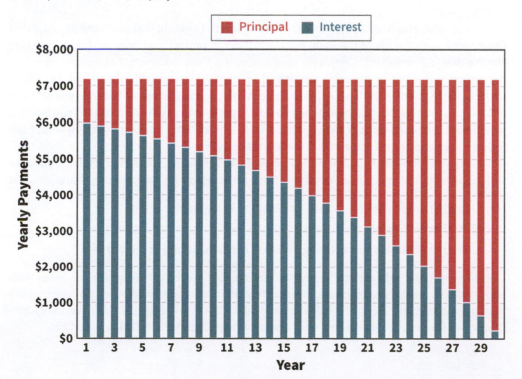

The loan illustrated in Figure 6.7 requires fixed payments of $599.55 per month ($7,195 per year) for 360 months (30 years). A portion of the monthly payment pays interest on the balance owed, and the remainder is applied to repayment of principal. In the first month, interest is calculated as 0.5 percent (6 percent divided by 12 months) of the mortgage amount ($100,000), or $500. The remaining $99.55 goes toward repayment of the principal, reducing the outstanding balance to $99,900.45. The next month, interest is $499.50 (0.5 percent interest on the new lower balance), so $100.05 ($599.55 − $499.50) goes toward repayment of principal. The interest continues to decline over time as the balance owed gradually declines. Because the monthly payment is fixed, more of it is applied to reducing the principal balance in each successive month.

To help certain home buyers qualify for mortgages, the U.S. Department of Veterans Affairs (VA) and the Federal Housing Administration (FHA) offer insurance for conventional loans under certain circumstances. These agencies do not provide the mortgage financing money—they simply guarantee to pay lenders (usually banks and savings institutions) the promised interest and principal if the borrower defaults. This guarantee makes lenders more willing to provide favorable financing terms to buyers with higher loan-to-value ratios and lower incomes. The minimum down payment can be lower, and these loans commonly require the payment of points, which are discussed below.

- **Adjustable rate mortgages** An **adjustable rate mortgage (ARM)** has an interest rate that changes over time with market conditions. Because the lender is less exposed to the risk of rising rates, the initial rates on ARMs are usually lower than those on conventional mortgages. Changes in the rate over time are governed by the terms of the mortgage contract. Most commonly, adjustments are made every one or two years and are based on changes in a specific index or market rate, such as the 10-year Treasury bond rate.

The amount that the rate on an ARM can change is limited by **interest rate increase caps** after an initial fixed period, commonly five or seven years. The caps apply to both the change per year and the total change over the life of the loan. Suppose, for example, you have an ARM with an initial rate of 5 percent, an annual rate increase cap of 1 percent, and a lifetime rate increase cap of 5 percent. With this loan, you'll never see the interest rate increase by more than 1 percentage point per year, and the highest interest you'll ever pay is 10 percent per year. The downside to this type of loan is that the payment might grow to be more than you can afford. If you borrow $100,000, your payment at 5 percent is only $537 per month. But if rates rise steadily over the next five years, the payment could increase to $877 by year 5.

Some ARMs also have a payment cap, which limits the amount that your monthly payment can change over the life of the loan. Although this will protect you from payment increases like the one just described, a payment limit that is less than the amount of interest owed for the period will result in **negative amortization**—that is, the unpaid interest will be added to the balance owed on the loan. In the example above, suppose there had been a payment cap of $700 on your ARM. That's all you would have paid per month in year 10, but your loan balance would have increased by $177 each month. If rates stayed high for a long time, you would still have a balance to pay off at the end of the mortgage term.

Many variations on ARMs have been developed over the last several years. In addition to variations in interest rate caps and payment caps, some ARMs have the following characteristics:

- ARMs that are convertible to fixed-rate loans at some point
- ARMs that are fixed for several years (five to seven) at the outset of the loan
- ARMs that adjust only once during the life of the loan, usually at around year 7

These innovations help reduce lender risk and enable borrowers to qualify for loans with affordable payments. In some cases, though, they also encourage home buyers to borrow more than they should, increasing the risk of default. Although the mortgage industry certainly contributed to the problem, borrowers were also at fault, as discussed in **Ethics in Action**.

Ethics in Action

Who Is to Blame for Mortgage Loan Defaults?

Leading up to the 2008 financial crisis, there was a boom in subprime lending to less creditworthy borrowers, who often had lower credit scores, higher levels of debt, and insufficient income relative to the amount of the mortgage payment. To help borrowers qualify for larger homes, many mortgages were ARMs with lower initial monthly payments. During the crisis, housing values fell, people lost their jobs, interest rates—and ARM payments—increased.

Still feeling the sting from so many mortgage defaults, most mortgage lenders have focused on prime lending in recent years, applying much stricter lending standards than before. But this may be changing. There has been an uptick in what is now called the "nonprime" market, representing about 16% of new mortgages. Some experts worry about this trend, particularly as the economic expansion slows and interest rates continue to rise.

If a bank customer borrows more than he or she can afford, underestimates the impact of rising rates on ARM mortgage payments, or ends up "under water" on their mortgage because they took on too much debt relative to the value of their home, whose fault is it? Although the knee-jerk response may be to place the onus on borrowers who should know better than to contract for a loan they cannot afford, lenders and secondary market participants probably need to share some of the blame. Both types of firms have a greater understanding of the risks, and lenders are in a good position to be the gatekeepers and to educate borrowers about these risks. However, because banks usually sell a loan in the secondary mortgage market within a few days of finalizing the contract with the borrower, they have little incentive to be watchdogs.

So what about the firms who buy the loans in the secondary market? These firms set standards that determine which loans they are willing to buy from banks (e.g., minimum FICO score, debt payment ratio). But they need to keep their loan volume high to be profitable. With rising rates, the mortgage market began to slow in 2018, so Fannie Mae announced that it was increasing the maximum debt payment ratio for loans it would purchase, from 45% to 50%. Not surprisingly, the volume of loans from borrowers with ratios greater than 45% increased right away. Would you be surprised if default rates increase as well?

Does the average borrower understand the risks? With an ARM, initial payments are often quite affordable, but they can rise substantially over the life of the loan. The terms of an ARM are very complex, and it is likely that borrowers are focused on the immediate gratification of buying a larger and nicer home. It's also true that most people are overly optimistic. They may underestimate future rate increases, overestimate future pay raises, or assume that they can refinance or sell their home if the payment gets too expensive. All of these factors worked out poorly for subprime borrowers in the financial crisis. By May 2009, about 25 percent of those borrowers were at least 90 days behind on their payments and many of them ultimately experienced foreclosure.

- **Balloon mortgages** A balloon mortgage is a loan for which the final payment is much larger than the earlier, regular payments. The payments are usually calculated based on a 30-year amortization schedule like conventional fixed-rate mortgages, but the payments don't continue for the full length of the schedule. Instead, the entire remaining balance is due at a prespecified point, usually five to ten years after the mortgage begins. This type of mortgage reduces lenders' risk of rate decreases. It may also result in lower rates for buyers who don't expect to stay in a home long enough for the balloon to come due.

- **Graduated payment mortgages** Another innovation in the mortgage market is the graduated payment mortgage, which carries a fixed rate of interest but allows payments to be lower in the early years and increase over the life of the loan. Because the costs are shifted to later years, you may be able to qualify for a larger loan balance with this type of loan. However, this type of arrangement always results in negative amortization in the early years of the loan. As in the case of the payment caps on certain ARMs, the mortgage balance will increase in any month where the payment is lower than that month's interest owed on the mortgage balance.

- **Growing equity mortgages** Total annual payments on a growing equity mortgage are greater than those on a conventional loan of the same amount, but the added amounts are applied to the principal, so the loan balance can be paid off more quickly. A common form of this type of loan is the biweekly mortgage, sometimes called the 26-pay mortgage. Here, you make payments every two weeks in an amount equal to half the amount you would have paid per month on a comparable fixed-rate, fixed-payment loan. Because there are 52 weeks in the year, you make the equivalent of an extra monthly payment each year. All of the extra payment is applied to paying down the principal. Of course, you can generally accomplish this result on your own by making extra principal payments throughout the life of the loan.

- **Reverse annuity mortgages** If you have a lot of equity in your home and would like to apply the money to something else, you may be able to access it through a **reverse annuity mortgage**, also known as a home equity conversion mortgage. A financial company will take the equity in your home and convert it to tax-free cash. The Federal Housing Administration, which insures these mortgages, requires that you be at least 62 years old and use the home as your primary residence. You can receive the funds in a lump sum, as a credit line, or in a stream of monthly payments. The amount you will receive depends on your age, because the lender will not get to take possession of the home until you die. Older homeowners who need cash but don't want to sell their homes can use this as a method of financing their living expenses or health care costs. When the homeowner dies, the loan must be repaid, but if there is equity left in the home, the deceased homeowner's heirs receive a payment after the home is sold.

Factors That Affect Mortgage Payments

With what you already know about the valuation of annuities, you can probably guess the factors that will affect mortgage payments. The extent to which your payments will be affected by each of the factors may not be quite as obvious. You should compare loans based on interest rate, term to maturity, and discount points. In addition, economic conditions, the location of your property, and your credit history may influence your payments.

Interest Rate

ONLINE CALCULATOR DEMONSTRATION VIDEO

See **Online Calculator Demonstration Video: Mortgage Payment Calculator** in **WileyPLUS**.

All else being equal, the higher the annual percentage rate (APR) charged on a mortgage, the larger the mortgage payment. For a rough estimate, an easy rule of thumb is that your monthly payment of principal and interest will increase about 10 percent for every percentage point increase in your fixed 30-year loan rate. **Demonstration Problem 6.6** shows how you can use a financial calculator to more precisely determine the effect of rates on your payment. **Online Calculator Demonstration Video: Mortgage Payment Calculator** in WileyPLUS shows you how to use an online calculator to estimate monthly mortgage costs.

DEMONSTRATION PROBLEM 6.6 | Calculating the Impact of APR on Monthly Mortgage Payments

Problem

You are considering a $100,000 loan for 30 years, or 360 months. If the quoted APR is 6 percent, what is the monthly payment? How much difference will it make if the rate is 7 percent instead?

Strategy

Recall from Chapter 2 that the monthly payment on a loan can be solved for using present value of an annuity calculations on a financial calculator or a spreadsheet. If you know the amount of the loan, the number of periods, and the rate, you can solve for the payment.

Solution

Calculator solution: Using a financial calculator, enter PV = loan amount = $100,000, N = 30 × 12 = 360, I = APR % /12 = 6/12 = 0.5, and FV = 0. Solve for PMT = −$599.55. If you change the interest rate to I = 7/12 = 0.5833, you can solve for the new PMT = −$665.30. The payment increased $65.75, a little more than 10 percent, when the rate increased by 1 percentage point.

    Figure 6.8 illustrates the payments for a wider range of interest rates. The payment increases about 10 percent per one point increase in APR.

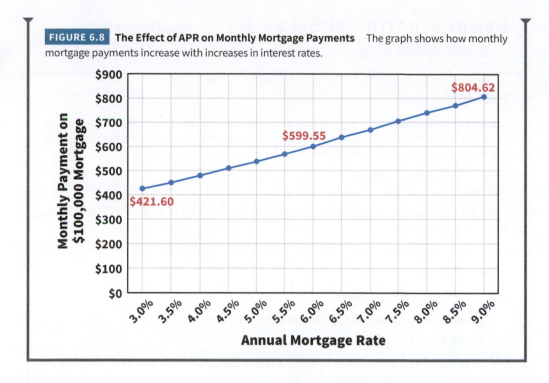

FIGURE 6.8 **The Effect of APR on Monthly Mortgage Payments** The graph shows how monthly mortgage payments increase with increases in interest rates.

Term of the Loan

All else being equal, the longer the term of the loan, the smaller the monthly mortgage payment and the more interest you will pay over the life of the loan. Lenders usually offer mortgages that are amortized over either 15 years or 30 years. **Figure 6.9** shows the monthly payments for a $100,000 mortgage with a 15-year term and a 30-year term. As shown in the figure, the monthly payment for a 15-year mortgage is 30 to 50 percent greater than that for a 30-year mortgage, even though the interest rate is the same. This is because the principal is being paid back over a shorter period of time.

FIGURE 6.9 **The Effect of Loan Term on Monthly Payments** Monthly payments are always higher for equivalent-sized 15-year loans than for 30-year loans. But you'll pay off the loan in half the time.

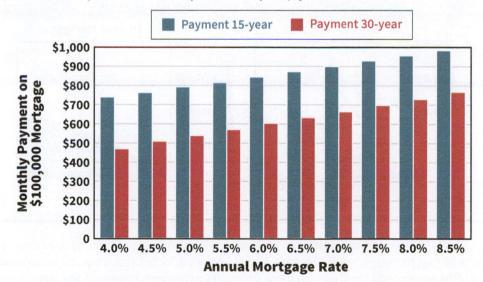

Demonstration Problem 6.7 shows how the choice between 15-year and 30-year mortgages affects the total interest you'll pay over the life of the loan. Total interest paid on a mortgage over the life of the loan can be estimated using **Equation 6.2**:

$$\text{Total interest} = (\text{Number of payments} \times \text{Monthly payment}) - \text{Loan amount} \qquad (6.2)$$

DEMONSTRATION PROBLEM 6.7 | Comparing 15-Year and 30-Year Mortgages

Problem

You need to borrow $100,000 to buy a home and are considering whether to obtain a 15-year or a 30-year mortgage. If the interest rate on both is 5 percent per year, how much more interest will you pay over the life of the loan if you take the 30-year option?

Strategy

First, use your calculator to find the payments. Then use Equation 6.2 to estimate the interest paid over the life of each loan.

Solution

Step 1: Calculate monthly payments:

15-year loan: PV = $100,000; N = 180; I = 5/12; solve for PMT = $790.79

30-year loan: PV = $100,000; N = 360; I = 5/12; solve for PMT = $536.82

In this example, the monthly payment for the 15-year mortgage ($790.79) is 47 percent more than the payment for the 30-year mortgage ($536.82).

Step 2: Calculate total interest:

$$\text{Total interest paid} = \text{Total payments} - \text{Original loan amount}$$

15-year loan: Total interest = ($790.79 × 180) − $100,000 = $42,342.85

30-year loan: Total interest = ($536.82 × 360) − $100,000 = $93,255.20

The shaded areas in **Figure 6.10** show the cumulative amounts of interest paid over time on these two loans.

FIGURE 6.10 **Cumulative Total Mortgage Payments and Interest Paid for 15-Year and 30-Year Mortgages at 5 Percent Interest** For mortgages that are equivalent in other ways, you will pay more than twice as much interest for a 30-year loan than for a 15-year loan.

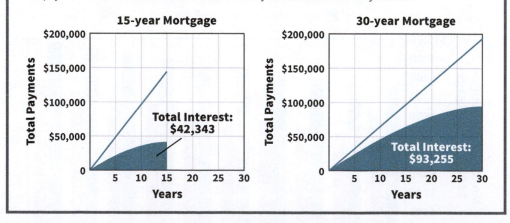

As you see from the demonstration problem, you'll pay more than twice as much interest on the 30-year mortgage, mostly because you are borrowing for twice as long. The opportunity cost is the amount you could earn on those dollars. If you can earn more than the interest cost of the mortgage, it would make financial sense to invest the money instead.

Points

Lenders often give you the opportunity to pay **discount points** to reduce your loan interest rate, commonly referred to as a rate "buy-down." A "point" is 1 percent of the loan amount. Thus, if you're borrowing $100,000, one point is equal to $1,000 paid at the time you get the loan. The points required for a specific rate reduction vary with competition and market conditions. In deciding whether to pay points in return for a lower rate, you need to evaluate the up-front cost against the present value of future payments. **Demonstration Problem 6.8** shows you how to do this calculation.

DEMONSTRATION PROBLEM 6.8 | Should You Pay Points to Get a Lower Mortgage Rate?

Problem

Suppose a lender offers you a 6.5 percent mortgage rate with no points (monthly payment $632) or a 6 percent rate if you pay one point up-front (monthly payment $600). Your loan value is $100,000. Does it make sense to lower your rate by paying the point?

Strategy

Divide the up-front cost of paying the point by the reduction in the monthly payment to determine how long it will take to regain the cost of the point.

Solution

The cost of the point is 1 percent of your loan value, or 1% × $100,000 = $1,000. The reduction you get in your monthly payment is $632 − $600 = $32. Therefore, it will take $1,000/$32 = 31 months to recoup the up-front cost, almost three years. If you expect to own the home that long and you have sufficient cash to do so, then it may be worthwhile to pay the extra amount up front in this case.

In comparing your mortgage choices based on rate, term, and up-front costs, you may want to create a chart to summarize your choices. **Excel Worksheet 6.7** (Personal Financial Planner: Mortgage Comparison) allows you to compare mortgages based on payments, total interest, and term. **Figure 6.11** shows an example.

EXCEL WORKSHEET

See **Excel Worksheet 6.7** (**Personal Financial Planner: Mortgage Comparison**) in **WileyPLUS**.

FIGURE 6.11   **Sample for Excel Worksheet 6.7: Mortgage Comparison**

	A	B	C	D	E
1	Mortgage Information				
2	Amount of Loan		$ 70,000		
3					
4	Annual Rate	6.00%	5.50%	6.50%	6.00%
5					
6	Points	0	1	0	1
7	Upfront cost of points	$ 0.00	$ 700.00	$ 0.00	$ 700.00
8	Term of Mortgage (Years)	15-Year Mortgage		30-Year Mortgage	
9	Mortgage payment				
10	Monthly	$ 590.70	$ 571.96	$ 442.45	$ 419.69
11	Annual	$ 7,088.40	$ 6,863.50	$ 5,309.37	$ 5,036.22
12	Total	$ 106,325.96	$ 102,952.52	$ 159,281.14	$ 151,086.73
13	Cumulative Interest Paid				
14	1 year	$ 4,119.23	$ 4,472.86	$ 4,526.96	$ 4,876.62
15	5 years	$ 18,648.36	$ 17,719.80	$ 22,074.54	$ 21,019.17
16	15 years	$ 36,325.96	$ 32,952.52	$ 60,431.97	$ 55,977.56
17	30 years	N/A	N/A	$ 89,281.14	$ 81,786.73
18	Principal Balance Remaining				
19	1 year	$ 67,030.83	$ 66,909.36	$ 69,217.59	$ 69,140.39
20	5 years	$ 53,206.37	$ 52,702.30	$ 65,527.68	$ 65,138.05
21	15 years	$ −	$ −	$ 50,791.40	$ 49,734.19
22	30 years	N/A	N/A	$ −	$ −

Other Factors

As mentioned earlier, several other factors may affect your mortgage payments, including economic conditions, property value, and creditworthiness.

- **Economic conditions**   Mortgage rates go up and down over time with economic conditions. In the last few decades, mortgage rates have ranged from more than 18 percent back in 1982 to 3.5 percent in 2019. When rates are very low, home buyers can afford more expensive homes, and existing homeowners can refinance their original mortgage loans to free up cash for other purposes. Current mortgage rates are still low by historical standards, and most experts expect rates to increase in the future.

- **Property value**   Many lenders will offer better rates on loans with smaller loan-to-value ratios. If home values go down in your area, having a lower loan-to-value ratio makes it less likely you'll end up "under water," owing more than the value of the home. When that happens, a homeowner may decide to walk away from the loan or try to sell the home in a **short sale** for less than the amount they owe. To ensure that the value of the property is sufficient to guarantee coverage of the mortgage amount, lenders require independent appraisals of property values before approving mortgages. You may be required to make a larger down payment if the home doesn't appraise high enough.

- **Location**   Although the mortgage market is increasingly national in scope, rates may still be lower in some areas of the country than in others. For this reason, you shouldn't limit yourself to local lenders. You might get a little more personal service locally, but remember that the local lender will probably sell your loan anyway, so it's more important to focus on your costs.

- **Your creditworthiness**   Your mortgage payment is also affected by your credit history. As you learned in Chapter 5, lenders use credit bureau reports to check your creditworthiness. If you have a poor credit history—prior loan defaults, late payments, or too much debt—you won't be eligible for favorable mortgage terms.

Lenders will also limit your borrowing based on your capacity to repay the loan. They commonly use the debt payment ratio and the mortgage debt service ratio to assess this aspect of the loan. These are the same debt ratios we considered in Chapter 2. Although the minimums can vary substantially from lender to lender, a common requirement is that the mortgage debt service ratio be no more than 28 percent (31% for FHA loans). You can improve these ratios by minimizing your debt payments as a proportion of your total budget. **Demonstration Problem 6.9** reviews these ratios and shows how they can affect whether you qualify for a loan. You can use **Interactive: Maximum Mortgage Payment Calculation** to find out the maximum mortgage payment you could qualify for.

INTERACTIVE

To find out the maximum mortgage payment you can qualify for, see Interactive: Maximum Mortgage Payment Calculation in WileyPLUS.

DEMONSTRATION PROBLEM 6.9 | Qualifying for a Mortgage Based on Lender Ratios

Problem

Your gross monthly income is $3,400. You are applying for a mortgage that will have a $760 monthly payment of principal and interest. In addition, property taxes will be $150, and homeowner's insurance will be $30. Your other monthly debt payments are $300 (car loan) and $125 (minimum payments on credit cards). Will you qualify for the mortgage loan if your lender requires mortgage debt service ratio be no more than 28 percent of gross income and that total debt payments be no more than 36 percent of gross income?

Strategy

Calculate the ratios and compare the results with the minimum lender requirements.

Solution

Recall from Chapter 2 that the mortgage debt service ratio is defined as follows. Substituting the values given above yields the ratio:

$$\text{Mortgage debt service ratio} = \frac{\text{Principal} + \text{Interest} + \text{Taxes} + \text{Insurance}}{\text{Gross monthly income}}$$

$$= \$760 + \$150 + \$30 = \$940$$

$$= \frac{\$940}{\$3,400}$$

$$= 0.276, \text{ or } 27.6\%$$

Because this value is just a bit lower than the 28 percent maximum, you qualify based on this ratio. Similarly, you can calculate the debt payment ratio as follows:

$$\text{Debt payment ratio} = \frac{\text{Total monthly debt payments}}{\text{After-tax monthly income}}$$

$$= \frac{\$940 + \$300 + \$125}{\$3,400}$$

$$= 0.401, \text{ or } 40.1\%$$

Because this value is greater than the 36 percent maximum, you don't qualify based on this ratio.

Note that for simplicity, lenders commonly use gross monthly income rather than after-tax monthly income for the denominator of this ratio and adjust their requirement accordingly.

When to Refinance

Mortgage loan rates change over time with market conditions. If you originated your loan in a high-interest-rate environment and the rate later decreases significantly, you may want to **refinance** by getting a new mortgage at a lower rate and paying off the old one. If you refinance a 7 percent mortgage with a 6 percent one, you'll be able to reduce your mortgage payment and pay less in total interest over the remaining life of the loan.

Why Refinance?

Some good financial reasons to refinance include the following:

- **To save money**   If you can lower your monthly payment and the total interest paid on the loan, it may make sense to refinance.

- **To access your home equity**   Although you can do this with a second mortgage, it's often cheaper to do so by refinancing your first mortgage for a larger amount.

- **To reduce the term of your mortgage**   If you have 25 years to go on your current mortgage and the lower rate will allow you to reduce the term to 15 years for a similar monthly payment, you can reduce the total interest paid over the life of the loan.

Costs of Refinancing

While it might seem like a simple decision—exchanging the old rate for the new rate to get a lower payment—the costs of refinancing may sometimes outweigh the benefits of the lower rate. Because a refinance results in a completely new mortgage, you will incur most of the same mortgage-related finance charges and closing costs as with the original mortgage. (These costs are discussed in the next section.) In addition, some loans carry a prepayment penalty, which means that you will have to pay a fee if you pay off the loan prior to the end of the original term. In some cases, lenders may allow you to add the up-front costs to the loan balance so that you don't have to pay anything out of pocket for the refinance. This option may seem attractive, but it is not necessarily a good idea, because it will add to the loan balance on which you'll be paying interest for many years.

If you've been making mortgage payments for several years, you'll have paid off some of the original mortgage, so you can refinance a smaller amount. You can find the remaining balance on your most recent mortgage statement. To estimate the payoff yourself, use

Excel Worksheet 6.8 (Personal Financial Planner: Mortgage Amortization Schedule) to create an **amortization schedule** showing the payment, principal, interest, and loan balance in each month of the loan. A portion of such a schedule is reproduced in **Figure 6.12** for a 7 percent mortgage with an original balance of $70,000. The highlighted value ($68,786.56) is the loan balance after 20 monthly payments have been made.

FIGURE 6.12   Sample for Excel Worksheet 6.8: Mortgage Amortization Schedule

	A	B	C	D	E	F	G	H
1	Number of Payments Made	Beginning Balance	Monthly Payment	Monthly Interest	Principal Repaid	Total Cumulative Interest	Total Principal Repaid	Ending Balance
2	1	$70,000.00	$ 465.71	$ 408.33	$ 57.38	$ 408.33	$ 57.38	$ 69,942.62
3	2	69,942.62	465.71	408.00	57.71	816.33	115.09	69,884.91
4	3	69,884.91	465.71	407.66	58.05	1,223.99	173.14	69,826.86
5	4	69,826.86	465.71	407.32	58.39	1,631.32	231.53	69,768.47
6	5	69,768.47	465.71	406.98	58.73	2,038.30	290.26	69,709.74
7	6	69,709.74	465.71	406.64	59.07	2,444.94	349.33	69,650.67
8	7	69,650.67	465.71	406.30	59.42	2,851.24	408.75	69,591.25
9	8	69,591.25	465.71	405.95	59.76	3,257.18	468.51	69,531.49
10	9	69,531.49	465.71	405.60	60.11	3,662.79	528.62	69,471.38
11	10	69,471.38	465.71	405.25	60.46	4,068.03	589.09	69,410.92
12	11	69,410.92	465.71	404.90	60.81	4,472.93	649.90	69,350.10
13	12	69,350.10	465.71	404.54	61.17	4,877.47	711.07	69,288.93
14	13	69,288.93	465.71	404.19	61.53	5,281.66	772.59	69,227.41
15	14	69,227.41	465.71	403.83	61.89	5,685.49	834.498	69,165.52
16	15	69,165.52	465.71	403.47	62.25	6,088.95	896.72	69,103.28
17	16	69,103.28	465.71	403.10	62.61	6,492.05	959.33	69,040.67
18	17	69,040.67	465.71	402.74	62.97	6,894.79	1,022.31	68,977.69
19	18	68,977.69	465.71	403.37	63.34	7,297.16	1,085.65	68,914.35
20	19	68,914.35	465.71	402.00	63.71	7,699.16	1,149.36	68,850.64
21	20	68,850.64	465.71	401.63	64.08	8,100.79	1,213.44	68,786.56
22	*	*	*	*	*	*	*	*
23	*	*	*	*	*	*	*	*
24	*	*	*	*	*	*	*	*

A simple rule of thumb for deciding whether it's worthwhile to refinance a mortgage is to divide the estimated costs of refinancing by the monthly payment savings from the refinance. That will tell you how many months it will take to recoup your costs. If you plan to stay in the home for at least that long, you will break even on the costs of refinancing. Note, however, that if you refinance for a longer period than the remaining number of years on your current mortgage, then the difference in payment is not just from the lower rate, but also from extending the repayment period. **Case Study 6.2** presents an example illustrating how one couple made the refinancing decision.

Case Study 6.2

Michele Oenbrink/Alamy Stock Photo

The Nguyens Consider Refinancing Their Mortgage

Nam and Quynh Nguyen currently have a 30-year mortgage on their condominium. The original loan was for $70,000 at 7 percent, and the monthly payment is $465.71. They purchased their condo 20 months ago and have made all their payments on time. They can now refinance with a 30-year mortgage at 6 percent. The lender has provided them with an estimate of $2,000 for the costs of refinancing. Is it worthwhile for them to refinance?

Strategy

Apply the following steps to determine whether it is worthwhile for the Nguyens to refinance their existing mortgage loan:

1. Determine the remaining balance on the current loan.

2. Calculate the payment for the new loan.

3 Estimate the change in monthly payment.

4. Divide the additional up-front costs by the payment savings to get the number of months it will take to recoup the closing costs.

Solution

1. **Remaining balance:** Using the amortization schedule (shown in Figure 6.12) for their $70,000 loan, the Nguyens look down the last column to the 20th month—this shows that the remaining balance on their loan is now $68,786.56. You can usually get this information from your lender or online.

2. **Payment on new loan:** Using a financial calculator or Excel Worksheet 6.8, calculate the new mortgage payment. Financial calculator solution: enter N = 360, I = 6/12 = 0.5, and PV = $68,786.56, and solve for PMT = $412.41.

3. **Monthly savings:** The Nguyens' monthly savings after the refinance will be $466 – $412 = $54 per month.

4. **Months to break even:** It will take approximately $2,000/$54 = 38 months to recoup the closing costs. However, the Nguyens will have added another 20 months to their mortgage term.

In addition to considering the reduced monthly payments, your refinancing analysis should take into account the following:

- The additional years you'll be paying interest if you refinance for a longer period than remains on your old loan

- Any prepayment penalties on your previous mortgage

- How long you expect to stay in your home

6.5

Completing a Real Estate Transaction

LEARNING OBJECTIVE 6.5
Identify factors that affect home prices, and explain the other costs of completing a real estate transaction.

Once you've determined how much you can allocate to buying a home and understand your financing alternatives, the final steps in the purchasing process will be easier. In this section, we explain the process and costs of buying a home. First, though, we discuss the factors that affect home prices—a topic based on **Figure 6.13**, touched on earlier in the discussion of what affects the size of mortgage payments.

Determinants of Real Estate Value

Although your home purchase decision will no doubt be made based on many factors, including affordability and personal preference, you shouldn't forget that your home is also an investment. Thus, you should consider each alternative property's potential for appreciation in value. A real estate broker can help you better understand an area's market, but you should also do your own homework.

We noted earlier that the location of a property affects its cost. In fact, in the real estate business, it's a common joke to say that the three determinants of real estate value are (1) location, (2) location, and (3) location. This isn't entirely true, of course, but location is a very important factor.

Home prices across the United States vary widely. Two identical houses will have a different values depending on their location. A beautiful mansion with all the amenities will be worth

FIGURE 6.13 Average Home Price by State, 2018

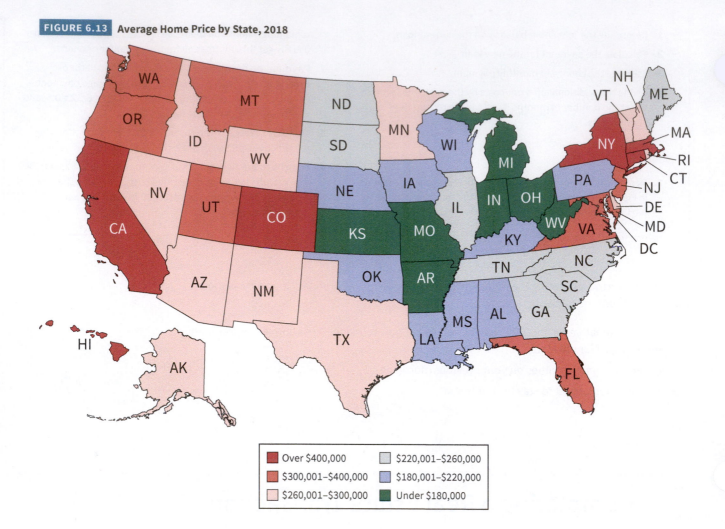

▮ Over $400,000	▮ $220,001–$260,000
▮ $300,001–$400,000	▮ $180,001–$220,000
▮ $260,001–$300,000	▮ Under $180,000

practically nothing if it's located next to a smelly landfill. And a small, run-down bungalow on the Florida beachfront may be worth a million dollars. A home in a good location will appreciate more quickly, and you'll have an easier time reselling it later. Based on Figure 6.13, how do home prices in your state compare with those in other states?

Various aspects of location affect property value, including the following:

- The desirability of the state and town in which the home is located
- The values of surrounding properties
- Proximity to (and quality of) schools
- Proximity to transportation, including bus routes, highways, and airports
- Zoning—commercial versus residential—of the property and nearby lots (If you have a house that backs up to a large vacant lot zoned for future commercial use, you could end up with a Wal-Mart in your backyard.)

Qualitative factors other than location also influence home prices. These factors include:

- The type of structure (single or multifamily)
- When the home was built and whether it's been maintained and modernized over time
- Characteristics of the property, such as number of rooms and baths, square footage and acreage
- Curb appeal (attractiveness from the street, landscaping)
- Interior appeal (height of ceilings, carpet and flooring condition, decor colors)

Perhaps most important, real estate values are determined by what a reasonable buyer is willing to pay for the property. This factor is highly dependent on market conditions and mortgage rates at a given time. When there are many foreclosures in an area, the result is lower values for other properties in the same neighborhood. Therefore, before you buy a home, you need to check out recent sales and foreclosures nearby.

The Home-Buying Process

A **real estate broker** (or **real estate agent**) is a licensed professional who helps match up buyers and sellers. Most people use a real estate broker when they buy or sell a home, although you aren't legally required to do so. Because you'll probably buy or sell a home only a few times in your life, having an experienced broker to guide you through the process will make it easier. A broker's familiarity with real estate in the area and available financing options, as well as the negotiation process, can be invaluable to you, and brokers' fees are typically paid by the seller. When you sell your home, a broker can also help you price it more realistically.

Choosing a Broker

How do you select a broker? When considering any professional services, you should evaluate the person's qualifications and professionalism. What if you look at some houses with a particular broker but decide you don't like her? You're not legally obligated to continue to work with her, but the industry rule is that the first broker to show you a particular property is the one who should get the selling commission. Therefore, it pays to assess a candidate's qualifications *before* he or she does any work for you. **Table 6.6** shows you some helpful questions to ask an agent.

TABLE 6.6	Questions for Real Estate Agents or Brokers

Real estate agents and brokers don't make any money unless they facilitate the sale of a house, either for the buyer or for the seller. Consider asking prospective agents these questions to assess whether their qualifications will meet your needs.

1. **Can you give me a reference from former buyers or sellers you've worked with?**
   You'll want to ask the references about service, dependability, personality, and professionalism.

2. **How long have you sold real estate in this area?**
   More experienced agents will be better informed about area amenities and value determinants.

3. **Is real estate your primary profession?**
   If it's a second job, you may get lower-quality service, and this might be an indication that the agent can't make a living selling real estate full time.

4. **What is your sales track record, and what is the average price of the homes you have sold?**
   Many agents specialize in certain market segments.

5. **How many realtors work for your brokerage firm?**
   Larger offices may have more in-house listings. When the market is "hot," the best properties may be sold before they can be advertised.

How a Broker Is Paid

Real estate agents and brokers are paid a **commission** by the seller. The commission is typically 5 to 7 percent of the negotiated sale price of the house, but the seller can negotiate the amount of the commission. Several national real estate chains are now advertising much lower rates, such as 1 percent for listing a property. When more than one broker is involved, the commission is split.

Let's say that you buy a condo for $100,000. Two agents are involved in the sale—Pete represents the seller, and Sandra works for you. Pete is called the *listing broker*. In a standard listing contract, Pete's office will be entitled to one-half of the full commission, to be split between himself and the supervising broker in his office. If the full commission is 6 percent, Pete's commission will be 1.5 percent of the sale price, and his boss will also get 1.5 percent. Your broker, Sandra, who helped you find the home and negotiate the sale price, is a *cooperating broker*. She will normally receive the other half of the 6 percent commission, to be shared with her office. If the sale price is $100,000, the listing broker, the cooperating broker, and their managing offices will each receive $1,500, all paid for by the seller out of the money received from the sale of the home.

Your Legal Relationship with a Broker

Although many buyers believe that their brokers are acting as their agents—after all, the brokers are taking them to look at houses and then shepherding them through the negotiation and transaction—this is not actually the case. The seller is the one who pays the broker the commission and is therefore the one to whom the broker owes a primary legal duty. The objective of the seller is to sell the house for the *highest* possible price, and the objective of the buyer is to pay the *lowest* amount possible. Brokers obviously cannot act in the best interests of both parties. The law concerning the duties of brokers who are helping buyers in the real estate process differs by state, but a good rule of thumb is to never reveal information to your broker that you don't want the other party to know.

In some states, you may be able to contract with a **buyer broker**, a real estate agent who works exclusively for the buyer and owes no legal duty to the seller. Of course, these brokers still need to be paid. A buyer who wants this type of service may have to pay for it separately, with fees ranging from hourly rates to 3.5 percent of the sale price. In some states, a buyer broker can share the seller's commission as a cooperating broker.

Reflection Question 3

If you were buying a house, would you want to pay for the services of a buyer broker? Why or why not?

Negotiating the Contract

Once you find a home that you want to buy, you must initiate the negotiation process. Although your broker may be helpful in this process, you should use your own judgment on whether the "price is right" because the real estate agents are more likely to be interested in closing the deal than in getting you the lowest price. In addition, although price is obviously the most important term of the purchase agreement, other factors may affect it. Here are the most common negotiation points for a real estate contract:

- **Price**   Most initial offers are less than the asking price, and sellers factor this into their initial asking price. The seller may counter your offer with a new price somewhere between the two amounts. Understanding the market conditions in the area will help you to determine how tough a negotiator you can afford to be on price. When the market is "hot," you may need to make a full-price offer or even offer more than the asking price.

- **Conditions**   Most purchase offers for houses are made contingent on the buyer's ability to get mortgage financing at favorable rates. Your purchase agreement will usually give you 15 to 30 days to find financing. Buyers may also make their offers contingent on selling their existing home. Although this is clearly in the buyer's best interest, sellers are not generally willing to wait very long.

- **Other terms**   There are many other terms you might want to negotiate. If you don't specify what is included with the house, certain conventions will apply. Although furniture and personal property of the seller are obviously not included (and must be removed from the premises prior to sale), most appliances (except the washer/dryer and sometimes the refrigerator) are included. Light fixtures, window treatments, wall-to-wall carpeting, and landscaping stay with the house unless otherwise agreed. If you inspect the home before closing and find that the seller has removed, say, the dining room chandelier without prior agreement, you can request compensation for that item at the closing.

- **Closing**   You can also negotiate on the split of certain closing costs, when and where the closing will occur, and what circumstances will allow you to get out of the agreement.

If your offer is accepted, a contract will be drawn up, and you will be required to make an initial good faith or earnest money deposit, which will be applied to your down payment at the closing. The next step is to get approval for a mortgage within the allowed time limit.

Arranging Mortgage Financing

After finalizing a purchase contract and shopping around to evaluate your mortgage options, you need to select a lender and make a formal loan application. In very competitive housing markets, buyers often get prequalified by a lender in order to make their offer more attractive to the seller. Although you may be most concerned with the rates a lender offers, the lenders with the lowest rates may also be slower at processing loans. As mentioned earlier, the location of the lender is probably not very important, since your loan will likely be sold in the secondary market. Most people trying to get a mortgage now use online resources to identify potential lenders, but 75 percent still finalize their applications in person. This is likely to change as Internet security improves and more lenders develop web-based applications.

The application can usually be processed within a few days but may take longer during very busy times (as when rates have recently fallen and many homeowners are refinancing) or if you have complicated financials, such as small business income. In October 2015, a government initiative called "Know Before You Owe" resulted in new regulations that require lenders to provide prospective borrowers with fair estimates of the costs associated with the transaction, including the APR, all fees, and all costs they will incur in closing the loan. Before being required to pay any fees, borrowers must receive a "Loan Estimate" that clearly lays out the APR, monthly payment, estimated closing costs, and cash to close. A few days before the closing, lenders must provide a "Closing Disclosure" that includes the same information for easy comparison with the original estimates.

Mortgage rates may change, favorably or unfavorably for you, between the time you apply for a loan and the time you complete the transaction. If rates are rising, you may want to lock in your rate with the lender to guarantee that you won't be subject to a higher rate at closing. Some lenders will lock in within 30 or 45 days of closing at no charge, but others may require that you pay a point (1 percent of the loan amount) or a portion of a point for a lock-in. What if rates fall? With most lock-in agreements, you won't be entitled to a reduction if rates fall before the closing.

The Closing

The date of the closing is set by mutual agreement among buyer, seller, and lender. As noted, prior to the closing date, your lender will give you a detailed accounting of the mortgage-related costs, and you will receive an accounting of the other purchase-related funds that will be collected and disbursed at the closing, such as prepayment of property tax and insurance. The lender at that time will confirm the cash needed to close and notify you of the method of payment, commonly wire transfer. Before the closing—usually earlier on the same day—you'll have an opportunity to inspect the property to be certain that the sellers have removed all of their belongings and that it's in the agreed-upon condition. Any problems you find can then be negotiated at the closing. The location of the closing is also agreed upon in advance and is usually at the office of a title insurer, realtor, or lawyer who is involved in the transaction.

At the closing, which will usually take about an hour, you, the seller, and the lender or the lender's legal representative will sign all the necessary legal documents to transfer property ownership to you by **deed**, record the transaction, and finalize the mortgage. In most cases, an escrow agent or title insurer collects and disburses the funds and ensures that all the closing costs are paid to the appropriate parties and governmental units.

A number of expenses must be paid by the buyer and the seller during the closing process. These closing, or settlement, costs will be summarized by your lender on the required

"Closing Disclosure." Closing costs include prepayments of homeowner's insurance and property taxes, to be held in an **escrow account** from which the lender will make payments on your behalf. **Title insurance** ensures that the seller is giving you the ownership rights for which you have contracted. **Table 6.7** details the common closing costs you can expect to pay. The exact amounts are difficult to pinpoint, because every purchase and financing transaction is unique.

TABLE 6.7   Summary of Closing Costs

Cost	Explanation	Paid by Seller	Paid by Buyer
Down payment	The purchase price less the mortgage		X
Mortgage-related costs	Daily interest to the end of the current month, application fee, credit report, points, loan origination fee, recording fee for public recording of deed and mortgage		X
Home inspection fee	Cost of having the home inspected for structural, electrical, and mechanical defects		X
Escrows	Two to six months property taxes and homeowner's insurance held in an account on your behalf so the lender can pay these as they come due		X
Title search	Cost of verifying that the seller actually owns the property and that there aren't any other claims on the property that might interfere with buyer's future ownership		X
Title insurance	Insurance to protect buyer and lender from financial losses resulting from problems with the title to the property that might interfere with future ownership; cost is a percentage of home value	X (can differ by state of residence)	
Commission	Percentage of sale price, paid out of seller's proceeds unless buyer uses separate buyer broker	X	
Attorney's fee	Fee for advice on legal aspects of the transaction; not required, because the title company's lawyer usually prepares documents	X	X
Closing charge	Payment for use of the room in which the closing occurs and preparation of documents for closing; shared between buyer and seller	X	X

Summary

Learning Objectives Review

LEARNING OBJECTIVE 6.1   Evaluate your household automobile needs and budget.

Before making any purchase, you should evaluate your needs and the impact on your financial plan.

- Your cost analysis should include **fixed expenses**, such as your loan or lease payment and insurance, and **variable expenses**, such as gasoline and repairs and maintenance. One type of fixed expense is **depreciation**, the expected decrease in the value of the vehicle over time.

- Your choice of automobile should be based on careful consideration of alternatives, using predefined criteria. Normally, these will include your price limitations as well as size, equipment, fuel economy, safety, reliability, and any **warranty** offered by the seller.

- You should be able to pay less than the **sticker price** for a new car. However, a dealer will expect to make a profit over the **dealer's invoice price** paid for the vehicle. Dealers may also make additional profit on installed accessories, from manufacturer rebates, or by selling you an **extended warranty** on the car.

- You can calculate annual gasoline costs using **Equation 6.1**:

Annual gasoline costs = Gallons per year × Price per gallon
= (Annual miles driven/MPG) × Price per gallon

LEARNING OBJECTIVE 6.2   Decide whether to lease or buy a vehicle, and negotiate the terms for purchase and financing.

In deciding whether to lease or buy a car, with cash or with a loan, you should carefully analyze the terms of alternative contracts to determine which is financially more attractive, given your expected use of the vehicle and its financing costs.

- An auto lease is an agreement to rent the vehicle for a period of time instead of buying. Lease payments are generally lower than loans for a similarly priced vehicle because you do not have **equity** in the vehicle. At the end of the lease, you must return the car to the lessor.

- Lease payments are determined by amortizing the expected depreciation of the vehicle over the lease term, including finance charges.

- With a **closed-end lease**, the **lessee** can walk away from the lease at the end of the term, subject only to a penalty for exceeding the mileage limitation. The **lessor** takes the risk that the value of the car may decline more than was originally estimated.

- Whether you lease or buy a vehicle, it's important to negotiate the best possible terms. A lower price will reduce the amount to be financed, so it will reduce loan or lease payments. You will also want to evaluate the finance charge, purchase option, and mileage penalty.

- To negotiate effectively, you should research the market value of the vehicle. If you are buying from a dealership, you should understand the components of dealer profit. Dealers may be willing to give you more attractive terms on price or financing if they are making profit on other elements of the transaction.

- If you buy a defective vehicle from a dealer, state **lemon laws** may provide a remedy.

LEARNING OBJECTIVE 6.3   Evaluate your housing needs and budget.

Your housing needs, whether you want a single-family home, rental apartment, or **condominium,** will change over your life cycle and with changes in life circumstances, such as marriage or divorce. The decision to buy or rent should be made in light of your household budget and prioritized financial goals. You should carefully evaluate the advantages and disadvantages of each alternative.

- Renters pay an up-front **security deposit**, are not usually responsible for property maintenance, and will not be able to take any tax deductions for housing costs.

- If you decide to buy a home, you should determine the price range you can afford in advance by considering your budget allocation to housing costs and taking into account the nonfinancing costs associated with home ownership, such as **property tax**, homeowner's insurance, association dues, and repairs and maintenance.

- The up-front costs of buying a home include **closing costs** and the **down payment,** which should be at least 20 percent to avoid paying extra **mortgage insurance.** These costs mean that renting is usually cheaper in the short run. However, the tax-deductibility of mortgage interest and property taxes and the fixed amount of a mortgage payment over time make buying a home preferable when considered over a longer time period.

LEARNING OBJECTIVE 6.4   Evaluate mortgage financing alternatives.

There are many sources of mortgage financing, and terms can vary substantially. Therefore, it pays to shop around for the best terms and rates and to carefully compare your total costs.

- Most home purchases are financed with a long-term loan called a **mortgage**.

- Borrowers normally make mortgage payments that include both interest and repayment of principal. The total mortgage interest you will pay over the life of the loan can be calculated using **Equation 6.2**:

$$\text{Total interest} = (\text{Number of payments} \times \text{Monthly payment}) - \text{Loan amount}$$

- In deciding whether to lend to you, mortgage lenders consider several key financial ratios and whether the loan will have FHA or VA payment guarantees.

- A **conventional mortgage** is a fixed-rate, fixed-term, fixed-payment loan. Lenders usually sell these loans in the **secondary mortgage market**.

- **Adjustable rate mortgages** (ARMs) usually have a fixed rate for a period of time, and then the rate is adjusted at set intervals subject to **interest rate caps**.

- There are many other types of mortgages, including graduated payment mortgages, which may include **negative amortization**, growing equity mortgages, and balloon mortgages.

- A **reverse annuity mortgage** allows a homeowner to convert the equity in his or her home into a lump sum or a series of annuity payments.

- Many factors can affect your mortgage payment. You should carefully evaluate all of your mortgage choices based on maturity, rate, **discount points**, and other closing costs. In addition, you may end up paying higher rates due to economic conditions, the location of your property, and your credit history.

- If mortgage rates decrease, it may be financially worthwhile to **refinance** your mortgage. The decision should be made by comparing the payment savings to the refinancing costs. You can determine your remaining balance on a loan by using an **amortization schedule**.

- If a home's value falls below the amount that is owed on a mortgage loan and the owner fails to make payments, lenders have the right to take the property in a foreclosure. In some cases, they may allow a **short sale**, in which the lender accepts a lower sales price in satisfaction of the debt.

LEARNING OBJECTIVE 6.5   Identify factors that affect home prices, and explain the other costs of completing a real estate transaction.

- In the process of finding a home to buy and negotiating a purchase price, many people use the services of a **real estate broker** or **agent**. The listing contract usually specifies a **commission** of 5 to 7 percent of the purchase price, which will be shared by the brokers working for the buyer and the seller. Buyers can sometimes arrange to use a **buyer broker** who will exclusively represent their interests.

- The buyer and seller negotiate the price and other aspects of the contract. The market value of the home will depend on the value of similar properties in the area and on the home's attributes—where it is located, its size, and its characteristics.

- When you apply for a mortgage, the lender will provide you with an estimate of the costs related to the transaction and the monthly payment you will have to make on the loan.

- The transfer of ownership by **deed** and the mortgage financing are finalized at a real estate **closing**. At that time, you will incur a number of different costs related to the mortgage and the legal transaction. **Title insurance** ensures that the seller is giving you the ownership rights you have contracted for. In most cases, you will be required to pay property taxes and homeowner's insurance in advance to the lender, who will hold the funds in an **escrow account** and disburse payments when they are due.

Excel Worksheets

6.1 Personal Financial Planner: Auto Costs Log

6.2 Personal Financial Planner: Maximum Affordable Car Price

6.3 Personal Financial Planner: Auto Features Comparison

6.4 Personal Financial Planner: Costs of Leasing versus Buying a Car

6.5 Personal Financial Planner: Costs of Renting versus Buying a Home

6.6 Personal Financial Planner: Calculating an Affordable Home Price

6.7 Personal Financial Planner: Mortgage Comparison

6.8 Personal Financial Planner: Mortgage Amortization Schedule

Key Terms

adjustable rate mortgage (ARM)   6-24
amortization schedule   6-32
buyer broker   6-36
closed-end lease   6-10
closing   6-20
closing costs   6-20
commission   6-35
condominium   6-16
conventional mortgage   6-23
dealer's invoice price   6-6
deed   6-37
depreciation   6-5

discount points   6-28
down payment   6-19
equity   6-10
escrow account   6-38
extended warranty   6-9
fixed expenses   6-4
interest rate increase caps   6-24
lemon laws   6-14
lessee   6-10
lessor   6-10
mortgage   6-22
mortgage insurance   6-19
negative amortization   6-24

property tax   6-18
real estate broker or
   agent   6-35
refinance   6-31
reverse annuity mortgage   6-26
secondary mortgage market   6-22
security deposit   6-17
short sale   6-30
sticker price   6-6
title insurance   6-38
variable expenses   6-4
warranty   6-9

WileyPLUS

Practice Questions to check your understanding, Peer-to-Peer Videos, Interactives, and many other resources are available in WileyPLUS.

Concept Review Questions

1. Look up the manufacturer's suggested retail price (MSRP) for a vehicle that is available in both gasoline and hybrid models. What is the price differential between the two models? How should you evaluate whether the difference in cost is worth the potential fuel savings?

2. Describe the process for negotiating a new car purchase.

3. Explain why a dealer might be willing to sell you a new car at only a few dollars over its cost.

4. Manuel bought a new car two years ago. The car has had electrical system problems ever since he bought it. He has taken the car back to the dealership for servicing under his warranty several times, but they have been unable to solve the problem. What should he do?

5. If all else is equal, explain how your decision to lease or buy a car will be affected if you tend to drive more than 15,000 miles per year.

6. If all else is equal, explain how your decision to lease or buy a car will be affected if you want a lower monthly payment.

7. If all else is equal, explain how your decision to lease or buy a car will be affected if the car you want is one that loses market value quickly.

8. If all else is equal, explain how your decision to lease or buy a car will be affected if you don't have much money for a down payment.

9. Explain why lease payments are usually less than loan payments for the same vehicle.

10. What are the advantages and disadvantages of renting as compared with owning a home?

11. How would you expect your housing needs to change over your life cycle?

12. Why might some buyers prefer to purchase a condominium instead of a single-family home even though they will have to pay monthly condominium fees?

13. What are some reasons you might want to spend less on housing costs than the maximum you can afford?

14. Explain how your other credit obligations, such as credit card debt and personal loans, can affect your ability to qualify for a mortgage loan.

15. Why are lenders required to provide mortgage applicants with a "Loan Estimate" prior to charging them any loan fees?

16. Mortgage lenders often require you to pay additional funds into an escrow account along with your principal and interest payments. What are these funds for, what does your lender do with the money, and why do lenders have this requirement?

17. What factors should you consider when deciding whether to refinance your existing home mortgage?

18. What are the pros and cons of using a real estate broker to help you sell your home as opposed to selling it yourself?

19. Your college roommate has recently obtained his real estate license. What factors should you consider when deciding whether to use him as your real estate broker?

20. What are the primary qualitative factors that affect the value of the house or apartment you currently live in? Do you think your home is worth more or less than other nearby homes? Why?

21. Describe the process of making a consumer purchase, and explain why it is important to follow this process when making large purchases such as houses and cars.

Application Problems

1. You are paying $20,000 for a car. If the loan amount is $12,000, the loan term is 48 months, and the APR is 8 percent, what is your loan payment?

2. If you drive 10,000 miles per year, your car gets 22 miles per gallon, and the average cost of gasoline is $4 per gallon, how much will you spend on gasoline per year?

3. Given the following information about the costs of automobile ownership, what is the total cost of ownership for the first year?

- First-year depreciation: $3,000
- Auto insurance cost: $200
- Registration and license: $250
- Regular oil changes: $120
- Monthly loan payment: $293
- Gasoline: $1,818

4. Assume that you own a car that gets 20 miles per gallon (MPG) on average. If you typically drive 16,000 miles per year and the price of gasoline goes from $2.00 per gallon to $3.00 per gallon, what is your additional cost per year?

5. Your three-year auto lease includes a mileage penalty of 25 cents per mile in excess of 12,000 miles per year. At the end of the lease, your mileage is 40,000. How much will you owe to the lessor?

6. Assume that you are considering the purchase of a used car for $6,000. Your lender is allowing you to finance the entire purchase price. What is the monthly payment, assuming that the lender is offering you a 48-month loan at 6 percent APR?

7. If you buy a car and finance it with a $6,000, 36-month loan at 5 percent APR, how much interest will you pay over the entire term of the loan?

8. What factors should you consider when deciding between a 48-month loan at 6 percent APR and a 36-month loan at 5 percent APR?

9. You bought a car three years ago for $20,000 and financed $16,000 at 6 percent APR for 60 months. You are now thinking about trading in that vehicle for a new one and would like to know how much you still owe on the loan. Assuming that you have already made 36 payments, what is the balance remaining on your loan?

10. Maria is comparing two housing alternatives: renting an apartment or buying a condo. She can rent an apartment for $800 per month. The security deposit is $1,200 (one and a half months' rent). Renter's insurance is $140 per year. She earns 1 percent on her savings account after tax, and her marginal tax rate is 25 percent. What is Maria's total first-year cost of renting? You may find it helpful to use Excel Worksheet 6.5 to answer this question.

11. Greta has decided to buy a condominium instead of renting. She estimates the following costs: purchase price, $103,000; down payment, $3,000; mortgage payment, $599.55 per month ($7,195 per year, of which $5,967 is interest in the first year); property tax, $1,300; homeowner's insurance, $500; repairs and maintenance, $500; closing costs, $2,000. The annual increase in the condo's value is estimated at 4 percent. She earns 1 percent on her savings account after tax, her marginal tax rate is 25 percent, and she does not itemize deductions. What is Greta's total first-year cost of buying? You may find it helpful to use Excel Worksheet 6.5 to answer this question.

12. Suppose you need to finance $100,000 for the purchase of a home, and you're deciding between a conventional 30-year mortgage at 6 percent and an ARM at an initial rate of 4 percent, an annual interest rate cap of 1 percentage point, and a lifetime cap of 5 percentage points. If you choose the ARM, how much less will your monthly mortgage payment be in the first year?

13. If you have an adjustable rate mortgage with an initial rate of 4 percent, an annual interest rate cap of 1 percentage point, and a lifetime cap of 5 percentage points, what is the maximum annual interest rate you could end up paying on the loan?

14. Calculate the monthly mortgage payment for a 30-year conventional mortgage at 6 percent, assuming a loan amount of $150,000.

15. Calculate the monthly mortgage payment for a 15-year conventional mortgage at 5 percent, assuming a loan amount of $150,000.

16. Your current mortgage interest rate is 7 percent, and your monthly mortgage payment (principal and interest) is $800. Rates have declined, and you estimate that you could reduce your payment to $750 by refinancing at a lower rate. You estimate that your total closing costs will be $3,500. Is it worth it to refinance? What factors will you consider in making this decision?

17. Jane's gross monthly income is $3,300. She is applying for a mortgage loan that will have a $800 monthly mortgage payment (principal and interest). In addition, property taxes will be $100 per month, and homeowner's insurance will be $50 per month. Jane's other debt payments are $250 (car loan) and $200 (minimum payments on credit cards). Will she qualify for the mortgage loan if her lender requires the mortgage debt service ratio to be no more than 30 percent and the debt payment ratio to be no more than 40 percent?

18. Suppose you are shopping for a mortgage and would like to finance $200,000. A lender offers you a conventional 30-year mortgage at 6 percent with no points (monthly payment = $1,199) or a 5.5 percent rate with one point (monthly payment = $1,136). How would you decide whether it makes sense to buy down your rate by paying the point?

19. You want to buy a home, and you have $15,000 available to cover the down payment and closing costs. Based on your household budget, you estimate that you can afford to allocate $1,200 per month to housing costs. Your real estate agent has given you the following estimates for the monthly nonfinancing costs of home ownership: property taxes, $200; homeowner's insurance, $75; repairs and maintenance, $50. Your lender has provided an estimate of $3,000 for closing costs. What is the maximum you can afford to pay for a home, assuming current mortgage rates are 6 percent? You may want to use Excel Worksheet 6.6 in solving this problem.

Case Applications

1. Annette Thoreson is a single mother of two. Her children are getting older, and she wants to replace her old car with a new minivan. In addition to extra room for camping gear and car pools, Annette wants safety features, such as dual front airbags and antilock brakes. She has decided that the best choice is a Honda Odyssey, for which she has negotiated a purchase price of $25,000. She has $4,000 to put toward the purchase and has prearranged for a car loan with her bank at 7 percent APR for 48 months. At the last minute, the car dealership's financing department pressures her to consider leasing the van for four years at $199 per month. The lease terms are as follows:

- Capitalized cost reduction: $3,000
- Security deposit: two lease payments
- Mileage limit: 12,000 miles per year
- Over-mileage penalty: $0.25 per mile
- Purchase option: $14,000
- After-tax APY on savings account: 2% (assume annual compounding)
- Estimated value of the car at the end of 4 years: $13,000
- Number of miles per year Annette typically drives: 13,000

a. What would Annette's monthly loan payment be if she decides to buy the car and finance it with the 7 percent 48-month bank loan?

b. What is the total cost of leasing the minivan for the four years? You may want to use Excel Worksheet 6.4 to solve this problem.

c. What is the total cost of buying the car by financing it with the bank loan? You may want to use Excel Worksheet 6.4 to solve this problem.

d. What does the auto dealership have to gain by encouraging Annette to lease instead of buy the minivan?

2. Rami and Sara Sayed are young married professionals. They have been renting a two-bedroom apartment in a major metropolitan area for the last two years. Their landlord has recently informed them that he will be increasing their rent to $1,500 per month for the coming year. Although they consider this amount an affordable housing expense, Rami and Sara are seriously thinking about buying a home instead of continuing to rent. They have collected the following information to use in making their decision:

Combined gross income:	$6,000 per month
After-tax income:	$5,000 per month
Car loan payments:	$550 per month
Credit card payments:	$150 per month
Student loan payments:	$230 per month
Available down payment:	$20,000
Expected closing costs:	$3,000
30-year fixed mortgage rate:	6 percent, 0 points
Estimated property tax:	$1,800 per year
Estimated homeowner's insurance:	$600 per year
Estimated maintenance costs:	$150 per month
Additional utilities:	$60 per month

a. Assuming that the Sayeds do not want to spend more than $1,500 per month on total housing expenses, calculate the maximum price that they can afford to pay for a home. You may want to use Excel Worksheet 6.6 to solve this problem.

b. The Sayeds have applied for a home mortgage from a lender. If they are approved, their monthly payment will be $1,100 per month for principal and interest. Use the Sayeds' financial information to calculate their mortgage debt service ratio and debt payment ratio (both as a percentage of gross income). If the Sayeds' mortgage lender requires that total debt payments be no more than 41 percent of gross income, and that mortgage debt service be no more than 28 percent of gross income, will the Sayeds qualify for the mortgage? Explain your reasoning.

c. Assume that the Sayeds buy a home in January and borrow $200,000 to finance it. The mortgage interest and principal payment is $1,199.10 per month. In the first year, they pay $11,933 in interest, $2,456 in principal, $1,800 in property taxes, and $8,000 in state income taxes. Their marginal tax rate is 25 percent.

Assuming that they do not have any other itemizable deductions, will they be able to save money by deducting mortgage interest and property taxes on their federal income tax return? If so, how much will this save them in taxes?

d. Based on your analysis, would you advise the Sayeds to buy a home? What other factors should they consider?

3. Jonas was reading the paper and saw an advertisement for a 30-year mortgage at 4 percent APR. The advertisement promised very quick processing and minimal closing costs. Jonas currently owns his home, which he financed a few years ago with a 30-year conventional mortgage at 5 percent APR. His monthly mortgage payment is $429.46. Assume that the current lowest quoted rate on 30-year conventional mortgages is 5.5 percent.

a. Why is it likely that the advertised rate is for an ARM?

b. How can lenders afford to offer rates as low as 4 percent? Would you expect that the interest rate caps and annual caps will also be low? Why or why not?

c. Assume that Jonas calls the lender and finds that the 4 percent is a teaser rate for the first year. The lender also charges 1.5 points. After the first year, the loan rate will be calculated by adding 2 percentage points to a particular index (which is currently at 3.8 percent). The annual interest rate increase cap after the first adjustment is 1 percent per year, and the lifetime interest rate increase cap is 5 percentage points over the original rate. If the index goes up to 4 percent next year, what is the maximum rate that this loan could carry in the future?

d. Assuming that Jonas's current loan balance is $77,579, what would his first-year monthly payments be if he takes the 4 percent ARM, and how much will he save per month?

e. Assuming that Jonas's current loan balance is $77,579, and that the lender charges 1.5 points, how many months would it take

Jonas to recoup his mortgage financing costs if he took out the new loan and rates remained the same?

f. Discuss the factors that Jonas should consider in deciding whether to take advantage of the 4 percent ARM.

4. Carrie and Brad Crenshaw are refinancing their home to take advantage of falling mortgage rates. Their current rate is 7.5 percent on a 30-year conventional mortgage, originated four years ago in the amount of $130,000. They have two options for refinancing: First, for a $250 fee, their current lender (Bank A) is willing to reduce their rate to 6 percent on a new 30-year conventional mortgage with no points as long as they don't increase the amount of their loan. Their only closing costs will be an updated appraisal and title insurance certificate, for a total of $500. The Crenshaws' second option is to take out a conventional loan with Bank B, which is offering 5 percent with 1 point. This lender's application fee is $250, and appraisal and credit report fees total $300. Bank B will allow them to finance the remaining balance on their loan plus an additional $15,000, and some of this can be used to pay their closing costs so that they will have no up-front costs.

a. What is the Crenshaw's current mortgage payment?

b. Calculate the balance owed on the Crenshaws' current mortgage.

c. If the Crenshaws refinance $130,000 with a new 6 percent loan from Bank A, what is their new monthly payment?

d. If the difference between their previous mortgage payment and the new payment on the Bank A's refinanced loan is $100, how many months will it take to recoup the financing costs?

e. Calculate the monthly payment for the new Bank B loan (5%, one point, $250 application fee, $300 appraisal and credit report fee), assuming the Crenshaws borrow a total of $140,000.

f. Discuss the pros and cons of each of the Crenshaws' loan options.

g. Explain to the Crenshaws why they might want to consider a shorter-term mortgage rather than refinancing for another 30 years.

CHAPTER 7

Insuring Cars and Homes

David Burkholder/Shutterstock.com

Feature Story

Although we may know for certain that the southeastern coastal states will experience hurricanes and that the Midwest will have tornadoes, there is always uncertainty about exactly when and where they'll strike and how much damage they'll cause. Since 2010, the east coast has averaged about 8 hurricanes and 15 tropical storms per year. The costliest hurricane season on record was 2017, in which several category 4 hurricanes made landfall. These storms caused a record total of $300 billion in damages to homes, businesses, and vehicles.

Does everyone have insurance to cover this type of damage? Not necessarily. Many people are inadequately prepared for the devastation resulting from natural disasters. It can be very expensive to insure homes and cars in hurricane-prone regions. And even if you have insurance, it may not be the right type, or it may be insufficient to cover your actual replacement or repair costs. In this chapter, we consider several categories of risks that households face and identify strategies for managing them. Risk management methods include, but are not limited to, the purchase of insurance.

LEARNING OBJECTIVES	TOPICS	DEMONSTRATION PROBLEMS
7.1 Apply the risk management process to identify risks and decide how to manage them.	**7.1 Managing Personal Risks** • The Risk Management Process • Identify and Evaluate Property and Liability Risks • Risk Management Methods	**7.1** Calculating Expected Losses
7.2 Explain how risk pooling works, and define common insurance policy terminology.	**7.2 How Insurance Works** • Risk Pooling and Insurance • Insurance Premiums • Insurance Policy Terminology	

(continued)

(continued)

LEARNING OBJECTIVES	TOPICS	DEMONSTRATION PROBLEMS
7.3 Describe the loss coverage provided by homeowner's and renter's insurance and the factors that affect premiums.	**7.3 Managing Homeowner's and Renter's Risk** • What Risks Do Homeowners and Renters Face? • Insuring Your Home • Pricing of Homeowner's Insurance • Umbrella Liability Insurance	
7.4 Understand your choices for auto insurance coverage and what factors are likely to increase your premiums.	**7.4 Auto Insurance** • State Auto Insurance Laws • Policy Coverage • Auto Insurance Pricing	
7.5 Compare insurers based on quality, service, and price before buying a policy.	**7.5 Buying Insurance and Making Claims** • Steps to Buying Property and Liability Insurance • The Role of Agents and Brokers • Comparing Insurance Policies • Using Online Resources to Evaluate Your Insurance Options • Making a Claim on Your Insurance	

7.1 | Managing Personal Risks

LEARNING OBJECTIVE 7.1

Apply the risk management process to identify risks and decide how to manage them.

You're exposed to risk in nearly everything you do. In its most general sense, risk is simply another word for uncertainty. From a financial planning perspective, you should be concerned about risks to yourself, your family, your property, and your investments.

A distinction is often made between a **pure risk**—a risk that produces only bad outcomes (car accident or fire)—and a **speculative risk**—a risk that involves the possibility of either loss or gain (gambling or investment). Because pure risk events happen at random, insurance is often available to help spread the cost of losses across the population, as we explain later in this chapter. In contrast, investment risks affect large groups of investors at the same time. For this reason, the strategies for managing investment risk, covered in later chapters, are quite different from those discussed in this chapter.

Although your financial plan needs to account for both pure and speculative risks, we focus our attention in this chapter on developing a plan for managing certain pure risk exposures—those that result from property ownership. In particular, we focus on auto and homeowner (or renter) risks. In later chapters, we apply these concepts to other pure risks as well, including health, disability, and mortality risk.

Because the potential losses can be large, having a plan for managing auto and home risks is an essential component of your financial plan and one that you can't afford to ignore. With careful planning, you can identify your risk exposures in advance and select appropriate and cost-effective ways to manage them. In the case of cars and homes, this often involves the purchase of insurance. In this chapter, you'll learn how to include the risk management process in your financial plan, how to identify your property and liability insurance needs, and what to look for in homeowner's, renter's, and automobile insurance. You'll also learn how to make a claim on your insurance in the event that you experience a loss.

The Risk Management Process

To a certain extent, you can control your exposure to the risks inherent in modern life through the choices you make. For example, you may choose not to smoke cigarettes, or you may choose to avoid risky sports. There are many risks, however, that you cannot control. Your house could be hit by lightning, or you might be the victim of a drunk driver. When you invest in risky assets, such as stocks and bonds, you are also exposed to the risk of financial loss. In this section, we more precisely define what we mean by risk, introduce the risk management process, and identify the most commonly applied risk management methods.

The risk management process is a series of steps that help you to organize your decision making with respect to risk exposures and their management. **Figure 7.1** summarizes the key steps in the process, and **Interactive: Applying the Risk Management Process** gives some examples in the context of auto and property risks. We discuss these steps in more detail in the sections that follow.

INTERACTIVE

Test your understanding by going to **Interactive: Applying the Risk Management Process** in **WileyPLUS.**

FIGURE 7.1 **The Risk Management Process**   Follow the steps in this process diagram to more effectively manage the risks that you are exposed to.

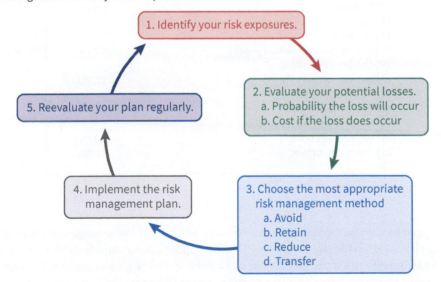

Identify and Evaluate Property and Liability Risks

The first step to managing a risk is to recognize that it exists. Although it may seem that most risks are obvious, some of the biggest risks are not. In general, people are not very good at recognizing and evaluating their own risk exposures. You're likely to overlook risks that occur infrequently, even when there are potentially serious financial consequences. At the same time, you may overestimate certain risks because extensive media attention leads you to believe that they occur more often than they actually do. For example, many people buy overpriced accident insurance policies at airport kiosks, despite the fact that plane crashes are extremely rare events.

Reflection Question 1

What personal risks worry you the most? In what ways do you think you have been influenced by risks you hear about in the media?

EXCEL WORKSHEET

See **Excel Worksheet 7.1** (Personal Financial Planner: Property Risk Exposure Checklist) in **WileyPLUS**.

One way to be sure you haven't overlooked risks related to property that you own is to use a checklist such as the simple one in **Excel Worksheet 7.1** (Personal Financial Planner: Property Risk Exposure Checklist). A completed version of this worksheet is shown in **Figure 7.2**. A financial planner is likely to ask you to complete a more extensive risk exposure checklist as a component of developing a financial plan.

FIGURE 7.2 Sample for Excel Worksheet 7.1: Property Risk Exposure Checklist

	A	B	C
1-2	**Types of Real and Personal Property**	**Do You Own?**	**Value**
3	**Real Property**		
4	House	✓	$150,000
5	Outbuildings	✓	$20,000
6	Pool		
7	Driveway		
8	Fence/retaining wall		
9			
10	**Personal Property**		
11	Clothes	✓	$10,000
12	Furniture	✓	$4,000
13	Jewelry/watches		
14	Firearms		
15	Dishes/silver/household goods		
16	Artwork/collectibles		
17	Musical instruments	✓	$2,500
18	Money/securities		
19	Office equipment	✓	$1,000
20	Business inventory and tools		
21	Vehicles and boats	✓	$13,000
22	Sports equipment	✓	$2,000
23			

Compared with property risk, it can be more difficult for the average person to identify **liability risk**, which is the risk of being held legally responsible for someone else's losses. You're exposed to liability risk if you own or operate a vehicle. You're also exposed to liability risk if other people visit your home. In a later section, we explain some legal rules that will help you better understand these risks.

After you've identified your risk exposures, the next step is to evaluate the expected financial consequences of each. To do this, you should consider both the **frequency of loss** (the likelihood or probability that a loss will occur) and the **severity of loss** (the dollar value of the loss if it does occur).

Although you obviously can't estimate the frequency of loss precisely, the point is to consider the *relative* likelihood that a loss will occur within a particular period of time (highly likely, not very likely, or very unlikely). You should also consider the relative severity of loss (enough to bankrupt you, a significant amount relative to your resources, or a budgetable amount). If you itemize your valuables on a risk exposure checklist, as described previously, it will be easier to estimate the potential severity of loss.

The choice of risk management tools and the expense you're willing to incur to manage each risk should depend on the combination of relative frequency and severity of loss. For example, certain types of losses occur with great frequency (your pen is stolen), but the severity of such a loss is so small that you shouldn't spend too much time worrying about it. In contrast, the theft of your laptop might cause you financial hardship and interfere with your studies, so it's a risk that you'd want to address in your risk management plan.

Mathematically, you can estimate the cost of your expected, or average, loss by multiplying the expected frequency of loss times the expected severity of loss using **Equation 7.1**:

$$\text{Expected loss} = \text{Expected frequency} \times \text{Expected severity} \tag{7.1}$$

For example, let's say you estimate that you have a 25 percent chance of having a car accident within the next year (and therefore a 75 percent chance of having no accident). You further estimate that the cost of an accident, if one occurs, will be $2,000. Based on Equation 7.1, the expected cost of the loss to your vehicle is $500 (0.25 × $2,000). You can think of this result as the average over a longer period of time. A 25 percent chance is equivalent to an accident happening once every four years. When it happens, it costs you $2,000, and in the other years it costs you zero. Over the course of four years, this equals $500 per year.

Although this simplified example suggests that the expected, or average, cost of the accident is a single value, the severity of loss can take on many values, and they don't all have equal likelihood of occurring. In the case of auto accidents, for instance, you have a much greater likelihood of experiencing a small fender bender than of being in a major crash that totals your car and seriously injures you. **Demonstration Problem 7.1** shows how to calculate risk when you have several possible levels of severity of loss that are not equally likely.

DEMONSTRATION PROBLEM 7.1 | Calculating Expected Losses

Problem

You've just built a mountain cabin and are deciding whether to buy fire insurance coverage. You've heard there's a 1-in-25 chance of fire in that area. If there is a fire, you estimate that there are three possible outcomes:

Damage	Cost	Probability
Minor smoke damage	$2,000	60%
Exterior fire damage	$10,000	30%
Everything ruined	$100,000	10%

You've been quoted a price of $700 per year for coverage. Should you buy the fire insurance?

Strategy

Estimate your expected loss and compare it with the insurance premium. Decide whether the insurance is reasonably priced relative to your expected loss and whether you're willing to take the risk of being uninsured.

Solution

The 1-in-25 chance of fire translates into an expected frequency of 4 percent (1/25 = 0.04). The expected severity is the weighted average of the three possible loss scenarios, taking the probability of each outcome into consideration. Multiply the dollar loss for each possible loss amount by the probability that it will occur and add the results.

$$\text{Expected severity} = (\$2,000 \times 0.6) + (\$10,000 \times 0.3) + (\$100,000 \times 0.1)$$
$$= \$1,200 + \$3,000 + \$10,000$$
$$= \$14,200$$

Now, you can calculate the expected loss using Equation 7.1:

$$\text{Expected loss} = \text{Expected frequency} \times \text{Expected severity}$$
$$= 0.04 \times \$14,200$$
$$= \$568$$

Although the $700 premium is greater than your expected loss of $568, you probably should buy the insurance. Whereas you might be able to pay for smaller losses out of pocket or even delay fixing the damage, the worst-case scenario would be financially devastating.

Risk Management Methods

The next step in the risk management process, after you've identified and evaluated your risks, is to formulate an organized plan for managing them. Risk management methods include various ways to reduce the frequency and severity of the risk or to pay for a loss if you do experience one. The most common methods are risk avoidance, risk reduction, risk transfer, and risk retention. Although risk transfer, through insurance, is probably the first method that comes to mind, it isn't always the most appropriate way to deal with risk. Sometimes, for example, complete insurance is unavailable or too expensive.

Avoid the Risk

You can manage some types of risk by simply avoiding the situation that produces it. For example, you can avoid losing your valuables by locking them in a safe deposit box. You can avoid being in an airplane crash by never flying. You can avoid smoking-related health risks by not smoking cigarettes. Although risk avoidance is effective for some risks, it's impossible to avoid property and liability risks completely. For example, to avoid being injured in an auto accident, you could decide to walk or bike everywhere instead of driving. Even then, you could be injured by another driver. In short, some risks are unavoidable.

Reduce the Risk

You can reduce the frequency or severity of your risk exposures by engaging in actions aimed at **loss control**. Wearing a seat belt significantly reduces the severity of injuries sustained in auto accidents, for example. Using fire-resistant materials in home construction can lessen the amount of damage to the home in the event that a fire occurs. Note that these particular examples of loss control can reduce the severity of the loss, but don't actually affect the likelihood that it will occur in the first place. In contrast, some risk reduction methods are directed at reducing the frequency of loss. To reduce the frequency of auto accidents, you can drive more defensively, avoid speeding, and equip your car with snow tires and antilock brakes. Promptly shoveling your driveway and sidewalks after a snowfall can decrease the likelihood of visitors slipping and falling (and, hence, your risk of being sued for their injuries). Some loss control strategies, such as healthy eating habits and regular exercise, can reduce both the frequency and severity of risk.

Transfer the Risk

The most common method for dealing with pure risks is to transfer them to someone else—usually an insurance company. By pooling the risks of many policyholders, insurers are able to spread the risk so that no single individual is faced with a catastrophic loss. Risk can also be transferred to others by contractual arrangements. If your child plays high school football, the school will require you to sign a form that releases it from liability for sports injuries. The school is transferring its liability risk to you. Other than by purchasing insurance, it's not that easy to transfer your risk. Although you could ask everyone who visits your home to sign a release of liability before allowing them on the premises, you probably wouldn't have many friends if you did.

Retain the Risk

As an alternative to buying insurance, you can pay for losses out of pocket, a risk management method known as **risk retention**. Risk retention is sometimes called "self-insurance," although in fact it's not insurance at all because there is no sharing or pooling of risk. Retention is a particularly appropriate risk management method when the potential losses are small, predictable, and budgetable. When you buy an insurance policy, the policy contract will often require that you retain some of the risk by paying for part of the losses that occur. You might also choose to retain a risk if you're wealthy enough to cover a loss or if the insurance costs too much. Insurance for risks with both high frequency and high severity—such as floods and earthquakes—can be very expensive. Although risk retention has a place in any insurance plan, many people retain risks not by choice but by oversight—they simply fail to recognize the risks and therefore make no conscious decision about how to manage them.

For each of the types of risks you are exposed to, you'll need to make decisions about how to manage the risk. Whether you decide to avoid, reduce, transfer, or retain each risk will depend on your assessment of its relative frequency and severity and also on your financial situation. You can test your ability to match risks with the appropriate risk management methods in **Interactive: Risk Management Methods**. In the next sections, you'll learn more about how to use insurance to manage auto and home risks.

INTERACTIVE

See **Interactive: Risk Management Methods** in **WileyPLUS** for practice with these concepts.

7.2 How Insurance Works

> **LEARNING OBJECTIVE 7.2**
> Explain how risk pooling works, and define common insurance policy terminology.

Once you've identified your risks and decided how to manage them, you must implement your plan. For auto and homeowner's risks, implementation will nearly always mean buying insurance. This section explains how risk pooling allows insurers to spread risk across many policyholders and what factors are important in insurance pricing.

Risk Pooling and Insurance

Insurance companies are financial institutions that provide a valuable risk-spreading service by pooling premium dollars and using the money to pay losses incurred by policyholders during the policy period. Just how does risk pooling work? The concept is based on the **law of large numbers**, which holds that as the size of a pool of identical risks increases, the loss per person becomes more predictable. This means that an insurer can charge each customer a premium that is pretty close to the expected loss and still break even.

To understand how an insurance pool works, consider a group of 1,000 homeowners, all in different cities in the United States. Each owns a home worth $150,000. We'll assume that for each homeowner, the risk of his or her home being destroyed by a fire is the same: 1 in 1,000. Based on that probability, we expect that one of these 1,000 homeowners will suffer the devastating loss of a home in the coming year.

Now suppose that all the homeowners got together at the beginning of the year and each contributed an amount of money equal to his or her share of the pool's total expected loss of $150,000 (the value of one home). The cost to each homeowner would be only $150 ($150,000/1,000). At the end of the year, the unlucky homeowner whose home was destroyed by a fire would be reimbursed from the pool. If, however, two houses happened to burn down that year, the pool would not have enough funds to cover the $300,000 total loss. In that case, would it be reasonable to ask each homeowner to chip in another $150? Do you think everyone would pay up?

Suppose, instead, that the pool is even larger, perhaps 100,000 homeowners or more, as is the case with many insurance company risk pools. The average individual share of the cost is still the same: $150. But the larger the size of the pool, the lower the risk of having insufficient funds to pay the expected claims each year. You'd expect 100 of the 100,000 homes to have a fire, but if another home did burn, the additional cost per person to the pool would be very small, only $1.50 per person. By charging each homeowner a little more than the expected loss, the insurer can cover all the losses even when they exceed the original estimate.

Insurance Premiums

The amount an insurer charges a policyholder for insurance protection is called a **premium**. In determining how much to charge, insurers estimate the expected loss by classifying policyholders according to their risk characteristics and looking at past loss experience for similar risks. Thus, for homeowner's insurance, people in rural mountain areas will have a different **risk classification** than those whose homes are near the local fire station. If you have a history of auto accidents or speeding tickets, you'll be classified as riskier than a driver who has a clean record. If an insurer thinks your expected losses will be higher than average, it will normally charge you a higher premium.

By accurately classifying policyholders and predicting losses, insurers can charge each policyholder a premium that is fairly close to that person's individual expected loss. In addition to charging for expected losses, insurers need to cover their expenses and make a profit. Some insurers can offer more competitive prices because they have lower agent commissions or advertising expenditures. Others may be less expensive because they have lower expected losses, as in the case of insurers that are stricter in their screening of potential customers' risk characteristics.

In actual practice, it isn't always easy for insurers to estimate the average expected risk for a pool of policyholders. There are three types of risks for which insurance is generally in short supply because the nature of the risk makes it more difficult to estimate expected losses or limits how well risk pooling works:

- **Correlated risks**   Risks that affect large numbers of policyholders in the same area (flood and earthquake, war, terrorism).
- **Nonrandom risks**   Risks that are within the control of the policyholder (intentional acts such as arson and suicide).
- **Unpredictable risks**   Risks with potentially unlimited severity, which makes it impossible to estimate the pool's expected loss with any certainty (for example, terrorism, mold contamination, environmental damage).

Insurance Policy Terminology

An **insurance policy** is a contract, between you (the insured) and a financial institution (the insurer), in which you promise to pay a certain amount of money in return for the insurer's promise to pay for certain covered losses that occur during the policy period. The policy explains all the rights and responsibilities of the parties to the contract.

It's important to read your insurance policies and understand your coverage. Insurance contracts are required by law to be written clearly and in language that can be understood by people who don't have expertise in law or insurance. Nevertheless, these documents can be relatively difficult to comprehend. Many people make the mistake of failing to read their policy until they want to make a claim, only to find out that their loss isn't covered.

Insurance policies often include terms and conditions that increase the predictability of the loss to the insurer and reduce premium costs to the insured. These include exclusions and limitations, incentives for hazard and loss reduction, and deductibles. An **exclusion** specifically identifies losses that are *not* covered under the policy at all. For example, your automobile insurance might exclude coverage for hail damage. In addition, limitations may be placed on specific categories of losses, as in the case of a homeowner's insurance policy that covers a maximum of $1,000 for lost or stolen jewelry. For an additional premium amount, most insurers offer supplemental coverage for limited or excluded items in the form of a contract addendum called a **rider**. Property and liability policies commonly also include an upper limit on total losses, although you can usually increase the limit by paying a higher premium.

The basic purpose of insurance is to restore you to the financial condition you were in before the loss occurred. The principle of **indemnity**, which underlies insurance law, says that you should never be able to recover more from your insurance than what you've lost. Thus, even if you insure your $100,000 home for $120,000, the most you can recover from your insurance is $100,000. Similarly, if you have health insurance policies with two insurers, you can't collect for the same health expenses from both of them.

Home and auto policies commonly include a **deductible**, which is an amount that you must pay out of pocket before the insurance company is obligated to pay anything. A policy with a higher deductible will have a lower premium because the deductible reduces the insurer's expected claims payments. If your deductible is $250 and you have a $1,000 loss, you'll pay the first $250, and the insurer will reimburse you for the remaining $750 loss. Some types of insurance (auto and homeowner's insurance) apply the deductible to each individual loss. Others (health insurance) have an aggregate deductible that you pay only once per year, after which the insurer will compensate you for all of your losses, subject to any copays, as explained in a later chapter. You can check your understanding of these contract terms in **Interactive: What Contract Terms Apply?**

INTERACTIVE

See **Interactive: What Contract Terms Apply?** in **WileyPLUS** to test your understanding of insurance contract terms.

7.3 | Managing Homeowner's and Renter's Risk

LEARNING OBJECTIVE 7.3

Describe the loss coverage provided by homeowner's and renter's insurance and the factors that affect premiums.

As shown in **Figure 7.3**, home equity is the single largest household asset. In addition to providing necessary shelter, home ownership has allowed U.S. households to benefit from increasing real estate values over time.

FIGURE 7.3 **Home Equity as a Percentage of Total Household Assets** Your home is likely to be your most valuable asset, so you need to protect it.

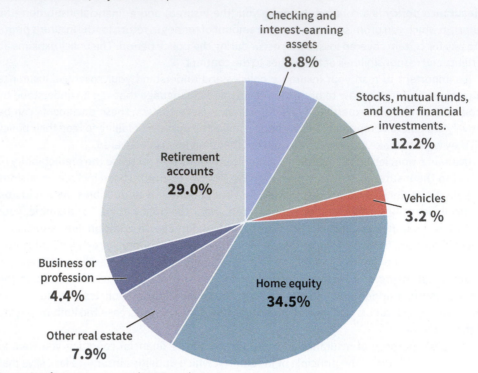

Source: Data from www.census.gov (2014 Census).

Home ownership is not risk free, however. In addition to the financial risk of fluctuating real estate values (which can provide either loss or gain), homes are exposed to many pure risks. These include the risks of loss or damage (from theft, fire, wind, and rain) as well as the risks of financial losses arising out of legal rules that hold homeowners responsible for injuries to visitors.

Insurance can help both homeowners and renters to deal with property and liability risk. **Homeowner's insurance** covers a broad range of property and liability risks. Renters can purchase **renter's insurance**, which has coverage and terms that are similar to homeowner's insurance, except that the policies cover a more limited number of risks.

Although most homes are insured because lenders require it as a condition of getting a mortgage or home equity loan, it is estimated that about 60 percent of the 80 million renters in the United States do not carry renter's insurance, even though this coverage is very inexpensive. In this section, we review homeowners' and renters' risks in detail, explain the financial protection provided by standard homeowner's and renter's insurance policies, and discuss the factors that can be expected to affect premiums.

What Risks Do Homeowners and Renters Face?

Figure 7.4 summarizes the risks faced by homeowners and renters. Note that, although homeowners are exposed to all of these risks, renters have only personal property risk and liability risk. For renters, the risk of damage to real property—the structure itself—is borne by the landlord.

Property Risk

Both real and personal property can be damaged by fires, hurricanes, and other natural phenomena. Either type of property can also be damaged by others. Factors to consider in evaluating your exposure to property risks include:

- The safety of the neighborhood you live in (crime rate, proximity to fire and police protection)

- Your home's safety features (locks, alarms, smoke alarms, sprinklers)
- Your geographic location (wildfire area, hurricane zone, flood zone)

Liability Risk

Estimating liability risk is a little more complicated than estimating property risk because it requires that you have some additional knowledge about the law. If a visitor or a visitor's property is injured on your premises, you may be legally responsible for the loss. This usually occurs when the person sues you in a court of law to get you to pay for their injuries or losses. The fact that you are sued, however, doesn't automatically mean you'll be held responsible. Generally, you are only legally responsible for losses that are caused by your **negligence**. Establishing negligence requires that the injured person prove three things:

- You had a duty to that person.
- You didn't fulfill your duty.
- Your failure to fulfill your duty directly caused the other person or the person's property to suffer a loss.

For example, you have a duty to keep your premises reasonably safe for visitors. If you fail to clear your sidewalk of snow and your neighbor slips on an icy spot on the way to your front door, you may be responsible for the resulting medical costs.

In a few rare situations, you might be held to an even higher duty. Most states have a special standard called **strict liability** that applies whenever children are injured by an "attractive nuisance" on someone else's property—defined as a dangerous environment that might be attractive to children, such as a swimming pool or construction equipment. Strict liability holds the property owner responsible for a child's injuries in this situation, even if that person wasn't negligent. Similarly, pet owners are generally held strictly liable for injuries caused by pets that are known to be dangerous. Some homeowner's insurance policies exclude this risk, as discussed in **Ethics in Action**.

FIGURE 7.4 **Homeowners' and Renters' Risks**   Homeowners and renters are exposed to real and personal property risks and also the risk of legal liability to others.

Defenses to Liability Claims

In some cases, you might be able to defend yourself against a negligence lawsuit by claiming that one of two legal rules applies: contributory negligence or assumption of risk. **Contributory negligence** exists when the injured person actually contributed to his or her own injury. If the person bears some fault for the injury, he or she may not be able to hold you financially responsible. Similarly, if the injured person knew about the risk and voluntarily

Ethics in Action

Dog Owner's Dilemma

Almost five million people are bitten by dogs in the United States each year, and about 15 percent of these injuries require medical treatment. Although many breeds of dogs have been known to bite, fatalities and serious injuries have been more frequently associated with certain breeds. If you own a pit bull, Rottweiler, or wolf breed, you might not be able to obtain liability insurance coverage for injuries they could cause.

Most states apply a strict liability standard for injuries inflicted by animals known to be dangerous. In the past, dog owners often used the excuse that they didn't *know* their dog was dangerous because the dog had never bitten anyone before. An old rule of thumb was "Every dog gets one bite." This won't always get you off the hook today, at least for certain dog breeds that are commonly known to be extremely aggressive. Because of this, many insurers now exclude coverage for injuries caused by certain dog breeds. Some will even refuse to sell homeowner's insurance to owners of these dogs.

What if you own a dangerous pet and your homeowner's policy doesn't cover injuries caused by the pet or places restrictive limits on the coverage? You can retain that risk and practice other risk management techniques, such as adequately fencing your yard, investing in training, and limiting access to the pet. Alternatively, you can purchase personal umbrella liability insurance (discussed later in the chapter). In addition, for people who cannot find coverage elsewhere, such as those with a history of such claims, some insurers sell specialized dog-bite liability policies.

exposed himself or herself to it, you may be able to use the defense of **assumption of risk** to avoid legal liability.

Consider again the example in which you neglected to shovel your sidewalk after a snowstorm and your neighbor slipped on the ice and was injured. The direct cause of the injury was your negligence in failing to clear the snow. However, if your neighbor was running up the sidewalk in high-heeled shoes texting on a smartphone at the time, you could claim that she contributed to her own injury. And if the ice was clearly visible, you could argue that she had assumed the risk by voluntarily stepping on the ice—in which case she wouldn't be able to hold you financially responsible.

As a homeowner, it's important to understand the legal rules in effect in your state so that you can protect yourself in advance from potential liability. If, for example, you have a temporarily dangerous condition on your property, such as a pothole or a broken step on your porch, it's a good idea to warn your friends and neighbors or put up a sign.

Insuring Your Home

As just discussed, homeowners and renters are exposed to many property and liability risks that could result in financial losses or financial obligations to others. Although you can take certain actions to reduce the potential frequency and severity of losses (such as installing smoke alarms and clearing snow from your sidewalk), you can't eliminate risks entirely. For this reason, you should plan to transfer some risk by buying insurance.

How do you choose the right insurance policy for your circumstances? How much insurance should you buy? How much will it cost? Like many other types of insurance contracts, homeowner's insurance contracts are standardized, making it easier to comparison shop. In this section, we first compare the standard policy forms and then look at the factors that affect prices of homeowner's insurance policies.

Property Coverage

The most common homeowner's policy forms (commonly labeled HO forms) are summarized in **Table 7.1**, including what type of home they apply to and what risks they cover. Note that unless you have replacement cost coverage, the insurance will pay you the depreciated value of what you have lost, which is often insufficient to replace your property following a loss.

TABLE 7.1   **What Risks Do Homeowner's Policies Cover?**

Homeowner's Policy Type	Coverage under Each Policy
All Policies	Personal liability, medical payments for guests, additional living expenses during repair
	Losses due to fire, lightning, windstorm, hail, explosion, riots, damage from aircraft or vehicles, smoke, vandalism, theft, glass breakage, volcanic eruption, falling objects, weight of ice/sleet/snow, discharge of water/steam, pipes bursting from heat/cold, electrical surge
HO-3 All-Risk	Covers all perils, including those listed above, except flood, earthquake, war, nuclear accident
HO-4 Renter's Contents	Covers loss to personal belongings caused by perils listed for HO-3
HO-5 Comprehensive	Similar to HO-3 but includes replacement cost coverage on contents and buildings
HO-6 Condominium	Similar to HO-4; covers personal belongings and additions to the living unit

Personal property is covered regardless of where it is located at the time it is lost, damaged, or stolen. Suppose you go to the bookstore at the beginning of the semester and purchase all your textbooks for the semester, spending $800 in total. During the day, your backpack is stolen with all your books in it. Your homeowner's or renter's insurance would cover your loss, subject to the applicable deductible. If your parents still claim you as a dependent, their homeowner's insurance will probably cover the loss, even if you don't live with them. Personal property coverage is limited to 50 percent of the amount of insurance on the house, and specific categories of personal property may have individual limits as well. Pets are not considered to be personal property.

Additional Losses Covered

If you're forced to leave your home because of an insured loss (such as fire or smoke damage), your policy will cover reasonable living expenses and personal property loss during repairs, up to a limit of 20 percent of the amount of insurance on the home. For example, if your insurance has a $200,000 limit for the home, you'd have $40,000 in living expense coverage. In addition, if you normally receive rental income from your property, the insurance will cover the lost rent. Policies also cover losses from credit card fraud, the cost of temporary repairs or emergency removal of property to prevent further damage, and fire department fees.

Liability Coverage

The United States has experienced an explosion of litigation in recent decades, making it more important than ever to purchase insurance protection to cover potential liability risks. Most homeowner's insurance policies provide $100,000 in basic personal liability coverage. For minor injuries and accidents, policies include no-fault medical coverage in the amount of $1,000, as well as no-fault property coverage of $250. *No-fault coverage*, in this context, means the insurer will pay the loss without requiring that the injured party prove negligence.

To illustrate how the no-fault provision might apply, suppose your friend is visiting and trips on a rock in your driveway, breaking her arm and ripping her jacket, resulting in medical costs of $1,000 and property loss of $100. Your friend will be reimbursed for her expenses without having to file a lawsuit. If your friend's injuries turn out to be more severe, perhaps resulting in the long-term loss of function of her arm, she may decide to sue you, in which case your policy will cover the liability judgment up to the limit of $100,000.

Pricing of Homeowner's Insurance

If you have a mortgage on your home, your lender will require that you carry homeowner's insurance. You can save money by shopping around for the best rates. Prices vary substantially from insurer to insurer but are related to the following factors, which we examine in this section:

- Location and property characteristics
- The amount and type of coverage purchased
- Deductibles and discounts
- Risk characteristics of the policyholder

Location and Property Characteristics

Your risk of property and liability loss has a lot to do with where your property is located. For example, wildfires are more common in the West; wind damage in areas where tornadoes and hurricanes are more likely; and theft in certain urban areas. Once you own a home that has high risk factors, you can't do much to change them, so it makes sense to consider them *before* purchasing the home. However, if you live in a high-risk area, you can also investigate how best to reduce the severity of potential losses. The Insurance Institute for Business and Home Safety provides tips for managing various types of risk, including fire, hurricane, earthquake, and tornado risks, at **www.disastersafety.org**. For examples of wildfire risk reduction, see **Interactive: Take Steps to Reduce Wildfire Risk to Your Home**.

A recent development in homeowner's insurance involves mold risk—the risk that mold contamination in a home may cause damage to the structure and contents, as well as significant health problems for residents (such as asthma and migraines). Mold contamination is usually caused by continued moisture and heat. Homes in high-humidity areas, such as Texas, Florida, and California, have cost insurers millions of dollars in claims and litigation costs, resulting in increasing homeowner's premiums in those states. For this reason, more than half of all states have approved revised homeowner's policy forms that specifically exclude coverage for mold, even when it is caused by an event that was otherwise insured.

Coverage Purchased

All else being equal, a more expensive home will cost more to insure than a less expensive home. Because the market value of your home includes both the building and the land (which can't be destroyed), you should buy insurance based on the value of the structure and contents rather than the total market value of the property.

What happens if you buy only $80,000 in coverage when you should buy $120,000? Most policies include a coinsurance requirement that the **face amount**, or the amount of insurance coverage purchased, must be at least 80 percent of the actual value. If not, the insurer will proportionally reduce how much it reimburses for a covered loss. For example, if you bought insurance that was two-thirds of the correct amount ($80,000/$120,000) and you incurred fire damage of $60,000 during the policy period, the insurer would reimburse you for only two-thirds of the damage, or $40,000.

Recall that we previously discussed limitations on coverage for certain personal items, such as the $1,000 limit on jewelry losses. Retaining the risks associated with jewelry, art, and collectibles (such as comics and antiques) will reduce your homeowner's insurance premium. If you do decide to pay the extra premium cost, you will probably need to provide a specific list of the insured property. In some cases, you may need to get an appraisal of the property to verify its value. The property on such a list is called **scheduled property**.

In deciding whether to buy extra coverage for jewelry or other personal property, you should evaluate the probability of loss and the replacement cost to determine whether the additional coverage is justified. For example, suppose it will cost you $50 per year to insure your wedding ring, but you never take it off your finger, so the probability of loss is pretty low. You may decide the insurance isn't worth it. One of the factors to consider is that, in the event of a

INTERACTIVE

See **Interactive: Take Steps to Reduce Wildfire Risk to Your Home** in **WileyPLUS**.

loss, the value placed on the claim will be the resale value of the item. Sentimental value will not be considered.

Recall that supplemental coverage such as extra coverage for your jewelry is provided in contract additions called riders. **Table 7.2** identifies common extras that can be added to your homeowner's coverage and a range for the additional premium cost for the increased coverage.

TABLE 7.2   Cost of Riders

Type of Property	Usual Limits	Cost for Increased Coverage
Jewelry	$1,000	1–4% of appraised value of scheduled personal property; available from primary insurers and specialty insurers (through jewelry stores and appraisers)
Home office furniture and equipment	$1,000	$75–$100 per year for $10,000 worth of coverage
Recreational vehicles	Excluded	Sold by specialty insurers; price depends on age and condition of vehicle, usage, and other factors; average cost $1,000 per year
Art and antiques	50–75% of face value of policy	$0.25 per $100

Deductibles and Discounts

It's a good idea to retain the risk of smaller losses if you can afford to budget for them. Recall from our earlier discussion that a deductible is the amount of a loss that you are responsible for paying before the insurer will pay any losses. A deductible is a form of risk retention. The higher the deductible, the lower the premium, all else being equal.

The minimum deductible on a homeowner's policy is $250, but the annual premium cost will be about 10 percent lower with a $500 deductible and about 30 percent lower with a $1,000 deductible, so many people opt for higher deductibles. The reason that the premium drops so dramatically is that many claims on homeowner's insurance policies are for fairly small dollar losses. The deductible provision effectively removes these from coverage, so the insurer expects to pay out fewer claims on your policy.

Insurers often give premium discounts for factors that lower your risk of loss. For example, if your home includes features such as smoke detectors, sprinklers, or fire extinguishers, it will be judged to have a reduced risk of damage from fire. If your home has a security system, you may qualify for a discount, because your risk of theft is lower. Most insurers also give discounts to customers who have more than one type of insurance with the same company.

Your Risk Profile

Your own characteristics can affect your premium as well. If you and other members of your household are nonsmokers, for example, you may get a lower rate, because so many house fires are caused by careless smokers. Your previous loss history is also relevant. When you apply for property or liability insurance, your insurer will commonly look up your loss history on the Comprehensive Loss Underwriting Exchange (CLUE). This is a national electronic database where insurers report insurance claims paid by them on property and liability insurance policies, as well as inquiries regarding losses that did not result in paid claims. If you have a clean record, the insurer will consider you a better risk and may offer you a lower premium. If you've had a lot of losses and claims in the past, you might have difficulty getting insurance or, at a minimum, will pay a higher rate.

In addition to your past claims history, your credit score will affect an insurance company's assessment of your risk. Why would insurers use your credit score as part of your risk profile? A credit score measures how responsibly a person handles certain aspects of his or her finances. Insurers have found that the credit score is also correlated with claims activity—people with low credit scores tend to make more claims. The Texas Department of Insurance studied the claims records of two million insurance policies to see if this was a reasonable proxy to use for underwriting auto and homeowner's policies. They found that policyholders in the lowest 10 percent, based on credit scores, were 1.5 to 2 times more likely to file a claim than policyholders in the top 10 percent. This result applied to both auto and homeowner's insurance claims. Those with the best credit scores were also 40 percent less likely to be in auto accidents than those with the worst scores.

Insurers generally don't penalize people for poor credit scores, but they do reward customers for good credit scores. **Case Study 7.1** provides an example of how credit scores can affect your insurance premiums.

Case Study 7.1

g-stockstudio/Shutterstock.com

How Does a Bad Credit History Affect Insurance Premiums?

Problem

Joel has not always been very timely in paying his bills, and as a result his FICO credit score has fallen to 550. Now that Joel is graduating from college, he and his roommate, Kris, are shopping for auto and renter's insurance separate from their parents' policies. Joel is surprised to find that his premium quotes are higher than his roommate's. Kris has been very responsible with his credit, and his FICO score is 700.

If neither Joel nor Kris has a prior claim history, and they have applied to the same insurance companies for quotes, what is the most likely explanation for the lower quotes Kris is getting? Is there anything that Joel can do to improve his chances of qualifying for lower-cost insurance?

Strategy

Consider the factors that determine insurance policy premiums, and evaluate which is most likely to have made Joel's premium higher than Kris's premium. Once Joel identifies the cause, he can investigate methods of reducing his insurance cost.

Solution Recall that the factors affecting homeowner's and renter's insurance are related to the property characteristics, the insurance coverage purchased, and the characteristics of the policyholder. If Joel and Kris are similar in all other dimensions, the most likely explanation for Kris's getting a better rate is that the insurers are giving him a discount for having a better credit score.

As discussed in Chapter 5, the factors that affect your credit score are your history of timely or untimely payments, the total of your current credit balances, the length of time you have had credit accounts, the number of new credit accounts you may have opened recently, and the types of credit you use. Joel can therefore improve his score over the next 12 months by paying his bills on time and paying off outstanding debt. Eventually, this will allow him to get a better rate, either with his current insurer or with a competitor.

Umbrella Liability Insurance

If your negligence causes someone to be severely injured on your property and the person sues to recover, a jury might well give the person an award in excess of the $100,000 liability limit on the standard policy. In that case, you could be personally liable for the remaining amount. For this reason, it's often advisable to purchase **umbrella insurance**, which comes with a limit of $1 million or more, to supplement your basic coverage, particularly if you have significant net worth. Umbrella coverage supplements your other liability coverage and also includes coverage for personal injury claims against you that wouldn't be normally covered under your homeowner's insurance, such as libel, slander, and invasion of privacy.

7.4 | Auto Insurance

LEARNING OBJECTIVE 7.4

Understand your choices for auto insurance coverage and what factors are likely to increase your premiums.

Unless you're into extreme sports, your riskiest behavior is probably driving an automobile. Even if you're a very careful driver, each time you get behind the wheel, you're exposing yourself to others who are driving while talking on cell phones, eating lunch, speeding to make it to an appointment, or—worst of all—intoxicated. Car accidents result in approximately 3.1 million injuries and 40,000 fatalities each year. Although automobile injuries and fatalities had been declining due to better vehicle safety, traffic experts are concerned because the rates for both injuries and fatalities have increased in the last few years, perhaps due to the use of cell phones while driving. **Figure 7.5** provides a visual summary of how legal and regulatory changes have improved vehicle and highway safety.

FIGURE 7.5   **Legal Reform and Auto Fatalities over Time**   Aggressive legal reforms have significantly reduced auto fatalities over time.

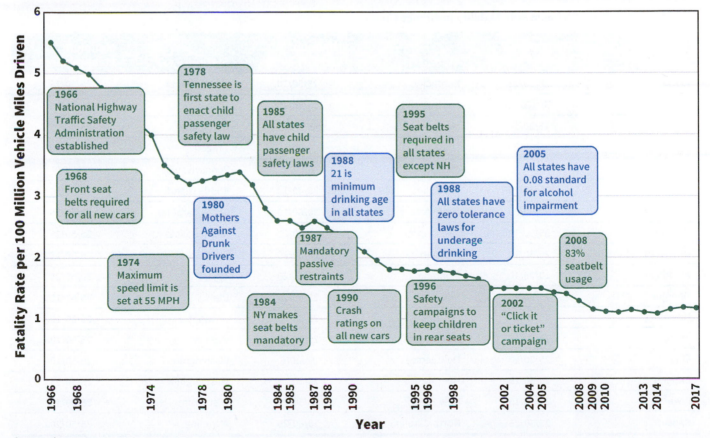

Source: nhtsa.gov.

When you drive a vehicle, you're exposed to the risk of injury to yourself, your passengers, and your vehicle, due to either your own negligence or that of other drivers. Since you probably don't have the choice of not driving, your risk management plan should include strategies for protecting yourself physically by owning a safe car, not driving when intoxicated, refraining from using your cell phone while driving, and obeying traffic laws. You should also protect yourself financially by carrying sufficient auto insurance.

State Auto Insurance Laws

Most states have **compulsory automobile insurance laws**, which require proof of liability insurance as a prerequisite to car registration. In addition, all states have **financial responsibility laws**, which require drivers who have been in a traffic accident to show proof of insurance or the ability to pay a claim.

The minimum auto liability coverage varies by state but is generally fairly low to ensure auto insurance is affordable for most drivers in the state. As a result, the minimum policy limits may not be enough to cover expected losses due to a serious traffic accident. If you don't have enough insurance, you can be held personally liable for the difference between your insurance coverage and the actual loss. To ensure that your personal assets are not at risk, you should carry more than the minimum level of liability insurance, and consider buying umbrella insurance if you have significant assets.

Table 7.3 details the minimum auto liability limits of the various states. The minimum limits listed in the table identify the required liability coverage for injury per person, total injuries to all people in the accident, and property damage. For example, as illustrated in **Figure 7.6**, the state of Maine requires liability coverage of $50,000 for injury per person, $100,000 for injury per accident, and $25,000 for property damage per accident. And note that this is liability coverage—that is, it covers only the injuries you cause to other people. For damage to your own person, vehicle, or property, you need additional coverage.

TABLE 7.3   **State Minimum Auto Liability Insurance Limits**

State	Minimum Liability Limits	State	Minimum Liability Limits	State	Minimum Liability Limits
Alabama	25/50/25	Kentucky	25/50/10	North Dakota	25/50/25
Alaska	50/100/25	Louisiana	15/30/25	Ohio	25/50/25
Arizona	15/30/10	Maine	50/100/25	Oklahoma	25/50/25
Arkansas	25/50/25	Maryland	30/60/15	Oregon	25/50/20
California	15/30/5	Massachusetts	20/40/5	Pennsylvania	15/30/5
Colorado	25/50/15	Michigan	20/40/10	Rhode Island	25/50/25
Connecticut	25/50/20	Minnesota	30/60/10	South Carolina	25/50/25
Delaware	25/50/10	Mississippi	25/50/25	South Dakota	25/50/25
District of Columbia	25/50/10	Missouri	25/50/25	Tennessee	25/50/15
Florida	10/20/10	Montana	25/50/20	Texas	30/60/25
Georgia	25/50/25	Nebraska	25/50/25	Utah	25/65/15
Hawaii	20/40/10	Nevada	25/50/20	Vermont	25/50/10
Idaho	25/50/15	New Hampshire	25/50/25	Virginia	25/50/20
Illinois	25/50/20	New Jersey	15/30/5	Washington	25/50/10
Indiana	25/50/25	New Mexico	25/50/10	West Virginia	25/50/25
Iowa	20/40/15	New York	25/50/10	Wisconsin	25/50/10
Kansas	25/50/25	North Carolina	30/60/25	Wyoming	25/50/20

Source: Insurance Information Institute, iii.org (June 2019).

FIGURE 7.6   **Interpreting Minimum Auto Liability Limits**   State auto insurance laws have separate minimum auto liability insurance limits for people and vehicles.

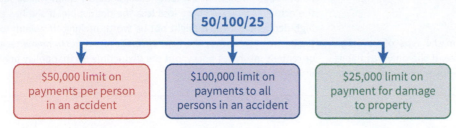

50/100/25

| $50,000 limit on payments per person in an accident | $100,000 limit on payments to all persons in an accident | $25,000 limit on payment for damage to property |

Policy Coverage

Although states commonly have relatively low minimums for auto insurance to keep it afford-able, you'll probably want to pay a little more for better protection. Next, we examine the cover-age available under typical auto insurance policies.

The Personal Automobile Policy (PAP)

Each state has a standard automobile insurance contract form—the personal automobile policy (PAP) for individual coverage or the family automobile policy (FAP) to cover several people in a fam-ily who are driving the same car. The standardization of contracts helps make coverage compara-ble across companies. **Figure 7.7** summarizes the components of coverage available under the categories of bodily injury coverage and property damage coverage. Consider the example in **Case Study 7.2** to see if you can determine which type of coverage would be necessary for that loss.

FIGURE 7.7   **Categories of Auto Insurance Coverage**   Auto insurance coverage varies by category, as the figure shows.

Bodily Injury Coverage

Bodily Injury Liability: Covers legal defense costs and judgments against you if you lose in court.

Medical Expenses: Covers medical costs to you and any passengers injured in an auto accident.

Uninsured Motorists: Covers costs for you and your family from injuries caused by an uninsured motorist or a hit-and-run driver.

Property Damage Coverage

Property Damage Liability: Covers liability for damage to property of others.

Collision: Covers damage to your own vehicle due to auto accident, regardless of fault.

Comprehensive Physical Damage: Covers you for risks caused by perils other than collision, including theft, vandalism, fire, wind, hail, tornado, lightning, earthquake, falling objects, hitting a deer, regardless of fault.

Case Study 7.2

iStock.com/dolgachov

Which Auto Policy Will Cover the Loss?

Problem

Serena was in a hurry and left her car unlocked while she ran into a store. When she returned, she found that her laptop had been stolen from the front seat. What should she do? Will her insurance cover any of the loss?

Strategy

Serena should first report the theft to the police. Although they are unlikely to find the thief, insurers will not consider claims for theft loss without documentation such as a police report. Next, Serena needs to consult her insurance policy to see how much, if any, of the loss be covered.

Solution Serena's recovery depends on the type of coverage she has and the amount of her deductible. If she only has liability insurance, she will have no coverage for this loss. If she has comprehensive physical damage coverage, it will cover the theft of personal belongings. In the latter case, Serena's claim will be for the actual cash value of the loss less the deductible. If she has a high deductible level, it might not be worth making this claim to the insurer. Serena may also have coverage under her homeowner's or renter's insurance policy, but the deductible on that policy may also limit her recovery.

If your vehicle is collateral for a loan, your lender will require that you carry **collision coverage**, which insures against loss or damage to your vehicle in an auto accident, and **comprehensive physical damage coverage**, which covers loss or damage to your vehicle from any other peril. The lender will usually also require that it be named as an insured party on the policy.

Consistent with the principle of indemnity discussed earlier in the chapter, the amount an insurer will pay for vehicle damage is always limited to the actual cash value of the vehicle. If the damage exceeds the vehicle's value, the insurer will "total" the car—that is, will pay you the actual cash value and take the car. For this reason, it's not always a good idea to carry physical damage coverage on an old but reliable vehicle.

No-Fault Auto Insurance

Suppose you're in an accident that was caused by the negligence of another driver. You sustain significant neck and back injuries, you miss work for several weeks, and your car is totaled. If the other driver's insurer decides to challenge the claim, how long do you think it will take to settle the dispute and get your losses paid? Your immediate medical costs may be covered by your own insurer. It could be much more difficult to recover for property damage, lost earnings, and long-term disability, however. It can take years for cases to move through the overcrowded court system. For some people, particularly those with the most serious injuries and those without other sources of reimbursement, such a delay can result in a significant financial burden.

Beginning in the 1970s, many states attempted to help auto accident victims receive prompt compensation for their injuries by enacting laws establishing **no-fault automobile insurance** laws. With this type of auto insurance system, your own insurer pays your economic losses, regardless of who is at fault in the accident. The objectives were to reduce the incentives for lawsuits and to compensate victims quickly and efficiently, resulting in reduced insurance costs.

As of 2019, only 12 states still have compulsory no-fault laws in place. The largest potential cost savings under a no-fault system would have been from reduced litigation-related expenses. Unfortunately, many states allowed the injured parties to collect from their own insurer *and* sue the other driver if the injury exceeded a verbal threshold ("accidents resulting in serious bodily injury") or a monetary threshold ("economic loss in excess of $2,000"). As a result, litigation and claims payments increased, insurance premiums increased, and state legislators eventually gave up on no-fault coverage and reverted to a negligence-based system.

Auto Insurance Pricing

As with other types of insurance, auto insurance premiums are intended to cover the insurer's expected losses and expenses and generate a reasonable amount of profit. Expected losses are determined by the company's assessment of each policyholder's risk level. Risk is assessed based on several rating factors, but not all companies weight them the same. Factors that will usually affect your auto insurance premiums include how much you drive, how well you drive, your risk characteristics, where you drive, where you park your car, and what vehicle you drive. Your choice of insurer can also make a difference in the premium you pay.

How Much You Drive

The more you drive your car, the higher your probability of being in an auto accident. If you drive only occasionally, you should pay a lower premium than if you're a salesperson who puts 30,000 miles on your car each year. Many new vehicles have global positioning system (GPS) technology, and some insurers are offering discounts to customers who agree to allow the insurer to track the number of miles they actually drive per year. Absent such reliable data, insurers often use other factors that are a proxy for miles driven.

For example, you probably already know that young female drivers pay lower auto insurance rates than young males. What's less commonly known is that this isn't because women are inherently better drivers. It's because teenage girls drive less than teenage boys—about half as many miles per year on average. Because insurers can't accurately measure how much a policyholder drives (and people, if asked, would be likely to underreport their actual mileage to save on insurance costs), gender acts as a proxy for miles driven for this age group. For the same reason, most insurers give discounts for multiple cars in the same household on the principle that each one will be driven less than if the household only had one car.

How Well You Drive

If you've had previous accidents or traffic tickets, this history will result in higher future auto insurance premiums. The more serious the violation, the greater the impact on your premium. For example, charges for driving under the influence (DUI) or driving while intoxicated (DWI) are treated very seriously. A second offense in either of these categories will likely result in cancellation of your policy. In general, insurers will look back only three years, so you'll eventually be able to enjoy lower premiums if you don't continue to violate the law.

Parents are often surprised at how expensive it is to buy auto insurance for teenage drivers. Insurers charge higher rates for teens because age and experience are strong factors in claims. As you can see in **Figure 7.8**, teenage drivers are far more likely to be involved in fatal car accidents than drivers in general. Teen drivers engage in many of the same risky driving behaviors as adults—eating or texting while driving, for instance, or failing to wear a seat belt—but their inexperience makes these behaviors more dangerous. Discounts are available for students with good grades, but rates can go up dramatically once a teen has had an accident.

FIGURE 7.8   **Auto Fatality Rate by Age and Gender**   Teens and people in their early 20s, especially males, are much more likely to be involved in fatal auto crashes, both as drivers and as passengers, than older people, though fatality rates climb again for people in their 70s.

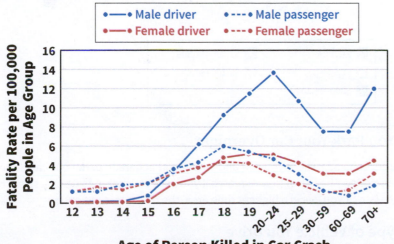

Source: Insurance Institute for Highway Safety, www.iihs.org.

Your Risk Characteristics

Insurers have found that people who act responsibly in other areas of life are also better drivers. For years, they've given good-student discounts to students who have a B average or higher and to new drivers who successfully complete a driver education course. Married couples often get lower rates than singles. Many insurers give better rates to nonsmokers as well. As is the case for homeowner's insurance, having a good credit rating can reduce your auto insurance premium.

Where You Drive

Auto insurance rates are also affected by where you live. If you regularly drive the congested roadways in New Jersey, you'll pay higher rates on average than if you're a rural customer in Idaho, where there are few other cars on the road at the same time as yours. Although the average annual auto insurance premium for the United States in 2018 was $1,365, **Figure 7.9** shows the wide range of prices. Average premiums in the high-cost states are more than double those in the low-cost states.

FIGURE 7.9   **Average Auto Premiums by State**   How do auto insurance rates in your state compare with rates in other states?

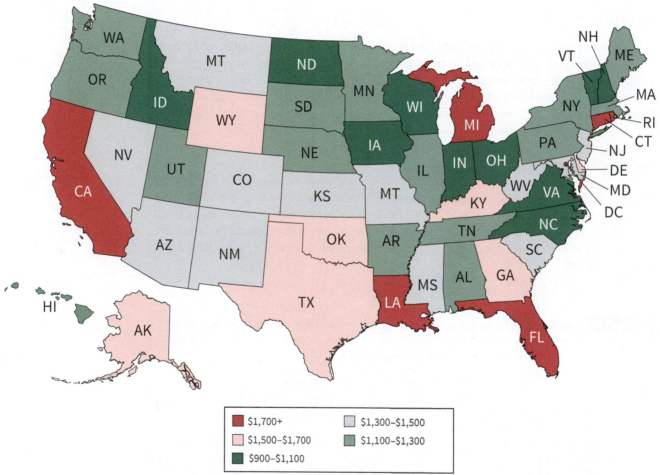

Legend:
- $1,700+
- $1,500–$1,700
- $900–$1,100
- $1,300–$1,500
- $1,100–$1,300

Source: insure.com, 2018.

Where You Park Your Car Overnight

Auto insurers consider where you live and where you generally park your car to be factors in pricing your policy. The risk of loss increases if you park your car outside on a street rather than in a garage. Also, if you live in a higher-crime area, the risk of loss increases.

What Type of Vehicle You Drive

Certain makes and models of cars are more likely to be stolen than others, but it's not always the fancy sports cars that get stolen. In fact, the most commonly stolen cars are popular lower-priced models, such as the Toyota Camry and the Honda Accord, which are easy to resell or dismantle for parts. In addition to theft risk, some cars—such as foreign makes and rare collectibles—are more expensive to repair, and, thus, property damage coverage for those cars costs more. On the positive side, you may be eligible for discounts if your vehicle has airbags, antilock brakes, antitheft devices, or other safety features.

Who Your Insurer Is

In addition to state-by-state variation, premiums for auto insurance can vary widely from insurer to insurer. If you shop around, don't be surprised to find that some insurers charge double what others charge for the same policy terms and limits. This range exists partly because companies have different costs, but it also results from the fact that insurance companies operate in a highly competitive market in which consumers are reluctant to switch insurers for small reductions in premiums. New companies entering an area must heavily undercut established firms to build their business. They know they'll lose money in the first few years, but expect that they'll make up the difference in investment returns and be able to charge higher premiums later on without great risk of customer cancellation. Although such heavy competition might seem to offer you an opportunity to get a good deal on auto insurance, keep in mind that any firm pricing its policies at a loss runs the risk of going bankrupt before it can make it to the profitable years. It may skimp on service or deny otherwise payable claims in an effort to cut costs. Thus, reputation and financial solvency ratings should always factor into your decision.

> **Reflection Question 2**
>
> Based on the auto insurance rating factors identified in this section, how would an insurer assess your risk in each of the categories in this section? Is there anything you can do to improve your risk rating?

7.5 Buying Insurance and Making Claims

> **LEARNING OBJECTIVE 7.5**
> Compare insurers based on quality, service, and price before buying a policy.

Steps to Buying Property and Liability Insurance

Property and liability insurance plays an important role in your financial plan. The risks you face from driving a car and owning or renting a home are the type that can be transferred to an insurer at relatively low cost. Many people make the mistake of buying this insurance without adequately evaluating their needs and their alternatives. In developing your insurance plan, you should follow the steps in **Figure 7.10**. Notice that, as with all elements of the financial planning process, the last step is always to reevaluate on a regular basis.

The Role of Agents and Brokers

People often buy insurance from insurance agents, also called brokers or producers. An insurance agent who works directly for a specific insurer and sells only that insurer's products is known as an **exclusive** or **captive agent**. In contrast, an **independent agent** sells insurance products for a number of different insurers. You also have the option of buying insurance directly from an insurance company through the company's website. You can learn more about how to compare insurance prices online by watching **Online Calculator Demonstration Video: Shopping for Auto Insurance**.

ONLINE CALCULATOR DEMONSTRATION VIDEO

See **Online Calculator Demonstration Video: Shopping for Auto Insurance** in **WileyPLUS** to learn about comparison shopping.

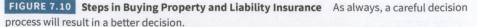

FIGURE 7.10 **Steps in Buying Property and Liability Insurance** As always, a careful decision process will result in a better decision.

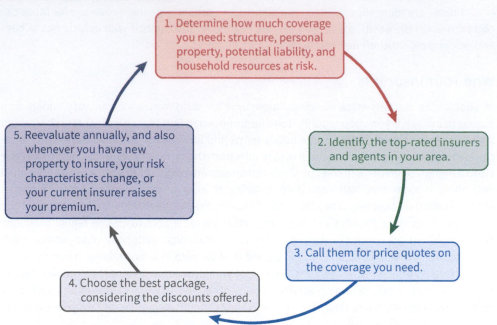

In deciding among these options, consider the trade-off between service and cost, as well as the ability of the agent to offer a greater variety of products to meet your insurance needs. Selling insurance directly to you is cheaper for the company than selling through an agent, who must be paid a commission. But you may find that a commissioned agent will provide you with better, more personalized service, helping you through the claims process and making sure that you maintain adequate insurance over time. In deciding between insurance agents, consider the recommendations of friends, relatives, and colleagues, as well as the agents' experience and certifications.

If you need more information about insurance and the insurance-buying process, there are many resources available. For example, the Insurance Information Institute (**www.iii.org**) is a nonprofit organization that maintains a consumer-friendly website.

Comparing Insurance Policies

EXCEL WORKSHEET

See **Excel Worksheet 7.2** (**Personal Financial Planner: Comparing Homeowner's/Renter's Insurance Policies**) in **WileyPLUS.**

EXCEL WORKSHEET

See **Excel Worksheet 7.3** (**Personal Financial Planner: Comparing Auto Insurance Policies**) in **WileyPLUS.**

One way to get insurance price quotes is to call local agents and insurers. In addition, there are many Internet sources for price quotes on auto and homeowner's insurance. In comparing your alternatives, be sure that the price quotes you receive are all comparable. In order to do this, you must provide each insurer with the same information about yourself, your car, and the limits and deductibles you're interested in. A company **underwriter** or an automated underwriting system will evaluate this information to provide a price quote. You can use **Excel Worksheet 7.2** (Personal Financial Planner: Comparing Homeowner's/Renter's Insurance Policies) and **Excel Worksheet 7.3** (Personal Financial Planner: Comparing Auto Insurance Policies) to compare quotes and coverage from different insurers.

Using Online Resources to Evaluate Your Insurance Options

Once you've collected all your information, you'll need to weigh the price quotes against differences in company financial strength, quality, and service. A company that consistently scores high ratings is unlikely to become insolvent in the near future and so will be around to pay your future claims.

Several websites, including **www.insure.com**, **www.insweb.com**, and **www.insurance.com**, provide insurer ratings and allow you to compare price quotes from participating insurance companies. Some insurers, such as GEICO and Progressive, will provide you with their own quote and other competitors' quotes for comparison. The difference between the highest and lowest quotes can sometimes be a lot of money. You should also investigate each company's financial health, rather than basing your decision on price alone. You can check the financial strength and credit ratings of various insurers and learn more about the rating process at **www.ambest.com**, the website of A. M. Best Company, one of the three major rating agencies. **Table 7.4** summarizes the results of a recent survey of customers of large auto insurers and also provides the A. M. Best financial strength rating for each of the firms.

TABLE 7.4	**Survey Rankings and A. M. Best Financial Strength Ratings for Various Insurers**		
Company	**Overall Survey Rating (out of 100)**	**% Who Would Recommend to a Friend**	**Financial Strength Rating, A.M. Best**
USAA	90.0	92	A++
American Family Insurance	88.3	93	A+
Allstate Insurance Group	88.3	89	A+
AAA Insurance/CSAA Insurance Group	88.1	94	A+
Auto Club of Southern California	87.8	94	A+
Mercury Insurance Group	87.7	93	A+
Liberty Mutual	87.2	86	A
Progressive	86.6	85	A+
Erie Insurance	86.3	89	A+
GEICO	86.0	89	A++
The General Automobile Insurance Services	85.8	87	A−
Farmers Insurance	85.2	81	A+
State Farm	84.8	86	A++
esurance	84.6	85	A+
Nationwide	84.4	85	A+
Metlife Personal Lines Group	84.3	85	A+
The Hartford	83.4	83	A+
Travelers	81.3	79	A++

Source: insure.com, "Best Insurance Companies 2018." The survey included 3,160 customers of the largest 20 auto insurers.

Making a Claim on Your Insurance

Even if you have so far avoided any losses due to auto or home risks, the odds are that eventually you'll experience one. Because it's not unlikely that at some point you'll be involved in an automobile accident, we first consider what to do in that situation. Then we summarize the steps in filing an insurance claim.

What to Do if You Have an Auto Accident

If you're involved in an automobile accident, whether it's a simple fender bender or a more serious accident, taking the correct steps can save you trouble and make the process of filing an insurance claim simpler. At the time of the accident, you should:

- Stop your vehicle and wait at the scene of the accident for a police officer.
- Call 911 to report the accident, and seek medical assistance for anyone who is injured.
- Exchange names, addresses, phone numbers, and insurance information with the other driver or drivers.
- Obtain contact information for any witnesses.

- When police officers arrive, provide information that they request, but do not admit fault.
- Get the case number while still at the accident scene, and obtain a copy of the police report after it's been prepared.
- Notify your insurer.

Steps in Filing a Claim

If you have suffered a loss that you think is covered under your insurance policy, you must decide whether you want to file a claim. Unless it's a very small loss, it's probably worthwhile to do so, but you'll need to consider the impact the claim will have on your future insurance premiums.

If you decide to make a claim, you should take the following steps:

- Promptly notify your insurance agent or insurer, and follow the directions provided. This will usually involve filling out required forms, providing a copy of the police report in the case of an accident or theft, and taking steps to minimize further damage or loss.
- Document your losses. Documentation can include photos, receipts for lost or stolen items, a written description of the event, names and addresses of witnesses, and other information that will verify your loss. It's a good idea to document your possessions before a loss occurs. One way to do this is to walk through your home with a video camera, being sure to open all your closets and drawers to capture their contents on tape.
- Document the progress of the claim. Keep copies of all records, phone calls, letters, and other materials that you submit to the insurer and anything that supports your claim.
- Don't sign any documents that may limit your ability to receive further payment from the insurer until you're satisfied that the entire claim has been paid. The insurer will commonly designate a person, called a **claims adjuster**, to assess whether the loss is covered under your policy and to assign a dollar amount to the loss. If you disagree with that assessment, you may need to provide independent evidence of the value of your loss (such as a repair estimate from your local auto body shop).

It's not uncommon for a claims adjuster to offer to settle a homeowner's claim promptly following a fire or theft loss by writing a check on the spot. Although it may be tempting to take the money and run, once the excitement of the initial loss event has passed, homeowners often later discover that additional items have been damaged or stolen, so it's advisable to let some time pass before agreeing to a final settlement amount.

Summary

Learning Objectives Review

LEARNING OBJECTIVE 7.1   Apply the risk management process to identify risks and decide how to manage them.

The risk management process consists of five steps: (1) identify risk exposures, (2) evaluate potential losses, (3) choose the most appropriate risk management method, (4) implement the risk management plan, and (5) reevaluate the plan regularly.

- Homes and autos expose you to property risk and **liability risk**.
- Evaluating risk requires that you estimate both **frequency of loss**, the probability that a loss will occur, and **severity of loss**, the cost of the loss if it does occur.
- You can estimate the cost of an expected loss using **Equation 7.1**:

Expected loss = Expected frequency × Expected severity

- Based on the expected loss, you can decide whether it makes sense to buy insurance. Insurance is generally available for **pure risks**, but not for **speculative risks**.
- The most common methods for managing risk are risk avoidance, **risk retention**, risk reduction (investing in **loss control**), and risk transfer (usually involving the purchase of insurance).

LEARNING OBJECTIVE 7.2   Explain how risk pooling works, and define common insurance policy terminology.

Insurers spread the risk of loss across many policyholders using the **law of large numbers**. As an insurance pool gets very large, losses per person in the pool become more predictable, so an insurer can charge its customers a **premium** that is close to their expected loss. In return for your premium payment, the insurer promises to reimburse you for covered losses that occur during the policy period.

- Insurance companies use **risk classification** to ensure that each policyholder pays a premium that is appropriate for his or her expected loss.

- Risk pooling does not work well for some types of risks, such as those that are unpredictable, highly correlated, or within the control of the policyholder.

- It is important that you read your **insurance policy** carefully because you will usually be bound by its terms.

- A **deductible** is an amount the insured must pay on a loss before the insurance company is obligated to pay anything. Deductibles and other limits on coverage help insurers keep premium costs down.

- In some cases, you may need to purchase a **rider** to cover a type of loss that would otherwise be subject to an **exclusion** or a limitation on coverage.

- The principle of **indemnity** says that you cannot recover more from your insurance than your actual loss.

LEARNING OBJECTIVE 7.3   Describe the loss coverage provided by homeowner's and renter's insurance and the factors that affect premiums.

If you own or rent a home, you are exposed to the risk of loss or damage to your property. You're also exposed to the risk that visitors to your property could sue you for injuries to themselves or their property. **Homeowner's insurance** and **renter's insurance** cover financial losses that arise from legal claims against you and from covered perils in the policies, such as theft, wind, rain, and fire.

- Homeowners and renters can reduce their risk of legal claims by understanding liability rules, such as those governing **negligence** and **strict liability**, and defenses to liability claims, such as **contributory negligence** and **assumption of risk**. Renter's insurance covers liability and personal property risk, but not damage to the building itself.

- The amount of coverage you need should be based on the value of your home and personal property. You can also purchase supplemental coverage for earthquake, flood, and personal property. **Umbrella insurance** is available to cover liability in excess of the regular policy limits.

- The major determinants of homeowner's insurance premiums are the location and characteristics of the home being insured, the **face amount** and type of coverage purchased (limits, deductibles, **scheduled property**), the characteristics of the insured person (past claim history, credit score), and the amount of coverage purchased.

LEARNING OBJECTIVE 7.4   Understand your choices for auto insurance coverage and what factors are likely to increase your premiums.

Operation of a motor vehicle exposes you to risks of bodily injury and loss of property, as well as liability risk for injuries or damage caused by you to the person or property of others.

- Most states have **compulsory automobile insurance laws**, which require proof of liability insurance as a prerequisite to car registration, and all states have **financial responsibility laws**, which require drivers who have been in a traffic accident to show proof of insurance or the ability to pay a claim.

- Standard auto liability insurance covers claims for bodily injury and property damage caused by you, medical expenses for you and any of your passengers injured in an accident, and losses caused by uninsured motorists. Optional coverage for damage to your own vehicle or for its theft requires the purchase of **collision coverage** or **comprehensive physical damage coverage**.

- Some states require insurers to offer **no-fault automobile insurance**, which means that each person relies on his or her own insurer for payment of losses, regardless of fault.

- The major determinants of auto premium costs are how much you drive, your driving record, your risk characteristics, your geographic location, the type of car you drive, and the insurance company you choose.

LEARNING OBJECTIVE 7.5   Compare insurers based on quality, service, and price before buying a policy.

There are five steps involved in buying property and liability insurance: (1) determine how much coverage you need, (2) identify the top-rated insurers and agents in your area, (3) call them for price quotes, (4) choose the best package, and (5) reevaluate annually or as necessary.

- You can buy insurance through an **exclusive** or **captive agent**, through an **independent agent**, or directly from an insurance company. An insurance **underwriter** will evaluate your application and provide a price quote.

- Comparison shopping is very important because prices and service can differ substantially between different insurers. As with other areas of your financial plan, you should reevaluate your coverage on a regular basis or if there are any changes in your circumstances.

- If you have a loss, you should promptly notify your insurer and document your losses carefully. The insurer will typically assign a **claims adjuster** to assess whether the loss is covered under your policy and to assign a dollar amount to the loss. Any payment to you will be made after applicable deductibles have been subtracted from the total loss.

Excel Worksheets

Key Terms

assumption of risk 7-12	financial responsibility laws 7-18	pure risk 7-2
claims adjuster 7-26	frequency of loss 7-4	renter's insurance 7-10
collision coverage 7-20	homeowner's insurance 7-10	rider 7-9
comprehensive physical	indemnity 7-9	risk classification 7-8
damage coverage 7-20	independent agent 7-23	risk retention 7-7
compulsory automobile	insurance policy 7-9	scheduled property 7-14
insurance laws 7-18	law of large numbers 7-7	severity of loss 7-4
contributory negligence 7-11	liability risk 7-4	speculative risk 7-2
deductible 7-9	loss control 7-6	strict liability 7-11
exclusion 7-9	negligence 7-11	umbrella insurance 7-16
exclusive or captive agent 7-23	no-fault automobile insurance 7-20	underwriter 7-24
face amount 7-14	premium 7-8	

WileyPLUS

Practice Questions to check your understanding, Peer-to-Peer Videos, Interactives, and many other resources are available in WileyPLUS.

Concept Review Questions

1. Describe the steps in the risk management process, and compare them with the steps in the financial planning process.

2. Explain why it is sometimes better to retain certain risks rather than purchase an insurance policy that would cover them.

3. Zelda is considering the purchase of a BB gun for her son. Apply the steps in the risk management process to this decision.

4. Why is it better to have large numbers of people in a risk pool?

5. Explain why risk pooling doesn't work well for correlated risks such as earthquakes.

6. What effect does a higher deductible have on your insurance premium, if all else is equal?

7. Explain what it means to identify a state's minimum auto liability coverage requirement as 50/100/25.

8. Describe three ways a consumer can reduce his or her auto insurance premiums.

9. Describe three ways a consumer can reduce his or her homeowner's insurance premiums.

10. Based on your driving record, personal characteristics, and type of vehicle, what auto insurance discounts might you be eligible for? Explain your reasoning.

11. What is the difference between collision coverage and comprehensive physical damage coverage?

Application Problems

1. For each of the following risks, suggest a method for reducing the frequency of loss.

  a. Injury to a person who slips on your sidewalk after a snowstorm

  b. Damage to your vehicle from hitting a deer while driving at dusk

2. For each of the following risks, suggest a method for reducing the severity of loss.

  a. Bodily injury in an automobile collision

  b. Fire damage to your home

3. Imagine that you have a $600 smartphone and that there is a 25 percent chance that it will be lost or stolen this year.

  a. What is the expected loss?

  b. Is it worth it to pay for replacement insurance on the phone? Explain.

4. For each of the following risks of loss, identify whether it is high or low in frequency and high or low in severity. Then suggest one or more methods for managing the risk.

  a. Getting a dent in your car door

  b. Complete destruction of your home in a fire

  c. Theft of your laptop from your dorm room

5. One of your classmates suggests that you can save money on renter's insurance by forming a risk pool. All 100 students in the class agree to contribute money to the pool and agree that anyone who experiences loss or damage to personal property in his or her place of residence can make a claim on the pool's funds over the course of the year.

    a. How would you decide how much money to charge each person in the class?

    b. Is it fair to charge everyone the same amount? Explain your reasoning.

    c. If, at the end of the year, it turns out that the total losses to the group are larger than the amount of money in the pool, what can you do?

    d. What are some potential problems with this pooling arrangement?

6. Mindy Stern currently insures her home for 100 percent of its replacement cost with an HO-3 All-Risk policy, providing her with $200,000 in dwelling coverage.

    a. What is Mindy's maximum coverage for personal property in the home?

    b. What is Mindy's maximum coverage for the cost of staying in a motel while her home is being repaired following a loss?

7. Imagine that you spend $20,000 to refinish your home's basement. How would this affect your homeowner's insurance premium at your policy renewal date, and why?

8. Imagine that your credit rating has improved because you've been doing a much better job of paying your mortgage and credit card bills on time. How might this affect your homeowner's insurance premium at your policy renewal date, and why?

9. Imagine that you make a large claim on your homeowner's insurance. How might this affect your homeowner's insurance premium at your policy renewal date, and why?

10. Imagine that you decide to buy your auto insurance from the same company that provides you with homeowner's insurance. How might this affect your homeowner's insurance premium at your policy renewal date, and why?

11. When Ernie Franklin originally bought his home for $150,000, he followed the advice of his agent and purchased homeowner's insurance in the amount of $120,000 to cover the value of the dwelling, not including the land. His home value has now increased to $210,000, of which $168,000 is the value of the dwelling, not including the land, but he has not increased the amount of coverage. If Ernie's insurer requires that its policyholders have at least 80% of the value insured, and his home is completely destroyed in a fire, will his loss be completely covered? Explain your reasoning.

12. Bonita Baca has a personal auto policy with coverage limits of 20/40/15. Bonita has collision coverage with a $250 deductible. She runs a red light and causes an auto accident in which three people are injured. Each of them sues her for $20,000 in personal injury and $5,000 for vehicle damage (there is no injury to Bonita or her car). How much will Bonita have to pay out of pocket, and how much will her insurer pay? Explain.

13. Harrison Hartel has a personal auto policy with coverage limits of 25/50/10. Harrison has collision coverage with a $500 deductible. He backs into his neighbor's garage door, causing $1,000 damage to the garage and $2,000 damage to his car. How much will Harrison have to pay out of pocket, and how much will his insurer pay?

14. Patrick O'Hara owns a 10-year-old car in great running condition. It is currently worth $4,000. Patrick has just taken a part-time job delivering pizza, and he is concerned about his increased risk of having an accident. He estimates that he has a 50 percent probability of having an accident within the next year. If he does have an accident, he estimates that there is a 25 percent chance it will cause significant damage to his vehicle ($3,000) and a 75 percent chance it will cause only minor damage ($500).

    a. What is Patrick's expected frequency of loss?

    b. What is Patrick's expected severity of loss?

    c. What is Patrick's expected total loss?

    d. If Patrick asks your advice about whether to purchase collision coverage for an extra $100 per year with a $500 deductible, what would you suggest, and why?

15. The tenants in the apartment above Blake's apartment left the water running in their bathtub, and it leaked through the ceiling onto his bed. If Blake does not have renter's insurance, who will pay for his damages, and why?

Case Applications

1. Ken and Erika Zumwalt are buying a new home in southern California. The property is in a lovely wooded community outside of San Diego, not far from an area that experienced a serious wildfire the previous year. The home is valued at $400,000, not including the land, and the Zumwalts estimate that they have about $100,000 in personal property, including $10,000 in jewelry. Their net worth, including their home equity, is about $250,000.

    a. What type of homeowner's insurance is best for the Zumwalts?

    b. What is the minimum amount of homeowner's insurance the Zumwalts should purchase?

    c. If the Zumwalts' homeowner's policy requires that the face amount be 90 percent of the actual value and the Zumwalts insure for less than that amount, what financial risk do they face?

    d. Should the Zumwalts consider additional coverage for their personal property? Why or why not?

    e. Should the Zumwalts consider purchasing an umbrella policy? Why or why not?

    f. What other risk management tools should the Zumwalts employ to reduce their risk of losses due to wildfire?

2. Over the holidays, David and Mary Costanza's Christmas tree caught fire, and they sustained significant damage to their home and personal property. They had to clean and repaint their living room and replace the living room carpet and furniture, at a cost of $7,000. While the work was being done, the family stayed in a motel for three days at a total cost of $300. The Costanzas had an actual cash value homeowner's insurance policy with a deductible of $250. The insurance company's claims adjuster came to the Costanzas' home and looked at the damage. He estimated actual cash values of $750 for the furniture, and $350 for the carpet, which had needed replacing for some time.

a. How much do you estimate that the insurer will pay the Costanzas?

b. If the Costanzas had purchased replacement cost insurance, how much would they have received from their insurer after the loss?

c. If the Costanzas were concerned about the effect of replacement cost insurance on their homeowner's insurance premium, what other suggestions could you offer that would help reduce their premium?

3. Carrie Richmond is 30 years old and single. She is achieving success as a professional photographer and now earns $50,000 before taxes. Carrie has been fairly diligent about establishing a financial plan and working toward achieving her financial goals. Two years ago, she bought a condominium, and it has appreciated in value to the point that she has $40,000 in home equity. She also has accumulated $25,000 in savings and paid off her student loan. Recently, Carrie paid off the remaining balance on the car loan for her four-year-old vehicle. After looking at Carrie's financial situation, her insurance agent suggested that she consider increasing her automobile coverage. Her current coverage is $25,000 bodily injury liability per person, $50,000 bodily injury liability per accident, and $15,000 property damage liability. She also has medical expense coverage of $10,000 per person and uninsured motorist protection of $25,000 per person, and $50,000 per accident. Because she previously had a bank loan on the car, she has been carrying comprehensive property damage insurance on the car.

a. Given the value of Carrie's household assets, what auto insurance liability limits would you recommend? Explain your reasoning.

b. Under what circumstances would Carrie need uninsured motorist protection? Is she adequately insured for this risk? If not, what limits would you recommend?

c. Assuming that her car is in fairly good condition and is worth $10,000, should she continue to carry comprehensive physical damage coverage, and, if so, in what types and amounts?

CHAPTER 8

Life Insurance and Long-Term Care Planning

LWA/Dann Tardif/Age fotostock

Feature Story

When Jackie Reynolds's husband died at 28 with barely enough life insurance to pay for his funeral, Jackie realized she had to do a better job of planning for the financial needs of her young daughters, Makayla and Trinity. She purchased a $500,000 term life insurance policy on herself and named the girls as her beneficiaries. When her girls were 10 and 15, Jackie was diagnosed with terminal lung cancer. Fortunately, her policy included an accelerated benefits provision that allowed her to use the money accumulated in the policy to finance her hospice care, pay off loans on the family home and car, and set up an education fund for her daughters. Today, Makayla, a recent college graduate, and Trinity, a high school senior, live in the home their mother purchased for them.

Everyone dies someday. The only question is when, and it can happen when we least expect it. Without advance planning, the death of a parent can cause serious financial hardship for the surviving family members. Because illness and death are difficult topics to talk about, however, many people avoid taking them into consideration as part of their financial plan until it's too late.

This chapter describes how life insurance works and how to determine whether you need any. The basic contract types and features are explained to help you make informed choices. Jackie's choice of a life insurance policy with an accelerated benefits clause, for example, allowed her some flexibility in making end-of-life decisions. We also consider the financial impact of both your own and your parents' long-term care needs and how you can use long-term care insurance to help pay future costs of a nursing home or home health care.

LEARNING OBJECTIVES	TOPICS	DEMONSTRATION PROBLEMS
8.1 Determine how much life insurance you need.	**8.1 Life Insurance and Your Financial Plan** • Life Insurance Compared with Auto and Homeowner's Insurance • Life Insurance Needs Analysis • Factors Affecting Your Life Insurance Needs	

(continued)

(continued)

LEARNING OBJECTIVES	TOPICS	DEMONSTRATION PROBLEMS
8.2 Select the type of life insurance that best meets your needs.	**8.2 Buying Life Insurance** • Choosing the Type of Policy • Choosing an Insurer • Choosing an Agent	
8.3 Define key terms used in life insurance policies.	**8.3 Reading Your Policy** • Policy Declarations • Key Provisions in a Life Insurance Policy • Settlement Options	
8.4 Explain the choices for funding long-term care needs.	**8.4 Planning for Long-Term Care Costs** • Long-Term Care Needs Analysis • Sources of Funds for Long-Term Care • Long-Term Care Insurance	

8.1 | Life Insurance and Your Financial Plan

LEARNING OBJECTIVE 8.1

Determine how much life insurance you need.

A wise person once said that the only things we can be sure of are death and taxes. Even though few would disagree with this statement, many people fail to adequately prepare for their death. Like Jackie Reynolds in the chapter opener, they avoid this part of their financial plan until they see what happens when someone dies without adequate coverage to meet their family's financial needs.

Clearly, illness and death are unpleasant to think about. When you're young and healthy, these risks may seem like remote possibilities that can easily be ignored. If you have dependents, however, you need to evaluate how their financial needs will be taken care of in the event of your death. In this section, we'll first examine the similarities and differences between life insurance and other types of insurance covered earlier. Then we'll consider whether you should include purchasing life insurance in your financial plan and, if so, how much you need to buy, given your household characteristics and life circumstances.

Life Insurance Compared with Auto and Homeowner's Insurance

The basic risk management principles underlying auto and homeowner's insurance apply to life insurance as well. Like other insurance products, life insurance is based on the concept of risk pooling. People die with a certain degree of predictability, and each person's death is, in general, independent of the deaths of others. Therefore, mortality is a type of pure risk for which the pooling mechanism is particularly well suited.

Unlike other types of insurable risks, death occurs with 100 percent certainty. The very certainty of the insured event makes life insurance inherently different from property, liability, and health insurance. Life insurance policies also tend to be longer-term in nature than other policies. In this section, we consider the effects of these differences by comparing life insurance with auto and homeowner's insurance based on three important dimensions: factors that affect premiums, the role of insurance company investments, and the intended use of the policy proceeds.

Factors That Affect Premiums

As with other types of insurance, the premium you're charged for life insurance depends on several factors:

- Expenses incurred by the insurer (for commissions to agents, underwriting, investigation and payment of claims, and management of the firm)
- Profit to the insurance company owners
- Your risk classification

Expenses and profit can be quite different from insurer to insurer. Remember the law of large numbers discussed in Chapter 7? As you might expect, larger insurers can often provide lower rates than small insurers because they can spread their costs across a bigger group of policyholders. Some insurers spend more money and time on deciding which applicants to accept. For example they might require more extensive medical exams. If they can limit their pool of policyholders to those with a lower-than-average risk of dying during the policy period, they can charge each insured person a lower premium.

Your life insurance risk classification is based on the insurer's estimate of the probability that you will die during the policy period. Because your risk of dying is related to your age, health, and family history, the information required by an insurer to underwrite your policy (decide whether to insure you and how much to charge) is similar to that required for individual health and disability insurance. For example, you'll commonly be asked about your family health history. For larger amounts of insurance, you'll usually have to undergo a medical exam and blood test. Obviously, if you have a terminal illness, insurers will not want to sell you a life insurance policy.

Our discussion of risk management in Chapter 7 began with an estimate of expected loss based on frequency and severity. The same principles apply to managing your mortality risk. What are your odds of dying in the next year, or 10 years, or 20 years? In other words, what is your **mortality risk**? In the life insurance business, a person's risk of dying is estimated using standardized mortality tables. These tables, based on many years of statistical data on millions of lives, provide yearly probabilities of dying and surviving based on current age.

Women tend to live longer than men, on average, so there are separate tables for males and females. The standard tables are regularly updated to account for improvements in life expectancy due to medical advances, better health care, and nutrition. It's also common for life insurers to use different tables to estimate mortality risk for smokers versus nonsmokers. At any age, a smoker's risk of dying is equivalent to that of a nonsmoker who is 5 to 10 years older. Excessive alcohol consumption has a similar impact on life expectancy and can factor into life insurance underwriting decisions. A portion of a mortality table is reproduced in **Table 8.1**, and **Case Study 8.1** illustrates how to use it. To learn how your longevity is affected by health and lifestyle factors, watch the **Online Calculator Demonstration Video: Estimate Your Personal Longevity**.

ONLINE CALCULATOR DEMONSTRATION VIDEO

See **Online Calculator Demonstration Video: Estimate Your Personal Longevity** in **WileyPLUS**.

The Role of Insurance Company Investments

An important difference between life insurers and property insurers is that the average term of a life insurance policy is much longer—about half of all life insurance policies sold today are long-term policies that accumulate cash value over time. Life insurers collect annual premiums

TABLE 8.1   **Excerpt from a Mortality Table**

Age	Male			Female		
	Deaths per 1,000	Life Expectancy (Years)	Probability of Living to This Age	Deaths per 1,000	Life Expectancy (Years)	Probability of Living to This Age
Newborn	1.0	76.6	0.9990	0.5	80.8	0.9995
1	0.6	75.7	0.9984	0.4	79.9	0.9991
2	0.4	74.7	0.9980	0.3	78.9	0.9988
3	0.3	73.8	0.9977	0.2	77.9	0.9986
4	0.2	72.8	0.9975	0.2	76.9	0.9984
5	0.2	71.8	0.9973	0.2	76.0	0.9982
6	0.2	70.8	0.9971	0.2	75.0	0.9980
7	0.2	69.8	0.9969	0.2	74.0	0.9978
8	0.2	68.8	0.9967	0.2	73.0	0.9976
9	0.2	67.9	0.9965	0.2	72.0	0.9974
10	0.2	66.9	0.9963	0.2	71.0	0.9972
11	0.3	65.9	0.9960	0.2	70.0	0.9970
12	0.3	64.9	0.9957	0.3	69.1	0.9967
13	0.4	63.9	0.9953	0.3	68.1	0.9964
14	0.5	63.0	0.9948	0.3	67.1	0.9961
15	0.6	62.0	0.9942	0.4	66.1	0.9957
16	0.7	61.0	0.9935	0.4	65.1	0.9953
17	0.9	60.1	0.9926	0.4	64.2	0.9949
18	0.9	59.1	0.9917	0.4	63.2	0.9945
19	1.0	58.2	0.9907	0.5	62.2	0.9940
20	1.0	57.2	0.9897	0.5	61.3	0.9935
21	1.0	56.3	0.9888	0.5	60.3	0.9930
22	1.0	55.3	0.9878	0.5	59.3	0.9925
23	1.0	54.4	0.9868	0.5	58.3	0.9920
24	1.1	53.5	0.9857	0.5	57.4	0.9915
25	1.1	52.5	0.9846	0.5	56.4	0.9910
26	1.1	51.6	0.9835	0.6	55.4	0.9904
27	1.2	50.6	0.9824	0.6	54.5	0.9898
28	1.2	49.7	0.9812	0.6	53.5	0.9893
29	1.2	48.7	0.9800	0.7	52.5	0.9886
30	1.1	47.8	0.9789	0.7	51.6	0.9879
31	1.1	46.8	0.9778	0.7	50.6	0.9872
32	1.1	45.9	0.9768	0.8	49.6	0.9864
33	1.2	45.0	0.9756	0.8	58.7	0.9856
34	1.2	44.0	0.9744	0.9	47.7	0.9847
35	1.2	43.1	0.9733	1.0	46.8	0.9837
36	1.3	42.1	0.9720	1.0	45.8	0.9827
37	1.3	41.2	0.9707	1.1	44.8	0.9817
38	1.4	40.2	0.9694	1.2	43.9	0.9805
39	1.5	39.3	0.9679	1.2	42.9	0.9793
40	1.7	38.3	0.9663	1.3	42.0	0.9780
50	3.8	29.2	0.9397	3.1	32.7	0.9578
60	9.9	20.6	0.8787	8.0	24.1	0.9063
70	25.8	13.3	0.7335	17.8	16.4	0.7974
80	70.1	7.5	0.4571	43.9	9.9	0.5866
90	187.7	3.8	0.1166	121.9	5.3	0.2503
100	363.2	2.1	0.0050	275.7	2.6	0.0261

Case Study 8.1

iStock.com/laflor

When Will Carson Die?

Problem

Carson is a 20-year-old male. What is the probability he will live until his 21st birthday? What is his life expectancy?

Strategy

Use the following data from **Table 8.1** to find Carson's death risk for his 20th year, as well as his life expectancy.

Solution   According to the mortality table, 1 out of every 1,000 20-year-old males will die before reaching age 21. A 0.1 percent (1/1,000) chance of dying means that Carson has a 99.9 percent chance of living through the year. This might seem like pretty good odds, but keep in mind it's only an annual probability. To get to age 21, he will have had to survive to each previous age, which is why the table shows a probability of 0.9888, or 98.88 percent, of surviving from birth to age 21.

In this table, life expectancy is the additional years a person will live, on average, beginning at the age given in the row. So at age 20, Carson has a life expectancy of 57.2 more years for a total expected age at death of 20 + 57.2 = 77.2 years. As he survives each successive year, his life expectancy, measured as expected age at death, actually increases. At birth, it was only 76.6. If he makes it to age 40, his life expectancy will increase to 40 + 38.3 = 78.3 years.

	Male			Female		
Age	Deaths per 1,000	Life Expectancy (Years)	Probability of Living to This Age	Deaths per 1,000	Life Expectancy (Years)	Probability of Living to This Age
19	1.0	58.2	0.9907	0.5	62.2	0.9940
20	1.0	57.2	0.9897	0.5	61.3	0.9935
21	1.0	56.3	0.9888	0.5	60.3	0.9930
22	1.0	55.3	0.9878	0.5	59.3	0.9925

from policyholders who won't die until many years in the future. Some of the funds are used to pay claims for any policyholders in the risk pool who die in the current year. The remainder is invested to offset insurance costs in later years. Investment performance is therefore very important—insurers with better investment results can charge lower premiums.

Intended Use of Policy Proceeds

Another important difference between life insurance and other types of insurance is that it isn't intended to cover a financial loss incurred by you, the policyholder. Rather, it is intended to benefit someone else you've designated as a **beneficiary**. If you die while the insurance policy is in force, your beneficiary will be paid a sum of money by the insurer. Although the proceeds of your policy cannot be earmarked for a particular purpose, the intent is usually to help your beneficiaries cover any financial losses resulting from your death. The most common purposes for life insurance benefits are summarized below:

- **Cover end-of-life costs**   Funeral costs can easily exceed $10,000. In addition, many people run up extensive medical bills in the last few months of their lives, which can otherwise deplete household resources.

- **Replace your income and services**   A family might need to replace a lost salary if a breadwinner dies or pay for lost services (child care, housekeeping, or transportation) if a stay-at-home spouse dies.

- **Preserve household wealth**   If they receive money from your life insurance policy, your dependents won't have to sell the family home or deplete retirement savings to cover their living expenses.

- **Fund future family needs**   Even when a family doesn't need income replacement, the insurance can be used to fund the "extras" that might otherwise be unaffordable—for example, allowing a spouse to work part time until the children are grown or paying for children to go to college.

- **Cover business losses**   If you're a partner or key person in a business venture, life insurance that names the company as the beneficiary can offset some of the costs of finding a replacement and provide the cash necessary to help the business continue operating.

- **Produce tax-free retirement income**   The accumulated cash value of a life insurance policy can be withdrawn with no tax owed on the withdrawal up to the amount of premiums that have been paid in. Any amount in excess of the premiums paid can be taken out as a loan as long as the policy is kept in force, making such a policy a tax-favored source of retirement income.

- **Pay estate taxes**   The estates of wealthy individuals and family businesses are sometimes subject to significant estate taxes. Life insurance can help the heirs cover this cost without having to sell off other assets.

> **Reflection Question 1**
>
> Considering your current life circumstances, what types of financial losses to your beneficiaries would your life insurance proceeds pay for in the event of your death? How might your answers be different 10 years from now?

Life Insurance Needs Analysis

The process of determining the potential financial impact of your death on others is called **life insurance needs analysis**. To decide how much life insurance is necessary, you estimate your dependents' total financial needs and then compare them with the financial resources you currently have to meet those needs. In the event of your death, your existing wealth can obviously be a source of support for your survivors. But because you've already earmarked this wealth for specific purposes (such as a college fund for your children or retirement income for you and your spouse), you'll usually purchase life insurance to provide whatever else might be needed.

In this section, we discuss two approaches commonly used to estimate life insurance needs. Note that the income-multiple method is quicker and easier, but generally less accurate. The more sophisticated financial needs method takes more time, but is more likely to result in the purchase of an appropriate amount of life insurance.

Income-Multiple Method

The simplest approach, and one that is often used as a shortcut in analyzing life insurance needs, is the **income-multiple method**. With this method, you simply multiply your income by a factor of 5 to 10. If you have income of $40,000, for example, you need between $200,000 and $400,000 in life insurance, according to this approach. The idea behind this method is that the life insurance should be sufficient to replace your income for a period of time.

There are several problems with this approach. First, it assumes that "one size fits all." As with many financial rules of thumb, there's no scientific evidence that this is the "right" amount of insurance to carry. Some people need far more, and others don't need any at all. Another problem is that there's usually no good explanation for why you should be on the high end or the low end of the multiple. Finally, the income-multiple method doesn't take into consideration the resources you already have to meet your financial needs.

Despite its disadvantages, the income-multiple method does have the advantage of simplicity. In addition, because most people don't have even the minimum amount of insurance recommended by this approach, it serves the purpose of identifying a shortfall.

Financial Needs Method

A more effective method of determining your life insurance needs is the **financial needs method**. The steps are illustrated in **Figure 8.1**. You'll first estimate how much money your dependents will need after your death to replace lost income and services and to fund capital needs. Some of these needs can be met with existing household savings and income. The remainder is the amount that you'll fund with life insurance.

FIGURE 8.1   **Steps in the Financial Needs Method**   The goal is to buy enough life insurance to meet the financial needs of your surviving dependents.

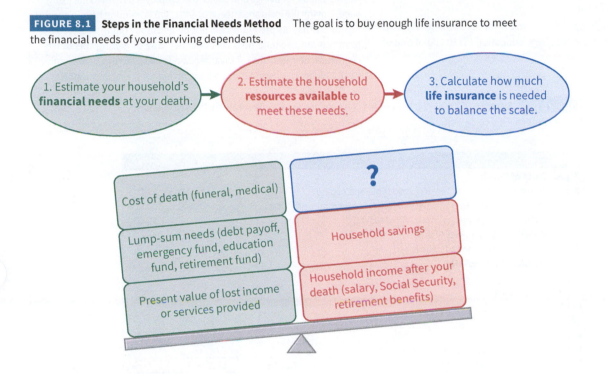

A financial planner can help you with this calculation, but it's not too hard to do on your own. For a quick estimate of your insurance needs, you can use one of the life insurance needs calculators that are available online. For a more precise calculation, you can use **Excel Worksheet 8.1** (Personal Financial Planner: Life Insurance Needs Analysis). **Case Study 8.2** illustrates the use of this worksheet to estimate one family's life insurance needs.

EXCEL WORKSHEET

See **Excel Worksheet 8.1 (Personal Financial Planner: Life Insurance Needs Analysis) in WileyPLUS.**

Case Study 8.2

szefei/Shutterstock.com

How Much Life Insurance Do Arjun and Tanya Chopra Need?

Problem

Arjun Chopra is 32 and married to Tanya, who is 30. Tanya is a stay-at-home mom to their two children, ages 1 and 4. The Chopras currently live on Arjun's salary of $80,000 (after taxes), and Tanya does not plan to return to work until their younger daughter goes to kindergarten in four years.

Use the following information about their available assets, insurance, and funding wishes to estimate how much life insurance Arjun and Tanya need, respectively:

- Arjun's employer provides $50,000 in group life insurance. Tanya does not have any life insurance.
- Based on the Social Security website, they estimate the family would be eligible for an annual maximum survivor benefit of $50,000 per year if Arjun dies. Because Tanya doesn't work, the family will not be eligible for a survivor benefit if she dies first.
- If he dies prematurely, Arjun wants to have enough insurance to cover household expenses for 10 years (which would be $20,000 lower than current expenses), pay off outstanding household debts, and provide $100,000 to establish a retirement fund for Tanya.
- They would like to add $10,000 to the family's emergency fund and fund the children's college education ($120,000) if one of them should die.

- If Tanya dies, she wants to have enough insurance for Arjun to be able to pay for child care ($10,000 per year) and housekeeping services ($5,000 per year) until the children are on their own.

Strategy

Enter Arjun and Tanya Chopra's information in Excel Worksheet 8.1 to estimate their life insurance needs.

Solution The Chopras' life insurance needs analysis, using Excel Worksheet 8.1, is shown in **Figure 8.2**.

Based on the worksheet, Arjun's survivors will need $456,500. He has $5,000 in savings and $50,000 in employer-provided life insurance, leaving life insurance needs of $401,500. Assuming he is in good health (so that his premiums will not be unusually high), $400,000 in term insurance would be a cost-effective way of getting this much life insurance protection. Tanya needs a lot less life insurance, only $141,000, because Arjun is not relying on her for financial support.

FIGURE 8.2 Sample of Excel Worksheet 8.1: Life Insurance Needs Analysis for Arjun and Tanya Chopra

	A	B	C
		Arjun	**Tanya**
2	**A. Costs of Death**		
3	1. Uninsured medical expenses (deductible and copay)	$1,000	$1,000
4	2. Funeral expense (average $10,000, but less for cremation)	$10,000	$10,000
5	3. Settlement of estate (estimate 4% of assets)	$5,000	$5,000
6	4. State inheritance taxes (if any)		
7	5. Counseling costs for adjustment to loss	$500	
8	**TOTAL COSTS AT DEATH** 1 + 2 + 3 + 4 + 5	$16,500	$16,000
9			
10	**B. Lump Sums**		
11	6. Outstanding debts		
12	a. Mortgage	$100,000	
13	b. Car loan(s)	$10,000	
14	c. Credit cards and other loans		
15	Total outstanding debt to repay 6a + 6b + 6c	$110,000	$0
16	7. Education fund for children or spouse	$120,000	$120,000
17	8. Spouse retirement fund	$100,000	
18	9. Household emergency fund (e.g., monthly household expenses × 3)	$10,000	$10,000
19	**TOTAL LUMP-SUM NEEDS** 6 + 7 + 8 + 9	$340,000	$130,000
20			
21	**C. Cost of Household Maintenance**		
22	10. Deceased's annual after-tax income	$80,000	$0
23	11. Annual cost of lost support services (child/eldercare, housekeeping)		$15,000
24	12. Reduction in family expense due to death (20-25%)	$20,000	$20,000
25	13. Annual Social Security survivor benefits	$50,000	$0
26	14. Net income shortfall 10 + 11 − 12 − 13	$10,000	($5,000)
27	**TOTAL HOUSEHOLD MAINTENANCE FUND NEEDS**		
28	Number of years you want to replace income shortfall	10	10
29	Line 14 × Number of years to replace	$100,000	$0
30			
31	**15. TOTAL FUND NEEDED** A + B + C	$456,500	$146,000
32			
33	**D. Available Resources to Meet Needs**		
34	16. Total savings and investments	$5,000	$5,000
35	17. Other life insurance (e.g., from employer)	$50,000	
36	18. Social Security lump sum benefit		
37	**19. TOTAL RESOURCES TO MEET NEEDS** 16 + 17 + 18	$55,000	$5,000
38			
39	**TOTAL LIFE INSURANCE NEEDS** 15 − 19	$401,500	$141,000

Let's look a little more closely at two items in the worksheet illustrated in Case Study 8.2. First, note that the worksheet uses a shortcut to calculate the present value of future cash flow needs by multiplying the current value times the number of years. This method works if the rate at which the cash flow needs will increase each year is equivalent to the rate that is earned on the invested lump sum. This same shortcut can also be used to estimate the amount needed for an education fund. If your education fund investments increase at approximately the same rate as college tuition, then today's annual college cost multiplied by four will be sufficient to fund four years of future college costs.

It is also worth noting that Social Security benefits can help offset life insurance needs for families with children. In Case Study 8.2, the Chopras estimated that, if Arjun died, Tanya and the children would receive $50,000 per year from Social Security. In addition to being a retirement program, Social Security pays benefits to the surviving spouse and children of qualified workers. Under current rules, benefits are payable for each child under the age of 18 and for a nonworking surviving spouse who stays at home with children, up to a specified family maximum. Financial planners often recommend that families extend the income replacement period to account for the reduction that will occur when the survivors are no longer eligible for Social Security benefits. However, nonworking spouses can usually offset this shortfall by returning to the workforce as their children become more independent. You can estimate the survivors' benefit on the Social Security website at **www.ssa.gov**. Alternatively, **Table 8.2** provides an estimate of annual survivor benefits for the family a fully insured worker who died in 2019.

TABLE 8.2   Estimated Annual Social Security Survivor Benefits (2019)

Worker Age at Death and Family Status	Current Income			
	$ 40,000	**$ 60,000**	**$ 80,000**	**$ 100,000**
Age 30				
Child under 18 or spouse with child	13,524	17,892	21,528	23,580
Family maximum	31,750	42,931	50,239	55,008
Age 40				
Child under 18 or spouse with child	12,672	16,596	20,520	22,572
Family maximum	28,656	40,621	47,889	52,658
Age 50				
Child under 18 or spouse with child	11,964	15,540	19,116	21,744
Family maximum	26,096	38,734	45,114	50,732
Age 60				
Child under 18 or spouse with child	11,388	14,644	17,940	21,048
Family maximum	23,968	35,862	43,009	49,124

Source: Social Security Administration Quick Calculator, available at www.ssa.gov. (August 2019)

Factors Affecting Your Life Insurance Needs

Previously, we identified many possible reasons to buy life insurance. Although both of the Chopras in Case Study 8.2 had some need for life insurance, not everyone does. And not everyone requires the same amount. For example, if no one relies on your income or services (no "significant other," no children, no pets, no business obligations), then the only financial cost due to your death will be your funeral expenses. If you have sufficient assets to cover those expenses, then you probably don't need life insurance. You might still *want* to buy it so that you can provide a larger inheritance to someone, but you don't *need* to buy it. Over your lifetime, however, your needs for life insurance are likely to change with your changing circumstances, so you should reevaluate your life insurance needs on a regular basis as a component of the financial planning process. Some of the factors that might change your life insurance needs include the following:

- **The number and age of your dependents**   The more dependents you have and the younger they are, the more life insurance you'll need.
- **Your age and life cycle stage**   You'll need more life insurance during the child-rearing years, particularly if you are the primary breadwinner, and less once your children are independent, unless you are using life insurance as an estate planning tool.
- **Your spouse's earning capacity**   If your spouse can't work or earns a lot less than you, you may need more life insurance.
- **Your financial wealth and obligations**   The lower your wealth and the higher your financial obligations, the more life insurance you'll need.
- **Your health**   If you have significant health problems, you may need more life insurance because your risk of dying prematurely is higher than average.
- **Your dependents' health**   If you have a spouse or a child with health problems, your death might make it difficult for him or her to maintain health insurance and to meet medical costs, so you could need more life insurance.

8.2   Buying Life Insurance

LEARNING OBJECTIVE 8.2
Select the type of life insurance that best meets your needs.

Once you've determined your life insurance needs, the next steps are to consider what type of policy will best meet those needs and to decide which insurer to buy it from. Because some insurers specialize in certain types of insurance policies, you should decide on the type of policy first. However, people who don't know much about life insurance usually decide on the insurer first and then rely on their agent to help them decide among policy types.

Choosing the Type of Policy

Although insurers are constantly trying to meet the needs of customers by creating "new and improved" life insurance policies, there are really just two basic types—term (or temporary) and permanent (or whole) life insurance. There are many variations on each general type, which can make the selection and comparison process somewhat confusing. But if you understand the fundamental differences, you'll be headed in the right direction. **Table 8.3** summarizes the primary features of the types of policies discussed in this section.

TABLE 8.3   **Comparison of Features of Common Types of Life Insurance**

Type of Policy	Premium Level	Period of Policy	Death Benefit	Cash Buildup	Choice of Investments	Proof of Insurability
Term insurance						
Regular term	Increase w/age	Usually 1 year	Fixed	N/A	N/A	Required
Increasing term	Increase w/age	1–10 years	Increase	N/A	N/A	Required
Decreasing term	Fixed	1–10 years	Decrease	N/A	N/A	Required
Level term	Fixed	5–10 years	Fixed	N/A	N/A	Rules differ
Renewable term	Increase w/age	5–20 years	Fixed	N/A	N/A	Required at application

(continued)

TABLE 8.3	Comparison of Features of Common Types of Life Insurance *(continued)*					
Type of Policy	**Premium Level**	**Period of Policy**	**Death Benefit**	**Cash Buildup**	**Choice of Investments**	**Proof of Insurability**
Permanent insurance						
Whole life	Fixed	Whole life	Increase w/cash buildup	Yes	No	Required at application
Universal life	Flexible	Whole life	Increase w/cash buildup	Yes	Yes	Required at application
Variable life	Fixed	Whole life	Increase w/cash buildup	Yes	Yes	Required at application
Single-premium life	Lump-sum payment	Whole life	Increase w/cash buildup	No	No	Required at application

Term Life Insurance

Term life insurance provides protection for a specific period of time, such as one year or five years. Term life is not an investment product, and there is no buildup of cash value. You pay an annual premium for the policy, sometimes in monthly installments. If you die during the contract period, your beneficiary will receive the **face value** of the policy—for example, the face value of a $100,000 life insurance policy is $100,000. If you don't die, then the contract concludes at the end of the policy period.

The primary determinant of the cost of term insurance is your probability of dying during the contract period. Death risk generally increases with age and health problems. Thus, the annual premium is fairly low when you're young and healthy and more expensive as you get older, as illustrated in **Figure 8.3**. For example, a 10-year renewable term policy for a 25-year-old woman can cost less than $150 per year for $500,000 in face value, whereas the price for the same face value and term can double at age 45 and be ten times as much at age 65.

FIGURE 8.3 **Cost of $500,000, 10-Year Renewable Term Life Insurance Policy for a Woman at Different Ages** Term life insurance premiums increase with age because, as you get older, your risk of dying in a given year is greater.

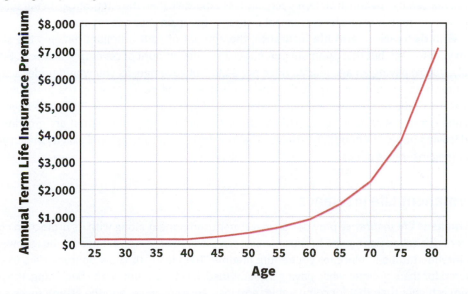

Term life insurance allows you to buy a fairly large amount of protection for a relatively low premium. Young families often have financial needs that are large relative to household resources, making this type of insurance particularly advantageous for them. As you get older, you can decrease your level of coverage as your wealth grows and your dependents' needs are reduced.

There are two primary problems with term insurance:

- **Premiums increase with age**   In fact, beyond a certain age limit (often age 65), you'll find that insurers are reluctant to sell term insurance to you at all.

- **Term life insurance remains in effect only for a specific period of time**   If the policy lapses, you might have to go through the complete application process all over again, including any required medical examinations. If your health deteriorates, the insurer could refuse to renew your policy, leaving you without life insurance coverage just when your family needs it most.

To address these problems, insurers make various features available with term insurance policies. Although you'll pay a higher premium for them, you should seriously consider features such as guaranteed renewability, level premiums, convertibility, and decreasing term when you purchase term insurance.

Guaranteed renewability is the right to renew the policy without additional proof of insurability, such as a medical exam. In renewable policies of this type, the face value usually remains the same over time, but the premium increases periodically. At each renewal date, the premium for the policy is adjusted upward to reflect the additional mortality risk for the insured person's older age group. The policy may be renewable annually, adjusted each year according to a predetermined schedule, or it may be renewable at longer intervals, such as every five or ten years. Although there are now some exceptions, in general you can renew term insurance only until you're 65 or 70. Even when it's possible to renew beyond these ages, the premium rates are prohibitively expensive.

Many insurers offer **level-premium term insurance**, which has a fixed premium rate for a period of years. Essentially, the insurer estimates the future premiums for the specified period of time, with increases for age-related risk, and then sets a fixed premium rate for the period that will be sufficient to cover those costs. The premiums will be higher than what you would otherwise have paid at the beginning of the period but lower than what you would have paid at the end.

In some cases, a term policy might be **convertible**, giving you the right to convert to permanent life insurance without additional proof of insurability. As you'll see in the following discussion, permanent life insurance is much more expensive than term insurance. The benefit of the convertibility feature is that it allows you to effectively lock in a premium rate based on a younger age while obtaining a larger amount of protection than you might have been able to afford if you were limited to permanent insurance. If you decide to exercise the convertibility option, you'll usually have to come up with the back premiums for the permanent coverage. Although this might not seem to be worthwhile, it's actually less expensive than the alternative—being subject to an annual premium rate for permanent insurance based on your current age.

With **decreasing-term life insurance**, the amount of your premium remains the same from year to year, but that premium purchases a smaller amount of coverage each year. Effectively, you're paying an age-related price per $1,000 of coverage, as you would under a standard term policy, but you're reducing the face value of the policy to keep the premium the same. This type of arrangement may make sense if you expect your life insurance needs to decline over time as your household wealth is increasing and your children are growing up and leaving home. It's doubtful, however, that the declines in coverage will exactly match your changing insurance needs.

Permanent Life Insurance

Permanent life insurance provides an investment component along with its protection component. It's called permanent because, unlike term insurance, it doesn't need to be renewed—it's intended to be in place for your entire lifetime. The idea is to allow policyholders to stay insured for their lifetimes while paying a guaranteed, level premium. In the beginning, the premium is higher than that for comparable term insurance coverage, and the insurer invests the difference. As the policyholder grows older and mortality risk increases, the premium stays the same. The extra cash invested in the policy, which will eventually be used to offset the increased costs of providing death protection at older ages, is known as the **cash value**. For this reason, permanent life insurance is also commonly referred to as *cash-value life insurance*.

The primary advantages of permanent insurance are that investment returns are not taxable and provide a mechanism for forced saving. However, it's important to carefully consider alternative investment options before deciding to buy permanent life insurance because the rates of return might be lower and expenses might be higher than for mutual funds of comparable risk.

The primary categories of permanent life insurance are whole life insurance, universal life insurance, and variable life insurance. All are similar in that the policies are long-term in nature and don't require renewal. The differences primarily relate to how premiums are determined and whether you can choose how your cash value is invested.

Whole Life Insurance   **Whole life insurance** provides death protection for a person's entire life. If the premiums are payable over the insured's whole life, the policy is **ordinary life insurance**. If the premiums are paid only for a specified period of time, after which the policy is paid up and still in force, the policy is **limited-payment life insurance**. Although it's common for people to purchase limited-payment life insurance that will be paid up at the time of retirement, typically age 65 or 70, these policies have a wide variety of payment options. For example, you can purchase **single-premium whole life insurance** with a one-time premium payment. Whatever the type of premium payment arrangement, your beneficiaries will be paid the face amount of the policy, regardless of when you die.

As an example of how whole life insurance works, suppose you purchase a $100,000 whole life policy with a level premium of $1,000 per year, payable for your whole life. By comparison, you could have bought one year of term insurance coverage for $100. This implies that $100 will be sufficient for the insurer to pay your share of the death claims for its pool of insured persons in the first year of the policy. The remaining $900 can be invested to help cover your death protection costs in the future, when you're older and your death risk is higher.

When you first buy a life insurance policy, as is illustrated in **Figure 8.4**, the insurer is providing death protection that is nearly equal to the face value of the policy. You haven't paid very much into the policy, so if you die, the insurer will be footing almost the entire bill. Over time, however, a larger share of the death protection will be covered by the policy's accumulated cash value, which is built up by your premiums. You won't be credited with much cash value for the first few years as the insurer recoups its issuance costs (commissions to agents, processing of your application). Eventually, however, you'll accumulate a cash reserve in the policy. This will be used to cover the cost of insuring your higher death risk when you're older. In addition, you can generally borrow against the cash value at a favorable interest rate, subject to a reduction in the death benefit to repay any unpaid loan balance at the time of your death.

FIGURE 8.4   **Components of Death Protection Provided by Ordinary Whole Life Insurance over Time**   In the policy's early years, death protection is provided primarily by the insurer. As time goes by, the proportion of protection provided by the policy's increasing cash value.

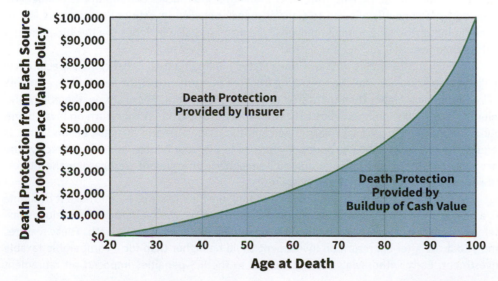

The policy illustrated in Figure 8.4 is an ordinary whole life policy. With a limited-payment life policy, after a certain point you'll no longer pay a premium. Your cash value will continue to earn investment returns, however, effectively increasing the amount that will be payable to your beneficiaries upon your death.

The concept of bundling death protection with an investment component makes sense only if the policy offers you a cost-effective way of achieving both objectives. Traditional whole life insurance has often been criticized for the low rates of return credited to policyholders, particularly during periods when the stock and bond markets have done well. For example, if the policy was priced assuming a 4 percent return on investment, but the insurer actually earned 12 percent, the policyholder didn't get to share in the good fortune—the insurer just made a larger profit. However, when markets are relatively flat, the guaranteed return on these products can look more attractive.

Another problem with traditional whole life insurance policies is that they're relatively inflexible regarding premium payments. If you have financial difficulties and miss a payment or two, your policy may be canceled. You'll still get most of the cash value back, but this can be far less than what you have invested in the policy.

Universal Life Insurance

Universal life insurance is a type of permanent life insurance that attempts to address the shortcomings of whole life insurance mentioned above. Universal policies promise death protection and a savings component, just as whole life policies do. The difference is that, in years where the insurance company earns greater-than-expected returns on its investment portfolio, the policyholder shares in some of that benefit, usually through a reduction in the following year's premium.

Universal life insurance also includes a flexible-premium option. A policyholder with sufficient cash reserves can choose not to pay the premiums, using accumulated cash value to meet mortality costs for the period, or to take some of the funds out of the policy entirely. On the one hand, this flexibility is a benefit in that the policy won't lapse if you run into some financial difficulties. On the other hand, it tends to undermine the savings component of the policy. If you don't put the money in and keep it there, you don't accumulate any savings.

Variable Life Insurance

The most popular types of permanent life insurance in recent years have been **variable life insurance** and **variable-universal life insurance**. Both of these products allow policyholders to decide how to invest the cash value accumulating in their policy. The insurer provides professional management of the accounts, and the policyholder selects from among several investment choices, similar to those in employer retirement plans. Because policyholders are exposed to risks of loss as well as possibilities for gain, the Securities and Exchange Commission has determined that variable life products are investment securities and must follow all the registration and disclosure rules applicable to securities.

The pricing of a variable life policy takes investment returns into account, so if your investments do well, you can benefit from lower premiums and quicker buildup of cash value. Policyholders are generally allowed to transfer money between investment options, subject to some timing restrictions. Variable-universal life insurance also includes the flexible-premium features of universal life.

Although most variable policies have a stated minimum death benefit, the expectation is that the cash value accumulation resulting from the performance of the selected investments will end up being higher than the stated death benefit amount. For example, the policy premium for a $100,000 policy might be determined assuming a 3 percent return on investment, but if the investments actually earn 8 percent, the cash value will increase beyond what is required to fund your $100,000 policy. If you were to die, your beneficiaries would receive the face value plus the extra accumulation. You'll generally get no guarantees regarding the interest rate or cash value for these policies, however.

If you maintain a variable life policy for a long time, its features might make it desirable as a combination death protection and investment vehicle. The buildup of cash value is tax-deferred, and the proceeds will be tax-free to your beneficiaries at your death. These features imply that the after-tax return on investment could be higher than for a comparable taxable investment. Early withdrawals are not subject to the IRS penalties imposed on retirement account withdrawals, but if you cash in your policy, you'll usually be subject to a penalty (surrender charges imposed by the insurer) and income tax liability on the excess of cash value over premiums paid.

There are two big downsides to variable life insurance: expenses and risk. Generally, the fees and expenses on these products are greater than on comparable-risk mutual funds. And even though all investments expose you to risk, it might not be appropriate to mix the protection-motivated purchase of life insurance with the wealth-building motivation of traditional investments. During the 1990s, when the stock market was climbing spectacularly, insurers found it difficult to entice customers to buy whole life insurance, but sales of variable products went through the roof. Many of those customers later found out the hard way that their cash values could actually go to zero. Perhaps more important, this risk was accompanied by much greater fund management expense than the policyholders would have incurred in comparable-risk mutual funds.

Now that you've read about the various types and features of life insurance, you know that certain features will make a policy more expensive to purchase. See if you can recall the effects of various factors on the policy premium in **Interactive: Which Policy Will Have the Lower Premium?**

INTERACTIVE

See **Interactive: Which Policy Will Have the Lower Premium?** in **WileyPLUS.**

Buy Term Insurance and Invest the Difference?

In deciding whether to buy term insurance (death protection only) or permanent insurance (death protection plus a savings/investment component), it's a good idea to compare the permanent insurance alternative with a "buy term and invest the difference" strategy. The annual premium for a given face amount of permanent insurance is much greater than the premium for the same amount of term insurance, especially when the insured is young and healthy.

Instead of paying a lot more for permanent insurance, you might consider buying decreasing term and investing the difference in a mutual fund. As the face value of the term insurance declines over time, the value of your investment portfolio will increase, so you can maintain relatively constant total protection plus wealth accumulation. Whether this is a good strategy depends on several factors:

- **Will you stick with your investment plan?**   A "buy term and invest the difference" strategy only works if you really do invest the difference. If you find other things to spend the money on, or if you dip into the investment portfolio on occasion, you'll end up with insufficient protection for your survivors.

- **Can you earn a comparable return on your investments?**   Obviously, you don't want to invest on your own and earn a lower return than you would have earned from a permanent insurance policy. Although life insurers are generally experts at investing, it's not very difficult to find mutual fund alternatives with comparable investment performance.

- **Is it cheaper to buy term and invest the difference?**   Whether you buy insurance with an investment component or you buy mutual funds on your own, you'll be exposed to some combination of investment commissions and management fees, as we explain in a future chapter. In deciding between these alternatives, you need to compare such costs.

Reflection Question 2

Assuming that you want to provide long-term protection for your family, what factors would you consider in deciding between buying whole life insurance versus buying term life insurance and investing the difference in premiums?

Choosing an Insurer

Life insurers are among the largest financial institutions in the world, but they're not all the same. Insurers differ in the products they offer, their financial arrangements with the agents who sell their products, how they underwrite and price their policies, and their financial solvency. Furthermore, recent financial deregulation has made it possible for financial institutions to offer products that were previously available only through specialized firms. Thus, you may find that even your bank sells some types of life insurance.

Financial Strength

In choosing an insurer, you should keep in mind that—unlike property and liability insurance contracts, which rarely extend beyond one year—life insurance is often a long-term arrangement. In addition, it involves potentially large sums of money. You don't want to take the chance that a company won't have sufficient funds to pay your beneficiaries the promised amount. For these reasons, the purchase of life insurance is a financial decision that requires some homework. Luckily, state regulators are also extremely concerned about the safety and soundness of financial institutions, and information resources are widely available.

Table 8.4 shows the ratings for a selection of top-rated life insurers in 2019. You can look up insurance company financial strength ratings at **www.insure.com, www.ambest.com** (A.M. Best Company), **www.moodys.com** (Moody's), **www.standardandpoors.com** (S&P Global Ratings), or **www.fitchratings.com** (Fitch Ratings). Although the rating agencies have different rating systems and criteria, the same life insurance companies rise to the top of each list. The two highlighted firms, New York Life Insurance Company and Northwestern Mutual Life Insurance Company, received the highest ratings from all three rating agencies in 2019. In general, the ratings don't change much from year to year.

TABLE 8.4 Financial Strength Ratings from Various Rating Agencies, 2019

Life Insurance Company	Rating Agency		
	A. M. Best	Standard & Poor's	Moody's
Allstate Life Insurance Company	A+	A+	A1
First Penn-Pacific Life Insurance Company	A+	A–	A1
Great-West Life Assurance Company	A+	AA	Aa3
Guardian Life Insurance Company of America	A++	AA+	Aa2
Jackson National Life Insurance Company	A+	AA	A1
John Hancock Life Insurance Company	A+	AA–	A1
Lincoln National Life Insurance Company	A+	AA–	A1
Massachusetts Mutual Life Insurance	A++	AA+	Aa2
Metropolitan Life Insurance Company	A+	AA–	Aa3
Nationwide Life Insurance Company	A+	A+	A2
New York Life Insurance Company	A++	AA+	Aaa
Northwestern Mutual Life Insurance Company	A++	AA+	Aaa
Principal Life Insurance Company	A+	A+	A1
Protective Life Insurance Company	A+	AA–	A1
State Farm Life Insurance Company	A++	AA	Aa1
TIAA-CREF Life Insurance Company	A++	AA+	Aa1
Transamerica Life Insurance Company	A+	AA–	A1
USAA Life Insurance Company	A++	AA+	Aa1

Notes: A. M. Best Ratings: A++ and A+ (Superior); A and A– (Excellent); B++ and B+ (Very Good). Standard & Poor's Ratings: Aaa (Extremely Strong); AA (Very Strong); A (Strong); BBB (Adequate); plus (+) and minus (–) show relative standing within the rating category. Moody's Ratings: Aaa (Exceptional); Aa (Excellent); A (Good); Baa (Adequate); 1, 2, and 3 show relative standing within the category.

Source: ambest.com, standardandpoors.com, and moodys.com.

Stock versus Mutual Companies

Another distinction among life insurers is their organizational form. A life insurer can be either a stock company or a mutual company. As explained in Chapter 3, a stock company is owned by the stockholders, who expect to make a profit on their investment in the firm. In contrast, a mutual insurance company is owned by its policyholders. Policies issued by a mutual company are called **participating policies**. Owners participate in the good performance of the company by receiving a dividend at the end of the year that can be used to reduce the premium for the next year. Dividends aren't guaranteed, so the net premium you end up paying each year will vary based on the financial performance of the mutual company. In some cases, stock companies offer participating policies as well.

Choosing an Agent

Insurance products are sold through many different distribution channels. You may be able to buy a policy directly from a company, or you may need to go through an agent. As you may remember from Chapter 7, there are two types of insurance agents. An exclusive agent sells insurance for a single company, whereas an independent agent sells insurance for a number of different insurers. Although it's often a little less expensive to buy from companies that sell directly to you—on the Internet or through direct mail, for example—you can't expect to get much personalized service unless you work with an agent. In general, the more complex the product, the better it is to deal with a well-informed agent who can explain the intricacies of various policies. An independent agent will offer a wider selection of products from which you can choose. However, that doesn't guarantee that you will get a lower price.

In selecting an agent, you should consider the following factors:

- **Education**   Look for appropriate education, professional credentials, certifications, and continuing education.
- **Experience**   The more years an agent has been in the business, the more likely he or she will be able to understand and evaluate your needs.
- **Reputation**   Ask your friends, colleagues, and other trusted professionals (financial planner, lawyer, banker) for recommendations. Ask about professionalism, experience, and service provided.
- **Responsiveness**   A good agent should provide you with the information necessary to make appropriate decisions—for example, a realistic analysis of your insurance needs, informative answers to your questions, and clear explanations of product details.
- **Ethical behavior**   An agent is paid a commission for selling you a policy, and thus may have incentives that aren't compatible with your best interests. Watch out for these red flags: (1) using high-pressure sales tactics, (2) using highly optimistic rates of return and/or policy dividends when illustrating the expected premiums and cash value of a policy, (3) encouraging you to replace an existing cash-value policy with a new one, (4) promising that cash-value buildup will cause your premiums to "vanish" within a few years, and (5) suggesting that you should borrow from a whole life policy to buy a variable annuity or other investment product.

8.3 | Reading Your Policy

LEARNING OBJECTIVE 8.3
Define key terms used in life insurance policies.

Your life insurance policy is a legal contract. Thus, as an informed consumer, you need to be aware of the terms to which you're agreeing. Although some policies are relatively straightforward and easy to understand, others involve more complex rights and obligations. Furthermore, you generally do not have the right to negotiate for more favorable contract language.

Fortunately, there are some protections for policyholders. State insurance laws require that insurance contracts be written in clear and unambiguous language that can be easily understood by consumers. In the event of a dispute over the meaning, any ambiguities in the contract will be interpreted in the light most favorable to the policyholder.

Unlike homeowner's insurance contracts, life insurance contracts are not standardized. However, if you understand the common features, terms, and clauses discussed here, you should be able to interpret your policy effectively.

Policy Declarations

All life insurance policies have a policy declarations page, which includes basic information about the policy, such as the following:

- The name of the insurance company
- The name of the insured and policyholder (you)
- The face amount of the policy
- The policy issue date
- The type of insurance and key features
- The period of time in which the policyholder can back out of the contract, often called the "rescission period" or "free look period"
- The insurer's promise to pay your beneficiaries upon your death

Although the placement of the information may differ from policy to policy, the items included in the declarations section are fairly consistent.

Key Provisions in a Life Insurance Policy

By state law, a life insurance policy may be required to include certain provisions, such as a grace period, the ability to borrow against any accumulated cash value, and a time limitation on the insurer's ability to get out of the contract. Many other provisions are optional. A policy may thus include one or more of the following components.

Grace Period

If you don't pay your premium on time, your policy will lapse on its anniversary date. However, insurers are required to give you a grace period for payment of the premium, usually one month for fixed-premium policies and two months for flexible-premium policies. Generally, insurers don't charge interest or penalties on overdue payments. If you haven't paid by the last day of the grace period, some insurers will allow you to reinstate your policy, but they aren't required to do so. If your policy lapses, you might have to provide proof of insurability to reinstate it, which could be a problem if your health status has changed since your first application. About 15 percent of permanent life insurance policies lapse in the first two years after issue.

Policy Loans

If you have a cash-value policy, you're allowed to borrow from your accumulated funds without terminating the policy. Outstanding loans accrue interest, usually at an attractively low rate, and there's no set schedule for repayment. However, the death benefit paid on the policy will be reduced by any outstanding amounts due, so you should take out a policy loan only if you've carefully considered your other borrowing options and your family's need for protection.

Incontestable Clause

Under general contract law, a contract is voidable by one of the parties if that party entered into it as a result of misrepresentations made by the other party. Suppose, for example, that you have a serious medical condition or that you regularly smoke cigarettes and you deliberately do not disclose this information on your life insurance application when asked about your medical history. Suppose also that, if the insurer had known the true facts about your health, it would not have issued the policy. If the policy is issued and you subsequently die (from any cause), the insurer has the right to refuse to pay the benefit to your survivors on the grounds that the policy was void due to your misrepresentation.

Because voiding the policy has the effect of leaving your beneficiaries without protection, insurers are given a limited time during which they can use misrepresentation to contest a claim or refuse payment—often one or two years from the policy issue date. The rationale for the **incontestable clause** is that, without such a limitation, insurers might be tempted to do very limited underwriting investigations, collect premiums for years, and then use misrepresentation as a reason to refuse to pay when the policyholder dies. By making the policy incontestable after a certain amount of time has passed, insurers are given incentives for more careful up-front investigation when they are making their underwriting decision.

Policyholder Dividends

As mentioned previously, policies issued by mutual companies are participating policies, which means that the policyholders are entitled to dividend distributions, much like stockholder dividends. The IRS treats these dividends as a return of premium, so they aren't taxable to the policyholder. Participating policies must include a clause that describes how and when dividends will be paid—usually on the policy anniversary and conditional on the policyholder's timely payment of premiums. These dividends are not guaranteed in the contract but depend on the insurer's financial performance. Although it's common to apply the dividend to reduce future premiums, policyholders might be given several options for receipt of a dividend, such as taking it as cash, putting it in an interest-bearing account, or using it to purchase small amounts of additional paid-up insurance or one-year term insurance.

Entire Contract Clause

Most policies include a so-called entire contract clause, which explicitly states that the written contract is the entire agreement between the insurer and the insured. This rule applies whether or not the policy explicitly states it, however, and is designed to prevent the insurer from imposing its own interpretation or changing the agreement in some way after the contract has been issued without the knowledge of the insured person.

Based on what you've read about the legal rules relating to life insurance, see if you can determine the outcome of the case described in **Interactive: You Be the Judge**.

INTERACTIVE

See **Interactive: You Be the Judge** in **WileyPLUS**.

Nonforfeiture

As described earlier, with level-premium permanent insurance, the premiums in the early years build up a cash reserve in addition to covering mortality risk in the current period. Nonforfeiture laws require that, if your contract lapses before maturity but after some minimum amount of time, such as three years, the insurer must refund a fair amount of the cash reserve. You have several options for receiving the refund:

- In cash
- As a paid-up policy in whatever amount the cash value is sufficient to purchase
- As a term life policy with the same face value as the lapsed policy, but for a period the cash value is sufficient to purchase, given your current age
- As an annuity for retirement income

Many people find the retirement annuity alternative attractive because they can purchase appropriate life insurance protection during their child-rearing years and later convert the accumulated cash value to a cash flow stream to be received in retirement.

Reinstatement

In some cases, you might be entitled under the terms of your policy to reinstate the policy if it has lapsed. For example, suppose you purchased a whole life policy ten years ago and it now has a cash value of $20,000. You're laid off from work and can't afford to make the required premium payment for the coming year. Although you could surrender the policy for its cash value, it might be preferable to allow the policy to lapse and then reinstate it once your financial situation allows it. If your policy permits reinstatement, you'll normally have to provide proof of insurability (commonly, a blood test and physical examination) and pay any missed premiums with interest.

Beneficiaries

You'll be required to designate a primary beneficiary for any life insurance policy—the person(s), estate, or business entity to receive the proceeds of the policy upon your death. You normally should also name a contingent beneficiary in case the primary beneficiary dies before you do. In naming your beneficiaries, you should be as specific as possible in order to avoid problems in identifying the recipients at a later date. It's also a good idea to review your policies regularly to ensure that you always have at least one living beneficiary and that you've included everyone you intended. For example, if your policy names "my sons, James and Robert," but you now have a third child, Jessica, you'll need to add her to the beneficiary list to ensure that she gets a share of the proceeds when you die.

Suicide Clause

If an insured person commits suicide, his or her beneficiaries might still be entitled to payment under the policy. This will depend on the terms of the suicide clause, which allows the insurer to deny coverage if the insured commits suicide and the policy has been in force less than a specified period of time, usually two years. In a particularly sad case several years ago, a businessman who was in significant debt and could see no other solution to his problems purchased a large amount of insurance on his life, naming his wife as beneficiary. The policy included a one-year suicide clause, so he waited until the one-year anniversary and shot himself in his office. Unfortunately, he was mistaken about the effective date of the policy (which was one day after he made his application) and committed suicide one day too early.

Waiver of Premium

Many insurers offer a relatively inexpensive option called **waiver of premium**. A policyholder who has purchased this option is allowed under some limited circumstances, usually permanent disability, to keep the policy in force without further payment of premium.

Accelerated (or Living) Benefits

An **accelerated benefits** option allows terminally ill policyholders to receive a portion of their life insurance proceeds before their death (see the chapter opener for an example). More than half the states have adopted a model regulation governing this type of benefit. The regulation lists the conditions that will trigger the benefit, including AIDS, acute heart disease, permanent brain damage from stroke, and kidney failure. This option may be an automatic feature of a policy, or it may require an additional premium. Although you might envision using your life insurance under these circumstances for the trip to Europe you never got to take while you were healthy, in most cases the insurance proceeds are used to help pay for medical treatments and hospice care. Another way to access the value of your life insurance in advance of your death, if allowed in your state, is to sell the policy to someone else, through a viatical settlement agreement, as described in **Ethics in Action**.

Ethics in Action

The Ethics of Viatical Settlements

Did you know that you can actually buy an interest in someone else's life insurance policy? Under a viatical settlement agreement, an investor purchases the policy from its owner and becomes the beneficiary of the policy. The investor pays the original owner from 40 to 80 percent of the death benefit, depending on life expectancy and other factors (cash value, quality of the insurer, and premiums necessary to keep the policy in force), and the original owner gives up all rights to the policy. The investor pays the premiums and receives the death benefit when the original owner dies.

Viatical investors commonly pool their funds and purchase a large number of policies, thereby spreading their risk. Whereas insurers make more money on life insurance policies if their insureds *stay alive*, a viatical investor only makes money *when people die*. For this reason, some lawmakers have argued that we shouldn't allow this type of financial arrangement at all. Nearly all states impose limitations on these contracts. Most require that standardized disclosures be made and that the insurance be in force for between two and five years before the policy can be sold.

Why would an insured person want to sell her life insurance policy to an investor? It's often because the person needs the money for other purposes, such as to pay medical bills. In fact, nearly 90 percent of viatical settlements in the past have gone to terminally ill AIDs patients. Recently, however, some insurers have been criticized for marketing life insurance policies to older people with the specific purpose of having them sell their policies to viatical investors. This practice may at first seem to be unethical because the customers will not actually have life insurance protection for their families after they sell their policies. However, the price offered by the viatical investors can be quite attractive, and some customers may find it worth their time to fill out the application and have the financial resources to make the premium payments for a few years.

Accidental Death Benefit

Your life insurance policy may include a rider or amendment that doubles the face value payable under the policy if your death is a result of an accident instead of natural causes. For this reason, the **accidental death benefit** is sometimes referred to as the "double indemnity" clause. Since the percentage of deaths that occur from accidents is fairly small, this is an inexpensive benefit to provide. However, individuals tend to overestimate the probability of accidental death. See whether your intuition is correct regarding various causes of death in **Interactive: How Likely Is Accidental Death?**

INTERACTIVE

See Interactive: How Likely Is Accidental Death? in WileyPLUS.

Guaranteed Purchase Option

Although you might not need much life insurance right now, you'll probably want to increase your coverage over time as your family circumstances change. You could plan to buy additional policies in the future to meet your growing needs, but you run the risk that you might become uninsurable in the future. Diagnosis of a serious illness or development of a disability might make it impossible to find insurance or might make the insurance prohibitively expensive. A guaranteed purchase option gives you the right to purchase additional amounts of insurance in the future without proof of insurability and without "restarting the clock" on the suicide and incontestable clauses. (Many group life insurance plans offered by employers also include this feature, allowing you to increase your insurance from $10,000 to $25,000 per year as long as you have continuous coverage.)

Settlement Options

Settlement options are choices regarding how the beneficiaries are to receive the proceeds of the policy. As the policy purchaser, you can make this choice in advance, but most people leave it to their beneficiaries to decide after their death. Suppose you have a term life insurance policy with a face value of $200,000, and your husband is the sole beneficiary. Your husband's choices for receipt of the funds after your death might include some or all of the following:

- **Lump sum**   Your husband can receive the entire $200,000 benefit as a tax-free lump sum. He can invest this money or purchase an annuity with it (without being limited to choices offered by your insurer). If he could earn 5 percent after taxes on the lump sum, he could spend $10,000 per year without touching the principal.

- **Periodic interest only**   Your husband can leave the money with the insurer, who will pay him taxable interest on the accumulated value. Because he will not deplete the principal, it will become part of his estate when he dies.

- **Income for a period of time**   If your husband needs more money than interest alone can provide, he can receive the funds from your insurer as a series of payments for a specified period. The payments can be calculated as an annuity that will completely deplete the principal over a period of time. This option will produce higher payments than the interest-only option, and the interest component of the payments will be taxable. It is possible, however, that your husband will outlive the payment stream.

- **Income of a specific amount**   Your husband can elect to receive a fixed amount per year until the principal and interest are exhausted. The interest portion of the payment is taxable.

- **Income for life**   If your husband wants to be sure he doesn't outlive his income stream, he can elect to receive a life annuity. We discuss life annuities in detail in Chapter 10. For now, you only need to know that the amount of income payable will depend on your husband's life expectancy, and the risk of his outliving his assets will be borne by the insurer. A portion of each payment will be taxable until your husband lives beyond his life expectancy, after which the full payment will be taxable.

8.4   Planning for Long-Term Care Costs

LEARNING OBJECTIVE 8.4
Explain the choices for funding long-term care needs.

So far in this chapter, we've focused on planning for the costs that would be incurred by your family in the event of your death. A related risk that many people fail to plan for is the risk of being incapacitated in old age. Because people are living longer, an increasing proportion of the population will eventually need nursing home care. This risk is not limited to the elderly, but it's clearly age-related. Although only 4 percent of people aged 65 and older reside in a nursing home at any given point in time, 43 percent of those who reach 65 (33 percent of men and 52 percent of women) will eventually require institutionalization.

This was not always the case. In earlier generations, the elderly and infirm could often rely on home care provided within an extended family. It's still true that the elderly are often cared for by a family member, usually female, but the demand for alternative caregiving is increasing. This is primarily the result of a dramatic change in the structure of households—more single parents, more working women, fewer children, and greater geographic dispersal of family members.

Long-term care (LTC) is a term that is broadly used to describe all supportive medical, personal, and social services needed by people who are unable to meet their basic living needs for an extended period of time because of accident, illness, or frailty. LTC involves receiving the assistance of another person to perform the essential activities of daily living (bathing, dressing, eating, and household chores) and may be performed at home (by paid caregivers, such as home health aides, or by informal unpaid caregivers, such as family members or friends) or in a nursing home or assisted living facility.

The length of time that a person requires long-term care obviously depends on the person's health and age at the time of illness or incapacity. On average, you can expect to live into your 80s, but you might live much longer. Today, many nursing home residents are victims of Alzheimer's disease, a brain disorder that results in significant mental incapacity. A patient who enters a nursing facility at age 70 with Alzheimer's, but who is otherwise in good health, could conceivably survive for another 20 years at a cost of more than $1,000,000.

The risk of incapacity, like the risk of death, is difficult to talk about and deal with. The prospect of being unable to take care of oneself is not pleasant. It's no wonder that, as with other financial decisions they'd rather avoid, many people ignore this component of their financial plan. A survey by the National Council on Aging shows that 67 percent of Americans believe that the cost of long-term care is the greatest threat to their standard of living, but only 35 percent have done any planning for long-term care. It's important to remember that you're not really planning for yourself, but rather for those who will be burdened in the event that you're some-day incapacitated. Having a plan in place will not completely relieve your family of the personal cost of your incapacity, but it will at least lessen the financial cost.

Long-Term Care Needs Analysis

Most people first confront nursing home expenses when an older relative—perhaps a parent or a grandparent—can no longer live alone. Often, the initial step is to have them move in with another family member. Perhaps the family will need to hire a medical professional to provide home health and personal care at a cost of $10,000 to $20,000 per year. Eventually, escalating medical needs or mental incapacity will force the family to consider a nursing home facility. The shock of finding out what these facilities cost can be tremendous.

The average annual cost of nursing home care in a semiprivate room in the United States was $89,297 in 2018, but costs vary widely from state to state. In Texas, for example, the average annual cost of such care was $57,579 in 2018, whereas Alaskan residents paid an average of $351,495, according to the survey results reported in **Table 8.5**. Other factors that affect costs include the level of medical care required (nursing homes are about twice as expensive as assisted living facilities), room type (private room versus semiprivate), and how long the person will be in the facility (the average stay is 2.4 years). **Table 8.6** shows the range of costs for different levels of care.

Many families find themselves in the unfortunate position of having to make the decision to move a relative to a nursing home. Perhaps, for example, a relative has been living with your family for a few years, but she's become a danger to herself or others. Or perhaps there are medication issues that you can't deal with at home. To add to the stress level, this person may

TABLE 8.5	Median Annual Cost of Nursing Home Care (Semiprivate Room) in 2018, by State				
State	**Annual Cost**	**State**	**Annual Cost**	**State**	**Annual Cost**
Alabama	$75,347	Kentucky	$82,125	North Dakota	$132,320
Alaska	$351,495	Louisiana	$62,780	Ohio	$85,410
Arizona	$77,928	Maine	$113,150	Oklahoma	$55,663
Arkansas	$64,240	Maryland	$110,778	Oregon	$111,325
California	$100,375	Massachusetts	$144,175	Pennsylvania	$115,340
Colorado	$94,703	Michigan	$102,748	Rhode Island	$105,850
Connecticut	$151,475	Minnesota	$109,500	South Carolina	$77,015
Delaware	$125,925	Mississippi	$80,300	South Dakota	$79,388
D.C.	$109,500	Missouri	$60,225	Tennessee	$76,650
Florida	$97,820	Montana	$84,067	Texas	$57,579
Georgia	$76,103	Nebraska	$82,855	Utah	$73,000
Hawaii	$146,000	Nevada	$98,733	Vermont	$113,698
Idaho	$90,885	New Hampshire	$124,100	Virginia	$89,425
Illinois	$70,993	New Jersey	$127,750	Washington	$104,025
Indiana	$82,308	New Mexico	$87,418	West Virginia	$123,370
Iowa	$73,000	New York	$141,073	Wisconsin	$100,010
Kansas	$64,970	North Carolina	$83,403	Wyoming	$86,140

Source: *Genworth Financial 2018 Cost of Care Survey*, www.genworth.com.

TABLE 8.6   U.S. Median Costs and Growth Rates for Different Types of Long-Term Care

	Median	Median Annual Rate	5-Year Annual Growth Rate
Licensed home health aide services	$22/hour	$50,336	2.5%
Assisted living (1 bedroom, single occupancy)	$4,000/month	$48,000	3.0%
Nursing home (semiprivate room)	$245/day	$89,297	3.4%
Nursing home (private room)	$275/day	$100,375	3.6%

Source: *Genworth Financial 2018 Cost of Care Survey*, www.genworth.com.

be openly resistant to moving to a long-term care facility. And don't be surprised if you find yourself someday having to make difficult decisions related to aging parents at the same time you're dealing with the complexities of getting your children through their teen years.

Fortunately, many sources of information are available to help you assess the quality, price, and appropriateness of various facilities. Based on a physician's recommendation, you'll need to first determine what level of care will be required. Many facilities offer graduated care options that allow you to opt for lower levels of care (at lower prices, though still expensive) at first and gradually increase the level of care (and the annual cost) as the need arises. Once you've narrowed your selection based on availability, services provided, location, and quality, you should visit each of the facilities in person.

Sources of Funds for Long-Term Care

How can the average family afford the expected future costs of long-term care? Instead of waiting for the need to arise, it's advisable to do some advance planning to determine how your family will finance the cost. Some options to consider include family caregiving, household and community resources, Medicaid, and long-term care insurance. The largest share of the costs for long-term care is currently paid by state-administered Medicaid programs for the poor, as illustrated in **Figure 8.5**.

FIGURE 8.5   Funding Sources for Long-Term Care Costs   Total spending for long-term care is more than $350 billion, about 10 percent of all U.S. health-care spending.

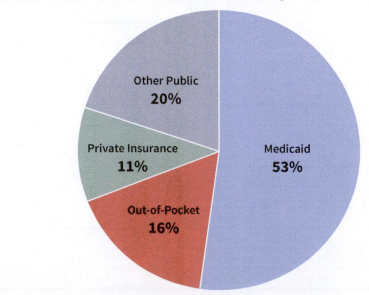

Source: Kaiser Family Foundation, "Medicaid's Role for Seniors" (June 2017), www.kff.org.

Family Caregivers

Although about half of all women and a third of all men will eventually require nursing home care, their care will initially be provided by family. About 9 million Americans are currently in long-term care, but the National Alliance for Caregiving estimates that about 34 million individuals in the United States (14 percent of the adult population) are providing unpaid care to a person age 50 or older (with the average age being 75). Nearly 61 percent of caregivers are women. The Congressional Budget Office estimates that the value of the "free" care provided by families is nearly as much as the total amount of Medicaid spending on long-term care.

Household Resources

If you're wealthy, you may be able to fund all your long-term care needs from your household resources. One of the problems associated with this strategy is that one spouse may need nursing home care before the other. The nursing home expenses of the spouse who is "first to care" might exhaust household resources, leaving the survivor with inadequate wealth to finance retirement. Some experts believe that the large percentage of elderly widows living at or below the poverty level is at least partially attributable to this problem.

Community Resources

Because the most expensive long-term care is institutional care, it makes sense to try to maximize home health care options before resorting to nursing home care. Community resources can help an infirm person—particularly one who needs a relatively low level of care—to remain at home or in a relative's home for a longer time. Services that might be available in your community include Meals on Wheels, which delivers regular meals to elderly people; household chore services; visitation programs; and caregiver respite services. For more information about these services, use the Eldercare Locator sponsored by the U.S. Administration on Aging at **www.eldercare.gov**, or call 1-800-677-1116. Many religious institutions offer services for elderly members as well.

Medicare

If you're over 65, Medicare Part A will provide benefits for skilled nursing care, home visits by nurses, and related medical expenses for up to 100 days following a hospital stay of at least three days. The Medicare program spends about $50 billion per year on nursing home and home health care services. However, Medicare does not provide coverage for assistance in the activities of daily living and therefore is not really a source of coverage for long-term care needs.

Medicaid

Medicaid is a federally authorized and state-administered health insurance program for the poor. People who meet low-income guidelines or who have exhausted all or most of their financial assets may be eligible for Medicaid coverage of nursing home expenses. In the past, examples of Medicaid fraud arose in which relatively wealthy individuals attempted to qualify for Medicaid coverage of nursing home care by transferring all their assets to their children. Today, new rules make this unethical practice more difficult and impose sanctions on those who attempt it. In recent years, state governments faced with budgetary shortfalls have been considering ways to curb Medicaid costs, either by capping payments to providers or tightening eligibility standards.

Life Insurance Policies

Many insurers are now offering accelerated benefits options with life and disability income policies to provide benefits for long-term care. Recall from the chapter opener that accelerated benefits are a way for people who are seriously ill to access the cash value of their life insurance policies before they die. These funds could be used to pay for long-term care. An extension rider increases the amount of funds available for long-term care costs beyond the amount of the death benefit. Depending on the face value of the life insurance policy, the amount that can be withdrawn each month might be more or less than actual costs of the care.

Other Insurance Options

In addition to the options just discussed, you should consider the purchase of long-term care insurance. Most long-term care insurance is purchased in the form of a stand-alone policy, as described in the following section.

Long-Term Care Insurance

Long-term care (LTC) insurance is a financial product that pays health-care expenses associated with incapacity. Because LTC insurance is a relatively new product, future claim costs are difficult to predict, and many insurers have lost money on these policies. Over the last decade, low interest rates on insurers' investments and rising nursing home costs have necessitated steep rate increases, even for policyholders who thought they had bought fixed-premium policies (but hadn't read the fine print). Several large insurers have recently decided to exit the market entirely, finding that they couldn't make a profit on LTC policies. As a result, as part of the American Taxpayer Relief Act, Congress commissioned a bipartisan Commission on Long-Term Care in June 2013 to investigate the issue and to propose a comprehensive solution to managing and financing long-term care costs in the United States. Although the Commission recommended the creation of a public program to supplement private options, no major policy changes have resulted from the Commission's recommendations. In this section, we explain the private insurance products that are currently available, but it is possible that, in the future, we'll see changes in the market and in consumers' choices for dealing with this risk.

Because there are many possible terms and conditions, and because premiums—even for the same level of coverage—vary dramatically across insurers and in different states, it pays to shop around and carefully evaluate what each policy covers. Obviously, the LTC policies that provide the greatest amount of coverage will cost more. Your age and health will also affect your premium costs and might even prevent you from being able to find coverage. As with other types of insurance, you'll need to consider the financial soundness of the provider as well.

When Is the Best Time to Buy Long-Term Care Insurance?

Unfortunately, there's no magic answer to the question of when to buy LTC insurance. As with other types of long-term insurance products, premiums may be fixed for a period of years. This implies that you'll pay a smaller annual amount if you buy the policy at a younger age because the insurer estimates you'll be paying the premium for more years. The quoted premiums can rise dramatically with age. But because you'll pay premiums until you go into long-term care, which might be never, your lifetime cost for the insurance may end up being much higher if you purchase the insurance at too early an age. The American Health Care Association—a federation of 50 state health organizations representing assisted living facilities, nursing facilities, long-term care facilities, and other care providers—recommends that you buy LTC insurance between ages 50 and 55 to obtain the optimal price.

Tax Considerations

Under the provisions of the Health Insurance Portability and Accountability Act, you can take an itemized deduction both for long-term care costs you pay out of pocket and for premiums you pay for long-term care insurance. Medical expenses are deductible on your federal income taxes to the extent that they exceed 10 percent of adjusted gross income. LTC insurance premiums can be included in this calculation but the allowed deduction depends on your age at the end of the year, as shown in **Table 8.7**. Self-employed individuals can deduct 100% of the premium up to the limit on this table.

TABLE 8.7	Limits on Tax Deductions for LTC Insurance Premiums
Age	**2019 Limit on Deduction (Indexed for Inflation)**
40 or younger	$420
41 to 50	$790
51 to 60	$1,580
61 to 70	$4,220
71 or older	$5,270

Benefits received from a qualified long-term care policy are generally not included in taxable income. IRS rules also allow you to take an early withdrawal from your 401(k) plan or IRA without incurring the usual 10 percent penalty if the funds are used to purchase long-term care insurance or to pay for medical expenses. You will still owe income taxes on any amount withdrawn from a tax-deferred account.

Features to Look for in Long-Term Care Insurance

If you decide to buy long-term care insurance, you'll want to consider the features summarized in **Table 8.8**.

TABLE 8.8	LTC Policy Provisions
Key Feature	**Considerations**
Benefit amount	Usually paid as a dollar amount per day of qualified care, such as $100 or $150 per day, or a percentage of actual expenses. You should select a benefit amount that corresponds to the average cost of care in the area where you live, less an amount that you can afford to pay out of pocket.
Inflation protection	The cost of care will increase over time, so your policy benefits should be inflation-protected. Although this feature may be expensive, it's very important because LTC costs have been rising faster than the prices of other goods.
Benefit period	The average nursing home stay is less than three years, and 75 percent of admissions are for less than one year. Your annual premium will be as much as 30 percent lower if you opt for a three-year benefit period instead of lifetime benefits.
Waiting period	The waiting period is the number of days you must pay for care before the LTC insurance begins to pay for it, typically 30, 60, or 100 days. Because Medicare pays for the first 100 days, this is the period most often selected.
Services covered	The policy can cover nursing home care only or can include home health care providers such as in-home therapists and nurses. Some policies provide benefits for in-home care provided by family members, which can be important if a family caregiver has to give up paid employment.

Talking with Older Family Members about Long-Term Care Insurance

Many students taking a course in personal finance are far too young to be thinking about buying LTC insurance for themselves. The purpose of covering this topic now is to alert you to issues you'll be facing with your parents in the coming years. If you're currently 20 to 30 years old and your parents are 40 to 60 years old, it's not too early to start talking with them about their plans concerning long-term care. You might even consider broaching the subject by mentioning what you've learned in this text. Although most people find it difficult to talk about these issues, they generally feel better once they've done so. You might also expand the conversation to include questions about your parents' plans for life insurance, retirement, and estate planning.

> **Reflection Question 3**
>
> Why do you think it's so hard for adult children to talk with their parents about life insurance and long-term care? How would you approach this topic with your own parents or grandparents?

Summary

Learning Objectives Review

LEARNING OBJECTIVE 8.1 Determine how much life insurance you need.

Adequate life insurance protection is an important component of most financial plans because it provides a relatively inexpensive way of protecting your loved ones from the financial consequences of your **mortality risk**.

- The process of determining the potential financial impact of your death on others is called **life insurance needs analysis**. There are two methods commonly used to assess life insurance needs: the **income-multiple method** and the **financial needs method**.

- Although it's simpler to apply the income-multiple method to roughly determine how much insurance you need, the financial needs method estimates the financial costs that will actually arise upon your death and balances them against existing household resources.

- The financial needs method takes into consideration the costs of death; any lump sums needed to fund future expenses, such as education costs, retirement funds, and debt repayment; and the future cost of household maintenance.

LEARNING OBJECTIVE 8.2 Select the type of life insurance that best meets your needs.

Before buying life insurance, you'll need to decide on the type of insurance, which insurer to buy a policy from, and whether to use an agent. There are many different types of life insurance to choose from.

- **Term life insurance** provides death protection only. Policies are usually short-term with premiums based on the policyholder's age and the policy's **face value**. Variations include policies with **guaranteed renewability**, **level-premium term insurance** policies, **decreasing-term life insurance** policies, and policies that are **convertible** to permanent insurance.

- **Permanent life insurance** is a long-term contract that includes an investment component that builds **cash value**. The premiums in the early years are invested to help cover the increased cost of death protection in the later years.

- The main categories of permanent life insurance are whole life insurance, universal life insurance, and variable life insurance.

- **Whole life insurance** that requires the payment of premiums over the insured's lifetime is known as **ordinary life insurance.** Alternative arrangements include **limited-payment life insurance** and **single-premium whole life insurance**.

- **Universal life insurance** adjusts premiums based on the insurer's performance. Universal life insurance also has a flexible-premium option that allows policyholders to pay their premiums from accumulated cash value without causing the policy to lapse.

- **Variable life insurance** and **variable-universal life insurance** allow policyholders to allocate their cash value to specific investments.

- Policies issued by a mutual company are called **participating policies**, because policyholders participate in the good performance of the firm by receiving a dividend at the end of the year that can be applied to reduce their future premium.

- In selecting a life insurer, you should pay careful attention to the company's financial strength. If you decide to buy through an agent, you should consider the agent's educational credentials, experience, reputation, and responsiveness to your needs, and you should avoid agents who engage in unethical sales practices.

LEARNING OBJECTIVE 8.3 Define key terms used in life insurance policies.

An insurance policy includes many important terms and clauses that policyholders should understand.

- Important terms include the provisions for payment of premiums, cash value accumulation, settlement options, policy loans, and designation of **beneficiaries**.

- Some policies include special features such as **accidental death benefits** or options such as **waiver of premium** or **accelerated benefits** under special circumstances.

- Policyholders are required to provide truthful information in their application or risk having their policy voided. The **incontestable clause** limits the insurer's right to void a policy for misstatements made in the application.

- An important requirement for your life insurance to remain in force is that you pay the premium when due or, if late, within the grace period. In some cases, following a lapse of coverage due to nonpayment, you may be able to reinstate your policy.

- The sources of funding for long-term care usually include existing household resources, public programs, and long-term care insurance.

- **Long-term care insurance** is a financial product that pays for qualified health-care expenses associated with incapacity, typically with daily or monthly limits.

- Long-term care insurance policies differ substantially, so you should understand the key contract features of these policies and know when and how to purchase such insurance.

LEARNING OBJECTIVE 8.4   **Explain the choices for funding long-term care needs.**

Many people eventually require nursing home care or home health care in old age, and these **long-term care** services can be very expensive. You should therefore have a plan for how these costs will be paid.

Excel Worksheet

8.1 Personal Financial Planner: Life Insurance Needs Analysis

Key Terms

accelerated benefits   8-20
accidental death benefit   8-21
beneficiary   8-5
cash value   8-12
convertible   8-12
decreasing-term life insurance   8-12
face value   8-11
financial needs method   8-7
guaranteed renewability   8-12

income-multiple method   8-6
incontestable clause   8-19
level-premium term insurance   8-12
life insurance needs analysis   8-6
limited-payment life insurance   8-13
long-term care (LTC)   8-22
long-term care (LTC) insurance   8-26
mortality risk   8-3
ordinary life insurance   8-13

participating policy   8-17
permanent life insurance   8-12
single-premium whole life insurance   8-13
term life insurance   8-11
universal life insurance   8-14
variable life insurance   8-14
variable-universal life insurance   8-14
waiver of premium   8-20
whole life insurance   8-13

WileyPLUS

Practice Questions to check your understanding, Peer-to-Peer Videos, Interactives, and many other resources are available in WileyPLUS.

Concept Review Questions

1. How does life insurance differ from property insurance with regard to each of the following factors?

   a. Predictability of loss

   b. Term of contract

   c. Factors that will result in an increase in premium

2. Explain why life insurance is an important component of financial planning.

3. Does everyone need life insurance coverage? Why or why not?

4. What categories of financial costs might be incurred by a family with dependent children upon the death of the primary earner?

5. What are the two approaches used to estimate the amount of life insurance needed, and is one preferable to the other? Explain your reasoning.

6. How do life insurers assess your probability of dying within the policy period? Explain why this estimate is likely to be very accurate on average for a large pool of policyholders.

7. Explain how each of the following factors might affect the amount of life insurance you need.

   a. Number of children you have

   b. The age of your children

   c. Your age

   d. Your spouse's earning capacity

   e. Your financial wealth

   f. Your outstanding debt

   g. Your health

8. How can life insurance be used to help your survivors reach household financial goals in the event of your death? For what types of goals would the purchase of life insurance be an appropriate risk management strategy?

9. If you are a stay-at-home parent and don't contribute any earnings to the household budget, why might you still need to have some amount of life insurance?

10. Compared with a standard term life insurance policy, will a policy with a decreasing term result in a premium that is higher, lower, or the same? Explain your reasoning.

11. Compared with a standard term life insurance policy, will a policy with guaranteed renewability result in a premium that is higher, lower, or the same? Explain your reasoning.

12. Compared with a standard term life insurance policy, will a term life insurance policy that is convertible to permanent insurance result in a premium that is higher, lower, or the same? Explain your reasoning.

13. Compared with an ordinary life insurance policy, will a limited-payment policy result in a premium that is higher, lower, or the same? Explain your reasoning.

14. Compared with a level-premium life insurance policy, will a policy with a premium that increases over time result in an initial premium that is higher, lower, or the same? Explain your reasoning.

15. Compared with a standard term life insurance policy, will a policy with a face value that decreases over time result in a premium that is higher, lower, or the same? Explain your reasoning.

16. Why are premiums for permanent insurance so much more expensive per dollar of coverage than premiums for term life insurance?

17. Compare the purchase of permanent life insurance with the strategy "buy term and invest the difference" with regard to risk, tax consequences, and flexibility.

18. In what ways is the cash value of permanent life insurance similar to a savings account? In what ways is it different?

19. What are the common criticisms of whole life insurance, and how does universal life insurance address these issues?

20. Why did variable life insurance become so popular in the 1990s?

21. Identify the criteria you should use in choosing a life insurance agent.

22. Identify the criteria you should use in choosing which life insurance company to buy insurance from.

23. Why do so many people fail to plan adequately for long-term care costs?

24. Why is it probably not cost-effective to buy long-term care insurance at an early age?

Application Problems

1. Your current income is $50,000. If your financial planner recommends an income multiplier of 5, how much life insurance should you have?

2. Keisha is a single parent who earns $40,000 per year. Her household expenses are $28,000 per year. If she were to die, she estimates that death costs would total $10,000. She has not participated in Social Security long enough to be fully insured. She wants to provide $50,000 for an education fund for each of her twin children, who are currently 10 years old. She also needs to provide for their care, which she estimates will cost $15,000 per year until they are 18.

   a. Would an income-multiple approach result in Keisha's purchase of sufficient life insurance? Why or why not?

   b. Using a financial needs approach, how much life insurance would you recommend that Keisha buy? Explain.

   c. If Keisha was fully insured under Social Security and her children were eligible for annual benefits of $15,000 each, how much difference would this make in her life insurance needs?

3. Elaine has just graduated from college, is single, and has no dependents except for her chocolate lab, Rufus. She's accepted a job with a starting salary of $50,000, and she has $10,000 in student loan debt. Her employer doesn't provide any group life insurance. Does Elaine need any life insurance? Why or why not?

4. Carrie and Brad are a young couple with no children or pets. Both are attorneys who earn more than $100,000 per year. Because they're relatively frugal, they have only a small mortgage on their jointly owned condo, and they have no outstanding debt. With their high net cash flow and some wise investment decisions, they've accumulated

sizable net worth, and both have good retirement plans with their employers. Does either of them need life insurance? Why or why not?

5. You have been quoted a premium of $120 per year for $100,000 in term life insurance, with the premium fixed for five years, and a premium of $1,120 per year for a permanent life insurance policy with an equivalent face value. Explain what you should do if you want to implement a "buy term and invest the difference" strategy. What else would you need to know about the term life insurance policy?

6. Suppose that you implemented the "buy term and invest the difference" strategy, investing $1,000 per year at the beginning of every year for the next five years, and earning 6 percent per year after taxes. How much would you accumulate after five years?

7. For each of the following characteristics, identify the type of life insurance (term, ordinary, universal, variable) to which it applies.

   a. Flexible premium

   b. Premium increases with age

   c. Investment choices for the policyholder

   d. Death protection for policyholder's entire life

   e. No cash value

8. What are some explanations for why the cost of nursing home care is so much more in some states than in others?

9. Your grandmother needs to go into a nursing home. She currently lives in Illinois and you live in North Carolina. You're deciding whether it will be cost-effective to move her to North Carolina. A facility in Illinois will cost $60,000 per year, and one in North Carolina will cost $70,000 per year. You estimate that it would cost you $5,000 to move your grandmother to North Carolina or $3,000 per year to travel back and forth to visit her in Illinois.

    a. What is the difference in cost between these two strategies for the first year?

    b. If you estimate that your grandmother will stay in the nursing facility for five years and the cost difference between the two facilities will stay constant over time, which is the better choice? What if she stays in the facility for only three years?

10. Your after-tax income is $40,000. Your spouse's after-tax income is $20,000, and you have one child under the age of 18. Your family's annual expenses are $60,000. Your average indexed earnings for Social Security benefit calculations are $40,000. You are 30 years old. If you died today, your family expenses would drop by 20 percent.

    a. If you died, how much extra income would your family need to meet their expenses (not taking Social Security survivor benefits into consideration)?

    b. Will your family be eligible for Social Security survivor benefits, and, if so, will the benefits be enough to make up for your lost income? (Hint: Consult Table 8.2 in the text.)

    c. If Social Security benefits are sufficient to cover the family's income shortfall, will you need to have any life insurance?

11. Under what circumstances might it be advisable to buy long-term care insurance for your parents, paying the cost out of your own pocket?

12. May-Yun, age 45, estimates that she needs to buy $300,000 in life insurance to protect her dependent children from suffering adverse financial consequences in the event of her death. As a single parent, she's on a pretty tight budget. Will term or permanent life insurance be more appropriate to meet her needs right now? Explain your reasoning.

13. Richard, age 35, is married and childless. He and his wife are both employed full time. He would like to have $100,000 in life insurance coverage and is interested in a policy that will also give him some low-risk investment earnings. Should he consider term insurance? Why or why not?

14. Cathy, age 50, is working on her financial plan. Mary, her mother, is 80 years old.

    a. Based on average life expectancy for her age, about how old will Cathy be when she dies, rounded up to the nearest year? (Hint: Consult Table 8.1 in the text.)

    b. Based on average life expectancy for her age, about how old will Mary, Cathy's mother, be when she dies, rounded up to the nearest year? (Hint: Consult Table 8.1 in the text.)

    c. Why isn't their life expectancy the same?

Case Applications

1. Vanna and Patrick O'Hara, ages 30 and 40, respectively, are considering the purchase of additional life insurance. They're both employed full-time, and they have two children who are 7-year-old twins. Vanna's after-tax income is $30,000, and Pat's is $50,000. Currently, Vanna has a $30,000 term life insurance policy paid for by her employer, and Pat has a $75,000 individual term life insurance policy. Each of the O'Haras would like to have enough life insurance so that, in the event of either's death, it would cover the lost cash flow to the household, help pay off some household debts, and fund their children's college costs. They have estimated these costs as follows:

College fund for children	$130,000
Pay off existing mortgage on home	150,000
Pay off credit cards	10,000
Costs of death	15,000

In addition, they estimate that their household expenses of $60,000 will be about 10 percent less if either one of them dies. If Vanna were to die, the cost of replacing her services to the household would be $10,000 per year for the next 11 years (until the children go to college). If Patrick were to die, this annual cost would be $5,000. They don't anticipate that either of them would qualify for Social Security survivor benefits, but the children would be eligible for combined benefits of $2,000 a month until they reached the age of 18. The O'Haras currently have $50,000 in home equity and $35,000 in savings.

    a. What would be the financial consequences for the O'Haras' children in the event of a tragic car accident in which both parents were killed?

    b. Using the income-multiple method, what is the minimum amount of life insurance that Patrick should have? What is the minimum amount that Vanna should have?

    c. Apply the financial needs method to determine how much life insurance Vanna and Patrick each should have.

    d. What type of insurance policy would you recommend for each? Explain your reasoning.

    e. If the O'Haras choose to buy term life insurance, what risks do they face, and are there any contract terms that could reduce this risk?

2. Kurt Nelson is 63 years old and has been retired for several years. Two years ago, his wife of 40 years passed away after two years of battling cancer. During her entire illness, Kurt provided the in-home care she required. Shortly thereafter, his mother became incapacitated and moved in with him. He hired a nurse to come in for a couple of hours each day to cook dinner and help with his mother's personal needs, but otherwise he took care of her himself. His mother died six months ago. Kurt has five surviving adult children and ten grandchildren, all of whom are financially secure. He would like to leave the bulk of his estate to his family but is worried that, should he require long-term care, the costs would rapidly deplete his hard-earned capital. He also wants to ensure that his beloved dog, Lucky, will be well cared for in the event that he cannot take care of Lucky himself. Lucky isn't particularly good with children and is accustomed to a lot of personal attention. Kurt knows that none of his children would be willing to take the dog, so he wants to set up a fund for this purpose. He estimates that he could hire someone to perform this service for $5,000 per year. Kurt is considering the purchase of additional life insurance as well as long-term care insurance. At his age, he finds that both will be relatively expensive despite the fact that he's in good health. He estimates that his investments are worth $500,000 and that they earn an average of 4 percent per year. He has a defined benefit pension that provides $32,000 in after-tax annual income. He started receiving Social Security benefits at age 62, and his current benefit is $18,000 per year. His annual expenses, excluding those related to Lucky, are $40,000.

a. If Kurt required long-term care for three years beginning this year, would his current income and assets be enough to pay for it, assuming the annual cost is $60,000 per year? If he goes into long-term care, he estimates that his other annual expenses would drop to $20,000, including the expenses for Lucky.

b. What would his situation be if he didn't need long-term care until he reached the age of 88 (25 years from now)? Assume that long-term care costs grow at 4 percent per year.

c. Does Kurt need life insurance? Explain your reasoning.

d. Assume that long-term care insurance premiums are $12,000 per year. If Kurt expects to enter a long-term care facility at age 73 (10 years from now) for one year, would he be better off investing the money or buying the long-term care insurance? What impact does the number of years of required long-term care have on his decision?

e. Should Kurt consider buying a life insurance policy with a long-term care accelerated benefits option instead? Explain your reasoning.

CHAPTER 9

Employee Benefits: Health, Disability, and Retirement Plans

Stephen Coburn/Shutterstock.com

Feature Story

Lori Yoshihama majored in marketing and public relations at a large public university. In her senior year, she sent out resumés and was interviewed by several prospective employers. A few months prior to graduation, she was excited to receive three interesting job offers. Although the working conditions in the positions were similar, the compensation and benefits packages were quite different. Lori realized that she didn't know enough about health insurance and retirement plans to make an informed decision. She would need to do some background research to be able to make the wisest choice from among her job offers.

In considering different employment opportunities, it's important to evaluate all the competing factors, including the nature of the job itself, the locations, and the compensation packages the employers offer. The most obvious component of these packages is, of course, the salary or hourly wage, but many jobs offer much more in the form of employee benefits, sometimes called *fringe benefits*. It's essential to take into account all the components of an employment opportunity and estimate the value of the total package before making your decision. This analysis requires that you carefully evaluate your employment preferences and that you understand the basic features and costs of the different types of employee benefits. In this chapter, we provide an overview of the range of options you might encounter at different companies and spend a little more time on the most valuable benefits, including health, disability, and retirement plans. We'll revisit Lori's decision process as we consider each of these important components of compensation.

LEARNING OBJECTIVES	TOPICS	DEMONSTRATION PROBLEMS
9.1 Explain the value of employee benefits as a component of compensation.	**9.1 The Value of Employee Benefits** • Why Benefits Are Preferable to Cash Compensation • Comparing Job Offers Based on Salary and Benefit Packages	**9.1** Calculating the Tax Savings from Pretax Employee Benefits

(continued)

(continued)

LEARNING OBJECTIVES	TOPICS	DEMONSTRATION PROBLEMS
9.2 Evaluate your health-related costs, and select appropriate health insurance to meet your needs.	**9.2 Health Insurance and Your Financial Plan** • Health Insurance Needs Analysis • What Happened to Health-Care Reform? • Types of Health Insurance Plans • Government-Sponsored Health Insurance Plans	**9.2** Comparing Deductibles and Coinsurance
9.3 Analyze your disability income needs, and identify sources of disability income.	**9.3 Planning for Disability Income** • Disability Income Needs Analysis • Sources of Disability Income	
9.4 Explain the benefits of participating in employer-sponsored retirement plans.	**9.4 Employer-Sponsored Retirement Plans** • Tax Advantages of Qualified Plans • Defined-Benefit versus Defined-Contribution Plans • Features of Defined-Benefit Plans • Features of Defined-Contribution Plans	

9.1 | The Value of Employee Benefits

LEARNING OBJECTIVE 9.1

Explain the value of employee benefits as a component of compensation.

Although you'll often find that the differences in wage and salary compensation between similar jobs in a given geographical area are fairly small, the same cannot be said about working environment and fringe benefits. Some employers are very generous in what they offer their employees, and others are more stingy. The types of benefits provided will often depend on the size of the company and the management's attitude about compensation and employee satisfaction.

Employee benefits include both tangible and intangible elements. Tangible benefits are those that have a financial or dollar value. They may include any or all of the following:

- Wage or salary compensation, commissions, and bonuses
- Cash-equivalent benefits, including contributions to retirement plans, health and life insurance, paid vacation, sick leave, paid maternity or paternity leave, personal leave, and education reimbursement
- Noncash benefits, such as the use of a company car, unpaid vacation, sick leave and personal leave, wellness programs, and access to child-care facilities or a health club membership

Although this chapter focuses on tangible benefits, your employment choices may also differ in important ways that are not readily quantifiable in money terms. Intangible benefits, which may still have an actual cost to your employer and a significant value to you, may include any or all of the following:

- Flexible work hours
- Opportunities for training and advancement
- Job location
- Pleasant working environment
- Quality and personality of coworkers

Although some employers offer more comprehensive packages, employee benefit packages commonly include vacation and sick days, various types of insurance (health, dental, vision, disability, and life), and retirement plans. Some employers offer a **cafeteria plan**, in which they provide a sum of money that can be applied to purchase benefits from a menu of options that they have selected. What options your employer will offer depends on the company's size, the type of position you hold, benefit packages being offered by competing firms, and competition in the labor market for qualified workers.

Benefits are sometimes completely paid for by the employer, in which case they're said to be noncontributory. If, instead, you're required to pay some or all of the cost yourself, the benefit plan is called a **contributory plan**. Many employers provide their employees with access to health coverage on a contributory basis, which means that the employee must pay some or all of the cost. If you have employer-based health insurance, the total annual premium and the amount of that premium that you are required to pay may be more or less than what you'd pay in the individual market.

The U.S. Department of Labor's Bureau of Labor Statistics regularly surveys employers to see what types of benefits they offer to employees. The key results of a recent survey are summarized in **Table 9.1**.

TABLE 9.1   **Employee Benefit Plan Participation, Civilian Workers, 2018**

Benefit Type	Percent Participation by Size of Firm		Benefit Type	Percent Participation by Size of Firm	
	<100 Employees (%)	100+ Employees (%)		<100 Employees (%)	100+ Employees (%)
Insurance			**Retirement Plan**		
Health	41	64	Any	40	71
Prescription drugs	40	63	Defined-benefit	10	33
Dental	24	47	Defined-contribution	34	51
Vision	14	28	**Paid Time Off**		
Life	42	76	Paid holidays	71	83
Long-term care	9	26	Paid vacation	69	81
Health savings account	19	38	Paid personal leave	35	56
			Paid family leave	13	22
Disability			Unpaid family leave	82	95
Paid sick leave	63	84	**Quality of Life**		
Short-term	29	43	Child care	5	16
Long-term	27	43	Subsidized commuting	5	10
Flexible Savings Accounts					
Child care	24	60	Wellness programs	24	63
Health care	19	38	Employee assistance programs	32	76

Note: This table reports the percentages of employees participating in the plan. In many cases, employers offer access to a benefit, but employees do not choose to participate because they do not need the benefit or don't want to pay for it.

Source: U.S. Department of Labor, Bureau of Labor Statistics, www.bls.gov.

INTERACTIVE

See **Interactive: Differences in Employee Benefits by Worker Characteristics** in WileyPLUS.

One thing to note from Table 9.1 is that employees at medium- and large-sized firms (100 or more employees) are more likely to have access to and participate in employee benefit plans. As an example, 64 percent of employees at medium and large firms participate in a health insurance plan, compared with only 41 percent of those at small firms. Employees at large firms are also more likely to have access to vision, dental, disability, and retirement plans. In addition, in both small and large firms, some types of workers are less likely to have access to benefits. You can learn more about these differences in **Interactive: Differences in Employee Benefits by Worker Characteristics**.

Differences in employee benefit offerings across firms are largely due to costs. It's very expensive for employers to provide and administer benefit plans. It is less cost-effective for small employers because they can't spread the administrative costs across a large group. Similarly, the record keeping involved in benefits administration makes it less practical to offer benefits to part-time or temporary employees. Approximately 8.3 percent of compensation costs are for legally mandated benefit programs, including Social Security, Medicare, unemployment, and workers' compensation insurance. When you add on generous employee benefit plans, total compensation costs can be 25 to 30 percent higher than cash wages and salaries.

If benefits cost so much, why do employers provide them at all? Why don't they just give you the extra money and let you choose to buy the benefits or keep the cash? Employers with less generous plans essentially do just that. But some employers recognize that offering an attractive fringe benefit package can pay off in the long run.

> **Reflection Question 1**
> Would you prefer that your employer give you a higher salary or a more generous employee benefit package? Why?

Why Benefits Are Preferable to Cash Compensation

Although some employers offer benefits to employees for altruistic reasons, competition is often the driving force. If a firm provides desirable benefits, it will be able to attract the most highly qualified workers. Other advantages may include reduced turnover, as well as increased employee loyalty, productivity, and job satisfaction. Employees who participate in such plans may gain the benefits of lower costs, greater convenience, better coverage, and lower taxes. We discuss these advantages in more detail in this section.

Lower Underwriting Costs

Group insurance is insurance purchased by an employer for the benefit of a group of employees. Recall from earlier chapters that insurance companies normally consider your individual risk characteristics before selling you an insurance policy, using a process called underwriting. For example, if you have higher risk of being in an auto accident, you pay a higher rate for your auto insurance. This is not the case with **group underwriting**. When an insurer provides health insurance to a group of employees through an employee benefit plan, the contract is with the employer rather than with the individuals, so there's a single application for the entire group. The insurer's pricing and coverage decisions are based on the risk of the group as a whole, rather than on risk characteristics of individual group members. Group underwriting therefore may allow you to have access to benefits that you could not qualify for on your own.

Lower Administrative Costs

In general, managing a group insurance plan is cheaper for an insurer than managing many individual policies, and these cost savings can be passed on to the employer and employee. The cost savings might result from consolidation of premium collection, claims management, and record keeping. The insurer also might have lower average claims because the group will likely include a balanced mix of healthy and unhealthy, young and old individuals.

Lower Taxes

Compared with cash compensation, employee benefits offer significant tax advantages to employees. To employers, there's no real tax difference. Subject to some limitations, employers can deduct both types of compensation as a business expense. However, the tax law *does* allow you, as an employee, to receive certain benefits without reporting the value as taxable income. If the plan is contributory and you have to pay for the benefits out of your employment income, your employer will subtract the amount of the benefit from your salary or wages before calculating taxes owed. This means you'll pay less federal and state income tax as well as less Social Security tax. You're eligible for this tax treatment even if you don't itemize deductions. The rule applies to all qualified group benefits, such as medical, dental, vision, and contributions to FSAs and HSAs. Typically, life and disability insurance premiums are paid with after-tax income so that the benefits will be tax-free when received.

To roughly estimate your tax savings from tax-deductible employee benefits, multiply your marginal tax rate by the cost of the benefit. Note, though, that this will understate your true tax savings. For a more precise estimate, you can use **Equation 9.1**:

$$\text{Tax savings from pretax employee benefits} = \frac{\text{Benefit cost}}{1 - \text{Marginal tax rate}} - \text{Benefit cost} \qquad (9.1)$$

The first part of this equation measures the amount of pretax income required to produce after-tax income sufficient to pay the benefits. **Demonstration Problem 9.1** illustrates this calculation and explains how to use **Excel Worksheet 9.1** (Personal Financial Planner: Tax Savings from Pretax Employee Benefits) to estimate the tax savings from your employee benefits.

EXCEL WORKSHEET

See **Excel Worksheet 9.1 (Personal Financial Planner: Tax Savings from Pretax Employee Benefits)** in **WileyPLUS.**

DEMONSTRATION PROBLEM 9.1 | Calculating the Tax Savings from Pretax Employee Benefits

Problem

Suppose your marginal tax rate for state, federal, and Social Security taxes is 30 percent. Through your employer, you can purchase health insurance in a group plan for $4,000 per year. Assuming that you could buy individual coverage in the health insurance market for the same price, how much will you save in taxes by getting your insurance through your employer?

Strategy

Use Equation 9.1 to calculate tax savings from pretax employee benefits.

Solution

Calculate the savings as follows:

$$\text{Tax savings from pretax employee benefits} = \frac{\text{Benefit cost}}{1 - \text{Marginal tax rate}} - \text{Benefit cost}$$

$$= \frac{\$4,000}{1 - 0.3} - \$4,000 = \$5,714 - \$4,000 = \$1,714$$

Unless you qualify for itemized deduction of medical expenses (limited to medical expenses in excess of 7.5 percent of adjusted gross income), your after-tax cost for individual insurance is $4,000. You would need $5,714 in gross income to have enough left after taxes to pay the $4,000 premium. Therefore, by purchasing insurance through your employer for $4,000 pretax, you're saving $1,714 ($5,714 − $4,000)—the amount in taxes you would otherwise have had to pay. Your net health insurance cost after tax savings is $2,286 ($4,000 − $1,714).

You can use Excel Worksheet 9.1 to estimate tax savings and net cost for any qualified employee benefit, as illustrated in **Figure 9.1**. Enter your total marginal tax rate (including federal, state, and Social Security payroll taxes) and the stated cost of the benefit to calculate the tax savings.

| FIGURE 9.1 | Sample of Excel Worksheet 9.1: Tax Savings from Pretax Employee Benefits |

	A	B
1		
2	1. Enter your marginal tax rate, including federal income tax,	30.0%
3	state income tax, and Social Security payroll tax.	
4		
5	2. Enter the dollar cost of the employee benefit.	$4,000
6		
7	3. Pretax income needed in order to have sufficient after-tax	
8	income to pay for the benefit on your own.	
9	= Benefit cost divided by (1 – Tax rate)	$5,714
10		
11	4. Tax savings from employee benefit (= line 3 – line 2)	$1,714
12		
13	5. Net cost of employee benefit (= line 2 – line 4)	$2,286
14		

In Demonstration Problem 9.1, we assumed you would have to pay the full $4,000 premium for the health insurance offered through your employer's plan. However, employers often pay some or most of the cost of employee benefits as part of their overall compensation package, so the actual advantage is even greater.

The chapter opener introduced Lori Yoshihama, a college senior who was deciding between competing job offers. **Case Study 9.1** illustrates how she can compare alternative job offers that differ in salaries, out-of-pocket benefit costs, and tax savings.

Case Study 9.1

Stephen Coburn/Shutterstock.com

Lori Evaluates Tax Savings from Employer-Provided Health Insurance

Problem

Lori Yoshihama has three job offers that are identical except for the following:

Company A: Starting salary $36,000 plus noncontributory health insurance costing the employer $4,000.

Company B: Starting salary $40,000, no health insurance.
Company C: Starting salary $40,000, fully contributory health insurance at a cost of $4,000.

Assume that Lori can purchase individual health insurance on her own at a cost of $4,000 per year and that her marginal tax rate, including all applicable taxes, is 30 percent. Which job offer should she choose?

Strategy

Recall that noncontributory benefits are paid for by the employer, whereas contributory benefits require the employee pay some or all of the cost. To determine which of these job offers is a better deal, Lori should evaluate the after-tax value of the salary and benefits for each one. She can use Equation 9.1 or Excel Worksheet 9.1 to estimate the tax savings. However, she also needs to take into account that the salaries for the three jobs are not all the same.

Solution   Table 9.2 details the calculation of the after-tax value of the salary and benefits from the three companies. Notice that when Lori pays the cost of the benefit through the employer plan, she gets to deduct it from her taxable income, resulting in a reduction in income and payroll taxes.

TABLE 9.2   Lori's After-Tax Salary and Benefits Comparison

	Company A ($36,000 Noncontributory Health Insurance Benefit)	Company B ($40,000, No Health Insurance Benefit)	Company C ($40,000 Fully Contributory Health Insurance Benefit)
Salary	$36,000	$40,000	$40,000
Less: Benefit deduction	$0	$0	$4,000
Net taxable income	$36,000	$40,000	$36,000
Less: Tax (30%)	$10,800	$12,000	$10,800
After-tax salary	$25,200	$28,000	$29,200
Out-of-pocket health insurance cost	$0	$4,000	$4,000
Salary after tax and health insurance costs	$25,200	$24,000	$25,200

Based on this analysis, Lori concludes that the cost of salary and benefits to each employer is exactly equivalent—$40,000. Essentially, there is no difference between the Company A and Company C job offers, because the health insurance paid for through the contributory plan at Company C will reduce Lori's taxable income.

If she goes to Company B, Lori will pay the insurance on her own and will not get a tax deduction. The tax savings of choosing Company A or Company C is $1,200. However, Lori will probably be better off choosing Company A because it pays the full cost of health insurance. Health insurance premiums tend to increase over time at a faster rate than salary, as we'll see later in this chapter.

Although the $4,000 difference in salary in this example is equivalent to the pretax cost of individual health insurance, this isn't always the case. When you're young and healthy, individual insurance can be a cheaper alternative. But if you're older, are in poor health, or need family coverage, the cost can be a lot higher. Furthermore, employers who do not offer full benefit packages may not offer equivalent cash compensation.

Case Study 9.1 considers only health insurance, but your employer may offer many types of benefits that will provide you with similar cost and tax advantages. For example, many employers offer the opportunity to set up a **flexible spending account (FSA)**. These arrangements allow you to set aside up to $2,700 of pretax income for the payment of qualified medical expenses and $5,000 per family for qualified child-care expenses (as of 2019). The health account funds can be used to cover insurance deductibles and copayments as well as a wide range of medical, dental, and vision expenses that might not be covered under your health-care plan.

Although you use your own money to pay expenses with FSAs, you'll pay less than if you'd had to first pay taxes on that income. The tax savings are the same as those calculated for pretax group benefits above. Suppose, for example, you regularly spend $2,500 per year on child care and your marginal tax rate is 30 percent. Based on Equation 9.1, you will save $1,071 in taxes ($2,500/0.7) − $2,500 per year by putting $2,500 in an FSA and getting reimbursed for those expenditures. So your net cost of $2,500 for child care is actually $1,429 ($2,500 − $1,071).

The downside to flexible spending accounts is that the IRS limits the amount you can roll over at the end of the year if you have not spent all of the funds. To be sure you don't leave money on the table, you should fund your FSA each year based on out-of-pocket expenses that are fairly certain to occur, such as the cost of new eyeglasses or contacts, orthodontics, plan deductibles, and other regular expenses not covered by insurance. Consider using online tools such as the one described in **Online Calculator Demonstration Video: How Much to Put in Your FSA?**, to figure out how much to contribute to your FSA.

Your employer may alternatively offer the opportunity to set up a **health savings account (HSA)** (formerly called a *health reimbursement account* or *medical savings account*). An HSA is connected with an employer health plan and can be used in the same way as an FSA for current medical expenses. Unlike an FSA, however, the HSA allows you to save for medical

ONLINE CALCULATOR DEMONSTRATION VIDEO

See **Online Calculator Demonstration Video: How Much to Put in Your FSA?** in **WileyPLUS**.

expenses that may occur far in the future. It is the only type of savings account that offers triple tax advantages: tax-free contributions and investment earnings, with no tax on withdrawals. If your employer offers this type of plan, you should consider funding it to the maximum allowed as part of your retirement planning.

Comparing Job Offers Based on Salary and Benefit Packages

With an understanding of some of the elements of employee benefit plans, you'll be better prepared to compare the compensation packages you might be offered by prospective employers. The world is a smaller place today than it was for previous generations of job seekers. It's not uncommon to be considering jobs with vastly different companies in several geographic areas—perhaps including countries other than the United States. Even if you're already employed, it's likely that you'll change jobs, and even careers, several times over your working life. When you're considering different job opportunities, you'll want to take into account a variety of factors, including the culture of the workplace, opportunities for advancement, and the fit with your interests and abilities. Here, we consider two financial elements of this decision: cost-of-living differences and the value of different employee benefit packages.

Comparing Salaries Based on Cost of Living

If you've traveled around the country much, you know that the prices of food, clothing, housing, child care, and transportation can vary greatly by geographic area. In general, it's more expensive to live on the East or West coasts than in the middle of the country, and it's also more expensive to live in urban areas than in rural areas. Although salaries are a little higher in expensive areas, you'll probably find that they're not sufficiently higher—a high salary in New York City will likely result in a lower standard of living than a lower salary for the same job in a small Midwest town.

In Chapter 1, we discussed how to use the consumer price index (CPI) to measure changes in prices over time. Although the CPI is based on national trends, regional differences in prices are regularly tracked as well, in the form of cost-of-living indexes (COLIs) for various locations. A COLI tells you how the cost of goods and services in a particular geographic area compares with the national average. Once you find the COLIs for two locations, you can use **Equation 9.2** to easily compare salary offers:

EXCEL WORKSHEET

See **Excel Worksheet 9.2 (Personal Financial Planner: City Cost-of-Living Comparison)** in **WileyPLUS**.

$$\text{Equivalent salary in City 1} = \frac{\text{COLI}_1}{\text{COLI}_2} \times \text{Salary in City 2} \qquad (9.2)$$

where COLI_1 is the cost-of-living index for City 1 and COLI_2 is the cost-of-living index for City 2. **Case Study 9.2** walks you through an example.

Case Study 9.2

Stephen Coburn/Shutterstock.com

Lori Compares Salary Offers Based on Cost of Living

Problem

Lori Yoshihama is comparing two job offers at public relations consulting firms. One is in Atlanta at a starting salary of $40,000, and the other in Minneapolis at a starting salary of $43,000. Lori looks up the cost-of-living index for each city and finds the following information:

- Atlanta's cost-of-living index is 95.6 (costs are 95.6 percent of the national average).

- Minneapolis's cost-of-living index is 111 (costs are 111 percent of the national average).

Are the two salary offers comparable? If not, which one is better?

Strategy

Lori can use Equation 9.2 to determine the level of salary in Minneapolis that would give her purchasing power equivalent to the $40,000 salary in Atlanta:

Solution   Lori calculates the following:

$$\text{Equivalent salary in Minneapolis} = \frac{\text{COLI}_{\text{Minneapolis}}}{\text{COLI}_{\text{Atlanta}}} \times \text{Salary in Atlanta}$$

$$= \frac{111}{95.6} \times \$40,000 = \$46,444$$

Based on this calculation, Lori concludes that the salary offer in Minneapolis isn't enough to compensate for the higher costs in that area. She would need to earn $46,444 there to have a salary equivalent to $40,000 in Atlanta.

You can also use **Excel Worksheet 9.2** (Personal Financial Planner: City Cost-of-Living Comparison) to check on cost-of-living differences between two cities.

Comparing Employee Benefit Packages

The next step in comparing job offers is to evaluate the employee benefit packages. As we've seen, the benefits offered by employers and the value of these benefit packages vary widely. This is a good application of marginal analysis, a decision-making technique we discussed in Chapter 1. When there are a lot of things to compare, you should focus only on the differences between two choices. You can also simplify the problem by considering only the benefits that are valuable to you at your current stage in the life cycle. There may be some benefits you really don't need right now and others that are particularly important to you. **Interactive: Employee Benefits and the Life Cycle** will help you to better understand which benefits are likely to be most important for your particular life circumstances.

In Case Studies 9.1 and 9.2, Lori Yoshihama compared her job offers based only on differences in taxes and cost of living. The final step is to compare the job offers against each other, considering all the other components of the compensation package. **Case Study 9.3** shows how Lori decides between two competing job offers using a job comparison worksheet like the one provided in **Excel Worksheet 9.3** (Personal Financial Planner: Job Comparison Worksheet).

INTERACTIVE

See **Interactive: Employee Benefits and the Life Cycle** in **WileyPLUS**.

EXCEL WORKSHEET

See **Excel Worksheet 9.3** (**Personal Financial Planner: Job Comparison Worksheet**) in **WileyPLUS**.

Case Study 9.3

Stephen Coburn/Shutterstock.com

Lori Compares Job Offers Based on Salary and Benefits

Problem

Lori Yoshihama has two competing job offers in Atlanta and Minneapolis. The Atlanta salary offer is $40,000, and the Minneapolis salary offer is $43,000. Lori has collected the following benefits package information from each firm's human resources department:

- The Atlanta employer provides fully paid health insurance, $20,000 in life insurance, four paid personal days, and a fully equipped on-site gym for employee use, and it contributes 3 percent of salary to a retirement plan.

- The Minneapolis employer provides fully paid health insurance, no life insurance, six paid personal days, and free child care for employees, and it contributes 7 percent to a retirement plan.

Strategy

Lori should use marginal analysis by focusing on the differences between job offers rather than trying to value all the benefits. For example, the two offers have comparable health insurance benefits, so she can ignore this benefit in her decision making. She also should focus on the benefits that are valuable to her.

Solution
Lori is single and has no dependents. Therefore, she decides to ignore the life insurance and child-care benefits in her comparison of the two jobs. However, she estimates that free access to a gym would save her about $500 per year. She completes the job comparison worksheet as illustrated in **Figure 9.2**.

FIGURE 9.2   Sample of Excel Worksheet 9.3: Job Comparison Worksheet

	A	B	C	D
1	Job Offer			
2	Components	Atlanta Job	Minneapolis Job	Difference
3	Salary	$40,000 (equivalent to	$43,000	= $46,444 – $43,000
4		$46,444 in Minneapolis		= $3,444
5		based on calculation in		
6		Case Study 9.2)		
7	Health Insurance	Fully paid	Fully paid	0
8				0
9	Life Insurance	$20,000 face value	0	(Lori doesn't need life insurance)
10				= ($46,444/250) per day
11	Personal Days	4 paid	6 paid	× 2 = $372
12		3% contribution	7% contribution	
13		= $40,000 × 0.03	= $43,000 × 0.07	$1,200 – $3,100
14	Retirement Plan	= $1,200	= $3,010	= –$1,810
15	Employee Gym	None	Fully paid	–$500
16				0
17	Child Care	None	Free	(Lori has no children)
18				
19	Net Difference			= $3,444 – $372 – $1,810 – $500
20				= $762

Lori first calculates the value of each day's work in Minneapolis by dividing the Minneapolis equivalent salary by the 250 days she expects to work per year. The two extra paid personal days for the Minneapolis job are worth $372. The Atlanta employer will contribute 3 percent of her salary toward a retirement plan, for a dollar value of $1,200, while the Minneapolis employer will contribute 7 percent, for a dollar value of $3,010. Note we use the actual dollars contributed rather than the Minneapolis cost-of-living equivalent, because this money is being allocated to an investment program rather than to spending on goods and services. Although Lori ignores the child-care benefit because she doesn't have children, the gym membership will save her $500 per year, so she takes this into consideration in making her comparison.

After considering these differences, Lori concludes the Atlanta job is still financially preferable to the Minneapolis job. Although the benefits package is less favorable, the difference in the cost of living more than makes up for it.

Comparing job offers isn't always as straightforward as demonstrated in Case Study 9.3. Sometimes, prospective employers, particularly those without large human resources offices, will not provide complete benefits information until you actually accept a job offer. Even those with relatively comprehensive information on their websites may limit access to that information to current employees. If you have a job offer in hand, don't be afraid to call the human resources or benefits office and ask for the information you need. If those employees are not very helpful, that might be a piece of qualitative information to consider in your employment decision.

You might also find that it's difficult to place a dollar value on certain benefits or to easily determine the difference in value for different types of health and retirement plans. In the next sections, you'll learn more about health, retirement, and disability benefits.

9.2   Health Insurance and Your Financial Plan

LEARNING OBJECTIVE 9.2

Evaluate your health-related costs, and select appropriate health insurance to meet your needs.

Health insurance is a benefit often found in compensation packages. Whether you participate in an employer plan or purchase individual insurance, health insurance is an important component of your financial plan. If you don't have insurance, illnesses and injuries can place a tremendous financial burden on your family. In this section, we consider how to evaluate your health insurance needs, identify your insurance alternatives, and suggest methods for selecting the most appropriate coverage and minimizing your future out-of-pocket health-care costs.

Health Insurance Needs Analysis

Health insurance provides protection against health-care costs incurred due to illness, accident, or disability. This type of insurance works in the same way as property, liability, and life insurance. Because a particular individual's health-related expenses are not usually correlated with those of other individuals, insurers can pool these risks and spread the cost over many policyholders. Insurers use statistical data to estimate future costs and charge premiums sufficient to cover their expected losses and expenses.

Health insurance decisions require that you begin with a realistic estimate of your expected health-care costs, taking into consideration your family situation and national trends in the costs of medical care.

Expected Health-Care Costs

In 2019, more than 28 million nonelderly people in the United States had no health insurance. Although this represents an improvement compared with the peak uninsured rate in 2012, the number of uninsured Americans has increased in the last few years.

Young, healthy people sometimes forego the expense of health insurance on the principle that "it won't happen to me." While it's true that your risk of a major health event is relatively small, even regular, predictable medical expenditures, such as annual diagnostic tests, prescription drugs, and office visits for minor illnesses, can rapidly deplete household resources. As with other types of insurance, it is often preferable to budget for small, predictable costs rather than insure against them. However, budgeting for more serious health costs is another matter. Specialists commonly charge $250 or more for office visits. Regular ambulance services might cost $2,000 or more, and a helicopter ambulance can run as much as $10,000 for one trip. If you require hospitalization, you can expect to pay several thousand dollars per day—and more for intensive care. If you have or plan to have children, you can expect to incur costs every year for illnesses, injuries, and wellness care.

It's also important to consider that, for some people, expected health-care costs are higher than average because of a family history of cancer, diabetes, or heart disease. In assessing your potential health-care needs, you should consider your family history, even if you haven't been diagnosed with a particular condition or illness. A relatively inexpensive genetic test can tell you more about your risks of certain diseases.

National Trends in Health-Care Costs

Even if you're relatively healthy, you can expect your medical care and health insurance costs to increase over time. For a variety of reasons, including increased quality of care and escalating prescription drug prices, medical costs and health insurance premiums have increased faster than wages and inflation, as illustrated in **Figure 9.3**.

Health insurance premiums for family coverage at small firms increased almost 200 percent between 1999 and 2018, significantly outpacing wage growth, which saw a cumulative increase of less than 70 percent over that period. Because small firms are less likely to completely subsidize health insurance, this implies that health-care costs have taken an increasingly larger bite out of family budgets over the last decade.

FIGURE 9.3 **Cumulative Increases in Health Insurance Premiums, Wages, and Consumer Prices, 1999–2018** Over the last two decades, health insurance premiums have increased at a much faster rate than wages or other consumer prices.

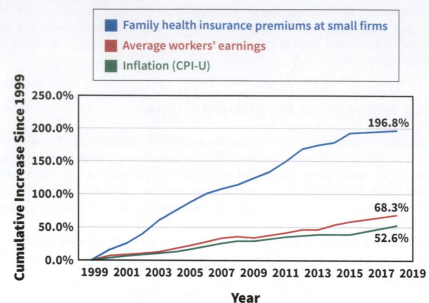

Note: CPI-U is the consumer price index for urban consumers.

Sources: Kaiser Family Foundation, 2018 Employer Health Benefits Survey; Social Security National Average Wage Index; Bureau of Labor Statistics.

Although health insurance premiums have been rising steadily, the share paid by employers has so far remained relatively stable. **Figure 9.4** shows the total costs for different types of health plans and the proportions paid by employers and employees, respectively.

FIGURE 9.4 **Average Costs for Different Types of Health Plans, 2018** Employers differ in the types of health plans they offer and also in the amount of the cost that they subsidize for their employees.

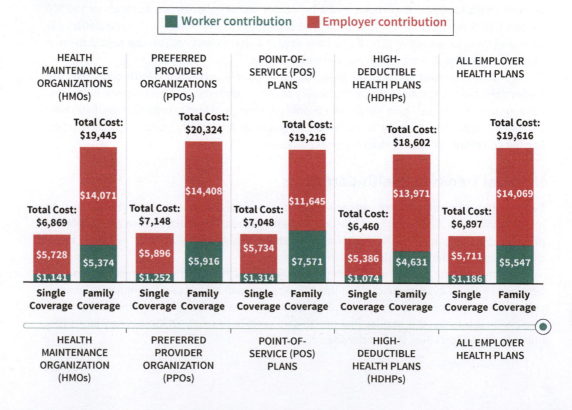

The average proportion of health insurance premiums paid by employers has declined over time, particularly as smaller employers are finding it increasingly difficult to absorb the rapidly increasing costs. In addition, employers have added cost-saving measures to their plans, such as larger deductibles and limitations on prescription drugs.

What Happened to Health-Care Reform?

In response to concerns about the rising cost of health care in the United States as well as the number of uninsured Americans, in March 2010 Congress passed the Patient Protection and Affordable Care Act, commonly called "ObamaCare." The law, which was politically controversial, included provisions to expand coverage, control health-care costs, and improve the health-care delivery system. Many of its key elements, which are summarized in **Table 9.3**, have since been repealed.

TABLE 9.3	**Major Provisions of the Patient Protection and Affordable Care Act of 2010 (and Its Current Status)**
Individual mandate	All U.S. citizens and legal residents must have qualifying health coverage or be subject to a tax penalty. The U.S. Supreme Court reviewed the constitutionality of the individual mandate in 2012 and did not overturn it, but this provision was repealed in 2018.
Employer mandate	All employers with more than 50 full-time employees must provide health coverage or pay a penalty. This provision was never enforced and has now been repealed.
Medicaid expansion	Originally, the law required all states to expand their Medicaid programs to cover individuals with adjusted gross incomes up to 133 percent of the federal poverty level or lose federal funding. The objective of this provision—to cover a large proportion of the uninsured—was significantly undermined by the Supreme Court's ruling that states could opt out of the expansion without loss of their existing funding. Thirty states and the District of Columbia decided to participate in the Medicaid expansion, resulting in a lower percentage of uninsured in those states.
Premium credits and subsidies	Individuals and families who earn less than 400 percent of the federal poverty level receive a federal tax credit if they buy insurance through an exchange. Small businesses are also given a tax credit to offset the cost of paying the premiums for their employees.
Health insurance exchanges	Many states developed electronic exchanges through which individuals and small businesses can comparison shop for health insurance plans with specific coverage options. In most states that do not offer exchanges, individuals are able to purchase insurance through a federally-facilitated exchange. The federal exchange is located at **www.healthcare.gov**. Although some states are still operating their own exchanges, many have switched to the federal exchange.
Coverage	All health insurance plans offered through the exchanges were required to offer certain types of coverage. Insurers cannot deny coverage based on a preexisting condition, which is an illness or injury that began prior to application, such as diabetes or heart disease. Children are allowed to stay on their parents' family plans until they reach age 26. Many of these requirements are still in effect, but insurers can now offer plans with less generous coverage.
Pricing	Insurers are restricted in their ability to increase premiums. The only underwriting factors that are allowed are age, family size, smoker status, and geographic location.

Note: For a more detailed summary, go to the Kaiser Family Foundation website at www.kff.org

By now, you should understand enough about insurance to see that in order to cover the costs of high-risk individuals who now cannot be denied coverage, a significant number of low-risk people need to buy insurance. The original provisions requiring individuals to have insurance and businesses to provide coverage, were designed to ensure that more young, healthy individuals would be in the pools. To encourage more people to sign up for coverage, the law includes tax subsidies to make the premiums more affordable. To fund the costs of the health-care reform program, the law imposes various additional taxes on individuals and businesses. Rather than repealing the entire law, Congress left in place some of the more costly provisions (such as coverage for preexisting conditions) and repealed the coverage mandates that would have resulted in more low-risk individuals in the pool. At this point, failure seems inevitable and health insurance premiums will continue to climb.

Reflection Question 2

What effect, if any, has ObamaCare had on your family's health insurance situation? How expensive would health insurance have to be for you to consider becoming one of the uninsured?

Types of Health Insurance Plans

Many types of group and individual health insurance plans are available in the marketplace today. You might have several to choose from at your place of employment. If your employer doesn't provide access to health insurance, you'll find hundreds of insurers that sell individual policies in the private market. People who have low incomes or are over age 65 may qualify for state or federal health insurance programs.

To select the right type of health insurance for you and your family, you'll first need to understand the similarities and differences among the various types of plans. All types of health insurance have certain features in common. All provide a mechanism for paying health-care providers (doctors, hospitals, and labs), whether through reimbursement to the policyholder for costs incurred or, more commonly, through direct payment to the provider. These plans differ in the limitations they place on membership, the services they cover, and the physicians they include. In this section, we examine the features of common types of health insurance plans.

Fee-for-Service Plans

Private health plans are usually categorized as either traditional fee-for-service plans or managed-care plans. A **fee-for-service plan**, sometimes called an *indemnity plan*, reimburses for the actual medical costs incurred. So, for example, if you have an X-ray or a blood test, the bill is submitted to the insurer, who either pays the provider or reimburses you if you have paid the cost out of pocket.

Traditional fee-for-service medical expense coverage is usually divided into two categories: basic health-care and major medical insurance.

- **Basic health-care insurance** **Basic health-care insurance** covers hospital, surgical, and physician expenses. These plans commonly limit the types of expenses covered and have relatively limited protection. For example, a basic health-care plan will typically pay for X-rays and lab tests if they're done in connection with hospitalization, but not if they're done in connection with an outpatient procedure.

- **Major medical insurance** **Major medical insurance** adds to the protection offered by basic health-care insurance by providing coverage for additional expenses and a wider range of medical services.

Critics of fee-for-service plans argue that they encourage (1) health-care providers to order too many tests and treatments and (2) consumers to ignore costs when they make health-care decisions. One approach to addressing these problems encourages consumers to take on more of their medical costs through deductibles and coinsurance, thereby becoming more sensitive to these costs. In contrast, a **managed-care plan** controls consumers' access to or use of medical services in an attempt to reduce plan costs.

Managed-Care Plans

The overall objective of managed-care plans is to keep health-care costs down by providing cost-saving incentives to providers and patients. Many types of managed-care plans are available today. Although the lines separating the different types are blurring, they are still primarily distinguishable by their financial arrangements with health-care providers. Three common types of managed-care plans are health maintenance organizations, preferred provider organizations, and point-of-service plans.

- **Health maintenance organizations**   A **health maintenance organization (HMO)** controls health-care costs by providing relatively comprehensive health insurance, encouraging preventive medicine (checkups, diagnostic tests, and immunizations), and giving health-care providers financial incentives to control costs. For example, a doctor who contracts with a plan might be given a fixed fee per participant per year regardless of the number of office visits, tests, and procedures. The HMO physician also commonly serves as a "gatekeeper" to other medical services. In other words, if you are an HMO member, you must get a referral from your regular HMO physician to see a specialist or to be hospitalized. HMOs normally charge a modest copay but do not require any deductible. The primary disadvantage of the HMO model of health care is that the patient often has a limited choice of physicians and limited access to specialist care.

- **Preferred provider organizations**   A **preferred provider organization (PPO)** gives you financial incentives to use "preferred" or "participating" providers who have contracted with the insurer to provide services at a reduced rate. If you choose to use other providers, you'll pay a larger share of the cost. The insurer might, for example, pay 90 percent of your expenses when you use a participating provider but only 80 percent if you use a nonparticipating provider. A PPO is similar to a traditional fee-for-service plan because it pays for services provided, but it's also similar to an HMO due to the limitations on choice of provider.

- **Point-of-service plans**   A **point-of-service (POS) plan** has elements of fee-for-service, HMO, and PPO plans in that you must choose a so-called primary physician. This physician, in turn, monitors your health-care needs and refers you to other providers. You commonly pay a small copay for office visits, as is the case with an HMO, but other services will be billed on a fee-for-service basis, with cost-sharing incentives for utilizing in-network providers.

Deductibles and Coinsurance

Fee-for-service plans, as well as some managed-care plans, may include deductibles and coinsurance requirements. As discussed in Chapter 7, a deductible is the amount of a loss that you must pay before the insurer pays any of the loss. With health insurance, these are commonly annual limits and can range from as low as $250 per person to $2,000 or higher. Premiums are generally lower when deductibles are higher. A **high-deductible health plan (HDHP)** is often referred to as a catastrophic health insurance plan, because it covers only major health expenses. It may also be called a consumer choice plan.

With **coinsurance**, you pay a percentage of medical costs after the deductible, often 10 to 30 percent, or a fixed fee, such as $10 to $25. This requirement applies until your total covered out-of-pocket costs reach a stated annual dollar amount. After that, the insurer will cover 100 percent of covered charges. Your required contribution is sometimes called a **copay**, but this term is more appropriately used to describe the dollar charge that some managed-care plans require you to pay for specific services, such as a $10 copay each time you visit the doctor or a $30 copay for prescription drugs.

The objective of deductibles and coinsurance is to deter the overuse of medical services by making insured people responsible for some of the cost. No one would ever intentionally break his arm, but a person might consider going to the doctor for a stuffy nose if they know that insurance will cover all of the cost. These measures keep down the overall costs of insurance by reducing the number of small claims. Such claims involve disproportionately high administrative costs for processing and record keeping—costs that must be passed on to policyholders.

Demonstration Problem 9.2 shows how to compare your out-of-pocket costs when choosing between participating and nonparticipating providers.

DEMONSTRATION PROBLEM 9.2 | Comparing Deductibles and Coinsurance

Problem

Your health insurance plan has a $500 annual deductible. Its coinsurance share is 90 percent for participating providers and 80 percent for nonparticipating providers. On a recent snowboarding trip, you took a bad fall and tore a ligament in your right knee. You would like to go to a well-known sports medicine specialist for the required surgery. In addition to being more expensive ($5,000 compared with $4,000 for a general surgeon), the specialist is not a participating provider in your plan. What should you consider when deciding between the two?

Strategy

Consider factors such as the qualifications and experience of each physician and the convenience of the location, in addition to your out-of-pocket cost (calculated by taking into consideration your deductible and coinsurance).

Solution

The table below shows the calculation of your out-of-pocket cost for each provider. As you can see, your out-of-pocket cost will be higher by $550 ($1,400 − $850) if you go to the specialist.

Description	Participating Provider	Nonparticipating Specialist
Total Charge	$4,000	$5,000
Deductible to Be Paid by You	500	500
Remainder after Deductible	$3,500	$4,500
Coinsurance to Be Paid by You	× 10% = $350	× 20% = $900
Amount Paid by Insurer = Total Charge − Deductible − Coinsurance	= $4,000 − $500 − $350 = $3,150	= $5,000 − $500 − $900 = $3,600
Your Out-of-Pocket Cost = Deductible + Coinsurance	= $500 + $350 = $850	= $500 + $900 = $1,400

Another factor you should consider is whether your insurance plan incorporates "usual and customary" limits on allowed provider charges for services. In such a case, the amount paid by the insurer will be a percentage of the standard cost for the procedure, rather than the specialist's actual charge. Suppose that the participating provider's charge of $4,000 is the usual and customary charge. In that case, your plan will subtract the deductible from the usual and customary charge and then pay 80 percent of the remainder (since your coinsurance share is 20 percent). Thus, the provider's insurance reimbursement will be ($4,000 − $500) × 0.8 = $2,800. This will leave you with a bill of $5,000 − $2,800 = $2,200. Even if your out-of-pocket cost is greater for the specialist, you may still decide that qualitative factors, such as the surgeon's reputation and experience, outweigh this extra cost.

Dental and Vision Insurance Plans

Medical costs associated with dental and eye care are normally excluded from health insurance policies. Your employer may, however, offer dental expense insurance, vision care insurance, or discount programs that will help you to cover these costs on a pretax basis.

- **Dental expense insurance**   Dental expense insurance, which is primarily available as a group benefit, is very similar to health insurance in that you pay a premium in return for being reimbursed for qualified expenses. You'll normally have to pay deductibles and coinsurance as well, and you will be subject to limits on some procedures, such as root canals and crowns. Most dental plans provide coverage for annual cleanings, X-rays, and checkups without a deductible, but they often cover only 50 percent of other services and place a relatively low limit on annual benefits, sometimes as low as $1,000. Cosmetic dentistry and orthodonture expenses are typically excluded. Thus, if you're considering paying for a contributory plan, you need to determine whether your typical out-of-pocket dental expenses will exceed the policy limit less the annual premium cost. And don't forget human nature—many people skip regular dental checkups even when they've paid for dental insurance simply because they hate going to the dentist.

- **Vision care insurance**   Vision care insurance provides reimbursement or discounts on eye examinations, glasses, and contact lenses. Normally, your regular health insurance will cover care related to diseases of the eye, such as glaucoma or macular degeneration, but not well care. This implies that vision care insurance policies essentially cover an annual expense that you can easily estimate and budget for. Although nearly every person over the age of 40 requires eye correction of some sort, vision insurance is often expensive relative to the benefit received. As with dental expense insurance, you should look carefully at what the plan offers before agreeing to pay for it, particularly in the case of "vision discount plans," which charge a fee in return for special discounts at participating merchant locations. Many consumers have found that the discounts are also available to people who don't participate in the plan, so they've paid the premium for nothing. Furthermore, typically only people who need glasses get vision insurance. This means the insurance company has to charge higher premiums, since almost everyone who signs up needs glasses.

Trends in Plan Type

In 1988, three out of four employment-based health plans were fee-for-service plans. As illustrated in **Figure 9.5**, by 2018 nearly all were managed-care plans. Such a large change in just three decades resulted from the efforts of employers to find lower-cost alternatives for providing health insurance benefits.

FIGURE 9.5   **Distribution of Health Plan Enrollment for Covered Workers by Plan Type, 1988 and 2018**
Once popular fee-for-service plans are disappearing in favor of plans that better control costs.

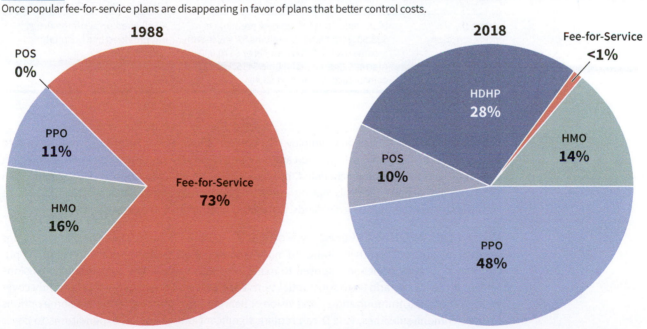

Source: Data from Kaiser Family Foundation, 2018 Employer Health Benefits Survey.

Government-Sponsored Health Insurance Plans

Like other developed countries, the United States has made efforts to protect the health and well-being of its most vulnerable citizens. Government-sponsored and government-subsidized insurance plans are intended to improve the health of the nation and to reduce national health-care expenditures through greater efficiency. There are two major government-sponsored health insurance programs: Medicare, which is for older Americans, and Medicaid, which covers the poor.

The Medicare Program: Health Insurance for Seniors

Medicare is a federally mandated health insurance program for individuals age 65 and over, individuals receiving Social Security disability benefits, and individuals with end-stage renal disease. More than 34 million seniors and 6 million disabled individuals are currently enrolled in the program. The components of the Medicare program, its coverage, and its premium costs are summarized in **Table 9.4**.

Table 9.4	Medicare Program Coverage	
Medicare Program	**Out-of-Pocket Costs in 2019 (Premiums and Deductibles Increase Annually)**	**Coverage**
Part A (Hospital Care)	No premium for those who are fully insured under Social Security. $1,364 hospital deductible plus daily coinsurance after 60 days and for nursing facilities.	Hospital room and board, pre-scription drugs furnished by the hospital, post-hospitalization extended care services for up to 100 days.
Part B (Supplemental Medical Coverage)	Monthly premium $135.50 for enrollees who earn less than $85,000 if single or $170,000 if married, more for higher-income enrollees (maximum 460.50). Rates increase annually with inflation. $185 annual deductible.	Physicians and surgeons, home health services, X-rays, lab test, medical equipment, ambulance service.
Part C (Medicare Advantage)	Insurance plan offered by private insurers that substitutes for Medicare Parts A and B (and sometimes D), usually offered as an HMO, PPO, or high-deductible plan.	Same health care services as Medicare Parts A and B. Most plans also include prescription drug coverage similar to Medi-care Part D. Sometimes also covers vision and dental.
Part D (Prescription Drugs)	Plans differ, but the average premium is $33.50, with higher premiums for those with income over $85,000 if single or $170,000 if married. Annual deductible $415, with 25% coinsurance for the next $3,405.	All allowed prescription drugs not provided in a hospital.

Medicare Taxes While you're employed, a portion of your Social Security payroll tax goes to Medicare (2.9 percent, split between you and your employer). The tax applies to all earned income, such as wages, salaries, and Schedule C business income. In addition, couples earning more than $250,000 per year and individuals making more than $200,000 pay an extra Medicare tax of 3.8 percent on unearned income, including dividends, real estate investments, and capital gains.

What Costs Are Not Covered by Medicare? Although the Medicare program provides a valuable source of health insurance to many who would otherwise be uninsurable in the private market, participants are exposed to many gaps in coverage. The coinsurance provisions and deductibles can add up to substantial sums each year, and the plan doesn't currently cover routine checkups, immunizations, and vision or hearing care. Although there are some options for government subsidies, Part D can require significant out-of-pocket expenditures to cover the deductible and coinsurance; this gap in coverage is often referred to as the "donut hole."

To fill in the gaps in Medicare coverage, many private insurers offer one or more Medicare supplement plans, commonly called **Medigap policies**, for participants in the Part A and B plans. Most of these plans include prescription drug coverage, so you don't have to pay an extra premium for Part D. The *Medicare Supplement Buyers Guide*, available free of charge from sellers of these products, provides detailed information on the various plan types and coverage.

When it's time for you to retire, it's important that you purchase a Medigap policy within six months of enrolling in Medicare Part B, especially if you're in poor health. After the six-month period has passed, your eligibility for Medigap insurance isn't guaranteed. Medicare Advantage plans don't have the same gaps in coverage as the basic Medicare program, so you don't need Medigap insurance if you belong to one of these plans. In fact, it's illegal for an insurer to sell you a Medigap policy under those circumstances.

If you're one of the lucky few, you might be eligible for group Medigap coverage through a former employer. This type of benefit is increasingly rare, and employers have been tightening eligibility requirements (for example, requiring more years of service) and reducing their subsidy of premium costs.

Future Prospects for Medicare   Medicare is currently in financial trouble due to the aging of the U.S. population and rising health-care costs. Without major changes, the system can't survive in its current form because the taxes it takes in are insufficient to cover the expected future benefits. It follows that benefits will have to be reduced and/or taxes and supplemental premiums will have to be increased in the future. What does this mean for your financial plan? As with other areas of your finances, you need to take personal responsibility for ensuring your future welfare. Instead of assuming that the government will take care of all your medical costs in retirement, you should include additional savings targeted to the payment of those future costs in your financial plan.

Medicaid: Health Insurance for the Poor

Medicaid is a federally authorized, state-run program that provides health-care coverage and premium subsidies for low-income families. The federal government funds much of the cost of Medicaid through state block grants, but allows each state to determine eligibility and benefits beyond some minimum requirements. The number of people covered under Medicaid increased substantially after the Affordable Care Act expanded eligibility standards. There are now more than 74 million people covered by this program, about 40 percent of whom are children.

COBRA Continuation Coverage

The Consolidated Omnibus Reconciliation Act of 1986 (COBRA) is a federal law that applies to all employers with 20 employees or more, with the exception of the federal government and religious institutions. Under this law, if you lose or quit your job, you're eligible to purchase coverage through your previous employer's plan for a period of 18 months (extendable under some circumstances to 36 months). To elect this coverage, you must notify your employer no later than 60 days after your last day of work. COBRA continuation coverage may also be used to obtain coverage following divorce, death of the covered worker, or loss of dependent status. If you elect to obtain COBRA coverage, you will be responsible for paying the entire premium, and your former employer can add up to 10 percent for administrative costs, so your health insurance costs most likely will increase substantially.

Divorce or Death   A disproportionate percentage of divorced women, whether employed or not, have inadequate health insurance or are uninsured. This is the case largely because women are more likely to work for employers that offer limited employee benefits. If you participated in a spouse's employment-based health plan before a divorce, you can elect to pay for the COBRA continuation coverage after the divorce (unless your former spouse worked for the federal government, a religious institution, or a firm with fewer than 20 employees). This rule also applies to widows and widowers who previously were covered under their deceased spouse's plan. In some cases, though, this coverage might be more expensive than buying individual insurance. Health insurance continuation should be a factor in divorce settlements, at a minimum requiring continued coverage for the children under the employed parent's plan and fair division of their uninsured medical costs, deductibles, and copays.

Loss of Dependent Status   COBRA also allows continuation coverage under a parent's health insurance plan for a child who is no longer eligible for family coverage. Under provisions of the Affordable Care Act, children can remain on their parents' plan until age 26, even if they are not dependents for tax purposes. Unless the child has health issues, this coverage is likely to be more expensive than individual health insurance.

9.3   Planning for Disability Income

> **LEARNING OBJECTIVE 9.3**
> Analyze your disability income needs, and identify sources of disability income.

A **disability** is an illness or injury that prevents you from earning your regular income or reduces how much you can earn. Most people underestimate their risk of becoming disabled. The fact is that you have a 33 percent chance of being disabled for at least three months during your working life. In any given period, your risk of disability is much higher than your risk of death. Unless you have sufficient financial resources, the loss of income during a period of disability can be financially devastating to your family. You might be unable to work, but you'll still have to meet the expenses of daily living. Understanding your disability income needs and your sources of disability income is therefore an essential component of your financial plan.

There are a variety of insurance programs and policies that provide replacement income during periods of disability, although they can differ in their definition of the degree of disability that triggers coverage. One may define disability as the inability to perform the regular requirements of your current job, for example, while another may define it as the inability to work at any job for which you are reasonably suited by education and experience. In this section, we look at how much disability income you might need and how you can prepare to meet those needs.

Disability Income Needs Analysis

The process of disability income needs analysis includes three steps:

1. Estimate your income needs.
2. Consider existing sources of funds to meet those needs.
3. Determine whether you need any additional disability income protection—for example, if you have an insufficient emergency fund.

What if, for example, you were injured in a car accident and couldn't work for a month or more? How much income per month would you need to meet your basic needs? You can begin to answer this question by referring to your personal cash flow statement, developed in Chapter 2. You could temporarily reduce your cash outflows by cutting out discretionary spending on clothing, gifts, and entertainment. If you were out of work for a very long period, you could consider more drastic cost-saving measures, such as moving in with your parents or selling your car. Once you've estimated the amount of income you would need, you can determine how best to fund these needs.

Sources of Disability Income

In earlier chapters, we discussed the importance of having a household emergency fund sufficient to cover several months of household expenses. Maintaining an emergency fund is an important method of managing the financial risk of disability. This type of fund and additional sources of disability income replacement are listed below:

- Household emergency fund
- Employment income from another member of the household
- Employee paid sick days, personal days, or vacation days
- Income from investments
- Group or individual disability insurance
- Government program benefits, such as state disability insurance, workers' compensation, or Social Security

---

Reflection Question 3

If you experienced a short-term disability and could not work for three months, what sources of income replacement would you have, and which would you use first?

Employer-Sponsored Disability Income Protection

Employers may provide disability income protection in several ways, including personal days, paid vacation time, sick leave, and group short- and long-term disability income insurance. **Disability income insurance** replaces lost income during a period of disability and is available from a number of sources including government, employer, and individual insurance. If you become ill or are injured and expect to be away from your job for more than a few days, you should consult with your employer's benefits department. There are often specific requirements regarding qualification and waiting periods.

- **Short-term disability insurance**   Some employers provide short-term disability (STD) insurance for workers with a qualifying disability. This type of insurance pays a portion (commonly 60 or 70 percent) of your pretax earnings after you've exhausted your sick and personal days and you've been unable to work for a specified waiting period (commonly 15 to 30 days). Although plans differ, these policies usually replace income for 6 to 12 months.

- **Long-term disability income insurance**   Long-term disability (LTD) income insurance is often an optional contributory group benefit under employee benefit plans, although it can also be purchased by individuals directly from an insurer (as discussed below). Even under a group policy, the premiums are usually age-related, so that older employees will pay more per month to participate in the plan. Like short-term disability insurance, long-term disability plans specify the definition of disability under which you qualify for income replacement, the waiting period before you're eligible to receive benefits (often three to six months of continued disability), the percentage of pre-disability income that will be replaced (usually 60 percent), and the length of time benefits will be paid. Many such policies pay benefits to age 65 if the policyholder is permanently disabled. It's advantageous to purchase group disability insurance if your employer offers it because individual insurance will be harder to buy at older ages or as your health condition becomes less favorable.

- **Taxation of disability insurance benefits**   When you purchase disability insurance through your employer, you're usually given the option of paying for it with either after-tax dollars or pretax dollars. Although it's generally preferable to use pretax dollars for other types of benefits, *you should buy disability insurance on an after-tax basis*. If you pay for the insurance with after-tax income and later are disabled, the income benefit you receive while disabled will be tax-free. In contrast, if you use pretax dollars for the insurance premium, you'll have to pay tax on the disability income when you receive it.

Individual Disability Insurance

If you don't have employer-sponsored disability insurance, or if you believe you need additional disability income protection, you can purchase coverage in the individual market. Although there are many variations on individual disability insurance policies, the best types are those that replace lost income if you're unable to perform the duties of your particular job—often called "own occupation" insurance. For example, a musician who has a hand injury could receive replacement income even if he or she could still work in another profession.

Individual disability policies are usually sold based on a dollar amount of income replacement with limits on what percentage of pre-disability income will be replaced. For example, you might buy a policy that will pay you $1,000 per month as long as that doesn't exceed 30 percent of your pre-disability income. Obviously, the more disability income coverage you purchase, the higher your premium will be. Other factors that increase the cost of individual disability income insurance are your profession, your age, and your existing health status.

Key features to look for in disability income insurance policies include the following:

- **Waiting period**   How long do you have to be disabled before you can begin receiving benefits? This period can be anywhere from 30 days to one year.

- **Benefit duration**   How long can you continue to receive benefits, assuming you continue to meet the definition of disability? A policy might pay benefits for a short time, such as two years, or until age 65, or for life. The longer the coverage the higher the premium will be.

- **Income replacement**   How much will the benefit be? Your objective is to meet your expenses, but you need to consider that if your disability continues for a long period of time, these costs might rise with inflation. A cost-of-living increase is therefore a desirable feature.

- **Renewability**   If your health deteriorates, can the insurer drop your disability insurance policy? You should look for policies with a guaranteed renewability feature. Some policies also waive your premium if you are disabled.

- **Treatment of other disability benefits**   Some policies will subtract other disability benefits, such as those received from workers' compensation and Social Security, from your benefit.

Workers' Compensation

All states have laws that make employers financially responsible for employment-related injuries or illnesses, regardless of fault. If you experience a job-related illness or injury, you don't have to sue your employer to recover your costs, and it won't matter if it was your fault you were injured. In fact, many state workers' compensation laws actually limit your right to sue your employer for additional damages, such as pain and suffering.

Most employers purchase **workers' compensation insurance**, either through private insurers or state-run programs, to cover claims associated with job-related illness or injury. In some cases, larger employers can self-insure these costs. Although state laws differ, all provide for payment of medical expenses, rehabilitation costs, lost wages, and specific lump sum benefits for death and dismemberment. However, waiting periods and benefits, such as the percentage of income that will be replaced, can vary substantially from state to state.

Social Security Disability

If your disability is serious enough, you may be eligible for Social Security disability insurance. To qualify for Social Security disability, you must have been out of work at least five months, expect to remain disabled at least one year, and be unable to work at *any job*. Eligibility for Social Security disability benefits also depends on your participation in the Social Security system and your average income over your working career. Payments from other disability insurance plans are usually reduced by any amounts you receive from Social Security.

In 2018, nearly 9 million disabled workers were receiving Social Security disability income and the average monthly benefit was $1,197. In addition, about 2 million disabled spouses, widows/widowers, and children of disabled workers were eligible for supplemental income, which averaged around $350 per month. To see if you're eligible and how much your benefits would be, you can consult your annual Social Security statement or go to **www.ssa.gov** and use the disability income calculator.

Case Study 9.4 illustrates the disability income needs analysis process. In the case, Mateo Rivera, introduced in earlier case studies, uses **Excel Worksheet 9.4** (Personal Financial Planner: Disability Income Needs Analysis) to determine whether he has enough resources to cover his disability income needs.

EXCEL WORKSHEET

See **Excel Worksheet 9.4 (Personal Financial Planner: Disability Income Needs Analysis)** in **WileyPLUS**.

Case Study 9.4

ESB Professional/Shutterstock.com

Mateo Rivera Estimates His Disability Income Needs

Problem

Mateo Rivera wants to be sure that his family's expenses would be covered if he were to become disabled for a period of time. When we considered the Riveras' household budget in Chapter 3 (Case Study 3.2), we saw that they estimated household expenses for the coming year to be approximately $4,800 per month. Mateo thinks that, if necessary, they could temporarily cut expenditures for job-related expenses ($50), savings ($725), and other discretionary spending ($700). His wife Rosa is a stay-at-home mom, so one alternative would be for her to return to work. However, she might not be able to earn enough to cover the additional child-care expenses. Mateo's employee benefit plan includes some paid leave days, as well as short-term and long-term disability insurance. Mateo also has a small individual long-term disability policy. If the family has an emergency fund of $5,000, does Mateo have sufficient disability income protection?

Strategy

Mateo enters all his information into Excel Worksheet 9.4 to estimate his disability income needs. The result is shown in **Figure 9.6**:

FIGURE 9.6   Sample of Excel Worksheet 9.4: Disability Income Needs Analysis

	A	B
1	**Monthly Income and Expenses**	
2	**1. Enter current pretax income**	$5,300
3	**2. Enter current household expenses**	$4,800
4	**3. Subtract any expenses that you can omit during a period**	
5	**disability**	
6	**a. Job-related expenses**	$50
7	**b. Contributions to savings**	$725
8	**c. Extras, such as entertainment, travel, clothing,**	
9	**charity, gifts**	$700
10	**d. Other**	
11	**4. Expected expenses while disabled (#2 – #3)**	$3,325
12	**Sources of Disability Income**	
13	**5. Continuation of employment income**	
14	**a. Unused vacation days**	5
15	**b. Unused personal days**	4
16	**c. Unused sick days**	1
17	**d. Total days before income is needed**	10
18	**6. Sources and amounts of after-tax income**	
19	**a. Spouse's income**	$0
20	**b. Income from investments**	$0
21	**c. Workers compensation**	$0
22	**d. Social Security disability insurance**	$0
23	**e. Short-term disability insurance**	
24	**Waiting period (days)**	30
25	**Replacement of pre-disability income**	70%
26	**Days of income replacement**	120
27	**Monthly income from STD**	$3,710
28	**f. Long-term disability**	
29	**Waiting period (days)**	180
30	**Days without coverage before LTD**	50
31	**Replacement of pre-disability income**	50%
32	**Monthly income from LTD**	$2,650
33	**g. Other monthly disability insurance**	
34	**Waiting period (days)**	180
35	**Income replacement (per month)**	$500
36	**7. Total income for long-term disability**	$3,150
37		
38	**8. Remaining monthly income shortfall (#4 – #7)**	$175

Solution Mateo estimates that, for a limited time, the family could get by on $3,325 per month to cover groceries, housing and auto expenses, utilities, and insurance without making any other major changes in lifestyle. In the event of a long-term disability, they could take more drastic steps, such as downsizing their house and cars, but this would take time. For now, the family needs to be sure its emergency fund is sufficient to cover expenses during gaps in coverage. If Mateo were disabled, his short-term disability policy would pay out from days 30 to 120, and his long-term policy coverage would begin on day 180. This means that, after using his 10 days of paid leave, Mateo would need to fund 20 days before the short-term policy kicked in and 60 days between the coverage periods for the short-term and long-term policies. Even for a relatively short period of disability, the $5,000 emergency fund wouldn't last long. The Riveras need to consider adding to their emergency fund. They have enough for a little more than one month of expenses, whereas the usual recommendation is to have enough for several months.

9.4 Employer-Sponsored Retirement Plans

> **LEARNING OBJECTIVE 9.4**
>
> Explain the benefits of participating in employer-sponsored retirement plans.

Arguably the most important employee benefit is a retirement or pension plan. The number of employer-sponsored retirement plans has increased steadily since Congress passed the Employee Retirement Income Security Act (ERISA) in 1974. About half of all workers are now covered by some type of employer retirement plan, and about 75 percent of households include at least one spouse enrolled in an employer-sponsored plan. Employer plans can differ substantially in generosity, so having one doesn't necessarily mean you'll be on track for retirement. We discuss retirement planning in detail in the next chapter. Here, we explain the tax advantages of employment-based retirement plans and the types that are commonly offered.

Tax Advantages of Qualified Plans

If your employer's plan meets certain requirements, it's said to be a **tax-qualified retirement plan**, which entitles the firm and you to the following tax benefits.

- Contributions to the plan are tax-deductible by your employer in the year in which the contributions are made.
- Your own contributions to the plan are not subject to current federal, state, or local income tax.
- Taxes on contributions, earnings on plan assets, and benefit accruals are deferred until withdrawal of funds at retirement.

As discussed in Chapter 4, tax deferral means that you don't have to pay taxes until some point in the future. For retirement plans, taxes will usually be due in the year the funds are withdrawn during retirement. When tax payments are deferred to the future, the present value of that future cash outflow is less than if the taxes were due in the current year. It's also possible that your income will be subject to a lower marginal tax rate when you receive the funds during retirement.

The powerful effect of tax-deferred contributions and earnings is illustrated by the following example: Suppose you have $100 in pretax income to invest and you put it in a tax-deferred account earning 8 percent per year. After 40 years, your $100 investment, with compound interest, will have grown to $100 × $(1.08)^{40}$, or $2,172. Compare that with the amount you'd have if your contribution and earnings were not tax-deferred but were instead subject to a marginal tax rate of 25 percent. In that case, you'd have only $75 to invest after paying 25 percent tax on the $100 in income. And on each year's interest earnings, you'd have to pay tax of 25 percent, so you'd net a return of only 6 percent on the investment after taxes. The final outcome after 40 years would be $75 × $(1.06)^{40}$ = $771, about one-third as much! Of course, you'd eventually owe taxes on the $2,172 when you withdraw it in retirement, so the net difference wouldn't be quite this large. But, even after taxes, you'd be about twice as well off with the benefit of tax deferral.

Given the tax advantages, you can see why you need to take full advantage of opportunities for tax-deferred investment. If you don't work for an employer that offers a plan, you should consider tax-deferred investment opportunities for private savings, like IRAs, discussed in the next chapter.

There are generally two approaches to employer retirement plans—the employer can make either a *benefit promise* or a *contribution promise*. In the sections below, we compare these two approaches and then describe specific retirement plan types in more detail.

Defined-Benefit versus Defined-Contribution Plans

In a **defined-benefit (DB) plan**, sometimes called a pension plan, the company promises that it will pay you a benefit in retirement determined by a particular formula. In the simplest case, the formula is a lump sum. DB formulas usually are based on the salary you're making when you retire and the number of years you've worked for the firm (commonly called "years of service"). For example, suppose your employer plan promises to pay you a retirement benefit equal to 2 percent of your final salary for each year of service. If you work for that employer for 25 years, your annual benefit will be 50 percent (0.02 × 25) of your final salary.

An important element of a DB plan is that all the financial risk is on your employer. It must invest money today in order to have sufficient funds to pay promised benefits to you in the future. If the stock market slumps immediately before you retire, the employer is still obligated to pay your promised benefit.

As an alternative to a defined-benefit plan, your employer might offer a **defined-contribution (DC) plan**. Under a DC plan, the employer promises to make periodic contributions to your retirement account but makes no promise about the benefit that might result from these contributions. The contribution made by the employer is determined by a formula, often a percentage of salary, such as 3 percent. Alternatively, the contribution may be a specific dollar amount or shares of employer stock, or it may vary with the profitability of the firm, with larger contributions in good years and smaller or no contributions in bad years. The actual benefit you'll receive at retirement will depend on the accumulated value of the account at the retirement date, which in turn depends on the amount of contributions made and the investment returns over time. Depending on the type of plan, investment decisions might be made by the employer, or they might be your responsibility. Either way, the risk of poor investment performance falls on you, the employee.

Recently, some employers have tried to combine the features of these two approaches in what is called a **cash-balance plan**. Here, the employer makes a benefit promise (as in a DB plan), but the actual benefit depends, in part, on the performance of an investment account kept on behalf of the plan participant (as in a DC plan). This type of plan places some of the investment risk on the employee.

Over the last several decades, retirement plan coverage for private-sector workers has remained steady at about 45 percent. As illustrated in **Figure 9.7**, however, the types of plans being offered by employers are increasingly of the defined-contribution type. The percentage of workers covered by defined-benefit plans has declined from 39 percent to 14 percent since 1980.

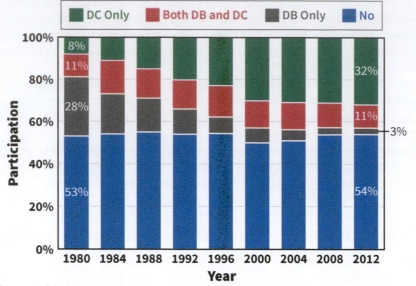

FIGURE 9.7 **Participation in DB and DC Plans as a Percentage of All Private-Sector Workers, 1979–2013** The proportion of workers participating in defined-benefit (DB) plans has been declining, while the proportion participating in defined-contribution (DC) plans has been increasing.

Source: Data from www.ebri.org.

It's easy to see why employers might prefer DC plans, which enable them to shift investment risk and longevity risk to employees. However, employees may also prefer DC plans, in spite of the added risk. DC plans are easier to understand, and employees may like having an account in their name and making their own investment decisions. Some may even think they can achieve better returns than their employer would. In addition, younger employees who do not plan to stay at the same firm very long might prefer to have their contribution dollars in cash or in an account they can more easily take with them to another employer.

Reflection Question 4

Which type of employer plan would you prefer, a DC plan or a DB plan, and why?

Like many other types of employee benefits, a retirement plan may be noncontributory, in which case it is funded entirely by the employer, or contributory, in which case employees are allowed or required to make contributions to the plan. In many DC plans, the employer promises to match employee contributions up to a certain percentage of salary. For example, your employer might offer to contribute 1 percent of salary for every 1 percent contributed by you, up to a 3 percent maximum employer contribution. In that case, if you make no contribution to the plan, the employer will have no obligation to contribute. But if you make contributions equal to 3 percent of your salary, the employer will match your contribution with an additional 3 percent, for a total of 6 percent. *You should always contribute enough to your retirement plan to qualify for a matching contribution from your employer*. A one-to-one match is equivalent to getting a 100 percent return on your investment in the first year.

Features of Defined-Benefit Plans

If your employer offers a defined-benefit plan, there are several of its features that you should understand. These include the benefit formula, vesting rules, portability, normal retirement age, and any insurance incorporated in the plan.

Benefit Formula

As we've already seen, the benefit formula for a DB plan is likely to be based on salary and years of work for that employer. The salary used in the formula might be your final salary, your highest salary, or an average of the salary in three to five of your highest-salary years. The percentage of salary per year of service might be fixed, or it might increase for longer service periods. For example, you might get 0.5 percent per year for the first 10 years and 1 percent for each additional year. You should also consider whether the plan includes a regular cost-of-living adjustment (COLA) to the benefit you receive. Although your initial benefit might be plenty to live on, inflation will gradually make it more difficult to make ends meet. With the exception of plans offered for government workers, most DB plans don't promise specific COLAs.

Vesting Rule

Pension plans have **vesting rules** that determine the number of years of employment required before an employee will have a legal right to accrued retirement benefits. Employees who are fired or leave their jobs without being vested have no right to contributions already made on their behalf and will not receive any retirement benefit from the employer. Your employer's vesting rule must be at least as favorable as one of the following:

- **Five-year cliff vesting**   Under this rule, you have no rights to benefits if you've worked less than five years at the firm. At the five-year mark, you'll be 100 percent vested—fully entitled to the benefits that have accrued in the plan (even though you won't be eligible to receive them until retirement).

- **Three- to seven-year graded vesting**   Under this rule, you'll accrue rights to 20 percent of the accrued benefit for each year of service from three to seven years. For example, if you leave the firm with six years of service, you'll be entitled at retirement to 80 percent of the accrued benefit (20 percent after three years, 40 percent after four years, and so forth).

Portability

Portability refers to the ability to take plan assets from one employer to another. Traditionally, DB plans were never portable, but the trend is toward increased portability. When an employer's plan isn't portable, the employer must keep records of the benefits due vested employees who leave the company before retirement, because these employees have the right to request benefit payments when they reach the eligible retirement age. Many defined-benefit plans have large numbers of unclaimed benefits because former employees have forgotten about small entitlements or failed to file the paperwork necessary to receive the benefits. Contributions that you make yourself are always immediately vested and portable.

Retirement Age

Each plan defines the normal retirement age at which an employee will be entitled to receive full benefits. Because of IRS rules for tax-qualified plans, the minimum is commonly age 59½, but the retirement age in your plan may be higher or lower. In most cases, if you take a disbursement from a retirement plan before age 59½, you'll have to pay a 10 percent penalty to the IRS in addition to any income taxes owed.

Government-Guaranteed Benefits

What happens if your employer has promised you a retirement benefit but then goes out of business before you retire? The Pension Benefit Guarantee Corporation (PBGC), a quasi-governmental organization established under ERISA, guarantees pension benefits to participants in most private DB plans. Thus, if your employer goes bankrupt, you'll still be entitled to vested benefits at retirement. In plans using salary and service formulas, though, the PBGC benefit will be calculated based on your salary and service at the time of termination of the plan rather than at the time of your actual retirement, so the guaranteed benefit may be much less than what you would have received if the plan had not prematurely terminated.

Disability, Survivors, and Retiree Health Insurance

Many DB plans include various types of insurance, such as the following:

- If you become disabled before you're eligible for retirement, you may be entitled to a disability benefit payment, commonly 50 to 70 percent of your retirement benefit.
- If you die before retirement age, your spouse may be eligible to receive a survivor benefit from the plan. Depending on the terms of the plan, he or she might receive a lump-sum distribution or a series of payments.
- Some DB plans, particularly those in the public sector, include a promise of health insurance for retirees up to age 65 (when they qualify for Medicare). Due to increasing health costs, many DB plans have dropped this benefit in recent years.

Features of Defined-Contribution Plans

Under current law, there are several types of DC arrangements, which are subject to different rules and limits. The differences among the types are based on: (1) the type of contribution promise being made by the employer, (2) whether employee contributions are also permitted, (3) who makes investment decisions, and (4) whether participants are employees or self-employed.

What Is Your Employer's Contribution Promise?

Defined-contribution retirement plans include money-purchase plans and profit-sharing plans. In a **money-purchase plan**, the employer promises to contribute a set percentage of salary. For example, your employer might promise to add 3 percent of your salary to a retirement account each year. In a **profit-sharing plan**, the employer's contributions are discretionary but are often a percentage of either profits or salary. As with a money-purchase plan, the employer might pay 3 percent per year into your account, but if profits are down, management can choose to not make a contribution at all.

Can You Contribute to the Plan?

In a **cash-or-deferred arrangement (CODA)**, in addition to your employer's money-purchase or profit-sharing contribution, you can make tax-deferred contributions to the account out of your pretax income. The 401(k) plan, named for the section in the IRS code that outlines the rules for CODAs, is by far the best-known type of defined-contribution plan. A 401(k) might be purely a salary deferral plan, with no employer contribution, or the employer may provide a matching contribution to encourage employee participation. A 403(b) plan—another type of CODA, sometimes called a tax-sheltered annuity (TSA) plan—is similar to a 401(k) plan but is sponsored by a nonprofit organization such as a government entity or religious group. Two relatively recent additions to the menu of DC plan options include Roth 401(k) and Roth 403(b) plans. Similar to Roth IRAs, discussed in Chapter 4, these options require that contributions be made with after-tax dollars, but allow tax-free withdrawals at retirement.

Who Makes the Investment Decisions?

Some DC plans allow participants to specify how they want their account balances invested—for example, the percentage to be placed in risky versus less risky assets. Others may hire professional investment managers or specify the investment allocation. In either case, DC plan participants face much more uncertainty about retirement income than do DB plan participants. If your plan allows investment choice, it's important that you take the time to learn about your investment alternatives so that you can make informed investment allocation decisions.

Stock bonus plans and **employee stock ownership plans (ESOPs)** are special types of profit-sharing plans that invest in stock of the employing company. These types of plans are very popular with larger companies because they can give participants company stock rather than cash to meet contribution promises. One of the most common mistakes that individuals make with their retirement funds is to invest too heavily in their employer's stock when they have other alternatives. While it might seem like a good idea to "invest in what you know," you run the risk of losing your job and your retirement nest egg at the same time if the company fails.

Retirement Plans for Small Businesses

Several types of retirement plans are specifically intended to meet the needs of self-employed individuals and small business owners. These plans include:

- Simplified Employee Pension (SEP) plan
- Savings Incentive Match Plan for Employees of Small Employers (SIMPLE)
- Keogh plan

SEP plans are defined-contribution plans with simplified administrative rules. Employees can contribute through salary deferral, and employers have the option of making matching contributions of up to 3 percent of their salaries. Many small employers like the fact that they are not locked into a particular contribution level. SIMPLE plans allow employees at small businesses (up to 100 employees) to contribute to a retirement account through payroll deductions, with or without employer matches. They are similar to 401(k) plans but have lower limits, as we discuss next. If you have income from self-employment, you can make tax-deferred contributions to a Keogh plan, also known as an HR-10 plan, even if you're participating in a qualified plan through your primary employer. Keogh plans can be set up to cover partners and employees as well.

Limits on Contributions

All qualified retirement plans are subject to maximum contribution limits for the employer and the employee. Under the Economic Growth and Tax Relief Reconciliation Act of 2001, the maximum tax-deductible employer contribution is 25 percent of compensation, applicable to both DB and DC plans. The limit on your own tax-deferred contributions to DC plans is $19,000 in 2019, increasing annually with inflation in increments of $500. If you're age 50 or over, a catch-up provision in the law allows you to contribute an additional $6,000 in 2019. This maximum is applied to the total of all contributions you make to tax-deferred arrangements in a given year, even if the contributions are made to several different plans.

The 2019 SEP and Keogh limit is the lesser of $56,000 or 25 percent of compensation. The SIMPLE limit on employee contributions is $13,000 in 2019 (increasing with inflation in increments of $500) through payroll deductions (plus $3,000 catch-up for individuals age 50 or over).

Summary

Learning Objectives Review

LEARNING OBJECTIVE 9.1 **Explain the value of employee benefits as a component of compensation.**

Compensation packages often include valuable employee benefits in addition to cash compensation.

- Employee benefits might be tangible, such as various types of insurance and retirement contributions, or intangible, such as flexible hours and a pleasant working environment. In choosing among employment opportunities, you should consider the total value of all components of compensation.

- In some cases, employers offer a **cafeteria plan** that allows you to choose from a menu of benefit options.

- With a **contributory plan**, you'll have to pay for some of the benefits out of your earnings.

- In general, benefits are preferable to equivalent cash compensation because you can buy benefits with pretax dollars and because

group insurance has lower costs for **group underwriting** and administration.

- The tax savings from pretax employee benefits can be calculated using **Equation 9.1**:

Tax savings from pretax employee benefits

$$= \frac{\text{Benefit cost}}{1 - \text{Marginal tax rate}} - \text{Benefit cost}$$

- **Flexible spending accounts (FSAs)** and **health savings accounts (HSAs)** allow you to pay for healthcare costs with pretax dollars.

- When considering competing job offers, you can use **Equation 9.2** to compare the cost of living in different locations:

$$\text{Equivalent salary in City 1} = \frac{\text{COLI}_1}{\text{COLI}_2} \times \text{Salary in City 2}$$

where COLI_1 is the cost-of-living index for City 1 and COLI_2 is the cost-of-living index for City 2.

- In deciding between job offers, you should complete a comparison worksheet that includes not only the salaries offered, adjusted for cost-of-living differences, but also the value of the benefits provided.

LEARNING OBJECTIVE 9.2 Evaluate your health-related costs, and select appropriate health insurance to meet your needs.

Whether you participate in an employer plan or purchase individual insurance, health insurance is an important component of your financial plan because illnesses and injuries can place a tremendous financial burden on your family. In evaluating your expected health-care costs, you should consider your life circumstances as well as national trends in health-care costs. Your plan should include strategies for funding these costs and minimizing future out-of-pocket expenditures.

- Health-care reform is increasing the availability of insurance to those who might previously have been uninsured or uninsurable. Although some changes have been made since it was first adopted, key elements of the Affordable Care Act (ObamaCare) included individual and employer mandates, development of online exchanges where consumers can shop for health insurance, and expansion of Medicaid. In addition, children under the age of 26 can remain on their parents' plans.

- Two major approaches to health insurance are **fee-for-service plans** and **managed-care plans**. **High-deductible health plans (HDHPs)** encourage participants to reduce claims costs and are therefore increasingly popular choices for employers. Although all types of plans include mechanisms for paying medical service providers, they differ in what services they cover, whether you have a choice of service providers, and how much you'll pay out of pocket in premiums, deductibles, **coinsurance**, and **copays**.

- Fee-for-service plans include **basic health-care insurance** and **major medical insurance**.

- Examples of managed-care plans include **health maintenance organizations (HMOs)**, **preferred provider organizations (PPOs),** and **point-of-service (POS) plans**.

- Other types of health insurance that may be available through an employer include dental expense insurance and vision care insurance.

- **Medicare** and **Medicaid** are two government-sponsored health insurance plans for people over 65 and low-income people, respectively. Medicare beneficiaries commonly purchase **Medigap policies** to cover the expenses that are not covered under the basic Medicare program.

LEARNING OBJECTIVE 9.3 Analyze your disability income needs, and identify sources of disability income.

Your financial plan should include strategies for dealing with the financial difficulties you'd face in the event that a **disability** limits your capacity to earn your regular income. In calculating your disability income needs, you should consider the minimum amount of income necessary to pay your expenses while disabled. Sources of disability income include the following:

- Household emergency fund

- Employment income from another member of the household

- Paid sick days, personal days, or vacation days

- Income from investments

- Group or individual **disability income insurance**

- Government program benefits, such as **workers' compensation**, in the case of work-related injury or illness, or Social Security

---

LEARNING OBJECTIVE 9.4 Explain the benefits of participating in employer-sponsored retirement plans.

The financial benefits of tax deferral make employer retirement plans an important component of your financial plan. Subject to certain limits, participants in a **tax-qualified retirement plan** can receive employer contributions and make their own contributions on a pretax basis, and they can earn investment returns on plan assets without owing current taxes.

- The two general types of retirement plans are **defined-benefit (DB) plans**, in which the employer promises the employee a benefit at retirement, usually based on a formula that incorporates salary and years of employment, and **defined-contribution (DC) plans**, in which regular contributions are made to an investment account. **Cash-balance plans** combine features of both DC and DB plans.

- In the last several decades, the percentage of workers covered by traditional DB plans has declined and the percentage in DC plans has increased.

- Important features of DB plans include the benefit formula, **vesting rules**, **portability**, age requirements, government guarantees, and insurance benefits.

- A DC plan can be a **money-purchase plan**, a **profit-sharing plan**, a **cash-or-deferred arrangement (CODA)**, or an **employee stock ownership plan (ESOP)**. Important features of DC plans include the type of contribution promised, whether employees can make contributions to the plan, and how the funds in the account can be invested. The most common type of CODA is a 401(k) plan, which allows employees to make tax-deferred contributions to the account.

- Tax laws place limits on the amounts that employers and employees can contribute to the various types of plans on a tax-deferred basis.

Excel Worksheets

9.1 Personal Financial Planner: Tax Savings from Pretax Employee Benefits

9.2 Personal Financial Planner: City Cost-of-Living Comparison

9.3 Personal Financial Planner: Job Comparison Worksheet

9.4 Personal Financial Planner: Disability Income Needs Analysis

Key Terms

basic health-care insurance   9-14
cafeteria plan   9-3
cash-balance plan   9-25
cash-or-deferred arrangement
   (CODA)   9-28
coinsurance   9-15
contributory plan   9-3
copay   9-15
defined-benefit (DB) plan   9-25
defined-contribution (DC) plan   9-25
disability   9-20

disability income insurance   9-21
employee stock ownership plan (ESOP)   9-28
fee-for-service plan   9-14
flexible spending account (FSA)   9-7
group insurance   9-4
group underwriting   9-4
health maintenance organization (HMO)   9-15
health savings account (HSA)   9-7
high-deductible health plan (HDHP)   9-15
major medical insurance   9-14
managed-care plan   9-14

Medicaid   9-19
Medicare   9-18
Medigap policy   9-19
money-purchase plan   9-28
point-of-service (POS) plan   9-15
portability   9-27
preferred provider organization (PPO)   9-15
profit-sharing plan   9-28
tax-qualified retirement plan   9-24
vesting rules   9-27
workers' compensation insurance   9-22

WileyPLUS

Practice Questions to check your understanding, Peer-to-Peer Videos, Interactives, and many other resources are available in WileyPLUS.

Concept Review Questions

1. Explain why it's important to consider all of the components of compensation, not just salary, when evaluating a job offer.

2. What is the difference between a contributory employee benefit plan and a noncontributory plan? Which would you prefer, and why?

3. Explain why it's often better to receive group insurance through your employer than to receive equivalent cash compensation out of which you must purchase the insurance on your own.

4. What are the national trends in health-care costs and insurance coverage, and what are some explanations for these trends?

5. What were the key features of the Affordable Care Act ("ObamaCare") and which components have been repealed? What was the purpose of this law?

6. Identify several ways you can reduce your expected future out-of-pocket costs for health insurance.

7. Which type of health insurance plan would you prefer, fee-for-service or managed care? Why?

8. What are the different ways to cover disability income needs?

9. What are the key features of disability income insurance? Explain each. Why is it important to consider the definition of disability in the policy?

10. Under what circumstances does Social Security provide disability income replacement?

11. What is the difference between a defined-benefit plan and a defined-contribution plan?

12. Which type of retirement plan places more risk on the employee? What kind of risk?

13. What are the tax advantages of a qualified retirement plan?

14. If your employer offers to match your 401(k) contributions up to 3 percent of your salary, why is it important to contribute enough to get the maximum match amount?

15. Why is it important to pay disability insurance premiums on an after-tax basis instead of a pretax basis?

Application Problems

1. Job A pays a salary of $40,000, and Job B pays a salary of $35,000. The cost of living in the Job A area is 102 percent of the national average, and the cost of living in the Job B area is 88 percent of the national average. If all other factors are equal, which of the two salary offers is better? Explain your reasoning.

2. Job A pays a salary of $40,000, and the firm will contribute 5 percent of your salary to a retirement plan. Job B pays a salary of $42,000, and the firm doesn't offer a retirement plan. They are both located in the same area. If all other factors are equal, which job opportunity is better? Explain your reasoning.

3. Job A pays a salary of $50,000 but does not provide health insurance. You can buy health insurance on your own for $5,000 per year. Job B pays a salary of $44,000 with fully paid health insurance. Your marginal tax rate is 20 percent. If all other factors are equal, which compensation package is better? Explain your reasoning.

4. Your health insurance requires payment of an annual deductible of $500 per person or $1,000 per family. After meeting the deductible, you must pay 20 percent of covered charges until you reach $5,000 out of pocket, after which the insurer will pay 100 percent of the costs. Assume that your family has had no other claims during the year and that your child requires emergency surgery. If the total covered charges for the surgery are $20,000, all incurred in the same plan year, how much will you end up paying out of pocket?

5. Your employer offers two health plan choices and requires that employees pay part of the premium cost. The fee-for-service option will cost you $100 per month for single coverage, does not cover preventive care, and imposes a $300-per-person annual deductible and 20 percent coinsurance to a limit of $2,000. The fee-for-service plan also covers prescription drugs after a copay of $30 per prescription. The managed care option (an HMO) will cost you $200 per month, covers all medical services (including preventive care and prescription drugs), and requires a $10 copay for each office visit or prescription.

  a. Over the course of a year, if you have an annual physical ($200), visit the doctor twice for illness ($50 per visit), and incur prescription drug costs of $500 (10 prescriptions at $50 each), how much would your out-of-pocket expenses be under both the fee-for-service plan and the managed-care option?

  b. Over the course of a year, if you have an annual physical, surgery for a skiing injury ($3,000 covered charges), and prescription drug costs of $200 (four prescriptions at $50 each), how much would your out-of-pocket expenses be under both the fee-for-service plan and the managed care option?

  c. What factors would you consider when choosing between the fee-for-service plan and the HMO plan?

6. Your employer offers a defined-benefit plan with the following formula: 1 percent of final salary for each of the first 15 years of service, 1.5 percent of final salary for each of the next 15 years of service, and 2 percent of salary for each of the next 20 years of service.

  a. If you work for the firm for your entire 45-year career and your final salary is $100,000, how much will you receive annually as a benefit?

  b. If you work for the firm for only five years, but are fully vested, how much benefit will you be entitled to receive at retirement, assuming that your final salary at the company is $40,000?

  c. If you work for the firm for only five years, but the firm has three- to seven-year graded vesting, how much benefit will you be entitled to receive at retirement, assuming that your final salary at the company is $40,000?

7. You've been laid off by your employer where you had been participating in a contributory health-care plan. Your share of the premiums, $200 per month, was 50 percent of the actual cost to the employer.

  a. Under what circumstances should you consider getting COBRA continuation coverage through your employer's plan, and how soon do you need to decide?

  b. If you opt for COBRA continuation coverage and your employer adds a 2 percent administrative charge, how much will you have to pay per month for the coverage?

  c. What alternative sources of health-care coverage do you have, and are they likely to be more or less expensive?

8. You are offered a job in Urban City that will pay $50,000 per year. You currently have a comparable job with comparable benefits in Rural Town, but it pays only $40,000. If the cost of living for Urban City is 105 percent of the national average and the cost of living in Rural Town is 85 percent of the national average, which job will give you more purchasing power?

9. Allison currently earns $3,000 per month and takes home $2,300. Her monthly expenses total $2,000. Her employer provides 5 sick days per year and a short-term disability policy that will pay benefits after 30 days of disability. The policy will pay 60 percent of her gross income for up to 12 months. The disability income payments aren't taxable because she used after-tax dollars to pay the premiums.

  a. If Allison wants to have sufficient liquid assets to cover the short-term disability needs that aren't met by her employer's plan, how much should she set aside for this purpose, assuming she might be disabled for a period of one year?

  b. If Allison is considering purchasing long-term disability insurance to cover a disability that lasts for more than 12 months, and assuming that she wouldn't qualify for Social Security disability, what would the monthly benefit need to be, assuming that she will pay the premiums with after-tax dollars?

Case Applications

1. Anna Trebuca, age 40, has just accepted a job as a legal secretary in a large law office. The law firm has a cafeteria plan and gives each employee $4,000 in pre tax dollars to spend on a menu of benefit options. Any dollars that are not spent can be received as cash compensation. Anna has the following options to choose from:

Benefits	Monthly Premiums
Health plan A: Fee-for-service (FFS) plan including basic and major medical; $250 annual deductible and 20 percent coinsurance; $5,000 maximum out-of-pocket; and no lifetime limit.	Employee only: $150 per month Employee + 1: $200 per month
Health plan B: Preferred provider organization (PPO) covering most services from in-network providers at 100 percent after a $100 deductible; out-of-network providers require a 25 percent copay.	Employee only: $200 per month Employee + 1: $300 per month
Dental insurance: Pays 100 percent of checkups and cleaning; 50 percent of additional services up to a maximum annual benefit of $1,000.	Employee only: $40 per month Employee + 1: $60 per month
Long-term disability insurance: Pays 60 percent of pre-disability income for up to two years if unable to perform the duties of current job; 12-month waiting period.	$15 per month

a. If Anna is single and childless and has no other group health insurance available, explain why she should participate in one of the health plans, even if she could find individual insurance for a slightly lower premium.

b. What factors should Anna consider in deciding between the fee-for-service and the PPO plans?

c. Which health plan would result in a lower total out-of-pocket expense for the year if Anna incurred $10,000 in medical expenses for a surgical procedure, assuming that she used a participating provider? Explain.

d. If Anna is married and her husband's employer provides a health insurance plan at a lower out-of-pocket premium cost, what should Anna consider when allocating her benefit dollars?

e. Is the dental insurance a good deal if Anna normally incurs very low dental costs each year ($150 for checkup and cleaning)? How much would her dental costs have to total for her to break even on the cost of the dental insurance?

2. Juan Morales is a single father and is worried about what would happen to his family finances if he were to become disabled. His total household expenses are $3,000 per month, although he estimates that, in a pinch, they could be cut to $2,200 per month. Juan currently earns $4,000 per month before taxes at his job as a retail store manager. His employer provides 5 sick days per year, 10 days of paid annual leave, and a short-term disability policy (purchased with after-tax dollars) that, after 30 days of continuous disability, will pay 55 percent of pre-disability gross income for 12 months. He is wondering whether he should also buy long-term disability income insurance through his employer's group plan

(after 12 months of continuous disability, the plan pays 60 percent of pre-disability gross income for up to 5 years of continued disability).

a. What are Juan's short-term disability income needs?

b. Suppose Juan can't work due to an injury at home. If he hasn't yet used any of the current year's paid leave or sick days when he became injured, how long will he continue to receive income, and how much will he get? If Juan is disabled for 12 months, does he have sufficient disability income protection? Explain why or why not.

c. Explain why Juan should look carefully at the definition of disability in both the short-term and long-term insurance policies.

d. If Juan permanently injures his back and is no longer able to perform the duties of his current job, will he be eligible for Social Security disability income? Why or why not?

e. Suppose Juan estimates that he would be eligible for a Social Security disability benefit of $500 per month. How should he incorporate this in his long-term disability planning?

3. Clare Deluna is in her last semester at a major public university, where she is completing a double major in finance and construction management. Her hard work has paid off, and she has been offered two jobs at different civil engineering firms. Matheson, Inc., a Denver-based firm, has offered her a $40,000 starting salary with an expected annual bonus of $5,000. Brandis Construction, a Seattle-based firm, will pay a starting salary of $48,000 but doesn't give annual bonuses. The firms have also provided Clare with some information about their company benefit packages, which include 401(k) defined-contribution retirement plans and health insurance. The major differences between the two benefit packages are as follows:

- Matheson pays the full cost of employee-only or family health insurance, whereas Brandis pays $200 per month toward the total cost of employee-only health insurance (currently $240 per month for single coverage, $420 for employee plus one, and $600 for a family).

- Matheson matches employee contributions to the 401(k) in cash, up to 3 percent of salary, while Brandis matches employee contributions to the 401(k) in company stock, up to 3 percent of salary.

a. Compare the two salary offers, assuming that the Denver cost of living is 105 percent of the national average and the Seattle cost of living is 110 percent of the national average. How should Clare take the bonus offered at Matheson into account?

b. Are the retirement plan benefits at the two employers comparable? Why or why not?

c. Complete a comparison table or worksheet to help Clare decide between these two offers, and explain your observations.

d. How would Clare's decision change if she needed family health insurance coverage—for example, if she were a single parent?

CHAPTER 10

Saving for Distant Goals: Retirement and Education Funding

Anna Swanson Herring, 1926, reprinted by permission from her granddaughter Vickie Herring Bajtelsmit

Feature Story

In this chapter, we consider the two biggest-ticket items of your financial plan: retirement and education funding. As you learned in the last chapter, some types of employers provide pretty generous retirement plans. If you're lucky enough to work for this type of firm, you might find that retirement planning is fairly easy.

As an example, consider the story of Anna Swanson. She was born in 1902 in Sweden, but faced with few prospects at home, left her family and friends behind in 1920 to make a new life for herself in the United States. Ultimately, she married and settled in Northern Virginia, where she went to work for the U.S. Census Bureau in 1935. Like many others in her generation, she worked for the same employer until she retired. As a federal civil servant with only a high school education, Anna was never paid a stellar salary. In fact, her gross income in 1960, when she retired at age 58, was only $7,000. After putting her son through college on her own, she had very little retirement savings, but she was eligible for an annual pension benefit of $3,500 (when adjusted for inflation, equivalent to about $30,000 in 2019). The pension automatically increased with inflation every year, so by the time Anna died in 1999, she was receiving approximately $18,000 per year. Anna enjoyed good enough health to live independently until the year before she died, and she loved to tell her family and friends what a wonderful deal she'd gotten from the federal government. She worked for only 25 years and received a pension for 40 years. She certainly got her money's worth!

Anna's story illustrates an important concept about retirement planning—you need a plan that will last your *whole life*, no matter how long that might turn out to be. Without her pension, Anna would have ended up like so many older women—dependent on financial support from family or public assistance.

Many people also discover that it's difficult to pay for their children's or their own college expenses while building up their own retirement savings at the same time. Although workers like Anna in previous generations often had access to defined-benefit pensions, you know from the previous chapter that these types of plans are no longer very common. In this chapter, you'll develop strategies for accomplishing long-term goals related to retirement and education.

LEARNING OBJECTIVES	TOPICS	DEMONSTRATION PROBLEMS
10.1 Estimate your retirement income needs, and develop savings goals.	**10.1 Developing a Retirement Plan** • What Are Your Retirement Goals? • How Much Will You Need to Save for Retirement? • Why Do So Many People Avoid Retirement Planning?	**10.1** Estimating Total Retirement Wealth Needed
10.2 Explain how employer-sponsored retirement plans and Social Security can help you meet your retirement goals.	**10.2 Retirement Income from Employer Plans and Social Security** • Income from Employer-Sponsored Plans • Income from Social Security	
10.3 Explain why individual retirement accounts (IRAs) offer advantages over taxable savings accounts and annuities.	**10.3 Individual Retirement Savings Alternatives** • Individual Retirement Accounts • Taxable Accounts • Annuities • Not on Track to Retire?	
10.4 Develop a plan for funding current or future education costs.	**10.4 Planning for Education Costs** • How Much Will Future Education Cost? • How Much Will You Need to Save? • Financing Higher Education with Student Loans • Government Programs to Help Fund Education Expenses	**10.2** Student Loan Costs After Graduation

10.1 Developing a Retirement Plan

LEARNING OBJECTIVE 10.1

Estimate your retirement income needs, and develop savings goals.

For most college students, retirement undoubtedly seems pretty far off in the future. After all, how can you think about retirement when you haven't even started your career? Similarly, if you're in the middle of funding your own education, your future children's education is unlikely to be on your immediate list of priorities. Nevertheless, retirement and education funding are likely to cost you a *lot* of money in the future, so it's important for you to begin planning for these goals as early as possible.

Figure 10.1 illustrates the planning process we use for both retirement and education funding. As with other goals we've considered, you'll identify your needs, develop goals, decide on the most appropriate strategies to meet your goals, implement your plan, and reevaluate on a regular basis. In the first few parts of this chapter, we focus on this process as it relates to retirement planning. In the last section, we consider education funding.

FIGURE 10.1 **Retirement and Education Planning Process** Careful planning for retirement and education funding will enable you to achieve your goals for those components of your financial plan.

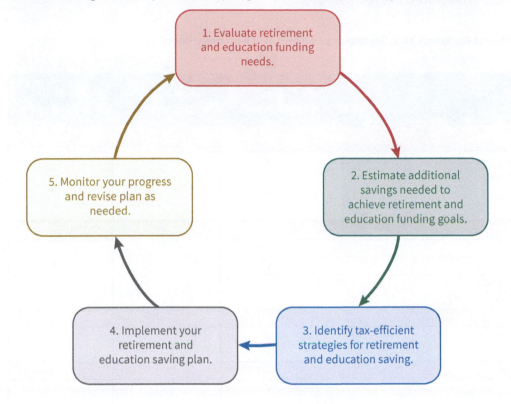

What Are Your Retirement Goals?

One person's ideal retirement isn't the same as another's. If you want to retire young enough (and wealthy enough) to travel to exotic places around the world, you'll need to sacrifice some current spending to achieve your retirement goals. But if you'll be content with having a lower standard of living in retirement, you won't have to save as much to accomplish your retirement goals.

When do you plan to retire? Obviously, the younger you retire, the longer your retirement period and the shorter the time you have to accumulate the wealth necessary to support yourself during your retirement. When surveyed, most people say they want to retire "early," which usually means in their middle to late 50s. Given increasing longevity, this is extremely optimistic, and many people have to revise their expectations as they approach their target retirement age. Although the average age of retirement has declined slightly over time, particularly for men, the most common retirement age is still age 65, the age of eligibility for Medicare. The normal Social Security retirement age is gradually being increased to 67, so it's likely that more people will delay retirement to that age in the future. Nevertheless, it's not a bad idea to have an optimistic target date if this means you'll be more aggressive about saving to achieve that goal.

Do you have any idea how much money you need to save for retirement? Many people aren't sure of the answer to this question, and this uncertainty affects their confidence about when they'll be ready to retire. Take a few minutes to answer the retirement confidence survey questions in **Interactive: Retirement Confidence**. It might be interesting for you to revisit these questions after you've had a chance to learn more about retirement planning in this chapter.

INTERACTIVE

See Interactive: Retirement Confidence in WileyPLUS.

EXCEL WORKSHEET

See **Excel Worksheet 10.1** (Personal Financial Planner: Developing and Prioritizing Retirement Goals) in **WileyPLUS.**

Before you can determine how much money you'll need in retirement, you have to develop and prioritize your retirement goals. To do so, create a list such as that in **Excel Worksheet 10.1** (Personal Financial Planner: Developing and Prioritizing Retirement Goals). **Figure 10.2** shows a sample list. For each item, indicate whether it's very important to you, somewhat important, or not important at all. If you have any additional goals, add them to the list. Keep in mind that your goals and priorities will likely change between now and your retirement date, so this is a step in the process that you must revisit.

FIGURE 10.2   Sample of Excel Worksheet 10.1: Developing and Prioritizing Retirement Goals

	A	B	C	D
1	**Retirement Goal**	**Very Important**	**Somewhat Important**	**Not at All Important**
2	Economic Security			
3	Maintain standard of living	✓		
4	Improve standard of living			✓
5	Financial independence	✓		
6	Afford to keep home		✓	
7	Family			
8	Bequests to heirs			✓
9	College costs for kids	✓		
10	Support children or parents		✓	
11	Continue family business			
12	Health			
13	Cover health-care costs	✓		
14	Cover long-term care costs	✓		
15	Extras			
16	Vacations	✓		
17	Hobbies	✓		
18	Charitable giving		✓	

Unless you're independently wealthy or expect to receive a large inheritance prior to retirement, you're not likely to achieve your goals unless you take steps today to accumulate sufficient wealth in time for retirement. Unfortunately, most households have unrealistic expectations about the retirement they can afford, given their current savings patterns. Recent studies on the adequacy of retirement funding conclude that both the Millennial and the Baby Boom generations are saving at about one-third the rate necessary to meet their retirement goals. Unless they increase their savings rates substantially, they will find themselves delaying their retirement date, relying on their children, or having a much lower standard of living in retirement.

Once you've established some goals for the kind of retirement you'd like to have, the next step is to estimate how much it will cost you. This isn't a particularly easy task because there are so many factors to consider. As a result, many people simply omit this step in their retirement planning. That's a mistake, though, and is likely to lead to poor planning and insufficient saving. If you don't know how much you'll need, how will you know if you're saving enough to get there?

In the next section, you'll learn how to set savings goals that will allow you to achieve your retirement goals. If you consult with a financial planner, he or she will help you with this process, but it doesn't hurt to know how to do it yourself.

How Much Will You Need to Save for Retirement?

The basic steps in estimating how much you'll need to save for retirement are listed below. After we discuss the steps, we apply them in a case study.

- Step 1: Estimate retirement expenses.
- Step 2: Estimate expected income from employer defined-benefit pension plan(s).
- Step 3: Estimate expected income from Social Security.
- Step 4: Calculate income shortfall for the first year of retirement.
- Step 5: Use time value of money calculations to estimate the total retirement wealth you'll need to have saved by the time you retire to cover your income shortfall.
- Step 6: Estimate the future value of any current retirement savings you have accumulated, and subtract that amount from total wealth needed to determine how much additional wealth you need to accumulate.
- Step 7: Estimate monthly savings required to meet the wealth accumulation goal.

Step 1: Estimating Retirement Expenses

The first step in figuring out how much you'll need to save is to estimate your future retirement expenses. The two methods most commonly used are the replacement ratio method and the adjusted expense method.

Replacement Ratio Method   The **replacement ratio method** assumes that your retirement expenses will be some fixed proportion of your preretirement expenses, often 70 to 80 percent. For example, suppose you've estimated that your current household expenses are $40,000 per year. If you assume that your expenses after retirement will be 70 percent of current expenses, the replacement ratio method will yield an estimate of $28,000 in today's dollars. You can then apply an average inflation rate to estimate what your expenses would be in future dollars. Although this simplified method is commonly used, your expenses may actually be lower or higher in retirement.

Adjusted Expense Method   The **adjusted expense method** for estimating retirement expenses will take a little more time but will result in a more accurate forecast. Here, you take your current expenses by category and adjust each one based on your estimates of changes that will occur in retirement. For example, if you expect to have a lower mortgage payment in the future (if you downsize or pay off your mortgage prior to retirement, for instance), you will adjust the mortgage expense amount accordingly. If you expect your health-care costs to be higher, you will add the additional cost to your forecast. You should use the goals that you developed earlier to help you identify the necessary adjustments. Keep in mind that you're doing this estimate in today's dollars, so if it would cost you $5,000 a year for a golf club membership today, that's the figure you'll use.

Adjusting for Inflation   Once you've estimated your expenses in current dollars by either of the methods above, you need to adjust this amount for expected inflation between now and retirement to determine your expenses for the first year of retirement. To do this, you'll use the time value of money formula to calculate the future value of a lump sum: $FV = PV \times (1 + i)^n$. The present value (PV) is your annual expenses in today's dollars, and you'll solve for the future value (FV). The future value is your estimate of what your expenses will be when you retire n years in the future compounded at the estimated rate of inflation (i). Although the rate of inflation has been lower in recent years, you can use 3 percent as a reasonable long-run average.

Let's assume that you've estimated your retirement expenses at $28,000 in today's dollars, you expect to retire in 40 years, and you expect inflation to average 3 percent over that time period. Substituting these values into the future value equation, your income requirement for the first year of retirement will be $28,000 \times (1.03)^{40} = \$91,337$. This means that, 40 years from now, you'll need $91,337 to have spending power equivalent to $28,000 today.

How much difference will it make if inflation over the next 40 years is more or less than what you've estimated? The short answer is—*a lot*. If, for example, inflation averages 4 percent instead of 3 percent, the future value of your expenses is $134,429, about 47 percent more than the first estimate. This is why it's so important to take inflation into account.

Adjusting for Income Taxes Some or all of your income in retirement may be subject to federal and state income taxes. We can't predict how the tax code will change in the future, but it's essential to consider the effect of taxes as best you can. Because the expenses you've estimated in the previous section will be paid primarily from after-tax dollars and most of your retirement income will be taxable if you've taken advantage of tax-deferred savings plans, you need to determine the before-tax income that will be necessary to meet these expenses. This is easily calculated using **Equation 10.1**:

$$\text{Pretax income} = \frac{\text{After-tax income}}{1 - t} \tag{10.1}$$

where t is the expected average tax rate.

Thus, if you need \$91,337 in after-tax income to meet your first year's retirement expenses, and you estimate that you'll pay 25 percent in taxes, then you'll need \$121,783 [\$91,337/ (1 − 0.25)] in pretax income. The higher your marginal tax rate in retirement, the more pretax retirement income you'll need to have.

Steps 2, 3 and 4: Estimating Expected Income and Income Shortfall

Once you know how much income you'll need in total, the next step is to subtract any income you know you'll receive from other sources to arrive at your retirement income shortfall. This step requires that you estimate retirement income you'll receive from employer defined-benefit (DB) pension plans and Social Security.

If your employer has set up a DB pension plan, you'll receive information about the plan from your employer at least annually. These reports will include an estimate of the benefit you're likely to receive from the plan under current assumptions. As you learned in the last chapter, the likelihood of having a DB plan is fairly low, but it might be your primary source of retirement income if you work in the public sector. Although we'll discuss Social Security benefits in more detail later in the chapter, an easy way to estimate your benefit is use the "Quick Calculator" on the Social Security Administration website (**www.ssa.gov**). **Online Calculator Demonstration Video: Estimating Social Security Benefits** shows you how to do this.

ONLINE CALCULATOR DEMONSTRATION VIDEO

See **Online Calculator Demonstration Video: Estimating Social Security Benefits** in **WileyPLUS**.

Once you have estimated your Social Security and DB plan benefits, you can subtract the total estimated benefits from your before-tax retirement income needed to arrive at the retirement income shortfall, as follows:

> Before-tax income needed in first year of retirement
>
> Minus: Expected income from employer DB plans
>
> Minus: Expected Social Security benefit
> ———————————————————————————————
> Equals: Retirement income shortfall in first year of retirement

Continuing the earlier example, suppose that you expect Social Security to pay you a benefit of \$3,000 per month, or \$36,000 per year and you anticipate receiving an annual benefit of \$30,446 from your DB plan. In this case, your retirement income shortfall in the first year of retirement will be \$55,337 (\$121,783 − \$36,000 − \$30,446).

Step 5: Estimating Retirement Wealth Needed

The next step is to figure out how much wealth would be sufficient to generate \$55,337 per year in pretax income. This might seem like a fairly straightforward present value of an annuity problem, but it's actually a bit more complicated, for two reasons:

- **Inflation** To maintain your standard of living, you'll have to spend a little more each year. The amount \$55,337 will be sufficient for the first year of retirement, but the purchasing power of this amount will gradually decline over your retirement years.

- **Risk of living long**   The number of years you'll live in retirement is uncertain. If you use the average expected life span to estimate the number of years for which you'll need retirement income, you have a 50 percent chance of outliving your assets.

There are two approaches you can use to estimate the total retirement wealth you'll need. In the first approach, you estimate an amount of wealth that would allow you to meet your income needs using only the interest earnings on your investments, thus preserving the principal. The lump sum you would need at retirement under this approach can be estimated using **Equation 10.2**:

$$\text{Wealth necessary to generate constant income without depleting principal} = \frac{\text{Income}}{r} \quad (10.2)$$

where r is the investment rate of return.

The advantages of this approach are that you won't outlive your assets and, upon your death, you'll have the remaining principal to pass on to your heirs. The disadvantage is that your savings will produce less current income than if you were willing to deplete the principal over time.

A variation of this method in which you still keep the principal intact but can increase the amount you withdraw each year for inflation is given by **Equation 10.3**. You'll need to save quite a bit more to accomplish this outcome.

$$\text{Wealth necessary to generate inflation-adjusted income without depleting principal} = \frac{\text{First-year income}}{r - i} \quad (10.3)$$

where i is the inflation rate.

Alternatively, you might want to have your income increase with inflation but be willing to spend down your principal over time to accomplish this objective. This strategy is called an **inflation-adjusted annuity**. You can calculate the required amount of wealth for a given starting income using **Equation 10.4**:

$$\text{Present value of an inflation-adjusted annuity} = \frac{\text{First-year income}}{r - i} \times \left[1 - \left(\frac{1 + i}{1 + r} \right)^{n} \right] \quad (10.4)$$

where n is the number of years in retirement. As a shortcut to this calculation, you can multiply the income shortfall by the appropriate factor from **Table 10.1**, given your expected return on

TABLE 10.1   **Retirement Wealth Factors for Estimating Retirement Savings Goal, Assuming 4 Percent Inflation**

To calculate your retirement savings goal, multiply your retirement income shortfall by the "retirement wealth factor" from the table, given your estimated years in retirement and expected annual investment return.

	Retirement Wealth Factor				
	Investment Return during Retirement				
Years in Retirement	5%	6%	7%	8%	10%
5	4.67	4.54	4.42	4.30	4.08
10	9.13	8.67	8.25	7.86	7.16
15	13.37	12.43	11.58	10.81	9.48
20	17.42	15.84	14.46	13.25	11.24
25	21.28	18.94	16.96	15.27	12.57
30	24.96	21.76	19.13	16.94	13.57
35	28.46	24.33	21.01	18.33	14.33
40	31.80	26.66	22.65	19.48	14.90

DEMONSTRATION PROBLEM 10.1 | Estimating Total Retirement Wealth Needed

Problem

You estimate that your retirement income shortfall after Social Security is $55,337 in the first year of retirement, and you expect your income needs to increase by 4 percent per year (i) due to inflation. You anticipate earning an 8 percent return on your invested assets (r) for your 20-year retirement period (n). How much money do you need to have at retirement to fund your estimated income needs if:

a. you plan to live on interest income alone, or

b. you plan to use both interest income and principal?

Strategy

Use Equations 10.3 and 10.4 to calculate the wealth needed for each approach.

Solution

a. *If you plan to live on interest income only,* you can use Equation 10.3 to estimate the amount of wealth you need, assuming that annual income will increase with inflation and that you will not deplete principal:

$$\text{Retirement wealth needed} = \frac{\text{First-year income}}{r-i} = \frac{\$55,337}{0.08-0.04} = \$1,383,425$$

b. *If you plan to use both the interest earnings and the principal to fund your income needs* but will fully deplete your assets by the end of the period, you should calculate the present value of an inflation-adjusted annuity using Equation 10.4:

$$\text{Retirement wealth needed} = \frac{\text{First-year income}}{r-i} \times \left[1 - \left(\frac{1+i}{1+r}\right)^{n}\right]$$

$$= \frac{\$55,337}{0.08-0.04} \times \left[1 - \left(\frac{1.04}{1.08}\right)^{20}\right]$$

$$= \$1,383,425 \times (1 - 0.47) = \$733,075$$

Note that your answer could be slightly different if you rounded at any of the steps of the calculation. Note, too, that since the problem assumes a 4 percent inflation rate, you can use Table 10.1 to find the answer. If you expect to earn 8 percent on your investment and live 20 years in retirement, then multiply $55,337 × 13.25 = $733,215. This is the same answer you got using the equation (with some rounding error).

invested assets and the number of years you expect to live in retirement. This table assumes inflation will be 4 percent per year during your retirement period, so if you think it will be more or less, you should use the formula approach. This method is illustrated in **Demonstration Problem 10.1**.

Steps 6 and 7: Estimating Monthly Savings Target

You now have an estimate of the total funds you'll need to have saved by the time you retire. You might have already begun saving toward this goal, or you might have an employer-sponsored savings program that will provide a sum of money at retirement. If you assume that your current wealth will remain invested until retirement, you can calculate its future value and subtract that from the total retirement wealth needed to arrive at a retirement savings goal. For example, if you currently have $50,000 in an employer-sponsored 401(k) plan earning 6 percent per year and will retire in 40 years, you can estimate that account will be worth $50,000 \times (1.06)^{40} = $514,286 when you retire, assuming no further contributions are made.

Once you have a lump-sum goal, you can again use a time value of money calculation to estimate the monthly savings that will get you there. If retirement wealth needed is $733,075 and current savings will be worth $514,286 in 40 years, you'll need to accumulate only an additional $218,789 ($733,075 − $514,286). To translate this additional lump sum to a monthly amount, you can use your financial calculator. Enter FV = $218,789, I = 6/12, and N = 40 × 12 = 480, and solve for PMT = $110. This is the amount you need to save each month until retirement to accumulate $218,789 by the time you retire. If you and your employer are already contributing to a 401(k) plan each month, you might already be on track to save this amount.

We've now gone through all seven steps in determining how much to save for retirement. Next, we'll apply them to an example in **Case Study 10.1**. This case study illustrates how to use **Excel Worksheet 10.2** (Personal Financial Planner: Retirement Planning Worksheet) to develop a monthly retirement savings target.

In the case study, Camilla found that she needed to increase her retirement saving to be on track for retirement. You can use **Interactive: Effect of Increased Retirement Savings** to see the impact of increased savings on how much wealth you can accumulate and how long it will last.

EXCEL WORKSHEET

See **Excel Worksheet 10.2** (Personal Financial Planner: Retirement Planning Worksheet) in **WileyPLUS**.

INTERACTIVE

See **Interactive: Effect of Increased Retirement Savings** in **WileyPLUS**.

Case Study 10.1

monkeybusinessimages/iStock/Getty Images

Camilla Hardin Develops a Plan for Retirement Saving

Problem

Camilla Hardin is 47 years old. She is worried that she might not be on track in terms of saving for retirement. She has been contributing to a 401(k) plan through her employer for most of her career and has accumulated $200,000 in total retirement wealth, but she wonders whether she needs to be saving more.

Strategy

Camilla completes Excel Worksheet 10.2 to determine her retirement saving needs.

Solution   Camilla's worksheet is shown in **Figure 10.3**. To complete Step 1, she estimates that, when she retires, she will no longer have certain expenses, resulting in savings of about $15,000 per year. However, she expects other expenses to increase by $4,000. Expected expenses for her first year of retirement in today's dollars thus total $49,000. She enters her expectations for 20 years in retirement, 3 percent inflation, and a 20 percent tax rate to arrive at $110,624 as her needed pretax retirement income.

Step 2 isn't relevant to Camilla, since she has no defined-benefit plan. In Step 3, she estimates that she will receive $40,000 per year from Social Security. This leaves her with a retirement income shortfall of $70,624 per year in Step 4.

The results of Step 5 show that the retirement wealth she will need, assuming that she spends both interest and principal, is $1,028,398. This is an eye-opener for Camilla, who realizes that she truly hasn't been saving enough to meet her goal of retiring at age 67.

The good news is that Camilla's current retirement account balance of $200,000 will help to meet her retirement wealth needs. In Step 6, she calculates that her current balance will triple in value by the time she retires, assuming a 6 percent average rate of return on her investments. This leaves her with a much more manageable savings goal of $386,971 over the next 20 years. Given that she and her employer are already contributing $500 per month, she estimates that she only needs to save another $338 per month. Under her new plan, she'll be able to retire in 20 years and completely meet her inflation-adjusted income needs for a 20-year retirement period.

FIGURE 10.3 Sample of Excel Worksheet 10.2: Retirement Planning Worksheet

	A	B	C
1	**STEP 1. Estimate before-tax income needs.**		
2	a. Enter current household expenses.		$60,000
3	b. Adjust for changes in expenses in retirement.		
4	Possible reductions:		
5	Employment expenses	$5,000	
6	Retirement savings	$6,000	
7	Housing expenses	$4,000	
8	Total reductions	$15,000	
9	Possible increases:		
10	Health care/insurance	$2,000	
11	Leisure activities	$2,000	
12	Gifts/donations		
13	Total increases	$4,000	
14	c. Adjusted expenses in current dollars		
15	= Expenses − Reductions + Increases		$49,000
16	d. Adjust for inflation to future dollars		
17	Expected annual inflation rate between now and retirement	3.0%	
18	Years until retirement	20	
19	After−tax expenses in first year of retirement	$88,499	
20	e. Calculate before−tax total income needed:		
21	Expected tax rate in retirement	20%	
22	Before−tax income needed = After−tax income needed ÷ (1 − tax rate)		$110,624
23	**STEP 2. Estimate annual retirement income from defined-benefit retirement plan(s).**		
	Total income from defined-benefit plans		$0
24	**STEP 3. Estimate annual retirement income from Social Security.**		
25	Estimated Social Security benefit (in future dollars)		$40,000
26	**STEP 4. Retirement income shortfall in first year of retirement.**		
27	Before-tax income needed less expected benefits from pensions = Step 1 − Step 2 − Step 3		$70,624
28	**STEP 5. Estimate total retirement wealth needed.**		
28	a. Expected rate of return on retirement savings	6.0%	
29	b. Expected annual inflation rate during retirement	3.0%	
30	c. Expected number of years you will be retired (until death)	20	
31	d. Inflation-adjusted discount rate	2.9%	
32	e. Retirement wealth factor	14.5615	
33	f. Retirement wealth needed		$1,028,398
34	**STEP 6. Estimate retirement savings goal.**		
35	a. Total value of current retirement savings (DC, IRA, other savings)	$200,000	
36	b. Future value of current retirement savings with no additional funding (assumes return on investment and years to retirement as above)		$641,427
37	c. Retirement savings goal		$386,971
38	**STEP 7. Estimate monthly savings required to meet savings goal.**		
39	a. Current monthly contribution to employer retirement plan	$500.00	
40	b. Additional monthly savings to reach retirement savings goal		$338

Why Do So Many People Avoid Retirement Planning?

INTERACTIVE

See **Interactive: Behavioral Biases and Retirement Planning** in **WileyPLUS.**

Unfortunately, many people tend to avoid planning for retirement. Why is this so? As with many aspects of personal finance, inadequate planning can be traced to innate psychological factors. Some of the more common behavioral biases are discussed below. Before you read this section, take the quick psychology quiz in **Interactive: Behavioral Biases and Retirement Planning** to see if any of them apply to you.

Myopia

Many people claim that they don't have enough money to save for retirement. But they may just be prioritizing current over future spending. More than ever, our society embraces a "live for today" ethos. Myopia, or near-sightedness, is the term used by economists to describe the tendency of people to overemphasize short-term goals and outcomes. Households are constantly bombarded with advertising that reinforces natural tendencies for current spending and immediate gratification. Taking an extra vacation or buying a new car might seem worth it at the moment, but it inevitably reduces the amount that you can allocate to retirement savings. Don't forget how important it is to start saving early so that the power of compound interest can work to your advantage.

Ignoring Inflation

Most people don't understand inflation. As a result, they underestimate how much more savings it will take to generate inflation-adjusted income in retirement. If you only save enough to produce a constant income, your standard of living in retirement will consistently decline as you get older.

Focusing on Averages

People tend to focus on averages rather than looking at the full range of possible outcomes. This mistake can create a number of difficulties, particularly in estimating life expectancy and investment returns. Based on average life expectancy, you probably think that you'll live into your mid-80s. But if you use this age to estimate how much you need to save for retirement, you have a 50 percent chance of saving too little. As medical treatments continue to extend life, it will become increasingly common for people to live to 100 years of age, approximately doubling the average retirement period. In Case Study 10.1, what impact would it have on Camilla if she ended up living to age 100 instead of to 87 as she estimated?

It Won't Happen to Me

A common psychological bias is the tendency to think that bad things happen to everyone but you. Despite the high rates of divorce, widowhood, and disability, most people don't have a plan for how they'll deal with these events if they come up. Any of them can produce income and expense shocks that inevitably affect the ability to accumulate funds for retirement. In many states, for example, retirement account balances and pensions are split between the divorcing spouses regardless of whose employment income they came from.

Even when you know about the behavioral biases we've just discussed, they are so ingrained that you may find yourself making bad decisions anyway. The best strategy is to establish your retirement plan based on reasonable and conservative assumptions, such as longer life, lower investment return, and higher inflation. Automating your savings and spending plans can help reduce the "human error" component.

10.2 | Retirement Income from Employer Plans and Social Security

LEARNING OBJECTIVE 10.2

Explain how employer-sponsored retirement plans and Social Security can help you meet your retirement goals.

Once you have an estimate of your retirement savings goal, the next step is to consider the various ways you can reach that goal. To achieve the greatest level of retirement security, you should plan on multiple sources of retirement income, including:

- Employer-sponsored retirement plans
- Social Security
- Personal savings

This is sometimes referred to as the "three-legged stool of retirement income," as illustrated in **Figure 10.4**. This visual metaphor originated in the Congressional discussions that led up to the creation of Social Security many decades ago. Policy makers were interested in creating a public safety net for seniors but emphasized the importance of having multiple sources of income in retirement.

FIGURE 10.4 **The Three-Legged Stool of Retirement Income** A retirement plan that relies too heavily on only one leg, such as Social Security, will be wobbly and will not provide reliable and stable retirement income.

How balanced is the retirement stool in reality? In the aggregate, **Figure 10.5** illustrates that Social Security makes up a little more than one-third of all income for households whose members are age 65 and over. However, the aggregate numbers disguise a serious problem: more than one-third of all households receive 90 percent or more of their income from Social Security benefits. This is likely one explanation for the relatively low median income of over-65 households. In addition, many seniors find it necessary to supplement their retirement benefits

FIGURE 10.5 **Aggregate Household Retirement Income, Age 65+, 2015** For over-65 households as a group, the "three-legged stool of retirement income" is out of balance, because too few have sufficient savings.

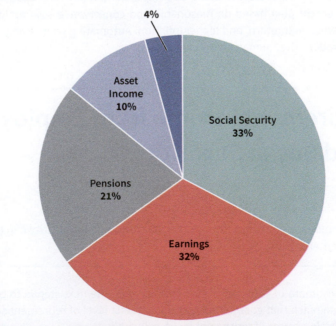

Source: Social Security Administration, *Fast Facts and Figures About Social Security, 2017,* www.ssa.gov.

with employment earnings, either by delaying retirement or working part-time during retirement. It's clear that the legs of the retirement income stool are pretty different from what was envisioned by Congress in the last century. And today's workers face additional challenges to retirement savings, including high levels of student loan debt and stagnant investment markets.

Another disturbing aspect of retirement income is the contrast between married-couple households and single households. Compared with married-couple household income of $55,108 in 2015, single retirees had less than half the household income ($20,825) and were more likely to be relying on Social Security as their primary source of income and more likely to be living in poverty.

To have a financially secure and independent retirement, it's therefore extremely important to make decisions today that will maximize your access to multiple sources of income in retirement. For example, you might want to seek employment with a firm that sponsors a generous retirement plan for its employees. This, combined with Social Security benefits, will reduce the amount of income shortfall that you'll have to finance from your investments or from continued employment after retirement. In this section, we look more closely at your potential income from employer-sponsored retirement plans and public pension benefits.

Income from Employer-Sponsored Plans

As you might recall from Chapter 9, the two major types of employer-sponsored retirement plans are defined-benefit (DB) plans and defined-contribution (DC) plans. Although you can't estimate income from such plans with much certainty until you get closer to your retirement date, you'll find it useful to understand the factors that enter into these estimates. We discuss these factors below.

Income from DB Plans

Because DB plans have been declining steadily, it is unlikely you will be lucky enough to be enrolled in one unless you work in the public sector (for example, as a teacher, police officer, or firefighter). Your future benefit from a DB plan is usually based on a formula that takes into account the number of years you've worked for the employer and how much you earn. For example, an employer might use the following formula: 1.5 percent of final salary for each year of service up to a maximum of 70 percent. If you work for this employer for 35 years, you'll receive a benefit equal to 52.5 percent of your salary at retirement. If you have a generous plan that also adjusts your benefit for inflation during retirement, your risk of outliving your assets will be significantly reduced.

Even though your employer provides a benefit estimate each year, you'll need to adjust the amount given, because it will be based on your current salary and years of employment (rather than your projected final salary and years of employment at retirement). In addition, there's no guarantee that you'll continue to work for the same employer. For this reason, a more precise estimate of your expected income shortfall requires that you take the time to project your future salary and apply the appropriate percentage. For example, suppose your current salary is $40,000 and you'll retire in 20 years, at which time you will have 35 years of service. When we apply the future value equation as before, if your salary increases at a rate of 4 percent, your salary at retirement will be $87,645 ($40,000 × 1.04^{20}). Using this salary amount, you can then estimate your projected benefit. For the plan described above, your future benefit would be $46,014 (52.5 percent × $87,645) per year. Note that, if you have a vested benefit from a previous employer's plan that uses salary in its formula, the benefit amount from that employer will be calculated based on your final salary at the time you quit working there, not on your earnings when you actually retire.

Income from DC Plans

If you work for an employer that sponsors a 401(k) or other type of DC retirement plan, contributions to your account can be expected to continue, and even to increase, until you retire. When you retire, you'll probably convert this fund to an income stream, either by purchasing an annuity or by spending the investment earnings and principal during retirement. Unlike a DB plan, the amount of income this fund will generate for you in retirement is fairly uncertain because it depends on how much is contributed each year and the rate of return on invested assets for many years into the future. This is why the retirement planning worksheet treats these funds as part of your total savings rather than as a projected benefit amount. Obviously, the greater the contributions to the plan and the higher the average investment return, the more money you'll have at retirement.

Income from Social Security

Social Security is clearly an important source of retirement income. For about two-thirds of retirees, Social Security provides more than half of their retirement income. For some retirees, it is their *only* source of income. In this section, we describe the Social Security retirement system and consider how to factor its benefit promises into your retirement plan.

What Is Social Security, and How Is It Funded?

Social Security is a public defined-benefit program administered by the U.S. Social Security Administration (SSA). In addition to the health and disability benefits described in previous chapters, the program is intended to provide at least subsistence-level retirement income to program participants, who include nearly all workers in the United States. About 45 million people are currently receiving retirement benefits from the program.

Social Security is referred to as a "pay-as-you-go" system because the money received from payroll (FICA) taxes assessed on the wages of current workers is used to pay benefits to qualified recipients. As the number of workers per retiree has decreased over the years (from 42 in 1945 to fewer than 4 today), the payroll tax rate has gradually increased to keep the system in balance. Currently, the tax burden is shared by employers and employees, as summarized in **Table 10.2**.

TABLE 10.2 **FICA Payroll Tax Rates for Social Security and Medicare Programs, 2019**

Program	Employee Payroll Tax Rate	Employer Payroll Tax Rate	Self-Employed Tax Rate	Maximum Income Subject to Tax
Retirement, Survivors, and Disability	6.20%	6.20%	12.40%	$132,900 (increases annually with inflation)
Medicare	1.45%*	1.45%	2.90%	No limit
Total	7.65%	7.65%	15.30%	

*As noted in the preceding chapter, the Affordable Care Act added a 3.8% Medicare tax to investment earnings and increased the Medicare payroll tax rate by 0.9% on income over $200,000 ($250,000 for married couples). These additional taxes are not included in the tax rates on this table.

Who Is Eligible and When Can You Receive Benefits?

To be eligible to receive Social Security benefits based on your own earnings history, you must be "fully insured," as defined below. You might also be eligible to receive Social Security retirement benefits based the earnings history of a fully insured spouse or former spouse.

Fully Insured Status   You will be fully insured at retirement if you earned at least a specified minimum dollar amount ($1,360 in 2019) in at least 40 three-month periods (10 years) over your working career, and paid FICA payroll taxes on that income. Fully insured participants who retire at the normal retirement age are entitled to benefits as defined by law.

Normal Retirement Age   The normal retirement age is 67 for anyone born 1960 or later. Older participants are subject to the normal retirement ages specified in **Table 10.3**.

TABLE 10.3 Social Security Normal Retirement Age

Year of Birth	Retirement Age
1943–54	66 years
1955	66 years, 2 months
1956	66 years, 4 months
1957	66 years, 6 months
1958	66 years, 8 months
1959	66 years, 10 months
1960 and later	67 years

Early or Delayed Retirement   Participants can opt for early retirement at age 62, in which case they receive a reduced benefit to account for the reduced years of payroll tax contributions and increased years of expected benefit receipt. For example, a worker born in 1960 or later who would be eligible for full retirement benefits of $2,000 per month at age 67 will get only $1,400 if he or she retires at age 62. About half of all retirees opt for early receipt of benefits despite the significant reduction in monthly benefit.

Participants can also delay retirement, choosing not to begin receiving benefits at the normal retirement age of 67. In this case, their benefits will increase by 8 percent for each year of delay up to age 70.

Spousal Benefits   Because Social Security was designed in an era when single-earner households were the norm rather than the exception, Congress included some protections for nonworking spouses in the program. If you've been married at least 1 year to a fully insured worker and you are at least age 62, you're eligible to receive a Social Security benefit of up to 50 percent of your spouse's Social Security benefit *or* a benefit based on your own earnings history, whichever is greater. Divorcées who haven't remarried are eligible for retirement benefits equal to 50 percent of their ex-spouses' benefits as long as the marriage lasted at least 10 years. Conceivably, for example, one man could have been married four times, each time for 10 years, and all four of his ex-wives could receive benefits at retirement equal to 50 percent of his benefit, as long as they hadn't remarried. This does not reduce what he can receive from Social Security. When your spouse dies, your 50 percent benefit is replaced by a survivor benefit equal to 100 percent of the higher earner's benefit. These significant protections for nonworking and underemployed spouses have resulted in reduced poverty rates for single elderly people over time.

Consider an example: Barbara didn't work outside the home until her last child went to college and she was 57 years old. At age 65, she had only contributed to Social Security for eight years—not enough time to achieve fully insured status. Barbara's husband, Dave, also age 65, was eligible for a monthly benefit of $1,900 based on his earnings history. Under the current system, Barbara is eligible for a spousal benefit of $950 per month. If Dave dies before her, she'll receive a survivor benefit equal to 100 percent of Dave's benefit.

How Much Will Social Security Pay Me?

Social Security benefits are based on a multistep calculation. The SSA first calculates your **average indexed monthly earnings (AIME)**, using your top 35 years of earnings (up to the taxable maximum for each year), adjusted for inflation to current-year dollars. If you've worked for less than 35 years, you'll have some zeros averaged in. The AIME is then used in a formula to calculate your **primary insurance amount (PIA)**, the monthly benefit you'd be entitled to if you retired at the normal retirement age (age 67 for anyone born 1960 or later). **Equation 10.5** shows the 2019 calculation. The dollar amounts in the formula are adjusted annually for inflation.

$$\text{PIA for 2019} = [0.9 \times (\text{First } \$926 \text{ of AIME})] + [0.32 \times (\text{AIME up to } \$5{,}583 - \$926)]$$
$$+ [0.15 \times (\text{AIME} - \$5{,}583)] \tag{10.5}$$

This formula is designed to have a redistributive effect by replacing a larger percentage of preretirement income for low-income retirees than for average- and high-income retirees. A low-income person (AIME = $1,200) retiring in 2019, for example, would have been eligible for the following monthly primary insurance amount:

$$PIA = (0.9 \times \$926) + [0.32 \times (\$1,200 - \$926)]$$
$$= \$833.40 + \$87.68$$
$$= \$921.08$$

This would have replaced about 77 percent of his or her preretirement income.

At the other end of the spectrum, consider a higher-income retiree. Recall from Table 10.2 that the maximum income subject to Social Security tax in 2019 is $132,900. A person who earned that amount would have monthly income of $11,075 ($132,900/12). But the maximum monthly benefit under the program for workers retiring at the normal retirement age in 2019 was $2,861 per month. That would replace only 24 percent ($2,861/$11,075) of the higher earner's preretirement income. For those who earned more than the Social Security income limit on average, the benefit would be an even smaller percentage of preretirement earnings.

On average, Social Security beneficiaries received a retirement benefit of $1,461 in 2019. The benefit amount is annually adjusted for inflation, a feature that ensures that a retiree's purchasing power will not decline during retirement.

You can use your annual Social Security statement or the retirement calculator on the SSA website (**www.ssa.gov**) to calculate your expected Social Security benefit more precisely based on your earnings history. Alternatively, **Table 10.4** provides benefit estimates for a range of age and salary combinations, assuming average wage increases and retirement at age 67. For example, if you were 25 in 2019 and earned $40,000, your annual Social Security benefit at age 67 is estimated to be $87,948 in future dollars. This might seem like a lot, but it's not. In the year 2061, when you retire, that amount will be roughly the equivalent in purchasing power of $25,000 in 2019.

TABLE 10.4 **Annual Social Security Retirement Benefit Estimates, 2019**

2019 Income	Age in 2019						
	25	**30**	**35**	**40**	**45**	**50**	**55**
$40,000	$87,948	$72,804	$60,156	$49,392	$40,140	$32,316	$25,644
$50,000	$102,252	$84,648	$69,912	$57,348	$46,548	$37,392	$29,592
$60,000	$116,544	$96,480	$79,668	$65,316	$52,956	$42,480	$33,552
$70,000	$130,836	$108,312	$89,424	$73,284	$59,364	$47,568	$37,500
$80,000	$138,816	$114,960	$95,112	$78,408	$64,212	$52,260	$41,460
$90,000	$145,512	$120,504	$99,672	$82,140	$67,212	$54,636	$43,896
$100,000	$152,208	$126,048	$104,256	$85,872	$70,224	$57,024	$45,756

Source: Values in future dollars obtained from the Social Security Administration Quick Benefit Calculator at www.ssa.gov, assuming retirement at age 67.

Will Social Security Be Around When You Retire?

Your eligibility for Social Security benefits makes a big difference in the amount of income shortfall you'll need to fund, so the question of whether the program will still be around when you retire is an important one. Many public opinion polls show that young people are much more skeptical about the prospects for Social Security than those nearer to retirement. Although Social Security is unlikely to be completely dismantled, it is possible that it won't be quite as generous in the future as it is today. You need to understand a little about how the financing works to see why this is the case.

Financing of the System

As mentioned, Social Security is a pay-as-you-go system—current payroll taxes are used to fund current benefit payments. When payroll taxes collected exceed the total being paid out in benefits to current retirees, the Social Security Administration invests the extra money in special-issue government bonds. The accumulated value of these bonds is called the Social Security Trust Fund. In the future, when payroll taxes are insufficient to cover benefits being paid out, the trust fund's assets will be used to cover the shortfall.

Causes of Projected Insolvency

Until the members of the Baby Boom generation reached their peak earnings years, the Social Security Trust Fund was really just a short-term parking place for funds, as Congress tweaked the benefit formula and payroll tax percentage to ensure that the money coming in was just enough to cover the benefits to be paid. Unfortunately, the Social Security Administration expects that the retirement of the Baby Boomer generation will place a corresponding drain on program funds over the next two decades. Assuming no major changes to the program, current projections suggest that the trust fund will be depleted (meaning all the bonds will have been cashed in) by 2034. And this doesn't even take into account the fact that the federal government is somehow going to have to come up with the funds to make good on its pile of IOUs to the Social Security Trust Fund, most likely by raising income taxes or selling investors new government bonds. This does not, however, mean that the Social Security program will go away. Forecasts indicate that payroll taxes would still be sufficient to cover 75 percent of promised benefits, so the worst-case scenario is simply a reduction in future benefits.

Several factors are contributing to Social Security's problems. One is simply that people are living longer and are therefore receiving retirement benefits for more years. Another, as already suggested, is that the Baby Boom generation is larger than the generations that preceded and followed it. This means that, as members of this generation retire, more and more retirees will be receiving benefits, and there'll be fewer workers paying taxes to cover those benefits. In another 20 years, when the bulk of the Baby Boomers have retired, there could be only two workers paying into the system for every retiree receiving benefits. It doesn't take a math genius to figure out that this won't work. Congress has aggravated the problem by responding to voters who want benefits and eligibility requirements to be more generous, rather than less. For example, even though the average number of years that retirees collect benefits has more than doubled since the program's inception, the normal retirement age remained at 65 until recently and is slowly being increased to 67. Many experts suggest that it should be 70 or higher.

Prospects for Reform

It has become apparent that some type of Social Security reform is necessary, and various proposals have been discussed. When the stock market was booming, many thought a defined-contribution approach was the way to go. In this type of plan, a portion of each worker's payroll tax would be deposited in an investment account, and his or her benefits would depend on the growth in value of this account over time (much like a 401(k) plan sponsored by an employer). There are several problems with switching to this type of system. First, older participants don't have the time to accumulate enough in an investment account to replace their current benefit promise, so they'll have to continue under the old program rules. Increasing federal budget deficits make it unlikely that the government will be able to help fund the transition period, so the younger participants' payroll taxes will have to be sufficient to cover the projected benefit obligations under the revised benefit and insurance formulas, their own account contributions, and the "grandfathered" retirees under the old system. Last but not least, it doesn't seem like a good idea for a "safety net" program to allow retirees to invest their retirement funds in risky stocks.

Reflection Question 1

Do you think it's important to have a Social Security system that provides a base level of income to retirees? How confident are you that Congress can enact reforms to ensure it will be there when you retire?

Instead of introducing a major reform of Social Security, it's much more likely that politicians will choose to take small steps—perhaps raising the normal retirement age a little more, tweaking the PIA formula, limiting benefits or benefit increases, or raising tax rates for the wealthy. In striving not to alienate older voters who are counting on the current system to remain unchanged, politicians prefer to dodge the bullet, even when most would agree that it is one of the most significant issues on their plate. In light of this, as you consider your personal retirement plan, you should probably be conservative about your estimated Social Security benefit so that you don't underestimate your retirement income shortfall.

10.3   Individual Retirement Savings Alternatives

LEARNING OBJECTIVE 10.3
Explain why individual retirement accounts (IRAs) offer advantages over taxable savings accounts and annuities.

Now that you know how much you need to save for retirement, you need to decide what form your personal retirement savings will take. Possibilities include investments in taxable and tax-deferred accounts, annuities, investments in income-producing real estate, and home equity. We focus on tax-deferred savings options here, but you'll learn more about other investment options in later chapters.

Congress has established several programs designed to encourage increased personal retirement saving. These programs generally provide tax incentives to low- and middle-income individuals and small business owners who make contributions to certain types of retirement plans. Recall that we defined and briefly discussed individual retirement accounts (IRAs) in Chapter 4. In this section, we review the differences between the types of IRAs, explain the rules for using them, and cover the tax advantages they offer to individual savers in more detail. We also compare these savings plans to taxable accounts and annuities.

Individual Retirement Accounts

Beginning in the early 1980s, individuals have had the opportunity to make tax-deferred contributions to individual retirement accounts. IRAs can be easily set up through many different financial institutions. The Tax Reform Act of 1986, the Tax Relief Act of 1997, and the Economic Growth and Tax Relief Reconciliation Act of 2001 together define the types of individual retirement accounts that are available, the tax preferences involved, and the contribution limits. The two main types of savings vehicles are the traditional IRA, sometimes called the "deductible IRA," and the Roth IRA.

Traditional IRAs

Traditional IRAs are subject to rules that are very similar to those governing qualified defined-contribution plans offered by employers. Contributions are deductible from income for the tax year in which they are made (contributions are allowed up to the April 15 tax filing deadline in the following year). If you have a deductible retirement plan through your employer, your ability to deduct IRA contributions will be phased out if your adjusted gross income exceeds certain limits. The 2019 allowable contributions and income limitations for deductibility are given in **Table 10.5**.

TABLE 10.5   IRA Contribution and Income Limits, 2019

	Traditional IRA			
	Single		**Married Filing Jointly**	
	No Employer Plan	**Participate in Employer Plan**	**No Employer Plan**	**Participate in Employer Plan**
Contribution limit	$6,000 + $1,000 catch-up for 50+	$6,000 + $1,000 catch-up for 50+	$6,000 + $1,000 catch-up for 50+	$6,000 + $1,000 catch-up for 50+
Income range over which deductibility is phased out	No income limit	$64,000 – $74,000	No income limit	$103,000–$123,000 (if both have plans) $193,000–$203,000 (if one spouse has plan, the other can make deductible contributions)

	Roth IRA	
	Single	**Married Filing Jointly**
Contribution limit	$6,000 + $1,000 catch-up for 50+	$6,000 + $1,000 catch-up for 50+ $6,000 + $1,000 catch-up for 50+
Income range over which eligibility to make contributions is phased out	$122,000 – $137,000	$193,000 – $203,000

Source: www.irs.gov.

In 2019, for example, a married couple who did not have a plan at either of their places of employment could make deductible contributions of $6,000 each (or $7,000 if they were age 50 or over). However, if both spouses had tax-deferred employer plans, they could make the full contribution only if their AGI was less than $103,000. For AGIs between $103,000 and $123,000, the deductibility is phased out. Similarly, if one spouse had an employer plan, the other could make fully deductible contributions as long as the couple's combined AGI was less than $193,000. If your income is greater than the highest end of the range given in the table, you can't deduct your IRA contribution at all, but you can still make contributions to the account with after-tax dollars. The earnings on the account will be tax-deferred until withdrawal, at which time they're taxed as ordinary income. If you withdraw funds before you reach age 59½, however, the withdrawal is subject to a 10 percent penalty in addition to any taxes owed, unless you use the funds to pay for qualified educational expenses, medical expenses, or a first-time home purchase.

Roth IRAs

A Roth IRA takes a different approach, requiring that contributions be made with after-tax dollars, but allowing investments to accumulate tax-free with no tax due on withdrawal, as long as the taxpayer has reached age 59½ or is using the proceeds for qualified educational or medical expenses or a first-time home purchase. The contribution limits for the Roth IRA are the same as for the traditional IRA ($6,000 in 2019, plus $1,000 catch-up for individuals age 50 and over), but some income limits are higher, making this an option for middle-income households. Full contributions can be made by singles with an adjusted gross income of no more than $122,000 in 2019 and by married joint filers with an adjusted gross income of no more than $193,000. Above that income level, the contribution is phased out up to the income limits of $137,000 for singles and $203,000 for joint filers.

Taxes on Benefits Received

In general, payouts from employer plans and traditional IRAs will be taxable when they're received. In contrast, you might have other sources of cash flow, such as Roth IRAs, that you can access without owing taxes. Tax rules require that you begin taking payouts from tax-deferred employer plans and traditional IRAs by April 1 of the year after you reach age 70½. Until then, you can wait to claim taxable benefits and annuities, and live off your Roth IRAs and taxable accounts. You'll eventually have to take the income from the other plans and pay the tax, of course. But better later than sooner.

Reflection Question 2

Which type of IRA would better meet your needs, and why?

Taxable Accounts

IRAs offer some tax advantages, but in return for these advantages you give up some financial flexibility because your retirement assets are not very liquid. Although you can cash them out before retirement in an emergency, you'll be subject to a penalty for doing so except under some limited circumstances. Suppose, for example, that your marginal tax rate is 25 percent and you have a financial emergency that requires withdrawal of $10,000 from a deductible IRA account. In the year of withdrawal, you'll pay $3,500 to the government—$2,500 goes to taxes and $1,000 is the 10 percent penalty for withdrawing before age 59½. This represents a substantial drain on your retirement funds. For some individuals, IRAs provide the discipline they need to leave their money alone for a long period of time. For others, it might be advisable to put some investment funds in taxable accounts.

The Importance of Starting Early

Many people don't get started on their retirement planning as early as they should. The fewer years you have to accumulate the retirement funds you'll need, the more you'll have to contribute each month to meet your goal. In some cases, the goal will be out of reach, given your household income and expenses. Your plan may require that you save less now and increase your savings rate later. However, as we've seen before, the power of compound interest will be greatest for your earliest contributions.

To illustrate this concept, let's consider the impact of getting a late start on your investments for retirement. Suppose that you've determined that you need to save $500,000 by the time you retire in 40 years. If you can earn 8 percent on your investments, you'll need to save $143.23 per month, a manageable goal. (To solve this future value problem on your financial calculator, enter FV = 500,000, N = 40 × 12 = 480, I = 8/12, and solve for PMT = 143.23) If you wait 10 years before starting to save for retirement (N = 360 instead of 480), to accumulate the same $500,000, you'll need to save $335.49 per month for 30 years—more than twice as much per month. But if you manage to save only $50 per month for the first 10 years, you can reach your $500,000 goal with an investment of only $268.37 per month for the last 30 years. Clearly, early contributions make a big difference in the end.

Earnings on Investment Make a Big Difference

Another reminder: Along with an early start, the rate of return on your investments makes a big difference in your accumulated wealth. In the example above, you saw that a monthly amount of $143.23 invested at 8 percent would result in a retirement nest egg of $500,000 in 40 years. What if you could only earn 6 percent? In that case, you'd need to save almost twice as much: $251.07 per month. In the next chapter, you'll learn more about investment alternatives.

Annuities

Annuities can be particularly valuable for retirement planning because they can produce lifetime income and thus reduce the risk of outliving retirement assets. They are commonly sold by life insurance companies because, like life insurance, pricing depends on life expectancy. Whereas life insurance provides income to your beneficiaries when you die, annuities pay income to you while you're living. In addition to buying directly from life insurance companies, annuities may be an option for your employer retirement plan, or you might have the option of converting all or part of your retirement account to an annuity when you retire.

Key Features of Annuities

In Chapter 2, we defined an annuity as a series of constant payments for a period of time. Although this is true of the "plain vanilla" annuity, many variations of this type of financial product are sold in the market today. Some key features to consider before buying an annuity are the following:

- **Period of benefit payment**   A life annuity pays benefits for life, whereas some annuities pay for a specified number of years. A **joint and survivor annuity** pays a married couple a benefit until the second spouse dies. For a given amount of wealth, a joint and survivor annuity will always result in a lower monthly payment than a single life annuity because it will pay out for a longer period of time. The payment reduction depends on the ages of the beneficiaries.

- **Payment amount**   A **fixed annuity** is constant over time. A **variable annuity** payment varies with the performance of invested assets. Some annuities increase with inflation. Joint and survivor annuities offer options to pay the surviving spouse a percentage, commonly 50 percent of the original benefit. This allows the couple to have greater income while they are both living, but might put the survivor at greater financial risk, particularly if he or she lives to a very old age.

- **Purchase options**   You can invest in annuities by making premium payments over time or by paying a single lump-sum premium. You can also pay today for a **deferred annuity** that will begin making payments at some point in the future.

- **When benefits begin**   An immediate annuity begins making payments when you purchase it. A deferred annuity will begin payments at some point in the future, often at retirement, as illustrated in **Figure 10.6**.

FIGURE 10.6   **Timeline for a Deferred Annuity**   This deferred annuity begins making payments when the annuity holder is 67—standard retirement age.

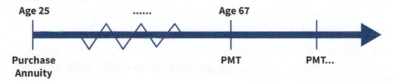

Taxes and Expenses

Two important considerations for investing in an annuity are taxes and expenses. An advantage of annuities is that the earnings on investment are tax-deferred until benefits are received. If the annuity is purchased with after-tax dollars, only a portion of the benefit payment will be taxable (the portion that represents the investment earnings). If it is purchased through a tax-deferred retirement account or IRA, the full benefit will be taxable when received, similar to other tax-deferred investments.

Compared with other investments, annuities will usually give you a lower rate of return, in part because sales commissions, fees, and expenses erode some of the investment earnings. As an alternative, you can invest in mutual funds at much lower expenses, as you'll learn in Chapter 13. The trade-off is that fixed annuities are a fairly safe investment when purchased from a highly rated insurance company. Variable annuities are riskier because they expose you to investment risk.

Health and Life Expectancy

In deciding whether to include annuities in your retirement plan, you should take your health status and age into account. If you buy a life annuity and then die after receiving only a few years of benefits, you certainly won't have gotten your money's worth. Although some insurers offer annuity products that guarantee to pay some of the benefits to your heirs if you die too soon, the guarantee might not be worth what you have to pay for it.

Home Equity Loans and Reverse Annuity Mortgages

If you've paid off your mortgage or you have substantial home equity at retirement, another option for generating tax-free retirement income is to convert your home equity into cash flow. If you have good credit, it's relatively easy to get a home equity loan or a home equity line of credit. These will require that you make loan payments, but you might be able to spread out the payments for a fairly long time. Unfortunately, the interest you pay on a home equity loan (unless used for home improvements) is no longer tax-deductible, but you'll still benefit from any increase in the value of your property while you continue to own it.

Another alternative you might consider is a reverse annuity mortgage, defined in Chapter 6. You may recall that, in this type of arrangement, you trade your home equity for an income stream. You're allowed to remain in the home for the period of the annuity, which might be a period of years or for life, after which the lender assumes ownership of the home or you have to pay off the loan. Depending on your home's value, a reverse annuity mortgage might not provide a big enough income stream to risk losing your equity if you die prematurely. If you are eligible for a $150,000 reverse annuity mortgage that pays out over 20 years, for example, you'll get around $12,000 per year. The percentage of home value that you can apply to a reverse annuity mortgage is typically much lower than the maximum allowed for home equity loans based on a loan-to-value ratio.

Not on Track to Retire?

Many people approach what they originally imagined would be their retirement age, but discover that they can't afford to retire yet. Whether this is due to children's college costs, bad investments, divorce, health issues, or some other cause, the end result is still unpleasant. If this happens to you, you might need to consider some of the following options:

- **Reduce expenses**   Downsizing housing and cars and cutting back on vacations and other expenses will make it possible to live on a more modest income.

- **Continue to work**   If your health permits, delaying retirement will allow you to continue your retirement savings program and will reduce the number of years of retirement income that your nest egg must support. Working after you've begun to collect Social Security may result in reduced benefits, but only if you retired before you reached your full retirement age.

- **Increase savings**   If you still have a few years to go before retirement, you can attempt to increase your savings rate. Taking an extra job and allocating all of that income to retirement saving may be an option.

- **Get help from family and government**   Although this is less common than it was in previous generations, family members sometimes provide monetary support, or older family members might actually move in with younger ones to stretch retirement savings. In addition, elderly people who live below the poverty level may qualify for public assistance, such as food stamps.

It's to be hoped that none of these outcomes will apply to you. If you start planning for retirement now, establish goals, and work toward meeting those goals, you'll have a better chance of funding a comfortable retirement.

10.4 Planning for Education Costs

LEARNING OBJECTIVE 10.4

Develop a plan for funding current or future education costs.

Like retirement funding, saving and paying for college takes advance planning. It is increasingly common for students to be paying for their own education while also trying to save for their children's future education costs and their own retirement. These are all large expenditures, and it's therefore extremely important to have a plan and to budget accordingly. For those who are planning ahead for future education costs, education funding is remarkably similar to retirement funding, so the methodology for estimating the monthly amount to be saved is the same. You'll first estimate how much you'll need and then calculate the monthly contribution you should make to meet your savings goal.

Many adults pay for their own undergraduate or graduate education, relying on employment income and student loans to pay their costs. Although student loans were introduced in Chapter 5 as a type of consumer credit, in this section, we'll consider student loan options in more detail.

How Much Will Future Education Cost?

Although higher education costs have risen at a faster rate than inflation over the last few decades, the rate of increase has slowed recently. For the 2018–2019 academic year, the average cost of one year of on-campus undergraduate education (tuition, room, board, transportation, books, and supplies) increased by less than 3 percent over the prior year to $25,890 at a public in-state university and $52,500 at a private university. For each of these types of schools, room, board, and transportation costs account for about $12,000 of the total.

Figure 10.7 estimates college costs for full-time students by projecting annual increases at 3% and 5% per year. The value graphed in the figure is the cost for the first year of college, assuming that the student begins school in that year. To estimate the required college fund to cover four years of school, before any sources of funding or financial aid, you can simply multiply by 4. For example, if your child will start school in 2026 and the annual cost for a full-time student living on-campus at a public university will be about $30,000, a college fund of $120,000 will cover the full 4 years.

Four ways to significantly reduce the total cost are (1) select an in-state public school, (2) live at home rather than on campus (assuming that family members will subsidize living costs), (3) go to a community college for the first two years, and (4) take advantage of employer tuition reimbursement plans. Full-time tuition and fees at community colleges in 2019 averaged only

FIGURE 10.7   **Estimated Future First-Year Cost for Higher Education (tuition, fees, room, board, transportation) Assuming Annual Inflation Rate of 3% or 5%**

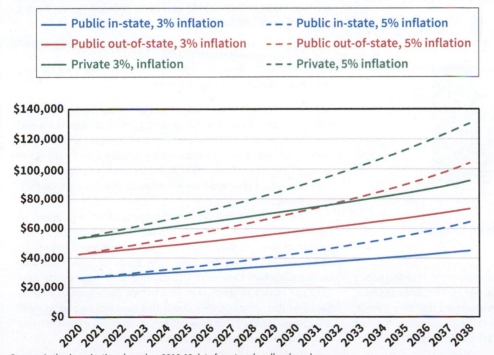

Source: Author's projections based on 2018-19 data from trends.collegeboard.org.

$3,660, about one-third as much as at public universities. For many students, the smaller class sizes and more individualized attention provided at community colleges are a better recipe for success. Many employers will pay for classes that lead to job-relevant degrees or certifications.

How Much Will You Need to Save?

EXCEL WORKSHEET

See **Excel Worksheet 10.3** (Personal Financial Planner: Education Funding Worksheet) in **WileyPLUS**.

So far, we've seen that college is expensive. Many students are able to qualify for loans, grants, and scholarships that can offset some of the costs of their education. About two-thirds of full-time students at four-year institutions pay less than the published rate for tuition and fees. **Case Study 10.2** shows you how to estimate your education funding goal and monthly savings objective by using **Excel Worksheet 10.3** (Personal Financial Planner: Education Funding Worksheet).

Financing Higher Education with Student Loans

It isn't always possible to fund higher education completely from savings, so many students and families include student loans in their education funding plan. In 2018, 69 percent of college seniors graduated with student loan debt, owing an average of about $29,800 (less for public university graduates). In addition, about 14 percent of parents took out federal loans, averaging $36,600.

Borrowing for college is a decision that should not be made lightly, as student loans can impose a substantial financial burden that will impact household finances for many years after graduation. To keep your monthly student loan payment manageable, your total student loan debt should not be greater than your expected first-year salary after graduation. At current loan rates, the monthly payment on that much debt would be about 10 percent of your take-home pay. **Demonstration Problem 10.2** shows how you can estimate the monthly payments on student loan debt after graduation.

Case Study 10.2

Indigo Fish/Shutterstock.com

Funding Jake Johnson's College Education

Problem

Holly and Gary Johnson's son Jake is 12 years old in 2019 and hopes to attend an in-state public university at age 18. The Johnsons have saved only $2,000 for college so far, which means that they are getting a late start on their goal of establishing an education funding plan for Jake. His grandparents have set up a college fund for him

that will be worth $20,000 by the time he starts college, and Jake plans to contribute $3,000 per year while he is in college from his savings and part-time employment. The Johnsons expect that Jake will receive $7,500 per year in scholarships and/or other financial aid. How much do they need to save per month in order to fund his remaining costs without borrowing?

Strategy

The Johnsons use Excel Worksheet 10.3 to calculate their funding objective and monthly savings amount.

Solution Consulting **Figure 10.7** and assuming 3 percent annual inflation between now and when Jake goes to college, Holly and Gary estimate that the annual total cost of one year at a four-year public university will be approximately $30,000 when Jake starts college. They are conservative investors with a relatively short time horizon, so they estimate a 4 percent rate of return on their investments.

The Johnsons college funding calculations are shown in **Figure 10.8**. Assuming that Jake will use student loans for a small portion of the cost, they estimate that they will need to fund an additional $43,469 by the time Jake starts college. With only six years in which to save for this expenditure, they need to save $535 per month to reach that goal before Jake goes to college. Based on their finances, they doubt that they will be able to meet this goal, so it's likely that Jake will end up with more student loans than they have estimated in the worksheet.

FIGURE 10.8   Sample of Excel Worksheet 10.3: Education Funding Worksheet

	A	B	C	D
1	Number of years until child goes to college?	6		
2	After-tax return on college fund investments?	4%		
3				
4	**Step 1. Estimate total college costs for four years of college.**			
5	Estimated first year college costs	$30,000		
6	Total for all years = Annual cost × 4			$120,000
7				
8	**Step 2. Subtract other sources of funding.**			
9	Grants and scholarships	$30,000		
10	Child's own savings or employment income	$12,000		
11	Support from other family	$20,000		
12	Amount saved so far	$2,000		
13	Future value of current savings	$2,531		
14	Total from other sources			$64,531
15				
16	**Step 3. Additional college funding needed by the time child starts school**			
17	Total college costs minus total from other sources (Step 1 – Step 2)			$55,469
18	Student loans	$12,000		
19	Funding goal (after student loans)			$43,469
20				
21	**Step 4. Calculate monthly savings needed to reach funding goal.**			
22	(Note: You can use these inputs in your financial calculator.)			
23	FV = Additional college funding needed (Step 3)	$43,469		
24	N = Number of months to save	72		
25	I = After-tax monthly investment return (= Annual return / 12)	0.33%		
26	Solve for PMT			$535
27				

DEMONSTRATION PROBLEM 10.2 | Student Loan Costs After Graduation

Problem

Karina is a recent university graduate. She financed her education costs as follows:

Employment during school and vacations	$5,000
Parents' savings	10,000
Scholarships	5,000
Grants	16,000
Student loans	24,000
Total costs	$60,000

Although there are a variety of repayment plans for student loans, assume that Karina's student loans must be repaid over a 10-year period at an interest rate of 5.05% (the 2018–2019 fixed rate for federal direct loans). How much she will have to pay per month?

Strategy

You can use a financial calculator or **Excel Worksheet 10.4** (Personal Financial Planner: How Much Is the Loan Payment?) to estimate the monthly payment for this loan.

EXCEL WORKSHEET

See **Excel Worksheet 10.4** (Personal Financial Planner: **How Much Is the Loan Payment?**) in **WileyPLUS.**

Solution

Karina is fortunate that she received so much support from scholarships and grants because these forms of financial aid do not have to be repaid. To determine the payment on her $24,000 in student loan debt using a financial calculator, enter N = 10 × 12 = 120, I = 5.05/12 = 0.4208, and PV = 24000, and solve for PMT = $255.14 per month. This is a significant burden on an entry-level salary, but will be manageable if Karina budgets appropriately. If she has difficulty repaying the loan, she may be eligible for a program that will allow her to make lower monthly payments.

Federal Student Loans   The application, borrowing, and repayment process for federal student loans is extremely easy because the federal government is the direct lender. The U.S. Department of Education provides more $50 billion in new loans each year to undergraduate students and their parents.

- **Eligibility**   To be eligible for a federal student loan, you must:
  1. Be a U.S. citizen with a valid Social Security number and a high school diploma or the equivalent.
  2. Be taking courses to fulfill requirements for a degree or certificate.
  3. Meet satisfactory progress standards set by your school.
  4. Certify that you will use the funds only for educational purposes.
  5. Certify that you are not in default on any other federal student loan.
  6. Comply with Selective Service registration, if you're a male aged 18 through 25.

- **Application**   Most student aid requires that you first submit the Free Application for Federal Student Aid (FAFSA), available at **www.fafsa.ed.gov**. Although there are firms that specialize in helping students through the application process for a fee, you can complete and submit this application yourself on the secure website at no cost. The results are emailed to you by the next business day. If you print the form and submit it by mail, you will receive the results in two to three weeks. Based on the household and financial information you provide, the Department of Education determines your expected family contribution (EFC) and reports it to participating colleges and universities. The EFC is the amount of your educational costs that you and your family will be required to pay out of your own resources. Obviously, you will be eligible for more financial aid if you have lower income and fewer assets. The Department of Education applies very strict criteria to prove independence, so the EFC for most college-aged students will consider potential contributions from both parents, even if they aren't planning to help with education costs. Participating colleges and universities take total expected annual education costs, including tuition, fees, room, and board, and subtract the EFC to determine eligibility for scholarships, grants, loans, and work study programs. A school may provide you with an award package that includes some combination of these sources of funding. Because scholarships and grants don't have to be repaid, they are more desirable, but they are also harder to come by, because each school has limited funds to award. The total award package you are offered may be more financial aid than you need, so you shouldn't automatically borrow the maximum allowed by your school. Instead, you should carefully assess how much you need.

- **Loan programs**   Loans under the William D. Ford Federal Direct Loan Program, including subsidized and unsubsidized Stafford loans, PLUS loans to parents or graduate students, and consolidation loans, are made directly by the federal government. Subsidized loans are awarded on the basis of need, carry a lower interest rate, and do not require the payment of interest or repayment of principal until six months after you graduate, withdraw, or drop to less than half-time. Key features of these loan programs are provided in **Table 10.6**.

- **Reduced payments, deferrals, and forgiveness of student loans**   In addition to their other benefits, federal student loans generally allow borrowers to defer loan payments under certain circumstances. Loan payments can be deferred for up to three years for economic hardship, postsecondary study (at least half-time), unemployment, or service in the military or the Peace Corps. In addition to fixed monthly repayment plans, the

TABLE 10.6   **Student Loan Types and Characteristics**

	Direct Subsidized Loan	Direct Unsubsidized Loan	Plus Loan for Graduate Students and Parents of Dependent Undergraduates	Private Loans
Lender	U.S. Department of Education	U.S. Department of Education	U.S. Department of Education	Bank, credit union, etc.
Interest rates for loans disbursed July 1, 2018–June 30, 2019 (maximum rate for future years)	Undergraduate 5.05%* (maximum 8.25%)	Undergraduate: 5.05%* Graduate: 6.6%* (maximum 8.25%)	7.6%* (maximum 9%)	Varies by lender and depends on credit of borrower
Annual loan limits for dependent (independent) students	Undergraduate: Yr 1: $3,500 Yr 2: $4,500 Yrs 3+: $5,500	Undergraduate: Yr 1: $5,500 ($9,500) Yr 2: $6,500 ($10,500) Yrs 3+: $7,500 (12,500) Graduate: $20,500	Cost of attendance not covered by other financial aid (subject to same maximums as direct unsubsidized loan)	Varies by lender and depends on credit of borrower
Maximum total debt for dependent (independent) students (graduate student limits include undergraduate totals)	Undergraduate: $23,000 Graduate: $65,500	Undergraduate: $31,000 ($57,500) Graduate: $138,500	Cost of attendance not covered by other financial aid	Varies by lender and depends on credit of borrower
Time limit for receiving loans	150% of degree length (6 years for 4-year degree)	150% of degree length (6 years for 4-year degree)	150% of degree length (6 years for 4-year degree)	
Repayment begins	6 months after graduation, withdrawal, or attending less than half-time	6 months after graduation, withdrawal, or attending less than half-time	6 months after last attendance	Usually upon disbursement
Interest accrues	When repayment begins	From date of disbursement	From date of disbursement	Usually upon disbursement
Fees	1.062% origination fee	1.062% origination fee	4.248% origination fee	Varies by lender and depends on credit of borrower
Repayment period	10 to 25 years	10 to 25 years	10 to 25 years	Varies by lender and depends on credit of borrower
Loan consolidation and income contingent repayment plans	Yes	Yes	Yes	No

*Interest rates for federal loans are fixed for the life of the loan. Rates are set each year on July 1 based on market rates for disbursements occurring July 1–June 30.

Direct Loan Program offers several repayment plans that can make it easier for graduates to repay the loans:

1. Extended payment plan allowing up to 25 years for borrowers with larger balances.

2. Graduated payment plan with reduced payments in the beginning, increasing every two years. If the payment is less than the interest owed for a period, the amount is added to the balance of the loan.

3. Income-driven repayment plans based on ability to pay. In these programs, borrowers can request a lower payment and extended time to repay. The remaining balance, if any, is forgiven at the end of 20 or 25 years (depending on the forgiveness program) or 10 years for those working in certain public service professions. There is a helpful calculator at **studentaid.ed.gov** that will estimate the lower payment you may qualify for.

Private Student Loans In addition to federal student loan programs, students and their parents have private loan alternatives. Generally, these loans from private lenders have much less favorable rates and repayment requirements. Interest begins to accrue as soon as you take out the loan and you'll usually have to make payments while you're still in school. Interest rates can be much higher than on federal loans, sometimes as high as credit card rates. As shown in **Figure 10.9**, nonfederal student loans represented one-quarter of all student loans through the mid-2000s, but that proportion had fallen to less than 10 percent by 2018. Although total student debt had been rising steadily, it has declined a little over the last decade.

FIGURE 10.9 **Growth of Undergraduate Student Loans, 1990–2018**   Total undergraduate student loan debt is more than 9 times what it was in 1990, mostly due to expansion of federal student loan programs.

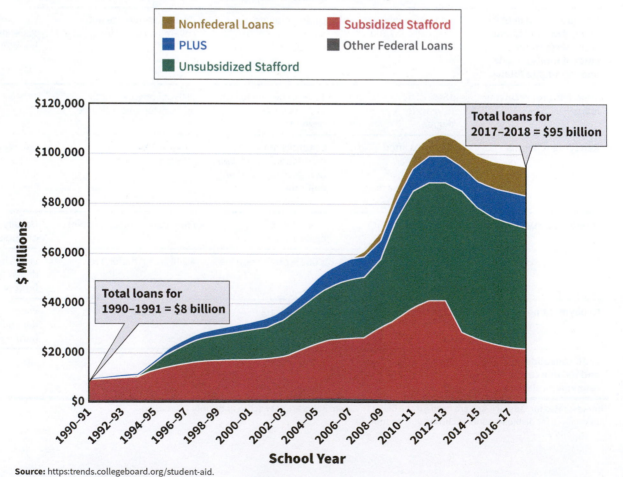

Government Programs to Help Fund Education Expenses

As with retirement, there are state and federal programs that include tax incentives designed to encourage saving for educational expenses. These incentives fall into the general categories of tax-preferred savings plans and tax credits. In Case Study 10.2, we didn't explicitly consider how tax deductions or credits could help lower the after-tax cost of Jake Johnson's higher education.

Tax-Preferred Education Savings Plans

Both the federal government and state governments offer methods for tax-preferred education saving. Three of the most important of these are summarized in **Table 10.7**. For example, the federal government has authorized **Coverdell Education Savings Accounts**, previously called Education IRAs. The tax treatment of these accounts is similar to that of Roth IRAs—contributions are made with after-tax dollars, but interest earnings aren't taxed, and no taxes are due when the funds are withdrawn. Subject to income limitations ($110,000 for singles, $220,000 for married couples), you can contribute up to $2,000 per year per child. Funds can be used for K-12 expenses as well, and families can have both Coverdells and 529 plans in place.

TABLE 10.7   Key Features of Education Savings Plan Programs

Features	Coverdell Education Savings Account	Section 529 Prepaid Tuition Plan	Section 529 Savings Plan
Available from	Financial institutions	States	States
Contribution limit	$2,000 per child under age 18 per year	Depends on plan and age of student; up to $15,000 per person per year (2019) free of gift tax	Depends on plan and age of student; up to $15,000 per person per year (2019) free of gift tax
Income limits	Phases out from $95,000 to $110,000 ($190,000 to $220,000 filing jointly)	None	None
Taxation of contributions	Taxable	May be exempt from state income tax	May be exempt from state income tax
Tax benefits	No tax on growth or withdrawals	No tax on growth or withdrawals	No tax on growth or withdrawals
Qualified expenses	All education costs including K-12: tuition, fees, room, board, and books	Most states allow use for all higher education costs: tuition, fees, room, board, and books. A few limit to tuition and fees.	All higher education costs: tuition, fees, room, board, and books
Transferability	Can transfer to different 529 plan	Can transfer to a different fund or to 529 plan	Depends on plan
Effect on eligibility for tax credits	Can still take the credit if withdrawal is used for different expenses	Can still take the credit if withdrawal is used for different expenses	Can still take the credit if withdrawal is used for different expenses
Effect on eligibility for financial aid	Considered asset of the student so will reduce eligibility	Considered asset of the student so will reduce eligibility	Considered asset of the account owner, so may reduce eligibility if owner is a parent
Account control	Parent or guardian for benefit of child	Contributor	Contributor
Maximum age to use funds	Any unused funds are disbursed when beneficiary reaches age 30	Depends on plan	Depends on plan
Investment choices	Made by account owner; broad selection of allowed investments	Made by plan administrator	Depends on plan
Ability to change Beneficiary	Yes, to another member of the beneficiary's family	Yes, to another member of the beneficiary's family	Yes, to another member of the beneficiary's family
Penalty for nonqualified withdrawal	Earnings subject to income tax plus 10% penalty	Earnings subject to income tax plus 10% penalty	Earnings subject to income tax plus 10% penalty

Most states offer **Section 529 plans** for funding college education costs. A Section 529 plan can be either a prepaid tuition plan or a savings plan. Both types of plans require after-tax contributions, although some states allow state residents to deduct the contribution from income in calculating state taxes owed.

The prepaid tuition plans enable you to pay in advance for college costs by either paying a lump sum or making a series of payments. Although rules may vary from state to state, most plans are open to residents of any state, and many allow the transfer of tuition credits to institutions outside of the state.

The amount you'll have to pay for a given number of units of tuition depends on current education costs, expected future increases, and the age of the child. For example, if four years of tuition at an in-state public institution costs $35,000 today, a Section 529 plan might allow you to pay $35,000 (or more) today to prepay for four years of tuition 18 years from now when you expect your child to go to school. The plan administrators invest the plan assets. When your child reaches college age, you can request reimbursement from the plan for qualified education expenses (which include room, board, tuition, and books), and you won't owe any taxes on the amount received. If the fund's investments earned at least as much as the rate of tuition increase, the plan will have enough to cover your child's future tuition at the then-applicable cost.

Note that despite being called "prepaid," these plans are not guaranteed. That is, there's no guarantee that the fund's investments will cover actual costs. In addition, many of the plans charge pretty hefty fees. Therefore, you should carefully compare plans before investing.

In contrast to Section 529 prepaid tuition plans, Section 529 savings plans are more similar to IRAs and Coverdell Education Savings Accounts. You choose how much to invest, and you might be able to allocate your money to particular investment vehicles. The amount you accumulate in your account will depend on how your investments do over time. As with the tuition plans, you can apply the money to any qualified education expenses.

In evaluating the various tax-preferred plans, you should consider several important questions, including limits on contributions to the various types of plans, transferability of accounts, and the effect on your child's eligibility for financial aid. Some of the account choices described above will technically be considered an asset of your child, which means that contributions to the account will be treated as gifts that are subject to gift tax if they exceed an annual limit. Because the accumulated funds belong to your child, he or she is less likely to qualify for financial aid. Finally, you need to think about what will happen if your child decides not to go to college. With Coverdell accounts, your child has control over the account when he or she reaches age 18, whereas Section 529 plans leave control with the contributor.

For more detailed information on all of the savings alternatives discussed in this section, **www.savingforcollege.com** is an excellent resource. The site allows you to compare state plans and other college savings options based on important features.

Tax Credits for Education Expenses

There are two federal income tax credits that can be claimed for education expenses, although you can't use both at the same time for the same qualifying dependent.

- You can claim the **American Opportunity tax credit** for up to $2,500 per year of a dependent child's tuition and fees (100 percent of the first $2,000 of expenses and 25 percent of the next $2,000). The student must be enrolled at least half-time and be in the first four years of a degree program. This credit phases out for adjusted gross income from $80,000 to $90,000 for singles and from $160,000 to $180,000 for married couples filing jointly.

- The **Lifetime Learning tax credit** is 20 percent of the first $10,000 of tuition and fees, including graduate school, up to a maximum of $2,000 for every eligible dependent who has incurred these expenses during the year. There is no limit on the number of years that you can claim this credit. In 2016, the credit was phased out for AGIs from $52,000 to $62,000 ($104,000 to $124,000 for married couples filing jointly).

Reflection Question 3

How well did you and/or your parents plan for your education costs? If you had it to do over, what would you do differently?

Other Education-Related Tax Breaks

If you have begun paying back student loans, you might be able to deduct the interest on these loans. You can deduct up to $2,500 in student loan interest paid for yourself, your spouse, or a qualified dependent, although the deduction is phased out for incomes from $65,000 to $80,000 ($130,000 to $160,000 for married couples filing jointly). This deduction is available even if you do not itemize deductions.

Scholarships and grants spent on tuition, school expenses, and books are tax-free, as is education assistance provided by an employer for graduate school (up to $5,250). For more information on the tax rules related to education expenses, see Publication 970 at **www.irs.gov**.

Summary

Learning Objectives Review

LEARNING OBJECTIVE 10.1 Estimate your retirement income needs, and develop savings goals.

The planning process to use for retirement and education funding is a variant of the general financial planning process: evaluate funding needs, estimate savings needed to reach goals, identify strategies for saving, implement the saving plan, and continually monitor progress.

- Two methods for estimating expenses in retirement are the **replacement ratio method**, in which you apply a fixed ratio to your current expenses and then adjust for expected inflation, and the **adjusted expense method**, in which you attempt to more accurately forecast the changes in spending patterns you can expect in retirement.

- In adjusting your income estimates to take income taxes into account, you can use **Equation 10.1**:

$$\text{Pretax income} = \frac{\text{After-tax income}}{1-t}$$

- Your retirement income shortfall is your estimated expenses in retirement less any income you expect to receive from existing pension plans and Social Security.

- Retirement wealth needed is the amount you'll need at retirement to fully fund your retirement income shortfall.

- If you want to live off the interest on your wealth and not touch the principal, you can estimate retirement wealth needed using **Equation 10.2**:

$$\text{Wealth necessary to generate a constant income without depleting principal} = \frac{\text{Income}}{r}$$

- If you want your retirement income to increase with inflation each year, but don't want to deplete your principal, you can estimate wealth needed using **Equation 10.3**:

$$\text{Wealth necessary to generate inflation-adjusted income without depleting principal} = \frac{\text{First-year income}}{r-i}$$

- If you want inflation-adjusted income in retirement, known as an **inflation-adjusted annuity**, and are willing to use both principal and interest, you can estimate wealth needed using **Equation 10.4**:

$$\text{Present value of an inflation-adjusted annuity} = \frac{\text{First-year income}}{r-i} \times \left[1 - \left(\frac{1+i}{1+r}\right)^{n}\right]$$

- In planning to accumulate sufficient wealth to meet your expenses in retirement, you'll need to make assumptions about how long you'll be retired, how much your investments will earn, and what the rate of inflation will be.

- From the total retirement wealth you need, you subtract the estimated future value of any current savings to arrive at your retirement savings goal. From this, you can calculate the necessary monthly contribution to your savings using the time value of money methods from Chapter 2. The longer you have to save and the greater your return on investment, the less you'll need to save each month.

LEARNING OBJECTIVE 10.2 Explain how employer-sponsored retirement plans and Social Security can help you meet your retirement goals.

Retirement planning should incorporate funding from multiple sources, including employer-sponsored plans, Social Security, and individual savings. In some cases, you may also plan to fund your income needs through continued employment in retirement.

- You can estimate income you expect to receive from defined-benefit (DB) pension plans by consulting your employer's annual report to you or by using the benefit formula.

- Retirement income from a defined-contribution (DC) pension plan depends on the amount of contributions, investment allocation, and investment performance over the investment period.

- Social Security is a pay-as-you-go public defined-benefit retirement program that uses payroll taxes from current workers to pay benefits to retirees. Workers and their employers each contribute a percentage of the payroll tax, currently 6.2 percent each (plus an additional 1.45% each for Medicare).

- Fully insured workers who retire at the normal Social Security retirement age will receive a monthly benefit that depends on **average indexed monthly earnings (AIME)** over their working career. The AIME is used in a formula to calculate the **primary insurance amount (PIA)**. The calculation for 2019 is given by **Equation 10.5**:

$$\text{PIA for 2019} = [0.9 \times (\text{First } \$926 \text{ of AIME})] + [0.32 \times (\text{AIME up to } \$5{,}583 - \$926)] + [0.15 \times (\text{AIME} - \$5{,}583)]$$

- You can use your annual Social Security statement or the Social Security website to estimate your future retirement benefits from this plan. This amount is reduced for early retirement and increased for delayed retirement. Social Security also provides benefits to spouses of fully insured workers and children of deceased or disabled workers.

- Social Security faces future challenges due to increased longevity and the shift toward an older population. Reforms are necessary to ensure the long-term viability of the program.

LEARNING OBJECTIVE 10.3 Explain why individual retirement accounts (IRAs) offer advantages over taxable savings accounts and annuities.

Options for retirement investing include investments in taxable and tax-deferred accounts, annuities, investments in income-producing real estate, and home equity.

- Individual retirement accounts offer the opportunity to save for retirement on a tax-deferred basis. Traditional deductible IRAs allow you to make contributions with pretax dollars and to defer payment of taxes until funds are withdrawn during retirement. Roth IRAs require that contributions be made with after-tax dollars, but you won't owe any tax when you make withdrawals in retirement.

- Both types of IRAs impose penalties for early withdrawal prior to age 59½ unless the funds are used to pay for certain qualified expenses.

- Retirement plan payouts can often be taken as a lump sum or an annuity. An annuity can be a **fixed annuity** or a **variable annuity**. It can pay out for a specific period of time or for life. With a **joint and survivor annuity**, it can even pay out over two lives. A **deferred annuity** can be purchased in advance but payments will begin at some point in the future, such as during retirement, and will grow tax-deferred until that time.

- If you've accumulated substantial home equity, you can access it to pay for postretirement expenses with a variety of types of mortgages.

LEARNING OBJECTIVE 10.4 Develop a plan for funding current or future education costs.

Funding your own or your child's education is similar to funding retirement, except that you have less time to save.

- Forecasts of future college costs can help you to develop a plan for saving for education. The amount you'll need must take into account future increases in the cost of higher education as well as your estimates of after-tax returns on investment accounts.

- If you do not have sufficient savings to fund education costs, you can take out student loans, either from the federal government or from private lenders. Federal loans tend to have more favorable rates and repayment terms.

- There are a variety of education savings programs that have tax advantages, such as the **Coverdell Education Savings accounts** (federal) and **Section 529 plans** (state). Both are similar to Roth IRAs in that you invest after tax, but you can withdraw tax-free as long as the funds are used for qualified education expenses.

- Federal tax credits include the **American Opportunity tax credit** and the **Lifetime Learning tax credit**. You need to be aware of the maximum contribution amounts and income limitations of the various options.

- Other tax incentives include tax deductions for tuition, fees, and student loan interest.

Excel Worksheets

Key Terms

WileyPLUS

Practice Questions to check your understanding, Peer-to-Peer Videos, Interactives, and many other resources are available in WileyPLUS.

Concept Review Questions

1. In what ways should you take inflation into account in your retirement planning?

2. In what ways should you take income taxes into account in your retirement planning?

3. What is meant by the "three-legged stool of retirement income"?

4. Do most retirees receive income from all three sources of the "three-legged stool of retirement income"? Why or why not? Are there any other sources of income in retirement?

5. How can you estimate the income you'll receive from an employer-sponsored defined-benefit plan?

6. How can you estimate how much income you'll receive from an employer-sponsored defined-contribution plan?

7. What financial problems are projected for the Social Security system, and what are the causes of these problems?

8. Explain the similarities and differences between a traditional deductible IRA and a Roth IRA.

9. What is the penalty for withdrawing your money from a tax-deferred retirement account prior to retirement age? Are there any exceptions to this rule?

10. Use an example to illustrate how investing in a tax-deferred account can give you a better outcome than investing in a taxable account.

11. Comment on the validity of the following statement: "Once I retire, I won't have to worry about my investments anymore."

12. Describe the process you should use in planning for funding your children's education. How is this similar to the retirement planning process?

13. Explain the similarities and differences between Roth IRAs and Coverdell Education Savings Accounts.

14. What types of tax incentives are offered for funding higher education?

15. When is the best time to begin planning for your children's education? Explain.

16. Al and Janet Fernandez have two alternatives for financing their son Joel's college costs: an unsubsidized federal student loan with a variable rate of 5.05 percent or a fixed-rate home equity loan at 6 percent. Assume that both loans will have 10-year terms for repayment. What factors should the Fernandezes consider in deciding between these two alternatives?

17. What are the differences and similarities between subsidized and unsubsidized federal student loans?

Application Problems

1. Alonzo plans to retire at age 67. His current expenses are $40,000, and he expects 3 percent inflation from now until retirement. Use the replacement ratio method to estimate Alonzo's pretax retirement income needs in the first year of retirement, assuming that he is now 22 years old and will need to replace 80 percent of his final salary.

2. Sophia plans to retire at age 67, and she expects 3 percent inflation from now until retirement. Her current expenses are $40,000. Use the adjusted expense method to estimate Sophia's pretax retirement income needs in the first year of retirement (in future dollars), assuming that she is currently 22 years old. Assume that the reduction in expenses for employment costs and mortgage payments will save her $15,000 per year in current dollars and that her additional costs for insurance and vacations will be $10,000.

3. Mark is a 30-year-old professional who earns $50,000 per year and will retire at the normal Social Security retirement age for his birth date (67). Use Table 10.4 to estimate Mark's first-year Social Security benefit in future dollars.

4. Larissa worked as a homemaker until she was 50. Since then, she has worked part-time as a retail clerk, and she is now ready to retire at age 65. Based on their individual earnings histories, her husband's Social Security PIA is $2,000, and hers is $500. What will Larissa's Social Security benefit be?

5. Janelle's estimated retirement income shortfall is $18,000, and she expects to live 40 years in retirement. If she can earn 6 percent per year on her investments during retirement and wants her retirement income to increase by 4 percent per year during retirement to offset inflation, how much does she need to have saved by the time she retires? You can use Equation 10.3 to solve this problem, or refer to Table 10.1.

6. What annual contribution will you need to make to your retirement fund, assuming that your retirement wealth goal is $500,000 and you'll earn 6 percent on your investments for the next 40 years?

7. Fred has just started a new job. His employer requires that he contribute 2 percent of his salary to a qualified retirement plan and will match any additional contributions up to 3 percent. Fred's salary isn't very high ($32,000), so he's thinking about contributing just the 2 percent minimum. What percentage of his salary does Fred need to contribute to get the maximum contribution from his employer?

8. Tom is contributing 2% of his $32,000 salary to an employer-sponsored retirement plan. Calculate the future value of Tom's first-year contribution, assuming that his account will earn 10 percent per year until retirement in 40 years.

9. Miguel has just opened a Section 529 plan to save for his daughter's college education. If he contributes $1,600 per year and earns a 6 percent annual rate of return, how much will he have accumulated by the time she starts college in 13 years?

10. You are currently 37 years old, and you plan to retire in 30 years. You've estimated that you need to accumulate an additional $1 million by the time you retire in order to fund your retirement income shortfall.

    a. If your invested funds will earn 6 percent per year, how much do you need to save each month?

    b. If your invested funds will earn 8 percent per year, how much do you need to save each month?

11. Based on your estimates, you'll need $40,000 per year to cover your expenses after you retire this month. You expect your expenses to increase with inflation at 4 percent per year, and you hope to live 30 years after retiring. How much retirement wealth do you need to have now if you'll invest your funds to earn 5 percent per year?

12. Loveta has saved $250,000 and is ready to retire. She expects to earn 5 percent per year on her investments.

    a. How much annual cash flow will this investment generate, assuming that Loveta doesn't want to touch the principal?

    b. How much annual cash flow will this investment generate, assuming that Loveta wants to withdraw equal annual payments over the next 20 years and have zero left at the end?

13. Tom decides to get an early start on retirement saving. Beginning at age 22, he invests $3,000 per year in a Roth IRA for 10 years in a row. At that point, he stops contributing to the account but leaves the money invested until age 65 (a period of 33 years). Harry doesn't start investing until he's 32 but from then on invests $3,000 in a Roth IRA each year for 33 years until retirement at age 65. If both men earn 10 percent per year on their investments, compounded annually, which one has more in the account when he reaches age 65?

14. Your child is 8 years old. You anticipate that he'll go to an in-state public university in 10 years. The current cost of one year of school is $25,000, and you estimate that costs will increase by 6 percent per year for the next 10 years. Estimate the cost of education when your child starts his first year of college.

15. Your college-funding target is to accumulate four times the expected cost of college when your child starts school. You estimate that the first year of school will cost $43,000. Calculate the amount you would need to save each year for 10 years to fully fund this future cost, assuming that you will earn 8 percent on a tax-deferred investment.

16. Assume that the first-year cost of attending college is currently $15,000 and that this cost is increasing at a rate of 5 percent per year. What is the amount needed now to fund four years of college, assuming that your invested funds earn 5 percent per year after taxes and you plan to begin school this year?

17. You estimate that you will need to have accumulated $80,000 by the time you start college in six years. How much do you need to save each year to meet this goal, assuming that your savings will earn 5 percent per year?

18. You estimate that you'll need to have saved $90,000 to fund your child's future college education in 12 years. How much do you need to save each month to reach this goal if you expect your savings to earn 6 percent per year?

19. Assume that you are ready to retire at the normal retirement age in 2019. Your average indexed monthly earnings (AIME) is $6,000. What is your primary insurance amount (PIA) using the 2019 Social Security benefit formula, and what percentage of your preretirement income will be replaced by Social Security, assuming that you earned $5,000 per month in your last year of work?

20. Rich was laid off three months ago and has exhausted his emergency funds. His new job doesn't pay enough to cover his expenses, so he's had to withdraw $15,000 from his IRA. If his marginal tax rate is 20 percent, how much of this money will he actually have available to use after penalties and taxes?

21. Luciana has just graduated from college and will have to begin making student loan payments soon. If her total debt is $20,000 and the loan rate is 6% for 10 years, how much will her monthly payment be?

Case Applications

1. Ernie Chu, currently age 27, has just taken a job as an instructor at a large public university. His starting salary is $50,000, and he has been told that salary increases have averaged 4 percent per year. After looking at the benefits package, he learns that the state recently changed its retirement plan from a defined-benefit plan, which paid retirees up to 70 percent of final salary with cost-of-living adjustments, to a defined-contribution plan. Participants contribute 8 percent of their salary to the plan, and the state contributes another 9 percent, all of which can be invested in a variety of mutual funds. Assume that Ernie and his employer contribute a combined 17 percent of his salary each year until he retires. He also finds that his employer is exempt from Social Security, so he won't have to pay the retirement portion of the payroll tax. Assume that Ernie works for a total of 40 years.

   a. How much is his salary at years 10, 20, 30, and 40, respectively, if salaries at the university continue to grow at 4 percent per year?

   b. If Ernie had been able to participate in the defined-benefit plan and was eligible to receive the maximum benefit, how much would it be?

   c. Assuming that he started work on January 1, what is Ernie's first-year contribution to his retirement plan, including funding from both himself and his employer?

   d. Estimate the amount Ernie will have in his retirement account in 40 years, assuming that his investments earn an average rate of 4 percent per year (the same as the rate of increase in his contributions to the account) and he makes beginning-of-year contributions. To do this, you can use the following shortcut: if a contribution increases each year at the same rate as the annual investment return on the account, the future value of the account can be calculated as $FV = n \times \text{Initial PMT} \times (1 + i)^n$ (for beginning-of-year contributions) and $FV = n \times \text{initial PMT} \times (1 + i)^{n-1}$ (for end-of-year contributions).

   e. Assuming that Ernie will live for 25 years in retirement and will continue to earn 4 percent on his investments, what constant level of income could he generate if he had retirement wealth of $1.6 million and wanted to spend down both interest and principal? What difference would it make if he wants to increase his withdrawals by 3 percent each year for inflation?

   f. Based on this analysis, is Ernie better off with the defined-contribution plan? Why or why not? What risk does he face now that he wouldn't have faced with the defined-benefit plan?

2. Henry decided to take early retirement at age 55 to care for his wife, Ada, who was in poor health. Because he was certain he'd outlive Ada, he convinced her that they should take the pension payout as a single life annuity for his lifetime instead of a joint and survivor annuity. The difference in the monthly payment was substantial—he'd get $2,500 per month instead of only $1,700 with the joint and survivor annuity. To save money, Henry also reduced the amount of his life insurance policy. When he was 57, Henry had a heart attack during his daily five-mile run and died.

   a. What benefit will Ada be eligible for under Henry's pension?

   b. Were the assumptions on which Henry based his pension annuity decision reasonable?

   c. If Ada is also 57 years old, can she qualify for Social Security benefits?

   d. If Ada can't qualify for Social Security and has no other sources of income, what are her options?

3. Margaret Bradford is 66 years old and has been widowed for 12 years. She was married to her second husband, Charles, for 15 years. Because they hadn't expected him to die so young, the couple hadn't gotten around to doing much retirement planning before his death. She did receive a life insurance settlement of $100,000, which she used to pay the uninsured medical expenses from Charles's illness and to repay the remaining balance on her home mortgage. Charles's pension plan gave her a lump sum benefit of $250,000,

which she rolled into an IRA. This has been invested in government bonds for the last 12 years. Her average annual return has been 4 percent, and the bond fund is now worth $400,000. After Charles's death, Margaret took a job as an office manager in a law firm, where she earns $30,000 per year, and she's been contributing to a 401(k) plan in which she has accumulated $115,000. Margaret would like to retire when she turns 67 next year. She knows she'll qualify for Social Security benefits based on her deceased husband's earnings history, and her home is worth $200,000.

   a. If Margaret had invested a little less conservatively and earned 6 percent instead of 4 percent per year for the last 12 years, how much would her account be worth today?

   b. Margaret's annual expenses are currently $18,000 per year. Use the replacement ratio method to estimate her postretirement expenses beginning one year from now, assuming that inflation is 4 percent and she will need to replace 80 percent of her preretirement income.

   c. Estimate the monthly Social Security benefit Margaret will receive, assuming that Charles was fully insured, that he had average indexed monthly earnings equal to $2,917 per month in today's dollars, and that she will make her claim based on his earnings history. (Round to the nearest dollar.)

   d. If Margaret continues to earn 4 percent on her invested assets throughout retirement, can she afford to retire? Does she face any risk of outliving her assets? Explain.

4. Rosanne and Benjamin Carter married young and had two children by the time they were 25. They had trouble making ends meet until Rosanne returned to work when Kaitlyn, their younger child, was in school full-time. Rosanne currently earns $25,000 per year after taxes, and the couple estimates that they can allocate a substantial portion of her income to their children's college fund. The Carters are now 31 years old, and their children are 10 and 7. They want to begin a savings program to help them pay for their children's college education at an in-state public university, which currently costs $24,000 per year. Assume that the education costs will increase at a rate of 4 percent per year.

   a. What will annual costs be when each of the two children start college at age 18?

   b. If the Carters' children can contribute one-fourth of the costs and they qualify for student loans and financial aid to cover another one-fourth of the costs, how much will the family need to save for each of the children? Estimate each separately.

   c. If the Carters estimate that they will need to have saved $65,000 in 8 years for their older child and $75,000 in 11 years for their younger child, is it realistic for them to think they'll be able to afford to send their children to college if they can earn 6 percent on their investments after taxes?

   d. Should the Carters consider setting up a Section 529 plan for each of the college funds? What are the pros and cons of doing this?

   e. Assuming that current tax laws remain in place, what effect will the Carters' education expenses have on their taxes?

   f. If the Carters haven't yet thought about retirement planning, what effect will education funding have on their ability to adequately fund their retirement? Will it be possible for them to work toward both long-term goals simultaneously?

CHAPTER 11

The Fundamentals of Investing

ambenvalee/Shutterstock.com

Feature Story

Florida residents John Rowles, Jim Cole, and Wayne Minton decided to supplement their regular nine-to-five incomes by starting a worm farm business. They paid $50,000 for a franchise from B&B Worm Farms of Oklahoma and invested another $100,000 in start-up costs. In return for the franchise fee, B&B promised to buy all the worms they produced, for $7 a pound, to sell to chicken farms, dairies, and agricultural facilities that need worms to process compost. At that price, the three friends estimated they'd recoup their initial investment in less than a year. The worms seemed like a no-risk investment.

Jim's garage was soon too small for their operation, so they expanded to a greenhouse. Before long, they had more than 200 manure-filled bins and lots of wiggly merchandise. Things went downhill fast when the entrepreneurs discovered that B&B was being investigated by the Oklahoma Department of Securities for securities law violations and would not be able to buy the 11 million worms they had ready for market.

Fortunately, Jim, John, and Wayne eventually found buyers for the worms, so they didn't lose all their money. They also learned some hard lessons about investing. First, there's no such thing as a "no-risk" equity investment. Second, it isn't a good idea to have everything tied up in a single investment. Finally, always do your homework before investing your cash—a call to the Department of Securities at the outset would have prevented the three partners from getting into a business arrangement with a firm that was not transacting business legally.

In this chapter, you'll read about the fundamentals of investing. When you understand how to develop an investment plan and what your investment choices are, you'll be able to better select investments that are consistent with the returns you want and the amount of risk you can tolerate.

Sources: "Lots of Wiggle Room," *Tampa Tribune*, January 16, 2003; "Worm Ranch in Sticky Situation," *Tampa Tribune*, April 15, 2003; Paul Monies, "States Sue Worm Buy-Back Scam Companies," *The Oklahoman*, April 15, 2003.

LEARNING OBJECTIVES	TOPICS	DEMONSTRATION PROBLEMS
11.1 Develop a realistic investment plan to meet your long-term financial goals, taking into account budgetary constraints, transaction costs, and taxes.	**11.1 Developing a Realistic Investment Plan** • First Things First: Establishing a Firm Foundation • Establishing Investment Goals • Key Strategies for Investment Success	

(continued)

(continued)

LEARNING OBJECTIVES	TOPICS	DEMONSTRATION PROBLEMS
11.2 Identify and define the major types of investments.	**11.2 Understanding Your Investment Choices** • Investing by Lending and by Owning • Major Asset Classes	
11.3 Compare investment alternatives based on return and risk.	**11.3 The Risk–Return Trade-off** • Rate of Return • Risk • How Risk-Averse Are You? • Factors Affecting Risk Attitudes • Types of Investment Risk	
11.4 Evaluate portfolio performance relative to a similarly diversified benchmark index.	**11.4 Diversification and Performance Evaluation** • How Diversification Works • Asset Allocation • Evaluating Performance Against a Benchmark • Active versus Passive Investing	

11.1 Developing a Realistic Investment Plan

LEARNING OBJECTIVE 11.1

Develop a realistic investment plan to meet your long-term financial goals, taking into account budgetary constraints, transaction costs, and taxes.

As you've learned in other chapters, achieving your financial goals often requires that you develop a plan for saving and investing. As with other aspects of financial planning, you'll need to develop goals and investigate your options for achieving those goals. The entrepreneurs in the Feature Story were attempting to build their financial wealth by starting a small business growing worms, but they made the mistake of not being fully informed about their risks and ended up losing a lot of their invested funds. In this chapter, you'll learn how to develop your investment plan and select from broad categories of investments to build a portfolio that's consistent with your risk tolerance. In Chapters 12 and 13, you'll learn more about stocks, bonds, mutual funds, and real estate investments.

First Things First: Establishing a Firm Foundation

Although it might sound like fun to jump right in and start investing, there are a few things you should take care of first. As you already know, a comprehensive financial plan has many components, some of which have priority over others. Before you begin to develop an investment plan, you should make sure that you have a secure foundation to build on. Have you established the necessary foundation elements of your plan, prioritized your financial goals, and developed a budget that will allow you to set aside sufficient funds for investing? If so, you can move ahead in the investment planning process. To see if you're ready for this step, ask yourself the questions in **Figure 11.1**.

FIGURE 11.1   **Am I Ready to Start an Investing Plan?**   Before you start work on your investment plan, check to make sure that other elements of your financial plan are in place.

✓	Have I established my financial goals?
✓	Am I living within my budget and meeting my basic needs?
✓	Have I paid off high-interest credit?
✓	Have I established an emergency fund?
✓	Do I have adequate insurance coverage?
✓	Are my housing needs being adequately met?

If you can answer "yes" to all these questions, then you're ready to begin your investment planning. That doesn't mean you should immediately call a broker and buy 100 shares of Netflix stock. Before you take any specific action, you'll need to establish your investment objectives and educate yourself about the investment marketplace and your investment alternatives. The investment planning process is summarized in **Figure 11.2**. We discuss the steps in this process in more detail in later sections of this chapter.

FIGURE 11.2   **The Investment Planning Process**   As in other areas of your financial life, planning for your investments is the key to success.

1. Identify your investment goals.

2. Learn about your investment choices.

3. Evaluate your risk tolerance.

4. Select investments consistent with risk tolerance, time horizon, and investment objectives.

5. Monitor the plan.

Establishing Investment Goals

In developing your investment plan, you should first ask yourself, "Why am I investing?" There are many possible investing goals. Some might be short-term, such as accumulating funds to buy a car or take a vacation. In previous chapters, we've discussed long-term investment goals such as buying a home, saving for retirement, and funding education. If you have more than one investment goal, you'll need to prioritize them and develop a plan for meeting each of them over time.

How Much Do You Need, and When Do You Need It?

In Chapter 1, we discussed the process of goal setting and encouraged you to write down and prioritize long-term goals. Many of these goals require that you save money over time in order to achieve them. To be most successful in this part of your plan, you should try to make sure that your investment goals are realistic, specific, and measurable. For each of your goals, you'll need to answer these questions:

- When will you need the money?
- How much money must you accumulate to meet each goal?
- What will your monthly or annual budget allocation to each investment goal be?

EXCEL WORKSHEET

See **Excel Worksheet 11.1** (Personal Financial Planner: Setting Investment Goals) in **WileyPLUS**.

In the last chapter, you learned how to estimate funds needed and monthly savings goals. At this point, you should be ready to develop a complete list of your investment goals, with specific savings allocated to each. **Case Study 11.1** illustrates how to use **Excel Worksheet 11.1** (Personal Financial Planner: Setting Investment Goals) to help quantify your investment goals.

In this chapter, we look at where to invest the funds you have allocated to meeting your goals. Different types of investments have different average returns over time, so the amount you'll need to invest to achieve your goals will depend on your choice of investments. You'll also need to consider the riskiness of different investments relative to your preferences and time horizon. If you're saving for a long-term goal, you might be able to weather some ups and downs in the stock market, but if you need the money relatively soon, like the newlyweds in Case Study 11.1, you can't afford to take much risk.

Case Study 11.1

Marilyn Volan/
Shutterstock.com

Newlyweds Set Their Investment Goals

Problem

Ben and Abby are newlyweds. Their number-one financial goal is to buy a home within the next five years. Based on home prices in the area, they estimate they will need about $20,000 to cover the down payment and closing costs. They hope to reach this goal by saving their $4,000 tax refund and sticking to a regular monthly savings plan. They need to estimate how much to save per month, assuming that their investment fund will earn 4 percent after taxes.

Strategy

To find out how much they need to save each month, Abby and Ben use Excel Worksheet 11.1. This worksheet has built-in time value of money calculations and can be used for any financial goal. The worksheet allows you to enter the amount you need, how long you have to save, and the rate of return you can expect to earn on your investments. You can do the same calculation with a financial calculator using the methods explained in Chapter 2.

Solution   Ben and Abby's completed worksheet is shown in **Figure 11.3**. Based on the information they have entered in the worksheet, they will need to save $278.70 per month for five years to reach their goal of accumulating $20,000 to put toward the purchase of a house.

FIGURE 11.3 Sample of Excel Worksheet 11.1: Setting Investment Goals

	A	B
1	**Financial goal (in words)**	Down payment for house
2		
3	**Risk tolerance: (high, medium, low)**	Low
4		
5	**Amount needed**	$20,000
6		
7	**When needed (in years)**	5
8		
9	**Amount of initial investment (if any)**	$4,000
10		
11	**Annual after-tax return on investment**	4%
12		
13	**Future value of initial investment**	$4,867
14		
15	**Amount remaining to reach goal**	$15,133
16		
17	**Monthly payment necessary to reach goal**	$228.26
18		

Obtaining the Money to Invest

The actual process of investing is not especially difficult. The most common stumbling block is lacking the necessary funds to invest. An essential element of your financial plan must therefore be to prioritize your spending so that investing for the future receives sufficient attention. You'll probably have to sacrifice current spending to have money available to devote to your investment plan. Depending on where you are in your career and life cycle, you might need to start out small and build your investment program as your income increases. Even if you can only invest a fairly small amount at first, the time value of money and the power of compound interest will help you move toward achieving your long-term goals. As we've noted in other chapters, the earlier you start, the less you'll need to save each month to achieve a specific goal. Taking the first step is the toughest part—once you get started, you'll find it easier to continue.

Table 11.1 gives common tips from professional financial planners for making it less painful to find the money in your budget for investing. In **Interactive: How Much Difference Does a Little More Saving Make?**, you'll be able to see how much difference each investment strategy will make to the success of your plan.

INTERACTIVE

See Interactive: How Much Difference Does a Little More Saving Make? in **WileyPLUS**.

TABLE 11.1   Financial Planners' Tips for Finding the Money to Invest

1. **Pay yourself first.**   Most people find that, if they wait until the end of the month to invest, the funds are no longer there—they were whittled away by small and often unnecessary expenditures. Take a predetermined amount right off the top at the beginning of the month, and you'll be more likely to stick to the plan.

2. **Save half your raise.**   Make a deal with yourself that you'll allocate half of your annual raise to savings. If you don't let yourself become accustomed to the extra income, but instead immediately set it aside for your investment plan, it won't feel like you're cutting back on immediate consumption.

3. **Set aside bonuses, tax refunds, and other lump sums.**   When the money you're applying to investments has never been part of your regular income, it's even less painful to set it aside. Bonuses and other lump-sum windfalls such as birthday gifts, tax refunds, and inheritances can be immediately applied to your investment plan. And if these lump sums are fairly significant amounts to start with, you'll see that the dollars accumulate more quickly.

(continued)

TABLE 11.1	Financial Planners' Tips for Finding the Money to Invest *(continued)*

4. Continue a payment plan.　When you've finished paying off an installment loan, such as a car loan or student loan, consider shifting those dollars immediately to your investment plan. Because you haven't been spending that portion of your income on consumption, you can put it toward this new use without feeling the loss. Your $300 monthly car payment could put you closer to achieving your investment goals by $3,600 per year.

5. Maximize your employer match.　If your employer offers to match your contribution to a retirement plan, you'll get the benefits of tax deferral, and the employer contribution will make your account grow that much faster. The match is like a 100% return on investment of your own contribution for the first year.

6. Stop up a cash leak.　Careful evaluation of your budget sometimes reveals regular household expenditures that could be avoided or reduced. Examples include eating out instead of "brown bagging" your lunch a few days a week, taking books out of the library instead of buying them, and taking public transportation or biking to work instead of driving. Try allocating these dollars to an investment plan instead.

7. Go on a financial diet once or twice a year.　Many people find it easier to tighten their belts in short stretches. Try being a cheapskate for one or two months a year, trimming your budget down to just the necessities and banking the rest.

8. Take a second job.　Although you probably don't want to work two jobs indefinitely, taking a second job for one or two months is a good way to start a nest egg for investing.

Key Strategies for Investment Success

For your investment plan to be successful, you'll need to stick to your plan, minimize transaction costs and taxes that can erode your investment earnings, and work hard to be an informed consumer. We explain these strategies in more detail below.

Start Early and Be Consistent

The time value of money will benefit you the most if you get started investing as soon as possible. Even if you're a typical college-age student, it's not too early to start thinking about saving for future goals such as buying a home. Beginning the financial planning process while you're still in school will help you "hit the ground running" so that you'll be able to achieve your financial goals sooner.

Lots of people make New Year's resolutions to invest and save, but they aren't all successful. Remember the "pay yourself first" rule, and set up a regular savings and investment plan that comes right off the top, which will help you stick to your plan. Many investment advisors recommend a strategy called **dollar cost averaging**, which involves investing equal dollar amounts at regular intervals rather than making a large investment at one time. Because most individual investors attempt to make regular contributions to investments from current income, this strategy is a natural fit for their financial plans.

The logic behind dollar cost averaging is that you can't predict whether market prices today are high or low compared with what they'll be later. By spreading your investment purchases over time, however, you'll average out the ups and downs of purchase prices. When prices are rising, your dollars will purchase fewer units of the investment at the higher prices. When prices are falling, you'll be able to buy more, but at lower prices. Over the long term, the average purchase price per unit will be lower than the long-term average price for the investment.

Take Advantage of Favorable Tax Rules

Recall that it's always important to take taxes into consideration before making financial decisions. The higher your tax bracket, the more you'll benefit from tax-preferred methods of saving such as employer retirement plans, college savings plans, and IRAs. But there are costs as well. Most of these savings options place limitations on your ability to use the money, and some have income maximums.

ONLINE CALCULATOR DEMONSTRATION VIDEO

See **Online Calculator Demonstration Video: Does Dollar Cost Averaging Work** in **WileyPLUS**.

When you invest in a *tax-deferred* account such as a traditional IRA, you'll be able to defer paying tax on the earnings from income and growth until you withdraw the funds at retirement. At that time, your withdrawals will be taxed at your ordinary income tax rate. In contrast, a *tax-exempt* investment's returns are not subject to certain taxes at all. Interest on municipal bonds (debt issued by state and local governments) is exempt from federal income tax, and your interest earnings on these bonds will also be exempt from state income tax if you're a resident of the state that issued the bond. Similarly, interest on federal government debt securities is exempt from state and local income taxes.

Although tax-deferred and tax-exempt investments will obviously save you money over the long term, when you invest for shorter-term goals, it might be necessary to have your money in a taxable account so that you can withdraw funds without penalty. In this case, the taxes you'll pay on income from interest, dividends, and capital gains will reduce your annual returns and the cumulative value of your portfolio.

As you may recall from Chapter 4, current income from investments held in taxable accounts is taxable as ordinary income. In other words, you'll pay a tax on this income equal to your marginal tax rate. If you're subject to a marginal tax rate of 25 percent, for example, your interest income of $100 will net you $75 after taxes. In contrast, the tax on capital gains—gains from the sale of an investment—depends in part on how long you hold the investment before selling it. Profits on the sale of investments held for one year or less are taxed as ordinary income. However, if you hold an investment longer than one year, the gain on the sale is subject to a special lower tax rate. Dividend income from most US stock investments is also taxed at the lower rate. **Table 11.2** details the federal long-term capital gains tax rates applicable in 2019. The maximum tax on a long-term capital gain of $100 was $20.

TABLE 11.2	**2019 Federal Capital Gains Tax Rates on Investments Held for One Year or More**
Federal Income Tax Bracket	**Long-term Capital Gains Tax Rate**
10%, 12%	0%
22%, 24%, 32%, 35%	15%
37%	20%

Another advantage of capital gains over interest and dividend income is that the increase in an asset's value isn't taxed until the asset is sold, so if your investment has grown by $100 in value over the year but you haven't sold it, you won't owe any current tax on the gain. For this reason, while you're in the wealth-building stage of your life cycle, you'll do better to invest in growth assets, which provide a return to investors primarily in the form of increased value, rather than income assets, which pay potentially taxable interest and dividends.

Minimize Transaction Costs

Most individual investors buy investments through an intermediary, such as a bank or brokerage firm. Although full-service brokerage firms are available, your cheapest alternative is likely to be a **discount broker**. These firms now provide much the same level of online account management, investment research, asset allocation tools, and loan availability as their more expensive counterparts. Most can set up an IRA for you as well.

When you do business with a brokerage firm, you'll be required to open a **brokerage account** and keep a minimum amount there, in either cash or securities. Your funds may be insured against brokerage firm failure by the Securities Investor Protection Corporation (SIPC). Although your account records will include the specific shares you own, the actual documents that evidence your ownership interest—your stock, bond, or mutual fund certificates—will be held in the name of the brokerage firm and maintained at its office.

Competition has driven trading fees to all-time lows in recent years. **SmartMoney.com** reports that average costs per trade at discount brokers are now less than $8, compared with $28 in 1994, and trading is free at some firms. **Table 11.3** provides some details on online brokerage firms that were rated best for beginners by **NerdWallet.com** in 2019. Although this evaluation considered many factors, you should always do your homework before selecting a brokerage firm. All of the firms listed in Table 11.3 have low trading fees, for example, but some may add extra fees for making transactions over the phone, closing an account, or leaving an account inactive for a period of time.

TABLE 11.3   **Top-Rated Online Brokers for Beginners, 2019**

Online Broker	NerdWallet Rating (out of 5)	Commission per Trade	Account Minimum	Best Features
Ally Invest	5.0	$4.95	$0	Low costs Strong web-based platform Free research and data
E*Trade	4.5	$6.95	$500	Easy-to-use tools Large investment selection Extensive research and data Advanced mobile app
Fidelity Brokerage	5.0	$4.95	$0	Low costs Large selection of research Strong customer service
Merrill Edge	4.5	$6.95	$0	No account minimum Extensive research and data Free trades for large accounts
Robinhood	4.5	$0	$0	Low costs Streamlined interface Cryptocurrency Customizable mobile app
Schwab Brokerage	5.0	$4.95	$0	No inactivity fees Strong customer support Extensive research and data Mutual funds and ETFs
TD Ameritrade	5.0	$6.95	$0	No account minimum Excellent customer support Large investment selection Good mobile app

Source: www.nerdwallet.com, "Best Online Stock Brokers for Beginners March 2019."

Be an Informed Investor

In today's information-overloaded world, there are so many sources of financial information that it's easy to become overwhelmed. Nevertheless, to make good investment decisions, you'll need to take the time to learn about the financial markets and to stay informed. Useful sources of information include the following:

- **Internet resources**   The Internet is a tremendous resource for investors. On various financial websites, such as **finance.yahoo.com**, **google.com/finance**, and **cnbc.com**, you can easily find price histories for stocks, read analysts' reports, and track general market movements. In addition, you can also find financial calculators and tutorials on a variety of subjects related to personal finance.

- **Periodicals**   The *Wall Street Journal* and the *Financial Times* both provide up-to-date and well-written news coverage related to the securities marketplace and to individual securities in the market. If these newspapers seem a little too heavy-duty, financial magazines such as *Fortune*, *Money*, *Forbes*, *Barron's*, and *Kiplinger's Personal Finance* provide good-quality information targeted to the average consumer.

- **Brokers and financial advisors** If you use a discount broker to manage your investments, you'll have access to a wealth of online financial tools, tutorials, and news.

- **Annual reports** Publicly traded companies are required to report each year on their financial performance for the current year and prior years and to make projections about the company's future. These reports are available for free download at **www.annualreports.com** and on company websites. Publicly traded companies also must file quarterly and annual financial reports with the Securities and Exchange Commission, and these reports are available for free download at **www.sec.gov/edgar.shtml**.

- **Self-help books** At your local bookstore or Internet book distributor, you'll find literally hundreds of self-help resources for investors. As with online resources, some trade books are based on sound research and experience, and some are not. To choose the most helpful reading materials, look for reputable reviews in the financial press, and examine closely the credentials of the authors.

- **Investment clubs** Investment clubs are groups of individuals who get together on a regular basis to share information about investments and jointly manage an investment fund. The advantage of an investment club is that you can profit from the knowledge, experience, and time invested by others. The disadvantage is that you might find yourself in the proverbial situation of "the blind leading the blind." If you're interested in forming an investment club or learning more about them, go to **www.aaii.com** to find a local chapter of the American Association of Individual Investors.

Reflection Question 1

Given that there is so much information available on the Internet, what sources would you trust the most and why? What can you do to combat information overload?

Keep Accurate Records

Record keeping is an aspect of your investment plan that you can't afford to ignore. Not only must you keep records for tax purposes, but you also need to be able to make changes promptly if circumstances require it. Keeping thorough records doesn't have to be an onerous task. There are many ways to track your portfolio, ranging from worksheets that you update periodically to more complex investment-tracking software. Fortunately, much of the work will be done for you by your brokerage firm, and you'll be able to easily download trade confirmations, account statements, and tax documents from its website.

11.2 | Understanding Your Investment Choices

LEARNING OBJECTIVE 11.2
Identify and define the major types of investments.

There are many different investment alternatives, and it's very important to understand their characteristics before making any investment decisions. In the Feature Story, you saw the consequences of investing in something without full information. With so many complex and risky products available to investors today, it's easier than ever to lose money if you aren't careful.

In the next two chapters, we'll talk in greater detail about specific investment choices. In this section, you'll learn about several broad categories of investments, with specific focus on the types of cash flows they generate for investors. We begin with an explanation of the difference between investing as a lender and investing as an owner, and then we explain the most common types of investments in each of those categories. We also discuss some important differences in risk and return for each type of investment.

Today, most employer-sponsored and individual retirement savings are in the form of mutual funds. Recall from Chapter 3 that mutual funds are investment companies that invest in a variety of different types of assets, such as stocks and bonds. Because mutual fund investing is so common today, we cover it in more detail in Chapter 13. However, before investing in a mutual fund, you should have a basic understanding of the assets that the mutual fund might buy on your behalf. **Figure 11.4** compares the assets of mutual funds in 2000 and 2018. Most of these funds continue to be in stocks and bonds. In addition, funds' allocation to lower-return and safer money market securities has declined and their allocation to stocks has increased over this period of time.

FIGURE 11.4 **Mutual Fund Assets 2000 and 2018 (billions of dollars)** The total amount invested in mutual funds more than tripled between 2000 and 2018.

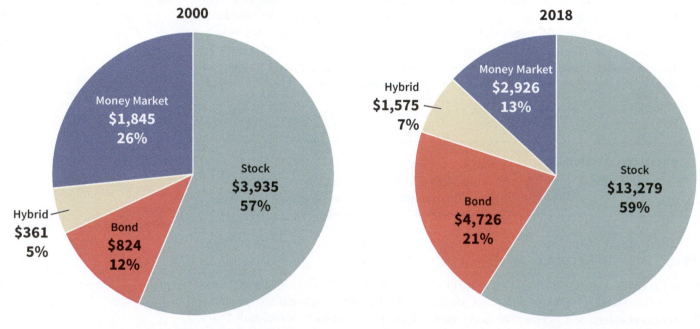

Source: Data from Investment Company Institute, *2018 Investment Company Factbook,* 58th ed., available at www.ici.org.

Investing by Lending and by Owning

There are generally two ways to invest—you can be either a lender or an owner. When you lend, whether it's to a government entity, financial institution, or other business, you're called a **debt investor**. When you own, you're an **equity or stock investor**. In either case, the return on your investment will come from some combination of the following:

- Regular cash flow, such as the payment of interest or dividends
- Growth in the value of your investment over time, also known as a **capital gain**

The amounts you earn and the risks you're exposed to with these two methods of investing differ in important ways.

The Advantages and Disadvantages of Lending

When you lend to others—whether to an individual, government entity, financial institution, or other business—your cash flows will generally include regular interest payments and the eventual repayment of your original loan. If you sell your debt investment to someone else before the loan is repaid, you might end up with either a capital gain or a capital loss, depending on the investment's value at the time you sell.

Debt investments are sometimes called **fixed-income investments**, because the interest is commonly paid in equal installments over time. The relative certainty of future cash flows is one of the advantages of debt investing. Yet, as many debt investors discovered during the recent financial crisis, these investments can still be risky if the borrower gets into financial difficulty and fails to make payments as promised.

There are many types of lending opportunities, and they differ in risk and return. The relationship between risk and return should be familiar to you from previous chapters. Recall that one of the basic principles of finance is that, generally, the lower the risk, the lower the return. Your bank savings account, for example, is a very low-risk, federally insured loan made to your financial institution. The bank, in return for your deposit, promises to pay you regular interest on your savings and to return your funds to you upon request; however, because the risk is so low, the rate of interest the bank pays is very low as well. In contrast, if you lend money to a governmental entity or to a business and commit your funds for a long period of time, you're exposed to greater risk and will therefore be paid a higher annual rate on the debt investment.

In short, debt investments offer the security of receiving regular interest payments. However, the trade-off for this safety is that you'll generally earn a lower investment return on debt investments than on other investment alternatives.

The Advantages and Disadvantages of Owning

If you're an entrepreneur at heart, you can invest by owning your own business. This, of course, requires certain skills and a substantial investment of time and money. It also exposes you to the risk of total loss in the event that your business is not successful. Alternatively, if you want to share in the profits of a business without having to run the business yourself, you can become an equity or stock investor. In this case, you're a partial owner of a company, but rely on others to manage it. As a stock investor, you expect to receive a return on your investment in the form of growth in the value of your investment over time and/or regular distribution of business profits as dividends.

Your cash flows as an owner are much less certain than your cash flows as a lender. If the company does very well, your income stream may increase over time, but you also run the risk that the company's profits will be less than expected or that the company will experience a loss or go out of business. Whereas the company is obligated to make payments to its debt investors, it has no similar obligation to its owners; in a bad year, there might be nothing left to distribute to equity investors.

Major Asset Classes

Although there are many investment choices, novice investors should generally stick to the basics—mutual funds that invest in stocks and bonds. In some cases, it might also make sense to invest in real estate. These broad categories of investments, commonly referred to as **asset classes**, are groups of investments that have certain characteristics in common. In this section, we review major classes of assets. As you gain experience, you might decide to branch out to more complex investments, but you need to start out simple and add to your knowledge base as you go. Your objective is to build a diversified portfolio, or collection, of investments that fulfills your objectives.

Some investments may also be called securities. By law, a **security** is created when investors contribute money to a common enterprise with the intention of earning a profit through the efforts of others. There are special regulatory and disclosure requirements for selling securities to investors. Stocks, bonds, and mutual fund shares are common examples of financial securities.

Common Stock

A share of **common stock** represents a share of ownership in a business. If you own a share in a company that has a total of 1,000,000 shareholders, your single share means you own

1/1,000,000 of the company. Your share entitles you to vote on major issues, such as election of the board of directors of the company or merger opportunities. If the board decides to distribute some of the company's profits to its shareholders, you're entitled to your proportional share.

As mentioned, stock investors generally expect to make a return on their investment in the form of **dividends**, which are periodic distributions of profits to equity investors, and capital gains, which are increases in the value of investors' shares over time. Neither form of return is guaranteed, however. In fact, both are fairly risky. Dividends can be paid only if the company has funds available after paying all its other obligations. Shares of stock have no maturity date, so the firm never has to pay you back the amount you've put into the firm, but you can sell your shares to other investors or pass them on to your heirs, assuming that the firm is still in existence at that time.

Bonds

The most common long-term debt investment is a **bond**. A bond generally has a fixed maturity date (often 20 years or more in the future), at which time the borrower promises to repay the loan in full. In addition, the bondholder is entitled to receive a fixed payment of interest periodically, usually semiannually (every 6 months). Unlike mortgage loans, this type of loan is not amortized, so the regular payments are interest only, and the full amount of principal is due when the bond matures. For example, a 20-year corporate bond with a $1,000 face value might promise a $60 interest payment per year, or 6 percent of the face value. The investor would receive half of this interest, or $30, every six months and be repaid the $1,000 in full on the maturity date, 20 years from the initial day of issuance.

Bonds are issued by federal, state, and local governments and by corporations to finance operations and expansion. Like stock investors, bond investors expect to make a return on their investment from both current income (periodic interest payments) and capital gains (change in value of the bond over time). Although the interest payments are usually fixed for the life of the bond, the bond *value* is not. As you'll learn in the next chapter, the value of a bond tends to change in the opposite direction from market interest rates. So when the Federal Reserve acts to reduce interest rates, as it did after the financial crisis, bond values will increase. If the Fed increases rates, bond values will decline.

Money Market Securities

Money market securities are another category of interest-earning investments. These investments offer very low interest rates and also have very low risk. They include Treasury bills (T-bills) issued by the federal government and CDs issued by banks. These investments are called "money market" securities because they are similar to cash in that they have very low risk of going down in value over short holding periods.

Preferred Stock

In addition to common stock, companies also sometimes issue **preferred stock**. This type of investment has characteristics that make it somewhat like a hybrid of a stock and a bond. Similar to common stock, preferred stock represents an ownership share in the firm and has no maturity date. Like a bond, a share of preferred stock produces a constant cash flow for the investor, because the dividend is a fixed dollar amount per share per year. Although the constant cash flow makes preferred stock resemble bonds, it's a riskier investment than bonds because it does, in fact, represent an equity interest. In the event of financial difficulties, the company must make its debt payments before paying any dividends to shareholders. Preferred shareholders do, however, have priority over common shareholders, which is why they are called "preferred."

Real Estate

In addition to owning your home, you might also want to consider investing in other real estate. As an owner of investment real estate, you can receive cash flows from net rental income and capital gains from the growth in the property's value. The risks include relatively high transaction costs and lack of liquidity. We discuss real estate investment in more detail in Chapter 13.

Derivatives

The investment marketplace has expanded in recent years to include a large number of complex and risky securities. Many of these fall into a general category of investments called **derivative securities** because they derive their value from the price movements of some other underlying assets. Common examples of derivatives include commodities, futures, and options. These assets are considered to be **speculative investments** because they don't pay dividends or interest income. Instead, investors hope to make a short-term profit based on changes in supply and demand. Although it's possible to make a large return on some types of speculative investments, you run the risk of quickly losing everything you've invested. Therefore, these types of investments generally are not a recommended financial planning strategy, particularly for inexperienced investors.

Commodities are raw materials (such as oil and precious metals) and agricultural products (such as corn, wheat, and sugar). Investors trade in these assets using futures and options. A **futures contract** allows you to buy or sell an underlying asset at a future date for a price that is set in advance. The underlying security can be a commodity, a financial security, or a currency. The buyers and sellers of futures contracts are making bets on which way prices will go in the future.

An **option contract** is like a futures contract except that the buyer is not obligated to go through with the contract to buy or sell in the future—he or she simply has the right to do so. A buyer of a *call option* has the right, but not the obligation, to purchase the underlying asset at a set price on or before the call's maturity date. A buyer of a *put option* has the right, but not the obligation, to sell the underlying asset at a set price on or before the put's maturity date. Although option contracts might seem a bit less risky than futures contracts, the buyer of an option has to pay a price up front for that right, so even if prices move in a favorable direction, the cost of the option itself might offset any profit made.

Mutual Funds

Mutual funds are not actually an asset class—they are a vehicle through which investors can invest in portfolios of stocks, bonds, and other assets. When you buy shares of a mutual fund, you are buying proportional ownership in all the assets held by that mutual fund. The mutual fund hires investment professionals to select and manage a portfolio of investments on behalf of the fund's shareholders. As a mutual fund investor, you're therefore entitled to share in the income and the growth of the investment pool. Most employer-sponsored retirement plans are invested in mutual funds. Mutual fund return and risk depends on the return and risk of the particular assets that the fund invests in.

11.3 | The Risk–Return Trade-off

LEARNING OBJECTIVE 11.3
Compare investment alternatives based on return and risk.

One of the most important concepts in investing is the relationship between return and risk. Almost all investments expose you to some amount of risk. In general, however, riskier investments provide you with higher average rates of return over time. Therefore, if you're investing for the long term, taking a little risk will help your savings grow more quickly. In this section, we define return and risk more precisely and explain how risk preferences might influence your selection of investments.

Rate of Return

Recall that investors expect to make money from current income generated by their investments (such as interest, dividends, or rents) and from the gains in the value of their investments over time. These are referred to collectively as the return on investment, which is usually expressed as a **rate of return**, or **yield**. The rate of return is the gain or loss on an investment over a particular period expressed as a percentage of the price paid for the investment. The rate of return is calculated as shown in **Equation 11.1**:

$$\text{Rate of return} = \text{Current yield} + \text{Capital gain yield}$$

$$= \frac{\text{Current income}}{\text{Beginning price}} + \frac{\text{End price} - \text{Beginning price}}{\text{Beginning price}} \tag{11.1}$$

$$= \frac{\text{Current income} + \text{End price} - \text{Beginning price}}{\text{Beginning price}}$$

As an example, suppose you buy a share of stock for $20. Over the course of a year, the stock pays you a cash dividend of $1. That amounts to 5 percent of your original purchase price ($1/$20). The stock also increases in value to $22 (a gain of $2, or 10 percent of the original purchase price). The combined value of the dividend income and the gain in value gives you a $3 return for the year, so you have earned a rate of return of 15 percent ($3/$20) on the stock investment.

Figure 11.5 illustrates long-term performance, including both capital gains and interest or dividends, of a $1 investment in Treasury bills, Treasury bonds, large-company stocks, and small-company stocks. Remember that Treasury bills and bonds are short-term and long-term debt securities issued by the federal government. For comparison, inflation in the value of a dollar over time is also included on the graph.

FIGURE 11.5 **Long-Term Performance of Various Investments** The graph shows how an investment of $1 would have grown over time. Over long periods, stock investments have outperformed Treasury bills and bonds by a large margin.

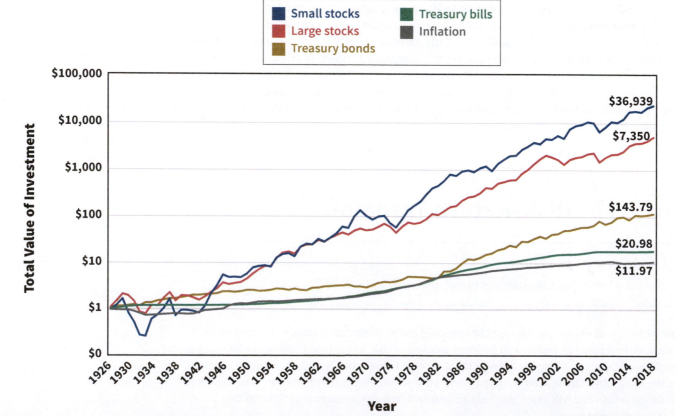

Source: Author calculations based on total return data series in *Ibbotson SBBA Classic Yearbook* (2018).

Do you notice anything unusual about the vertical axis in Figure 11.5? Because of the extreme differences between the ending dollar values for these investments, the graph is drawn on an exponential scale, with each higher gridline 10 times the one below it. If the graph was drawn on a regular scale, the bottom three lines would look like they were flat along the horizontal axis, and we wouldn't be able to see the difference between them.

Although the graph shows the cumulative value of the investment, investments are often compared based on *annualized* return on investment. **Table 11.4** shows the annualized returns over some specific periods of time.

TABLE 11.4   **Average Annual Returns for Different Periods of Time**

	Small Stocks	Large Stocks	Long-term Government Bonds	Treasury Bills	Inflation
1926–2017	16.52%	12.06%	5.99%	3.40%	2.81%
1988–2017	14.05	12.16	8.87	3.13	2.11
2008–2017	11.89	10.39	7.19	0.39	0.25

Source: Author calculations based on total return data series in *Ibbotson SBBI Classic Yearbook* (2018).

If you invested $1 in T-bills in 1926 and continually reinvested earnings each year, your initial investment would have been worth about $21 in 2018. That might not seem too bad until you compare it with your other choices. For example, $1 invested in large company stocks in 1926 would have been worth about $7,350 in 2018, and $1 invested in small company stocks would have grown to $37,000. During this time period, inflation took a bite out of spending power. It cost $12 in 2018 to buy the same goods that cost $1 in 1926. The stocks were clearly riskier, adversely affected by several stock market crashes (most recently in 2008), but the long-run performance was many times better.

> **Reflection Question 2**
>
> Since stock investments have consistently performed better than investments in other asset classes, should you put all of your money in stocks? Why or why not?

Risk

The amount of risk that you're willing to take depends, in part, on whether you expect to be adequately rewarded for taking that risk. Even if an investment were truly risk-free, you'd still expect to be compensated for investing your money instead of being able to spend it for current consumption. The additional return you earn from any investment is your compensation for bearing different types of risk.

Because there are two sources of return, current cash flow and capital gains, you need to worry about two kinds of risk that might adversely affect your ability to meet your financial goals:

- The risk that you won't receive expected cash flows from the investment
- The risk that the value of your investment will decline over time

Depending on the type of investment you make, you may have more or less exposure to these two types of risk. Small stocks are more prone to failure, so the risk of not receiving cash flows is fairly high. In contrast, the federal government has never defaulted on its obligation to pay interest to investors, so the risk of not getting paid is very low for Treasury bills or bonds.

Figure 11.6 illustrates the positive relationship between risk and return. Investments on the high end of the risk scale expose investors to much greater uncertainty regarding cash flows

FIGURE 11.6 **The Risk–Return Relationship for Various Asset Choices** An important investing principle is that taking on more risk should result in earning higher returns.

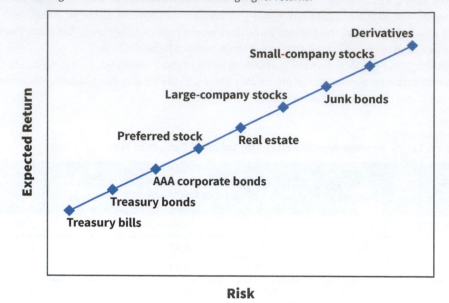

and price increases. Investors would not be willing to put money in those investments unless they offered a high enough rate of return on average to compensate them for the risk. You'll learn more about each of the investments on this chart in Chapters 12 and 13.

How Risk-Averse Are You?

Not everyone is comfortable with taking investment risk. For this reason, it's important that you make sure your investments are consistent with your risk preferences. Your investment risk exposure should not be greater than your desire and ability to bear risk. To make this decision, you'll need to be able to assess the expected returns and risks for each of your investment alternatives so that you can evaluate whether their expected performance is consistent with your risk tolerance.

You may already have a good feel for how much risk you're willing to take in your investments. Your first reaction might be "None at all!" In that case, we would say that you're very risk-averse, which just means that you don't like risk. Financial professionals often use a more precise definition of **risk aversion**, defining a risk-averse person as someone who prefers to receive a certain amount of money over a gamble that would, on average, produce the same amount of money.

For example, suppose you're offered the following gamble: We'll flip a coin. If it comes up heads, you win $100; if it's tails, you get zero. How much would you be willing to pay to play that game? Paying $50 would represent a "fair" gamble—that is, if you could play the game many times, on average you'd break even. Even so, a risk-averse person wouldn't usually be willing to pay $50 to play, because he or she would rather have the $50 for certain than take the risk. The risk-averse person might, however, be willing to pay $40 or $30 to play. The less you're willing to pay, the more risk-averse you are. In other words, a risk-averse person is only willing to take a gamble if he or she gets something extra for taking the risk. In an investment context, the "something extra" is a higher rate of return on investment.

Most of us are risk-averse to some extent, but we might be willing to accept a little more risk to get a little more benefit. Furthermore, all of us have a personal preference for just how much extra benefit we require. Investment advisors usually evaluate their clients' risk tolerance before recommending investment strategies, and they have an ethical obligation to recommend investments that are consistent with their clients' preferences and appropriate for their life circumstances. Don't be surprised to find that your attitudes toward investment risk taking might be very different from those of your friends or family members. Gender, ethnicity, age, and wealth are all factors that affect risk aversion. You'll also be influenced by your experience with risk taking, your education, and family circumstances.

Because risk preferences are so important to investment decisions, financial advisors commonly attempt to evaluate new clients' risk preferences, using either an oral or a written series of questions. This evaluation helps them to better recommend appropriate investment strategies. How comfortable are you with taking investment risk? To find out, complete the questionnaire in **Interactive: How Risk-Averse Are You?**

INTERACTIVE

See **Interactive: How Risk-Averse Are You?** in **WileyPLUS.**

Factors Affecting Risk Attitudes

Individuals demonstrate wide variation in the willingness to bear investment risk. Differences in risk tolerance arise from many factors, including these:

- **Life-cycle effects**   Although age is often associated with risk-taking tendencies, it's actually your life-cycle stage that makes the biggest difference. In the early life-cycle stages, you're working on developing a foundation for the future. During this period, you "invest" in your education and career, building your human capital—an asset that will provide returns to you in the form of increased earning potential. The focus on liquidity and safety during this period of your life means that you're less inclined to take substantial risks. During the wealth accumulation stage of the life cycle, individuals who have already established their foundations (insurance and emergency funds) tend to be more willing to take risks to accumulate the funds necessary to achieve their future goals. The focus shifts from building human capital to building financial capital. As individuals approach retirement their focus shifts to protecting their principal. They tend to gradually revert to being more risk-averse, probably because they realize that they have less time to recover from a loss in their investment portfolio.

- **Wealth and income**   Wealthier people tend to be more willing to take risk. If you have more, it makes sense that you can afford to risk losing some. Income has a similar effect, although stability of income is perhaps even more important than level of income. If you have a secure job—for example, if you're a tenured university professor—you might be more willing to take a little risk in your investments. In contrast, a salesperson with irregular income from commissions might not be able to commit to regular contributions and might be nervous about the possibility of losing money in his or her portfolio.

- **Family status**   In general, families with children tend to be less willing to take financial risk. This tendency may be due to their greater need for liquid emergency funds and to the high cost of raising children. Once the foundations for financial security are established, parents might be more willing to take investment risk.

- **Gender**   There is some evidence that women are less inclined to take risk than men, but this difference is less pronounced in younger generations, perhaps because the education and work experience of young men and women are more similar today than was the case in previous generations.

- **Education and experience**   The effect of education on risk tolerance is less clear-cut than that of some of the characteristics previously mentioned. For example, studies have not shown a significant difference between the risk-taking behavior of those with and without a college education. However, specific investment-related education might make people more comfortable with taking a little risk in their investment portfolios.

- **Consumer confidence**   Your willingness to take risk is also related to your confidence about the future. Whether you're worrying about the possibility of a future job loss or downturn in the economy, negative prospects for the future will make you less willing to bear risk. In the recent recession, when consumer confidence plummeted, households pulled out of the stock market in favor of less risky alternatives.

Types of Investment Risk

An easy way to think about the relationship between return and risk is that investors will require a certain amount of return, or a risk premium, for *each type of risk* to which they're exposed. For debt securities, these may include inflation risk, interest-rate risk, reinvestment risk, default risk, liquidity risk, and market risk. Equity investments expose investors primarily to inflation risk, reinvestment risk, and market risk. The bigger each of these risk components is, the greater the level of return that an investor will require. The risk components of debt securities are included in **Equation 11.2** and illustrated in **Figure 11.7**.

$$\text{Yield on debt security} = \text{Real risk-free rate} + \text{Inflation risk premium} \\ + \text{Interest-rate risk premium} + \text{Default risk premium} \\ + \text{Liquidity risk premium} \tag{11.2}$$

FIGURE 11.7 **Risk Premiums and Yields on Debt Investments**   Debt investments with greater exposure to more types of risk will generally offer higher rates of return.

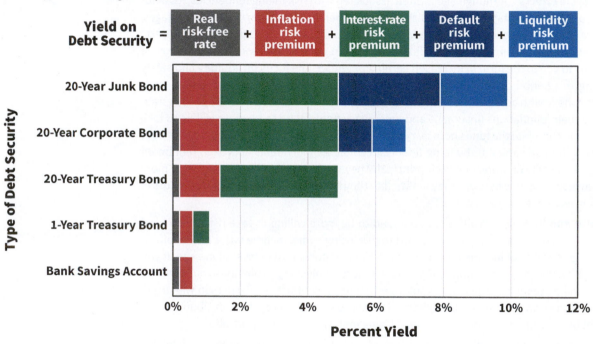

Inflation Risk

We noted earlier that, even if an investment were virtually risk-free, you'd require compensation for delaying consumption. This minimum return is referred to as the *real risk-free rate*. With most investments, you'll also be exposed to inflation risk—the loss in spending power over the investment period. Thus, the minimum rate of return you'd expect from any investment would include compensation for delaying consumption and for bearing inflation risk. This minimum rate of return, which is the sum of the real risk-free rate and the inflation risk premium, is usually called the **nominal risk-free rate**—a rate that is higher during periods of rising inflation than during periods of low inflation. The shortest-term debt security issued by the federal government, a 13-week Treasury bill, is an investment that is expected to earn the nominal risk-free rate because it doesn't expose you to any of the other types of risk we discuss below. Inflation risk normally increases with the term to maturity, so a 1-year Treasury bill will have a slightly larger inflation-risk premium than a 13-week Treasury bill.

Interest-Rate Risk

Although interest rates can have an effect on all investments, some types of securities—bonds and preferred stock—are more highly influenced by interest-rate changes. When interest rates go up, the present value of cash flows to be received in the future goes down. A decrease in the value of future cash flows causes prices to fall. When rates go down, prices go up. The longer the term to maturity, the more the price of the security is affected. This effect is commonly called **interest-rate risk**, although it's sometimes called maturity risk or price risk because of the strong interrelationship among interest rates, maturities, and prices. Investors expect to be compensated for this risk with an interest-rate risk premium. Short-term securities have a lower interest-rate risk premium—they provide a lower return on investment, all else being equal—than longer-term securities.

A corollary to interest-rate risk is **reinvestment risk**—the risk that you'll have to reinvest cash flows from an investment at a time when the rate of return has fallen. Whereas interest-rate risk is greatest for long-term debt securities, reinvestment risk is highest for short-term debt investments. This risk is greatest during periods of higher interest rates. After the 2008 recession, when the Federal Reserve was keeping rates at all-time lows, investors were not worried about reinvestment rate risk. Instead, they were wishing that rates would go up before they had to reinvest!

Default Risk

The risk that you won't receive expected cash flows from an investment is called **default risk**. Although any borrower can run into financial difficulties, some corporations and government entities are considered more likely to default than others. The issuers of risky bonds must offer investors a greater rate of return to compensate for greater default risk. For equity investors—who can't technically be defaulted on, because the company has not actually promised the investors any particular return—there's still the risk of business failure. In a bankruptcy proceeding, the value of an equity investment is likely to be zero.

Liquidity Risk

Liquidity risk is the risk that you won't be able to convert your investment to cash on short notice without losing value. This risk is lowest for securities that have active markets with lots of buyers and sellers, as is the case for publicly traded stocks and bonds. In contrast, real estate is fairly difficult to sell on short notice because there aren't as many buyers interested in any given property and it takes a while to finalize the transaction. If you need to sell in a hurry, you'll probably have to significantly discount the price. Other examples of illiquid investments include art, jewelry, and collectibles. Investors expect to receive a premium when they invest in less liquid assets, but it might be insufficient to offset the cost of not being able to sell when you need to.

Market Risk

In addition to the components of individual risk discussed above, all investments expose you to **market risk**, the risk associated with general market movements and economic conditions. In a recession, when businesses are cutting back on spending and unemployment rates are high, investment values tend to decline, resulting in a "bear market." When times are good, the result is a "bull market" characterized by increasing asset values fueled by high business profits, low interest rates, and economic growth. A period of time in which the United States had a bear market followed by a bull market is illustrated in **Figure 11.8**. Although both debt and equity markets are influenced by market conditions, they don't necessarily move together. You could, for example, simultaneously have a bull stock market and a bear bond market.

FIGURE 11.8 **Bear versus Bull Markets** The stock market was a "bear" from January 2008 to March 2009, but switched to a "bull" afterward.

Market risk is related not only to economic conditions in the United States but also to global risks. The recent financial crisis affected financial markets around the world and made it very apparent that global and political factors are important to investors. Although investing overseas is easier now than ever before, it's important to remember that many of the legal protections we take for granted in this country (such as information disclosure and standardized accounting practices) may not be applicable elsewhere. Investor fraud is commonplace in many areas of the world, so the caution "buyer beware" takes on new meaning in those contexts.

Even in calmer political times, exchange rates and the balance of trade can strongly influence the economic environment and the profitability of firms. Investors are also exposed to domestic political risk, such as changes in tax laws, tariffs, and other business legislation that might negatively affect future profits. For example, in late 2018, President Trump announced that he would increase tariffs on goods imported from China. Because so many companies in the United States expected higher input costs as a result of the tariffs, the stock market took a nosedive. Throughout 2019, the stock market rose and fell with sometimes positive and sometimes negative news about continuing trade negotiations.

11.4 Diversification and Performance Evaluation

LEARNING OBJECTIVE 11.4

Evaluate portfolio performance relative to a similarly diversified benchmark index.

If you could see the future and know with certainty which of your investments would perform best, you could put all your money there and never lose a dime. Contrary to the boasts of investment gurus on investment advice shows, though, no one can accurately predict the ups and downs of specific companies or even of broad asset classes. If you diversify your portfolio by spreading your money across a range of different investments and asset classes, you reduce the risk that one bad choice will cause you to lose everything. The principle of **diversification** is based on the same principle as the old proverb "Don't put all your eggs in one basket." In practice, deciding exactly which "baskets" to use and how many "eggs" to put in each isn't simple and may require that you seek the advice of a financial professional.

How Diversification Works

Suppose you have $10,000 to invest in a portfolio of stocks. At the beginning of the year, you put half the money in Stock A and half in Stock B. Both are expected to earn a return of 10 percent per year, on average. But these are risky investments, so the actual return in each year will not always be 10 percent. Rather, the returns will fluctuate around an average of 10 percent and may even, in some years, be negative. Over a two-year period, the actual annual returns for your investment portfolio, counting dividends and capital gains, are as shown in **Table 11.5**.

TABLE 11.5   **Comparison of Two Stock Investments over Time**

	Annual Return, Year 1	Annual Return, Year 2	Average Annual Return
Stock A	18%	2%	10%
Stock B	4%	16%	10%
50/50 Portfolio	11%	9%	10%

In this example, if you'd put all your money in Stock B, your return would only have been 4 percent in Year 1. Because Stock A earned 18 percent in Year 1, however, you were able to earn an overall return of 11 percent on your 50/50 two-stock portfolio. In Year 2, Stock A earned only 2 percent, but Stock B earned 16 percent, so your average return was 9 percent, a little less than the expected return of 10 percent. Splitting your money between these two stocks reduced the risk that your investment portfolio return would deviate too far from your expected return. As usual, though, there's a cost associated with reducing risk. Although your returns were higher than if you had all your money in the worst performer for each year, they were lower than if you had picked the higher-performing stock.

As you increase the number of investments in your portfolio, the variability of your overall returns will decline. That's because many of the things that affect a given firm's profitability are company-specific, and the ups and downs of individual investments will cancel each other out. One company might have a labor dispute when another introduces a new product. One company could be named in a product liability lawsuit when another expands its operations into South America. Your diversification objective is to have enough investments so that all the company-specific risks average out, resulting in reduced variability of return for your total portfolio.

Figure 11.9 graphically illustrates the risk-reducing effect of adding more stocks (or other investments) to your portfolio: The more you have, the lower your company-specific risk. Although the graph shows that random asset selection will negate most company-specific risk after you have about 40 stocks in your portfolio, there actually isn't a magic number of investments that will result in perfect diversification. Diversification depends on many factors, including your choice of specific investments, the relationships between the investments you hold in your portfolio, market conditions, and your own risk tolerance. It's also important to understand that, even if your portfolio is well diversified, it still isn't risk-free. After all company-specific, or diversifiable, risks are canceled out, what will be left is market risk—the risk of portfolio fluctuations caused by common market factors. If the stock market crashes, your stock portfolio is going to lose value regardless of how well diversified it is.

What if you're pretty sure that a single investment is going to do so well that you want to put all your money in it? For example, suppose you work at a terrific company that gives you company stock bonuses or retirement plan contributions. In the past, you've seen the value of your employer's stock rise at a rate faster than the market as a whole. Under those circumstances, is it necessary to diversify? Although financial advisors have for years warned individuals about the hazards of being completely undiversified, people like to invest in what they understand, or *think* they understand. The company you work for may seem like a wise investment, but you

FIGURE 11.9 **Risk-Reducing Impact of Diversification** As the number of different, randomly selected stocks in a portfolio increases, diversification reduces portfolio risk. However, the risk that is due to common market factors will still remain.

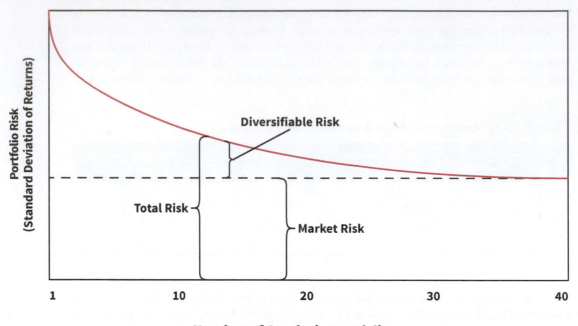

need to resist the urge to go overboard. If your employer goes out of business, you might find yourself losing both your job and your retirement fund at the same time. As a general guideline, financial advisors recommend that you invest no more than 10 percent of your total portfolio in any single investment.

Asset Allocation

Asset allocation is the process of deciding what proportion of your portfolio to invest in each of several broad investment classes, such as stock, bonds, real estate, and cash. Within each asset class, you should also spread your money among different securities. However, academic studies have shown that as much as 90 percent of the overall performance of a long-term portfolio is attributable to the broad asset allocation mix, as opposed to a selection of individual assets within each asset class.

Your allocation of funds between broad asset classes should change over your life cycle to be consistent with your investment objectives, family situation, time horizon, and risk tolerance. There's no hard-and-fast rule that applies to everyone, but most people want to allocate a higher proportion of their portfolio to stocks when they're younger. With a longer time to invest, you can afford to take more risk, and you should have more of your wealth in assets that have the potential for greater returns. As you approach retirement and your investment horizon shortens, it is advisable to gradually shift your portfolio toward lower-risk asset classes. Your goal at that point will be to maintain the wealth you've already accumulated, so you don't want to take too much risk. When you reach your retirement years, you'll be spending rather than saving, but you'll need to earn enough on your money to offset the eroding effect of inflation. Thus, even in retirement, you'll want to allocate some of your money to stocks. After all, if you retire at 65 and expect to live to be 90, you'll still have a fairly long investment horizon.

Although there's no one-size-fits-all formula for asset allocation over the life cycle, investment advisors commonly provide their clients with rules of thumb for asset allocation decisions. These rules aren't universally accepted and haven't been scientifically validated. But they do have the positive effects of discouraging overly conservative investment behavior at young ages and encouraging risk reduction at older ages. For example, an advisor might suggest the following rule: The percent of money you should invest in stocks is 110 minus your age, and the rest of your portfolio should be equally allocated to bonds and cash. By that rule, at age 25, you would invest 110 – 25 = 85 percent in stocks, and at age 65, you would invest only 45 percent in stocks. The remainder of your portfolio would be a combination of bonds and cash. **Figure 11.10** shows how this allocation strategy might evolve over a typical person's life cycle. Note, however, that a different financial advisor might advise you to allocate based on a different formula—perhaps 100 minus your age. In **Interactive: Whose Portfolio Is It?**, you can try applying the principles of life-cycle allocation.

INTERACTIVE

See **Interactive: Whose Portfolio Is It?** in **WileyPLUS.**

FIGURE 11.10 **Possible Asset Allocation over the Life Cycle** This allocation is based on a rule of thumb suggesting that the percentage of your investments allocated to stock should equal 110 minus your age, with the remainder equally divided between bonds and cash.

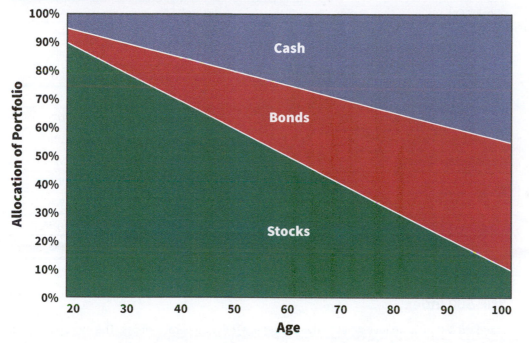

Evaluating Performance Against a Benchmark

Typically, investors compare the performance of their portfolio against an established benchmark, such as a stock or bond market index. An **index** tracks the performance of a particular group of stocks, bonds, or other securities. This is useful as a way of gauging general market conditions and is also commonly used to evaluate the performance of portfolio managers and mutual funds. Some portfolio managers specifically identify a certain index as their benchmark, which means that their goal is to perform at least as well as the group of stocks in the index while maintaining a similar level of risk. Several common stock market indexes are described below.

Dow Jones Industrial Average

When you hear in the news that the market has gone up or down, the newscaster is usually referring to the Dow Jones Industrial Average (DJIA), commonly called "the Dow." The Dow tracks the performance of the 30 very large company stocks listed in **Table 11.6** and is the most widely watched and reported index in use today. The companies included in the DJIA do not stay the same over time. During the past decade, several companies have been dropped from the index, replaced by others that were considered to be more representative of the mix of industries in the U.S. stock market. Given the large number of stocks in the marketplace, it might seem that too much emphasis is placed on this index of only 30. However, these 30 companies are so large and have so many investors that they represent a significant percentage of the value of the broader market.

TABLE 11.6 Stocks in the Dow Jones Industrial Average, 2019

Company Name	Ticker Symbol	Company Name	Ticker Symbol
3M Co.	MMM	J.P. Morgan Chase and Co.	JPM
American Express Co.	AXP	McDonald's Corp.	MCD
Apple	AAPL	Merck & Co.	MRK
Boeing Co.	BA	Microsoft Corp.	MSFT
Caterpillar Inc.	CAT	Nike Inc.	NKE
Chevron Corp.	CVX	Pfizer Inc.	PFE
Cisco Systems Inc.	CSCO	Proctor and Gamble Co.	PG
Coca-Cola Inc.	KO	Travelers Companies Inc.	TRV
Dupont De Nemours	DD	United Technologies Corp.	UTX
Exxon Mobile Corp.	XOM	United Health Group Inc.	UNH
Goldman Sachs Group Inc.	GS	Verizon Communications Inc.	VZ
Home Depot Inc.	HD	Visa Inc.	V
Intel Corp.	INTC	Walmart Stores Inc.	WMT
IBM Co.	IBM	Walgreens Boot Alliance	WBA
Johnson & Johnson	JNJ	Walt Disney Co.	DIS

S&P 500 Index

Standard & Poor's, an investment advisory service, offers several indexes. The most popular is the S&P 500 Index, which tracks the performance of 500 of the largest US companies, most of them traded on the New York Stock Exchange (NYSE). Because this index represents a broader cross-section of American businesses than the DJIA, the S&P 500 is a somewhat better indicator of general stock market performance. For this reason, the S&P 500 is the benchmark most commonly used by mutual funds and money managers to assess performance.

Other Stock Market Indexes

Both the Dow and the S&P 500 measure the performance of large company stocks. If your portfolio includes smaller companies or is weighted more heavily toward a certain sector, such as technology or financial services, you might want to compare its performance with that of a benchmark of similar stocks. Both Standard & Poor's and Dow Jones offer indexes that track other categories of stocks, for example by industry or by firm size. In addition, the NYSE Composite Index and the AMEX index track price movements for the groups of stocks that trade on their respective exchanges, the New York Stock Exchange and the American Stock Exchange. The NASDAQ Composite Index tracks the over-the-counter market, which includes a higher percentage of small company stocks. Another broad market indicator, the Wilshire 5000 Index, includes around 3,500 of the most actively traded stocks.

Figure 11.11 shows historical values of three popular indexes and their changes in value from 2008 through 2019. From this chart, you can see that these indexes tend to move up and down together even though the S&P 500 and the NASDAQ include many more stocks than the Dow. Notice also that, although all the indexes crashed together in late 2008 and recovered over the next few years, the NASDAQ rose more quickly than the other two in the recovery period and continues to outperform the others. Stock investors lost about 50 percent of their investments in 2008. But those who resisted selling out during the recession had recovered by 2011 and had doubled their 2008 value by 2019.

FIGURE 11.11   **Stock Index Performance 2008 to 2019, Dow Jones Industrial Average, NASDAQ Composite, and S&P 500**   The line for each index shows the cumulative change in value from the beginning of the time period. For example, the NASDAQ increased more than 80 percent from January 2008 to March 2019.

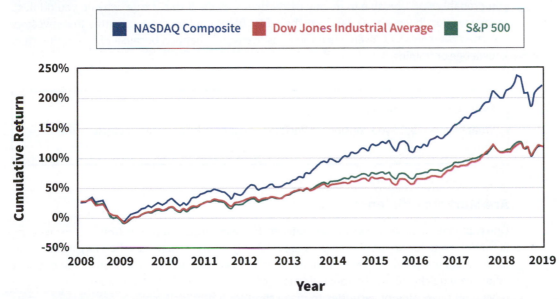

Other Asset Benchmarks

Although stock market indexes are commonly used for portfolio performance evaluation, there are indexes for every asset class. So if you have a portfolio of bonds or real estate, you can compare your performance to an index that tracks that particular sector.

Active versus Passive Investing

Recall that the fourth step in the investment planning process is to establish an investment strategy that's appropriate for you. In the next two chapters, we go into more detail on investing in specific stocks, bonds, and other assets, and we discuss asset-specific investment strategies. In this section, we describe the difference between active and passive investing strategies and explain why most individual investors will be better off taking a passive approach.

An **active investor** attempts to identify investments and asset classes that are undervalued in the short run and to make returns by buying those that are underpriced and selling those that are overpriced. In the extreme, an active investor might be what is called a day trader—one who makes many trades in a single day, attempting to capitalize on new information or temporary imbalances in supply and demand.

In contrast, a **passive investor** attempts to carefully select a combination of investments that will, *over the long term*, result in achieving his or her investment return goals. The objective of an active investor is to beat the market, or to make greater returns than would normally be expected for the level of risk in the portfolio. Passive investors are happy to do as well as the market on average, earning a return that is appropriate for the portfolio risk.

Can Active Investors Beat the Market?

As you learn more about investing, you might be tempted to capitalize on your newfound knowledge by doing some active investing. Before you do, however, carefully consider the evidence regarding the long-run performance of professionally managed funds. Many studies show that portfolios actively managed by professional money managers achieve lower annual returns, on average, than the market as a whole. This implies that investors have paid for the services of these professionals when they would have been better off simply buying shares of an indexed security (discussed below). But aren't some professional investors more successful than others? The evidence shows otherwise—the managers who achieve the highest returns in a given year are rarely at the top of the list the following year.

Because you're not as experienced or knowledgeable as these professionals, it follows that you probably won't be able to do any better than they do. If this is true, why do you think so many investors believe they can beat the odds? Behavioral research confirms that investors are often overconfident, even when their positive results happen because of luck rather than knowledge or training.

Reflection Question 3

What factors would you consider in deciding whether to be an active investor in the future?

Are Markets Efficient?

One explanation for why investors are unlikely to make consistent profits from active investing is that markets for financial securities are relatively efficient. **Market efficiency** means that, as investors use publicly available information to make buy and sell decisions, market prices adjust very quickly to be accurate reflections of security value. Active investors are essentially relying on mispricing of securities to make short-term profits. If markets are efficient, active investing should not be a successful strategy, because any mispricing should be very temporary. There is significant debate surrounding this issue. In fact, it is the most studied issue in financial economics. As you might expect, stock analysts and investment managers who attempt to make a living based on active trading strategies believe that markets are inefficient. Even if they are, however, it's possible that any potential profit from mispricing is minimal.

On a very basic level, market efficiency can be thought of as being related to how *quickly* prices react to news. Because information is so easily available today and there are so many investors in the marketplace who are all trying to identify undervalued securities, the window of opportunity for capitalizing on any new information is fairly small. If, for example, you hear that a company is coming out with an innovative new product and you believe that this will cause the stock price to go up, you might want to try to buy some shares at the current price and sell them after the price rises with the good news. But everyone else has heard the good news, too, so lots of investors will immediately start buying up as many shares as possible, and the price will rise. By the time you try to buy the shares, the stock price may already be high. The moral of this story is that market efficiency makes it difficult, though maybe not impossible, to make a profit on any new information. You just have to be at the front of the line.

Today, the efficiency of the market makes it riskier than ever to be an active investor. Prices of actively traded stocks and bonds react to information so quickly that they sometimes move in advance of any public announcement on the strength of expectations alone. Generally, if you see information reported in the financial press, it's already too late to act on that information to make a short-term profit.

Passive Investing Strategies

Although being a passive investor implies that you're not making regular changes in your portfolio, most passive investors continue to build their portfolios over time. Therefore, they must make regular investment contributions and selections. Common passive investing strategies include the following:

- **Buy-and-hold**   Most passive investment strategies are types of **buy-and-hold** strategies. When you use a buy-and-hold strategy, you select an asset allocation appropriate for your life stage and risk tolerance and then choose a diversified set of securities within each asset class. After making your investment selections, you hold them for the long term, making changes only as necessary to maintain your asset allocation and to reflect changes in information about the assets in your portfolio. The advantages of a buy-and-hold strategy are that you can capture the long-term gains for each asset class while avoiding most of the transaction costs associated with buying and selling securities. You pay less in brokerage commissions, and you defer the taxes on your gains until you choose to sell.

- **Indexing**   Recall that an index tracks the returns of a broad asset class, such as large company stocks. Because many passive investors are interested in getting returns comparable to the index, there are a variety of investments, discussed in more detail in Chapter 13, that are designed to mimic the performance of various indexes. For example, a mutual fund that is indexed to the Dow Jones Industrial Average will be invested in shares of all 30 stocks making up that index. Indexing is a good way for passive buy-and-hold investors to achieve their objectives with fairly low expenses.

- **Dividend reinvestment plans**   Another way to stick to your plan and, at the same time, avoid brokerage commissions on small trades is to have dividends from current investments automatically invested in new shares of the same fund or company. If you hold stock in a company or mutual fund that pays regular dividends, you can usually choose to reinvest your cash dividends in the stock through a **dividend reinvestment plan (DRIP)**. Such plans automatically use any cash distributions to buy additional shares for you. Suppose, for example, that you're entitled to a $20 dividend distribution on the 100 shares you own of a particular company's stock, which is currently valued at $10 per share. Under a dividend reinvestment plan, you'd receive two additional shares instead of the dividend.

- **Laddering**   **Laddering** is a type of buy-and-hold investment strategy in which you purchase a collection of bonds with different maturities spread out over your investment horizon. If, for example, you have a 10-year investment horizon, you could buy bonds that mature in 1, 2, 3, 4, 5, 6, 7, 8, 9, and 10 years. Then, when each bond matures, you'll use the money to buy a bond that matures in 10 years (so that you'll always have one bond of each maturity in the portfolio). The advantage of this strategy is that it balances the risk and return elements in the portfolio, because the bonds with shorter terms to maturity will not be as sensitive to interest rate changes, while the bonds with longer terms to maturity will give slightly higher yields.

- **Maturity matching**   **Maturity matching** is similar in concept to laddering, but it requires purchasing assets that have cash flows that coincide with the period in which you need the funds. Thus, if you need the funds 10 years from now, you'll purchase only bonds with 10 years to maturity. Zero-coupon bonds, explained in more detail in Chapter 12, are often used for this purpose because they don't pay any interest in the interim and you'll receive the full principal at maturity. Alternatively, you might buy bonds that will make interest payments for the period when you'll need the funds—let's say 20-year coupon bonds that will make interest payments over the expected 20-year period of your retirement.

Does Timing Matter to Passive Investors?

Just because you're a passive investor doesn't mean you should have blinders on and ignore what's going on around you. Some investors attempt to avoid general downturns and take advantage of general increases in particular markets by strategically reallocating their portfolios. This is a strategy called **timing**. For example, suppose you thought the stock market was about to take a nosedive. You could pull all your money out of stocks and put it into cash to avoid such losses. This is an example of *market timing*, in which you try to anticipate major moves in certain asset markets. Alternatively, you might try to implement a strategy called *business cycle timing*, in which you put more money into your investment portfolio when the economy is expanding and you cash out when the economy is contracting.

You can also apply a timing strategy to bond portfolio decisions. For example, if rates are currently fairly low relative to historical averages, you might not want to buy long-term bonds, because you'll be locking in a low yield to maturity. You could, instead, buy relatively short-maturity bonds in anticipation of future rate increases. When your bonds mature, if rates have since risen, you'll be able to purchase bonds with longer maturities at lower prices and lock in a more favorable yield.

The problem with timing strategies is that even the experts aren't that good at correctly predicting what the market is going to do. If markets are efficient, prices should quickly respond to changes in the economic outlook, so you could easily be too late to catch the wave. In practice, investors probably get it right less than half the time. In the late 1990s, for example, when the market moved continuously upward, many business cycle timers pulled money out of the stock market too soon and missed out on the strong returns at the end of the decade. Other individual investors waited too long to start investing in the stock market in the late 1990s, buying at the high point and shortly thereafter watching their portfolio values decline sharply. Even missing a few of the best days of a bull market can significantly reduce your portfolio's performance. From 1980 to 2002, if you'd missed the top 10 days, you'd have 40 percent less than if you had followed a simple buy-and-hold strategy. Although some timers have had good success over the long term, you'll probably find that you are better off selecting a diversified portfolio and letting it ride.

Summary

Learning Objectives Review

LEARNING OBJECTIVE 11.1 Develop a realistic investment plan to meet your long-term financial goals, taking into account budgetary constraints, transaction costs, and taxes.

If you've established a budget, paid off high-interest credit, and established an emergency fund, then you're ready to think about investing to meet your other long-term financial goals.

- The investment planning process begins with identifying realistic, specific, and measurable goals and finding the money in your budget to apply to these goals. Then you can investigate various alternatives for investing so that you can select investments that are appropriate for your risk tolerance, time horizon, and investment objectives. As with other areas of your financial plan, this process will need to be monitored and reevaluated on a regular basis.

- To meet your investing goals, it's best to start early and be consistent. Regular contributions to investment accounts offer the advantage of **dollar cost averaging**.

- Transaction costs and taxes can erode investment earnings. Therefore, taking advantage of tax-free and tax-deferred savings opportunities can be an important strategy. For taxable accounts, setting up a **brokerage account** through a **discount broker** can be an inexpensive way to invest.

- It's also important to keep accurate and thorough records and to take the time to learn about key features of the investment choices available to you.

LEARNING OBJECTIVE 11.2 Identify and define the major types of investments.

There are many different investment alternatives, and it's very important to understand their characteristics before making any investment decisions.

- There are generally two ways to invest—you can be either a lender or an owner. When you lend, you're a **debt investor**; and when you own, you're an **equity or stock investor**. In either case, the return on your investment will come from some combination of:

- Regular cash flow, such as the payment of interest or **dividends**

- **Capital gain**, or the growth in the value of your investment over time

- An investment is a **security** whenever investors contribute money to a common enterprise with the intention of earning a profit through the efforts of others. There are special regulatory and disclosure requirements that apply to selling securities to investors.

- Stocks, bonds, and mutual fund shares are common examples of financial securities that are in different **asset classes**. For example, government and corporate **bonds** are **fixed-income investments** that pay interest. **Common stock** and **preferred stock** are equity securities. **Derivative securities**, which include **futures contracts** and **option contracts**, are considered **speculative investments**.

- Instead of buying individual securities, many investors choose to buy shares of mutual funds that have professional managers who select the individual assets in the portfolio.

LEARNING OBJECTIVE 11.3   Compare investment alternatives based on return and risk.

Almost all investments expose you to some amount of risk. In general, however, riskier investments provide you with higher average rates of return over time.

- **Rate of return**, or **yield**, is usually measured by the cash flows from interest, dividends, and increases in price relative to the price at the beginning of the period, as calculated with **Equation 11.1**:

Rate of return = Current yield + Capital gain yield

$$= \frac{\text{Current income} + \text{End price} - \text{Beginning price}}{\text{Beginning price}}$$

- In general, the higher the risk, the higher the average rate of return. There are two kinds of risk that may adversely affect your ability to meet your financial goals:
- The risk that you won't receive expected cash flows from the investment
- The risk that the value of your investment will decline over time
- Investors differ in their levels of **risk aversion**, and they need to take this into account in making their asset allocation decisions.
- Over long periods of time, stocks have outperformed bonds, and small company stocks have outperformed large company stocks.
- Investors require a certain amount of return, or a risk premium, for each type of risk to which they are exposed. Types of risk include inflation risk, **interest-rate risk**, **reinvestment risk**, **default risk**, and **liquidity risk**.

- The risk-related yield on a debt security is calculated with **Equation 11.2**:

Yield on debt security = Real risk-free rate + Inflation risk premium + Interest-rate risk premium + Default risk premium + Liquidity risk premium

- The minimum rate of return, which is the sum of the real risk-free rate and the inflation risk premium, is usually called the **nominal risk-free rate**.
- All investments are exposed to some level of **market risk** due to common market factors that affect securities, such as economic and political conditions. A "bull market" occurs when stock prices are rising, and a "bear market" occurs when they are falling.

LEARNING OBJECTIVE 11.4   Evaluate portfolio performance relative to a similarly diversified benchmark index.

- Investors can reduce the risk of their portfolio through **diversification** across different asset classes.
- Through the process of **asset allocation**, investors determine what proportion of their portfolios to invest in the various asset classes.
- Investors often compare the performance of their portfolios against a benchmark, such as a stock or bond market **index**.
- A **passive investor** attempts to achieve return and risk comparable to a benchmark and consistent with their risk preferences through careful asset allocation. In contrast, an **active investor** attempts to identify and capitalize on short-term mispricing in the marketplace.
- **Market efficiency** means that, at any given time, prices of various investments fully reflect available information and risk. This efficiency implies that active investing and **timing** strategies are unlikely to be consistently successful.
- Several passive investment strategies include **buy-and-hold**, indexing, **laddering**, **maturity matching**, and **dividend reinvestment plans**.

Excel Worksheet

11.1 Personal Financial Planner: Setting Investment Goals

Key Terms

WileyPLUS

Practice Questions to check your understanding, Peer-to-Peer Videos, Interactives, and many other resources are available in WileyPLUS.

Concept Review Questions

1. Before you develop a plan for building your wealth, what elements of your financial plan should you consider? Why is this important?

2. What does it mean to "pay yourself first," and how can this strategy help you stick to your financial plan?

3. If you don't currently have excess cash flow in your budget to allocate to saving for future financial goals, what are some other strategies for finding the funds necessary to save or invest?

4. Why do riskier investments give investors the opportunity for a higher average rate of return?

5. Are all investors risk-averse? Why or why not?

6. Explain how each of the following factors can influence a person's risk preferences.

   a. Life-cycle stage

   b. Children

   c. Income and wealth

7. Identify the type of risk described in each of the following statements.

   a. Interest rates are expected to rise over the next several years.

   b. Prices of goods and services are rising rapidly.

   c. A company's management is indicted for fraud, and the company declares bankruptcy.

   d. The United States declares war on another country.

8. Why do investment advisors commonly recommend stocks for long-term investors?

9. How does the diversification of a portfolio help reduce its risk?

10. Should investors change their asset allocation over their life cycle? Why or why not?

11. Why is it important to evaluate the performance of your investment portfolio against an appropriate benchmark?

12. What are some arguments in favor of being a passive investor?

Application Problems

1. You own 100 shares of stock that you bought one year ago when the stock price was $30 per share. During the year, you've received dividends totaling $1 per share, and the stock is now worth $32 per share. What is your pretax rate of return for the year?

2. You own 100 shares of stock that you bought when the stock price was $30 per share. Assume that you sell your shares for $32 per share one year after you bought them, and you've received dividends during the year totaling $1 per share. If you're in the 24 percent federal income tax bracket and your dividends and capital gains both qualify for taxation at the capital gains tax rate, what is your after-tax rate of return?

3. You bought a corporate bond one year ago for $1,000. The bond is still worth $1,000, and you have received interest payments totaling $90 during the year. What was your pretax rate of return?

4. You bought a corporate bond one year ago for $1,000. The bond is still worth $1,000, and you have received interest payments totaling $90 during the year. If your marginal tax rate is 22 percent, what is your after-tax rate of return?

5. You want to save up to buy a new car in four years. If you expect to need $6,000 four years from now, and your investment earns 5 percent interest after taxes, how much do you need to contribute at the end of each month to achieve your goal?

6. You need to accumulate $100,000 for your child's college education 18 years from now. How much do you need to save each year if you can earn 2 percent after taxes on your investment, assuming that you will make annual end-of-year payments into the account?

7. Maria contributes $150 per month to her investment account at the end of each month, earning 4 percent per year after taxes. How much will she have in the account after six years?

8. Lavonne receives a divorce settlement of $100,000. Her marginal tax rate is 25 percent, and the capital gains tax rate is 15 percent. How much will her account be worth in 20 years under each of the following investment scenarios, assuming annual compounding of interest?

 a. Lavonne puts all the money in taxable bonds that earn 5 percent per year before taxes, and she reinvests the after-tax interest.

 b. Lavonne puts all the money in a tax-deferred account that earns 10 percent per year before taxes.

9. More than a year ago, George purchased 100 shares of Stock A for $5 per share and 50 shares of Stock B for $25 per share. During the current tax year, he sold the Stock A shares for $10 per share and the Stock B shares for $23 per share. Neither stock paid any dividends. How much will he owe in capital gains tax, assuming that he is in the highest marginal tax bracket for federal income taxes and that the applicable capital gains tax rate is 20 percent.

10. The nominal risk-free rate is currently 3 percent. You are considering investing in a 20-year corporate bond. The interest-rate risk premium is 2 percent, the default risk premium is 1.5 percent, and the liquidity risk premium is 1 percent. What should your yield on this bond be?

11. Your mother received a $50,000 settlement (after taxes) from a lawsuit, and she has asked you to recommend an asset allocation strategy for investing it. She is 45 years old, divorced, and in danger of being laid off from her job in the next two years. She has an emergency fund equal to three times her monthly expenses, she doesn't own a home, her high-interest credit card debt currently totals $5,000, and she owes $3,500 on a car loan.

 a. Should your recommend that your mother invest the entire $50,000? Why or why not?

 b. Would it be beneficial for your mother to pay for the services of an investment advisor? Why or why not?

 c. Assuming that she does have some funds left to invest, what proportion of the funds, if any, should she invest in stocks? Explain your reasoning.

12. Consider each of the following financial goals, and discuss whether stocks would be an appropriate investment choice for some or all of the funds allocated to that goal.

 a. Saving to go to graduate school in five years

 b. Building a college fund for your two-year-old child

 c. Funding your retirement in 40 years

 d. Establishing an emergency fund

Case Applications

1. Terrie and Jeff Sanders recently sold a vacant lot next to their home and have $35,000 available to invest. They've been married for three years and have two young children. Their combined after-tax income is $45,000 per year, and their net cash flow each month is close to zero. They have not established a household budget. Their home is worth $110,000, and they have a mortgage of $80,000. They have a $4,000 emergency fund. Both Terrie and Jeff contribute to employer-sponsored retirement plans, and they have adequate health and life insurance through employee benefit plans. Their two biggest investment goals are to buy a bigger house and to start a college fund for the kids. Terrie would like to take the $35,000 and invest it in a stock mutual fund, because she's heard that this will give them the biggest return on investment. Jeff thinks they should consider taking care of some of their other needs first. Even if they invest the money, he would like to put some of it in less risky assets. He also wonders whether it would make sense to pay off their credit cards and add to their retirement accounts, because they currently aren't contributing the maximum allowed.

 a. Based on the information provided, have Terrie and Jeff established all the foundation elements of their financial plan? If not, what do they still need to do?

 b. Do you agree with Terrie or Jeff regarding the way the money should be invested? Explain your reasoning.

 c. In this case, would it be advisable to invest some of the money in retirement accounts? Why or why not?

 d. Jeff suggests to Terrie that they use some of the money to pay $8,000 in credit card debt, on which they pay an average finance charge of 18 percent. Would this be a good use of their money? Explain why or why not.

2. Winken, Blinken, and Nod are triplets, but they have very different attitudes toward investing. Five years ago, each began an investment program with $10,000. Winken, a risk taker, invested the entire amount in a high-growth stock mutual fund. Blinken is extremely conservative and invested his $10,000 in a high-grade, low-risk, corporate bond fund. Nod took a personal finance class in college, so she's invested half her money in the stock fund and half in the bond fund. Taking into account both income and growth, the after-tax annual returns on the funds over the last five years have been as follows:

Year	Stock Fund (%)	Bond Fund (%)	50/50 (%)
1	5.0	8.0	6.5
2	−8.0	10.0	1.0
3	18.0	2.0	10.0
4	−2.0	7.0	2.5
5	25.0	4.0	14.5

 a. What was the average annual return for each fund and for the 50/50 combination? Which investment was riskiest? Explain.

 b. At the end of the five years, what was the value of each of the triplets' portfolios?

 c. Did diversifying across two funds provide any advantages to Nod? Explain.

3. The Herring family recently had dinner at Great-Grandma Anna's house. Present at the gathering were Great-Grandma Anna, age 96, Grandma and Grandpa Herring, both age 70; their five children, Vickie, Jill, Ron, Ken, and Holly (ages 30 to 50), with respective spouses; and grandchildren ranging in age from 5 to 25. The conversation turned to investment risk, and Anna, who is still sharp as a tack, commented that she would never have put any money in the stock market. "It's like gambling!" she said. "I'm not even sure you can trust the banks to keep your money safe. That's why I always keep some cash in my freezer." Grandma and Grandpa Herring chuckled, because they'd long ago given up on getting Anna to keep all her cash in the bank. Talking more to his kids than to her, Grandpa argued that everyone should invest in the stock market, citing how he'd been able to almost double the value of an inheritance received by Grandma from an elderly aunt several years before. "Why earn 5 percent when you can earn 10?" he asked. "Besides," said Grandpa, "assuming I live to be as old as Great-Grandma Anna, my investment horizon is pretty long, so I can afford to take a little risk." The adult children were amazed to hear their dad talk this way, because they all tended to be a bit more risk-averse in their investing. Not a single one had more than 50 percent of his or her investments in the stock market. But the oldest great-grandchild, Kristopher, said, "Way to go, Grandpa! If I had any money, I'd take your advice."

a. Did the members of each generation of the Herring family demonstrate typical attitudes toward investment risk for their age and life-cycle stage? Why or why not?

b. If it's true that Great-Grandma Anna has kept a significant amount of her cash savings in her freezer over the years, has she avoided all investment risk? If not, what kind of risk has she been exposed to?

c. Is Grandpa Herring right in saying that everyone should invest in the stock market? Why or why not?

d. If you knew that both Grandpa and Grandma Herring had government pensions that would provide them with a reasonable income for life, would this help explain Grandpa's risk attitude? Why or why not?

e. Should Kristopher follow through on his stock-investing strategy if he suddenly comes into some money? Why or why not?

4. A recent college graduate, Jeff Goldberg, is currently working as the manager of an office supply store. He wants to save money for a down payment on a home in a few years, and he's heard that investing in stocks will help him quickly build his investment portfolio. Jeff can invest about $3,000 at the end of each of the next three years, and he thinks he'll need to save $15,000 to $20,000 for the down payment. Jeff will hold this money in a taxable account, and his marginal tax rate is 15 percent.

a. If Jeff puts the money in a CD earning 5 percent per year, how much will he have accumulated by the end of five years after taxes?

b. An investment advisor has suggested that Jeff can earn at least 10 percent per year in stocks. If he earns 10 percent, how much will he have accumulated by the end of five years before taxes?

c. Would you advise Jeff to invest in stocks, given his investment objective and time horizon? Why or why not?

d. If Jeff does decide to invest in stocks, what types of stocks would you recommend? Explain.

CHAPTER 12

Investing in Stocks and Bonds

NicoElNino/Shutterstock.com

Feature Story

Although stocks, on average, have outperformed bonds over time, it doesn't always turn out that way. What if you had a crystal ball and could always predict exactly which asset class would have a higher return over a certain time period? Suppose, for example, that you start with $1,000 and, each year, move all of your money, including interest and dividends earned, to either an S&P 500 Index fund or Treasury bills based on which of those you knew would do better in the coming year? The answer will make you wish you knew a fortune teller with a reliable crystal ball!

A $1,000 investment in the S&P 500 fund at the beginning of 2000 would have grown to about $2,600 by the beginning of 2019. The same investment would have grown to only $1,400 if it had been invested in Treasury bills for the same period. But the "fortune teller" investment strategy, switching each year to the investment you know will have the highest return in that year, would have resulted in a portfolio value of almost $8,000, more than three times as much as the investment in the S&P 500 fund. If you used your crystal ball to pick the best performer monthly instead of annually, your portfolio could have grown to nearly $100,000 by 2019!

Perhaps not surprisingly, you probably haven't heard of any investment managers advertising that kind of growth. The reality is that no one is very good at predicting returns on stocks or bonds, so even when managers do shift portfolio allocations to take advantage of market movements, they are wrong as often as they are right.

For beginning investors, investing in individual stocks and bonds is not the best strategy for achieving financial goals. There are many factors that influence stock and bond values, and more sophisticated investors may have an informational advantage over you. As you saw in Chapter 11, diversification of your portfolio reduces your risk, so it is generally more appropriate to invest in well-diversified mutual funds rather than individual stocks and bonds. We discuss mutual funds in more detail in Chapter 13, but you still need to understand the basic characteristics of stocks and bonds in order to make good mutual fund choices for your portfolio. In this chapter, we describe the characteristics, classifications, and performance evaluation of common stock, bonds, and preferred stock in more detail.

LEARNING OBJECTIVES	TOPICS	DEMONSTRATION PROBLEMS
12.1 Describe the characteristics and classifications of common stock.	**12.1 Investing in Common Stock** • What Is Common Stock? • Advantages of Stock Investing • Disadvantages of Stock Investing • Classification of Common Stock • Measures of Common Stock Performance	**12.1** Comparing Returns on Different Stocks

(continued)

(continued)

LEARNING OBJECTIVES	TOPICS	DEMONSTRATION PROBLEMS
12.2 Describe the characteristics and classifications of bonds.	**12.2 Investing in Bonds** • What Is a Bond? • Types of Bonds • Bond Terminology • Bond Valuation • Why Do Investors Buy Bonds?	**12.2** Ken Calculates Bond Yield to Maturity
12.3 Compare the features of preferred stock with those of common stock and bonds.	**12.3 Investing in Preferred Stock** • What Is Preferred Stock? • Preferred Stock Valuation • Contract Terms Affecting Preferred Stock Cash Flows • The Benefits and Risks of Preferred Stock	**12.3** Calculating the Value of Preferred Stock
12.4 Describe the operation and regulation of the securities markets.	**12.4 Securities Markets** • Primary versus Secondary Market • Securities Exchanges • Buying and Selling Stocks and Bonds • Regulation of the Securities Markets	

12.1 Investing in Common Stock

LEARNING OBJECTIVE 12.1

Describe the characteristics and classifications of common stock.

Before you consider investing in common stock, there's a lot you need to know. Many beginning investors make the mistake of jumping in without really understanding what they're buying. If they're lucky, or if the economy happens to be in a growth phase, their investment portfolios might do well. Unfortunately, inexperienced investors have too often lost their life savings by making poorly-thought-out investment decisions.

What Is Common Stock?

You already know from Chapter 11 that when you buy shares of stock, you're actually becoming a part owner of a business. You wouldn't consider buying into a local business, even if it was owned by your best friend, without checking whether the business is in good financial shape. Is it making a profit? Does the company have the potential for future growth? If you invest in the company, will you make a reasonable return on your investment? Your decision to buy shares of stock isn't really much different, and it deserves the same careful deliberation. To evaluate your stock investment alternatives, you'll first need to understand the terminology used by stock investors and the rights and obligations of corporate stockholders.

Each share of common stock represents a proportionate share of ownership in a **corporation**, equal to the number of shares owned divided by the total number of shares owned by all investors in the firm. A corporation is a type of business organization that exists as a legal entity separate from its owners, the shareholders. The corporate form of organization enables the company to have many owners with limited rights and obligations. In contrast, the owners of companies organized as sole proprietorships and partnerships have more extensive rights (such as the ability to directly participate in the management of the business), but they also have greater responsibility (such as personal liability for the debts of the business).

Corporations can be classified as private or public. Shareholders of private corporations do not buy or sell their shares. This chapter focuses on publicly traded companies whose stock can be bought and sold by investors in the securities market.

Why Do Companies Issue Stock?

Even multibillion-dollar companies such as McDonald's, Inc., and Facebook, Inc., began as small private companies with only a few owners. Those owners eventually found it necessary to sell shares of stock to the public to acquire the funds they needed to grow their companies. After selling shares to the public, the original owners have a smaller proportional ownership interest in their companies, but they generally expect their return on investment to increase as a result of the expansion.

As a company continues to grow larger over time, it may again need funds, which can come from current earnings, borrowed funds, or the sale of additional shares of stock. Most large publicly traded companies have millions, or even billions of shares of stock outstanding, so each individual share represents only a very small ownership interest in the firm.

What Are the Rights and Obligations of Stock Ownership?

Investors who buy a company's stock are hoping to share in the future income and growth of that company. Their investment comes with very few strings attached. Shareholders have limited rights to influence the management of the firm, but they also have limited liability for the firm's losses. This section summarizes shareholders' rights and obligations.

- **Sharing the profits**   In return for providing equity capital to the firm, a common shareholder expects to share in the profits of the firm, either through dividends or through increases in the stock price. A common shareholder's claim on the firm is said to be a **residual claim**. That means the shareholder has a right to share in the assets and income of the firm only *after* higher-priority claims (such as interest payments on bonds) are satisfied. If the firm's revenues are greater than its expenses, the board of directors can decide to distribute a cash dividend to the shareholders, or it can decide to reinvest the funds for future growth. Shareholders benefit in either case. As a shareholder, if you receive dividend income, you have the immediate benefit of cash flow to spend or invest. Alternatively, if the firm reinvests the money instead of distributing it to you, the value of your shares should go up to reflect the firm's new investment in its earning power and the potential for future dividends. If you choose to sell at that point, you'll realize a capital gain—the difference between the price you get for your shares and what you paid for them previously.

In some cases, a firm issues a **stock dividend** in place of a cash dividend. Rather than receiving cash, you get additional shares of the firm's stock in proportion to the number of shares you already hold. While a stock dividend doesn't immediately provide as much benefit as a cash dividend or capital gain, it has the potential to produce benefits in the future. Because all stockholders receive these additional shares, everyone's percentage of ownership remains the same.

One of the risks of stock ownership is that firms are not required to pay dividends to shareholders. Even if a firm has issued dividends in the past, it may choose to reduce or eliminate them in the future. Conversely, firms that never issued dividends in the past may decide to begin doing so. This creates some inherent uncertainty, because you don't know in advance just how much current income you'll earn on your investment. You also take the risk that the firm might go bankrupt, in which case you'll be entitled only to a proportionate share of whatever is left over after all the firm's creditors are paid. But in return for bearing these risks, shareholders have the opportunity for unlimited gain. If the firm you've invested in does poorly, you might lose all of your initial investment. But if it does unusually well, you'll share in the bounty.

- **Voting rights** Each common stockholder has the right to vote for members of the board of directors at an annual meeting. The board is responsible for selecting the top-level management of the firm and for making major policy decisions. In general, corporations follow a one-vote-per-share system, so if you own 100 shares of a particular firm's stock, you'll be able to cast 100 votes in the annual election. Of course, your 100 votes won't make a huge difference in the outcome of an election when there are millions of shares outstanding. Often, a few shareholders hold large blocks of stock. Mark Zuckerberg, for example, owns about 12 million Class A and 400 million Class B shares of Facebook, Inc., which gives him 53.3% of the voting rights in the firm. If you own some shares, but can't go to the annual meeting, you're allowed to pass your voting right to someone else through a written agreement called a *proxy*. Generally, the current management team and opposing candidates will ask for your proxy vote before the election.

- **Limited liability** By state law, stockholders of corporations have the important protection of **limited liability**, which means that the most you can lose when you own a share of stock is the value of the share itself. Without the limited liability right, no one would be willing to buy shares of stock, because doing so would put their personal assets at risk of being taken to pay for corporate debts in the event of company failure.

- **Preemptive rights** When companies sell additional shares of stock, it's a bit like cutting the same pizza into a larger number of smaller slices. If you have only one slice, you'll have less of the total pizza. Similarly, if you have the same number of shares after the new stock is issued as you had before, your ownership interest in the company will be proportionately smaller.

  In some cases, shareholders are entitled to maintain their proportionate interest in a company as the number of shares outstanding increases with new issues. This is called a **preemptive right**. For example, suppose you own 100 shares in a company that currently has one million shares outstanding. If the company decides to issue another 250,000 shares, and if you have preemptive rights, you'll be able to buy 25 shares of the new issue before it goes on sale to the public in order to maintain your current percentage ownership $(100/1,000,000 = 125/1,250,000)$.

- **Stock splits** Corporations sometimes decide to declare a stock split, which is similar to a stock dividend in that each shareholder gets a number of new shares in proportion to the number of shares already held. The most frequent type of stock split is a two-for-one split, but three-for-one or three-for-two splits are also relatively common. The price of each share usually adjusts so that the total value remains the same. **Interactive: How Are Stock Splits Like Pizza Slices?** illustrates this with an analogy to slicing up a pizza.

INTERACTIVE

See **Interactive: How Are Stock Splits Like Pizza Slices?** in **WileyPLUS**.

Investors tend to view a stock split as favorable information about the company's prospects for future growth, so the company's market value often increases a little when a company announces a split. Why is a split good news? The logic is that management likes to keep the company's share price below some maximum value perceived as affordable to the company's investors. Announcement of a split is seen as a signal that management expects the stock price to continue to rise above this maximum value. To the extent that this is news to investors, they'll respond by buying the stock and driving up the price.

If it has occurred to you that this stock price reaction might create an opportunity to make a quick profit, you're not alone. A lot of investors buy shares just as the split announcement is made, hoping to sell them after the company's value increases in response to the announcement of the split. However, market efficiency implies that any price change will occur incredibly quickly. In fact, by the time you get your order in to buy the shares after the split, the price might have already gone up.

Advantages of Stock Investing

Chapter 11 introduced several of the advantages of investing as an owner rather than as a lender: no management responsibility, higher long-run returns, greater liquidity, less sensitivity to interest, and the ability to diversify a portfolio to reduce company-specific risk. Let's explore these advantages and a few others in a bit more detail.

No Management Responsibility

Stock investing allows you to participate in the profits of a firm without having to contribute anything except money to the venture. While you might earn as much or more by starting your own business and keeping all the profits for yourself, it would require a lot more effort on your part. Your stock ownership interest also protects you with limited liability—you can never be held personally responsible for losses incurred as a result of poor management.

Higher Long-Run Returns

Recall that riskier assets usually earn a higher rate of return. Over long time periods, large-company stocks have averaged a 12 percent return compared with about 6 percent for Treasury bonds. How much would that difference in investment return affect your long-term wealth accumulation? You can use your financial calculator to answer this question. Assume that you plan to put $1,000 in an investment account today. What will it be worth in 20 years if you invest in government bonds, earn 6 percent interest, and reinvest all your interest earnings? To find the answer, solve for the future value of a lump sum. With the financial calculator, you would enter PV = −1,000, N = 20, and I = 6, and solve for FV = $3,207. This is the amount you'd have in 20 years if you invested in government bonds. Now, what if you invest in stocks instead and earn 12 percent per year? Using the same method, you can determine that your $1,000 investment will be worth $9,646 at the end of 20 years—almost three times as much. (If your $1,000 is held in a taxable account, the after-tax investment returns will be lower for both asset classes.)

Even though stocks have yielded better returns than other investments over time, there can be fairly big differences between different stocks and over different time periods. **Figure 12.1** shows the stock price history for two familiar companies, Walmart (WMT) and International Business Machines Inc. (IBM). Although both increased in value from 2009 to 2019, WMT showed slow and steady growth, whereas IBM had a lot more ups and downs. That's because IBM is in a riskier industry. Technology companies are more strongly affected by economic conditions than discount department stores, which have steady customers regardless of the state of the economy.

FIGURE 12.1 **Walmart and IBM Monthly Stock Prices, 2009–2019** Investors in both IBM and Walmart enjoyed the benefits of a bull stock market between 2009 and 2019.

Demonstration Problem 12.1 shows how you can compare the rate of return on different investments.

DEMONSTRATION PROBLEM 12.1 | Comparing Returns on Different Stocks

Problem

Suppose you had $1,000 to invest at the beginning of 2009. At that time, Walmart stock was priced at $37 per share and IBM stock at $68 per share. If these stocks grew in value to $95 and $133, respectively, by January 1, 2019, including both capital gains and dividends, would Walmart or IBM have been the better investment?

Strategy

Calculate the rate of return for each stock for the 10 year period to find the growth in value of your $1,000 investment in both stocks. Because the prices are already adjusted for dividends, we can simply look at the change in each price over the period and then annualize it.

Solution

Substitute the new and old prices into Equation 1.1 (from Chapter 1) to find the rate of return for the two companies' stocks over the period in question:

$$\text{Rate of return (IBM)} = \frac{\text{New price}}{\text{Old price}} - 1 = \frac{\$133}{\$68} - 1 = 0.96, \text{ or } 96\%$$

$$\text{Rate of return (WMT)} = \frac{\text{New price}}{\text{Old price}} - 1 = \frac{\$95}{\$37} - 1 = 1.57, \text{ or } 157\%$$

These are cumulative returns over 10 years. The annualized return, calculated as $(1 + \text{Holding period return})^{1/10} - 1$, will be lower:

$$\text{Annualized return (IBM)} = 1.96^{1/10} - 1 = 0.07, \text{ or } 7.0\%$$

$$\text{Annualized return (WMT)} = 2.57^{1/10} - 1 = 0.099, \text{ or } 9.9\%$$

By either of these measures, we see that WMT stock turned out to be the better investment over this period of time. With IBM, you could have almost doubled your original investment over the decade, but with WMT, you would have ended up with about 2.5 times what you started with.

Liquidity

Another advantage of stocks is that they are fairly liquid investments. As you know, a liquid asset is one that can be converted to cash quickly without loss of value. Bad news, such as a product recall that will cost the firm millions of dollars, can cause a stock's value to decline rapidly, so we wouldn't place this asset in the same category as liquid savings and checking accounts. However, you can usually sell shares of stock quickly, easily, and at relatively low cost. This is an important factor if you need cash in a hurry.

Low Interest-Rate Sensitivity

Recall from Chapter 11 that the value of bonds and other debt securities is highly influenced by interest rates, creating interest-rate risk that increases with the term to maturity on the bond. When rates go up, bond prices fall, and vice versa. One of the advantages of stocks in a portfolio is that stock values are less sensitive to interest-rate movements. Even though higher discount rates can reduce the present value of future cash flows from stock investments, there are often offsetting factors. For example, if the reason interest rates are increasing is that the economy is in an expansionary period of the business cycle, the cash flows of the firm will increase as well, so the value of the firm will not necessarily decline.

Diversifiable Risk

One of the fundamental principles of investing is that you can lower your risk, as measured by variability of returns, by having a variety of investments in your portfolio. We introduced diversification in Chapter 11 in conjunction with the concept of asset allocation, because holding several different asset classes has a diversifying effect on your portfolio. But diversification can reduce risk *within* asset classes as well, as long as you select individual investments that aren't too similar. If you hold a portfolio of many different stocks, some of them will do well when others are doing poorly. Holding a number of stocks will therefore allow you to cancel out much of the company-specific variability in returns. What you'll be left with is market risk, the risk that can't be diversified away because it comes from factors common to all stocks.

As you saw above, the stock prices of both IBM and Walmart increased in value between 2009 and 2019, despite being in different sectors and having different sensitivities to economic conditions. If you look closely at the stock price chart in Figure 12.1, though, you can see that the ups and downs of the two companies' share prices were often opposite each other in a given month. This means that if you had owned shares of both companies in your portfolio, the IBM price declines would have been at least partially offset by Walmart price increases.

Figure 12.2 compares $1,000 investments in IBM, WMT, and a portfolio split equally between these two stocks over the years 2009–2019. You can see that at first IBM outperformed WMT and the 50/50 portfolio, though it began to lose value in 2013. By late 2014, all three investments had approximately doubled in value. Then IBM's value experienced another decline, while WMT's value increased, a trend that continued through 2019. The 50/50 portfolio ended up somewhere in the middle, earning an annualized 8.6% over the 10-year period. Although investing in the 50/50 portfolio resulted in slightly lower accumulated value than investing in

ONLINE CALCULATOR DEMONSTRATION VIDEO

See **Online Calculator Demonstration Video: Asset Allocation** in **WileyPLUS.**

FIGURE 12.2 **The Effects of Diversification** Investing in a 50/50 portfolio of WMT and IBM smoothed out some of the ups and downs associated with investing in only one of the stocks.

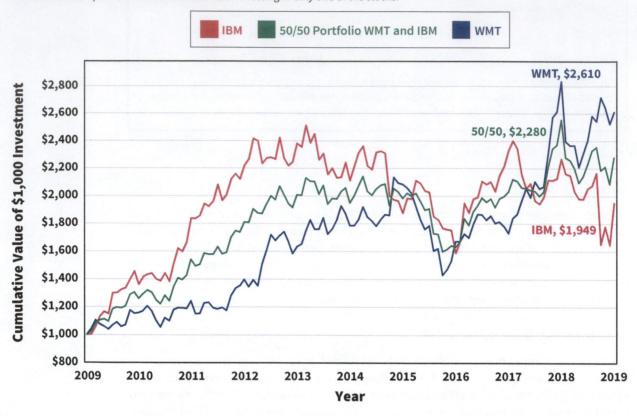

Walmart stock alone, it also smoothed out some of the ups and downs you would have experienced if you had invested in only one of the stocks.

Disadvantages of Stock Investing

Although stock investing clearly offers some advantages for long-run investors, it might not be for everyone. Investing in stocks exposes you to substantial risk that you cannot control, other than by selling your shares if you don't like the actions taken by the management of the company. Depending on your personal risk preferences, financial goals, and investment time horizon, you might not be willing or able to bear this level of risk in your portfolio.

Risk

An old saying warns, "If you can't take the heat, get out of the kitchen." Stock investors must be prepared to "take the heat" in the form of ups and downs in stock prices, as illustrated in **Figure 12.3**, which shows the price history of the S&P 500 Index over a span of 21 years, from 1998 to 2019. This was clearly a very volatile period for the stock market, with terrorist attacks, a global financial crisis, and political uncertainly resulting in two large stock market declines and subsequent recoveries. Investors lost about 40 percent of their wealth between 2000 and 2003, regained it between 2003 and 2007, then lost even more between 2007 and 2008, recovering again through 2014 and beyond.

The first decade of the 2000s was not kind to stock investors. In fact, a diversified portfolio from the early peak in 2000 through the end of 2012 would have earned you a whopping 0 percent return for more than a decade of investing. Clearly, this was not what investors expected to happen based on prior historical performance of the stock market. However, investors who were in for the long haul saw their portfolios almost triple in value between 1998 and 2019. This illustrates an important lesson about stock investing—even though stocks may be a good long-term investment, you'll have substantial risk of ups and downs in the short term.

FIGURE 12.3   **S&P 500 Index, 1998–2019**   The stock market has been on a roller coaster ride since the late 1990s.

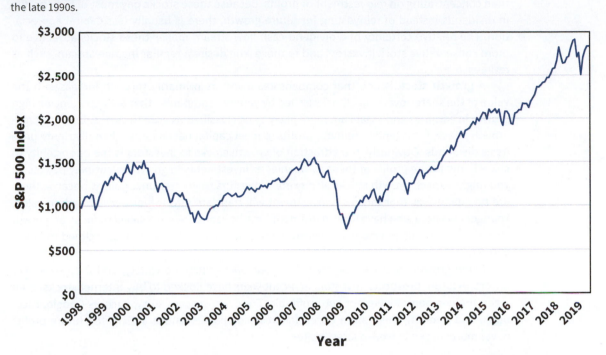

No Control

We've already seen that, as a stock investor—particularly in a large, publicly held corporation—you have little power to influence the actions of management. And management can do many things that cause your share value to decline. Top managers can make business decisions that increase the company's risk or reduce its competitive advantage. Their financial decisions might dilute your ownership interest if they issue more shares or decrease your residual interest if they take on more debt. In the extreme, they may make self-interested decisions that line their own pockets at your expense. Even if you know what they're doing and object to it, you have little recourse because your limited voting rights make it almost impossible to effect any managerial change. For this reason, it's commonly said that stockholders "vote with their feet." In other words, if you don't like what management is doing, you can walk away by selling your shares. Unfortunately, by the time you know what's wrong, the value of the stock will probably already reflect the bad news, so you're likely to lose money.

Classification of Common Stock

Common stock is usually classified according to broad, and sometimes overlapping, categories related to cash flow, risk, and line of business. Although these classifications have no official status, understanding the common lingo used by investment professionals will help you to better communicate with financial advisors, make allocation decisions for your employer-sponsored retirement plan, and comprehend what you read in the financial press. An important cautionary note if you are investing in individual stocks rather than mutual funds: Companies differ widely from one another, so it's always important to analyze the individual companies independently rather than to rely solely on these classifications to make judgments about the suitability of their stock for your portfolio. We look at some of the more common classifications of common stocks in this section.

Income versus Growth Stocks

As previously discussed, investors usually expect to receive some combination of current cash flow and price appreciation in return for providing capital to a firm. Stocks are often classified based on whether the company tends to reward its investors primarily with current income or with capital gains. An **income stock** is one that pays investors a regular dividend rather than concentrating on reinvestment of profits. Because these stocks pay most of their profits in dividends instead of reinvesting for future growth, there is usually less capital appreciation. The relative certainty of a dividend cash flow stream makes these stocks attractive to more conservative stock investors and to those who desire a regular income stream, such as retirees.

A **growth stock** is one that compensates investors primarily through increases in the value of the shares over time. Stocks issued by younger companies that are experiencing high growth in earnings and assets are more likely to be classified as growth stocks. During a high-growth phase, firms tend to reinvest profits to meet capital needs rather than distribute profits as dividends. Obviously, the attraction of growth stocks to investors is the opportunity to share in the future profits of these companies as investments in growth eventually pay off. As you might expect, growth stocks also expose investors to greater uncertainty, because there are no guarantees that today's reinvestment will translate into tomorrow's growth in value. Younger investors who have long investment time horizons are more likely to focus on growth stocks, while investors who want investment income and stability are less inclined to invest in them.

Some growth stocks are highly risky—their prices fluctuate widely, and they have very uncertain future prospects. Investors in recent years have flocked to buy Internet stocks, even when the companies were not yet profitable. For every success story, such as Google, Facebook, and Amazon, there are a dozen failures—companies whose anticipated future profits never materialized or were overestimated.

Blue Chip Stocks

A **blue chip stock** is one issued by a large, stable, mature company. The earnings and growth of these multibillion-dollar companies tend to track the overall market. As consistent performers, they're considered less risky than growth stocks; however, they don't offer opportunities for unexpectedly high returns. They are the slow and steady performers, often leaders in their industry, and they commonly pay dividends in addition to offering the opportunity for some growth in value over time. Examples of such companies include Anheuser-Busch, Procter & Gamble, and Coca-Cola.

Cyclical versus Defensive Stocks

In the earlier example, we saw that IBM's stock price was more sensitive to economic conditions than Walmart's stock price. A **cyclical stock** exhibits above-average sensitivity to the business cycle—that is, it tends to perform well during strong economic climates and poorly in downturns. Cyclical companies include firms that produce consumer durable goods and luxury items—automobiles, appliances, technology, furniture, and sporting equipment. Purchases of such goods can nearly always be put off when money is tight. Companies connected to the home-building industry (such as Home Depot) and companies that provide services or goods to other businesses (such as transportation and technology firms) are also cyclical, because during recessions, construction and investment projects tend to be put on hold.

The opposite of a cyclical stock is a **defensive stock**, such as Walmart stock, which is less sensitive to market ups and downs. These stocks might still go down in bear markets, but can be expected to lose less than others. As a result, they can help to stabilize your portfolio during market downturns. Stocks that are related to food and beverages (Anheuser-Busch and Coca-Cola) and to health care (Pfizer and CVS) are examples, because they are in industries that provide essential products and services that are in demand regardless of economic conditions.

A measure commonly used to estimate the risk of stock investments held in a diversified portfolio is the **beta**. A stock's beta measures its market risk, as discussed in Chapter 11, or how much it tends to move with the overall market. The risk measured by beta is also sometimes called nondiversifiable risk because it's the risk that remains when you've already diversified your portfolio. Cyclical stocks will usually have higher betas, and defensive stocks will have lower betas.

A beta equal to 1 means that the stock has the same degree of volatility as the overall market and is expected to earn a similar long-term rate of return if held in a diversified portfolio. A beta less than 1 means that the stock is less volatile than the market average and investors should expect a proportionally lower return. A beta greater than 1 means that the stock is more volatile than average and should provide a proportionally higher return. Because most stocks tend to go up and down simultaneously with the general market, just in different degrees, most beta values are between 0.5 and 1.5, and it is rare to find a stock with a negative beta.

Industry and Sector

Stocks are also categorized by the sector and industry of the issuing companies. **Table 12.1** provides sector classifications, along with some examples of representative companies and their industries. In this table, the "sensitive" classification includes companies with average sensitivity to the business cycle. Industries in the financial services sector include banks and insurance companies. Companies selling household and personal products are in the consumer defensive sector because people need to purchase their products even when the economy is in a slump. Beverage companies, such as Coca-Cola, are also considered to be defensive. Note that the table also lists the *ticker symbols* of the representative companies. These are the abbreviations used to identify the companies on the various securities exchanges.

TABLE 12.1 **Sector Classifications with Industry and Company Examples**

Sector	Industry	Representative Company	Stock Ticker Symbol
Cyclical			
Basic materials	Building materials	Owens Corning	OC
Consumer cyclical	Airlines	Delta Airlines, Inc.	DAL
Financial services	Banking	Wells Fargo & Company	WFC
Sensitive			
Communication services	Telecom services	Verizon Communications, Inc.	VZ
Energy	Oil and gas—diversified	Exxon Mobile Corporation	XOM
Industrials	Diversified industrials	3M Co.	MMM
Technology	Internet content/information	Alphabet, Inc.	GOOG
Defensive			
Consumer defensive	Household & personal products	Proctor & Gamble Co.	PG
Health care	Health-care plans	CVS Health Corporation	CVS
Utilities	Utilities—diversified	Public Service Enterprise Group, Inc.	PEG

Market Capitalization

Market capitalization is the total value of a company's shares at a share's current market price. It is calculated according to **Equation 12.1**:

$$\text{Market capitalization} = \text{Current market price} \times \text{Number of shares outstanding} \qquad (12.1)$$

On the basis of capitalization, companies are classified as large-cap, mid-cap, or small-cap. Here, we consider the general parameters for these classifications, but these definitions aren't engraved in stone—investors tend to include companies in these groups based on not only market capitalization but also revenue, growth potential, and past history.

- Large-cap companies have market capitalization of $10 billion or more. These are the largest firms in the country and include all the companies in the Dow Jones Industrial Average and the S&P 500 Index. Historically, large-cap stocks have been viewed as having lower risk than the stocks of small-cap and mid-cap firms. That rule of thumb doesn't really apply to large-cap technology and Internet companies, however, because many of them are still in a high-growth stage, which makes them riskier. The Coca-Cola Company (ticker: KO) traded at around $46 per share in early 2019 and had 4.3 billion shares outstanding, giving it a market cap of nearly $200 billion. In contrast to KO, which has been in existence for a very long time, Facebook, Inc. (ticker: FB) went straight to large-cap status after its first offering of stock to the public in 2012. In mid-2019, the stock traded at $199 per share, and the company had 2.8 billion shares outstanding, for a total market cap of more than $568 billion.

- Mid-cap companies have $2 billion to $10 billion in market capitalization—they're still large, but not giants. A few examples of mid-caps in 2019 include The Cheesecake Factory Incorporated (ticker: CAKE), Stitch Fix, Inc. (ticker: SFIX), and Etsy, Inc. (ticker: ETSY).

- A small-cap company generally has market capitalization of less than $2 billion. Although that might not seem very small to you, these firms are small relative to many others and generally are young, growing companies. You're less likely to recognize many of these companies by name, but one you might have heard of is BJ's Restaurants, Inc. (ticker: BJRI), which had a market cap of less than $1 billion in 2019. Although rates of return on small-cap stocks have been greater than the returns on other asset classes over time, their prices tend to be more sensitive to market movement, and the companies usually don't pay dividends. This means that small-cap investors are subject to a lot more risk. This effect is even more pronounced for the *micro-caps*—companies with less than $300 million in capitalization.

Reflection Question 1

If you had some money to invest in stocks, what types of companies would you choose? Would it make sense to invest in companies that produce products that you like? Why or why not?

Measures of Common Stock Performance

You should select individual stocks for your investment portfolio based on your evaluation of expected returns as well as an assessment of how much risk the investment will add to your portfolio. In addition to looking at historical rates of return on particular investments, investors commonly use earnings per share and the price-to-earnings ratios to help them estimate future rates of return. In this section, we explain how each of these measures is used to evaluate stock investments.

In Chapter 11, you learned that the annual rate of return on an investment comes from two components, the current income and the growth in value over the year. For stock investors, the current yield is usually called the dividend yield, because the current income to a stock investor is the annual dividend payment. The two components of a stock's rate of return, dividend yield and capital gains yield, are calculated according to **Equation 12.2** and **Equation 12.3**:

$$\text{Dividend yield} = \frac{\text{Annual dividend}}{\text{Beginning stock price}} \tag{12.2}$$

$$\text{Capital gains yield} = \frac{\text{Annual change in stock price}}{\text{Beginning stock price}} \tag{12.3}$$

As an example, suppose you're considering purchasing a stock with a market price of $50 per share. If the stock pays an annual dividend of $1 per share, you'll earn a dividend yield of 2 percent ($1/$50 = 0.02). Your total annual return on the stock will be the 2 percent dividend yield plus the expected capital gains yield. If, historically, the stock has increased in value an average of 10 percent per year, you might expect the price to rise to $55 by the end of the year. In this case, you'd earn a total rate of return of 12 percent on your stock investment for the year—2 percent in dividend yield and 10 percent in capital gains yield. Normally, the price that you'll use in the denominator of Equation 12.2 or 12.3 will be the price you paid, or expect to pay, for the shares.

Investors' expectations about future capital gains and future dividend income will have an impact on the value of stock. Because there are so many factors that enter into this assessment, there's no easy formula to determine the value of a firm or its future returns. However, investors commonly look at financial ratios that have been found to be good indicators of future performance.

Perhaps the most closely watched ratio is the company's **earnings per share (EPS)**, which is calculated according to **Equation 12.4**:

$$\text{Earnings per share} = \frac{\text{After-tax net income}}{\text{Number of shares outstanding}} \tag{12.4}$$

Stock investors own a proportionate share of the company, so they have an interest in a proportionate share of the firm's annual after-tax net income, commonly called earnings. The company can use those dollars to pay dividends, or it can reinvest them to grow the firm. Either way, stockholders stand to benefit if earnings go up. When a company reports better than expected earnings, its stock price tends to go up, because investors see that as a good sign for the future. When earnings are lower than expected, the stock price tends to go down.

EPS provides a rough measure of profitability and can be compared over time for a particular firm. However, it's not very useful as a decision-making tool, because there isn't a universally accepted "good" or "bad" value (as long as EPS is positive and increasing over time). To see why this is the case, consider two similar companies that had earnings per share equal to $2 last year. You can't conclude that they'd be equally profitable to you as an investor, because it depends on what you'd have to pay to get this level of earnings. If one company's stock is half as expensive as the other's, you'd have to conclude that the lower-priced stock was giving you a better relative level of earnings. Generally, differences in company size, industry, and share price all make it difficult to directly compare companies based on EPS.

To account for other company differences, investors typically consider EPS relative to some other variable. For example, you can use the **price-to-earnings (P/E) ratio**, which measures the relation of share price to earnings per share. We can calculate the P/E ratio using **Equation 12.5**:

$$\text{Price-to-earnings ratio} = \frac{\text{Price per share}}{\text{Earnings per share}} \tag{12.5}$$

The P/E ratio is seen as a measure of potential for future growth in earnings. A high P/E ratio, relative to those of other similar firms, is considered a positive indicator of a firm's potential for future growth. The implication is that investors perceive the firm as being "worth" the extra price. However, a high P/E ratio can also be an indication that a stock is currently overpriced relative to similar stocks that have lower P/E ratios.

Although P/E ratios differ over time and across industries, the average for large-cap stocks is usually between 10 and 25, whereas P/E ratios for high-growth stocks can be much higher. For example, the average P/E ratio for companies in the Consumer Discretionary sector in 2019 was 27, and **Amazon.com**, Inc., had a P/E ratio of 83. In contrast, the average P/E ratio for banks was 13, and the P/E for large bank Wells Fargo & Company was only 10.

Interactive: Stock Valuation Measures gives you an opportunity to test your understanding of stock valuation measures.

INTERACTIVE

See **Interactive: Stock Valuation Measures** in **WileyPLUS.**

12.2 | Investing in Bonds

LEARNING OBJECTIVE 12.2

Describe the characteristics and classifications of bonds.

To decide whether bonds fit into your investment plan, you need to know about the cash flows, risks, and tax implications of investing in bonds. In this section, we consider why bonds are issued in the first place, because the motivations of the issuers have an impact on the returns to investors and the differences in risk between bonds and stocks. We then discuss some basic bond terminology and explain various factors that affect bond values.

What Is a Bond?

Chapter 11 introduced the choice between investing as a lender and as an owner. When you buy stock in a company, you're an owner. When you buy bonds, you're a lender. Recall that a bond is a type of financial security that represents a long-term loan of money to a company or governmental entity. When you invest in a bond, you have the right to receive interest payments and to have your loan repaid in the future.

The Purpose of Bonds

In general, an organization seeks outside investors when it doesn't have enough current cash flow to support its needs. A business might need cash because it's growing rapidly or its revenue is insufficient to cover its costs. Similarly, a government entity—federal, state, city, or municipal—might need money to pay for a large construction project or to cover budgeted costs that exceed tax revenues.

Borrowing money to spread the cost of a large expenditure over time is sometimes a sound financial strategy. However, as is the case with household debt, using long-term borrowing to fund budget shortfalls can lead to future financial difficulties. Therefore, businesses and government entities commonly use long-term bond issues to fund projects that they expect to have a long-term payoff. If they need funds for only a short time, they're likely to issue short-term debt or take out a short-term bank loan instead.

You may wonder why organizations choose to borrow instead of selling stock. With government entities, of course, there isn't really a choice. These organizations don't have the option of selling shares to the public. Other than raising taxes, federal, state, and local authorities have no alternative but to borrow the money. However, businesses do have an alternative, so it's reasonable to ask why they would choose to issue bonds instead of stock. Bondholders expect to receive regular payments of interest and to be paid back when their bonds mature, whereas stockholders aren't entitled to dividends or repayment of their principal. The reasons for debt financing are related to cost, taxes, control, and the benefits of financial leverage.

- **Cost**   Debt financing is usually cheaper than equity financing. Because they bear more risk than bondholders, equity investors expect to earn a higher rate of return. This expectation puts greater pressure on management to generate profits and increase the value of the firm. In contrast, a company can afford to pay its bond interest even if it's only moderately profitable.

  Another cost-related factor is the expense associated with the actual issuance of the bonds. Bonds are issued in significantly higher denominations than common and preferred stock (usually $1,000 each), and they're often sold to a small number of large investors. This makes a bond issue less costly to the firm (in terms of advertising, legal, and accounting expenses) per dollar of capital raised than selling common stock to a large number of equity investors.

- **Taxes**   Another reason that companies like to issue bonds stems from the tax treatment of the cash flows they pay to bond and stock investors. Interest payments are tax-deductible to the firm; dividend payments are not. Therefore, the after-tax cost of bond interest payments, particularly for highly creditworthy companies, is fairly low. If, for example, the company issues bonds that require 5 percent annual interest payments and the firm's marginal tax rate is 30 percent, then the after-tax cost is only 3.5 percent [$5\% \times (1 - 0.3) = 3.5\%$]. In contrast, because dividend payments are not tax-deductible, the firm bears the full cost.

- **Control**   When a company sells additional shares of stock, the percentage ownership of existing shareholders is reduced. Issuing debt allows the company to raise the necessary funds for expansion without forcing current owners to reduce their percentage ownership.

- **Leverage**   Stockholders also benefit from the effects of financial leverage associated with using borrowed funds. Debt improves the returns to existing shareholders, so long as the debt is relatively cheap. That is, if a company can borrow money at a low rate and earn a higher rate of return, the profit accrues to the residual owners—the shareholders. In Chapter 6, you learned about the benefits that leverage can have on your personal finances.

If you buy a home and finance 80 percent of the cost with a home mortgage, the increase in the value of your home over time accrues entirely to you—you don't have to share the capital gain with the mortgage lender. This substantially increases your return on the small investment of your down payment. The same is true for businesses, although they generally are not as highly leveraged as homeowners. On average, businesses finance less than one-third of their assets with debt.

Types of Bonds

Bonds are commonly classified according to the type of issuer and certain characteristics of the bonds.

Classification by Type of Issuer

Bonds are issued by corporations and various government entities. Because these issuers have different prospects for the future and different sources of cash flow, their bond issues are distinctly different in risk characteristics. We explain the major classifications below.

- **Corporate bonds** Corporate bonds are long-term, interest-bearing debt securities issued by a corporation to help finance its long-term assets or operations. They are usually issued in denominations of $1,000 and promise semiannual interest payments based on a fixed rate. Terms to maturity can vary from 5 to 30 years or more, with the most common maturities being 20 and 25 years.

   With so many corporations in existence, there are many corporate bonds to choose from, and these bonds can differ substantially in cash flows and risks. Bonds may also incorporate special features or contract terms that make them more or less valuable. For example, a convertible corporate bond allows the bondholder to convert to stock in the future, and a callable bond allows the firm to buy back the bond under some conditions, at a predetermined price. Although most bonds have fixed interest rates, you'll sometimes see bonds with variable rates.

- **U.S. Treasury bonds** The U.S. government regularly issues debt with various terms to maturity. We've previously considered Treasury bills, which have maturities of one year or less. Although T-bills may be an appropriate choice for funds you've allocated to short-term objectives, such as an emergency fund, the rate of return is too low to be an option for your intermediate- and long-term investment plan. Treasury securities with original terms of 1 to 10 years are called Treasury notes, and those with longer terms are Treasury bonds. All Treasury securities are considered to be default-risk-free, because the federal government has the power to raise taxes to pay its obligations in the future. Some investors may also find these securities attractive because the interest paid on them, while federally taxable, is exempt from state and local income taxes. Because of the minimal risk and the tax benefits, the yield on this type of debt investment is lower than that on corporate bonds with similar maturities.

- **Municipal bonds**   A **municipal bond**, often called a "muni," is a long-term debt security issued by a state or local government entity. The money raised from a municipal bond offering might be earmarked to pay for airport construction, public schools, parks, infrastructure improvements (such as roads and bridges), or ongoing government expenditures.

   One of the most important features of municipal bond investments is that interest payments are exempt from federal income tax. If the investor lives in the state of issuance, the interest is usually exempt from state and local taxation as well. However, a capital gain earned on the sale of a municipal bond is still subject to tax.

   A muni can be either a general obligation bond or a revenue bond. If it's a general obligation bond, the interest and principal payments will come from the normal operating cash flows of the issuing entity, and the security for the bond is just the "full faith and credit" of that entity. Normally, general obligation bonds can be issued only by states, cities, and other entities that have taxing authority (the power to assess taxes on property, sales, or income). In contrast, a revenue bond will be repaid from the income generated by the project it is issued to finance. For example, for a bond issued to fund the building of a bridge, interest and principal repayments could be made from future tolls charged for the use of the bridge. In some cases, after the bond issue is repaid, the government might decide to keep the tolls in place to pay for ongoing repairs.

Municipal bonds can sometimes be fairly risky investments. State and local governments with serious budget problems may find it difficult to make good on their obligations. Sometimes, the projects financed by revenue bonds are subject to construction delays or fail to generate as much revenue as expected. When investors see an increased risk of default, bond prices can decline dramatically.

- **Agency issues**   An **agency issue** is a bond issued by a federal agency, such as the Government National Mortgage Association (Ginnie Mae), the Federal National Mortgage Association (Fannie Mae), the Federal Home Loan Mortgage Corporation (Freddie Mac), or the Student Loan Marketing Association (Sallie Mae). The agency funds the interest payments to its bond investors from regular interest and principal paid by the individuals who have home mortgages or student loans. We discuss the process of creating these securities and the role they played in the recent financial crisis in **Ethics in Action**.

Ethics in Action

Mortgage-Backed Securities

As noted, agency bonds are issued by federal agencies and backed by pools of loans, such as mortgages or student loans. Each agency specializes in a specific segment of the market, buying particular types of loans from banks and savings institutions. It finances the cost of buying the loans by borrowing the money from bond investors, such as pension funds and insurance companies, in large denominations (a minimum of $25,000).

When the portfolio is made up of home mortgages, as shown in **Figure 12.4**, the bonds are called mortgage-backed securities (MBS). Mortgage loans to homeowners are typically sold off by the original lenders into the MBS market where they are used to create MBS portfolios. Once they have sold the loans, the lenders no longer bear the risk of loan default. In the early 2000s, when the demand for traditional mortgages was lagging, government agencies, encouraged banks to loosen their credit standards to generate more mortgages to sell into the MBS market. While interest rates were low and house prices were rising, this all worked pretty well, and the MBS market grew rapidly. At the peak of the housing bubble in 2007–2008, lenders were making high loan-to-value loans without even requiring verification of income from borrowers, commonly called "no doc" loans and eventually "liar loans," since the borrowers essentially had to lie about their income in order to qualify. By 2007, these types of loans represented 9 percent of all outstanding mortgages.

Everything fell apart when interest rates began to increase, layoffs became more common, and housing prices went down. The rate of mortgage defaults increased and many people lost their homes. When people commit to larger loan payments than justified by their income, it doesn't take much to push them into default.

Financial regulations put in place after the Financial Crisis now require banks to verify that a borrower has "a reasonable ability to repay." The logical question to ask is "Why didn't they do that before?" Clearly, profit got in the way of common sense.

FIGURE 12.4   **The Process of Creating Mortgage-Backed Securities**
The interest payments on these bonds are backed by pools of home mortgage loans that have been sold by the originating banks to Fannie Mae or another agency.

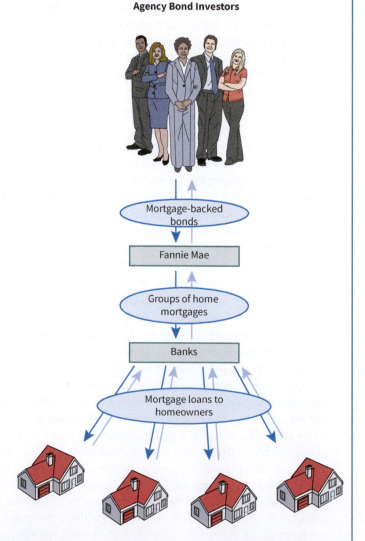

Agency Bond Investors

Mortgage-backed bonds

Fannie Mae

Groups of home mortgages

Banks

Mortgage loans to homeowners

Classification by Bond Characteristics

In addition to the major classifications based on type of issuer, bonds are sometimes classified based on differences in specific characteristics that affect their return and risk.

- **Secured versus unsecured bonds**   Most corporate and government bonds are unsecured bonds. This means that the promise of payment of interest and principal in the future is backed only by the creditworthiness of the company or governmental body. In contrast, a **secured bond** is one for which the issuer has pledged specific assets or future cash flows as collateral. In the event of nonpayment, the holders of a secured bond, through a trustee, have the right to take the pledged assets in payment of the debt. Examples of secured bonds include mortgage bonds, which are backed by pools of loans backed by real estate, and equipment bonds, which are backed by valuable equipment or vehicles.

  Although the existence of collateral for a loan can reduce the risk of default to bond-holders, the amount of risk reduction (and consequent reduction in yield) depends on the value of the security and its resulting cash flows. For example, we've already seen that municipal bonds might be secured by future revenue from a particular project. If the project fails to generate the expected net revenue (either through insufficient gross revenue or greater than expected costs), the bondholders are still exposed to default risk. Suppose, for example, that a city uses a bond issue to build a public aquarium, but it turns out that the planners had overestimated the number of annual visitors to the aquarium and underestimated the costs of running it. As a result, the city is losing money and decides to close the aquarium. The bond investors will be out of luck.

- **How interest is paid**   Bonds are also classified according to how interest is calculated and paid to investors. Most bonds pay a fixed rate of interest in semiannual installments, but there are variations on this arrangement. For example, with **floating-rate bonds**, interest payments are tied to current market interest rates and adjusted periodically, similar to an adjustable-rate mortgage. The issuer of floating-rate bonds gains the advantage of keeping the interest it pays on the bonds close to the market rate of interest. If rates go down, investors will get a lower interest rate, but they will not be subject to large fluctuations in price. When the interest rate is tied to a market index, the bond is called an **indexed bond**.

  A **zero-coupon bond** makes no interest payments but instead is discounted at the time of sale so that the gain in value over the life of the bond will provide the bondholder with an appropriate rate of return. With this type of bond, your entire yield comes from the increase in value from the purchase date to the maturity date. The price is the discounted present value of the face value, so the longer the time to maturity, the steeper the discount. Zero-coupon bonds are issued by both corporations and governments, with the U.S. Treasury being the largest issuer.

  If you aren't interested in current income but have a specific investment goal in mind, such as paying for your child's education 18 years from now, it might appear that a zero-coupon bond would be an attractive investment. The major problem with these bonds, however, lies in their current federal income tax treatment. Even though you don't receive interest in the form of regular payments, the IRS considers the annual appreciation in the value of the bond to be "undistributed interest" and requires that you treat it as taxable income each year. For example, suppose you bought a 20-year zero-coupon bond, with a face value of $1,000, one year ago for $240. Today, it has 19 years to maturity, and its value is $258. The $18 increase in value will be taxable as interest income to you, even though you haven't actually received it. For this reason, these bonds are best held in tax-deferred accounts or by minor children who are subject to low tax rates.

  Another disadvantage of zero-coupon bonds is that, because their only cash flow is the amount to be received many years in the future, they expose investors to greater interest-rate risk than interest-paying bonds. Although an increase in interest rates will cause all bond prices to decline, the prices of zero-coupon bonds tend to experience larger declines as a percentage of value. Nevertheless, zero-coupon bonds are very popular with buy-and-hold investors who plan to hold the bonds to maturity and therefore aren't concerned with interim swings in value.

- **Inflation protection** For investors who are worried about the risk of inflation, U.S. government **Treasury Inflation-Protected Securities (TIPS)** are an important investment alternative. These inflation-indexed bonds, available through **TreasuryDirect.gov** in units of $100, protect against inflation by adjusting the face value of the bond each year. For example, suppose you buy a $100 face value TIPS bond that promises to pay 2.5 percent over inflation. If inflation turns out to be 3 percent in the next year, the face value of the bond will increase by 3 percent to $103 and your coupon payment will be 2.5 percent of the adjusted value. If you're relying on your bond portfolio to pay regular expenses, the inflation adjustment means that the cash flows will continue to increase with the cost of goods so you never lose purchasing power. The interest on these bonds is taxable unless they are held in a tax-deferred account such as an IRA.

- **Risk** Because default risk is so important to bond investors, bonds are often classified according to risk. Several rating agencies, including Moody's, Standard & Poor's, Duff & Phelps, and Fitch Group, regularly evaluate large corporate and municipal bond issues and provide ratings based on risk. The two most popular rating systems—Moody's and Standard & Poor's—are described in **Table 12.2**. Bonds rated Baa and above in Moody's system and BBB and above in Standard & Poor's are called **investment-grade bonds**, whereas those with lower ratings are called **high-yield bonds**, or **junk bonds**. Although high-yield bonds gained in popularity in the last decade due to higher returns, these bonds are substantially riskier than higher-quality bonds. This is not only because of the difference in default risk, but also because of lower liquidity. Junk bonds are less actively traded and tend to be more sensitive to economic conditions. Certain financial institutions, such as pension funds and insurance companies, are heavily invested in bonds, but they're often required to hold only investment-grade bonds. For this reason, if a bond issue is downgraded, the value is likely to fall substantially as the investors sell their holdings to meet their investment requirements.

TABLE 12.2 **Bond Ratings and Their Meanings**

General Rating	Moody's	Standard & Poor's	Explanation
Very high quality	Aaa* Aa	AAA* AA	High-grade bonds. Extremely strong or very strong capacity to pay interest and principal. Profitable for many years and unlikely to default.
High quality	A Baa	A BBB	Medium-grade bonds. Strong or adequate capacity to pay but can be susceptible to adverse economic conditions or changing circumstances.
Speculative	Ba B	BB	Low-grade bonds. Capacity to pay interest and repay principal is speculative. Company may have some merits, but there is great uncertainty about its exposure to adverse conditions.
Very poor quality	Caa C	CCC D	Highest-risk bonds. Issuers are in default on paying interest and/or principal, with little chance of recovery.

*These are the primary categories of ratings, but finer gradations are sometimes given by adding 1, 2, 3 (Moody's) or +/− (Standard and Poor's) at the end of the letter grade.

Bond Terminology

As in other areas of investing, you'll need to master a few specific terms to understand bonds and bond investing. To discuss bond terminology, let's refer to the advertisement for the issuing of a hypothetical new bond, shown in **Figure 12.5**. The bond is formally referred to in the advertisement as a *debenture*, which is an unsecured bond.

FIGURE 12.5 **Advertisement for a Hypothetical New Bond Issue**   In this 2019 advertisement, Cavalier Corporation gives potential investors information about its new bond issue.

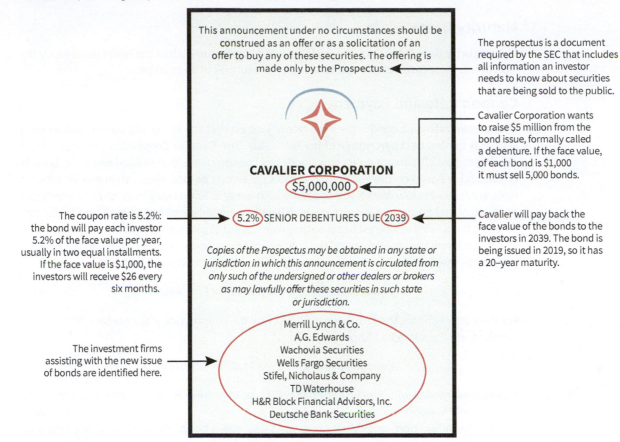

Prospectus

As with new stock issues, the Securities and Exchange Commission requires that a bond issuer provide all prospective investors with the pertinent information about the company and the security in a document called a **prospectus**. If you were interested in a particular company's bonds, you'd probably want to know, for example, what the company's primary business is, how the funds raised by the bond issue will be used, the financial strength of the issuer, and how the company plans to make good on its promise to pay interest and to repay the principal at maturity.

Trustee

The contract between a bondholder and the issuer of the bond specifies all the important terms of the bond agreement, including the rights and obligations of the bondholders and the issuer. A **trustee**, usually a bank trust department, is hired by the bond issuer to keep an eye on the company, making sure that the bondholders' rights are protected. The trustee enforces a bond indenture agreement that lists all of the issuing company's obligations. If, for example, the trustee finds that the company has violated a promise specified in the indenture, it can bring a legal action on behalf of all the bondholders to force the company to remedy the situation.

Face Value

The **face value**, or *par value*, of a bond is the amount that will be repaid to the bondholder when the bond matures, or comes due. Corporate bonds are usually issued with a face value of $1,000, but the face value can be larger. Unlike car loans and mortgages, bonds are not amortized. That means the issuer does not pay back any of the principal of the loan until the end, often 20 years or more from the date of issue. Over that period, the bonds can be bought and sold between bond market investors, just as common stocks are. No matter what happens to the price of the bonds in these transactions, however, the face value will remain at $1,000. Whoever owns the bond on the maturity date will receive that amount.

Maturity Date

The **maturity date** is the date on which the bond comes due—when the issuer must repay the loan in full. Most corporate bonds have original maturities of 20 to 30 years.

Coupon Rate and Payment

The **coupon rate** on a bond is the fixed rate of interest that the issuer will pay the holder each year. It is quoted as a percentage of the face value. The Cavalier Corporation, for example, is offering to pay 5.2 percent on its new bond. The coupon rate is determined when the bond is issued and is based on prevailing market rates for similar bonds. Thus, when market interest rates are relatively low, bonds will be issued with lower coupon rates than when market rates are high. At any given time, a company may have several outstanding issues of bonds that pay different fixed rates of interest because they were issued at different times.

If you know the face value and the coupon rate for a bond, you can calculate the **coupon payment**—the dollar amount paid in interest each year—using **Equation 12.6**.

$$\text{Coupon payment} = \text{Coupon rate} \times \text{Face value} \qquad (12.6)$$

For the Cavalier bond, the face value is $1,000, and the coupon rate is 5.2 percent. The coupon payment will therefore be $52 per year:

$$\text{Coupon payment} = 5.2\% \times \$1,000 = \$52 \text{ per year}$$

This annual interest will usually be paid in two equal installments, so investors will receive $26 ($52/2) every 6 months.

The term "coupon" originated many years ago, when bond certificates actually had tear-off coupons on the back. These bonds were called *bearer bonds*, because whoever had possession of a bond (the "bearer") could mail in a coupon to request an interest payment as it came due. Although some of these older bonds are still in existence, buyers of newer bonds don't even receive certificates, because their contact information is kept electronically. Nevertheless, the "coupon" terminology continues to be used.

Callable Bonds

In some cases, a bond issuer might want to repay the loan early. For example, suppose the issuer is currently paying a high fixed interest rate on a bond issue (because the bond was issued in a high-interest-rate environment), but the current rate on similar bonds is much lower (because market rates have declined). The company could reduce its interest costs by refinancing, similar to the way a homeowner reduces mortgage payments by refinancing a mortgage at a lower rate. However, a bond issuer can't require an investor to sell back a bond unless the bond contract includes a **call provision**—a contractual term that allows early repayment by the issuer, often at a slight premium over the face value.

Because callable bonds are advantageous to a company, most corporate bonds have call provisions, although some might include restrictions on the company's right to call—for example, specifying that a call can take place no sooner than five years after initial issuance. The call provisions also specify the price that the company will pay the investor to call the bond—an amount greater than the face value. Generally, investors aren't very happy when a company exercises its call rights. It usually means they'll no longer be earning a rate of interest higher than the going rate.

Convertible Bonds

Some bond issues include a special provision that allows the bondholders to convert their bonds to shares of common stock in the future. The contract will specify how many shares a bondholder can receive for each bond. For example, suppose you hold a bond with a face value of $1,000 and the bond is convertible to 50 shares of the firm's stock. If the stock is currently valued at $10, you wouldn't want to convert at the moment, because you'd give up a $1,000 bond for only $500 in stock. But if the stock price later rises to more than $20, you might want to convert. Because convertibility is an attractive feature, a convertible bond will usually pay a coupon rate that's one to two percentage points lower than a comparable nonconvertible bond. The lower annual interest is somewhat offset by the greater potential for capital gains—when the stock price rises, the market value of the convertible bond will also rise.

Use **Interactive: Bond Terminology** to see if you understand basic bond terminology.

INTERACTIVE

See **Bond Terminology** in **WileyPLUS.**

Bond Valuation

Before investing in bonds, you must understand the determinants of bond value. Bond valuation is a great application of the time value of money concepts discussed in Chapter 2. As with other investments, the value of a bond is determined by the present value of its expected cash flows, which come in two forms: periodic interest payments and repayment of the principal at maturity. In combination, these two components provide bond investors with their expected return on investment, or yield. The yield from regular payments of interest is often called the coupon yield, or current yield. The yield from the gain (or loss) on the purchase price relative to the sale price is called the capital gains yield.

Long-term investors commonly evaluate their bond investments using **yield to maturity (YTM)**, which incorporates both the coupon yield and the capital gains yield. The YTM is the annualized return on a bond, assuming that you hold the bond to maturity, receive all promised cash flows from the date of purchase, and reinvest annual payments at the same rate.

An important principle to remember here is that the present value of any future cash flow will go down when market interest rates go up, and vice versa. Because bond cash flows do not change over time, an increase in market interest rates will cause bond values to decline across the board. Similarly, a decrease in market interest rates will cause an increase in bond values. If you hold a bond to maturity, however, these interim changes in price will not affect you, and you will have earned the yield to maturity estimated at the outset of your investment period.

In the simplest case, where you pay exactly the $1,000 face value for a bond, the yield to maturity will be the same as the coupon rate. Because there is no difference between the $1,000 you pay at the beginning and the $1,000 you receive at maturity, your only income from the bond is the annual interest received. Therefore, your total yield is the current yield. However, if you pay less (or more) than the face value for the bond, the yield to maturity will include the gain (or loss) in value between the time you buy the bond and the maturity date. Thus, your yield to maturity will be the coupon yield plus the annualized capital gains yield. **Demonstration Problem 12.2** shows how to use a financial calculator to solve for yield to maturity. You can also use **Excel Worksheet 12.1** (Personal Financial Planner: Bond Yield to Maturity) to determine the yield to maturity.

EXCEL WORKSHEET

See **Excel Worksheet 12.1** (Personal Financial Planner: Bond Yield to Maturity) in **WileyPLUS.**

DEMONSTRATION PROBLEM 12.2 | Ken Calculates Bond Yield to Maturity

Problem

Ken is considering buying bonds issued by home improvement giant Lowe's because he has learned that the bonds have a relatively high coupon rate (6.5 percent). The face value is $100. The bonds are due to mature in 15 years and are rated "A" by Moody's. If Ken buys these bonds at $130 and holds them to maturity, what yield to maturity will he earn? Is this a good investment for Ken?

Strategy

You can use a financial calculator or Excel Worksheet 12.1 to determine the yield to maturity by entering the information you know about the bond and solving for what you don't know.

Solution

To use a financial calculator, enter the following information:

$$N = \text{Number of semiannual payments} = 2 \times 15 = 30$$
$$PV = \text{Price paid for the bond} = -130$$
$$PMT = \text{Semiannual coupon payment} = (6.5\% \times 100)/2 = 3.25$$
$$FV = 100$$

Solve for the semiannual yield I = 1.924. Multiplying by 2 gives the annual yield to maturity of 3.85%.

Whether this is a good investment for Ken depends on his risk tolerance, his other investment alternatives, and what happens to market rates of interest during the time that he holds the bonds. It is important for Ken to realize that even though he is getting a good coupon yield (6.5 percent), the total yield on these bonds will be much lower because it includes the capital loss incurred from paying more than the face value for the bond.

What yield to maturity should you expect to earn on bond investments over time? The general perception is that bonds are safe, but their values can vary a lot. Yields tend to track fairly closely with market interest rates, which vary over time with general economic conditions, and this can result in changes in prices. **Figure 12.6** shows how corporate bond yields have changed over time compared with Treasury bonds, notes, and bills.

FIGURE 12.6 **Yields on Debt Securities, 1998–2019** Yields on different types of bonds tend to go up and down together, but they can vary a lot over time.

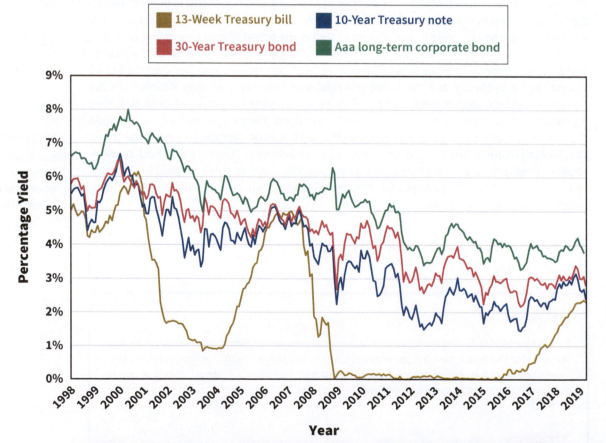

Source: Data series for monthly yields on 3-month Treasury bills, 10-year Treasury notes, and 30-year Treasury bonds: finance. yahoo.com. Data series for corporate bonds: Moody's Seasoned Aaa Corporate from Board of Governors of the Federal Reserve System.

Why Do Investors Buy Bonds?

Even if it makes sense for corporations and government entities to sell bonds, there wouldn't be a market for these securities unless investors were willing to buy them. As we've seen, bonds generally provide a lower rate of return over time than stocks. Despite this, fixed-income securities make up a substantial proportion of individual investors' portfolios. There are five primary reasons individual investors buy bonds:

- Predictable income stream
- Matching timing of cash flow needs
- Lower risk than other investment alternatives
- Portfolio diversification
- Profit on price changes

Predictable Income Stream

Some investors hold bonds because they need or want a steady stream of income. When you retire, for example, you could purchase long-term bonds and live off the interest. The interest payments are usually a fixed amount for the life of the bond, so you'll know with certainty how much income you'll be receiving. The downside is that the income stream will not increase with inflation. That's why we often say that retirees are living on a fixed income.

Matching Timing of Cash Flow Needs

Because bonds have a fixed maturity date, some investors like them because they can match the time horizon of their investment with their future needs for the funds. For example, a retired couple might buy 20-year bonds to provide 20 years of interest income during their retirement period. Or new parents might buy zero-coupon bonds that will pay them a lump sum at maturity coinciding with when their child starts college.

Lower Risk

If you've assessed your risk tolerance and find that you prefer to bear less risk, even though it might mean receiving a lower return, you might prefer bond investing to stock investing. Consistent with the general rule discussed in Chapter 11, bond investors earn lower returns primarily because they are taking less risk. When you buy a bond from a creditworthy company, you know that you'll most likely receive your promised interest payments and that your principal will be repaid at maturity. For many investors, this level of certainty is more important than the uncertain possibility of greater returns from a risky stock.

Diversification

Although both bonds and stocks are affected by market interest rates, they don't usually move together. Thus, holding both bonds and stocks in a diversified investment portfolio can reduce the risk of the portfolio. Over the last decade, an investor who maintained a 50/50 allocation between bonds and stocks would have had lower returns during the stock market run-ups than an all-equity investor. But a 50/50 allocation would have softened the blow of the market downturns, because the interest rate declines during those periods caused bond prices to rise. The net effect on the portfolio would have been slightly lower average return and significantly lower risk.

Profit on Price Changes

Bond prices go up and down over time in response to changes in market interest rates—when interest rates go up, bond prices go down, and vice versa. If you're a buy-and-hold investor, this won't matter to you because you'll be holding the bond to maturity and you'll receive the face value at that time regardless of what has happened in the meantime to interest rates. However, if you need to sell a bond before its maturity date, you might find that the market price is more (or less) than what you paid, resulting in a capital gain (or a capital loss). **Table 12.3** shows bond prices for several combinations of coupon rate, term to maturity, and investor-required return, and gives you an idea of how much the bond price might change for a given increase or decrease in interest rates.

TABLE 12.3   **Sensitivity of Bond Prices to Interest Rates**

Years to Maturity	Annual Coupon (Paid Semiannually)	Required Return		
		5%	7%	9%
1	$50	$1,000	$981	$963
1	$70	$1,019	$1,000	$981
1	$90	$1,039	$1,019	$1,000
5	$50	$1,000	$917	$842
5	$70	$1,088	$1,000	$921
5	$90	$1,175	$1,083	$1,000
10	$50	$1,000	$858	$740
10	$70	$1,156	$1,000	$870
10	$90	$1,312	$1,142	$1,000
20	$50	$1,000	$786	$632
20	$70	$1,251	$1,000	$816
20	$90	$1,502	$1,214	$1,000

Consider a bond that has a 7 percent coupon rate (paid semiannually) and 10 years to maturity (boxed in the table). If the current required rate of return on a bond of this type is 7 percent, then the price will be equal to the par value of $1,000. Immediately to the left and right of the boxed value, you can see what would happen to the price of this bond if the required rate of return decreased or increased by two percentage points. If rates decline by two percentage points, to 5 percent, the value of the bond will increase to $1,156, a 15.6 percent increase. But if rates increase to 9 percent, the value of the bond will decrease to $870, a 13 percent decrease.

Again using the table, compare the 10-year bond to a bond with the same coupon rate and only one year to maturity (in the first highlighted row). If market rates fell by two percentage points, to 5 percent, the value of the one-year bond would be $1,019, an increase of 1.9 percent. If market rates rose by two percentage points, the value of the bond would fall to $981, a 1.9 percent decrease. In other words, the effect of interest rate changes on price is much smaller for the 1-year bond than for the 10-year bond. Long-term bonds are considered riskier than short-term bonds because they have larger price changes for a given change in interest rates. This is why interest-rate risk, which we defined in Chapter 11, is sometimes called maturity risk.

We can also see from the table that the amount of the coupon payment makes a difference in the bond's maturity risk. For any given maturity, the price of the bond with the lowest coupon rate experiences the largest price decline with an increase in interest rates. For this reason, zero-coupon bonds can be expected to have the greatest maturity risk—their prices will exhibit the largest changes in response to increases or decreases in market interest rates.

We can summarize maturity risk factors as follows:

- The longer the time to maturity, the greater the percentage change in bond value for a given change in required return.
- The smaller the coupon rate, the greater the percentage change in bond value for a given change in required return.

Active bond investors may attempt to buy and sell bonds in anticipation of interest rate changes, hoping to profit on changes in price. As we've discussed, though, it isn't easy to predict the market, so these strategies are not always successful.

12.3 Investing in Preferred Stock

LEARNING OBJECTIVE 12.3
Compare the features of preferred stock with those of common stock and bonds.

In addition to common stocks and bonds, you might want to consider investing in preferred stock. As noted in Chapter 11, this type of security offers the advantage of paying regular, fixed dividends that take precedence over dividends to common shareholders. In this section, we review the most important features of preferred stock.

What Is Preferred Stock?

Preferred stock has similarities to both common stock and bonds. Like both bonds and common stock, preferred stock is issued by companies as a means of raising capital to fund ongoing operations or expansion. Like bonds, most preferred stock provides a fixed cash flow to investors. Like common stock, though, preferred stock has no set maturity date, and the company never has to repay the original investment amount.

To understand preferred stock well enough to decide whether this asset is suitable for your investment plan, you'll first need to understand the cash flows associated with this type of security. As with other investments, your cash flows from preferred stock will be some combination of income and a capital gain (or loss) upon sale of the stock. By design, preferred stock is primarily an income investment, and this means that its price will be sensitive to interest rate changes just as bond prices are.

Preferred stock usually pays a quarterly dividend based on a fixed percentage of its par value. **Preferred stock par value** is the term used for an arbitrary initial value assigned to the preferred stock shares at issuance, usually a round number like $25, $100, or $1,000. Unlike the face value of a bond, the par value of preferred stock is never owed to the investors. Note, too, that the current price of a share of preferred stock might be higher or lower than its par value and will depend on the dividend rate relative to market rates at the time.

Suppose that a company issues shares of preferred stock with a $100 par value and a 10 percent dividend rate. Each holder of a share of this stock will receive a dividend equal to $10 (10 percent of $100) per year, which will be paid out in installments of $2.50 per quarter per share. Because the shares have no maturity date, this payment stream is perpetual, continuing for as long as the company is in existence. The timelines in **Figure 12.7** show the income streams an investor might earn on an initial $1,000 investment in a bond with a 7 percent coupon rate, preferred stock with a 7 percent dividend rate, and common stock.

FIGURE 12.7 **Comparison of Cash Flows** These timelines compare the cash flows for a bond, preferred stock, and common stock.

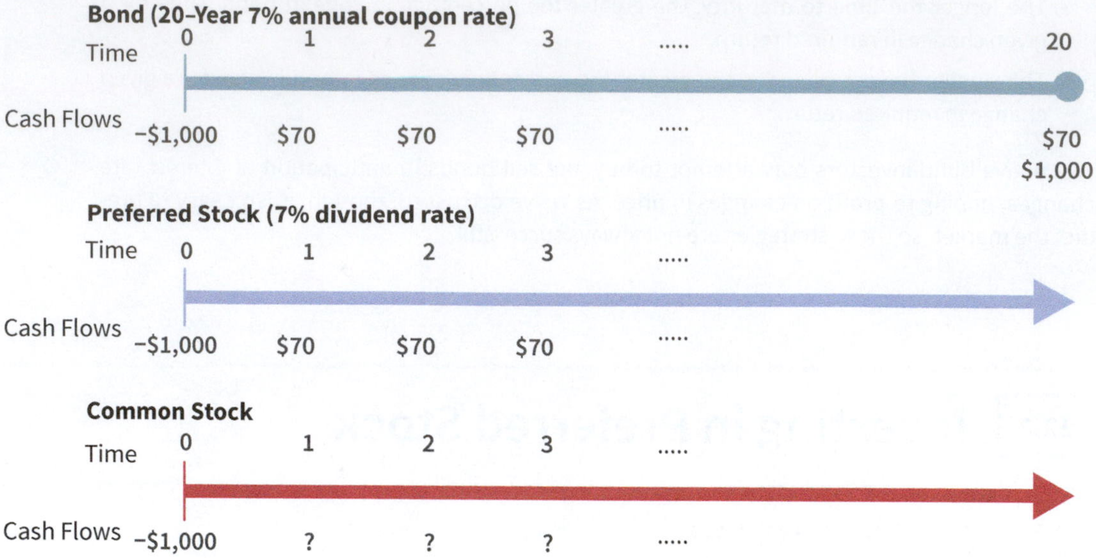

Bond (20–Year 7% annual coupon rate)

Time	0	1	2	3	.....	20
Cash Flows	–$1,000	$70	$70	$70	.....	$70 $1,000

Preferred Stock (7% dividend rate)

Time	0	1	2	3	.....	
Cash Flows	–$1,000	$70	$70	$70	.....	

Common Stock

Time	0	1	2	3	.....	
Cash Flows	–$1,000	?	?	?	.....	

For this comparison, the actual dollar amounts of the cash flows are not important. Instead, focus on the timing and certainty of the cash flows. Notice that the bond's cash flow stream has a specific end date, whereas the cash flows of the two types of stock extend indefinitely. Notice also that the owners of the bond and the preferred stock know exactly what payments they will receive, whereas the cash flow to common stockholders is uncertain.

Preferred Stock Valuation

As you know, the value of any asset is determined by the discounted present value of the cash flow it will generate. Because the dividend you will receive from preferred stock is known with a fair degree of certainty, we use that information to calculate the present value. Preferred stock dividends represent a special type of annuity known as a **perpetuity**. The series of equal payments for a perpetuity continue into infinity. We can use **Equation 12.7** to estimate the present value of this cash flow:

$$\text{Value of preferred stock} = \frac{\text{Annual dividend}}{\text{Required return}} \tag{12.7}$$

where required return is the rate of return that an investor expects to receive on investments of comparable risk. **Demonstration Problem 12.3** shows you how this seemingly simple equation is related to the time value of money.

Because prices are generally driven by the market, it's not usually necessary to calculate the value of preferred stock—you can just look up the market price you'll have to pay. Instead, investors evaluate preferred stock based on the expected yield. The yield for a buy-and-hold investor comes entirely from the dividend cash flows, so the appropriate yield to consider is the dividend yield that was defined in Equation 12.2 as dividend divided by price. Notice that this is essentially the same as Equation 12.7, but it solves for the rate instead of the price. If you observe that the price of an issue of preferred stock is $125, and you know that the dividend is $10 per year, then your dividend yield is 8 percent ($10/$125 = 0.08).

DEMONSTRATION PROBLEM 12.3 | Calculating the
Value of Preferred Stock

Problem

Suppose a company pays a $10 annual dividend on its preferred stock. Based on the risk of the company, you think you should earn 8 percent on this investment. What is the stock really worth?

Strategy

Use Equation 12.7 to estimate the value of the stock.

Solution

The value of this stock is $125 per share:

$$\text{Value of preferred stock} = \frac{\text{Annual dividend}}{\text{Required return}}$$

$$= \frac{\$10}{0.08} = \$125$$

This may or may not be the same as the current price of the stock. If the price is higher, you would choose not to buy it. If the price is lower, it looks like a good deal for you. To convince yourself that this shortcut equation makes sense, redo this calculation as a normal present value of an annuity problem. Preferred stock will pay that $10 dividend into infinity, but let's just assume a very large number of years, such as 100. On your financial calculator, enter PMT = 10, N = 100, and I = 8 and solve for PV = $124.94. Even though 100 years isn't infinity, you can see that, for this purpose, it's close enough.

Contract Terms Affecting Preferred Stock Cash Flows

What we've just described is the "plain vanilla" type of preferred stock arrangement. However, many contract variations are used by issuing firms to make their preferred stock more attractive to investors. Some firms offer many issues of preferred stock that differ in their contract terms and promised dividend rates. We explore several variations in this section.

Callability

Suppose a company issues preferred stock during a period when interest rates are relatively high, so the dividend rate is also high. Similar to call provisions on bonds, callable preferred stock gives the issuer the right to buy back its shares. Because this is better for the issuer, the company will usually pay a higher dividend rate than it would for comparable noncallable preferred stock.

Cumulative Dividends

What happens if a company doesn't have enough cash to pay the dividend on its preferred stock in a given year? Unlike bonds, the failure to pay under these circumstances doesn't put the company in default. Preferred shareholders have a little more protection from this downside risk if they hold **cumulative preferred stock**. With a cumulative feature, the company accumulates an obligation to its preferred stock investors that must be paid in subsequent years before any dividends can be paid to common shareholders. For noncumulative preferred stock, the missed dividends are lost and never need to be repaid.

Fixed versus Adjustable Dividends

Preferred dividends are normally fixed-rate payments. As noted, if market rates on comparable investments fall, the company may be required to call, or buy back, the issue in order to refinance at lower cost. This can be a fairly expensive and time-consuming process. In a relatively new variation, some companies are now issuing adjustable-rate preferred stock, which pays a dividend that is tied to a market interest rate. As an investor, you might not be happy to find that the rate on your stock has gone down, but at least you'll avoid the necessity of reinvesting the money due to the exercise of the call provision. And when rates go up, the dividend will rise as well.

Convertibility

Similar to convertible bonds, preferred stock can include a feature that allows investors to convert preferred shares to common stock under certain conditions. The number of shares for which each preferred share can be exchanged is determined by contractual agreement. This feature is beneficial to investors in that it gives them the option of participating in the future growth of the company if it becomes favorable to do so. The associated cost is that the dividend rate for convertible preferred stock is lower than that for preferred stock that isn't convertible.

The Benefits and Risks of Preferred Stock

The primary attraction of preferred stock is its steady dividend stream, which provides a yield that is usually greater than the pretax yield on long-term bonds with similar risk. Unless preferred stock is held in a tax-deferred account, the dividends are taxable income to the investor. A special tax rule allows corporations that hold the stock of other corporations to exclude 70 percent of the dividends from taxable income. Although this is good for corporate investors, it's a disadvantage to individual investors, because these tax-advantaged investors are willing to pay more for the stock, which drives up the price for all investors.

The most important risks faced by preferred stock investors are interest-rate risk, liquidity risk, call risk, and default risk. Like bond values, preferred stock values are sensitive to market rates of interest. Let's consider what happens to the value of preferred stock shares if interest rates go up. You previously saw that the value of preferred stock with a $10 annual dividend was $125 when the required yield was 8 percent. If preferred stock investors instead require a 9 percent return, the value of the share would fall to $111 ($10/0.09). The dollar amount of the dividend is constant over time, so the only thing that causes the value of the stock to change is the interest rate used to discount the cash flows. As we've seen, these rates depend on the return required by investors as compensation for the risk of the investment. Increases in the inflation rate or market interest rates can therefore increase the required returns of investors. Preferred stock values will move in the opposite direction of interest rates, just as bond values do.

What if interest rates decline? You might expect that falling rates would be good for investors because prices will increase. However, in the case of callable preferred shares, the issuing corporation is likely to exercise its call rights and retire the stock. Thus, the investor gets the worst of both worlds—the price declines when rates rise, and the stock is called when rates fall.

Default risk depends on the issuing firm's business risk. Riskier companies on average pay higher dividend rates than less risky companies. In the event the issuing company experiences a cash shortfall, preferred stock investors, particularly holders of cumulative preferred stock, are in a better position than common stock investors. Although bondholders still get paid first, preferred shareholders must be paid their dividends before the company can declare a dividend for the common shareholders. Therefore, preferred stock is generally less risky than common stock and more risky than bonds. As with bonds, rating agencies such as Moody's and Standard & Poor's regularly provide ratings of credit risk for issues of preferred stock.

Securities Markets

LEARNING OBJECTIVE 12.4

Describe the operation and regulation of the securities markets.

A given share of stock can change hands many times, and its price will change in response to company and market events. These transactions can occur on an organized exchange like the New York Stock Exchange on Wall Street in New York City or, more commonly today, through super-fast computers in an online trading environment. As an individual investor, it pays to be familiar with the different avenues for trading, the transaction costs associated with buying and selling, and the legal rules that govern and protect investor behavior.

In the past several years, many changes have occurred in the securities markets, forever altering the investment playing field. While competition—between global securities markets, between investors, and between financial institutions—is clearly a major driver, there have also been changes in response to the 2008 financial crisis and to well-publicized scandals. All of these developments have had important and, for the most part, positive impacts on the securities markets and on buying and selling within those markets. In this section, you'll learn about the markets in which stocks, bonds, and other securities are traded, the process by which investors buy and sell securities, and some important regulations that protect investors.

Primary versus Secondary Market

Stocks and bonds are bought and sold in the securities market. This market has two parts:

- The **primary market** is where stocks and bonds are sold to the public by the issuers for the *first time*.

- The **secondary market** is where stocks and bonds that have already been issued are traded *between investors*.

Even though most individual investors' transactions occur in the secondary market, it's useful to understand the role of both parts of the securities market.

When a company issues stock for the first time, we say that the company is "going public," and the stock issue is called an **initial public offering (IPO)**. Facebook, Inc., founder Mark Zuckerberg decided to take his company public in early 2012. On May 18, 2012, in the fourth-largest IPO in history, 421 million shares were sold at $38 each, for a total value of $16 billion.

The IPO process is usually handled, or underwritten, by one or more investment banking firms. For example, the underwriters for Facebook, Inc.—Morgan Stanley, JP Morgan, and Goldman Sachs—helped the company determine a price for the new issue, facilitated the paperwork, and managed the selling process. Sometimes, it's difficult to determine exactly how much a company is worth, particularly if it's expected to grow quickly after the infusion of cash from the sale of stock. The underwriter may guarantee a minimum price to the issuing firm or it may buy the entire issue itself and then resell it to the public. Before settling on the price of $38 per share for Facebook, the underwriters had to look very carefully at revenue and expense projections as well as risk exposures for the future. A summary of this information was included in a prospectus that was used to advertise the new stock. At first, it appeared that the Facebook underwriters had been overly optimistic about the company's prospects: By September 2012, the stock price had fallen to less than $18. Investors who held on, however, were hugely rewarded: The stock was worth nearly $200 a few years later, in July 2019.

Although you might someday have an opportunity to purchase shares directly from a company through an IPO, it's more likely that your transactions will be with other investors in the secondary market. The existence of an active secondary market makes stocks more attractive to investors because it reduces liquidity risk. Billions of shares change hands on any given day, so you can almost always find willing buyers and sellers to deal with. This means that, if you have money tied up in stock and you need the cash for something else, you can easily sell some of your shares at their current value. Trades in the secondary market don't result in any cash flows to the corporation whose stock is being bought or sold. A corporation only acquires cash for shares when it sells them for the first time in the primary market.

The issuance of new bonds also requires registration and a prospectus, but the process is somewhat simpler. In many cases, large institutional investors, such as life insurers and pension funds, buy large blocks of new bond issues to hold until maturity. Bonds are not as actively traded as stocks and some bonds might never be traded in the secondary market at all.

Securities Exchanges

Trading among investors can be accomplished through a **securities exchange** with a physical location where trading occurs or through an electronic marketplace, referred to as the **over-the-counter (OTC) market**. The world's largest and best-known securities exchange is the New York Stock Exchange (NYSE). A particular stock can be traded on more than one exchange.

The Rise of Electronic Trading

Not so long ago, most stock trading was accomplished on the floor of exchanges like the NYSE, where traders bought and sold stocks face to face. Today, though, high-frequency trading on supercomputers, executed in microseconds, makes up more than half of all trading volume.

Electronic trading offers some advantages for investors. Competition has driven down trading costs and increased the speed and efficiency of transactions. On the downside, the rise in high-frequency electronic trading executed by computers rather than people has increased risk and volatility. On April 23, 2013, a hoax tweet was posted on an Associated Press Twitter account saying that there had been an attack on the White House that left the President injured. This fictional tweet resulted in a quick drop in stock prices. The S&P 500 Index stocks lost $136 billion in value. Regulations are in place to limit this type of event from happening, but it's difficult to rescind millions of automated sell orders once they have been placed.

Listing of Securities

Each exchange has its own rules governing what it takes to qualify as a **listed security**, one that is offered for sale on the exchange. For example, the NYSE requirements for listing a stock is that the firm have at least 1.1 million shares outstanding, $40 million in market capitalization, a share price of at least a $4, and $10 million in pretax earnings over the last three years.

Unlike the NYSE, the over-the-counter market is not a formal exchange and doesn't have a physical location. Instead, it's a network of securities dealers communicating electronically to quote the prices at which they're willing to buy or sell securities. Multiple dealers in these stocks post offers on an electronic platform to buy or sell shares at particular prices. The most frequently traded OTC stocks trade on the **NASDAQ**, which is the second largest stock market in the world by market capitalization and was the first stock exchange to allow online trading. Generally, the smaller size and lower liquidity of stocks traded exclusively over the counter make them riskier investments than stocks listed on organized exchanges.

Similar to over-the-counter stocks, bonds are also traded through a network of dealers. Participating dealers post prices at which they are willing to buy or sell specific quantities of each bond issue.

Buying and Selling Stocks and Bonds

Buying financial securities isn't like making the consumer purchases we've discussed in previous chapters—you can't just go out and buy stocks or bonds directly from other investors.

Transactions in the secondary market require the services of a licensed broker. The brokerage firm pays fees to be able to transact business on an organized exchange or in the over-the-counter market on your behalf and will charge you for this service.

As discussed in Chapter 11, individual investors can easily set up an account with a discount broker such as E*Trade or Robinhood through which they can buy and sell stocks, bonds, and mutual funds. **Figure 12.8** describes a typical stock transaction, but the process is the same for other securities as well.

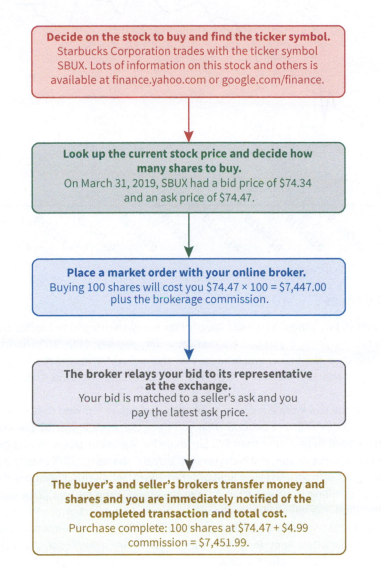

FIGURE 12.8 **The Process of Buying Shares of Stock** When you place a market order for shares of stock, you'll pay the current ask price plus a commission to the brokerage firm.

Bid and Ask Price

In this section, we walk through the process you'd follow if you wanted to buy some shares of a particular company. For example, suppose you'd like to buy 100 shares of Starbucks Corporation. To implement this transaction, you'll need to find out what the current price is and place a specific order with a broker. On various financial websites, such as **finance.yahoo.com** or **google.com/finance,** you can look up the latest **bid price** offered by other buyers and the latest **ask price** requested by potential sellers, but the posted prices will usually be delayed about 15 to 20 minutes. You can also find the **close price**—the last price at which the stock traded on the previous business day. **Figure 12.9** shows the close prices each day between January 2019 and March 2019 for Starbucks (SBUX).

FIGURE 12.9 **Starbucks, Inc., Daily Close Prices, January 2019–March 2019** The close price is the last price at which the stock traded on the previous business day.

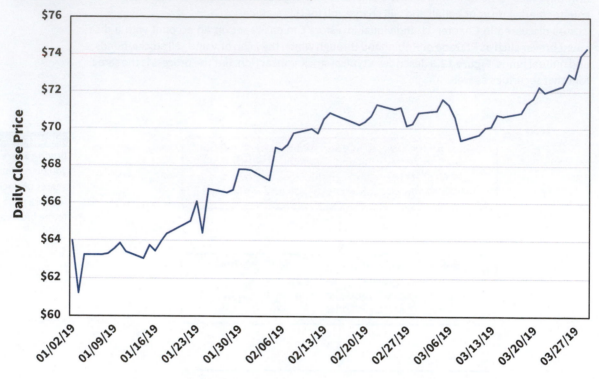

Types of Orders

When you offer to buy shares, you must specify how many shares you're buying, but you don't have to specify the price. If you place a **market order**, you say: "Buy 100 shares of SBUX at market." In this case, the broker will execute your trade at whatever the market price is at the time your trade is actually received. This means it could be higher or lower than the most recent price you saw online.

But what if the stock price is creeping upward and you're worried that it might increase beyond what you can afford or beyond what you think the stock is worth? For example, suppose you don't want to pay more than $75 per share for Starbucks stock. In that case, you can give a **limit order** to the broker, in which you say, "Buy 100 shares of SBUX as long as the price is no more than $75." You can also give a limit order when you sell shares, specifying the minimum price that you're willing to accept from a potential buyer. If the current price does not meet your specified limit, the limit order can be set up to remain in effect until you cancel it, so you might get the shares you want a few days or weeks later. If you don't want to leave your order open, you can place a time limit on it, the most common being a day order, in which your order expires at the close of trading for the day.

The third type of order is a **stop order**, which is commonly used to minimize losses or protect gains on a particular stock. For example, suppose you bought the Starbucks stock at $70 and it later goes up to $75 per share. You can sell it and take the profit of $5 per share, or you can hold on to it in the hope that the price will increase even more. If you hold on to it, though, you don't want to take the chance of losing all the profit you've gained on paper if it subsequently declines in value. To protect against that possibility, you can place a stop order with your broker that says, "Sell all my SBUX shares if the price drops to $72." If the price begins to fall, this order will be executed when the price hits $72, and you'll have locked in $2 profit per share.

Now suppose instead that your SBUX stock has dropped from its original $70 purchase price to $67 per share. You might not want to sell it now and take the $3 loss—perhaps you think there's a chance it will recover in value. But you also might not want to lose much more money. In this case, you can place a stop order instructing the broker to sell your shares if the price falls below, say, $63 per share. This type of stop order is often called a stop-loss order, for obvious reasons. If the order results in a sale at $63 per share, you'll have lost $7 on your original $70 investment, or about 10 percent, but you'll have cut off the risk of losing even more if the stock price continues its downward slide. With 20-20 hindsight, many investors regret their failure to use stop-loss orders during market declines.

Long versus Short

As a long-term investor, you'll primarily be a buyer of stocks rather than a seller. When you buy and hold stock in your portfolio, you're said to be "long" the stock. You'll make money when the stock price goes up and lose money when the stock price goes down. Your objective is to *buy low and sell high*, in that order.

You'll sometimes hear investors talk about making money on their investments by **selling short**. This happens when they issue a sell order to their broker but don't actually have the stock to sell; instead, they borrow it from their broker. They're betting that the price of the stock will go down so that they can buy the stock later at a lower price and make a profit on the difference. A short seller's objective is therefore to *sell high and buy low*, in that order.

Although short sellers can sometimes be quite successful, earning a return without putting up much cash of their own, the key factor is that they're counting on being right about the direction the price will move. What happens if the stock price goes up instead of down? They end up paying whatever the current market price is for the stock they borrowed from the broker as well as repaying the broker for any missed dividends and interest on the stock loan. **Interactive: The Ups and Downs of Selling Short** will show you how much you can gain or lose when you sell short.

INTERACTIVE

See **Interactive: The Ups and Downs of Selling Short** in **WileyPLUS**.

Types of Brokerage Accounts

Most brokers offer three types of accounts: cash accounts, margin accounts, and discretionary accounts. If you have a *cash account*, you're required to make payment in full within three days of a buy order. Because three days isn't enough time to mail in a check, you'll need to have an electronic transfer system between your bank and your brokerage account. If you have sufficient funds in your brokerage account, your broker can execute buy orders using those funds.

But what if you don't have funds on hand to buy the shares you want? A *margin account* allows you to borrow from the brokerage firm to pay for some of your stock purchase. This is called **buying on margin**. Although margin trading allows you to buy more stock than you could if you used only your own money, it's also riskier because you have to earn enough on the stock to pay back the loan plus interest. The advantage is that, if the stock goes up in value, you don't have to share the gain with the brokerage firm—you only owe the amount of the loan plus interest. This means that your return on investment is higher than it would have been if you had put up all the money for the stock. If you buy $2,000 in stock, paying only half of the amount with your own money and borrowing the rest, a $200 gain represents a 20 percent return on your investment of $1,000, whereas it would only be a 10 percent return if you'd had to invest the full $2,000.

The Federal Reserve requires that the margin—the equity in the account divided by the stock value—be at least 50 percent. To guard against the possibility that the value of the stock is less than the loan amount, brokers also set a maintenance margin (such as 30 percent). Thus, if stock prices fall sufficiently, you might get a **margin call** from your broker requesting that you deposit additional funds into your account so that you can meet the maintenance margin limit. For example, if you buy $5,000 in shares using $2,500 of your own money and $2,500 borrowed from the brokerage firm, you have a 50 percent margin. If the share prices fall, so that the shares in your account are worth only $3,500, your margin will be 28.6 percent $[(\$3,500 – \$2,500)/\$3,500]$, which is less than the 30 percent minimum. You'll need to deposit at least $50 to meet the required minimum. If you do not pay the amount needed for a margin call, your broker will sell enough of your shares (even at a loss to you) to reach the required maintenance margin.

The last type of brokerage account is a *discretionary account*, in which you delegate the decision-making authority for buying and selling to the broker. Brokers make more money when they make more trades, so you run the risk that the broker might make lots of trades just to get the commissions. There are ethical restrictions on excessive trading, sometimes called "churning," in discretionary accounts.

Regulation of the Securities Markets

The U.S. securities market is heavily regulated by the federal government, and as an individual investor, you reap many benefits from this regulation. As we've seen in other areas of personal finance, government regulations are designed to ensure that you have access to accurate information and to protect you from the fraudulent actions of others. To better understand the motivation for and importance of U.S. regulation of the securities market, you need to know a little bit about history. In this section, we provide some historical context for current securities law and summarize the most important elements of federal securities regulation.

In the early part of the last century, the U.S. securities market was very different than it is today. Investor fraud was commonplace, and a "buyer beware" environment prevailed. It was very difficult for stockholders to obtain financial information about potential investments or even about the companies whose stock they held. The worst economic downturn in U.S. history, now called the Great Depression, was precipitated by widespread mistrust of financial markets combined with an unusually large number of bank failures in the 1920s and the 1929 stock market crash. In the early 1930s, faced with thousands of business failures, double-digit unemployment rates, and related problems, Congress enacted far-reaching legislation in many areas, including banking and securities regulation. The overriding objective of the federal securities laws was investor protection, because it was generally believed that restoring investor confidence was a prerequisite for the nation's economic recovery.

Information Disclosure Requirements

Two acts passed by Congress in the 1930s, the Securities Act of 1933 and the Securities Exchange Act of 1934, are still in place today and form the foundation for federal securities regulation. In addition, each state has its own securities laws (commonly called *blue sky laws* in reference to the objective of giving investors a clear view of company finances). Because of the overlap in legal rules, state securities regulators don't usually deal with securities and trading issues, but instead focus on state licensing and registration of brokers and brokerage firms and on prevention and prosecution of other types of investment fraud.

Today, all traded securities must be registered with the Securities and Exchange Commission (SEC), an independent agency of the federal government charged with enforcement of the securities laws and broad oversight of the securities market, OTC trading, brokers, and dealers. Issuers of new securities are required to fully disclose all relevant information to prospective investors and to make periodic, detailed financial reports on their performance to the SEC, in a report commonly referred to as the 10-K, and to their stockholders, in an annual report. Information disclosure helps to level the playing field for small investors and makes it easier to compare companies based on financial performance. Many websites make information available to investors.

Insider Trading

In addition to requiring information disclosure, federal law protects investors by prohibiting fraud and misrepresentation in the sale of securities. Although the broad language of the law encompasses most types of misrepresentation, there are specific rules aimed at preventing price manipulation through **insider trading**. Insider trading is an illegal act in which company "insiders"—those who are privy to information about a company that isn't available to the general public—buy or sell company stock based on their inside information. Insider trading is bad for the financial markets because it causes other investors to lose confidence in the fairness of the system. After all, whenever an insider sells stock at a high price just before bad news about the company is going to come out, the loser is the buyer who didn't have the inside information.

Although the definition of "insider" obviously includes the officers and directors of a company, a recent Supreme Court case broadens the definition to include anyone who knowingly uses nonpublic information to deceive other investors. To make it easier to track these transactions, officers, directors, and major stockholders are required to report all transactions in their company's stock to the SEC. The Insider Trading and Securities Fraud Enforcement Act of 1988 increased the penalties for securities fraud.

Reflection Question 2

Suppose that your neighbor gives you a "hot tip" that the company he works for is about to make a public announcement that will cause its stock price to increase. Would it be unethical and/or illegal for you to buy the stock and make a big profit? Who would be hurt by your actions?

Despite the legal consequences of insider trading, including penalties and jail time, there is evidence that such activities persist. Stock prices often seem to react in advance of the release of public information, suggesting that insiders might have leaked the information, perhaps to family and friends. Furthermore, examination of the profits made by insiders on their reported trades compared with the profits made by other investors in the same stocks tends to indicate that these trades are motivated by better-than-average knowledge of the firm's future prospects.

Circuit Breakers

After the stock market crash in 1987, the securities industry made some changes to its system of self-regulation to protect against extreme market volatility. The stock market now has in place a set of so-called circuit breaker rules that stop trading for a short period of time when the market experiences a large drop. There are also some special rules for price changes on individual stocks during the first and last few minutes of the trading day, when volume is heaviest.

The longest period of market closure was seen during the week following the September 11, 2001, terrorist attack on the World Trade Center. The circuit breakers led to market closure that morning, and the market didn't reopen until the following Monday, September 17.

Other Regulations

Several additional statutes offer expanded protections for investors. For example, SEC registration and disclosure rules now apply to securities associations, securities dealers, mutual funds, and mutual fund advisors. Brokers also must pay into an insurance fund that will protect investors from loss of their investment securities if their brokers get into financial difficulty.

Summary

Learning Objectives Review

LEARNING OBJECTIVE 12.1   Describe the characteristics and classifications of common stock.

Common stock represents a share of ownership in a **corporation**. Shareholders have a **residual claim** on the assets and income of the corporation, but only after other claims have been satisfied.

- The size of a publicly traded company is often measured based on its **market capitalization**, which is calculated with **Equation 12.1**:

$$\text{Market capitalization} = \text{Current market price} \times \text{Number of shares outstanding}$$

- Investors earn money on stock from two potential sources: the growth in the value of their shares (capital gain) and dividends paid to them by the company, either in cash or as a **stock dividend**.

- The rate of return on a stock investment has two components, the dividend yield and the capital gains yield, as given by **Equation 12.2** and **Equation 12.3**:

$$\text{Dividend yield} = \frac{\text{Annual dividend}}{\text{Beginning stock price}}$$

$$\text{Capital gains yield} = \frac{\text{Annual change in stock price}}{\text{Beginning stock price}}$$

- In return for bearing equity risk, shareholders have some voting rights, but they enjoy **limited liability** and do not participate in the management of the firm. Some investors may have a **preemptive right** to keep their proportionate ownership interest when the company issues new shares.

- Stock investments are usually classified according to broad categories related to cash flow, size, risk, and line of business. For example, a stock may be classified by its industry group (technology or retail), method of compensating investors (**income stock** or **growth stock**), sensitivity to the business cycle (**cyclical stock** or **defensive stock**), risk (**blue chip stock**), or market capitalization (large-cap, mid-cap, or small-cap).

- Investors compare stocks based on ratios such as **earnings per share** (**Equation 12.4**) and the **price-to-earnings ratio** (**Equation 12.5**):

$$\text{Earnings per share} = \frac{\text{After-tax net income}}{\text{Number of shares outstanding}}$$

$$\text{Price-to-earnings ratio} = \frac{\text{Price per share}}{\text{Earnings per share}}$$

They may also evaluate the performance and risk of their portfolio relative to benchmarks such as the S&P 500. The degree to which a security moves with the market is measured by its **beta**.

LEARNING OBJECTIVE 12.2   Describe the characteristics and classifications of bonds.

A bond is a debt security issued by a corporation or a government entity to finance its operations and growth. For example, a state or local government might issue **municipal bonds**. **Agency issues** are bonds issued by federal government agencies such as Fannie Mae.

- Bond investors usually receive a fixed semiannual payment, called the **coupon payment**, and are repaid the **face value** at the **maturity date** of the bond. The coupon payment is based on the **coupon rate** of interest and calculated with **Equation 12.6**.

$$\text{Coupon payment} = \text{Coupon rate} \times \text{Face value}$$

- The terms of the bond contract are administered by a **trustee**.

- Some bonds also include other features that affect their value, such as **call provisions** that allow the issuer to buy back the bond in the future.

- Bonds are commonly classified according to the type of issuer (corporations, U.S. government, federal agencies, states, cities, and municipal authorities). They can also be characterized according to certain bond characteristics, such as the existence of collateral (unsecured versus **secured bonds**), how interest is calculated and paid (**floating-rate bonds**, **indexed bonds**, and **zero-coupon bonds**), inflation protection (**Treasury Inflation-Protected Securities**, or **TIPS**), and the risk level of the issuer (**investment-grade bonds** versus **high-yield bonds**, or **junk bonds**).

- Bond value is determined by the present value of the future expected cash flows, which include the interest payments to be received over time and the repayment of face value at maturity. Investors commonly evaluate bond issues based on **yield to maturity (YTM)**, which is the coupon yield adjusted for the price you paid for the bond.

- Investors buy bonds for several reasons, including the predictable income stream, lower risk, portfolio diversification, and the ability to match the timing of cash inflows with cash needs.

LEARNING OBJECTIVE 12.3   Compare the features of preferred stock with those of common stock and bonds.

Like both bonds and common stock, preferred stock is issued by companies as a means of raising capital to fund ongoing operations or expansion. Preferred stock has similarities to both common stock and bonds.

- Like bonds, most preferred stock pays a dividend equal to a fixed percentage of the **preferred stock par value**. If a company has insufficient income in a given year, the investors will not be paid unless the dividends are cumulative. With **cumulative preferred stock**, any unpaid dividends must be paid in subsequent years before dividends can be paid to common shareholders.

- Like common stock, though, preferred stock has no set maturity date, and the company never has to repay the original investment amount.

- Because the cash flow is constant over time, preferred stock can be valued as a **perpetuity** using **Equation 12.7**:

$$\text{Value of preferred stock} = \frac{\text{Annual dividend}}{\text{Required return}}$$

- Preferred stock is less risky than common stock because the dividend rate is fixed and preferred stockholders must be paid before common stockholders. But it is more risky than bonds because bondholders must receive their coupon payments before any dividends can be paid to either type of stockholder.

LEARNING OBJECTIVE 12.4   Describe the operation and regulation of the securities markets.

Common stock, bonds, preferred stock, and other securities are bought and sold in the securities markets.

- **Initial public offerings (IPOs)** are made in the **primary market**, whereas transactions between investors take place in the **secondary market**. The secondary market includes organized **securities exchanges**, which have specific requirements for **listed securities**, and the **over-the-counter (OTC) market**, which includes the **NASDAQ**.

- The securities market in the United States is highly regulated. The existing laws protect investors by requiring extensive information disclosure, including a **prospectus**, and public filings of financial statements with the SEC. The laws also prohibit fraud and **insider trading** in securities transactions and require licensing of investment professionals and insurance for brokerage accounts.

- Offers to buy (**bid price**) and sell (**ask price**) in the securities markets are matched up on the exchanges or in the OTC market. Many small transactions are now matched electronically. The price paid by a buyer in the last trade of the day is called the **close price**.

- When you offer to buy or sell, you can do so with a **market order**, **limit order**, or **stop order**.

- Some riskier trading alternatives include **selling short** and **buying on margin**. You must pay interest on a margin account and maintain sufficient equity in the account at all times. If you do not, you may get a **margin call** requesting that you deposit additional funds in the account.

Excel Worksheet

12.1 Personal Financial Planner: Bond Yield to Maturity

Key Terms

agency issue   12-16
ask price   12-31
beta   12-10
bid price   12-31
blue chip stock   12-10
buying on margin   12-33
call provision   12-20
close price   12-31
corporation   12-3
coupon payment   12-20
coupon rate   12-20
cumulative preferred stock   12-27
cyclical stock   12-10
defensive stock   12-10
earnings per share (EPS)   12-13
face value   12-19
floating-rate bond   12-17
growth stock   12-10

high-yield bond, or junk bond   12-18
income stock   12-10
indexed bond   12-17
initial public offering (IPO)   12-29
insider trading   12-34
investment-grade bond   12-18
limit order   12-32
limited liability   12-4
listed security   12-30
margin call   12-33
market capitalization   12-11
market order   12-32
maturity date   12-20
municipal bond   12-15
NASDAQ   12-30
over-the-counter (OTC) market   12-30
perpetuity   12-26
preemptive right   12-4

preferred stock par value   12-25
price-to-earnings (P/E) ratio   12-13
primary market   12-29
prospectus   12-19
residual claim   12-3
secondary market   12-29
secured bond   12-17
securities exchange   12-30
selling short   12-33
stock dividend   12-4
stop order   12-32
Treasury Inflation-Protected Securities
    (TIPS)   12-18
trustee   12-19
yield to maturity (YTM)   12-21
zero-coupon bond   12-17

WileyPLUS

Practice Questions to check your understanding, Peer-to-Peer Videos, Interactives, and many other resources are available in WileyPLUS.

Concept Review Questions

1. Why do companies issue stock?

2. What is the difference between a stock dividend and a cash dividend, and which is preferable?

3. What is a stock split, and why would a company take this action?

4. What is a blue chip stock, and why is it considered to be less risky than other classifications of stock?

5. What is a limit order, and under what circumstances would you want to place this type of order?

6. What is a stop order, and under what circumstances would you want to place this type of order?

7. What does it mean to sell short, and under what circumstances would an investor want to do this?

8. In what ways is short selling a riskier strategy than taking a long position in a stock?

9. Why is the securities market so heavily regulated?

10. Why is it illegal for insiders to trade on nonpublic information, and who gets hurt by this activity?

11. Why is debt financing cheaper than equity financing for a firm?

12. Why is a bond with a call provision less attractive to an investor than one without a call provision? What effect does a call provision have on the yield for a callable bond?

13. Under what circumstances would you want to have a bond with a convertibility feature? What effect does a convertibility feature have on bond yield? Explain.

14. Why do bond investors normally focus more on yield than on value in making their investment decisions?

15. In what ways is preferred stock similar to bonds, and in what ways is it similar to common stock?

16. If a firm gets into financial trouble and can't make good on all its obligations, what rights does a preferred stockholder have compared with the rights of bondholders and common stockholders?

17. What are the primary risk exposures for preferred stock investors? How do these risk exposures differ from the risk exposures for common stock investors?

18. How has electronic trading changed the securities market? In what ways has this benefited small investors?

19. What is the difference between the primary market and the secondary market, and in which market are you most likely to trade in the future?

Application Problems

1. You are considering three potential stock investments. Stock X is a blue chip stock issued by a company with $12 billion in market capitalization. Its dividend yield has been about 6 percent per year for several years, but its price hasn't appreciated much. It has a P/E ratio of 8. Stock Y has a $3 billion market cap, pays a very small dividend, and has seen an average annual price appreciation of 15 percent over the last several years. Its P/E ratio is 14. Stock Z has a $500 million market cap and pays no dividend. Although it has yet to show a profit since it went public three years ago, its price has increased 25 percent per year in each of the last two years.

Identify the capitalization and income/growth classification for each stock.

  a. Stock X is a _____-cap stock (large-, mid-, or small)

  b. Stock Y is a _____-cap stock (large-, mid-, or small)

  c. Stock Z is a _____-cap stock (large-, mid-, or small)

  d. Stock X is a(n) _____ investment (growth, income, or growth and income)

  e. Stock Y is a(n) _____ investment (growth, income, or growth and income)

  f. Stock Z is a(n) _____ investment (growth, income, or growth and income)

  g. Classify each of the companies as income or growth, if applicable.

  h. If you're an aggressive stock investor, which stock would be most appropriate for you, and why?

  i. If you're a conservative stock investor, which stock would be most appropriate for you, and why?

  j. If you have a five-year time horizon for achieving your investment objectives, would any of these investments be appropriate? Explain.

2. For each of the following companies, identify the classifications that apply to its stock—sector, industry, income versus growth, and market capitalization. If you don't have sufficient information about the company, check the company website for more details.

  a. The Gap (ticker: GPS)

  b. Intel Corporation (ticker: INTC)

  c. Ford Motor Company (ticker: F)

  d. Chipotle Mexican Grill, Inc. (ticker: CMG)

3. You bought 150 shares of ABC Corporation stock at $70 per share. When the stock price rose to $90 per share, the company management announced a three-for-one stock split. How many shares will you own after the split?

4. You bought 150 shares of ABC Corporation stock at $70 per share. When the stock price rose to $90 per share, the company management announced a three-for-one stock split. What will the price per share be immediately after the split?

5. Marian buys $3,000 in stock and holds the shares for one year. If she pays $50 per share in cash, receives no dividend, and sells the shares for $55 one year later, what will be her return on investment, ignoring transaction costs?

6. Juanita buys $3,000 in stock and holds the shares for one year. If she pays $50 per share, with a 50 percent margin, receives no dividend, and sells the shares for $55 per share one year later, what is her return on investment, ignoring transaction costs?

7. The current price of a stock is $25 per share. You place a market order for 100 shares with a discount broker who charges $10 per transaction. By the time the order can be executed, the price has risen to $25.50. How much will you pay per share, including any commission charge?

8. The current price of a stock is $25 per share. You place a limit order for 100 shares at $25.25 with a discount broker that charges $10 per transaction. By the time the order can be executed, the price has risen to $25.50. How much will you pay per share, including any commission?

9. A stock is currently selling for $30 per share, representing a price increase of $3 for the year, and there are 1 million shares outstanding. The company recently reported net income of $2 million. The annual dividend per share is $1. What is the company's earnings per share?

10. A stock is currently selling for $30 per share, representing a price increase of $3 for the year, and there are 1 million shares outstanding. The company recently reported net income of $2 million. The annual dividend per share is $1. What is the company's P/E ratio?

11. You bought a stock for $27 per share one year ago and the share price is now $30. There are 1 million shares outstanding. The company recently reported net income of $2 million. The annual dividend per share is $1. What is the dividend yield over the last year?

12. You bought a stock for $27 per share and the share price is now $30. There are 1 million shares outstanding. The company recently reported net income of $2 million. The annual dividend per share is $1. If you bought the stock one year ago, what was your total rate of return for the year?

13. You have the following information about several potential stock investments:

Company Name	Beta
Vixen, Inc.	2.5
Denicorp	1.2
Ferengi Oil	0.8
Luke Enterprises	0.5

  a. Which of these stocks has the most market risk?

  b. Which of these stocks has the least market risk?

  c. If the S&P 500 Index increased by 20 percent, which of these stocks would you expect to increase in value the most?

  d. If the S&P 500 Index declined by 20 percent, which of these stocks would you expect to decline the least?

14. You own 400 shares of a blue chip company's stock, which you bought last year for $65 per share. The company pays a quarterly dividend of $0.90 for a total of $3.60 per year. How much will your dividend check be this quarter?

15. You own 100 shares of a dividend-paying stock and receive total dividends for the year of $360. What tax rate will be applicable to these dividends if the stock is held in a taxable account and you're in the 12 percent federal income tax bracket in 2019?

16. You own 100 shares of stock for which you paid $65 per share. If the company pays a dividend of $3.60 per share this year, what is your dividend yield on this stock?

17. Ariel bought 100 shares of Puck Stores stock for $20 per share one year ago. Before the market opened today, she placed a limit order to sell her stock at a price of $26 per share. The stock price at the market open was $25.50; it hit a high of $27 at around noon but was back down to $25.50 by the close. Her trading costs were $10 per transaction, and the stock paid no dividends during the year. What was Ariel's return on investment on this stock for the year? If she had placed a market order instead, how much would she have sold her shares for, and what would her return on investment be?

18. A corporation issued a fixed-rate coupon bond that pays a coupon rate of 7.65 percent in semiannual payments and has a maturity date of March 2033. The face value of the bond is $1,000. How much will each bondholder receive every six months?

19. A corporation issues a fixed-rate coupon bond that pays a coupon rate of 7.65 percent in semiannual payments and has a maturity date of March 2033. The face value of the bond is $1,000. At maturity, how much will the bondholders be paid?

20. ABC Corp. has two coupon bond issues outstanding: each bond has a face value of $1,000 and semiannual coupon payments. Bond 1 has 20 years to maturity, a 5 percent coupon rate, and a current price of $850. Bond 2 has 10 years to maturity, a 6 percent coupon rate, and a current price of $1,000.

   a. Calculate the current yield for each bond.

   b. Given that both of these bonds are issued by the same company, why is the 20-year bond so much cheaper ($850) than the 10-year bond ($1,000)?

21. You buy a fixed-rate coupon bond that has a face value of $1,000 and 10 years to maturity. The current market price is $910, and the coupon rate is 8 percent with semiannual payments. What is the yield to maturity for this bond?

22. You are deciding between two bonds. Both are issued by the same highly rated company, have a coupon rate of 6 percent (with semiannual payments), and a face value of $1,000. Bond A has 10 years to maturity (current price $928.94), and Bond B has 20 years to maturity (current price $802.07).

   a. If both bonds are issued by the same company and pay the same coupon rate, why is one cheaper than the other?

   b. Calculate the yield to maturity for each bond.

c. Assume that one year later, the yields on comparable investments have risen to 8 percent and 9 percent respectively. Which of these two bonds would be expected to experience a greater decline in value?

23. Simone owns 10 bonds from the same bond issuer. Each has a $1,000 face value and a 6 percent coupon rate. If Simone has a marginal tax rate of 25 percent, what is her annual after-tax interest income from these bonds?

24. For each of the following investments, calculate the after-tax yield, assuming that the marginal federal income tax rate is 24 percent and the marginal state tax rate is 6 percent.

   a. Corporate bond held in a taxable account with an 8 percent pretax yield

   b. Municipal bond (issued in the purchaser's state of residence) held in a taxable account with a 7 percent pretax yield

   c. U.S. Treasury bond held in a taxable account with a 5 percent pretax yield

25. A company's preferred stock has a par value of $25 and a dividend rate of 7.5 percent. How much will be paid per share each year?

26. You are considering the purchase of shares of preferred stock that pay an annual dividend of $10.

   a. If the market price of the preferred shares is currently $111, what is the yield?

   b. If market interest rates increase so that investors in these securities now require 1 percentage point more in yield, how will this affect the price of the stock?

   c. If the market price goes down from $111 to $100 in one year, what is the capital gain or loss for investors?

27. Bonnie wants to buy zero-coupon bonds as a means of saving for retirement. She finds that the current price of a zero-coupon bond with a face value of $1,000 and 30 years to maturity is $231.40.

   a. If she buys this bond and holds it to maturity, what is Bonnie's annual yield to maturity before taxes?

   b. Explain why it is advisable that Bonnie hold these bonds in a tax-deferred or tax-exempt retirement account.

28. Lenore is subject to a 30 percent marginal tax rate. She has purchased 6.5 percent municipal bonds, which are exempt from federal and state taxes. What yield would she need to earn before tax on a taxable investment to obtain an after-tax interest yield equivalent to what she is earning on the municipals?

Case Applications

1. One year ago, Joe and Marissa Morini made several large-cap stock investments. They used no margin, and their trading costs were $8 per transaction. Their purchases included the following:

   100 shares of Stock A at $26 (annual dividend, $0.16)

   100 shares of Stock B at $35 (annual dividend, $0.60)

   100 shares of Stock C at $40 (annual dividend, $0.50)

   100 shares of Stock D at $15 (no dividend)

The current stock prices are as follows: Stock A, $29; Stock B, $33; Stock C, $41; and Stock D, $18.

   a. What was the total start-up cost for their investment portfolio?

   b. What is the current value of the Morinis' portfolio?

   c. Calculate the dividend yield and capital gains yield for each of the Morinis' stocks, ignoring transaction costs.

   d. Calculate the annual return on investment for the Morinis' investment portfolio.

e. Based on their stock selections, what index or market average would you recommend that the Morinis use as a benchmark for their portfolio?

f. Assuming that the return on the S&P 500 Index for the same period was 12 percent, how well did the Morinis do?

g. If the Morinis would like to add to their current stock portfolio, in what ways could they improve its diversification?

2. Ernie and Belinda Maxwell often tell people that they're "68 years young." They have an active lifestyle, playing golf, regularly volunteering at their church, and traveling around the country in their RV to visit their three children and five grandchildren. But as they approach their 50th wedding anniversary, they are beginning to worry about their finances. When Ernie retired 10 years ago, his retirement fund accumulation of over $1 million had seemed more than sufficient to support their lifestyle. Their home mortgage was paid off, and their children were grown. After investing all of the retirement fund in corporate bonds with a laddered maturity structure of 20 years (because they didn't want to risk their money in the stock market), they were happy to find that their nest egg produced income of about $80,000 a year before taxes. Ten years later, the Maxwells (who are in the 25 percent tax bracket) are finding that it's harder to live on that amount of income each year. They've gradually been selling bonds, so they now have less to invest.

Their portfolio includes bonds with about $850,000 in total face value, and it is generating only $60,000 in before-tax income. As they've reinvested money from maturing bonds, Ernie and Belinda have been dismayed to find that market yields have fallen since they originally retired, to a **current** level of 5.5 percent for 20-year corporate bonds. The Maxwells, who are in excellent health, expect to live into their 90s based on their family histories and are worried about outliving their money.

a. What was the average coupon rate on the original bonds in the Maxwells' portfolio? What is it now?

b. Why has the income from the Maxwells' portfolio fallen over the past 10 years?

c. If market interest rates rise, will the Maxwells' income rise accordingly? Why or why not?

d. Are the Maxwells correct to worry about outliving their assets? Explain.

e. Is the Maxwells' present asset allocation (100 percent corporate bonds) appropriate for their life-cycle stage and risk preferences? Why or why not?

f. Did the Maxwells make a good decision 10 years ago when they chose to invest exclusively in fixed-income securities?

g. If the Maxwells continue to buy and hold bonds, is their investment strategy fairly low-risk? What risk exposures do they still face?

3. Mike Hettwer was pleased to find that his great-uncle Clyde, who lived to the ripe old age of 87, had remembered all his nieces and nephews in his will. Instead of leaving them cash, however, Clyde's will said that he wanted them all to get a taste of investing. Clyde's bequest to Mike was a portfolio of bonds issued by different corporations, with a total face value of $60,000. Mike is 25 years old and earns $40,000 per year. His marginal tax rate is 15 percent, and he has no other investments at the moment. Mike asked you for advice on his investments, and you requested that he look up some information on them first. He has summarized the information as follows:

Bonds	Number of Bonds	Bond Rating	Coupon Rate	Term to Maturity	Yield	Price
1	10	Aaa	5.3	25	6.0	$910
2	10	Aaa	6.7	13	5.2	$1,140
3	10	Ba	7.5	20	7.5	$1,000
4	10	Ba	8.2	10	7.0	$1,085
5	10	B	9.0	17	8.5	$1,045
6	10	B	7.8	5	8.0	$992

a. Based on Mike's information about the bonds, estimate the market value of his portfolio.

b. Mike is pretty excited to find out how high the average yield on these bonds is. Do you agree that these are good investments for him? Why or why not? Explain your reasoning.

c. Mike asks you why the two bonds with Aaa ratings don't have the same yield. Explain.

d. Are the differences in yield between the Aaa-rated bonds and the other bonds reasonable?

e. How diversified is Mike's portfolio based on default risk? Assuming that he decides to stay invested in bonds, should he consider any changes in asset allocation?

CHAPTER 13

Investing in Mutual Funds and Real Estate

Hill Street Studios/DigitalVision/Getty Images

Feature Story

Jose Herrara is the owner and manager of a matador store in southern Texas. Although his business has provided only modest income for his family, he and his wife, Maria, have saved nearly $800,000 in a tax-deferred retirement plan and also own two rental properties, bringing their total nest egg to just over the million dollar mark. Only 2 percent of households age 55 and over have been able to save this much, so how did José and Maria do it?

Without any formal financial education, José read up on investing and decided that, with his busy work schedule, he would need to rely on professionals to do the actual investing. He and Maria decided to put half their savings in a stock mutual fund and half in a bond fund. In most years, they saved between 15 percent and 18 percent of their income. When Maria's mother died, they bought two rental units with their small inheritance and expect to have the mortgages paid off in a few years, leaving them with some supplemental monthly income.

In previous chapters, you've learned how to estimate your retirement wealth needs. If you found that your wealth target exceeds the million dollar mark, this may seem like a pretty daunting goal. It turns out that José and Maria had the right idea. The key success factors have very little to do with investment expertise and more to do with persistence. The "401(k) million-aires" are people who, like José and Maria, have saved a big percentage of their income over a fairly long period of time. This means they might have had to forego some luxuries during their working careers—maybe they made do with older cars and smaller homes, for example.

In this chapter, you'll learn how to invest in mutual funds and real estate. If you make the commitment to consistent savings and have a well-diversified portfolio, you could someday be a 401(k) millionaire like Jose and Maria Herrera.

LEARNING OBJECTIVES	TOPICS	DEMONSTRATION PROBLEMS
13.1 Distinguish different types of investment companies based on key characteristics.	**13.1 What Is a Mutual Fund?** • What Does a Mutual Fund Investor Actually Own? • Types of Investment Companies • Growth in the Market • Fund Classifications	**13.1** Calculating Net Asset Value

(continued)

(continued)

LEARNING OBJECTIVES	TOPICS	DEMONSTRATION PROBLEMS
13.2 Explain the advantages and costs of investing in mutual funds versus individual securities.	**13.2 Mutual Fund Investing** • The Advantages of Mutual Fund Investing • The Costs of Mutual Fund Investing • Selecting and Evaluating Mutual Funds	
13.3 Identify the advantages and disadvantages of direct and indirect real estate investments.	**13.3 Real Estate Investment** • Your Home as an Investment • Direct Real Estate Investment • Indirect Real Estate Investment	**13.2** Calculating Return on Investment for Income Properties
13.4 Explain why investments in precious metals, gems, collectibles, cryptocurrencies, and derivatives are speculative.	**13.4 Speculative Investments** • Precious Metals and Gems • Collectibles and Art • Cryptocurrencies • Financial Derivatives	**13.3** Estimating Return on Art and Collectibles

13.1 | What Is a Mutual Fund?

LEARNING OBJECTIVE 13.1

Distinguish different types of investment companies based on key characteristics.

In the Feature Story, José and Maria were able to invest in stocks and bonds without having to make the individual investment selections themselves. You can do this by purchasing shares of an **investment company** that pools small dollar amounts from many investors and invests those funds in a wide variety of assets. Each investment company must provide detailed background information for potential buyers, including the company's investment objectives, holdings, and track record.

Investors like José and Maria buy shares in the investment company, and the company uses the dollars to make investments on behalf of the investment pool. The term *mutual fund* is often used to refer to all types of investment companies, but technically, a mutual fund is a specific type called an open-end investment company, which we explain later.

Although the mechanism can differ across funds, the cash flows generated by the securities in the investment pool are later distributed to the investors. As with stock investments, this distribution can take the form of dividends or an increase in the value of investment shares. Investors who purchase shares in mutual funds are like other corporate shareholders—they have an equity interest in the pool of assets and a residual claim on the profits, but they have no say in day-to-day decisions about buying and selling the financial assets.

Until the enactment of comprehensive securities laws in the 1930s, investors didn't have a lot of confidence in this type of investment. Today, however, mutual fund shares are considered securities under the legal definition of the word, and shareholders are therefore entitled to all the protections afforded to owners of other financial assets. That means the investment company must provide all potential investors with detailed disclosure information, much like the information you'd get for a stock or bond investment. The company also must make regular reports to the Securities and Exchange Commission, which regulates mutual funds.

In this section, we first take a closer look at the mutual fund investor's ownership interest, usually measured as net asset value. You'll learn about the various types of investment companies and the advantages and costs associated with mutual fund investing.

What Does a Mutual Fund Investor Actually Own?

One measure of the value of an investor's claim on a mutual fund's assets is called the **net asset value**. This is calculated as assets minus liabilities, per share, as defined in **Equation 13.1**:

$$\text{Net asset value} = \frac{\text{Market value of assets} - \text{Market value of liabilities}}{\text{Number of shares outstanding}} \tag{13.1}$$

For example, suppose you own one share of a mutual fund that has 5 million shares outstanding. The fund portfolio is currently worth $100 million, and its liabilities include $2 million owed to investment advisors and $1 million in rent, wages, and other expenses. Your net asset value is therefore:

$$\text{Net asset value} = \frac{\$100,000,000 - \$3,000,000}{5,000,000} = \frac{\$97,000,000}{5,000,000} = \$19.40 \text{ per share}$$

If the securities that are held in a mutual fund increase in value or pay dividends, the net asset value of the shares of the mutual fund should also increase in value, even though these increases are technically unrealized capital gains. The objective of fund managers is therefore to invest in assets that will continue to grow in value over time. This is an important point to keep in mind as you learn more about this type of investment—mutual fund values will tend to track the performance of the assets they invest in. So if the stock market is down, mutual funds that invest in stock will typically decline in value as well, because the assets they have invested in will have lower market values. **Demonstration Problem 13.1** shows how to calculate net asset value.

DEMONSTRATION PROBLEM 13.1 | Calculating Net Asset Value

Problem

You want to calculate the net asset value for the Acme Balanced Growth and Income mutual fund. You have the following information from the January 1 balance sheet:

Assets: $150 million
Liabilities: $10 million
Shares: 12.3 million

Strategy

Use Equation 13.1 to calculate net asset value.

Solution

$$\text{Net asset value} = \frac{\text{Market value of assets} - \text{Market value of liabilities}}{\text{Number of shares outstanding}}$$

$$= \frac{\$150,000,000 - \$10,000,000}{12,300,000} = \frac{\$140,000,000}{12,300,000} = \$11.38 \text{ per share}$$

A mutual fund investor earns a return on their investment in the same way as stock and bond investors. They are paid dividends on their shares, and they benefit from an increase in the net asset value of their shares over time. As you learned in previous chapters, the rate of return on investment will be (Dividends + Change in value)/Beginning price. Suppose you bought the shares described in Demonstration Problem 13.1 for $11.38 per share and received a dividend during the year of $0.50 per share. If the shares are worth $12.50 one year later, you have earned a return of ($0.50 + $12.50 − 11.38)/$11.38 = 0.1424, or 14.24%.

Types of Investment Companies

Although different types of investment companies are often lumped together in a discussion of mutual funds, the Investment Company Act of 1940 identifies several distinct types that provide pooling opportunities for individual investors. Types of investment companies include open-end funds, closed-end funds, exchange-traded funds, unit investment trusts, and real estate investment trusts.

Open-End Funds

By far the most common type of investment company, an **open-end fund** is different from the other types discussed in this section in that: (1) it is required to buy back shares any time an investor wants to sell, and (2) it continuously offers new shares for sale to the public. As mentioned above, the term *mutual fund* typically refers to this type of investment company.

With open-end funds, the share price for purchases and sales is usually the net asset value plus trading costs. The issuing company provides the only market for the shares, and there is no secondary market for trading between investors. The investment company is free to issue new shares at any time to raise additional funds for investment and to meet investor demand for the shares.

Open-end funds can be very large, with many billions of dollars under management. This is the type of fund that is commonly available through employer-sponsored retirement plans. As more dollars flow into an open-end fund from retirement plan sponsors, the fund creates more shares and invests in more securities.

Closed-End Funds

A **closed-end fund** is an investment company that issues a fixed number of shares that trade on a stock exchange or in the over-the-counter market. The process of issuing shares is very similar to that discussed in Chapter 12 for stocks. The initial public offering of shares is sold directly to investors, after which the shares trade between investors in the secondary market. Like open-end funds, closed-end funds hire professional managers to use investor's money to buy a diversified portfolio of assets that will meet the investment objectives described in the fund prospectus.

Closed-end funds trade primarily on major stock exchanges, such as the New York Stock Exchange and the NASDAQ. The market values of shares traded on the secondary market fluctuate with supply and demand and may be greater or less than the net asset value per share. Closed-end funds make up only a small proportion of the total number of investment companies (around 500 in the United States, compared with more than 9,000 open-end mutual funds) and are declining in popularity relative to their close cousin, the exchange-traded fund.

Exchange-Traded Funds

An **exchange-traded fund (ETF)** combines some of the characteristics of open-end and closed-end funds. It is technically an open-end fund because the company is free to issue new shares or redeem old shares to increase or decrease the number of shares outstanding. But like a closed-end fund, an ETF is traded on an organized exchange, and share prices are determined by market forces. Investors buy ETF shares through a broker just as they would purchase shares of common stock of any publicly traded company.

Although the number of ETFs is still small relative to the numbers of open-end funds and unit investment trusts (discussed below), their size and popularity are growing rapidly. In fact, the number of ETFs has more than doubled to nearly 2,000 in the last decade. Many ETFs are designed as index funds, investing in a set of securities that mimic the performance of a particular market index such as the S&P 500 Index, but with lower expenses and a lower minimum required investment than for actively managed funds. For these reasons, the financial press has been strongly recommending this type of fund, since it originated, for individual investors seeking diversification and low costs. Investors who buy shares of an ETF based on the S&P 500 (called a "Spider" because its ticker is SPY) will see an increase in the value of their shares when the S&P 500 Index increases in value. Similarly, investors in a "Diamond" (ticker DIA), an ETF based on the Dow Jones Industrial Average, will benefit when the Dow goes up. For investors who want their portfolio to track large company stocks with low expenses, either of these ETFs is a good choice.

Not all ETFs today are simple index funds. Specialized versions include ETFs that use different trading strategies, such as leverage, to magnify returns (or losses), and those that track returns of much riskier asset classes, such as cryptocurrencies or precious metals. As with other investment company types, the return and risk characteristics of ETFs are totally dependent on the underlying portfolio.

Unit Investment Trusts

Another type of investment company is a **unit investment trust (UIT)**. A UIT buys and holds a fixed portfolio of securities for a period of time that's determined by the life of the investments in the trust (which usually are fixed-maturity debt securities). Because there isn't any change in the portfolio over the period of investment, this type of fund is essentially unmanaged. The manager of the pool, called the trustee, initially purchases the pool of investments and deposits them in a trust. Owners are issued redeemable trust certificates, which entitle them to proportionate shares of any income and principal payments received by the trust and a distribution of their proportionate share of the proceeds at the termination of the trust.

The investors in a unit investment trust generally pay a premium over what it costs the trustee to purchase the underlying assets, providing the equivalent of a commission to the trustee for his or her services (pooling the funds and distributing the income and principal). Because the funds are unmanaged, the fee should be lower than that for a comparable managed fund, but it still can be as high as 3 to 5 percent.

Why would an investor be willing to incur such a high cost? The answer lies in the type of securities that make up unit investment trusts. About 90 percent of these assets are fixed-income securities, primarily municipal bonds. Each trust specializes in a certain type of security, so one might hold only municipal bonds and another only high-yield corporate bonds. The high cost of individual bonds (usually $1,000 minimum) makes it otherwise difficult for individual investors to include these investment classes in their portfolios. The availability of unit investment trust shares means that small investors can still participate in a relatively diversified pool of specialized debt securities. Although there isn't an active secondary market for the trust certificates, the trustee will usually buy them back on request.

A unit investment trust continues in existence only as long as assets remain in the trust. Thus, a trust invested in short-term securities might exist for only a few months, whereas a trust holding municipal bonds might have a life of 20 years or more, depending on the maturities of the bonds held. The number of unit investment trusts and the total dollars invested in them have remained relatively stable over the last decade.

Real Estate Investment Trusts

A **real estate investment trust (REIT)** is a special type of closed-end fund that invests in real estate and mortgages. By law, a REIT must have a buy-and-hold investment strategy, a professional manager (the trustee), and at least 100 shareholders. The trustee initially issues shares and then uses the investors' money to buy real estate assets according to the terms of the trust, much like a unit investment trust. The difference is that the REIT doesn't have a limited life span, because most real estate investments don't have fixed maturities. An important factor for individual investors is that REITs must distribute 90 percent of their profits to shareholders each year, and this income will be taxable as ordinary income unless the shares are held in a tax-deferred account.

REITs offer individual investors the opportunity to diversify their investment portfolios into real estate. Many investors wouldn't otherwise have access to this investment class because of the high initial investment required and the liquidity risk involved. In many respects, REITs are similar to stock investments and closed-end mutual funds, trading on national exchanges and distributing profits to the investors through dividends. REITs often specialize in particular types of real estate investments. Equity REITs, which make up a large share of the market, specialize in making direct investments in income-producing real estate, such as office buildings and shopping centers. Mortgage REITs focus on mortgage investments, such as residential and construction loans.

REITs can provide diversification for your portfolio because their prices do not tend to go up and down at the same time as stock and bond prices. However, they aren't as liquid as stocks and are highly sensitive to the real estate market environment. In the early 2000s, REIT investors benefited from the real estate bubble, earning higher returns than investors in most other asset classes. But when real estate prices plummeted later in the decade, contributing to the 2008 financial crisis, REIT investors were badly affected. As shown in **Figure 13.1**, the average equity REIT lost about two-thirds of its value between April 2007 and February 2009, much more than the decline in the stock market over that period. Fortunately for investors, as the economy recovered and real estate prices stabilized, REIT shares returned to their pre-2008 values.

FIGURE 13.1 **Equity REIT Total Return Index** REIT investors were hard hit by the financial crisis, but the real estate market rebounded strongly from 2009 to 2019.

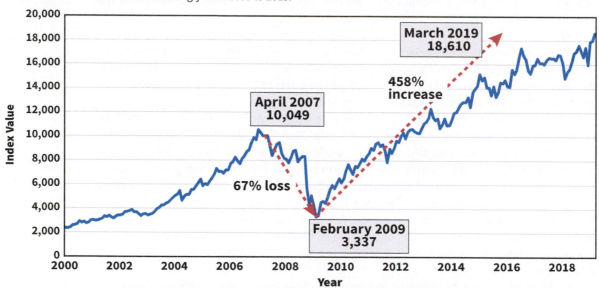

Source: FTSE NAREIT U.S. Real Estate Index Series for Equity REITs, nareit.com.

Growth in the Market

Mutual fund investing by individuals has dramatically increased over the last several decades. In 1980, fewer than 6 percent of households owned mutual fund shares. In 2018, as shown in **Figure 13.2**, nearly 44 percent were mutual fund investors, in large part due to the growth in defined-contribution retirement plans and IRAs. When asked why they invest in mutual funds,

94 percent say they are saving for retirement, and 48 percent say they are saving for emergencies. Although the number of mutual funds hasn't changed much, total investments have experienced tremendous growth since 1995, as shown in **Table 13.1**.

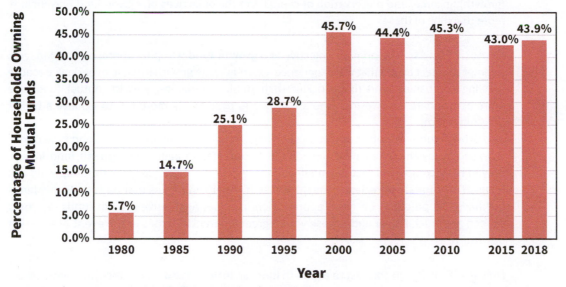

FIGURE 13.2   **Percentage of U.S. Households Owning Mutual Funds**   After growing fast for several decades, the proportion of households owning mutual funds has stabilized.

Source: Data from Investment Company Institute, *2019 Fact Book*, www.ici.org.

TABLE 13.1   **Growth in Number and Total Assets of U.S. Funds, by Type of Investment Company**

	Open-end Funds		Closed-end Funds		Exchange-traded Funds		Unit Investment Trusts	
	Number of Funds	Assets ($ billions)	Number of Funds	Assets ($ billions)	Number of Funds	Assets ($ billions)	Number of Funds	Assets ($ billions)
1995	5,761	$2,811	499	$143	2	$1	12,979	$73
2000	8,370	6,965	481	143	80	66	10,072	74
2005	8,449	8,891	634	276	204	301	6,019	41
2010	8,536	11,833	624	238	950	992	5,971	51
2015	9,517	15,652	559	261	1,644	2,101	5,188	94
2018	9,599	17,707	506	250	1,057	3,371	4,917	70

Source: Data from Investment Company Institute *2019 Factbook*, www.ici.org.

Fund Classifications

Mutual funds are usually classified based on investment objectives and portfolio composition. As the competition for investors' dollars has grown, mutual fund companies have attempted to distinguish themselves from competitors, creating so much diversity that it isn't always easy to categorize funds. The classifications suggested in this section aren't uniformly applied, but will familiarize you with the terms commonly used to describe mutual funds. In general, you'll find that the most important distinctions among funds are the type of investment (equity versus debt) and the investment objective (income versus capital gain).

Classification by Investment Objective

Each mutual fund has a specific investment policy, which is described in the fund's prospectus. For example, money market mutual funds, introduced in Chapter 3, consider the preservation of capital to be an important investment objective. To achieve this objective, the fund managers must invest in short-term, low-risk debt securities. Investors know this in advance and therefore have specific expectations about the performance of this type of fund based on its objective. The most common general investment policy categories are capital appreciation (growth), income, and preservation of capital, but the objectives of a given fund may include more than one of these.

Growth Funds   The primary objective of a **growth fund** is capital appreciation. Managers attempt to select assets that will experience above-average growth in value over time. Because growing companies tend to be riskier than stable companies, growth mutual funds are more appropriate for investors who are willing to bear a little more risk to achieve a higher long-run return.

   Growth funds are often placed in subcategories depending on the level and type of risk represented by the investment portfolio. For example, an aggressive growth fund invests only in risky companies that pay no dividends, whereas a moderate growth fund, while still focused on capital appreciation, might invest in larger companies that pay stable dividends but have the potential for good appreciation in value. Aggressive growth funds, as you'd expect, are much riskier and expose you to greater potential losses in the event of a market downturn.

Income Funds   In contrast to a growth fund, an **income fund** holds stock and bond investments that provide high current income, either in dividends or interest. These funds tend to be viewed as less risky than growth funds, because the investor is realizing immediate gains rather than taking the risk of waiting for future gains. As with growth funds, there are various subcategories within this group, most commonly based on the source of the income (interest versus dividends) and the risk level (high-quality debt versus junk bonds).

Growth and Income Funds   Some funds try to straddle the fence, providing reasonable income to investors while still investing in companies that have good potential for growth in value. Primarily invested in growth-oriented blue chip stocks, these funds have generated respectable returns over time and have been more stable than the market as a whole.

Balanced Funds   A **balanced fund**, sometimes called a hybrid fund, provides investors with the opportunity to benefit from investments in both stocks and bonds. Because they are better diversified than funds that are entirely invested in stocks and because they tend to focus on high-grade securities, balanced funds tend to have stable returns over time. These funds are similar to income funds but focus more on reducing investment risk.

Value Funds   A **value fund** invests in companies that its managers believe to be currently undervalued by the market—companies with good fundamentals whose stock prices are low relative to their perceived potential. As there are always many other investors seeking these same undiscovered gems, the risk of being wrong is fairly high. Value funds are a little less risky than aggressive growth funds but still offer fairly good returns.

Life-Cycle and Target-Date Funds   A **life-cycle fund** allocates fund assets based on the age of the investor. A fund for 30-year-olds will be invested in riskier assets than a fund for 60-year-olds. A **target-date fund** adjusts the portfolio allocation to meet objectives related to a particular future need for cash, such as retirement or education funding. Funds of this type often have names like "Retirement 2040." Generally, life-cycle and target-date funds attempt to rebalance the portfolio to gradually reduce risk as the investor gets older. If you're 30 years old, you could select a life-cycle fund that is designed for your age group. However, if you plan to retire earlier or later than average for your age group, you might prefer a target-date fund instead. Given the financial planning emphasis on changing needs over the life cycle, the idea behind the design of these types of funds is sound, although there isn't always agreement on the optimal asset mix.

The number and variety of life-cycle and target-date funds increased substantially after the passage of the Pension Protection Act of 2006, which requires employers to offer a reasonable option to employees who are automatically enrolled in an employer-sponsored retirement plan. Because of their simplicity for the investor, these funds have become very popular choices for 401(k) plan assets. More than two-thirds of 401(k) plans now offer target-date and life-cycle funds as investment options, and more than 50% of plan participants allocate at least some of their savings to these funds.

Classification by Portfolio Composition

In addition to being classified by investment objective, funds are also commonly categorized based on portfolio composition. This can involve some combination of asset class, industry representation, and index benchmark.

Asset Class   Mutual funds commonly confine their investments to certain asset classes, such as stocks versus bonds, although as we've seen, some funds hold both stocks and bonds. Within each broad asset class, funds may be further classified according to such features as size of company (large-cap, mid-cap, or small-cap) or type of asset (long-term Treasury bonds, high-grade corporate bonds, or municipal bonds). When you invest in a mutual fund that is concentrated in a particular asset class, the performance of your fund is likely to mimic the overall performance of that asset class. Your share values will respond to economic conditions in much the same way as do investments in individual stocks and bonds.

Industry or Sector   A **sector fund** specializes in a particular industry or business sector, such as technology, financial services, telecommunications, or health care. These funds tend to focus on growth rather than income, and they enable investors to allocate more of their money to the sector believed to offer the most attractive returns. Because this strategy results in less diversification, sector funds tend to be riskier over time than those that cover more industry groups. For example, we saw earlier how REITs were stars in the early 2000s but had bigger losses than investments in other sectors during the financial crisis.

Geographical Focus   When the U.S. stock market is down, investors can benefit from global diversification. An **international fund** invests exclusively in securities from other countries. Some funds include securities from a particular region, such as Latin America or Asia. Others, commonly referred to as *country funds*, specialize in securities from a particular country. In contrast, a **global fund** attempts to diversify globally, investing in U.S. as well as foreign securities.

Index Funds   Many managed funds try to mimic the performance of a particular index, such as the S&P 500 Index, without necessarily buying every stock that is included in the index. The performance of such a fund is judged by how well it compares with the performance of its benchmark index. Many academic studies, however, have shown that it's difficult for an actively managed fund to beat its benchmark.

As an alternative, index funds attempt to buy and hold a selection of stocks that can mimic the market more exactly and at lower cost. If the index fund is targeting the Dow Jones Industrial Average or the S&P 500 Index, for example, it will usually buy all the stocks in that index in about the same proportions and will therefore be able to track the index almost exactly. For indexes that include a much larger number of stocks, such as the New York Stock Exchange Index, the index fund might try to buy a smaller selection of representative stocks. Because index funds buy and hold, trading costs and fund expenses are minimized.

Socially Responsible Funds   If the "bottom line" is not your primary focus, you might be interested in a **socially responsible investing (SRI) fund**. The manager of an SRI fund is charged with selecting stocks issued by companies that meet some predefined ethical and moral standards. Although the objectives of various funds differ, common issues that are considered are a company's policies toward employees and the environment. For this reason, companies are commonly rated based on ESG criteria (environmental, social, and governance), making it easier for investors to identify qualifying investments. SRI funds also commonly avoid securities of companies that are involved in "sin industries" such as tobacco, alcohol, and gambling. Note that there are also socially irresponsible funds (like the VICE Fund) that specifically invest in such industries.

Reflection Question 1

Is being a socially responsible investor important to you? Why or why not?

INTERACTIVE

See Interactive: Mutual Fund Classifications in **WileyPLUS.**

You can use **Interactive: Mutual Fund Classifications** to review the various types of mutual funds.

13.2 | Mutual Fund Investing

LEARNING OBJECTIVE 13.2

Explain the advantages and costs of investing in mutual funds versus individual securities.

In the chapter introduction, you read about an ordinary couple who had saved more than a million dollars by regularly investing in mutual funds over their working career. They might have been able to achieve the same results by investing directly in stocks and bonds, but in this section, we explain why mutual funds make investing easier and cheaper, and are a particularly good choice for novice investors.

The Advantages of Mutual Fund Investing

From the point of view of individual investors, mutual funds have some advantages that make them preferable to investments in stocks, bonds, and other financial assets. The advantages include increased portfolio diversification, reduced transaction costs, professional money management, and greater liquidity. Although these points apply to most types of investment companies, we focus on open-end funds in several of the examples because they represent such a large share of the total number of funds and invested dollars.

Diversification

Suppose you have $200 per month to invest. If you buy stocks or bonds directly, it will be difficult for you to buy more than one company's securities at a time. You might even have to save up for several months before you can make certain investments, such as bonds (which often cost around $1,000 each). Furthermore, if one of the companies you've invested in goes downhill, a big chunk of your investment portfolio will go downhill with it. Now, consider instead what will happen if you split the $200 and invest half in a diversified stock mutual fund and half in a diversified bond mutual fund. You'll not only be able to allocate your money between two asset classes, but you'll also become an owner (although admittedly a small one) of a diverse pool of investments in each asset class. If a single company's stock or bond price declines in value, it should have only a minimal impact on your portfolio.

Mutual funds are broadly invested in the financial markets. Indeed, mutual funds and other investment companies are major players in the financial marketplace. **Figure 13.3** shows the ownership percentage of various markets that are held by investment companies. For example, these companies own 30 percent of all U.S. common and preferred stock.

FIGURE 13.3   **Investment Companies' Ownership Percentage of Total Market Securities, December 31, 2018**   Investment companies own a large share of the total value of U.S. stocks and bonds.

Source: Data from *Investment Company Institute 2019 Factbook*, www.ici.org.

Figure 13.4 shows the investment allocation of funds held in U.S. mutual funds. As you can see, stocks make up the largest proportion of the total net assets of these funds. If you exclude money market funds, which have very short-term investment objectives, nearly two-thirds of mutual fund dollars are in stocks.

FIGURE 13.4   **Share of Total Net Assets for Mutual Funds, by Asset Class, December 31, 2018** Given the widespread use of mutual funds for retirement investing, it makes sense that these funds invest mostly in stocks.

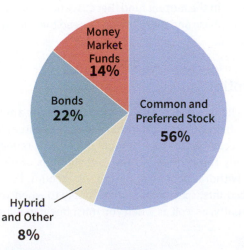

Source: Data from *Investment Company Institute 2019 Factbook*, www.ici.org.

INTERACTIVE

See Interactive: Diversification in a Large-Cap Growth Fund in WileyPLUS.

Although Figure 13.4 tells us about diversification of the aggregate mutual fund market-place, it doesn't tell us anything about the diversification within each fund. Given that mutual funds normally specialize in one or a few asset classes, they don't individually have the kind of asset allocation shown in the figure. To determine the asset allocation of a particular fund, you have to look at its annual report, which lists all the fund's holdings as of the end of the reporting period. **Interactive: Diversification in a Large-Cap Growth Fund** will help you better under-stand the asset allocation within a specific mutual fund.

Professional Money Management

One reason investors like mutual funds is that the individual investment selection decision is taken out of their hands. The investment company hires professionals whose job it is to man-age the fund, generally making use of the most current data and analysis tools available. Many of the largest companies (not including those that simply buy and hold) have a full-time staff of security analysts. Of course, even the experts aren't always right, so professional management is no guarantee of performance, but you can probably assume that the professional money manager knows more than you do and that his or her overall objective is the same as yours—to increase the value of your investment.

Liquidity

Recall that liquidity is the ability to convert an asset to cash without loss of value. Under this definition, we'd have to conclude that mutual funds are somewhat liquid. If you need access to your money, it's fairly easy to sell your mutual fund shares if you own a closed-end fund, but the price will depend on market supply-and-demand forces. If you own shares in an open-end fund, you can nearly always sell them back to the investment company, but the price you receive will depend on the net asset value per share at the time you sell. In either case, you might have to pay a transaction fee, which we discuss later in this chapter.

Although the shares of a mutual fund may not be quite as liquid as some of the stocks and bonds the fund invests in, they can be far more liquid than other investments you might make. Municipal bonds and real estate, for example, have fairly low liquidity, so holding shares in a mutual fund that invests in either of these types of assets provides you with much more liquidity than you'd have if you invested in the assets directly.

Dividend Reinvestment

Most mutual funds allow you to automatically reinvest dividends and capital gain distribu-tions, similar to the dividend reinvestment plans for stocks discussed in Chapter 11. Instead of receiving immediate cash flow, you use your dividends and capital gains distributions to buy additional shares in the mutual fund. Because most mutual fund investors are still in the wealth accumulation phase and therefore don't need the current cash flow, this is a very desir-able feature.

Withdrawal Options

Although you initially invest in a mutual fund to save for a future goal, the time will come when you want to start converting the shares to cash. Mutual funds provide several options for this process. You can receive a set amount per month, redeem a certain number of shares per month, take only the current income (distributions of dividends and capital gains), or make a lump sum withdrawal of all or part of the account. For funds designated as tax-qual-ified retirement accounts, specific limitations apply to when you can begin withdrawing the money without penalty, as well as when you must begin making minimum withdrawals from the account.

The Costs of Mutual Fund Investing

The benefits offered by mutual funds—such as liquidity, professional management, and diversification—don't come free. Fund investors can therefore expect to pay a variety of fees and expenses. As with other investments, you won't earn a profit on your investment until you've recouped your initial costs. However, for most investors, these costs are much lower than the costs of trading on their own. Because they make large-volume trades, the cost per trade for mutual funds is much lower than for individual investors.

Another cost saving to consider is the cost of your time. If you invest on your own, you'll need to educate yourself about your investment choices, make investment decisions, implement trades, and monitor your portfolio. Some investors enjoy doing these things. For those who don't, an investment company can probably do them more efficiently and professionally. The investment company also will provide you with regular reports to help you keep track your investments, including information on capital gains distributions, dividends, purchases, and sales.

By law, all funds are required to disclose fees and expenses in a standardized fee table at the front of the fund's prospectus, a document that must be provided to investors. The fee table must break out the fees and expenses. Generally these costs fall into two categories: those paid directly by shareholders and those paid for out of fund assets.

Shareholder Fees

Fees paid directly by shareholders may include one or more of the following:

- A one-time sales charge or commission assessed at the time of purchase
- A redemption fee when an investor sells shares back to the company
- An exchange fee when an investor transfers money from one fund to another
- An annual account maintenance fee charged to cover the costs of providing services to investors who maintain small accounts

Fund Expenses

In addition to the charges paid directly by investors, funds incur expenses that are deducted directly from the funds' assets before earnings are distributed. These expenses impose an indirect cost on investors, as they reduce the investors' returns. They may include some combination of the following:

- An annual management fee charged by the fund's investment advisor for managing the portfolio, usually calculated as a percentage of the assets being managed
- Annual distribution fees, commonly known as 12b-1 fees, to compensate sales professionals for marketing and advertising fund shares and, increasingly, to compensate professional advisors for services provided to fund shareholders at the time of purchase (limited to a maximum of 1 percent of fund assets per year)
- Other operational expenses, such as the costs of maintaining computerized customer account services, maintaining a website, record keeping, printing, and mailing

Comparing Costs

As mentioned, the prospectus for each fund must include a standardized fee table so that investors can compare the costs of investing in different funds. In addition, there are many other resources that can help you to make direct comparisons of those costs. Many websites also make this information available. In comparing the costs of different funds, it's useful to understand the differences between load and no-load funds and to be able to interpret the expense ratio.

Load versus No-Load   If you have to pay a commission or sales charge to buy mutual fund shares, this charge is called the *load*. Mutual funds are thus classified as either load, if they charge a fee, or no-load, if they don't.

Open-end mutual funds that are not offered through an employer-sponsored retirement plan often assess a **front-end load** at the time shares are purchased. The load can be as high as 8.5 percent of the purchase price of the shares. However, the average is around 5 percent, and some loads are as low as 2 percent. A fund with a load of 3 percent or less is sometimes called a *low-load fund*. Some load funds charge a **back-end load**, officially known as a *contingent deferred sales charge*, if you sell your shares back to the fund within a certain period after the date of purchase. Back-end loads often become smaller over time and are intended to encourage investors to hold onto their shares. For example, you might have a back-end load of 6 percent if you sell the first year, 5 percent the second year, and so on.

Paying a front-end load has the effect of reducing the amount of your investment. For example, if you have $1,000 to invest and the fund has a load of 5 percent, or $50, you'll be paying $1,000 but only getting $950 worth of shares. As with other types of transaction costs, you'll need to earn a rate of return on your investment that's sufficient to offset the costs and also compensate you for the risk that you bear. In other words, if you receive a dividend distribution this year in the amount of $50, you won't really have earned a positive return on your investment—you'll only be back to the $1,000 you started with. Because front-end loads are only charged at the time of purchase, a buy-and-hold investor is less affected by them. Over a 10- or 20-year holding period, a one-time $50 sales charge is relatively insignificant. But if you're an active investor, you should stick to no-load funds.

A **no-load fund** charges no commission at the time of purchase or at the time of sale. Although this is obviously going to save you money, you need to look carefully at what you're giving up by purchasing shares in this type of fund and at the fund's other expenses and charges to see if it is really a better deal than a low-load fund. Instead of charging investors at the time of purchase or sale, no-load funds tend to have higher management expenses. Whereas load funds generally provide investors with professional advice from brokers and financial planners (who receive a portion of the load charge), a no-load fund will have to either skimp on this service or charge you for it in a different way, often through 12b-1 fees. In order to be designated as no-load, however, a fund can't impose a 12b-1 charge of more than 0.25 percent.

Expense Ratios   You've seen that fund expenses include trading costs and operating expenses, as well as the costs of professional investment management, security analysis, and legal and accounting services. Even though all funds charge their investors for providing these services, some are much more efficient in managing costs than others and pass the savings on to investors. For this reason, it's important to take expenses into account when evaluating potential mutual fund purchases.

A fund's **expense ratio** is measured by the expenses per dollar of assets under management, as defined in **Equation 13.2**:

$$\text{Expense ratio} = \frac{\text{Total expenses}}{\text{Total assets in fund}} \tag{13.2}$$

All else being equal, the lower this ratio, the better. The expense ratio must be disclosed in the fund's prospectus. It's usually between 0.05 and 1.25 percent but can be as high as 2 percent. Because a fund's operating costs increase with its levels of research and trading, expense ratios for index funds are usually much lower than for actively managed funds. The average expense ratio for actively traded equity funds, as shown in **Figure 13.5**, is about 0.78 percent, compared with 0.09 percent for equity index funds. Similarly, actively managed bond funds have a 0.55 percent expense ratio compared with 0.07 for bond index funds. If the expenses generate higher returns due to the quality of analysis and security selection, or if they provide you with excellent investor advisory services and user-friendly website tools, it might be worth paying the higher cost.

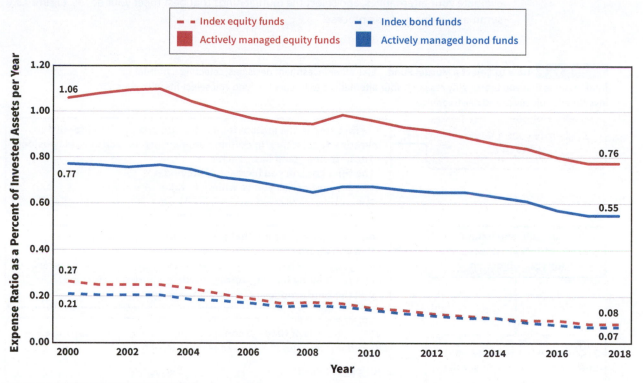

FIGURE 13.5 **Average Expense Ratios for Index Funds and Actively Managed Funds** Expense ratios have been steadily declining over time. Actively managed funds have higher expense ratios than index funds.

Source: Investment Company Institute, 2019 Factbook, www.ici.org.

Mutual funds held in employer-sponsored plans tend to carry relatively low expenses, in part because plan sponsors do the research and attempt to offer low-cost options for their employees. In 2018, for example, half of 401(k) equity funds had expense ratios less than 0.5 percent and 90 percent were less than 1.0 percent.

Mutual Fund Classes by Fee Structure

Just as a corporation can sell different types of stock (common and preferred), a mutual fund can offer a menu of share classes that differ in load and expenses. For example, Class A shares usually have front-end loads of 4 to 5 percent; Class B shares carry a back-end load and impose a 12b-1 fee; and Class C shares have no back-end load but carry a higher 12b-1 fee. Some funds also have Class D shares, which have a front-end load and a smaller 12b-1 fee.

If you like a particular mutual fund but aren't sure which class of shares to purchase, the most important consideration is your time horizon. Front-end loads are a one-time charge, whereas management fees and 12b-1 fees are incurred on an annual basis. Therefore, if you plan to hold the mutual fund shares for a long time, the class with a front-end load might be the best option, since you'll incur that charge only once. The back-end load is also less important if you plan to hold the shares beyond the point at which it disappears. A 5 percent load on Class A shares might seem like a lot, but you'll pay up to 1 percent per year in 12b-1 fees every year if you buy Class C shares instead.

Selecting and Evaluating Mutual Funds

Assume that you've decided to buy one or more mutual funds. Now comes the step that requires some homework on your part. With so many to choose from, how do you pick the funds that are best for you? The answer is to return to the basic decision-making process we've used throughout this course.

The Mutual Fund Selection Process

In selecting which mutual funds to purchase, you need to consider your goals, identify and evaluate your alternatives, and select the mutual funds that best meet your needs. **Figure 13.6** summarizes this decision process.

FIGURE 13.6 **How to Select a Mutual Fund** Like other investment decisions, selecting a mutual fund requires that you thoroughly research your alternatives to be sure the fund you select fits with your investment objectives and risk tolerance.

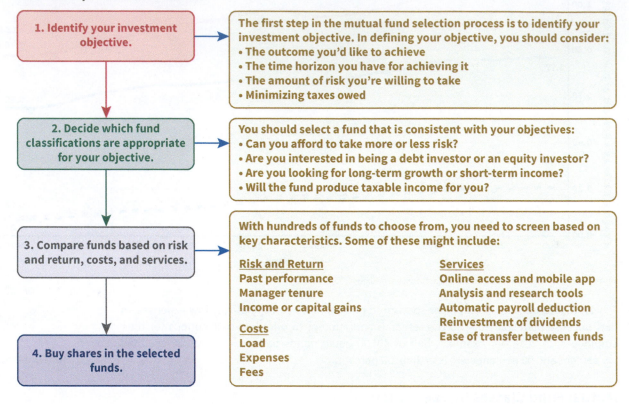

1. Identify your investment objective.

The first step in the mutual fund selection process is to identify your investment objective. In defining your objective, you should consider:
• **The outcome you'd like to achieve**
• **The time horizon you have for achieving it**
• **The amount of risk you're willing to take**
• **Minimizing taxes owed**

2. Decide which fund classifications are appropriate for your objective.

You should select a fund that is consistent with your objectives:
• **Can you afford to take more or less risk?**
• **Are you interested in being a debt investor or an equity investor?**
• **Are you looking for long-term growth or short-term income?**
• **Will the fund produce taxable income for you?**

3. Compare funds based on risk and return, costs, and services.

With hundreds of funds to choose from, you need to screen based on key characteristics. Some of these might include:

Risk and Return
Past performance
Manager tenure
Income or capital gains

Costs
Load
Expenses
Fees

Services
Online access and mobile app
Analysis and research tools
Automatic payroll deduction
Reinvestment of dividends
Ease of transfer between funds

4. Buy shares in the selected funds.

There are many resources to help you through the mutual fund selection process. For example, if you are making an investment decision for an IRA offered through a financial institution, you'll be provided with key comparison information, such as past performance and fees. In employer-sponsored plans, you'll usually be offered a selection of pre screened funds, so you'll primarily be making the Step 2 decision about investment classification. For personal investing, you'll need to do more of the homework on your own, and this can seem a little daunting. Fortunately, there are lots of Internet resources you can use. The mutual fund screener at **finance.yahoo.com**, for example, will identify a selection of funds based on your investment objective, ratings, and performance criteria.

Even after you have narrowed your selection to funds that meet your basic criteria, you will undoubtedly still have several funds to choose from. You might want to summarize the key information about each of the funds on your short list before making a final decision. You can use **Excel Worksheet 13.1** (Personal Financial Planner: Mutual Fund Comparison) for this purpose.

EXCEL WORKSHEET

See **Excel Worksheet 13.1** (**Personal Financial Planner: Mutual Fund Comparison**) in **WileyPLUS.**

How Many Funds?

Another issue to consider when you invest in mutual funds is the number of funds to invest in. Suppose, for example, that you've decided to invest $5,000 a year in mutual funds. If you have $5,000 invested in one fund, are you less diversified than if you have $2,500 each in two funds? The answer depends on what the funds are invested in. Many mutual fund investors assume that having several funds necessarily reduces their risk. If your money is in two large-cap growth funds, though, chances are good that the two funds are invested in many of the same stocks, so you won't actually be more diversified or less exposed to risk.

A **fund family** is an arrangement in which a single company, such as Fidelity Investments or Vanguard, operates a number of separately managed mutual funds with different investment objectives. Holding funds in different fund families can reduce the risk related to investment company failure or wrongdoing, though it may end up costing you a little more. Splitting your money between fund families won't reduce market risk, though, unless you invest in funds that include different asset classes and different securities within those asset classes.

There are some advantages to choosing a fund that is part of a fund family. Firms that offer families of funds often allow you to transfer money between funds within a family at little or no cost. So if you decide in the future that you'd like to invest some of your portfolio in a different type of fund, you can easily switch.

If you want to diversify your mutual fund holdings, instead of investing in a number of similar funds, you should buy shares in funds that focus on different areas. For example, you might invest in a large-cap equity fund, a small-cap equity fund, an international fund, an investment-grade bond fund, and a REIT. You might save money, either now or in the future when you want to rebalance, by sticking to the same fund family.

The Mutual Fund Transaction

Once you've decided what funds you want to buy, you must actually make the purchase. As you know, open-ended funds do not trade in the market, so you'll need to buy through a broker or from the company directly. The price you pay will be based on the net asset value, which is calculated at the end of the previous day.

Many investment companies keep their costs down by marketing their funds directly to consumers. You can contact these companies directly by phone or over the Internet to set up an account and purchase shares. About half of all funds are sold through brokers or through "financial supermarkets," such as Fidelity Investments or Charles Schwab & Co., which allow investors access to a large number of funds from different fund families under one umbrella. The greatest advantage of this type of arrangement for investors is that they can purchase from several fund families, switch money among them easily, and still receive a consolidated financial report from the supermarket company. In addition, many of these funds can be purchased without paying a sales commission because the supermarkets have made deals with the mutual fund companies to split the management fee. Not all funds sold in this way are offered on a no-fee basis, however, and some have relatively high fees.

Closed-end funds and ETFs are purchased like stocks and bonds through any brokerage trading platform. Each fund has a specific ticker symbol, and the price will change over the course of each day based on trading activity.

After Congress passed the Financial Services Modernization Act in 1999, banks and insurance companies obtained the right to create and market mutual funds. Today, most large financial institutions also have mutual fund holding companies, essentially corporations owned by the parent bank or insurer.

13.3 | Real Estate Investment

LEARNING OBJECTIVE 13.3
Identify the advantages and disadvantages of direct and indirect real estate investments.

Real estate can add value to your investment portfolio, increase your diversification, and provide less volatile returns over time. However, it's an asset class that requires a substantial amount of hands-on management and expertise, including legal knowledge, so it isn't for everyone. In this section, we consider your real estate investment alternatives, including your primary residence, investment properties, and indirect methods of participating in this market.

Your Home as an Investment

In Chapter 6, you learned how to select and purchase a home. Because housing is a basic need, we didn't approach buying a home as an investment decision in that chapter. Even if your home increases in value over time, the reality is that you can't easily access the returns from that investment without incurring substantial costs. If you sell the house, you'll have to buy another and incur the costs of the search and the move. If you access the built-up equity in the house by taking a home equity loan, you incur the costs of repayment and potential damage to your credit. Therefore, it's better to think of your home separately from your investment portfolio.

Even though we're not considering your home primarily as an investment asset, it clearly has investment characteristics that are both beneficial and risky to you. For example, during 2001 and 2002, when stock portfolios declined an average of 43 percent, home values in the United States increased 17.4 percent. For homeowners, increasing home equity served to reduce the impact of the stock market decline on aggregate household wealth. Unfortunately, many homeowners took advantage of low interest rates and easy credit availability to refinance their mortgages and access their equity for other purposes. Ultimately, this led to financial disaster when real estate values began to plummet in 2007 and many people found that their homes were worth less than what they owed on their mortgages.

We've seen in earlier chapters that home equity represents a large percentage of household wealth in America—probably too large a percentage from the standpoint of a diversified portfolio. However, if you think that your portfolio could benefit from additional investment in real estate, there are several alternatives for achieving this diversification. You can make a direct investment or one of several types of indirect investments, as we discuss next.

Direct Real Estate Investment

Real estate investments can be either direct or indirect. An investor who has made a **direct real estate investment** holds title to the actual property. By this definition, your home is a direct investment, but you can also invest directly in a second home, a rental apartment, vacant land, or commercial property. In contrast, you make an **indirect real estate investment** when you invest through a trustee or company that holds the title to the property. Earlier in the chapter, you saw an example of an indirect real estate investment—a real estate investment trust. Recall that a REIT investor buys a share in a trust and the trust manager uses the money to buy investment real estate. Mortgage-backed securities are another example of an indirect investment in real estate.

Advantages of Direct Real Estate Investment

ONLINE CALCULATOR DEMONSTRATION VIDEO

See **Online Calculator Demonstration Problem Video: Rental Property Investments** in **WileyPLUS**.

Your choices for direct real estate investment include many types of income-generating properties, as well as vacant land. An income property is one that will generate cash flows to you as the owner, usually in the form of rental income. As with other types of investments, investors in real estate generally expect to benefit from some combination of price appreciation and cash flow. Although non-income-generating real estate (such as a vacant lot) might still be expected to increase in value over time, it won't provide the positive cash-flow benefits you'd get with a rental property. For this reason, we concentrate our discussion on income properties.

After-Tax Cash Flows   When you invest in an income property, you hope it will produce a positive cash flow for you, either currently or in the future. You'll collect rents from your tenants, and you'll have to pay the expenses associated with the property from those dollars. These expenses are similar to those you incur as a homeowner—property taxes, repair and maintenance costs, insurance, and debt service on the mortgage, if any. Because the mortgage costs are usually fixed for the life of the loan, your property may begin with negative operating income, but it will eventually produce a positive cash flow as you raise the rent over time.

Your cash flow might also benefit from certain favorable tax rules that apply to rental properties. When you invest in rental property, you're allowed under tax laws to take a deduction against your net operating income for depreciation. Effectively, the IRS is allowing you to spread the cost of your initial investment in the building (not the land) over 27.5 years (39 years for commercial properties). If you purchase a residential rental property that includes a building worth $100,000, for example, you'll be able to deduct $100,000/27.5 = $3,636 per year from your rental income.

Other allowed deductions include interest expense (not including any repayment of principal on the loan), property taxes, insurance, utilities, and expenses for repairs and maintenance—basically any reasonable expenses that you incur in the management of the property. The net effect of all this is that many properties generate positive net cash flow to the investors but have negative taxable income. When you have *negative taxable income* (a tax loss) from an investment real estate property that you actively manage, you're allowed to deduct the losses against other taxable income up to a maximum of $25,000 per year, as long as your adjusted gross income (AGI) is less than $100,000. The allowed maximum loss deduction is phased out for AGIs between $100,000 and $150,000. If we assume that you meet the income limitation, the cash flow benefit of the tax deduction is the amount of the loss times your marginal tax rate.

The Tax Cuts and Jobs Act of 2017 gave residential rental owners a new tax benefit. Subject to some limitations, small business owners are allowed to deduct 20% of their net business income in calculating taxable income.

If you have a vacation home, you're allowed to rent it out up to 14 days per year without reporting the income. But if you go over the 14 days, the IRS considers the vacation home an investment property, and you must report the income. This can be an important rule if you occasionally rent out your home through **airbnb.com** or **vrbo.com**.

Price Appreciation and Leverage   As with any investment, you expect that the value of your direct real estate investment will increase over time. On average, the price of real estate has increased at a faster rate than the prices of other goods, making investing in it a good hedge against inflation. However, the appreciation of any individual property depends primarily on its location, which will determine its resale value and potential rental income. Therefore, your purchase decision must be made in light of surrounding real estate and, if applicable, the expected rental demand for the property in the future.

One of the great benefits of real estate investing is that you can often borrow a large proportion of the up-front cost at a fairly low interest rate. In general, if you can borrow at a low rate and invest in assets that earn more than they cost, you'll end up ahead of the game. The basic idea is that, if you have to put in only a small proportion of your equity investment up-front, your percentage return on investment will be larger than the actual change in value of the real estate. Financial professionals refer to the benefits of using low-cost debt as *leverage*. Because of leverage, you'll find that it's usually beneficial to finance the purchase of investment real estate with a mortgage. To calculate your return on investment, you can use **Equation 13.3**. We explain this calculation in **Demonstration Problem 13.2**. For more detailed analysis of a rental property, you can use **Excel Worksheet 13.2** (Personal Financial Planner: Real Estate Investment Return) to calculate your net cash flows and return on investment.

EXCEL WORKSHEET

See **Excel Worksheet 13.2** (Personal Financial Planner: Real Estate Investment Return) in **WileyPLUS**.

$$\frac{\text{Return on real}}{\text{estate investment}} = \frac{\text{Increase in value} + \text{Net rental income} - \text{Interest expense}}{\text{Beginning investment}} \qquad (13.3)$$

DEMONSTRATION PROBLEM 13.2 | Calculating Return on Investment for Income Properties

Problem

You purchased a condominium for $100,000, borrowing $75,000 of the cost (15-year amortized loan at 6 percent) and paying the rest from your own funds. You rent the property for $600 per month and incur no additional expenses the first year. By the end of the first year, the condo has increased 5 percent in value, to $105,000. Assuming that the total interest paid on your loan in the first year was $4,500, what is your total return on investment in the first year?

Strategy

To calculate your return on investment for the income property, use Equation 13.3.

Solution

Net rental income is your annual rental income less any expenses for maintenance and repairs, and interest expense is the total interest you've paid on your mortgage loan over the year. Note that this equation is almost the same as the equation for total yield we've used elsewhere. The differences are that you must deduct your continuing expenses and that you divide by your equity investment rather than the initial price of the property.

Calculate return on the investment as follows:

$$\frac{\text{Return on real}}{\text{estate investment}} = \frac{\text{Increase in value} + \text{Net rental income} - \text{Interest expense}}{\text{Beginning investment}}$$

$$= \frac{\$5,000 + (\$600 \times 12) - \$4,500}{\$25,000}$$

$$= \frac{\$7,700}{\$25,000} = 0.308, \text{ or } 30.8\%$$

Of course, in real life, you would probably have additional expenses to subtract, such as property taxes, repairs, homeowners' association fees, and other expenses. So your actual return would likely be somewhat lower than 30.8 percent.

Disadvantages of Direct Real Estate Investment

Direct real estate investments can earn high returns, but as you know, investments that earn higher returns usually do so because of their higher level of risk. Thus, you shouldn't be surprised to learn that direct real estate investment involves several disadvantages and that some of these disadvantages are related to risk.

Large Initial Investment   To invest in real estate, you have to pay a substantial amount of money up-front to cover the down payment (typically, 25 to 30 percent for investment properties) and closing costs.

Lack of Liquidity   Whereas stocks, bonds, and mutual funds can be traded fairly easily, there isn't an active secondary market where you can sell your direct real estate investments. In any given area, only a limited number of potential buyers exist, particularly for more expensive properties, and it typically takes three to six months to find a buyer and close the deal. Even if you do find a buyer, it will be difficult to say whether you've gotten a fair price for the property. The real estate market isn't as efficient as the stock and bond markets, where thousands of investors influence the market price of a given security. When only one or two people are interested in your property, you're likely to get a lower price than you'd like.

Reduced Diversification   Because real estate requires a large dollar investment, you'll inevitably be less diversified, particularly when you consider that you may already have a home in the same geographic area. This leaves you more exposed to risks related to the local economy. What if the major employer in your town suddenly decides to close its plant? Your home value will undoubtedly decrease as the workers pull up roots to move elsewhere, reducing the demand for housing in the area. At the same time, the value of your investment property will also decline, causing a double hit on your net worth.

If you make real estate investments in several geographic areas, you'll increase your diversification within this asset class. Nevertheless, your portfolio will still be overly exposed to risks that are peculiar to the real estate market.

Transaction Costs   Relative to other types of investments, real estate has very high transaction costs. Buyers incur substantial closing costs, as discussed in Chapter 6. Sellers, in addition to their closing costs, can usually expect to pay a commission of 6 to 7 percent on developed property and 10 percent on vacant land. Mortgage interest rates for investment properties also tend to be higher than those for owner-occupied properties, and lenders require lower loan-to-value ratios.

Hassles   If you own rental real estate, you must be prepared to deal with the hassles of day-to-day management of the property. These can include anything from legal liability for injuries to people on your property to eviction of problematic tenants. Although you can pay a real estate management company to do some of this for you, the costs of such services are usually fairly high—often one month's rent per year.

Even with the disadvantages, the returns generated by many direct real estate investments are a strong lure. One reason may be that people feel that they understand real estate better than they understand financial investments like stocks and bonds.

Reflection Question 2

What are the most important factors you would consider in deciding whether to own residential rental properties in the future, and why?

Indirect Real Estate Investment

You can get many of the benefits of real estate investment without incurring the costs and risks of direct investment by making indirect investments through real estate investment trusts, mortgage-backed securities, and limited partnerships. These investments provide better liquidity and, because you can make indirect investments in smaller increments, you'll be able to better diversify your holdings.

Real Estate Investment Trusts

Real estate investment trusts (REITs), introduced earlier in this chapter, are probably the most attractive indirect real estate investment alternative. However, like other mutual funds, REITs can be very different from one another, so you need to do your research to find out who is managing a particular fund and how well it has performed over the years. If you're interested in investing in REITs, you can get more information from the National Association of Real Estate Investment Trusts, an industry trade group.

Mortgage-Backed Securities

Another way to invest indirectly in the real estate market is by purchasing bonds that are backed by pools of mortgages. For example, many funds specialize in bonds backed by mortgages guaranteed by the Government National Mortgage Association (GNMA), or "Ginnie Mae." Note that although the funds are indirectly related to real estate, their performance is highly dependent on market interest rates, so they are more closely related to the bond market than the real estate market.

Limited Partnership

In a **limited partnership**, several investors (the limited partners) put up the money to buy a property, such as a shopping mall or apartment complex, and a general partner manages the investment. The limited partners are so called because they have limited liability—the most they can lose is their original investment, much like a corporate stockholder. At the same time, they have no right or obligation to participate in the management of the property. In return for their invested dollars, they receive a proportional distribution of the net cash flows generated by the investment. These cash flows may be similar to those of a direct real estate investment. The tax benefits of participating in a limited partnership are not as good, however, because real estate investors must *actively* manage their investments to be able to take deductions for tax losses.

13.4 Speculative Investments

LEARNING OBJECTIVE 13.4

Explain why investments in precious metals, gems, collectibles, cryptocurrencies, and derivatives are speculative.

If you're a novice investor, the investment alternatives discussed in this section are not a great choice for your portfolio. In general, they are too speculative. Your goal is to build your wealth over time so that you can achieve your financial goals, but speculation exposes you to the risk of losing it all. Even though higher risk often implies the potential for higher returns, there's a limit to how much risk you should take with your nest egg. Some people are wealthy enough that they can afford to lose, but most are not.

Speculative investments include precious metals and gems, collectibles and art, crypto-currencies, and derivative securities. In this section, we describe each of these categories of investments.

Precious Metals and Gems

Investments in precious metals such as gold, silver, and platinum or in precious stones such as diamonds, sapphires, and rubies can be made directly or indirectly. These investments involve high up-front costs and provide no regular cash flow, so their returns are unlikely to exceed those of other investment alternatives. They also are not very liquid assets because it may be difficult to find a buyer when you need to sell, and you may be exposed to high transactions costs for doing so.

Although it might seem like your personal jewelry collection is an investment when you consider how much you paid for each piece, the resale market for jewelry is relatively thin, so in most cases you probably won't be able to recoup what you paid. Furthermore, the potential for fraud is fairly high because most buyers can't tell a diamond from a cubic zirconium. For this reason, "buyer beware" is a warning that you should take to heart in this market.

Investments in gold and other precious metals are often marketed as good ways to achieve diversification. Gold values tend to increase during times of political uncertainty and inflation and decrease when economic conditions are more stable. In general, however, the average returns on these investments are so low that they drag down overall portfolio returns in good times.

Let's look at an example. During the recession of 2007–2009, gold sellers advertised that gold was the only "safe" place to invest money. They argued that investing in gold would provide protection against looming inflation, which they claimed would inevitably result from federal stimulus spending and rising debt.

Apparently lots of investors found this line of reasoning compelling—the price of gold rose from about $300 to more than $1,700 in about a decade, far surpassing returns on any other asset class. Unfortunately, inflation never turned out to be a problem, and many investors bought gold after its price had already gone up considerably. When the gold bubble eventually burst, many were left with significant losses.

To learn more about whether gold is a good investment if you're worried about inflation, see **Interactive: Gold versus Inflation**. You can use **Excel Worksheet 13.3** (Personal Financial Planner: Return on Gold Investments) to estimate how much you would have earned on a gold investment over different time periods.

If you want to invest directly in gold or other precious metals, you can buy coins or bars from dealers or banks, paying a commission of at least 2 percent. When you sell the metal, you'll pay another commission fee. Direct investment in metals also means that you'll need to pay for a safe place to store it—it's not a good idea to have gold bars sitting around the house, and your homeowner's insurance will not cover them if they're lost or stolen. Alternatively, you can participate in precious metals by purchasing shares of gold or silver mutual funds or stock in mining companies. However, keep in mind that the performance of these investments might not perfectly track the value of the underlying metals. Over the 2000s, gold mining stocks and mutual funds that invested in gold generally increased at a lower rate than gold prices.

INTERACTIVE

See **Interactive: Gold versus Inflation** in **WileyPLUS.**

EXCEL WORKSHEET

See **Excel Worksheet 13.3** (Personal Financial Planner: Return on Gold Investments) in **WileyPLUS.**

Collectibles and Art

Do you have a collection of rare comic books or perhaps some original pieces of art? Some people invest in rare coins, vintage cars, or antique quilts. These types of investments serve a dual purpose—you get enjoyment out of them today (think of it as a dividend that isn't taxed), and they might have value in the future. Like gold and gems, these collectibles don't generate any form of regular cash flow (unless you can charge people to come see them), so you're relying totally on their appreciation in value over time. This appreciation in value depends on supply and demand, as well as collector fads. In addition, investors who must go through dealers, as is often the case with art and antiquities, pay very high transaction costs. As with previous metals, investors are exposed to significant liquidity risk.

Although historically the resale market for collectibles was small, making them a fairly risky investment, the Internet has changed the collectible marketplace for the better. If you have a rare Spiderman #1 in mint condition or an original 1950s Barbie still in its original packaging, the odds are good that you can find an investor out there who will buy it from you. But what it's worth will be driven by a more efficient market, and there might be several other 1950s Barbies that are in better condition than yours. Although you can buy or sell just about anything on eBay and other auction sites, the Internet is still best suited for small items that don't require close examination to determine their value.

In deciding whether to invest in collectibles, you should consider the risk and return factors we've previously identified. And don't forget to take the time value of money into consideration when you evaluate your return on investment. If you bought a collectible Barbie in 1995 for $100 and it's worth $200 in 2020, you've doubled your initial investment, but your annualized return is much lower. After all, you've held the investment for 25 years.

As we've seen before, you can calculate the average change in value of a collectible, which is equivalent in this case to your annualized return on investment, using **Equation 13.4**:

$$\text{Annualized return on investment} = \left(\frac{\text{End price}}{\text{Purchase price}}\right)^{1/n} - 1 \qquad (13.4)$$

where n is the number of years you've held the investment. It's easier, however, to use your financial calculator to find the annual return. Enter the purchase price for PV, the current market value for FV, and the number of years for N, and solve for I. (Don't forget to enter the present value as a negative number, because it's an outflow to you.) Using this method, we find that the Barbie "investment" earned an average annual return of less than 3 percent, about as much as the inflation rate over that time period. If you had put the same $100 in a 25-year bond in 1995, your return would have been at least double that amount. **Demonstration Problem 13.3** offers more practice in using Equation 13.4.

DEMONSTRATION PROBLEM 13.3 | Estimating Return on Art and Collectibles

Problem

Sunflowers, the Van Gogh painting shown in **Figure 13.7**, was sold at auction in 1987 for a record price of $39.7 million. If the previous owner had purchased the painting in 1889 (98 years before) for $125, what was the rate of return?

FIGURE 13.7 **Van Gogh's *Sunflowers***
This well-known painting sold at auction for almost $40 million.

Universal History Archive/Universal Images Group/Getty Images

Strategy

Calculate the holding period return and annualized return on investment.

Solution

In previous chapters, you learned that Holding period return = (End price/Purchase price) − 1. The previous owner's original investment return is ($39,700,000/$125) − 1) = 317,599%. This is such a large multiple that it seems like a real windfall for the owner. However, using Equation 13.4, you find that he earned an average of 13.8 percent per year ($317,599^{1/98} - 1$). This is still a good return, but it might not be high enough to compensate for the risk of holding onto a piece of art for 98 years.

Cryptocurrencies

Cryptocurrency is a relatively new type of investment asset. Some well-known examples are Bitcoin, Ethereum, Litecoin, and Libra. Cryptocurrency is a digital asset originally intended to be a medium of exchange or a store of value similar to the U.S. dollar or the Japanese yen. Users can make transparent, yet anonymous, peer-to-peer transactions throughout the world with lower transaction costs than with some other electronic payment systems. Some people believe that increased privacy, security, and independence from government intervention make cryptocurrencies superior to existing currencies.

Individual investors can buy and sell various cryptocurrencies directly through specialty exchanges, or they can invest through mutual funds that hold the currencies. As with other speculative investments, currencies do not produce any current income to the investor, so the return on investment must come from an increase in the price of the asset. This might happen, for example, if the demand for the currency exceeded the supply. Prices might fall if investors lost trust in a particular cryptocurrency or the cryptocurrency market as a whole.

Since the initial creation of Bitcoin in 2009, more than 4,000 different cryptocurrencies have been introduced, and market prices have fluctuated wildly. For example, in 2017, the price of a Bitcoin increased from $800 to $18,000, but in the next year it fell below $4,000. There are very few investments that can expose you to that level of risk in such a short amount of time.

To be a viable medium of exchange, a currency needs to be widely accepted, and users need to be able to convert to other currencies or make purchases as needed without facing extreme price changes. Neither of these two criteria appear to be met, and the sheer number of different cryptocurrencies make it less likely that any one of them will emerge as a preferred replacement for cash in the United States. However, in some emerging economies and rural areas without access to reliable banking services, cryptocurrency may be preferable to local currencies.

Financial Derivatives

You may recall from Chapter 11 that there's a class of widely traded securities called derivatives, so named because they derive their value from some underlying asset. The best known of these are futures and options.

A futures contract is one in which you promise to buy or sell the underlying security at some point in the future at a price that is determined today. The underlying security might be a commodity, such as a bushel of corn, or a financial security, such as a Treasury bill.

An option contract is similar except that it gives you the *right* to buy or sell in the future at a specified price but doesn't require you to go through with the purchase or sale. The right expires on a future date specified in the option contract. A call option is the right to buy something in the future, and a put option is the right to sell something in the future.

Advantages of Investing in Derivatives

The advantage of investments in derivatives is that you can participate in the price movements of the underlying security without buying the security itself. For example, suppose that, for $2 per share, you can buy a call option that gives you the right to buy a particular stock for $100 per share when the actual price of the stock is $97. You're hoping the stock price will rise as much as possible over $102 (the price of the share plus the cost of the option) before the expiration of the option. Let's say that the price goes up to $103. You can then exercise the option to buy at $100 and immediately sell at the market price of $103, making $1 per share. Your return on investment is 50 percent, because you've made a profit of $1 on an investment of $2, which is what you paid for the option. If, instead, you had bought the actual stock for $97 and the price rose to $103, your return on investment would have been only 6.2 percent ($6/$97 = 0.062).

Risks of Investing in Derivatives

When the price of the underlying asset changes in your favor, you might realize a much greater return by investing in a derivative security than by investing in the underlying asset itself, because the amount you have to spend up-front is low relative to the cost of the underlying asset. However, the risk you take for this extra return is substantial. You actually risk losing your entire investment. In the example above, if the stock price had stayed at $97, you wouldn't have exercised the option, so you would have paid $2 and gotten nothing (a loss of 100 percent of your investment). If instead you'd bought the underlying stock, you'd still own the $97 share, and it might increase in value in the future.

Futures and options are financial investments that require in-depth understanding of the markets and of the investments that the derivatives are based on. Investors who get into this market without the appropriate expertise can lose a lot of money—and even supposed experts have lost billions of dollars (of other people's money, for the most part). In most of these cases, the losses occurred because the investors didn't fully understand what they were doing and became greedy after a few lucky investments. In other cases, additional investments were made to cover up losses made on earlier investments, and the problems snowballed.

Using Derivatives to Reduce Risk

Although trading in futures and options is often speculative, these securities can also be used to *reduce* risk in your underlying portfolio. If you invest in a derivative contract that will increase in value when something else in your portfolio decreases in value, you are said to be hedging. This is an investment strategy that reduces the overall risk of your portfolio by protecting your assets from big swings in value. For example, many farmers in the United States reduce their risks from uncertain future crop prices by selling futures contracts to lock in the price they will get for their crop at harvest time. For these investors, the futures contract is not speculative because they are promising to sell something they will actually have. For corn futures investors who are not farmers, however, selling a futures contract is just a way of speculating on the price of corn.

If the concept of derivative investing doesn't seem crystal-clear to you after reading this brief introduction, don't be surprised. Derivatives are complex and often risky securities that take many years to truly understand. Although greater risk might translate into greater returns, there is no guarantee that you'll earn those returns. You almost certainly will not be successful with these investments unless you invest in education.

Should you consider alternative investments? Before deciding to get into riskier investments as a means of making bigger profits, take a close look at your financial plan. Have you met all your security needs? Have you accumulated sufficient wealth toward your larger financial goals? Have you adequately diversified your portfolio into various other asset classes? What are the opportunity costs of making an investment in this area—the costs of liquidating other investments, the possibility of reduced diversification, the tax consequences? Do you have the time to educate yourself about these investments? And most important, can you afford to lose the money?

Summary

Learning Objectives Review

LEARNING OBJECTIVE 13.1   Distinguish different types of investment companies based on key characteristics.

An **investment company** sells shares to investors and uses the funds to purchase a portfolio of securities. The investors have an equity interest in the pool of assets and share in the cash flows generated by and the capital appreciation of the fund's assets.

- The value of a share in an investment company is usually reported as the **net asset value**, calculated using **Equation 13.1**:

$$\text{Net asset value} = \frac{\text{Market value of assets} - \text{Market value of liabilities}}{\text{Number of shares outstanding}}$$

- Types of investment companies include **open-end** and **closed-end funds, exchange-traded funds (EFTs), unit investment trusts (UITs),** and **real estate investment trusts (REITs)**.
- Funds are commonly classified by investment objectives, such as capital appreciation, income, and preservation of capital. Funds may be called **growth, income, balanced, value, life-cycle,** or **target-date funds**.

- Funds may also be classified based on portfolio composition, usually determined by asset class, industry representation, and index benchmark. Examples include **sector funds, international funds, global funds,** and **socially responsible investing (SRI) funds**.

LEARNING OBJECTIVE 13.2   Explain the advantages and costs of investing in mutual funds versus individual securities.

The process of mutual fund investing involves screening mutual fund alternatives to identify those with investment objectives that are a good match with your time horizon, wealth-building objectives, and tax preferences.

- Key characteristics for evaluating funds include risk and return, costs, and services.
- Investing in funds that are part of a **fund family** makes it easy to move money to other funds as your investment objectives change.

- The advantages of investing in mutual funds include increased diversification, reduced transactions costs, greater liquidity, and professional money management.

- Costs of investing in mutual funds include fees paid directly by shareholders, such as **front-end load** and **back-end load**, and fees paid by the fund before making distributions to shareholders. **No-load funds** do not charge these fees but may charge other kinds of fees.

- The fund costs are disclosed in the prospectus and are reported as an **expense ratio** measured according to **Equation 13.2**:

$$\text{Expense ratio} = \frac{\text{Total expenses}}{\text{Total assets in fund}}$$

LEARNING OBJECTIVE 13.3   Identify the advantages and disadvantages of direct and indirect real estate investments.

You can invest in real estate either directly, by purchasing and managing property yourself, or indirectly, by owning an interest in a **limited partnership** or REIT that invests in real estate.

- Real estate investing can provide a regular source of cash flow, potential tax deductions, price appreciation, and leverage benefits. Investing in real estate can be either a **direct** or an **indirect real estate investment**.

- The rate of return on a real estate investment in a given year can be calculated using **Equation 13.3**:

$$\text{Return on real estate investment} = \frac{\text{Increase in value + Net rental income − Interest expense}}{\text{Beginning investment}}$$

- The disadvantages of investing in real estate are large up-front costs, low liquidity, high transaction costs, and reduced diversification.

LEARNING OBJECTIVE 13.4 Explain why investments in precious metals, gems, collectibles, cryptocurrencies, and derivatives are speculative.

Investing in precious metals, gems, collectibles, cryptocurrencies, and derivatives is not usually recommended for the average investor. All of these investments are considered riskier than other investment alternatives and are deemed speculative.

- Investments such as metals, gems, collectibles, and art require high up-front costs, provide no regular cash flow, and incur storage costs. When you invest in them, you are simply hoping that the price will go up.

- When an investment does not generate any cash flow, you can estimate your annual return using **Equation 13.4**:

$$\text{Average annual return on investment} = \left(\frac{\text{End price}}{\text{Purchase price}}\right)^{1/n} - 1$$

- A cryptocurrency is a digital asset intended to be used for transactions around the world. The large number of different cryptocurrencies and lack of price stability makes cryptocurrency a very risky choice for individual investment portfolios.

- Derivative investments, such as option and futures contracts, have smaller up-front costs than buying the underlying asset directly. This can, in some circumstances, make it possible to earn a higher rate of return. The trade-off is that derivatives also expose you to the risk of losing your entire investment.

Excel Worksheets

13.1 Personal Financial Planner: Mutual Fund Comparison

13.2 Personal Financial Planner: Real Estate Investment Return

13.3 Personal Financial Planner: Return on Gold Investments

Key Terms

WileyPLUS

Practice Questions to check your understanding, Peer-to-Peer Videos, Interactives, and many other resources are available in WileyPLUS.

Concept Review Questions

1. Describe the similarities and differences between open-end and closed-end funds.

2. How is a mutual fund's net asset value calculated, and what is its relationship to share price?

3. Identify the main advantages of mutual fund investing for individual investors.

4. In what ways can a mutual fund provide better diversification of your portfolio than you can get by investing in individual stocks and bonds?

5. Identify the major categories of expenses paid by shareholders in mutual funds.

6. Why do some mutual funds have much higher expense ratios than other mutual funds?

7. What is the difference between a front-end load and a back-end load?

8. Explain the difference between each of the following pairs of mutual fund classifications:

   a. Growth versus value

   b. Large-cap versus small-cap

   c. Equity versus debt

9. What is a life-cycle fund, and why is this type of fund useful from a financial planning perspective?

10. Describe the process you should use to select mutual funds for your portfolio.

11. In what ways is your home an investment? What impact does your home have on your portfolio diversification?

12. What are the advantages and disadvantages of investing in rental properties?

13. Identify the various ways to invest indirectly in real estate. Explain why these might be better for the average investor, as compared with direct real estate investing?

14. Explain what it means to say that investments in precious metals, gems, collectibles, cryptocurrencies, and derivatives are speculative.

15. In what ways are investors in precious metals, collectibles, and gems exposed to liquidity risk?

Application Problems

1. The ABC Small-Cap Fund, a closed-end fund, has total assets of $240 million, total liabilities of $10 million, and 15 million shares outstanding. Calculate the net asset value per share.

2. You estimate that the net asset value per share of a particular closed-end fund is $15. If the current share price is $17, is this price a good deal? Explain your reasoning.

3. The Verity Large-Cap Value Fund has total assets of $50 million, total liabilities of $500,000, and 5 million shares outstanding. If you bought shares in this fund one year ago when the net asset value was $8 per share, what was the annual percentage increase in the net asset value?

4. Cruella owns shares in a fund that has a net asset value of $40 per share. The expenses are $1 per share. What is the expense ratio?

5. You are buying 50 shares of the Xavier Fund at $35 per share. The sales charge is 4 percent. How much commission will you pay?

6. You plan to invest $10,000 in a no-load fund that has a 0.5 percent expense ratio. The net asset value of the fund is $100 million. How much will you pay directly in shareholder fees?

7. You plan to invest $10,000 in a no-load fund that has a 0.5 percent expense ratio. The net asset value of the fund is $100 million. How much are the annual fund expenses (in dollars)?

8. You purchased $3,500 worth of shares in a mutual fund that does not have a front-end load. However, there is a back-end load of 5 percent if you sell in the first year, and it decreases one percentage point per year. You sell $1,000 worth of shares in the third year. How much will your back-end load be?

9. For each of the following people, suggest some mutual fund classifications consistent with the stated investment objective and time horizon. Explain your reasoning.

   a. 20-year-old woman saving for a down payment to buy a home within 5 years

   b. 60-year-old retired couple looking for a regular source of income

   c. 30-year-old couple saving for their 5-year-old child's college education

10. You bought 60 shares of a mutual fund one year ago for $50 per share. The front-end load is 5 percent. The fund paid $1.50 per share in dividends during the year. If the fund's net asset value increased 12 percent during the year, what is the percent return for the year?

11. You own 100 shares of a mutual fund that you purchased two years ago for $31 per share. The shares currently are worth $36 each, and the fund has paid you a dividend of $2 per year. What is your return on investment for the whole two-year holding period and your annualized return on investment?

12. You purchased a rental property for $180,000 at the beginning of last year. The net rental income for the year was $12,000. The value of the property increased to $190,000 by the end of that year. If you paid cash for the property (no mortgage), what is your return on investment for the first year?

13. You purchased a rental property for $180,000 at the beginning of last year. The net rental income for the year was $12,000. The value of the property increased to $190,000 by the end of that year. If you borrowed 50 percent of the purchase price from a local bank to finance the purchase, paying 6 percent, interest-only, what was your return on investment for the first year?

14. You purchased a rental property for $180,000 at the beginning of last year. The net rental income for the year was $12,000. What expenses will you probably incur if you choose to sell the property for $190,000, after one year. Assuming that you paid cash for the property, how will this affect your return on investment?

15. You bought an original painting at an art auction 10 years ago for $1,000. You have been offered a price of $2,500 for it today. If you sell it for that price, what was your annual return on investment?

16. You bought one bitcoin in January 2018 for $14,000 and sold it two years later for $10,000. What was your holding period return and your annualized rate of return?

Case Applications

1. Elena Musinski is divorced and has two daughters, ages five and six. Her ex-husband is paying $100 per child per week in child support in accordance with a court order. Because her daughters are in school full-time, Elena has returned to work as a high-school math teacher at a salary of $50,000 per year. Since her income is enough to support the family, she has decided to put the child support money in a college fund for the girls. For the last year, she's been depositing the money in a savings account earning only 1 percent annual interest, and she's accumulated $10,600. She realizes that she needs to invest this money to earn a better return.

    a. What is Elena's specific investment goal and what types of mutual funds might be appropriate to meet this goal? Should Elena consider tax-exempt investments? Explain.

    b. Elena is considering keeping the money in a bank savings account that earns 1 percent after taxes. Assuming that Elena's ex-husband will continue to pay the same amount of child support for each daughter until she reaches the age of 18, calculate how much Elena will be able to accumulate using this investment strategy. For ease of computation, you can assume end-of-year child support payments of $5,200 per year for each child. What is the risk of this type of investment strategy?

    c. What difference would it make if Elena chooses to invest in a balanced mutual fund that earns 6 percent after taxes? Assuming that Elena's ex-husband will continue to pay the same amount of child support for each daughter until she reaches the age of 18, calculate how much Elena will accumulate. For ease of computation, you can assume end-of-year child support payments of $5,200 per year for each child.

2. Right before the financial crisis that began in 2007, Gabe Lopez made the big decision to retire at the age of 60 from his 35-year career as manager of the auto parts department at a large dealership. He and his wife, Della, also 60, decided that she would continue to work until she would qualify for Social Security benefits at 62. Gabe took the money from his 401(k) retirement plan and bought shares in a long-term, AAA-rated corporate bond fund, because he wanted to be conservative with their retirement nest egg. Stock market declines earlier in the decade had reinforced his belief that stocks are too risky. At the time he made this decision, 20-year AAA corporate bonds were yielding about 5 percent. Because they owned their home free and clear, the Lopezes figured that the income from their bond fund, combined with Della's income, would be plenty to live

on. The first year, Gabe's mutual funds generated $30,000 in income before taxes. Although this was about of half what he had earned at his job, he was pleased to find that they didn't have to dip into the principal to support their lifestyle. As rates on AAA corporate bonds fell over the next few years, the value of his bond portfolio shares went up a little, but the annual interest income went down. He and Della were confused—they thought that bonds were safe investments. Gabe recently read an article that warned of a coming crash in bond values. He wondered if they should switch to a different type of investment.

    a. Does mutual fund investing make sense for the Lopezes, compared with investing directly in bonds or stocks? Explain.

    b. Is the asset allocation chosen by the Lopezes appropriate for their life situation and risk tolerance? Explain.

    c. Explain why the value of the Lopezes' bond mutual fund went up when interest rates went down.

    d. If the Fed acts to increase interest rates, will the Lopezes' bond portfolio value take a big hit? Why or why not?

    e. Would it be a good idea for the couple to move their money to a different type of investment? Why or why not? If you think they should, what would you recommend they invest in?

    f. Do you think that a financial planner would have recommended that the Lopezes put 100 percent of their money in a bond mutual fund in 2007? Explain.

3. Janelle McClatchey is a single lawyer, age 30. Her income is substantially more than her expenses, and she wants to begin an investment plan. Although she has considered investing in stocks, she doesn't feel that she has the expertise or time to make well-informed decisions. She has a 401(k) plan with her employer in which she has accumulated $50,000 in a diversified stock mutual fund. She thinks she'd like to leverage her knowledge of the legal aspects of real estate by using her savings to invest in some rental property. Janelle is considering the purchase of a small house that has two rental units and is located near the local university campus. She estimates that she'll need to invest about $10,000 for new carpet, paint, and a few repairs before she can rent the apartments. Her rental income will be $15,000 per year. The purchase price of the property is $145,000. She has $42,000 to cover the $3,000 closing costs, remodeling costs, and a 20 percent down payment. She'll finance the rest with a 6 percent mortgage. Interest on the mortgage for the first year will total $6,921.

a. How much will Janelle's mortgage payment be, assuming a fixed-rate mortgage with monthly payments for 30 years, not including property taxes and insurance?

b. Assuming Janelle incurs $2,500 in expenses per year, calculate her pretax net cash flow for the first year, after financing costs.

c. If the property increases in value to $165,000 after one year, and the apartments were rented for the full 12 months, what is Janelle's pretax return on investment, taking into account the additional investment she has made in the property?

d. Is this investment more or less risky for Janelle than stocks and bonds? Explain.

e. Given her life situation, is Janelle sufficiently diversified? Explain your reasoning.

4. Barbie is one of the most popular categories of collectibles. Although literally millions of "normal" Barbie dolls have been sold worldwide, Mattel, Inc., regularly produces "limited edition" Barbie collectibles, many of which cost $200 or more. These are marketed to collectors as "investments." Beverly has been collecting Barbies for the last ten years and estimates that she has more than 1,000 dolls. An investment advisor has suggested that she sell them all and invest in the stock market instead. Beverly shows him a Mattel, Inc., book that gives the current market values of her dolls and verifies that her "portfolio" has increased in value over time with no risk.

a. Explain to Beverly why the Mattel, Inc., book is not an accurate measure of the value of her portfolio.

b. Identify the risks Beverly is exposed to when she invests in Barbies.

c. Assume that Beverly bought a Holiday Barbie for $50 ten years ago. If she sells it this year for $75, incurring $5 in transaction costs, what is her holding period return and her annualized return on investment?

d. What are the advantages and disadvantages of a large auction market like ebay.com? Before eBay was created, how would Beverly have sold her dolls? Do you think that they would have been worth more or less?

e. If collectibles make up about 10 percent of Beverly's investments, with the rest invested in diversified tax-deferred retirement accounts, evaluate whether her investment in Barbies is a good use of her funds.

CHAPTER 14

Estate Planning

s5iztok/iStock/Getty Images

Feature Story

Charlie is a baby macaw. His owner, Sam, a second-year college student, bought him at a local pet shop last year. Although Sam didn't know it at the time, a bird like Charlie might actually outlive its owner. Unfortunately, thousands of people die every year without having made arrangements for the care of their pets. Fido and Fluffy might have several good years left, but if you don't provide for the costs of their care, your heirs may be inclined to give them away or have them put to sleep. As a responsible pet owner, Sam should develop an estate plan that will take care of Charlie's needs in the event of his death.

Sam doesn't need to go to the extremes of millionaire Leona Helmsley, who left her dog Trouble $12 million when she passed away in 2007. A judge later reduced the amount to $2 million. When Trouble died in 2011, the remainder went into the family trust for Leona's other heirs. However, Sam should identify a guardian who would be willing to take care of Charlie, and he should establish a modest trust fund for his care. At Sam's age, a small life insurance policy would be an easy way to take care of this cost. Believe it or not, pet estate planning is a growing business. There are even "pet retirement homes" for animals whose owners have enough money to spend on their furry and feathered friends.

When you're young, have no dependents, and haven't yet accumulated a lot of wealth, it's tempting to think that a chapter about estate planning won't be very useful or applicable to you. While it's true that some information in this chapter might be important only until you pass the final exam, there are a few topics that you should pay close attention to, particularly if you have any dependents, whether human or animal. You may also be interested in better understanding estate planning if you have parents or grandparents who need to do some advance planning. It's not always easy to get family members to talk about planning for death, but mentioning your class content to them may open the door to a productive family discussion.

In general, estate planning is about taking care of the needs of other people. After all, you'll be dead before any of your plan takes effect. Most people would prefer that their assets and wealth go to their intended beneficiaries rather than the government. So an important component of estate planning is taking steps that will transfer your assets according to your wishes and minimize post-death hassles for your loved ones. For wealthier people, estate planning is also about minimizing taxes that could be owed after their death. In this chapter, you'll get a broad overview of the estate-planning process and the key components of an estate plan. The chapter covers the basics, such as what you should include in your will and living will. Note, though, that you'll need to hire an estate-planning attorney to draft the final documents. The chapter also explains recent changes to federal estate tax law that make it highly unlikely that you'll be subject to estate taxes in the future.

LEARNING OBJECTIVES	TOPICS	DEMONSTRATION PROBLEMS
14.1 Identify key components of an estate plan, and determine whether you need one.	**14.1 What Is Estate Planning?** • The Estate-Planning Process • Who Needs an Estate Plan? • Key Components of an Estate Plan • Organizing Financial and Legal Documents	
14.2 Explain the importance of having a valid will and arranging in advance for easy transfer of assets to your heirs.	**14.2 Methods of Transferring Property** • Preparing a Valid Will • Passing Property Outside a Will	
14.3 Explain recent changes to federal estate and gift taxation laws that significantly reduce the number of estates that have to pay these taxes.	**14.3 Estate and Gift Taxes** • Federal Gift Taxes • Federal Estate Taxes • State Death Taxes	
14.4 Understand how trusts, gifts, and charitable contributions can reduce estate taxes.	**14.4 Reducing Taxes Through Trusts and Gifts** • When Are Trusts Useful? • Types of Trusts • Gifting Alternatives	

14.1 What Is Estate Planning?

LEARNING OBJECTIVE 14.1

Identify key components of an estate plan, and determine whether you need one.

In recent chapters, we've focused primarily on accumulating wealth to meet household financial goals. The objective of estate planning is to distribute your wealth according to your wishes after your death and to plan for the care and financial well-being of your dependents. In this context, your **estate** is your net worth at death—all your assets less all your debts, just as we defined net worth in Chapter 2. Federal estate and gift taxes have recently undergone an overhaul as part of the American Taxpayer Relief Act of 2013 and the Tax Cuts and Jobs Act of 2017. Although most households will now avoid estate taxes completely, wealthier households and those in certain states may still owe taxes unless they do careful planning. Thus, one of the additional objectives of estate planning is to avoid paying excessive estate taxes. In this section, we provide an overview of estate planning, why it should be a component of your financial plan, and the key components of an estate plan.

The Estate-Planning Process

Estate planning is the process of developing a plan for what will happen to your wealth and your dependents when you die. This involves both financial and legal considerations and, in most cases, will require the advice of a professional, such as an estate lawyer or a financial professional with specific knowledge and skills in this area. Nevertheless, you'll save both time and money if you've done some of the work before you seek professional guidance.

The estate-planning process is depicted in **Figure 14.1**. As with other elements of financial planning, your first step is to evaluate your financial situation. If you've been applying the concepts in this book to your own personal finances all along, this should be relatively easy. How would you like your assets to be distributed after you die? If you have children (or pets), who will take care of them? Do you have favorite charities you want to help after you die? In addition to writing a will, you might also want to consider several other legal documents discussed in this chapter to ensure that your wishes are carried out after your death. If you're wealthy, it makes sense to develop a plan that will minimize taxes due upon your death.

FIGURE 14.1   **The Estate-Planning Process**   The estate-planning process may not seem like a high priority to you right now, but it's something you will need to know about.

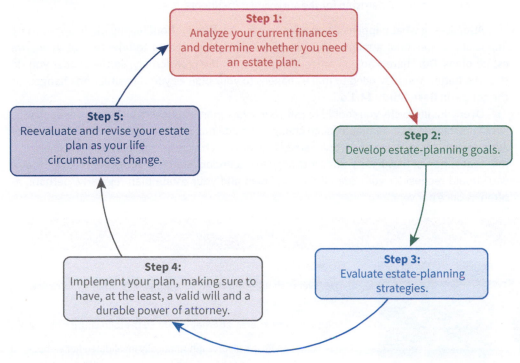

Step 1:
Analyze your current finances and determine whether you need an estate plan.

Step 2:
Develop estate-planning goals.

Step 3:
Evaluate estate-planning strategies.

Step 4:
Implement your plan, making sure to have, at the least, a valid will and a durable power of attorney.

Step 5:
Reevaluate and revise your estate plan as your life circumstances change.

Who Needs an Estate Plan?

Because everyone will eventually die, we all should have an estate plan. However, because people's needs—and their estates—differ, some estate plans are very simple, and others are necessarily more complex. If, on the one hand, you're a typical college student with no dependents and negative net worth, your plan will be simple. Your biggest problems might be: Do you want your roommate to have your iPad if you die unexpectedly? Who will take care of your cat? Do you want to be cremated? What kinds of life-extending measures should doctors to take if you're physically or mentally disabled in the future? If, on the other hand, you are relatively wealthy, have dependent children, or own property in multiple states, your plan will be more complicated and the consequences of failing to plan could be more serious.

The legal process of settling your estate—paying your debts and distributing your assets according to your wishes—is called **probate**. This process is supervised by a local court, which will appoint someone to administer the distribution of assets. Only certain assets have to be distributed through this process, so one of the objectives of your estate plan will be to arrange for as much of your wealth as possible to bypass the probate process. If you die without a valid will, or if your family can't locate necessary documents, the probate process can take a long time. Your family could end up being cash-strapped for many months (or years) if they get stuck in an extended probate process.

Most people in the United States have not adequately prepared for their death. In fact, only one-third of all Americans have valid wills, and the numbers are even lower for African Americans and Hispanics. Your first exposure to the problems created by failure to plan might be when a parent becomes terminally ill or dies. If one of your parents dies without an estate plan or a will, the value of the estate may be unnecessarily eroded by the following costs:

- Federal estate taxes (up to 40 percent tax on estates above the exemption amount)
- State inheritance taxes (0–20 percent, depending on the state of residence)
- Probate costs (2–5 percent)

Other personal costs may include:

- Delays in settlement of the estate
- Distress over having to make difficult health-care decisions and funeral arrangements without knowing the deceased's wishes
- Disagreements with family members regarding distribution of the deceased's personal effects
- Potential financial hardship for the surviving dependents

After seeing what happens when a family member dies without having made appropriate financial and personal arrangements, many people are motivated to take care of their own estate plans. But there's no guarantee that you won't die prematurely, so the sooner you do this, the better. You may need to make changes to your plan as your life situation changes, as the couple in **Case Study 14.1** do.

Over your life cycle, you should revisit your estate plan whenever you have a major change in circumstances. At a minimum, such changes include marriage, divorce, remarriage, birth or adoption of a child, death of anyone named in your will, change of state of residence, change of job, acquisition of new assets, and/or change in dependent status of your children. Optimally, you should reconsider your overall financial plan and your estate plan regularly, perhaps as often as once per year.

Case Study 14.1

ESB Professional/Shutterstock.com

Estate Planning Changes over the Life Cycle

Problem

Mateo and Rosa Rivera have not rewritten their wills since they married and have done no other estate planning. They have a new baby and a child from Rosa's first marriage. Mateo's will leaves everything to his brother, Manuel. Rosa's old will names her ex-husband as her primary beneficiary and names her ex-husband's mother, now deceased, as the guardian for her son Kyle. Neither Rosa's nor Mateo's will provides for additional children.

Strategy

The Riveras should consult an estate-planning attorney to review their wills.

Solution   The Riveras' attorney identified the following problems:

- Although Rosa's divorce automatically invalidated her ex-husband's status as beneficiary, the legal status of both old wills is questionable now that Mateo and Rosa are married, and clearly those wills are inconsistent with the couple's current intentions.

- Although Rosa's will included a provision for guardianship of her son, the designated guardian is deceased, and a backup guardian was not named in the will.

- Because their old wills did not provide for additional children, the Riveras' new baby daughter, Julia, would not be entitled to any of their estate should they die before executing new wills. In addition, if both parents died, the courts would have to assign a guardian for the baby.

The Riveras' attorney recommends drafting new wills that name an executor, name guardians for both children, and allow for the possibility of additional children in the future. She also recommends that they both write living wills and durable medical powers of attorney, as explained in the next section.

Although your estate plan will be fairly simple when you're young, it should grow in complexity with the complexity of your family circumstances and finances. Through your 40s and 50s, your primary estate-planning concerns will be the protection of your spouse and children, but as you age, it will probably shift to providing for your spouse's retirement and passing your wealth to your grandchildren or your favorite charities.

Key Components of an Estate Plan

Although estate plans can be very different from one another, most share certain key components. These may include a will, a living will and durable power of attorney, a letter of last instruction, and any trust instruments deemed necessary.

Will

The most important component of your estate plan is your **will**. A will is a legal document that specifies how you want your property to be distributed upon your death. A person or entity designated to receive something from your estate after your death is called your beneficiary or **heir**. If applicable, your will should also specify who will have responsibility for the care of your surviving minor children and other dependents.

Whether you have a will or not, state law requires that your assets be distributed after your death. If you die **intestate** (without a valid will), every state has legal rules that govern how a resident's property will be distributed. Although the manner of distribution differs depending on the state in which you are residing when you die, these rules will not necessarily divide up your assets in the way you would have chosen had you drafted a will yourself. Furthermore, without a will, you have no say in determining the guardian for your children. In most states, for example, your spouse gets no more than half your assets, with the other half going to surviving children or your parents. If you have no children, your spouse will likely have to share the wealth with other relatives, which might leave him or her in financial difficulty. If you die without a will and have no living relatives, all of your assets will become the property of the state government through a legal rule called **escheat**.

Living Will or Durable Power of Attorney

Most people should also have a living will and a durable power of attorney. Whereas wills have been around for thousands of years, the **living will** is a by-product of modern medical advances. In this document, you specify what kind of medical care you want to receive in the event that you can't make decisions for yourself due to terminal illness, physical disability, or mental disability. For example, some people do not want to have extraordinary measures taken to resuscitate them if they sustain an injury that leaves them without normal brain function. It is much easier for family members to make this difficult decision when they know it is in accordance with the wishes of the injured person. Because doctors are not bound to honor a living will, or may not be aware of its existence at the time of medical treatment, you may also want to ask your doctor to write a "do-not-rescusitate" order, or DNR, which will instruct health care providers not to perform cardiopulmonary resuscitation (CPR).

You've probably heard on the news about families who have kept their loved ones alive for years without much hope of improvement in condition, such as the case discussed in **Ethics in Action**. If you don't decide in advance how you want to deal with situations of this kind, your family might be unable or unwilling to make the tough decisions for you, instead bearing a significant and continuing financial and emotional burden themselves. Even if you have a living will that outlines your wishes, it doesn't force your loved ones to abide by them. Therefore, you also need a **durable power of attorney**, a document in which you appoint someone to make the specific medical decisions in accordance with your wishes when you are incapacitated. This document needs to be drafted by an attorney to be sure that it will satisfy legal requirements in your state.

The most difficult part of drafting a living will is deciding what limitations to place on the level of extreme medical care you're willing to receive. For example, you can be fairly vague and specify just that no "heroic measures" be taken to keep you alive by artificial means. In that case, it will be up to your family to decide exactly what constitutes a heroic measure (respirator,

Ethics in Action

Terri Schiavo's Life-or-Death Experience

Imagine that you suffer a heart attack, and the loss of oxygen to your brain leaves you in what your doctors term a "persistent and irreversible vegetative state" with no hope of recovery. This is what happened in 1990 to Terri Schindler-Schiavo of Tampa, Florida, at the age of 26. For several years, her family pursued rehabilitation and treatment options. By 1998, her husband, Michael, had petitioned the Florida courts to remove the feeding tubes that were keeping her alive. At this point, Terri's parents intervened, insisting that Terri was aware of her surroundings and responsive to them. They attempted to have Michael removed as Terri's guardian and took legal action to block Michael's attempts to have the feeding tubes removed.

Eventually, in 2001, a court ordered the removal of Terri's feeding tubes, but they were reinserted a few days later. Over the next few years, the Schiavo case made it through fourteen appeals, five suits in federal district court, the passage of a Florida law ("Terri's Law") giving Governor Jeb Bush the right to order reinstatement of the feeding tubes, a Florida Supreme Court reversal, four denied requests for review by the Supreme Court of the United States, and federal legislation signed by President George W. Bush. At the end of this very expensive appeals process, the original order was upheld, and Terri's tubes were removed on March 18, 2005, resulting in her death later that day.

By the time Terri died, the large trust fund for therapy and medical treatment, the result of a malpractice lawsuit, was depleted to about $40,000, which wouldn't have been sufficient to keep her alive for even one more year.

Although each individual is free to have his or her own opinion about whether Terri Schiavo should have been kept alive for 15 years through artificial means, only Terri could have told us her wishes. If she had had a living will or medical power of attorney in place, a lot of family feuding and expensive litigation could have been avoided.

kidney dialysis, feeding tubes?), and they might disagree with each other on this point. Or you might limit the living will's applicability to situations in which your brain function is severely reduced to the extent that you have no reasonable chance of living a productive life. Although greater specificity can be helpful to the members of your family who will be called on to make the difficult decisions, you'll need to be general enough to cover all the possible circumstances that might arise. You wouldn't necessarily want your living will to prevent you from benefiting from advances in medical knowledge or improved chances of survival in the future.

The format of living wills can vary greatly depending on your preferences, and many lawyers will draft one along with your regular will at no additional charge. Most states have a particular legal form that they recognize for this purpose, but other forms will be acceptable if they include the necessary elements. In general, this type of document should be witnessed and notarized. An example of a living will is provided in **Figure 14.2**. You may notice that the living will is focused on end-of-life matters. For issues related to medical treatment in other situations, you need to be sure that the person with your health-care power of attorney understands your wishes.

FIGURE 14.2 **Sample Living Will** This sample includes common elements found in a living will.

Declaration as to Medical or Surgical Treatment

I, _____ being of sound mind and at least 18 years of age, direct that my life shall not be artificially prolonged under the circumstances set forth below:

1. If at any time my attending physician and one other qualified physician certify in writing that:

   a. I have an injury, disease, or illness that is not curable or reversible and that, in their judgment, is a terminal condition; and

   b. For a period of seven consecutive days or more, I have been unconscious, comatose, or otherwise incompetent so as to be unable to make or communicate responsible decisions concerning my person, then

I direct that life-sustaining procedures shall be withdrawn and withheld pursuant to the terms of this declaration, it being understood that life-sustaining procedures not include any medical procedure to provide comfort or alleviate pain.

I also authorize my family to effectuate my transfer from any health care facility in which I may be receiving care if that facility declines or refuses to carry out the instructions in this document.

I hereby make an anatomical gift, to be effective on my death, of any needed organs or tissues.

Signed _____ Date _____

Address _____

Social Security Number _____

Witness _____ Date _____

Letter of Last Instruction

Although not a legal document, the **letter of last instruction** serves the purpose of helping your survivors through the process of your death. You could use this document to communicate your personal wishes regarding funeral arrangements, to identify people who should be notified of your death, and to list important information, such as account numbers, PIN numbers, passwords, online account challenge questions, contact information for insurance companies and brokerage firms, and safe-deposit box locations and numbers. Your survivors might also appreciate knowing your wishes regarding distribution of your minor personal assets (your old football jersey, comic book collection, or family memorabilia) that have sentimental but not financial value. (Note, though, that these instructions are nonbinding, in that specific bequests of your assets must be written into your will to be legally enforced.) The letter of last instruction should be copied and distributed to several people (including your attorney) to ensure that it is found in the event of your death. You should update the information regularly, particularly to ensure that your digital account information and passwords are accurately recorded.

Trusts

For many estate plans, it's desirable to set up legal arrangements called trusts. A **trust** is a legal entity that holds and manages assets on behalf of someone else. Trusts are commonly used in estate planning for a variety of purposes. We discuss trusts in more detail in a later section.

    Some components of an estate plan will be more important than others, depending on an individual's personal circumstances. See if you can identify which ones are most important for the different people described in **Interactive: Estate Planning Needs**.

INTERACTIVE

See **Interactive: Estate Planning Needs** in **WileyPLUS**.

Organizing Financial and Legal Documents

If you've ever suffered the death of a loved one and had to subsequently handle any of that person's affairs, you'll recognize how helpful it is when financial and legal documents are organized, accessible, and easy to understand. Unfortunately, this is the exception rather than the rule. In most families, one person takes responsibility for the bill paying and record keeping, and other family members don't have a clue where anything is. Depending on the organizational skills of the person in charge of these matters, it can be quite a challenge to piece things together after a death in the family. An important component of estate planning therefore includes the organization of your legal and financial records so that the right person (or persons)—spouse, trustee, trusted family member, lawyer, or estate planner—can easily find them. Not only will this make it more likely that the bills will be paid and that the most recent version of your will is the one that will be opened, but it's also simply a kind and thoughtful thing to do for your survivors. If you take the time to organize your financial affairs while you're living, your family will have one less source of stress to deal with in their time of grief.

    It makes sense to leave one copy of each important document with your estate attorney or planner and one copy at home in a fireproof file. Don't put wills, trust documents, or powers of attorney in a safe-deposit box, because that is often sealed at death (although it's okay to keep copies of such documents there). If critical information is stored on your computer, make a disk copy and a paper copy. In addition to your will, you should include copies of every current legal document related to your financial and personal life. You may recall from an earlier chapter that having organized and easily accessible financial records is an important component of your personal financial plan. **Excel Worksheet 14.1** (Personal Financial Planner: Estate-Planning Checklist) can be used to keep track of estate-related financial records, as illustrated in **Figure 14.3**.

EXCEL WORKSHEET

See **Excel Worksheet 14.1 (Personal Financial Planner: Estate-Planning Checklist)** in **WileyPLUS**.

FIGURE 14.3 Sample of Excel Worksheet 14.1: Estate-Planning Checklist

	A	B
	Done (✓) **Documents**	**Location of Documents/Notes**
2	✓ Will	Attorney's office, lockbox
3	✓ Living will	Attorney's office, lockbox
4	✓ Letter of last instructions	Attorney's office, lockbox
5	Trust documents	
6	Durable power of attorney	Need to draft
7	Medical durable power of attorney	Need to draft
8	✓ Personal legal records (Social Security number, prenuptial agreements, birth certificate, marriage certificate, divorce decree, court judgments, military records)	Lock box
9	✓ Bank account information (account numbers, address and phone of financial institutions)	Office file cabinet
10	✓ Investment information (brokerage accounts, mutual funds, CDs, annuities)	Office file cabinet
11	✓ Debt information (credit card and loan account numbers, balances, repayment terms)	Office file cabinet
12	Business interests (partnership and buy-sell agreements, articles of incorporation)	
13	✓ Retirement accounts (IRAs, 401ks, pension plans, Social Security records, small business retirement accounts)	Office file cabinet
14	✓ Insurance (account numbers and copies of policies)	Office file cabinet
15	✓ Real estate and personal property (deeds, mortgages, titles, title insurance, rental property records, timeshares, leases)	Office file cabinet

14.2

Methods of Transferring Property

> **LEARNING OBJECTIVE 14.2**
>
> Explain the importance of having a valid will and arranging in advance for easy transfer of assets to your heirs.

The failure to have a valid will can easily result in your assets being distributed contrary to your wishes. So why do only one-third of Americans have valid wills? Many people assume that their property will pass to their spouses or that they don't have enough assets to worry about having a will. What they might not realize is that the failure to have a will is sure to complicate the settlement process and create added hardship for their survivors. This section focuses on how you can ensure that your estate goes where you want it to go. Along with a valid will, your decisions regarding legal ownership of certain assets are important elements of this process.

Preparing a Valid Will

A will enables the person writing it, the **testator**, to direct the disposition of his or her assets to specific **beneficiaries**, those who will receive the assets. Wills can be very simple or very complicated but must satisfy certain legal requirements to be valid. If your will is declared to be invalid, the property will be distributed as if you had died intestate, so it is generally worthwhile to hire a lawyer to draft or at least review your will for legality. The cost of having a simple will drawn up may be as little as $200 but can be much higher for more complex estates. Read through the requirements for a valid will provided in **Table 14.1** and then see whether you can spot the problems with the sample will in **Interactive: Is This Will Valid?**

INTERACTIVE

See **Interactive: Is This Will Valid?** in **WileyPLUS**.

TABLE 14.1   Requirements for a Valid Will

Wills are governed by state law, and state laws vary. However, in many states, your will must meet the following criteria:

1. You must be of legal age (usually 18).
2. You must have the mental capacity to make a will:
   a. You must understand the *nature and extent* of your assets.
   b. You must understand to *whom* you intend your assets to be distributed.
   c. You must understand *how* you are distributing your assets.
3. You must intend for the document to be your will.
4. The will must be in writing and, with some limited exceptions, typed or printed.
5. The will must be dated.
6. The will must be signed in the presence of two witnesses who are not your relatives or named beneficiaries in the will.
7. The will must name an executor or personal representative.

Capacity to Make the Will

Even if all the other requirements are met, a will can be declared invalid if the testator did not have the legal **capacity** to make the will. For this reason, many wills begin with the language "I, [testator name], being of sound mind and body. . . ." In this context, "of sound mind" addresses the requirement of legal capacity. The testator is considered to be of sound mind if he or she understands the nature and content of the document, is mentally capable of making decisions regarding the distribution of his or her assets, and is not acting under threat or coercion from another person. Capacity is a requirement for making any legally binding contract, but in the case of a will, it is particularly important, because the elderly are often unwitting victims of greedy relatives or scam artists.

Common Elements of a Will

Figure 14.4 provides a sample will for Rosa Rivera to illustrate the common clauses and sections found in most wills. These usually include clauses or sections for the introduction, payment of debts and taxes, distribution of assets, appointment of executor, appointment of guardians and trustees, and execution, or signing. These elements are described in more detail below.

- **Introduction**   Wills usually begin with a set of introductory declarations in which you identify yourself and your state of residency and verify that the will replaces all previous wills you might have written. Because you might revise your will several times over the years, it's important to date it and to identify each new one as your last will. To ensure that a previous version of your will is not inadvertently identified, you should notify your attorney and your relatives when you write a new will, and destroy any old ones.

- **Payment of debts and taxes**   This clause instructs the estate to pay your debts and expenses, including funeral expenses, medical expenses, and any taxes due. Because creditors are generally protected by other laws, the important component of this clause is the instruction to pay taxes. In the absence of such a clause, most states have laws that will allocate the taxes among the beneficiaries based on their shares of the estate. Thus, if you want to be sure that the Girl Scouts get $20,000 from your estate, you need to include a clause that directs payment of taxes *before* distribution of specific bequests to ensure that your bequest isn't reduced by a share of the taxes owed.

- **Distribution of assets**   The distribution of assets is usually the primary purpose of a will. You can distribute your assets very simply, leaving everything to your spouse with no specific bequests, or you can provide a lot of detailed instructions. Some wills direct that specific personal effects be given to named beneficiaries before the distribution of the

Last Will and Testament

Article 1 Introduction

I, Rosa Rivera, Anytown, New Jersey, being of sound mind and body, declare this to be my last will and I revoke all wills and codicils made prior to this will. My husband is Mateo Rivera, also of Anytown, New Jersey.

Article 2 Payment of Debts and Expenses

I direct my Executor to pay my medical expenses, funeral expenses, debts, and the costs of settling my estate.

Article 3 Distribution of Assets

I give to the Girl Scouts of America the sum of $20,000. All the rest of my estate, real and personal, I give to my beloved husband Mateo Rivera. If my husband dies before me, I give my estate to be shared equally by my children Kyle Larson and Julia Rivera, also of Anytown, New Jersey.

Article 4 Appointment of Executor and Guardian

I hereby nominate my beloved husband Mateo Rivera to be the Executor of this Will. If he is unable to serve, then I nominate my sister Juanita Macera of Henniker, New Hampshire. If my husband dies before me, then I appoint my sister Juanita Macera of Henniker, New Hampshire, as Guardian of the person and property of my children Kyle Larson and Julia Rivera until they each reach the age of 18. If she is unable to serve as Guardian, then I appoint my sister Elisa Juarez of Marlboro, New Jersey.

Article 5 Power of Executor

The Executor of this Will has the power to receive payments, buy or sell assets, and pay debts owed and taxes owed on behalf of my estate.

Article 6 Payment of Taxes

I direct my Executor to pay all estate, inheritance, or other similar taxes imposed by the government on my estate.

Article 7 Execution

IN WITNESS THEREOF, I hereby sign and declare this to be my Last Will and Testament, which consists of two pages, each of which I have initialed, on this the 15th day of May, 2020.

Rosa Rivera   _May 15, 2020_
_____   _____
Rosa Rivera

Article 8 Witness Clause

The above-named person signed in our presences and in our opinion is mentally competent.

Witness 1 Name	Address	Date
Witness 2 Name	Address	Date

remainder of the estate. If you have a long list of specific items to be distributed, you may want to include this list with your letter of last instruction instead of in the will itself. That way, you can make changes as necessary over time without having to draw up a new will. After specific gifts have been distributed, the remainder of the estate, called the *residual estate*, will go to the residual beneficiaries as named in the will.

- **Appointment of an executor or executrix** In your will, you'll need to name the person who will handle the settlement of your estate, called the **executor** (if male), **executrix** (if female), or, in some cases, *personal representative*. This person has the legal and ethical obligation to distribute your assets as you have directed and to pay taxes according to the law. If your estate is complex, your attorney may suggest that you name a lawyer or bank trust department instead of a family member to fill this role. You should also be realistic about the other time commitments of any person you're considering naming as your executor and should consider whether the person lives close enough to handle the details of financial transactions related to settlement of the estate. In addition to naming your executor, your will can provide for the executor to be compensated for his or her services and expenses incurred in settling the estate. This compensation is commonly a small percentage of the total value of the estate.

- **Appointment of guardian**   If you have minor children, your will should identify a guardian who will take care of them and a **trustee** who will manage their inheritance until they reach the age you have designated in your will. The same person often serves as both guardian and trustee and is commonly the child's other parent or an adult sibling. Even if your children are old enough to be legal adults, however, your will can specify a later age for receipt of inheritance or require satisfaction of specific goals, such as graduation from college.

- **Execution**   Execution is a legal term for the process of signing and witnessing a document to make it legally valid. To be properly executed, a will generally must be in writing and signed by the testator in the presence of at least two witnesses. Because most challenges to wills are related to the question of *capacity*, it is recommended that the witnesses sign a statement in the presence of a notary public declaring their belief that the testator is acting with full mental capacity. The family of eccentric multi-billionaire Howard Hughes challenged a handwritten will that left substantial sums to various parties, including a very young female companion whom the family suspected of unduly influencing the elderly Hughes. After many years in court, the will was eventually ruled a forgery and his vast estate was split among 22 cousins.

Should a Lawyer Draft Your Will?

Although many websites, software packages, and self-help books suggest a do-it-yourself approach to writing a will, this is clearly an area where you don't want to be "penny-wise and dollar-foolish." It would be a shame for your will to be invalidated based on a legal technicality. Therefore, no matter how small your estate is, you'd be well advised to get professional help in drafting your will. Such assistance is particularly important if you have children for whom you need to appoint a legal guardian or establish a trust. To minimize the cost, assemble all the necessary information before meeting with the lawyer. Think through the important issues, such as whom to appoint as executor and guardian. You might even prepare a rough draft. Most lawyers will charge a flat price for preparing a simple will.

What if you truly can't afford the expense at the moment? Because it's clearly better to have a will than not to have one, you can at least draw up and properly execute a simple will on your own. Samples are available from the websites, software packages, and self-help books mentioned earlier. At the same time, though, you should add getting a legal review of your will to your short-term financial planning "to do" list.

Making Changes to Your Will

You can change or revoke your will at any time, as long as you still have the mental capacity to execute a new will. As mentioned before, you should review your will periodically as your circumstances change to make sure that it still accurately reflects your intentions. You may want to add or subtract beneficiaries, make additional charitable bequests, or name a different executor or guardian. For example, suppose that six years ago you wrote a will identifying your unmarried sister as the guardian of your three children. Since then, she has married and has had three children of her own. Although she might be a wonderful mother, six children to raise might be too great a burden. Instead, you could now name your unmarried brother as the guardian (subject to his agreement, of course).

To make small changes to your will, you can write a **codicil**, a short (usually single-page) document that reaffirms your original will except for a small provision that is being changed. A codicil can be used to change a named guardian or trustee, for example, or to add a new baby to your list of heirs. Because the codicil is a legal document, it should be drawn up, executed, and witnessed in the same way as a will. For larger changes, rather than adding a codicil to your will, your attorney will probably recommend that you make a new will and revoke the old one.

Passing Property Outside a Will

Any wealth transferred by will is part of your estate and must go through probate. Depending on the complexity of your estate, probate can be a lengthy process. Any assets of which you are the sole owner must go through probate. However, you can keep property out of probate by holding assets jointly with your heirs and by naming specific beneficiaries for life insurance and retirement accounts.

Ownership of Assets

Assets can be owned in various ways. When two people own property in a **joint tenancy with right of survivorship**, the ownership of the property automatically passes to the surviving owner upon the death of the other, without going through probate. The property will also be free of claims from creditors (except for collateralized loans such as mortgages), other heirs, or executors. Joint ownership of this type is not divided—all the owners share ownership of the entire property. Thus, if you and your brother own your parents' former home as joint tenants, you don't own half of the property separately, and you therefore can't leave your interest in the property to your wife or children. Total ownership of the property will automatically pass to your brother upon your death. In some states, a special form of ownership, called tenancy by the entirety, applies to married couples and is essentially the same as joint tenancy with right of survivorship.

Joint ownership has advantages and disadvantages. The primary advantage is that the survivor gets immediate ownership of the property without going through probate court to get the title transferred to his or her name. Consider, for example, what would happen if household checking and savings accounts were not owned jointly—the surviving spouse might not have access to the necessary funds to pay household expenses during the process of probate. Joint ownership of such accounts is easy and inexpensive to set up.

The disadvantages of joint tenancy with right of survivorship as an estate-planning tool are as follows:

- You do not have complete control over the property during your lifetime. While living, joint tenants have to agree on all decisions regarding the property, similar to a partnership.

- You have no say over what happens to the property after you die. If you die first, the property belongs to your joint tenant. If your joint tenant is your spouse, and you die first, your spouse can leave the entire property to children from a previous marriage.

- For very wealthy people, the transfer of property to the joint tenant might result in greater tax liability. Although the transfer to a spouse initially bypasses the estate tax, it may result in higher taxes later, if the combined estate held by your spouse is large enough to trigger the tax when he or she dies.

- You lose the ability to have the property pass to a trust. If the property is owned in joint tenancy, it is no longer yours to leave to others under the terms of your will.

For most married couples, the flexibility offered by joint tenancy with right of survivorship, in the form of immediate access to assets and avoidance of probate, outweighs the disadvantages.

An alternative to joint tenancy with right of survivorship is a type of ownership called **tenancy in common**. Here, each tenant retains the right to transfer his or her ownership interest independently. Your portion of the property will be included in your estate and passed by the terms of your will. If you and your spouse own your home as tenants in common, though, naming someone other than your spouse as your heir could create difficulties. Unless your spouse has sufficient funds to buy out the other person's ownership, the home might have to be sold.

Finally, some states have a form of property ownership for married couples called **community property**. In these states, it is assumed that any property acquired during the marriage is owned jointly by both spouses. One spouse's share of the property can be willed to someone other than the surviving spouse, however, as in a tenancy in common.

Beneficiary Designation

Various types of financial accounts, such as mutual funds, retirement accounts, and some savings accounts, will automatically transfer upon your death to the person you've named as the beneficiary for the account. Spouses who receive qualified retirement plan assets in this way can roll the funds over into another qualified plan or IRA. Given the tax advantages of qualified plans, it is sometimes advisable to name a younger child as the beneficiary in order to allow the funds to maintain their tax advantages for a longer period of time. To be sure that these assets avoid probate, you should also name a contingent beneficiary.

14.3 Estate and Gift Taxes

LEARNING OBJECTIVE 14.3

Explain recent changes to federal estate and gift taxation laws that significantly reduce the number of estates that have to pay these taxes.

If you have significant financial assets or a family business that you'd like to pass to your heirs, you can do so either while you are living, through gifts, or after you die, through bequests in your will. In either case, the money may be subject to taxes. Inheritances account for 40 percent of all wealth in the United States and 4 percent of annual household income, but under current law, 99.94 percent of estates pay no estate tax. Because gifts and bequests are alternative ways to pass your wealth to the next generation, estate tax and gift tax laws work together, so we discuss both in this section. The federal estate tax law was temporarily reformed in 2017 to apply only to the very wealthy, but this law is set to expire in 2025 unless Congress acts to make it permanent. In this section, we explain how gift and estate taxes are currently calculated and identify ways that you can minimize the amount paid by those who receive an inheritance or gift from you.

Federal Gift Taxes

Under federal law, you may be subject to a tax on gifts you make during your lifetime if they exceed certain limits. You and your spouse can each give up to $15,000 per person in 2019 and 2020 (increasing with inflation) to as many people as you like. If you give more than the allowed annual amount to anyone, you have to file a gift tax return (IRS Form 709), and the excess amount will be applied to reduce the amount of your estate that is exempt from the estate tax, as discussed below. Effectively, this means your estate will have a lower estate tax exclusion (reduced by the amount of taxable gifts at the time of your death).

There are two important exceptions to the limits on gifts. First, there is no limit on how much you can give your spouse. Second, there is no limit on gifts for the payment of medical expenses or certain educational costs, provided that you make the payments directly to the service provider or educational institution. This means that your rich great-uncle can pay the bill for your college tuition and fee expenses directly to the school without exceeding the gifting limit.

Federal Estate Taxes

If you don't give your wealth away while you're living, you can give it away at your death. The Tax Cuts and Jobs Act of 2017 significantly reduced the likelihood that you will personally be subject to the estate or gift tax. Under the current law, individual estates are allowed an exemption of $11.4 million ($22.8 million per married couple) in 2019, less any lifetime gifts in excess of the annual limits. This exemption is referred to as the *federal unified credit for estates and gifts*. The amount of your estate that exceeds the allowed exclusion (which will increase with inflation over the years) is subject to a progressive tax rate schedule with a maximum rate of 40 percent. You can see from **Figure 14.5** that the amount of wealth that is currently exempted from taxation is much higher than it was in the past, making it highly unlikely that you will be subject to this tax. However, unless Congress acts to make this rule permanent, the exemption amount is set to expire in 2025, at which time the tax-exempted amount will revert back to the 2017 level of $5.49 million.

FIGURE 14.5 **Federal Unified Credit for Estates and Gifts** For 2019, a total of $11.4 million per person is exempt from estate and gift taxes.

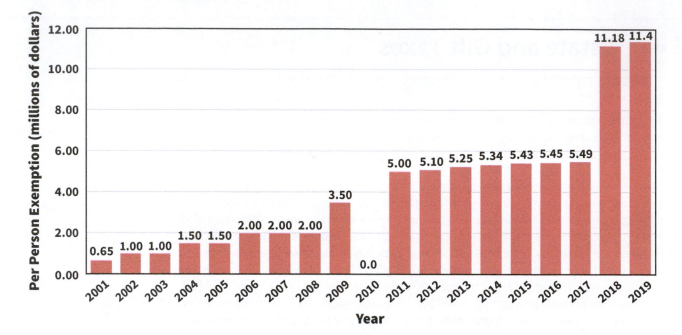

An important feature of estate tax law for married couples is that the surviving spouse can inherit the entire estate without paying any tax, regardless of the size of the estate. Therefore, the primary purpose of estate tax planning is actually to minimize the taxes payable by your surviving spouse's estate (or your estate if you leave your wealth to someone other than your spouse).

You can use **Excel Worksheet 14.2** (Personal Financial Planner: Calculating Estate Taxes) to estimate the estate taxes that might be owed at your death. **Case Study 14.2** shows how this could apply to a particular wealthy person's estate.

EXCEL WORKSHEET

See **Excel Worksheet 14.2** (**Personal Financial Planner: Calculating Estate Taxes**) in **WileyPLUS**.

Case Study 14.2

Hero Images/Getty Images

Lisa Calculates Her Taxable Estate

Problem

Lisa is a wealthy single entrepreneur (net worth of $15 million) and the primary shareholder in a successful Internet-based start-up company. She hasn't yet made a will, and if she were to die before marrying, her widowed mother would inherit under state law. Lisa has discussed with an attorney the possibility of gifting $4 million to her alma mater. Assuming that her estate expenses will total $40,000, how much difference would the proposed gift make to the amount of taxes that the estate would owe and the amount Lisa's mother would receive on her death?

Strategy

Complete Excel Worksheet 14.2 (Personal Financial Planner: Calculating Estate Taxes) under each of the two scenarios to determine the effect of Lisa's proposed gift.

Solution Lisa's estate could owe a lot in estate taxes if she dies without doing any estate planning. As shown in **Figure 14.6**, after the 2019 exemption, her estate will pay taxes on $3.56 million in wealth, significantly reducing what she can give to her heirs. However, because she is allowed to gift an unlimited amount to

charity through her estate, the gift to her alma mater will reduce her taxable estate by the amount of the gift. This will reduce her taxable estate to zero, saving almost $1.4 million in taxes owed by the estate. By using the charitable exemption, Lisa's estate will pay no taxes, resulting in all of her wealth going to her mother and her alma mater. If Lisa consulted an estate-planning professional, that person would also recommend that she execute a will and retitle some of her assets so that they will pass directly to her heirs rather than going through probate. This would result is lower estimated estate expenses and make things easier for her heirs.

FIGURE 14.6 **Sample of Excel Worksheet 14.2: Calculating Estate Taxes**

	A	B Before Estate Planning	C After Estate Planning
1			
2	**1. Calculate gross estate:**		
3	**Net worth**	$ 15,000,000	$ 15,000,000
4	Include only your share of jointly owned property		
5	**Excluded assets**		
6	Life insurance held in irrevocable trust		
7	Other irrevocable trust assets		
8	Assets transferred through family limited partnerships		
9	Gross estate = Net worth − Excluded assets	$ 15,000,000	$ 15,000,000
10			
11	**2. Calculate adjusted gross estate:**		
12	Estate expenses		
13	Funeral expenses	$ 15,000	$ 15,000
14	Executor's fee		
15	Legal fees	$ 10,000	$ 10,000
16	Court fees	$ 5,000	$ 5,000
17	Estate administration fees	$ 10,000	$ 10,000
18	Adjusted gross estate = Gross estate − Estate expenses	$ 14,960,000	$ 14,960,000
19			
20	**3. Calculate taxable estate:**		
21	Unlimited marital and charitable deductions		
22	Amount to spouse		
23	Amount to charity	$ -	$ 4,000,000
24	Adjustment for gifts in excess of annual or lifetime limits		
25	Taxable estate = Adjusted gross estate − Unlimited deductions + Excess gifts	$ 14,960,000	$ 10,960,000
26			
27	**3. Calculate estate tax:**		
28	Federal unified credit exemption ($11.4 million in 2019)	$ 11,400,000	$ 11,400,000
29	Taxable estate after exemption	$ 3,560,000	$ 0
30	**Estate taxes owed (based on progressive rate schedule)**	$ 1,369,800	$ 0

Each of the steps for calculating taxes included in the Excel worksheet is explained in more detail below:

1. **Calculate gross estate.**   Your gross estate is your net worth, as described in Chapter 2, less any excluded assets. Although you know the value of your net worth today, you

actually should consider what it might be in the future. Even if you have fairly little wealth today, by the time you die, your savings and investment portfolio will probably have grown substantially, and it pays to plan for that contingency. Checking and savings accounts, investment accounts, annuities, employment pension and retirement plan assets, IRAs, and other assets are all part of your gross estate even if you've designated a beneficiary in order to remove them from the probate process.

In completing the first step on the worksheet, you should enter your net worth and then subtract the value of any assets that you have effectively excluded from your estate. Because no estate tax is owed on amounts transferred to your spouse, exclusion strategies are important only if you list someone other than your spouse as the beneficiary on your life insurance policies or financial accounts. Life insurance proceeds will be included in your gross estate if you retained the right to change beneficiaries, turn in the policy for its cash value, or borrow against the cash value. You can remove those proceeds from your gross estate by placing them in certain types of trusts, as we explain later in this chapter.

2. **Calculate adjusted gross estate.** Your gross estate is reduced by funeral costs and settlement expenses to arrive at your adjusted gross estate.

3. **Calculate taxable estate.** To calculate your taxable estate, you'll start with your adjusted gross estate, subtract marital and charitable bequests, and add any taxable gifts (in excess of the annual and lifetime limits). Your spouse can inherit an unlimited estate without being subject to federal estate tax, and the deduction for charitable giving is also unlimited.

4. **Calculate estate tax.** Finally, subtract the exemption amount ($11.4 million in 2019). The remainder, which for most people will be zero, is subject to a federal estate tax rate schedule with brackets that range from 18 to 40 percent.

Reflection Question 2

In your opinion, should the United States get rid of the estate tax? Why or why not?

State Death Taxes

As we've seen, the federal unified exemption is now so large that very few taxpayers will have to pay any federal estate tax. In addition to the federal estate tax, however, a number of U.S. states impose estate or inheritance taxes. Federal estate tax law allows a deduction from your estate for state death taxes paid, which reduces, but does not eliminate, the effective cost of the state taxes. For this reason, some states are more expensive places in which to die than others.

As of 2019, the District of Columbia and 12 states imposed estate or inheritance taxes. Although several states set their exemption amounts at the same level as the federal exemption ($11,400,000 in 2019), some have lower limits. For example, both Oregon and Massachusetts exempt only $1 million. If you are a resident of one of those states when you die, your estate can owe state death taxes even if it is exempt from federal tax. Therefore, if you live in one of those states, you should consult an estate planner to be sure your heirs won't be hit with unexpected taxes upon your death. Or you could move to a different state.

As you can imagine, people don't generally like the idea of owing state estate taxes even if they don't owe federal estate tax. For this reason, several states have repealed their estate tax laws altogether in the last few years. In addition, several states have set their exemption amount at the same level as the federal unified credit, and others are gradually phasing in the increase. Another of the advantages of having the same exemption level as the federal estate tax is that state tax collectors don't have to spend a lot of time reviewing tax forms. Much as with state income tax, they simply adopt the federal calculation and apply their tax rate to that amount.

14.4 | Reducing Taxes Through Trusts and Gifts

> **LEARNING OBJECTIVE 14.4**
>
> Understand how trusts, gifts, and charitable contributions can reduce estate taxes.

The larger your taxable estate, the greater the likelihood that your heirs or your spouse's heirs could be subject to estate taxation. There are two general ways to reduce the size of your taxable estate. As mentioned, you can move money or assets to legal vehicles called trusts, or you can give away your assets, either as gifts before your death or through charitable bequests in your will. Gifts and trusts can also be used to achieve other goals, so they may be desirable even if you don't expect to be subject to estate taxes. In this section, we discuss these strategies in more detail.

When Are Trusts Useful?

You have learned that a trust is a legal entity that holds and manages assets on behalf of someone else. The **grantor**, the person putting the assets in a trust, transfers the assets to the trust, which is managed by a trustee for the benefit of the beneficiary of the trust. Trustee services are commonly provided by banks, financial institutions, and law firms. Trusts are used in estate planning for several purposes:

- To bypass probate, providing your heirs with immediate access to the property upon your death
- To remove property from the taxable estate, thereby minimizing taxes owed
- To ensure that the estate achieves certain purposes after the grantor's death, such as providing income to surviving dependents

If this all sounds very technical, it's because it is. Trusts are fairly sophisticated legal arrangements, so before attempting to implement one, you should consult with an experienced estate-planning lawyer. He or she can recommend the type of trust that will best meet your needs and draft the appropriate legal documents.

Types of Trusts

The type of trust that will best meet your needs depends on your objectives. Here, we briefly review some of the important distinctions among the various types of trusts and the ways in which they can help you meet one or more of the objectives identified in the previous section.

Revocable versus Irrevocable Trusts

If your primary purpose is to reduce estate taxes, then you'll need to set up an **irrevocable trust**, which means that you can't change the terms of the trust once it is established. Irrevocable trusts bypass probate and are not subject to federal or state estate taxes. If, instead, you create a **revocable trust**, you retain the right to change the terms of the trust during your lifetime. In that case, the trust will bypass probate but the assets will still be subject to any applicable state and federal estate taxes.

Living versus Testamentary Trusts

You can set up a **living trust** that takes effect now or a **testamentary trust** that is created by your will at the time of your death. A fairly common practice is to set up a revocable living trust that becomes irrevocable upon your death or incompetence. You place your assets in the trust, but you can still use them, receive income from them, or sell them while you're alive. If your total estate is less than the estate tax exemption amount, you don't need to worry about estate taxes, but placing them in the trust will bypass probate so that your assets are immediately transferred to your beneficiaries after your death.

Estate planners commonly recommend that wealthier clients establish trusts for children (or other family members) that, upon the grantor's death, will be funded with the maximum amount allowed under estate tax exemption rules, with the remainder going to the grantor's surviving spouse.

Charitable Trusts

Trusts can also be established for the benefit of charitable institutions. Your will can transfer wealth to charities free of estate tax, so the purpose of this type of trust is not to avoid estate taxes. Instead, the objective of a charitable trust is to allow a charity to benefit from your assets during your lifetime while allowing you to retain either the use of, or the income from, an asset and to take an income tax deduction for the charitable donation.

A **charitable remainder trust** allows you to give away an asset but retain the cash flow generated by that asset during your lifetime. It is called "remainder" because the charity gets the remainder of the trust assets after your death. In contrast, a **charitable lead** (or **income**) **trust** provides income to the charity during your lifetime or for a period of years, after which the property goes to a beneficiary of your designation. It is called an income trust because the charity gets the income, not the assets. If you set up this type of trust, you get an immediate income tax deduction for the present value of the expected future income to be received by the charity.

Gifting Alternatives

In making gifts, it's important to consider the tax consequences. If charitable giving is one of your estate-planning objectives, you should make the gifts in a way that will take advantage of income tax rules as well. Charitable gifts will never be subject to estate taxation. In addition, while you're alive, they are deductible from your current income in calculating your federal income tax liability if you itemize deductions instead of taking the standard deduction.

You can also reduce the taxes payable upon your death by gifting your tax-deferred retirement plan assets to a charity. Because the contributions to these accounts are made with pre-tax dollars, the assets will be subject to income tax when distributed (while you're alive or after you die). Such taxes can be avoided, however, if you specifically designate in your will that qualified retirement account assets will go to a charity. These organizations are tax-exempt, so you'll be effectively giving the charity the full amount of your account, whereas anyone else you gave it to would receive only the net after taxes.

Another way to reduce the taxes that will be payable upon your death is to give away some of your assets while you're alive. Remember that gifts you make to individuals during your lifetime are subject to annual and lifetime limits. But you and your spouse can each give the allowed annual amount ($15,000 in 2019) to any number of people in a given year. Therefore, individuals with sizable estates should seriously consider gifting during their lifetime. Not only will they have the immediate gratification of seeing the results of their gifts, whether to charities or individuals, but they will also reduce the likelihood that their estates will be eroded by taxes when they die.

Wealthy donors sometimes make transformative gifts to universities to establish new programs, build new stadiums, or endow professorships and scholarships. For example, in 1991, an Illinois State University alumnus made a large charitable donation that established the Katie School of Insurance and Financial Services, named in honor of his deceased daughter. As a result of his generous gift, the program now boasts hundreds of well-trained graduates.

> **Reflection Question 3**
>
> Suppose your financial plan is successful and you reach old age with a large amount of accumulated wealth. What factors would you consider in deciding whether to make large charitable gifts to reduce your potential estate taxes? Which organizations would you give your money to, and why?

Summary

Learning Objectives Review

LEARNING OBJECTIVE 14.1   Identify key components of an estate plan, and determine whether you need one.

Estate planning is the process of developing a plan for what will happen to your **estate** and dependents when you die.

- If you die **intestate**, without a will, your assets will be distributed as required by law. In some cases, even if you do have a will, your estate will go through a lengthy **probate** process. If you have no living relatives or **heirs**, your assets may revert to the state through **escheat**.

- The estate-planning process requires that you evaluate your financial situation to determine your needs, establish strategies that will accomplish your objectives, and regularly reevaluate your plan as your life situation changes. These steps require the assistance of an estate-planning attorney or other professional. Estate plans might include creating a **will**, a **living will**, a **durable power of attorney**, a **letter of last instruction**, and possibly various **trusts**.

- Your estate plan will need to be revised as you undergo life changes such as marriage, divorce, and parenthood.

- Your family will also benefit if you have your financial and personal records well organized and accessible, since that will allow the settlement of your estate to occur with a minimum of difficulty.

LEARNING OBJECTIVE 14.2   Explain the importance of having a valid will and arranging in advance for easy transfer of assets to your heirs.

Three methods for transferring property at your death include a will, **beneficiary** designation, and joint ownership of property.

- Having a valid will in place reduces family stress at the time of your death, ensures that your assets are distributed according to your wishes, and allows you to be the one to determine the guardianship of your children.

- To make a valid will, the **testator** must be of legal age, and have the intent and mental **capacity** to make a will. The will should be typed, dated, signed, and notarized in the presence of two witnesses, and an **executor** or **executrix** must be named. The will can also name a guardian and a **trustee** to take care of minor children and manage assets on their behalf.

- If you want to change your will, you can revoke the old one or write a **codicil** that amends it.

- If you own an asset as a **joint tenant with right of survivorship**, the asset can pass directly to the other owner when you die instead of becoming part of your estate. With a **tenancy in common**, each owner can transfer his or her ownership interest in his or her will. With regard to **community property**, it is assumed that any property acquired during the marriage is owned jointly by both spouses.

LEARNING OBJECTIVE 14.3   Explain recent changes to federal estate and gift taxation laws that significantly reduce the number of estates that have to pay these taxes.

You can transfer your property by gifting it while you are alive or passing it to your heirs after your death.

- You can gift up to $15,000 per year per person or entity in 2019 and 2020 (with the amount increasing with inflation) without being subject to gift tax. Amounts in excess of that will reduce your lifetime combined exemption from estate and gift taxes.

- Federal estate taxes are owed on taxable estates in excess of the $11.4 million exemption less any excess lifetime gifts (for 2019, increasing with inflation). The current exemption amount is more than double the exemption before the tax reform was passed in 2017. The maximum marginal tax rate is 40 percent, but a very small percentage of estates will owe estate taxes.

- You are allowed to leave an unlimited amount of your estate to your spouse or to charities.

- Your gross estate is your net worth less certain excluded assets that have been transferred to irrevocable trusts or through family limited partnership arrangements. The taxable amount of an estate is the gross estate less costs of administering the estate and the unlimited marital and charitable deductions.

- Some states also impose estate, inheritance, and gift taxes in addition to the federal tax.

LEARNING OBJECTIVE 14.4   Understand how trusts, gifts, and charitable contributions can reduce estate taxes.

You can reduce the size of your taxable estate by making gifts during your lifetime or by transferring some of your assets to trusts.

- Gifts are tax-exempt as long as they don't exceed the allowed annual and lifetime limits. In addition, you can transfer an unlimited amount of wealth to charity through your will without it being subject to estate or gift tax.

- Trusts are also ways to reduce taxes and avoid probate. Assets that are placed in **irrevocable trusts** by a **grantor** are removed from the estate. With a **revocable trust**, you'll avoid probate but the assets will be part of your estate.

- A **living trust** is established while you are still alive, and a **testamentary trust** is established after you die by the terms of your will.

- You can gift income, assets, or both to a charity and avoid gift or estate taxes. With a **charitable remainder trust**, you get the use of the assets while you're alive, and the charity gets what's left upon your death. With a **charitable lead** (or **income**) **trust**, you gift the income while you're alive, and the assets pass to your heirs upon your death.

Excel Worksheets

14.1 Personal Financial Planner: Estate-Planning Checklist

14.2 Personal Financial Planner: Calculating Estate Taxes

Key Terms

beneficiary 14-8
capacity 14-9
charitable lead (or income) trust 14-18
charitable remainder trust 14-18
codicil 14-11
community property 14-12
durable power of attorney 14-5
escheat 14-5
estate 14-2

estate planning 14-3
executor or executrix 14-10
grantor 14-17
heir 14-5
intestate 14-5
irrevocable trust 14-17
joint tenancy with right of survivorship 14-12
letter of last instruction 14-7
living trust 14-17

living will 14-5
probate 14-3
revocable trust 14-17
tenancy in common 14-12
testamentary trust 14-17
testator 14-8
trust 14-7
trustee 14-11
will 14-5

WileyPLUS

Practice Questions to check your understanding, Peer-to-Peer Videos, Interactives, and many other resources are available in WileyPLUS.

Concept Review Questions

1. What is an estate plan, and why is it important for everyone to include one in his or her personal financial plan?

2. What are some of the adverse consequences that can result from the failure to do any estate planning?

3. How might your estate plan be expected to change over your life cycle?

4. Identify and explain the key components of an estate plan.

5. What is a living will, and what are the advantages of having one?

6. What types of information would you probably want to include in a letter of last instruction?

7. If a letter of last instruction is not a legally binding document, why should you bother to draft one?

8. Why do so many people not have valid wills?

9. How are estate and gift taxes related to each other?

10. Does a husband ever have to pay estate tax on an inheritance from his wife? Why or why not?

11. What are the two primary ways of reducing the size of your taxable estate?

12. What is a trust, and what are the purposes of such an arrangement in the context of estate planning?

13. Make a list of estate-planning objectives, given your current life-cycle stage and family situation. Next, pretend that it's 20 years in the future. Redo the list for the life-cycle stage and anticipated family situation that will be applicable at that time.

Application Problems

1. Identify estate-planning goals that would be appropriate, considering life-cycle stage and family circumstances, for each of the following people:

   a. Single college student, age 20, with a negative net worth

   b. Married couple, both age 30, with two dependent children and a net worth of $500,000

   c. Retired couple with independent adult children and a net worth of $1 million

   d. Retired widower with dependent children and a net worth of $10 million

2. For each of the following estate-planning goals, indicate the type of estate-planning tool or strategy that could be used to help accomplish the goal:

a. Ensure that your daughter ends up with the family china (instead of your sister, who lives closer and who will likely come to help clean out your belongings after you die)

b. Ensure that you aren't kept alive by artificial means when there's no chance of your recovery from a terminal illness or mental incompetence

c. Provide for your children's college education after you die

d. Make sure your children don't have to pay estate taxes on their inheritance from you

3. For each of the following situations, identify what type of trust, if any, would be appropriate to accomplish the stated goal.

a. You want to be able to make changes to the trust while you are living.

b. You want to donate assets to a charity while you are living but continue to receive income from those assets while you are living.

c. You want to give income from your investment account to a charity while you are living and have the account pass to your heirs when you die.

4. Ryan Stern died in 2019 and left an estate valued at $13,000,000 after the payment of his debts. His will gave $50,000 to the Humane Society, $100,000 to the University of Missouri, $150,000 to the Boy Scouts of America, and the remainder to his sister Mindy. The expenses of settling the estate were $10,000 for the funeral, $5,000 to his brother as executor, and $3,000 to accountants and lawyers.

a. Calculate Ryan's gross estate.

b. Calculate Ryan's adjusted gross estate.

c. Calculate Ryan's taxable estate.

d. What is the applicable exemption amount?

e. What amount of Ryan's estate will be subject to federal estate tax?

5. Keira's rich uncle committed suicide and left behind a handwritten suicide note and a will stating that he left all of his wealth to his very attractive young nurse. A previous will had named Keira and her brother as the sole heirs. The new will was witnessed by the uncle's maid and butler, who were good friends of the nurse. On what grounds can the family contest the will?

6. If you don't currently have a will, write a first draft to present to a lawyer for finalizing. If you already have a will in place, review its terms and update it as necessary. To help you formulate the contents of your will, answer the following questions:

- To whom do you want to leave your assets in the event of your death? Do you have any special items that you would like to give to certain people?

- If you have children, whom would you like to be their guardian, should that be necessary? How will you provide (financially) for your children's care and education?

- If you have pets, how will they be taken care of after you die?

- Do you have adequate life insurance? Have you named a beneficiary and a contingent beneficiary?

- Have you named a beneficiary for your pension or retirement plan?

7. At the age of 30, Lotta Cache, a successful entrepreneur, has already accumulated $20 million in wealth. She has no husband or children, but she wants to minimize the amount of estate taxes her estate would owe upon her death, and she wants to have some control over the distribution of the wealth she has worked so hard to accumulate. She has decided to use her wealth to benefit her favorite charity Wikipedia. How can she use gifts and trusts to do this?

Case Applications

1. Mina Bhatti is a successful entrepreneur. She started a small bakery when she graduated from college and has turned it into a multi million-dollar business. Mina is divorced and has had sole custody of her daughter Naitra, age 10, since divorcing her ex-husband six years ago. He provides no financial support for Naitra. Mina has spent a great deal of time running her business—so much that she has sometimes neglected her financial plan. Recently, though, she consulted a financial planner, who was adamant that she immediately take care of a few very important elements of her financial plan. First and foremost, he wants her to make a will right away. Mina and her ex-husband had made wills many years ago, but they predated Naitra's birth. In her old will, Mina left all her wealth to her husband. Mina's current assets are as follows:

Equity in family home	$ 250,000
Business assets	$ 750,000
Retirement account	$1,250,000
Other investments	$ 500,000
Total net worth	$2,750,000

In the event of her death, Mina would want her sister Janna to be Naitra's guardian. Janna is aware of Mina's wish and has agreed to act in this capacity. Mina's brother Sanjay was named as the executor in her prior will and will probably be willing to continue in that role.

a. Does Mina need a will? What would happen if she died today (before drafting a new will)?

b. What should Mina include in her will?

c. Does Mina need to establish a trust in her will? Why or why not?

d. If Mina names Janna as Naitra's guardian but Janna dies before Mina does, who will end up being guardian?

e. What duties will Sanjay have to perform as executor of the estate?

2. Crystal and Richard Ball are wealthy retirees who have an estate worth $15 million. They have five adult children. Four of them, ages 32 to 40, are financially secure professionals, but their youngest child, Ricky, age 26, is a struggling rock musician. Since Richard always wished he had pursued a music career, Crystal and Richard have been providing continued support for their youngest in the hope that he might realize his dream. His siblings have not always been supportive of their parents on this issue, thinking that Ricky should "get a real job." Crystal's will currently leaves everything to her husband and names their five children as equal contingent beneficiaries. Richard's will similarly leaves everything to Crystal. The Balls have recently consulted an estate-planning attorney and would like to put in place an estate plan that will minimize the estate taxes that might be payable upon their deaths and also achieve some other goals:

- Provide continued support for Ricky as long as he is actively pursuing his music career
- Leave a modest inheritance ($100,000) to each of their ten grandchildren, currently ages 2 to 11, to be received when they reach the age of 30
- Provide for the income needs of the spouse who outlives the other
- Leave the remainder of their estate to the National Endowment for the Arts

a. Do Crystal and Richard need to write new wills to accomplish their objectives? Explain.

b. If they have done no additional estate planning and each has a life insurance policy with a face value of $500,000 and with the other as beneficiary, will any estate taxes be payable when one of them dies?

c. If the Balls simply rewrote their wills designating their grandchildren as the beneficiaries, would any estate tax be payable when either of them dies? Explain your reasoning.

d. What types of trusts, if any, would you recommend the Balls establish to meet their objectives?

e. What might be the Balls' motivation for not giving their grandchildren any inheritance until they reach the age of 30?

f. To minimize family strife that might occur later, would you recommend that the Balls discuss their estate plan with their children now? Why or why not?

3. Roberta and Harry Caruso have two children: Mary, age 5, and Harry Jr., age 15. They are in the process of writing their wills and need to decide whom to appoint as guardian for their children in the event that they both die. Roberta thinks that they should have her parents be the guardians. Harry would prefer to have his sister and brother-in-law as guardians because they have two children who are close in age to Mary and Harry Jr.

a. What factors should Roberta and Harry consider in making this important decision?

b. Do they need to get permission from the prospective guardians? Why or why not?

c. Harry Jr. is 15, and in a few years, he will be old enough to care for his younger sister. Would you recommend that the Carusos change their will at that time to allow Harry Jr. to be the guardian? Why or why not? Would your answer be different if the Carusos have a very large estate?

4. Buddy and Carol have recently married. It is Buddy's second time to the altar and Carol's third. Both Buddy and Carol are fairly wealthy, and they are understandably cautious about commingling their assets because their previous divorces were costly. To further complicate their situation, each of them has two adult children from previous marriages. Carol's estate is currently worth $1.5 million, and Buddy's is worth $2 million. In the event of the death of either of them, the surviving spouse would be able to support himself or herself because both Buddy and Carol are working professionals.

a. Do Buddy and Carol need to do any estate planning?

b. Assume that both Buddy and Carol want to leave their wealth to their own children, but not to the other's children. Suggest alternative ways this might be accomplished.

c. If Carol were to die today (without have done any estate planning), how much would her estate owe in estate taxes?

accelerated benefits An option under which a terminally ill policyholder can receive a portion of his or her life insurance proceeds before death.

acceleration clause A part of a loan agreement that requires immediate repayment of the total amount due on an installment loan that is in default.

accidental death benefit A life insurance contract provision by which the face value is doubled in the case of accidental death.

active investor An investor who actively buys and sells securities in an attempt to make short-run gains.

adjustable rate mortgage (ARM) A mortgage loan with an interest rate that, by contract, varies over time with market conditions.

adjusted expense method A method for estimating after-tax retirement expenses in current dollars by adjusting current expenses for changes expected in retirement.

adjusted gross income (AGI) Earned income and unearned income minus certain allowed adjustments to income.

agency issue A bond issued by a federal agency.

alternative minimum tax (AMT) Income tax recalculation designed to ensure that people who receive certain tax breaks pay their fair share of federal taxes.

American Opportunity tax credit A tax credit of up to $2,500 per year for eligible expenses incurred during the first four years of college.

amortization The process of calculating equal loan payments that include principal repayment and interest on the declining balance.

amortization schedule A table that details the payment, principal, interest, and balance owed over the life of a loan.

annual percentage rate (APR) The standardized annual cost of credit, including all mandatory fees paid by the borrower, expressed as a percentage rate.

annual percentage yield (APY) The amount of interest paid each year, given as a percentage of the investment; the APY is used to compare interest rates across accounts with different compounding periods.

annuity A series of equal payments made at regular intervals for a period of time.

annuity due An annuity with beginning-of-period payments.

ask price The stock price requested by a potential seller.

asset allocation The process of deciding what proportion of a portfolio to invest in each asset class.

asset class A broad category of investments that have certain characteristics in common.

assets Things a person or a household owns, including liquid assets, real and personal property, and investments.

assumption of risk A defense to a claim of negligence may be used when the injured party voluntarily took on the risk.

attitudes Opinions and psychological differences between people that affect their decisions.

average daily balance The average of the balances owed on each day of the billing cycle.

average indexed monthly earnings (AIME) The average of a person's 35 highest years of monthly earnings, adjusted for inflation, used in computing that individual's Social Security benefit.

average tax rate The percentage of a taxpayer's total taxable income that is paid in taxes.

back-end load A fee paid by mutual fund investors at the time they sell shares.

balanced fund A mutual fund that invests in both stocks and bonds.

balloon loan A loan for which the regular installment payments are calculated using a longer amortization period, but a single large payment is required after a shorter period of time to repay the balance in full.

bank credit card A credit card issued by a depository institution.

bankruptcy The legal right under the U.S. Bankruptcy Act of 1978 to be relieved of certain debts and obligations by a court of law.

basic health-care insurance Health insurance that covers hospital, surgical, and physician expenses.

beneficiary A person, estate, or business entity designated to receive the proceeds of a life insurance policy upon the death of the policyholder.

beneficiary An individual or entity receiving assets under the terms of a will.

beta A measure of the market, or nondiversifiable, risk of a company's stock.

bid price The stock price offered by a potential buyer.

billing date The last day of a billing cycle; credit card transactions made after that date appear on the next month's bill.

blue chip stock A stock that is issued by a large, stable, mature company.

bond A debt investment representing a loan to a governmental or business entity, which usually pays a fixed rate of interest for a fixed period of time.

brokerage account An investor's account at a brokerage firm, from which the investor pays for purchases and into which the firm deposits proceeds from sales.

brokerage firm A nondepository financial institution that helps its customers to buy and sell financial securities.

budget A plan for future spending and saving.

budget variance The difference between budgeted cash flows and actual cash flows.

buy-and-hold A passive investment strategy in which the investor identifies his or her target asset allocation and then selects appropriate securities to hold for the long run.

buyer broker A real estate broker who works exclusively for the buyer and owes no legal duty to the seller.

buying on margin Using borrowed funds from your broker to purchase stock.

cafeteria plan An employee benefit plan in which the employer provides a sum of money and allows employees to choose the benefits they want from a menu.

call provision A contract term that allows a bond issuer to buy back a bond issue before the maturity date.

capacity The mental competence to make a will, including understanding the nature and content of the document and not acting under threat or coercion from anyone.

capital gain Growth in the value of an investment over time.

capital gain Profit on the sale of an investment; subject to a lower tax rate if the investment has been held for more than one year.

cash advance A cash loan from a credit card account.

cash management The management of cash payments and liquid investments.

cash reserve The liquid assets held to meet emergency cash needs.

cash surrender value The amount the insurer will pay to the policy owner if a cash value insurance policy is canceled.

cash value The value of the investment component of a permanent life insurance policy that is accessible to the insured.

cash-balance plan A defined-benefit retirement plan that includes an investment component similar to that of a defined-contribution plan.

cash-or-deferred arrangement (CODA) A defined-contribution retirement plan in which employees can contribute some of their salary to the plan on a tax-deferred basis.

certificate of deposit (CD) An account that pays a fixed rate of interest on funds left on deposit for a stated period of time.

charitable lead (or income) trust A trust that enables the grantor to give income to a charity during his or her lifetime or for a period of years but transfer the asset upon his or her death to a chosen beneficiary.

charitable remainder trust A trust that enables the grantor to give an asset to a charity but retain the cash flow generated by that asset during his or her lifetime.

claims adjuster A person designated by an insurer to assess whether a loss is covered by a specific policy and to assign a dollar value to the loss.

close price The last price at which a stock sold at the close of the previous business day.

closed-end credit Credit that is extended by a lender for a specific purpose and that must be paid back in a specified period of time, usually with monthly payments.

closed-end fund An investment company that has a fixed number of shares, which are traded in the secondary market.

closed-end lease A lease in which the lessor bears the risk that the value of the property at the end of the term is less than originally estimated.

closing A meeting at which participants sign the required paperwork to finalize a home purchase and mortgage agreement.

closing costs Transaction costs paid at the closing of a home purchase.

codicil A legal amendment to a will.

coinsurance An arrangement providing for the sharing of medical costs by the insured and the insurer.

collateral Valuable assets or real property that can be taken by the lender in the event that a loan is not repaid.

collision coverage Insurance that covers loss or damage to a vehicle caused by an automobile accident.

commercial bank A depository institution offering a wide variety of cash management services to business and individual customers.

commission A percentage of the sales price paid to a broker who assists in the sale of a home.

common stock An investment security that represents a proportionate ownership interest in a company.

community property A form of property ownership established by law in some states by which any property acquired during a marriage is considered to be jointly owned by both spouses.

compounding The process by which interest is paid on both the original investment and the interest already earned.

comprehensive physical damage coverage Insurance that covers loss or damage to a vehicle caused by any peril other than an automobile accident.

compulsory automobile insurance laws State laws that require proof of liability insurance as a prerequisite to auto registration.

condominium A type of multiple-unit property in which each owner has control over the interior of his or her unit, but common areas, including the exterior of the building and landscaping, are centrally managed and funded by dues paid by unit owners.

consumer credit Credit used to buy consumer goods and services.

consumer finance company A nondepository institution that makes loans to riskier consumers.

consumer price index (CPI) A measure of the price of a representative basket of household goods and services in the U.S. market.

contributory negligence A defense to a claim of negligence that may be used when the injured party contributed to his or her own injury.

contributory plan An employee benefit plan for which the employee pays some or all of the costs.

convenience check A check supplied by a credit card lender for the purpose of making a cash advance.

conventional mortgage A fixed-rate, fixed-term, fixed-payment loan that is secured by a home and paid off with monthly payments.

convertible A feature of a term life insurance policy that allows the insured person to convert the policy to a permanent life insurance policy without providing additional proof of insurability.

copay The dollar amount paid by the insured under a coinsurance provision; required contribution for specific services under some types of health plans.

corporation A type of business organization that exists as a legal entity separate from its owners, who have limited liability for corporate losses.

cosigner A person who agrees to take responsibility for repayment of a loan if the primary borrower defaults.

coupon payment The annual dollar amount paid in interest on a bond, equal to the coupon rate times the face value, usually paid to investors in two equal installments.

coupon rate The annual rate of interest on a bond, quoted as a percentage of the face value.

Coverdell Education Savings Accounts An option for education savings that allows after-tax contributions of $2,000 per year per child and tax-free withdrawals.

credit An arrangement to receive cash, goods, or services now and pay later.

credit bureau A company that collects credit information on individuals and provides reports to interested lenders.

credit card A plastic card printed with an account number and identifying the holder as a participant in a revolving credit agreement with a lender.

credit limit or credit line A preapproved maximum amount of borrowing for an open-end credit account.

credit union A nonprofit depository institution owned by its depositors.

cumulative preferred stock A preferred stock that gives holders the right to receive past unpaid dividends before any dividends can be paid to holders of common stock.

cyclical stock A stock exhibiting above-average sensitivity to the business cycle.

dealer's invoice price The price that a dealer pays to purchase a new vehicle from the manufacturer.

debt investor An investor who lends money to an individual, a government entity, a financial institution, or other business.

debt payment ratio The financial ratio that measures percentage of after-tax income required to make monthly debt payments.

debt ratio Total debts divided by total assets.

debts Amounts a person or a household owes to others, including unpaid bills, credit card balances, car loans, student loans, and real estate loans.

decreasing-term life insurance A type of term life insurance policy featuring a level premium and decreasing protection.

deductible The amount of a loss that must be paid out of pocket by an insured before the insurance company will pay anything.

deed A legal document that evidences ownership of real estate.

default Failure to meet the terms of a loan agreement, as when payments are not made in a timely fashion.

default risk The risk of not receiving expected cash flows from an investment.

defensive stock Stock that is relatively insensitive to the business cycle.

deferred annuity An annuity that begins payment at some point in the future, such as during retirement.

defined-benefit (DB) plan A retirement plan in which the employer promises employees a retirement benefit determined by a formula, commonly based on salary and years of service.

defined-contribution (DC) plan A retirement plan in which the employer promises to make regular contributions to employees' retirement accounts but does not guarantee the benefits that will result.

demand deposit A deposit account, such as a checking account, from which money can be withdrawn with little or no notice to the financial institution.

dependent A member of a household who receives at least half of his or her support from the head of the household.

depository institution A financial institution that obtains funds from customer deposits.

depreciation The decline in the value of an asset over time due to wear and tear, obsolescence, and competitive factors.

derivative security A type of investment that derives its value from changes in price of some underlying asset over time.

direct real estate investment A form of real estate investment in which the investor holds title to the property.

disability An illness or injury that prevents a person from earning his or her regular income or reduces how much he or she can earn.

disability income insurance Insurance that replaces lost income during a period of disability.

discount broker A brokerage firm that facilitates transactions at low cost to clients and provides online investment management tools and resources.

discount points Money paid up-front to a lender in return for a reduction in the annual rate on a mortgage.

discounting The process of calculating the present value of a lump sum or a series of payments to be received in the future.

diversification An investment strategy that involves spreading money across a range of investments in order to reduce the overall risk of the portfolio.

dividend Periodic distribution of profits to equity investors.

dividend reinvestment plan (DRIP) An investment strategy that allows investors to receive dividends in the form of additional shares of stock instead of cash.

dollar cost averaging An investment strategy in which equal dollar amounts are invested at regular intervals.

down payment The cash applied to a purchase, such as the purchase of a home, at the time the purchase is made.

due date The date by which payment must be received by the lender if the holder is to avoid late penalties and, in some cases, interest on new transactions.

durable power of attorney A legal document that allows you to specify someone you trust to make certain medical choices on your behalf when you are unable to make them for yourself.

earned income Income from salaries, wages, tips, bonuses, commissions, and other sources.

earnings per share (EPS) A measure of company profitability that is equal to after-tax net income divided by the number of shares outstanding.

economic cycle A pattern of ups and downs in the level of economic activity.

electronic cash Money in digitized format.

employee stock ownership plan (ESOP) A profit-sharing plan in which an employer makes contributions to employee accounts in the form of stock in the employing company.

equity The amount by which the value of an asset is greater than any outstanding debt secured by the asset.

equity or stock investor An investor who has an ownership interest in a business.

escheat The legal process by which the state government acquires the estate of a person who dies without a will and has no living relatives.

escrow account A reserve account held by a mortgage lender in which prepayments of property taxes and homeowner's insurance are held to be used to pay these costs.

estate A person's net worth at death.

estate planning The development of a plan for what will happen to your wealth and dependents when you die.

exchange-traded fund (ETF) An investment company with professionally, but not actively, managed assets, often intended to track a market index, and with shares that trade in the secondary market.

exclusion A potential loss that is explicitly not covered by an insurance policy.

exclusive or **captive agent** An insurance agent who sells the products of only one insurer.

executor or **executrix** A person designated to carry out the provisions of a will.

expansion A period in the economic cycle characterized by increased business investment and employment opportunities.

expense ratio The ratio of annual mutual fund expenses to total fund assets.

extended warranty A service contract agreement that, for a set price, extends an original warranty or adds services or coverage.

face amount The amount of insurance coverage purchased.

face value The dollar amount the bondholder will receive at the bond's maturity date.

face value The dollar value of protection payable to beneficiaries under the terms of a life insurance policy.

Federal Deposit Insurance Corporation (FDIC) A government-sponsored agency that insures customer accounts in banks and savings institutions.

federal funds rate The interest rate that banks charge each other for short-term loans.

Federal Reserve The central bank in the United States, which controls the money supply.

fee-for-service plan A health insurance plan that reimburses the insured for medical expenses incurred or pays the provider directly.

FICA payroll tax A tax levied by the U.S. government on earned income to fund Social Security and Medicare.

filing status An identification of household type for tax-filing purposes.

finance charge The dollar amount of periodic interest charged by the lender on a credit account.

financial needs method A method for estimating life insurance needs based on estimated capital and income needs of dependents net of current funds available to support those needs.

financial responsibility laws State laws that require proof of ability to cover the cost of injury to persons or property caused by an auto accident.

fixed annuity An annuity that makes a series of constant payments for a specified period of time or for life.

fixed expense An expense that remains constant each month.

fixed expenses Expenses that are a constant dollar amount each period.

fixed-income investment A debt investment that provides a fixed interest payment to the investor over the term of the investment.

fixed-rate loan A loan for which the rate of interest remains the same throughout the term of the loan.

flexible spending account An account maintained by an employer in which the pretax earnings of an employee are set aside and can be used for reimbursement of qualified medical and child-care expenses.

flexible spending account (FSA) An account maintained by an employer in which the pretax earnings of an employee are set aside for qualified medical and child-care expenses.

floating-rate bond A bond whose interest payments are adjusted periodically according to current market interest rates.

frequency of loss The probability that a loss will occur.

front-end load A commission or sales charge paid by mutual fund investors at the time they purchase shares.

fund family An arrangement in which a single company operates several separately managed mutual funds with different investment objectives.

futures contract A contract to buy or sell an underlying asset at a future date at a price set in advance.

future value (FV) The value a given amount will grow to in the future if invested today at a given rate of interest.

future value of an annuity (FVA) The amount to which a regular series of payments will grow, with compounding, if invested at a given rate of interest for a particular period of time.

global fund A mutual fund that invests in both U.S. and foreign securities.

grace period The time before interest begins to accrue on new transactions for cardholders who did not carry a balance from the previous billing cycle.

grantor A person or entity who legally passes ownership to another person or entity.

gross income Income before taxes and expenses.

gross income Income from all sources, including earned income, investment income, alimony, unemployment compensation, and retirement benefits.

group insurance Insurance purchased by an employer for the benefit of a group of employees.

group underwriting Underwriting in which the premium is based on the risk of a group as a whole rather than on characteristics of individual group members.

growth fund A mutual fund that focuses on capital appreciation.

growth stock Stock that compensates investors primarily through increases in value of the shares over time.

guaranteed renewability A feature of a term life insurance policy that gives the insured person the right to renew the policy without additional proof of insurability.

health maintenance organization (HMO) A managed-care plan that controls health-care costs by encouraging preventive care and requiring participants to use certain providers.

health savings account (HSA) An investment account in which an employer deposits pretax dollars allocated for payment of an employee's health-related expenses.

heir A person or entity designated to receive something from your estate after your death.

high-deductible health plan (HDHP) A health insurance plan that has a high deductible, designed to make insured individuals more cost-conscious when making health-care decisions.

high-yield bond, or **junk bond** A bond that pays a higher rate of return because it has a high risk of default and lower liquidity.

home equity The market value of a home minus the remaining mortgage balance.

home equity loan A loan that is secured by the value of the borrower's home equity.

homeowner's insurance Insurance purchased by a homeowner to cover property and liability losses associated with a home.

identity theft The use of another person's personal or financial information without permission to commit fraud or other crimes.

income fund A mutual fund that focuses on providing dividend and interest income.

income stock Stock that compensates investors primarily through the regular payment of dividends.

income-multiple method A method for estimating life insurance needs as a multiple of income.

incontestable clause An insurance contract clause stating that the insurer cannot contest a claim for misrepresentation after a policy has been in force for a specified period of time.

indemnity The principle that insurance will reimburse a policyholder only for actual losses.

independent agent An insurance agent who sells products for multiple insurers.

index An indicator that shows the average price movements of a particular group of securities and thus tracks the performance of a particular market segment.

indexed bond A bond whose interest payments are adjusted periodically according to a market index.

indirect real estate development A form of real estate investment in which an investment in property is made through a trustee or company that holds title to the property.

inflation An increase in the prices of goods and services over time.

inflation-adjusted annuity A series of payments at equal intervals that increase with inflation.

initial public offering (IPO) A company's first stock offering to the public.

insider trading Trading based on company information not available to the public, illegal under federal law.

insolvency The inability to pay debts as they come due.

installment loan A loan that requires repayment in equal periodic installments that include both interest and principal.

insurance policy A contract between an insured and an insurer in which the insured agrees to pay a premium in return for the insurer's promise to pay for certain covered losses during the policy period.

interest rate The cost of borrowed money or the return on invested money.

interest rate caps With respect to adjustable rate mortgages, limits placed on annual and lifetime increases in interest rates.

interest-only loan A loan in which the monthly payment is equal to the interest on the original loan balance, with no principal repayment.

interest-rate risk The risk of price changes due to changes in interest rates.

international fund A mutual fund that invests in securities from countries other than the United States.

intestate Without a valid will.

investment company A financial intermediary that pools investors' funds to purchase stocks, bonds, or other financial assets.

investment-grade bond A medium- or high-grade bond with a low risk of default on interest or principal.

irrevocable trust A trust that the grantor cannot revoke; it is not subject to probate or estate taxes.

itemized deductions An alternative to the standard deduction in which the taxpayer reports and deducts actual expenses in certain allowed categories to arrive at taxable income.

joint and survivor annuity An annuity that pays a regular benefit to a couple, often a married couple, until the second person dies.

joint tenancy with right of survivorship A form of property ownership in which, after the death of one owner, the property passes to the surviving owner without going through probate.

laddering An investment strategy in which the investor holds fixed-income securities with staggered maturities to diversify interest rate and reinvestment risk.

law of large numbers A principle holding that as the size of a pool of identical risks increases, the loss per person becomes more predictable.

lemon law A state law that protects consumers against chronically defective vehicles.

lessee A person who pays money for the privilege of using someone else's vehicle or real property for a period of time.

lessor An owner of an asset, commonly a vehicle or real property, who charges money for the use of that asset for a period of time.

letter of last instruction A nonbinding document that provides helpful information to survivors after the writer's death.

level-premium term insurance A term life insurance policy that has a fixed premium rate for a period of years.

liability risk The risk of being held legally responsible for injuries to another person or to another person's property.

lien Public notice of a right to real property.

life insurance company A nondepository financial institution that obtains funds from premiums paid for life insurance, invests in stocks and bonds, and makes mortgage loans.

life insurance needs analysis The process of determining the financial impact of a person's death on his or her dependents.

life-cycle fund A mutual fund that designs its asset allocation to meet the needs of individuals in a particular life stage.

Lifetime Learning tax credit A tax credit of 20 percent of the first $10,000 of college expenses up to a maximum of $2,000 for every eligible dependent who has incurred these expenses during the year.

limit order A request to buy stock at any price up to a given maximum or to sell stock at any price above a given minimum.

limited liability A statutory right of corporate shareholders that limits their potential losses to the value of the shares held.

limited partnership A partnership consisting of a general partner, who manages the investment, and limited partners, who provide investment funds, have limited liability, and share in profits.

limited-payment life insurance Whole life insurance that is paid up after a specified period.

liquid assets Cash and near-cash assets that can be easily converted to cash without loss of value.

liquidity ratio The financial ratio that measures ability to pay monthly expenses out of liquid assets in the absence of regular income.

liquidity risk The risk of not being able to convert an asset to cash on short notice without losing value.

listed security A security that is approved to be bought or sold on a particular exchange.

living trust A trust established during the grantor's lifetime.

living will A legal document that specifies a person's preferences as to medical care in the event that he or she becomes unable to make decisions because of illness or disability.

lockbox A fireproof, lockable box or safe kept in the home.

long-term care (LTC) Provision of medical and personal care to a person with an extended illness or disability.

long-term care (LTC) insurance An insurance policy that pays medical and personal care expenses associated with incapacity, such as home health care and nursing home costs.

loss control Actions taken to reduce the frequency or severity of expected losses.

major medical insurance Insurance that covers the costs of most medical services prescribed by a doctor, subject to deductibles and coinsurance.

managed-care plan A health insurance plan that attempts to reduce costs through contractual arrangements with providers and financial incentives for choosing low-cost alternatives.

marginal reasoning An analysis that considers the increased benefit that would result from a particular decision.

marginal tax effect The change in taxes owed as a result of a financial decision.

marginal tax rate A tax rate imposed on the taxpayer's next dollar of income.

margin call A request from a brokerage firm that the holder of a margin account add money to the account to maintain the required minimum.

market capitalization The total value of a company's stock at current market prices; calculated as the current market price times the number of shares outstanding.

market efficiency A theory that suggests prices immediately adjust to reflect all publicly available information.

market order An offer to buy stock at the market price.

market risk Investment risk associated with general market movements and economic conditions.

market value The price that an asset can be sold for today.

maturity date For a certificate of deposit (CD), the date on which the depositor can withdraw the invested amount and receive the stated interest.

maturity date The date on which the bond issuer makes the final bond interest payment and must pay the face value to the bondholder.

maturity matching An investment strategy in which the investor selects investments that have cash flows that match his or her investment goals.

Medicaid A federally-authorized and state-run program providing health-care coverage and premium subsidies for low-income people.

Medicare A federally-mandated health insurance program for people age 65 and over.

Medigap policy An insurance policy designed to pay deductibles and other costs that are not covered by Medicare.

minimum payment The minimum amount that must be paid by the due date to maintain good credit standing and avoid late payment penalties.

money market deposit account (MMDA) A savings account that pays interest that fluctuates with market rates on money market securities.

money market mutual fund (MMMF) A mutual fund that holds a portfolio of short-term, low-risk securities issued by the federal government, its agencies, and large corporations and pays investors a rate of return that fluctuates with the interest earned on the portfolio.

money-purchase plan A defined-contribution retirement plan to which the employer contributes a set percentage of the employee's salary.

mortality risk The risk of dying.

mortgage A long-term amortized loan that is secured by real property.

mortgage debt service The total monthly cost of a mortgage, including principal, interest, property taxes, and homeowner's insurance premiums.

mortgage debt service ratio The percentage of gross income used for mortgage debt service.

mortgage insurance Insurance charged to a mortgage borrower to protect the lender against the risk that the borrower will default.

municipal bond Long-term debt security issued by a state or local government entity.

mutual company A company that is owned by its customers.

mutual fund A nondepository financial institution that sells shares to investors and then invests the money in financial assets.

NASDAQ A completely electronic securities market that specializes in OTC stocks.

negative amortization An addition to a loan balance that occurs when the monthly payment is insufficient to cover the monthly interest charge.

negligence A failure to fulfill a legal duty to another that causes injury to that person or to his or her property.

net asset value The market value of a mutual fund's assets less the market value of its liabilities, divided by the number of shares outstanding.

net worth The difference between total assets and total liabilities.

no-fault automobile insurance A type of automobile insurance in which each insured driver involved in an accident collects the amount of his or her loss from his or her own insurer, regardless of who is at fault.

no-load fund A mutual fund that doesn't charge a front-end or back-end load.

nominal risk-free rate The expected return on a short-term risk-free investment such as a Treasury bill, equal to the real risk-free rate plus an inflation risk premium.

open-end fund An investment company that sells its shares directly to investors and buys them back on request.

open-end, or revolving, credit A preapproved amount of credit that can be used continuously for any purchases and usually requires monthly payments of at least part of the outstanding balance.

opportunity cost A measure of what has to be given up in order to take a particular action.

option contract A contract that gives the holder the right, but not the obligation, to purchase or sell a specified investment at a set price on or before a specified date.

ordinary annuity An annuity with end-of-period payments.

ordinary life insurance A whole life insurance policy with premiums that are payable up to the time of death.

overdraft protection An arrangement in which your financial institution automatically provides a short-term loan to your checking account if you have insufficient funds to cover a check or withdrawal.

over-the-counter (OTC) market An electronic network for trading securities through securities dealers.

participating policy A policy issued by a mutual insurer that pays a dividend to policyholder-owners to offset premium costs.

passive investor An investor who invests to receive long-term returns and doesn't actively engage in buying or selling.

payroll withholding The money regularly withheld by an employer from an employee's earned income for payment of the employee's taxes.

permanent life insurance A type of life insurance that provides both death protection and an investment component.

perpetuity A constant cash flow stream that continues into infinity.

personal balance sheet A financial statement that details the value of what you own and what you owe to others to arrive at an estimate of your net worth at a given point in time.

personal cash flow statement A summary of income and expenditures over a period of time, such as a month or a year.

personal finance The study of individual and household financial decisions.

personal financial planning The process of developing and implementing an integrated, comprehensive plan to meet financial goals, improve financial well-being, and prepare for financial emergencies.

personal financial statements The reports that summarize personal financial information.

point-of-service (POS) plan A managed-care plan in which participants have financial incentives to use in-network providers and services.

portability An employee's ability to take retirement plan assets from one place of employment to another when changing jobs.

preemptive right The right of a shareholder to maintain his or her proportionate ownership when the company issues additional shares of stock.

preferred provider organization (PPO) A managed-care plan that provides participants with financial incentives to use certain providers.

preferred stock A type of stock that pays a fixed dividend.

preferred stock par value An arbitrary initial value assigned to shares of preferred stock at issuance and used to calculate the dividend payment.

premium The amount an insurer charges a policyholder for insurance protection.

prenuptial agreement A written contract made in advance of a marriage that specifies how the assets will be distributed in the event of a divorce.

prepayment penalty A fee charged to the borrower when a loan balance is repaid before the end of the loan term.

present value (PV) The amount of money that would have to be invested today to grow to a given future value over a specified period at a specified interest rate.

present value of an annuity The lump sum amount that must be deposited today to provide equal periodic payments for a given number of periods in the future.

price-to-earnings (P/E) ratio A measure of a company's future earnings potential, calculated as market price divided by earnings per share.

primary insurance amount (PIA) The Social Security benefit payable to a program participant who retires at the normal retirement age.

primary market The market in which securities are sold to the public by the issuers for the first time.

principal The original amount borrowed or invested.

probate The legal process of settling an estate.

profit-sharing plan A defined-contribution retirement plan in which the employer's contributions are discretionary.

progressive tax A tax that requires higher-income taxpayers to pay proportionately more in taxes, through either higher tax rates or other rules.

promissory note A legal contract that specifies the terms and conditions of the borrower's agreement to repay a loan.

property tax A local tax based on the value of real estate owned by a taxpayer.

prospectus A document that summarizes financial information about a stock or bond issue and the issuing company for potential investors.

pure risk A risk that will produce only bad outcomes (losses).

rate of return The total income earned on an investment over a period of time, including capital gains and interest or dividends, divided by the original amount invested; also called the *yield*.

real estate broker or agent A licensed professional who assists home buyers and sellers, in return for a fee.

real estate investment trust (REIT) A type of closed-end fund that invests in real estate and mortgages.

recession A phase in the economic cycle characterized by reduced business investment and increasing unemployment.

reconciling a budget Adjusting income, expenses, and saving so that household spending does not exceed household income.

refinance To obtain a new mortgage to pay off a previous, usually higher-rate mortgage.

refundable tax credit A tax credit that can be claimed even when it is greater than total taxes owed, resulting in a cash payment to the taxpayer.

regressive tax A tax that places a disproportionate financial burden on lower-income taxpayers.

regular checking account A checking account that does not pay interest and requires the payment of a monthly service charge unless a minimum balance is maintained in the account.

reinvestment risk The risk that short-term investments will have to be reinvested at lower rates when they come due.

renter's insurance Insurance purchased by a renter to cover personal property and liability losses but not damage to the building itself.

replacement ratio method A method for estimating after-tax retirement expenses in current dollars by multiplying current expenses by a factor of 70 to 80 percent.

residual claim A common shareholder's right to a share of a firm's assets and income after all the other claimholders are paid.

retail credit card A credit card that can be used only at the sponsoring retailer's outlets.

reverse annuity mortgage An arrangement in which a homeowner sells equity in a home in return for a stream of income but retains the use of the home.

revocable trust A trust whose terms the grantor can change during his or her lifetime; it bypasses probate but is still subject to estate taxes.

rider An addendum to an insurance policy that requires payment of an additional premium in return for additional specified coverage.

risk An uncertainty about the potential outcome of a decision.

risk aversion A tendency to dislike risk and to be unwilling to invest in risky securities unless they earn higher investment returns

risk classification The categorization of policyholders by characteristics that affect their expected losses; insurers use risk classification to price policies fairly.

risk retention Planning to pay for losses out of pocket instead of purchasing insurance; sometimes called self-insurance.

Roth IRA An individual retirement account to which contributions are made with after-tax dollars, but investment earnings and withdrawals at retirement are tax-free.

Rule of 72 A method of calculating the time required for a sum of money to double by dividing 72 by the rate of interest earned on the money.

safe deposit box A secure, private storage area maintained at a remote location, usually a financial institution's place of business.

sales finance company A nondepository institution that makes consumer loans to buyers of products offered through its parent company.

savings and loan association (S&L) A depository institution that receives funds primarily from household deposits and uses most of its funds to make home mortgage loans.

savings ratio The financial ratio that measures the percentage of after-tax income allocated to savings.

scheduled property A specific list of valuable personal property that is insured under a rider.

secondary market The market in which previously issued securities are traded between investors.

secondary mortgage market A market in which lenders sell mortgages after their origination.

Section 529 plan A state-sponsored program that provides tax benefits for college saving.

sector fund A mutual fund that invests primarily in securities from a particular industry or business sector.

secured bond A bond for which interest and principal payments are backed by assets or future cash flows pledged as collateral.

secured loan A loan that includes a pledge of collateral.

securities exchange A physical location at which securities are traded; the largest is the New York Stock Exchange.

security An investment in which the investor contributes a sum of money to a common enterprise with the intention of making a profit through the efforts of others.

security deposit The dollar amount required at the beginning of a lease to cover unpaid rent and/or the costs of any damage to the property over the lease term.

selling short A strategy in which an investor borrows stock from a broker, sells the stock, and later buys stock on the market to replace the borrowed stock.

sensitivity analysis An estimation of the change in outcome that might result from a change in assumptions.

severity of loss The dollar value of a loss.

short sale A sale in which a home is sold for less than the remaining balance on the mortgage.

single-payment loan A loan that requires the repayment of interest and principal in a single payment at a specified date in the future.

single-premium whole life insurance A whole life insurance policy that is paid up with a one-time payment.

smart card A card that stores information and electronic cash in a computer chip.

socially responsible investing (SRI) fund A mutual fund that limits its holdings to securities issued by companies that meet certain ethical and moral standards.

speculative investment A high-risk investment made in order to obtain a short-term profit.

speculative risk A risk that involves the possibility of either loss or gain.

standard deduction The dollar amount based on filing status that is subtracted from adjusted gross income in calculating taxable income.

sticker price The manufacturer's suggested retail price for a new vehicle, including manufacturer-installed accessories and options.

stock company A company that is owned by outside stockholders.

stock dividend A dividend given to shareholders in the form of shares of stock instead of cash.

stop order An order to buy or sell shares of stock when the market price reaches a certain level.

stop payment order An order by which a financial institution promises not to honor a check that a depositor has written.

strict liability A rule of law that holds a property owner liable for damages without requiring proof of negligence.

target date fund A mutual fund that designs its asset allocation to be consistent with a future financial goal, such as retirement or education funding.

taxable income The amount of income on which taxes must be paid.

tax audit The process by which the IRS more carefully examines particular tax returns for errors and omissions.

tax avoidance The strategic use of knowledge of tax rules to avoid overpayment of taxes.

tax bracket The range of taxable income to which a particular marginal tax rate applies.

tax credit A reduction applied directly to taxes owed rather than to income subject to taxes.

tax evasion The deliberate nonpayment of taxes legally owed.

tax-qualified retirement plan A retirement plan that qualifies under federal law for tax deferral; that is, taxes on contributions made to the plan and earnings on plan assets are not due and payable until funds are withdrawn during retirement.

tenancy in common A type of ownership in which each person owns his or her share independently and retains the right to transfer that share by sale or will.

term life insurance A type of life insurance policy that provides death protection for a specified period of time, often one year, and no cash value.

testamentary trust A trust established by the terms of a will.

testator The writer of a will.

time deposit A savings account from which the depositor may not withdraw money without penalty until a certain amount of time has passed.

time value of money The principle that money received today is worth more than money to be received in the future because of the power of compounding.

timing An investment strategy in which the investor attempts to shift asset allocation to take advantage of upturns and avoid downturns in specific markets.

title insurance Insurance that covers the risk that the seller did not transfer clear ownership rights to the buyer as promised.

total income Gross income less certain exclusions allowed by the IRS.

traditional IRA An individual retirement account that allows the holder to subtract current contributions from income and to defer income tax until withdrawals are made in retirement.

transaction date The date on which a credit card purchase is made.

travel and entertainment (T&E) card A credit card that requires payment of the full balance each billing cycle.

Treasury Inflation Protected Securities (TIPS) U.S. government bonds with a face value that is adjusted annually for inflation to ensure that investors earn an inflation-adjusted rate of return.

trust A legal entity that holds and manages assets on behalf of someone else.

trustee A person or entity who manages assets on behalf of another.

trustee The legal representative for the owners of a bond issue.

umbrella insurance A supplemental personal liability insurance policy.

underwriter An insurance company employee who evaluates applicants for insurance and provides price quotes.

unearned income Income from investments, interest, dividends, capital gains, net business income, rents, and royalties.

unit investment trust (UIT) An investment company that buys and holds a fixed portfolio of securities for a period of time determined by the life of the investments in the trust.

universal life insurance A type of permanent life insurance that allows policyholders to benefit from the investment experience of the insurer and provides a flexible-premium option.

U.S. savings bond A bond issued by the U.S. Treasury that pays interest that fluctuates with current Treasury security rates and is exempt from state and local taxes.

value fund A mutual fund that invests in companies perceived to be undervalued by the market.

values Fundamental beliefs about what is important in life.

variable annuity An annuity in which the payments depend on performance of an underlying investment portfolio.

variable expense An expense that varies over time.

variable expenses Expenses that vary in amount from period to period.

variable life insurance Permanent life insurance that has a fixed premium and allows policyholders to choose from different investment alternatives.

variable-rate loan A loan for which the rate of interest varies periodically with a changing market rate, such as the prime rate.

variable-universal life insurance Permanent life insurance that includes a flexible-premium feature and allows policyholders to choose from different investment alternatives.

vesting rules The rules that define employees' rights to accrued retirement plan contributions and benefits.

waiver of premium An insurance option that allows the insured to waive premium payments under certain conditions, such as permanent disability.

warranty A written, oral, or implied promise by a seller regarding the qualities of the seller's product.

whole life insurance A type of permanent life insurance that provides death protection for the policyholder's whole life and includes a savings component.

will A legal document that transfers property upon the death of the property owner.

wire transfer The electronic transmittal of cash into an account from an account at another financial institution.

workers' compensation insurance State-mandated employer insurance coverage for lost wages and medical costs associated with job-related illness or injury.

yield The total income earned on an investment over a period of time, including capital gains and interest or dividends, divided by the original amount invested; also called the *rate of return*.

yield to maturity (YTM) The annualized return on a bond, if it is held to maturity and all interest payments are reinvested at the same rate.

zero-coupon bond A bond that doesn't provide interest payments to investors, but instead has a discounted price at the time of sale.

Index